Readings in Language and Mind

READINGS IN LANGUAGE AND MIND

Edited by
Heimir Geirsson and Michael Losonsky

BLACKWELL *Publishers*

First published 1996
2 4 6 8 10 9 7 5 3 1

Blackwell Publishers Inc.
238 Main Street
Cambridge, Massachusetts 02142, USA

Blackwell Publishers Ltd
108 Cowley Road
Oxford OX4 1JF
UK

Library of Congress Cataloging-in-Publication Data

Readings in language and mind / edited by Heimir Geirsson and Michael Losonsky.
 p. cm.
 Includes bibliographical references and index.
 ISBN 1-55786-670-8 (hardcover: alk. paper). – ISBN 1-55786-671-6 (pbk.: alk. paper)
 1. Language and languages – Philosophy. 2. Semantics. 3. Philosophy of mind.
4. Cognitive science. 5. Psycholinguistics. I. Geirsson, Heimir. II. Losonsky, Michael.
P106.M552 1996
401–dc20   95-12850
                        CIP

British Library Cataloguing in Publication Data

A CIP catalogue record for this book is available from the British Library.

Typeset in 10 on 11¹/₂ pt Ehrhardt
by Best-set Typesetter Ltd., Hong Kong
Printed in Great Britain by Hartnolls Ltd, Bodmin, Cornwall

This book is printed on acid-free paper

Contents

Preface

This is an anthology of 28 essays that document the close historical and conceptual ties between the philosophy of language, philosophy of mind, linguistics, cognitive psychology, and, more generally, cognitive science. Work in these areas is increasingly interdisciplinary and at this juncture it is no longer possible to introduce any of these areas without making references to results in the other areas. While there are a number of excellent anthologies in each of these disciplines, there are relatively few anthologies that bring them together and show their connection, and none brings them together around the theme of language.

The selections show how studies in semantics and pragmatics have led to and contributed to developments in philosophy of mind, psychology, linguistics, and cognitive science, including artificial intelligence, and how the latter disciplines have in turn influenced each other and semantics and pragmatics to the point that the disciplines now form a web of interdisciplinary studies.

The anthology is divided into three parts. The first part is devoted to the attempts to understand linguistic meaning. The second part is devoted to attempts to understand mental content. The third part is devoted to the scientific understanding of mind and language, including competing models of our linguistic capabilities. Most of the selections have already established themselves as classics in their respective disciplines, and all of them have contributed beyond their respective disciplines. Each part is further divided into several sections that are prefaced by introductions where we provide an overview of the selections, place them in a wider context, and suggest further readings.

From the beginning we intended the anthology to be a flexible tool for students as well as instructors. It is directed at upper-level undergraduate courses and graduate courses in philosophy of language, philosophy of mind, linguistics, cognitive psychology, cognitive science, and artificial intelligence, as well as courses which want to investigate recent developments in analytic philosophy. The selections appeal to and should draw students from a variety of disciplines and they are well suited to demonstrate for the students the importance of being attentive to advances in disciplines other than their own.

Finally, it would be a great source of satisfaction for us not only if students and instructors find this collection an aid in their academic pursuits, but if someone who simply is concerned with the way we have come to think about mind and language reaches for this collection.

H.G.
M.L.

Acknowledgments

The editors and publishers gratefully acknowledge the following for permission to reproduce copyright material in this anthology.

Tyler Burge, "Philosophy of Language and Mind, 1950–90," *Philosophical Review* 101 (1992). Copyright © 1992 by Cornell University. Reprinted with the permission of *The Philosophical Review* and the author.

Alfred Tarski, "The Semantic Conception of Truth and the Foundations of Semantics," *Philosophy and Phenomenological Research* 4 (1944). Copyright © 1992 the Estate of Alfred Tarski. Reprinted with the permission of Jan Tarski.

Donald Davidson, "Truth and Meaning," *Synthese* 17 (1967). Copyright © 1967 by D. Reidel Publishing. Reprinted with the permission of Kluwer Academic Publishers.

Robert C. Stalnaker, "Pragmatics," in G. Harman and D. Davidson, eds, *Semantics of Natural Language* (Dordrecht: D. Reidel, 1972). Copyright © 1972 by D. Reidel Publishing. Reprinted with the permission of Kluwer Academic Publishers.

Barbara H. Partee, "Semantics – Mathematics or Psychology?," in R. Baucrle, U. Egli, and A. von Stechow, eds, *Semantics from Different Points of View* (Berlin: Springer-Verlag, 1979). Copyright © 1979 by Springer-Verlag. Reprinted with the permission of Springer-Verlag.

H. P. Grice, "Meaning," *Philosophical Review* 66 (1957). In the public domain.

John R. Searle, "What Is a Speech Act?," in M. Black, ed., *Philosophy in America* (Ithaca, NY: Cornell University Press, 1965). Copyright © 1965 by Cornell University Press. Reprinted with the permission of the author and George Allen & Unwin Publishers Ltd.

H. P. Grice, "Logic and Conversation," in P. Cole and J. Morgan, eds, *Syntax and Semantics*, vol. 3 (New York: Academic Press, 1975). Copyright © 1988 by Mrs K. B. Grice. Reprinted with the kind permission of Mrs K. B. Grice.

David Lewis, "Languages and Language," in K. Gunderson, ed., *Language, Mind and Knowledge* (Minneapolis: University of Minnesota Press, 1975). Copyright © 1983 by David Lewis. Reprinted with the kind permission of the author.

Hilary Putnam, "The Meaning of 'Meaning'," in K. Gunderson, ed., *Language, Mind and Knowledge* (Minneapolis: University of Minnesota Press, 1975). Copyright © 1975 by University of Minnesota Press. Reprinted with the permission of the University of Minnesota Press and the author.

Roderick M. Chisholm, "Sentences About Believing," *Proceedings of the Aristotelian Society* 56 (1955–6). Reprinted with permission of the Aristotelian Society.

Wilfrid Sellars, "Language as Thought and as Communication," *Philosophy and Phenomenological Research* 29 (1969). Reprinted with permission of *Philosophy and Phenomenological Research*.

Donald Davidson, "Thought and Talk," © Oxford University Press 1975. Reprinted from *Mind and Language: Wolfson College Lectures 1974*, ed. by Samual Guttenplan (1975) by permission of Oxford University Press.

Alan M. Turing, "Computing Machinery and Intelligence," first appeared in *Mind* 59 (1950). Reprinted by permission of Oxford University Press.

John R. Searle, "Is the Brain's Mind a Computer Program?," *Scientific American* (January 1990). Copyright © 1990 by Scientific American Inc. Reprinted with the permission of Scientific American Inc.

Paul M. Churchland and Patricia S. Churchland, "Could a Machine Think?," *Scientific American* (January 1990). Copyright © 1990 by Scientific American Inc. Reprinted with the permission of Scientific American Inc.

Fred Dretske, "Representational Systems," ch. 3 of *Explaining Behavior* (Cambridge, MA: MIT Press, 1988). Copyright © 1988 by The MIT Press. Reprinted with the permission of The MIT Press.

Ruth Garrett Millikan, "Thoughts Without Laws: Cognitive Science with Content," *Philosophical Review* 95 (1986). Copyright © 1986 by *The Journal of Philosophy*. Reprinted with the kind permission of *The Philosophical Review* and the author.

Tim van Gelder and Robert S. Port, "It's About Time: An Overview of the Dynamical Approach to Cognition," in R. Port and T. van Gelder, eds, *Mind as Motion: Explorations in the Dynamics of Cognition* (Cambridge, MA: Bradford/MIT Press, 1995). Copyright © 1995. Reprinted with permission of The MIT Press and Tim van Gelder.

Jerry A. Fodor, "Methodological Solipsism Considered as a Research Strategy in Cognitive Psychology," *Behavioral and Brain Sciences* 3 (1980). Copyright © 1980 by Cambridge University Press. Reprinted with the permission of Cambridge University Press and the author.

Tyler Burge, "Individualism and Psychology," *Philosophical Review* 95 (1986). Copyright © 1986 by Cornell University. Reprinted with the permission of *The Philosophical Review* and the author.

George A. Miller, "Some Preliminaries to Psycholinguistics," *American Psychologist* 20 (1965). Copyright © 1965 by American Psychological Association. Reprinted with the permission of the American Psychological Association.

Noam Chomsky, "A Review of B. F. Skinner's *Verbal Behavior*," first appeared in *Language* 35 (1959). Copyright © 1959 by the Linguistic Society of America. Reprinted with the kind permission of the Linguistic Society of America and the author.

Eleanor Rosch and Carolyn B. Mervis, "Family Resemblances: Studies in the Internal Structure of Categories," *Cognitive Psychology* 7 (1975). Copyright © 1975. Reprinted with the permission of Academic Press and with the kind permission of Eleanor Rosch.

Dan Sperber and Deirdre Wilson, "Précis of *Relevance: Communication and Cognition*," *Behavioral and Brain Sciences*. Copyright © by Cambridge University Press. Reprinted with the permission of Cambridge University Press and the authors.

Jill Fain Lehman, Allen Newell, Thad Polk, and Richard L. Lewis, "The Role of Language in Cognition: A Computational Inquiry," in G. Harman, ed., *Conceptions of the Mind: Essays in Honor of George Miller* (Hillsdale, NJ: Lawrence Erlbaum). Copyright © 1993 by

Lawrence Erlbaum and Associates. Reprinted with permission of Lawrence Erlbaum and Associates and the authors.

David E. Rumelhart and James L. McClelland, "On Learning the Past Tenses of English Verbs," in J. L. McClelland, D. E. Rumelhart and the PDP Research Group, eds, *Parallel Distributed Processing*, vol. 2 (Cambridge, MA: MIT Press, 1986). Copyright © by The MIT Press. Reprinted with the permission of The MIT Press.

Jeffrey Elman, "Grammatical Structure and Distributed Representations," from *Connectionism: Theory and Practice*, edited by Steven Davis. Copyright © 1992 by Oxford University Press, Inc. Reprinted with the permission of Oxford University Press and kind permission from J. Elman.

Steven Pinker, "Rules of Language," first appeared in *Science* 253 (1991). Copyright © 1991 American Association for the Advancement of Science. Reprinted with the permission of the American Association for the Advancement of Science and the author.

The publishers apologize for any errors or omissions in the above list and would be grateful to be notified of any corrections that should be incorporated in the next edition or reprint of this book.

Philosophy of Language and Mind, 1950–90

TYLER BURGE

The last 40 years in philosophy of language and philosophy of mind have seen, I hazard to say, some of the most intense and intellectually powerful discussion in any academic field during the period.[1] Yet the achievements in these areas have not been widely appreciated by the general intellectual public. This is partly because they are abstract and difficult. But it is partly a reflection of the lamentably weak lines of communication between philosophy and the rest of culture, especially in America. In my view, this situation developed during the professionalization of philosophy in the positivist period. Indeed, positivism's harsh judgment of the cognitive value of most of nonscientific culture should probably be given much of the blame.

Logical positivism casts a long shadow. Its overthrow in the early 1950s is the central event at the outset of the period that I shall discuss. Elements from this movement motivated and colored much that followed. Philosophy's challenge has been to maintain the movement's clarity and respect for argument, while loosening its restrictions on method and subject matter.

Logical positivism aimed to make philosophy scientific – to end the succession of philosophical systems that seemed to promise no analogue of scientific progress. To support this aim, the movement presented an account of why philosophy had failed to be scientific and what its proper scope and limits are. This account rested on a theory of meaning coupled with a theory of knowledge.

The theory of meaning was the most original proposal of the movement. It consisted of two main principles. One was that the meaning of a sentence is its method of verification or confirmation (the *verificationist principle*). The other was that statements of logic and mathematics, together with statements that spell out meaning relations, are analytic in the specific sense that they are *true purely in virtue of their meaning and provide no information about the world: they are vacuously or degenerately true*. It was typically claimed that analytic truth is truth in virtue of conventions or other activities whose products are not rationally legitimated.

The verificationist principle was supposed to explain why philosophy, particularly metaphysics, had failed. The idea was that since philosophy associates no method of verification with most of its claims, those claims are meaningless. To be meaningful and produce knowledge, philosophy was supposed to imitate science in associating its claims with methods of testing them for truth.

The logical positivists saw both principles about meaning as underwriting an empiricist theory of knowledge, a theory according to which all nonvacuous knowledge is justifiable only by reference to sense experience. Science was supposed successful only because it checks and justifies its claims by reference to sense experience. Logic and mathematics, the traditional sources of difficulty for empiricism, were counted useful but vacuous in that they are analytic. Thus, all cognitively meaningful, nonvacuous claims about the world were supposed to be justifiable only by methods of verification that lead ultimately to sense experience.

This empiricism varies but slightly from that of Hume. The attempt to explain the limits of philosophy by reference to scientific method is an adaptation of Kant's broadly similar attempt. What distinguished the movement most sharply from its philosophical predecessors was its radical theory of meaning, represented by the verificationist principle, and its dispassionate, communal approach to philosophical discussion, practiced by its leading proponents – men like Carnap, Schlick, Neurath, Reichenbach, and Hempel. The theory of meaning gave philosophy a new focus and caught the attention of the intellectual public because of its radical implication that a lot that passed for serious intellectual discourse (outside philosophy as well as in it) was in fact "meaningless." The intellectual power, seriousness, and openness of the movement's leaders obtained for the movement a number of talented interlocutors.

Problems with the verificationist principle dogged the movement almost from the beginning. There was a difficulty with self-application. It is hard to cite a method of verification that is associated with the principle itself; and in the absence of such a method, the principle is "cognitively meaningless" by its own account. Some proponents counted the principle analytic, vacuously true. But this claim was difficult to make credible because the principle seemed so much more contentious than other purportedly analytic claims. Moreover, to admit that one's philosophy was cognitively vacuous was not to pay it much of a compliment. Among positivists, Carnap maintained the most sophisticated position on the issue. He recommended as a practical proposal, to be judged by its theoretical fruits, a linguistic framework within which the principle counted as analytic. He regarded the principle as a proposal for clarifying the informal meaning of "meaning." Given its allegedly practical cast, this position was not persuasive to those not already convinced. Moreover, it encountered problems with the notions of linguistic framework, analyticity, and the practical-theoretical distinction, some of which I shall discuss.[2]

There was also a difficulty in stating what counts as an admissible method of confirmation. Various proposals about the structure of confirmation were found to be revivals of traditional philosophical pictures (such as phenomenalism) in disguise. The proposals lacked scientific status. More generally, most of the more precise formulations either included parts of metaphysics as meaningful or excluded parts of science as meaningless. This problem led to a number of reformulations of the verificationist principle. But frustration with this difficulty finally led Hempel in 1950 to agnosticism about the truth of any suitably powerful verificationist principle.[3]

Quine's frontal attacks on both primary principles of logical positivism in the early 1950s marked the true end of the movement. His criticism of the verificationist principle aimed at the fundamental issue. Quine claimed that methods of confirmation in science could not be associated with single sentences, as the principle required. He held that sentences can be confirmed or disconfirmed only in relation to other sentences, in the context of theories. This general claim earned the loose title "holism." On this view, a method of confirmation cannot be uniquely associated with any one sentence as its meaning.[4] Holism, understood in this general sense, came to be buttressed by many examples from the practice of science. It has held the field in empirical domains ever since.

Quine also challenged the idea that the notion of analyticity had any application. The attack spilled over into a campaign against a variety of different notions associated with the specific notion of analyticity that I characterized. Since Quine himself often failed to distinguish among these notions, the attack on the original notion has been neglected in the controversy over the broader campaign.

Quine's primary and strongest point was that the claim that some sentences are vacuously true has no explanatory or cognitive advantage. He maintained that there is no ground for claiming that the relevant sentences are vacuously true, with no dependence on the way the world is, as opposed to true because of obvious and ubiquitous (in traditional terms, "necessary") features of reality. Quine's strongest point is not that the notion of meaning is incoherent or requires some special explanation. It is that there is no good argument for characterizing the distinction between the supposed instances of analytic truths (including logical truths and truths of "meaning analysis") and instances of other truths in terms of vacuous truth and subject matter independence.[5]

Carnap defended the claim that logic is analytic by holding it to be a practical proposal that is itself analytic – to be judged by its fruits in explicating meanings.[6] This defense paralleled his defense of the verificationist principle against the objection concerning self-application. Quine held that Carnap's notion of a practical proposal could not be distinguished from that of a theoretical proposal. For theoretical proposals in science are judged "pragmatically," by their theoretical fruitfulness.

Quine also criticized other attempts to spell out the claim that logic is analytic, or vacuously true. As against the view that logic is true by convention, he pointed out that logic has an infinite number of theorems. One might imagine, for the sake of argument, that individual axioms were true by conventional stipulation. But deriving the consequences of these axioms requires that one already assume logic. The main principles of logic seem prior to any activity that might be regarded as a laying down of linguistic meaning.[7]

Many positivists sympathized with Frege's logicist program of defining mathematical terms in logical terms, and deriving mathematical theorems from logical axioms together with the definitions.[8] Unlike Frege, they saw the program as aiding the empiricist cause of counting mathematics vacuously true. Many problems already clouded this vision. But Quine added to them by indicating that the vacuity of definitions is at best a passing trait. He noted that when definitions are incorporated into theories, they become subject to theoretical criticism and revision, thus not vacuously true. This point was subsequently substantiated by consideration of numerous theoretical definitions in science and mathematics, which had turned out to be false or theoretically inadequate.[9] By considering the practice of linguistic interpretation, Carnap tried to provide an empirical basis for distinguishing between meaning postulates and theoretical postulates.[10] Carnap's proposals are historically important because they motivated Quine to initiate his project of producing a theory of "radical translation" (discussed below). But quite apart from their great oversimplifications and their reliance on shaky psychological assumptions, Carnap's proposals are, I think, weak in that they never come to grips with the problem of defending analyticity. Although they may provide a start toward *some* distinction between meaning explications and ordinary theoretical postulates, they give no prima facie ground for distinguishing between nonvacuous and vacuous truth, or between true principles that are rationally legitimated and those that are not rationally legitimated. So they give no support to empiricist epistemology – the original motivation for invoking analyticity.

There was something more general than empiricism at stake in the dispute over analyticity. The positivists hoped "first principles," the boundaries of rational discussion, could be established as vacuously true and not subject to philosophical questions about legitimation. First principles included logic, but also other principles about the boundaries of rational discussion, such as the verificationist principle or the claim that certain truths are vacuously true and not subject to rational legitimation. If these principles were themselves analytic, they could be exempted from the traditional metaphysical and epistemological questions. Carnap maintained a principle of tolerance that allowed there to be different "first principles," which could be "adopted" for pragmatic reasons. But it was fundamental to his view, as well as the views of other less liberal positivists, that neither establishing nor changing a framework of such principles is subject to rational ("theoretical") considerations. Such changes were supposed to be "prompted" or "chosen" or were "merely practically" motivated. Quine's attack on analyticity calls this distinction into question. Indeed, what I regard as his fundamental criticisms of analyticity have never been satisfactorily answered: No clear reasonable support has been devised for a distinction between truths that depend for their truth on their meaning alone and truths that depend for their truth on their meaning together with (perhaps necessary) features of their subject matter. Similarly, neither Carnap nor anyone else has succeeded in distinguishing between nonrational grounds for adopting "first principles" and grounds that traditionalists (as well as Quine) might count as rational but obvious (or even rational but disputable). Quine thought that the grounds were covertly empirical. Traditionalists would think that the grounds were rational but a priori and relevant to deep structural aspects of the world. In any case, the relevant notion of analyticity has lost its central place in philosophical discussion. Quine's attack, somewhat against his own proclivities, reopened a path to traditional metaphysical and epistemological questions about "first principles" – a path to the traditional fundamental questions of philosophy. The positivists did not succeed in placing any questions – least of all those about their own two first principles – off limits from rational inquiry.

Quine argued against another notion called "analyticity," with no indication that it was distinct from the first. In this second sense, a statement is "analytic" (henceforth "*analytic-2*") if it is derivable from logic together with definitions.[11] Analyticity-2 is by itself clearly of no use to empiricism or to attempts to end traditional philosophy, for it is completely neutral on the metaphysical and epistemologial status of logical truth and definitions. The two notions were run together by many philosophers because of an assumption, common since Kant, that logic and definitions are vacuously true. Frege and Russell (not to speak of Aristotle and Leibniz) preceded Quine in rejecting this assumption.[12]

Quine ran together the two notions of analyticity for a different reason. He thought that both are useless. His complaint against analyticity-2 was that it has no clear explanatory value, and that all attempts to explicate the relevant notion of definition utilize notions that are equally useless. The key notion in explaining definitions was synonymy or sameness of meaning. Expanding on points about definitions mentioned earlier, Quine maintained that there is no explanatorily useful distinction between ordinary theoretical postulates and statements that give the meaning of terms, or between attributions of changes of meaning and attributions of changes of belief. Thus Quine proposed a general skepticism about the use of the notion of meaning itself.

The criticisms of analyticity-2 were more widely disputed than those of analyticity. I think them far less successful. But because of Quine's skepticism about the very notion of meaning, the issue over whether a notion of meaning could be clarified replaced the question of whether analyticity could be defended as the focus of discussion. Partly because clarifying the notions of meaning and logic sufficed for defending analyticity-2, this latter notion tended to obscure analyticity in the debate.

Many philosophers maintained that Quine's demands for a clarifying explication of the distinction were misplaced. They held that a distinction could be grounded in a practice rather than a principle – that the existence of a practice of explaining meaning, or giving dictionary definitions, gave credence to there being some distinction between meaning explication, or synonymy, and ordinary theoretical postulates.[13] Defenders of analyticity-2 commonly held that definitions or meaning explications could not turn out false. In this, I believe they were mistaken. But in their claims that there is a tenable distinction between explications of meaning and (other) theoretical postulates, defenders of analyticity-2 seem to me to be on stronger ground. Quine held, in effect, that a practice without a principle could not be justified. Moreover, he doubted that the distinctions that his opponents were pointing to need be explained by utilizing any notion of meaning.[14]

This dispute reflected a deeper division over ordinary practice. The division affected both linguistic and philosophical method. The positivist movement, influenced by Frege through Russell, Carnap, and Wittgenstein, had propagated the view that the study of linguistic meaning was the proper starting point for philosophy.[15] Language and meaning were supposed to elicit initial agreement better than other traditional starting points, such as the nature of concepts, or first metaphysical and epistemological principles. By the 1950s the linguistic turn had taken hold. It was filtered through two very different traditions.

One of these traditions derived from Frege's attempt to find a perfect language to express the structure of mathematics. This approach was taken up by the positivists, Russell, Wittgenstein, and eventually Quine. Frege's concern with mathematics was broadened by others to include all of science. The underlying idea was that though language was a reasonable focus for philosophy, it had to be understood in the light of reforms needed for scientific purposes.

The other tradition derived from G. E. Moore's insistence on the primacy of ordinary judgments and practices in dealing with philosophical problems. In Moore's ethical and epistemological writings, examples were given more weight than theory; and ordinary judgments were accorded priority over philosophical principles. Moore's emphases were taken up and applied to linguistic practice in Wittgenstein's highly original later work. In the late 1940s and the 1950s, before and after the publication of *Philosophical Investigations* (1953), concentration on the details and nuances of everyday linguistic practice became the watchword of "ordinary-language philosophy."[16] Proponents of this approach tended to assume that the wisdom of centuries was embedded in ordinary practices. Philosophical problems were seen to be either solvable or dissolvable by reference to ordinary practice.

Thus, both traditions took philosophy of language as the starting point for doing philosophy. In the 1950s both tended to be contemptuous of philosophy's past. But the tradition deriving from Frege took science, logic, or mathematics as the source of inspiration for linguistic and philosophical investigation, whereas the tradition deriving from Moore took ordinary practice as the touchstone for linguistic and philosophical judgment. The former tradition distrusted intuition and championed theory. The latter distrusted principles and championed examples.[17]

As approaches to understanding language and as starting points for doing philosophy, each tradition had its weaknesses. In both cases, impatience with standard philosophical problems led to attempts at quick fixes that in retrospect seem shallow.

The ordinary-language tradition produced some brilliant linguistic observation. It provided new tools for dealing with philosophical problems, and a sensitivity to linguistic distinctions. But as a philosophical method, it faced numerous difficulties, never adequately dealt with, in deriving philosophical conclusions from linguistic examples.[18]

As a way of understanding language, the tradition tended to be anecdotal, and its legacy of specific contributions is rather thin. Only a few works made durable contributions to linguistic understanding. Austin produced a taxonomy of speech acts (acts like asserting, promising, commanding) that embedded them in a larger view of human action. The taxonomy became a starting point for much work on pragmatics. Some of Strawson's early work on the speech act of referring and on presupposition bore fruit.[19] The tradition's primary contribution to the philosophy of language, its focus on details of usage, yielded better results when it later allied itself with systematic theory.

Influenced by the spectacular development of logic since Frege, the logical-constructionist tradition aimed at clarifying philosophical problems by formulating them in a precise logical system. Where ordinary notions were indefinite or vague, they were to be replaced by more precise analogues. The pressure to state precise rules of inference uncovered a vast array of distinctions. Logic itself may be regarded as a clarification of ordinary logical concepts. Logical constructionism yielded some notable early successes in producing new logics – particularly in the analysis of necessity and of temporal notions.[20]

As a philosophical method, however, it was limited by a tendency to assume that philosophical problems would disappear if they were replaced by logical problems or problems in constructing a scientific language. Many philosophical problems arise in nonscientific discourse and cannot be solved by laying down rules for the use of notions in a science. Even most of those problems closely related to the sciences are not solved merely by clarifying logical relations.

As an approach to understanding language, the tradition's method of replacement was calculated to ignore certain aspects of language use as detrimental to scientific purposes. Thus, vagueness, ambiguity, indexicality, singular reference, implicature, intensionality, and so on were ignored (by one writer or another) because of preconceptions about well-behaved logical systems or about the needs of science.

Frege's influence on the logical-constructionist tradition has already been mentioned. One of the most important developments in the 1950s was the upsurge of interest in Frege's own work, particularly his essays in the philosophy of language. Frege's name had been kept alive by Russell, Carnap, and Wittgenstein in the early part of the century, and by Church, Carnap, and Quine in the 1940s and early 1950s. But what provoked widespread consideration of his work was the publication in 1952 of *Translations of the Philosophical Writings of Gottlob Frege*, edited and translated by Geach and Black. Belatedly, during the 1950s, Frege came to be widely recognized as the father of twentieth-century philosophy.[21]

The philosophy of language became a vibrant, semi-autonomous discipline in the 1960s and early 1970s. In fact, it was considered by many to be the new "first philosophy."[22] The subject came of age, in my judgment, out of four primary sources. One was Frege's great influence and example. Another was the combination of the strong points of ordinary-language philosophy and logical constructionism: logical theory was brought to bear on ordinary language, with the aim of understanding it rather than reforming it. A third was the need to interpret the failure of the positivists' verificationist principle. And a fourth was a revival of traditional issues about singular reference. These sources fed discussion of three main problem areas: issues associated with logical form, issues associated with meaning, and issues associated with reference.

Frege's work was seminal in the discussion of all three problem areas. Each of the remaining three sources was primary for one of the three problem areas. I shall briefly mention some of Frege's contributions to the philosophy of language. Then I shall say something about the other sources of stimulation.

Frege made the first deep advance on the logic of Aristotle when in 1879 he stated the syntax and semantics for propositional calculus and first-and second-order quantificational logic. This work laid the groundwork for one of the great intellectual developments of the century – that of mathematical logic. This development gave philosophy a range of new problems and a new framework for discussing old ones. Influenced by Frege's work, as filtered through Russell and Wittgenstein, the development of formal semantics by Gödel, Tarski, Church, Carnap, and others in the 1930s and 1940s became the cornerstone for attempts in the 1960s and 1970s to provide an account of the truth conditions, logical form, and compositional structure of natural languages. Frege pioneered a method of finding logical form in natural languages by providing structures to account for actual inferences. His semantical explications of various linguistic constructions became both examples of how to theorize about language and contenders among competing accounts.

Frege also gave an argument for distinguishing between two semantical notions – sense and reference. The argument is so profound, despite its surface simplicity, that it has become a reference point for philosophical discussion of language and mind. He observed that a statement that Hesperus is Phosphorus has a different cognitive value from a statement that Hesperus is Hesperus. The one is potentially informative where the other is not. Since the referents of the component expressions of the two statements are the same, he located the difference in a difference in the sense, or cognitive value, expressed by the names "Hesperus" and "Phosphorus." Theoretical development and explication of the notions of reference and sense became fundamental problems for the philosophy of language.[23]

A second source of the flowering of the philosophy of language was a cross-pollination of the interests of ordinary-language philosophy with the methods of logical constructionism. Strawson and Quine provided a start at unifying these traditions. Trained in an environment that took ordinary language seriously, Strawson did significant work in the 1950s and early 1960s on referring, truth value gaps, and presupposition. He attempted to broaden the scope of logic to deal with insights derived from the ordinary-language tradition.[24]

Quine continued the logical-constructionist tradition. He aimed at providing a language adequate for the purposes of science. In *Word and Object*, a work of enormous influence, Quine argued that science could be formalized in first-order quantificational logic (without constant singular terms) together with set theory.[25] In carrying out this argument, Quine discussed a wide variety of linguistic constructions and showed a remarkable sensitivity to inferential patterns associated with them. Even where he ended by dismissing a possible account as useless to science, he frequently made it attractive to others whose purposes were less reformist.

Quine's *Word and Object* also influenced philosophical method. His ontological preoccupations indicated to many how philosophy of language could provide a framework for discussing traditional issues in metaphysics. Quine had advocated the view that a theory was committed to the existence of some sort of entity just in case entities of that sort had to be regarded as values of bound variables in irreducibly basic assertions of the theory.[26] In *Word and Object*, Quine (intentionally) blurred the distinction between language and theory. He then made natural assumptions about what sentences were true, considered various ways of paraphrasing or reducing those sentences into others with more perspicuous logical forms, and finally used the logical forms as bases for discussing pros and cons of admitting the existence of various sorts of entity – properties, stuffs, events, propositions, sets, numbers, mental states, sensations, physical objects, and so on. Quine advocated a broadly materialist position that was tempered by a reluctant platonism about sets. Quine's materialism was not new. But his defense of it in the context of a systematic investigation of language and logical form lent it new interest. Partly because of *Word and Object*, ontological issues became the dominant preoccupation of metaphysics, including the philosophy of mind, in the two decades that followed.

The approach to language through a study of logical form, illustrated in Frege's and Quine's work, was taken up and made prominent by Davidson. Davidson relinquished Quine's aim of reforming language and proposed a particular formal framework – that of giving a finitely axiomatized Tarskian truth theory – for displaying the logical form and "meaning" of natural language sentences. The question of in what sense Davidson's truth theories illuminate meaning is a complex and controversial one. But the contributions of his approach (and more generally of approaches that utilize classical logic) to studies of logical form are, I think, substantial and lasting.[27] Other philosophers proposed various types of intensional logic in the analysis of logical form.[28] Some of this work on logical form was conducted as applied logic. Some of it was directed to clarifying traditional philosophical investigations. Either way, much of it exemplifies high standards of creativity and argument.

The rise of generative linguistics coincided with the flowering of the philosophy of language.[29] In retrospect it is striking how little the two disciplines influenced one another in the 1960s. There were some significant exchanges about the sense in which one knows a language, about innate ideas, and about the proper subject matter of linguistics. There is no question that linguists were influenced by the methods of logic, and that philosophers were influenced by the notion of a level of language – then called "deep structure" – that is not immediately evident to ordinary speakers. But Chomsky's early emphasis on the relative purity of syntax matched poorly with philosophers' preoccupation with semantic and pragmatic issues. As linguistics took a more systematic interest in semantics and pragmatics in the early to mid 1970s (largely in response to philosophy), however, the two subjects began to come together. Much of the earlier work by philosophers on logical form has since been assimilated and modified within linguistics. This development surely counts as one of the successes of philosophy, in its traditional role as midwife to the sciences.

A third source of stimulation for the philosophy of language was the need to assimilate the failure of the verificationist principle. This source led to intense discussion of the form and prospects of a "theory of meaning." The discussion is so complex that glossing it without being misleading is impossible in a paper such as this one. I shall just mention a few strands of the discussion.

I noted that Quine criticized the verificationist principle by claiming that methods of confirmation cannot be associated with individual sentences. Roughly speaking, Quine accepted the positivist assumption that meaning is, if anything, a method of confirmation. But in view of the holistic nature of confirmation – the inability to associate confirmation with particular, definite linguistic sentential units – and the seeming impossibility of giving a general account of how disconfirmatory experiences lead one to revise theory, he concluded that there could be no theory of meaning. Indeed, he thought that the very notion of meaning had no place in a true account of the world. Even many who doubted Quine's radical skepticism about the cognitive value of the notion of meaning found this holism about meaning persuasive, and a source of doubt about a general theory of meaning. Some philosophers, like Dummett, accepted the verificationism and sought to limit the holism to scientific theory. He held that meaning in ordinary, nonscientific discourse was dependent on more atomistic criteria for applying terms. Others, like Putnam, rejected the verificationism but accepted a version of holism because of the variety of considerations that enter into determining constancy of meaning through changes of belief. Still others thought that the holism was restricted by considerations from the theory of reference, which I will discuss below.

Quine extended his criticism of the notion of meaning into arguments for the indeterminacy of translation.[30] He held that in any case in which one translates a natural language, there will be many equally ideal overall translations of the language which are so different that one translates a given sentence S into a true sentence while another translates S into a false sentence. Quine provided two sorts of argument for this position. One began with the claim that physical theory is underdetermined by all possible evidential considerations – so that two equally good but incompatible physical theories could be ideally but equally well justified. He then attempted to show that translation would be indeterminate even when one of these physical theories was fixed. Quine concluded that since physical theory is the proper standard for objective reality, translation does not concern anything definite that is objectively real. Quine's other argument took up Carnap's attempt to show that attributions of meaning (and analyticity) have an empirical basis. He provided a detailed theory of the method of translation. In this theory he attempted to show that our evidence for translation is too sparse even to underwrite determinate translations for terms that are ostensibly about ordinary macrophysical objects, like "rabbit."

Quine's thesis about translation was of profound philosophical value in that it opened a new area of philosophical discussion. His second argument stimulated discussion of the evidence and methods for interpreting such linguistically basic phenomena as assent, the logical connectives, observation terms. But his conclusion has not found wide support. The evidence Quine allows for translation in the second argument has been widely thought to be unduly restrictive. And the claim of the first argument (which informs the second as well) that the relevant sort of indeterminacy of translation relative to physical theory – i.e., physics, chemistry, biology, behavioral psychology, but not cognitive psychology or linguistics – would be damning to the cognitive status of translation has seemed to many to be unconvincing.[31]

Davidson's proposal that a Tarskian theory of truth provide the form for a theory of meaning provoked intense debate in North America and England.[32] As I have mentioned, the most stable result of this proposal was the work on logical form that it occasioned. The idea that a theory of truth simply is a theory of meaning has been widely disputed. Tarski's theory depends on a translation from the language for which the theory of truth is given to the language in which the theory is given. Many thought that unless one provided a theory of this translation, one would not have provided a *theory* of meaning. Davidson made some plausible suggestions for liberalizing Quine's strictures on translation. But the main theoretical upshot of his proposal was the idea that meanings are truth conditions – requirements whose fulfillment would constitute the truth of a sentence or proposition. Such truth conditions were to be systematically and informatively displayed in a theory of truth. Even though his idea captures relatively little of what many philosophers wanted in a theory of meaning, it does develop one major strand, initiated by Frege, in the notion of meaning – the idea that meanings, in one sense, are truth conditions. And it provided a systematic way of displaying deep inferential relations among truth conditions. Davidson held that this was as much system as one could hope for in a "theory" of meaning.

Influenced by mathematical intuitionism and by Wittgenstein, Dummett criticized the view that meaning should be understood in terms of truth conditions. He took proof rather than truth as a paradigm of linguistic "use," which he considered the basic notion in understanding meaning. He claimed that meaning could not "transcend" the conditions under which linguistic understanding could be put to use and manifested. Sentences outside of science were associated with criteria of application, useful in communication.[33] Dummett used these ideas in discussing a wide variety of profound metaphysical issues, which are outside the scope of this essay. Dummett's approach to meaning, though rich and deeply provocative, has not been widely accepted, partly because of its "anti-realist" metaphysical associations, partly because it has been seen by many as a recrudescence of verificationism. Understanding relations between confirmation, or use, and truth conditions remains, however, a complex and fundamental matter.

Concerned more with what makes expressions meaningful than with the structure of a language, Grice attempted to analyze linguistic meaning in terms of a special sort of communicative intention. He claimed that linguistic meaning is to be understood in terms of what a person means by an utterance. And this latter sort of meaning is to be understood in terms of the person's intending the utterance to produce some effect in an audience by means of the recognition of this intention. The linguistic meaning of the utterance is roughly the content of the intention.[34] Thus, certain mental states were taken to be analytically basic to understanding language. Mental states do appear to predate language. But it is difficult to see how some of our more sophisticated thoughts would be possible without language, or independent of language for their individuation. This issue about the relation between mind and language is extremely complex, and in need of further exploration.

Grice contributed another idea to the understanding of meaning. He pointed out that it is not always easy to distinguish between the linguistic meaning of an utterance and various contextual suggestions that might be associated with the meaning of the utterance – what Grice called "conversational implicatures." Grice produced an impressive theory of implicature that has been developed by linguists and philosophers.[35]

The fourth source of stimulation to the philosophy of language was major shift in the theory of reference. Frege had made some remarks that suggested that the reference of a proper name is fixed by definite descriptions that a speaker associates with the name. Thus the name "Aristotle" would have as its referent whatever satisfied a definite description like "the pupil of Plato and teacher of Alexander the Great." (Frege did not try to eliminate names from the descriptions.) Russell purified and generalized this sort of view. He claimed that reference could rest either on acquaintance – an immediate, infallible, complete knowledge of an object – or on description. Russell came to think that acquaintance was associated only with the expressions "I," "this" (as applied to a sense datum), and perhaps "now." All other instances of apparent singular reference, including reference with proper names and most demonstrative expressions, were based on description.[36]

This view of reference was questioned by Wittgenstein and in subsequent work by Searle and Strawson.[37] Searle and Strawson suggested that the reference of proper names was fixed by a cluster of descriptions associated with the name by a community of speakers. The effect of this suggestion was twofold. It loosened the relation between the reference of names and any one associated definite description. And it portrayed reference as dependent on more than descriptions in the mental repertoire of the speaker. Reference depended partly on the speaker's relations to others in the community.

These suggestions were radicalized in such a way as to produce a completely different picture of reference. In 1966 Donnellan pointed out that there is a use even of definite descriptions in which their meaning – the conditions laid down by the definite descriptions – does not fix the referent (or at any rate, *a* referent relevant to understanding the speaker). For example, a person can use the definite description "the man drinking the martini" to refer to a woman across the room who is sipping a soft drink.[38] Here the person picked out by the speaker seems partly independent of the description that the speaker associates with his act of reference.

The decisive further move was made in 1970 by Kripke and Donnellan, independently of one another. They produced a series of examples that indicated that the referents of proper names are in many cases not fixed by any set of descriptions the speaker associates with the name – or even by descriptions associated with the name by members of the speaker's community.[39] To use of Kripke's examples, "Jonah" might refer to a definite prophet, even though much of the descriptive material associated with the name is false, and even if not enough were known about the relevant historical figure to describe him in such a way as to distinguish him from all other historical figures. The speaker's whole community of contemporaries might be ignorant. Yet the name might still have a definite referent.

Implicit in the examples was a positive account of how the reference of names is fixed. The reference seemed to depend on relations between the speaker and his social and physical environments that are best understood not by investigating the speaker's mental repertoire but by inquiring into the chain of circumstances that led to the speaker's acquisition or present use of the name. These relations involve a mix of causal and intentional elements and include a person's reliance on others to fix a referent. Kripke sketched a picture according to which there was an initial dubbing or baptism, followed by a chain of uses of the name that are presumed by the users to maintain the referents of uses by those from whom they acquired the name. Such a chain of uses might maintain a referent even if descriptions associated with the name changed or became distorted. The conditions under which the chain maintains an initial referent, or changes to a new one, were subsequently found to be quite complicated.[40] But the rough shape of the account has come to be widely accepted.

Kripke embedded his account of names in a theory of necessity. He counted names "rigid designators" – expressions that maintained a certain constancy of reference through variation in the possible worlds by reference to which modal sentences might be evaluated. This theory revived a number of traditional questions about essence and necessity, which are outside the scope of this paper. In its enrichment of metaphysics as well as philosophy of language, however, Kripke's *Naming and Necessity* is a major landmark of the period.

Kripke and Putnam, independently, provided examples for thinking that natural kind terms are, like proper names, dependent for their referents not on a set of associated descriptions but on complex relations to the environment.[41] Putnam also sketched an approach to understanding the meaning of natural kind terms that was based on accounting for the fact that we can successfully explain to someone in short order how to use many common nouns. He proposed that the "meaning" of a term be conceived as a combination of the referent of the term with what he called a stereotype. The stereotype need not be complete enough to fix the referent by itself. It might even be untrue of the referent. Its role is to help another person in a given community to get on to the referent. This sketch has a number of problems. But it seems to me to be valuable in its attempt to explicate the success of dictionaries and other short, purpose-dependent explanations of meaning in our ordinary lives.

The main upshot of these papers on reference has been to portray reference as dependent on more than the beliefs, inferences, and discriminatory powers of the individual. Reference seems to depend on chains of acquisition and on the actual nature of the environment, not purely on the beliefs and discriminative abilities of the person doing the referring. This result suggests that reference cannot be reduced to psychological states of individuals, unless these states are themselves individuated partly in terms of the individual's relations to his community and/or physical environment.

Some philosophers have maintained that there is nothing more to the "meaning" or semantical value of certain expressions – for example, proper names and demonstratives – than their referents. Such expressions are counted "directly referential." Others have held that such expressions express a Fregean sense that indicates a unique referent, but that is not easily paraphrased in language. Yet others maintain an intermediate view.[42]

The terms of this dispute are, in my opinion, often less clear than they might be. Many of the differences hinge on what is to be meant by "meaning" or "semantics." Insofar as one sees these notions as applying to some communally common mastery of what is said – some idealized common denominator of understanding – then the direct reference views have substantial plausibility, at least as applied to some linguistic contexts. Insofar as one follows Frege in seeing these notions as applying to intentional cognitive content, something that individuals are expressing in thought in the use of these expressions, the direct reference views are inapplicable. Problems in this area, including several that survive clarification of the objectives of "semantics," remain a source of ferment.

Looking back over the last 30 years, I find the results on reference and some of those on logical from more substantial and durable than the results in the theory of meaning. The torrent of talk about a *theory* of meaning has even come to seem a bit naive. All the approaches to meaning seem to have some merit in bringing to light some aspect of the complex notion. The metadiscussion of what might be involved in a theory of meaning has been of genuine philosophical interest. But nothing that could be called a theory has elicited much agreement or shown many of the other sociological symptoms of systematic theoretical knowledge. It may be that the problem is too complex and simply needs more time. Or it may be that Quine (and implicitly Davidson) is right that a theory of meaning in anything like the accepted sense is not possible. Philosophers of language who have worked on meaning have usually wanted – and even presumed that they must have – a theory that reduces meaning to something more basic or scientifically "respectable." They have wanted a theory that explains what meaning is in other terms. But the notion may not be suitable to such explanation or reduction. It may be too multifaceted. There may be no general notion of meaning that will serve as explanadum. Various associated subnotions may be more suitable. Or the notion(s) of meaning may be too basic – so that a theory *of* meaning may be less appropriate than theories that make use of various notions of meaning.

However this may be, it seems unlikely that cognitive psychology and linguistics – much less philosophy and ordinary discourse – will do without some conception(s) of meaning. Some notion of intentional content is needed to talk about propositional attitudes. And the linguistic practices of paraphrase and semantical explication are too regular to make it credible that they are without cognitive import. The idea that there is something cognitively suspect about the notion of meaning – an idea that has been made common by Quine's doubts during the last 40 years – seems to me difficult to support. There are many such notions in ordinary life that do not enter into general laws of the sort found in the natural sciences. It would be absurd to suggest that all such notions are cognitively disreputable. Nevertheless, extreme care is required in the use of notions of meaning. Such notions will probably remain a topic of philosophical discussion for the foreseeable future.

Gradually but unmistakably, in the latter part of the 1970s, the philosophy of language lost its place as the dominant starting point for philosophical activity. No other area of philosophy assumed quite the status that the philosphy of language had had since the 1950s. But the degree of interest in relatively "pure" philosophy of language has certainly diminished. Moreover, there has been a perceptible shift of ferment toward issues in the philosophy of mind.

Some reasons for this change are internal to the subject. The discussions of meaning by Quine and Grice showed that there is a systematic interplay between meaning and propositional attitudes, like belief and intention. Although most discussion of language made some reference to this relation, there had been little concentrated reflection on the propositional attitudes. Therefore, dialectical pressure built toward a shift to the philosophy of mind.

Another internal reason was that some of the most difficult and persistent specific problems within the philosophy of language – accounting for Frege's puzzle about Hesperus and Phosphorus in the light of the new theory of reference, accounting for the cognitive value of demonstratives, giving an account of the truth conditions and logical form of sentences about propositional attitudes, explicating *de re* belief – all pointed toward the philosophy of mind.

A broader internal reason is that the philosophy of language seemed to have exhausted some of its promise in illuminating traditional philosophical questions, the questions that drew most philosophers into the subject. The original hope – among the positivists and among postpositivist philosophers of language – was that by clarifying issues about language, philosophy would put itself on a firmer footing for understanding the larger traditional problems. There is no simple account of how much of this hope was fulfilled. The philosophy of language improved methods of argument and sensitivity to relevant distinctions. It opened up perspectives on traditional issues that are new and worthwhile. And at least as regards the theory of reference, it laid the groundwork for a very different conception of many traditional issues. But by the late 1970s or early 1980s philosphy of language no longer seemed the obvious propaedeutic for dealing with central philosophical problems.

As I have intimated, one ground for this shift was that many philosophers felt that philosophy of language had done its job – that the natural development of philosophical reasoning led into the philosophy of mind, or other adjacent areas. Another ground was that some of the discussions, particularly of the theory of meaning and of what "semantics" should or should not do, seemed to be at impasses. There has been a paucity of important, large, new philosophical ideas in the subdiscipline for over a decade.

A further ground lay in the increasing specialization of the philosophy of language. One product of success was the development of a vocabulary and set of problems that had lives of their own – not directly dependent on issues in the rest of philosophy. Much of the work on logical form has passed into linguistics. Some of the work in the semantics of reference and on the (disputed) border between semantics and pragmatics seemed to gain in precision and systematic power by making idealizations that ruled many difficult philosophical problems out of court. This is sometimes the method of a successful science. But it reduces the motivation to study the philosophy of language for larger philosophical rewards.

An external reason for the shift was the rise of the computer paradigm in psychology, and the appearance of intellectually substantial findings in psychology that had apparent significance for philosophical problems.

I want now to sketch some of the main developments in the philosophy of mind since the 1950s.

Behaviorism dominated psychology during approximately the same period as logical positivism dominated philosophy. The principles of behaviorism are less easily stated than those of logical positivism. It is perhaps better seen as a method that eschewed use of mentalistic vocabulary in favor of terms that made reference to dispositions to behavior. Both movements aimed at banishing nonscientific speculation, and forcing theory to hew as closely as possible to methods of confirmation. Both methodological doctrines came to be seen as restrictive, even on the practice of science.

Behaviorism had a run of influence within philosophy. It was a favored view of some of the later positivists. They made use of the verificationist principle to attempt to dissolve the mind–body problem and the problem of other minds, declaring these problems meaningless. And they appealed to behavioral analyses of mentalistic terms as a way of maintaining strict experimental control on mentalistic language. The simplistic picture of confirmation associated with the verificationist principle, a picture that ignored the role of auxiliary hypotheses, paralleled and abetted the behaviorist blindness to the role of background assumptions in mentalistic attributions. As we shall see, this blindness led to the collapse of behaviorism. In postwar, postpositivistic philosophy, the early logical constructionists thought that behavioristic language was the most suitable way to "reconstruct" mentalistic language in scientific terms. Ordinary-language philosophers purported to find behavioristic underpinnings for ordinary language. Behaviorism influenced positivistic construals of psychology, Quine's theory of the indeterminacy of translation, Ryle's work on the concept of mind, and Malcolm's explications of discourse about dreaming and sensations.[43] These philosophers shared a tendency to think that theorizing in psychology or philosophy of mind should dispense with mentalistic vocabulary, or interpret it in nonmentalistic terms, as far as possible. They thought that such vocabulary should be largely replaced with talk about stimulations and about dispositions to behavior. Some philosophers thought that ordinary mentalistic terms could be defined or adequately explicated (for any cognitively respectable purpose) in these latter terms. Others thought that ordinary mentalistic terms were hopelessly unscientific or philosophically misleading, so no real explication was possible.

The demise of behaviorism in philosophy is less easily attributed to a few decisive events than is the fall of logical positivism. There was a series of influential criticisms of behaviorism beginning in the late 1950s and extending on for a decade.[44] The main cause of the shift seemed, however, to be a gradually developed sense that behaviorist methods were unduly restrictive and theoretically unfruitful. A similar development was unfolding within psychology, linguistics, and computer science, with an array of nonbehaviorist articles in the late 1950s and early 1960s.[45]

The attempts to provide behavioristic *explications* of mentalistic terms fell prey to various instances of a single problem. The behavioristic explications succeeded only on the implicit assumption that the individual had certain background beliefs or wants. As a crude illustration, consider an explication of belief as a disposition to assert. Even ignoring the fact that "assert" is not a behavioral notion, but presupposes assumptions about mind and meaning, the analysis could work only with the proviso that the subject wants to express his beliefs and knows what they are. Eliminating these mentalistic background assumptions proved an impossible task, given behaviorist methodological strictures. The problem, stated less methodologically, is that mental causes typically have their behavioral effects only because of their interactions with one another.

As behaviorism slipped from prominence in philosophy in the 1950s and early 1960s, it left two heirs, which gradually formed an uneasy alliance. One of these heirs was naturalism. The other was functionalism.

A doctrine I will call "naturalism" (and sometimes called "physicalism") emerged first as a distinctive point of view in the philosophy of mind in the early 1950s. This view maintains two tenets. One is that there are no mental states, properties, events, objects, sensations over and above ordinary physical entities, entities identifiable in the physical sciences, or entities that common sense would regard as physical. The formulation's vague expression "over and above" matches the doctrine's vagueness: the doctrine does not entail an identity theory in ontology. It does require some sort of materialism about the mind. Naturalism coupled this ontological position with an ideological or methodological demand. It demanded that mentalistic discourse be reduced, explained, or eliminated in favor of discourse that is "acceptable," or on some views already found, in the natural or physical sciences. Thus, we find repeated calls for "explaining" rationality or intentionality. In its materialism, naturalism emphasized ontology in a way that behaviorism did not. Its ideological program, however, continued the behaviorist attempt to make psychology and philosophy of mind more scientific by limiting the supposed excesses of mentalism.

As I have noted, many of the later logical positivists were naturalists. But issues about mind tended to be submerged in the general positivist program. The mind–body problem began to receive direct attention from a naturalistic point of view in articles by Quine, Place, and Smart, in the 1950s.[46] Place and Smart tried to identify mental states and events – primarily sensations and afterimages – with physical states and events. Smart thought that one could identify types of sensation in a "topic-neutral" way that would leave it open whether they were physical; he then predicted that each type of sensation would turn out to be a neural state of some kind. For example, he paraphrased "I am having an afterimage of an orange" as "I am in a state like the one I am in when I am seeing an orange." He thought that this translation would overcome any conceptual obstacles to identifying mental states with physical states. It would sidestep, for example, issues about the qualitative properties of afterimages. Science was supposed to settle the mind–body problem empirically – in favor of what came to be know as *type–type identity theory*, or *central state materialism*.

During the mid to late 1960s materialism became one of the few orthodoxies in American philosophy. It is difficult to say why this happened. No single argument obtained widespread acceptance. Perhaps the success in biochemistry during the 1950s in providing some sense of the chemical underpinnings of biological facts encouraged the expectation that eventually mental facts would receive a similar explication in neural terms. Moreover, there were some spectacular advances in animal neurophysiology during the period.[47] Perhaps the attempts of the positivists and behaviorists to make philosophy scientific had as a natural outgrowth the view that philosophical problems would eventually be solved by progress in the natural sciences – with the help of analytical clarification by philosophers. In any case, several philosophers in the 1960s defended either some form of the type–type identity theory or some form of eliminationism (the view that mentalistic talk and mental entities would eventually lose their place in our attempts to describe and explain the world).[48]

The most influential paper of this period was written several years before: Sellars's "Empiricism and the Philosophy of Mind" (1956). The article is a grand attempt to portray mental episodes as explanatory posits that hold a place in our conceptual scheme by virtue of their explanatory usefulness.[49] Sellars tried to undermine the view that knowledge of one's own mental events was intrinsically privileged or posed an obstacle to the empirical discovery that mental events are neural events. Although in my view the argumentation in this paper is not satisfyingly clear or convincing, the picture it paints of the status of mentalistic discourse is profoundly conceived.

Whereas materialism became widely accepted during the 1960s, issues surrounding naturalism's ideological demand remained intensely controversial. Putnam raised a serious objection to type–type identity theories of the sort that Smart had made popular. He suggested that it is implausible that a sensation like pain is identical with a single neural state in all the many organisms that feel pain, in view of their enormously varied physiologies. He also pointed out that it is even more implausible to think that any given type of thought – for example, a thought that thrice three is nine or a thought that one's present situation is dangerous – is realized by the same physical state in every being that thinks it. Not only the probable existence of extraterrestrials, the variety of higher animals, and the possibility of thinking robots (a possibility most materialists were eager to defend), but the plasticity of the brain seemed to make the type–type identity theory untenable.[50] Mental states seemed "multirealizable." Materialism maintained its dominance, but needed a new form. Putman's observation seemed to show that if mentalistic discourse was to be explicated in "scientifically acceptable" terms, the terms would have to be more abstract than neural terms.

Respones to Putnam's observation led to a more specific materialist orthodoxy. The response proceeded on two fronts: ontological and ideological. Most materialists gave up the type–type identity theory in favor of an ontology that came to be known as the token identity theory. Although a mental state kind or event kind was not identified with any one physical (neural) kind, each instance of a mental state and each particular mental event token was held to be identical with some instance of a physical state or with some physical event token. This claim allowed that the occurrence of a thought that thrice three is nine could be identical with the occurrence of one sort of physical event in one person, whereas a different occurrence of the same kind of thought could be identical with the occurrence of a different sort of physical event in another person.

Although this ontological position is still widely maintained, no one argument for it has gained wide acceptance. The commonest consideration adduced in its favor is its supposed virtue in simplifying our understanding of mind–body causation. Davidson gave a profound but controversial a priori argument along these lines.[51] He held, first, that there are causal relations between mental and physical events; second, that causal relations between events must be backed by laws of a complete, closed system of explanation ("backed" in the sense that the predicates of the laws must be true of the events that are causally related); third, that there are no psychophysical or purely mentalistic laws that form a complete, closed system of explanation. He concluded that since there can be no psychophysical or mentalistic laws that would provide the relevant backing for the causal relations between mental and physical events, there must be purely physical laws that back such relations. This is to say that physical predicates apply to mental events – that mental events are physical.

Davidson has not been ideally clear or constant in formulating and arguing for the third premise. But given the conception of "complete, closed system" that he usually adverts to, this premise seems plausible. The second premise is more doubtful. I do not think it a priori true, or even clearly a heuristic principle of science or reason, that causal relations must be backed by any particular kind of law. I think that we learn the nature and scope of laws (and the variety of sorts of "law") that back causal relations through empirical investigation. It is not clear that psychophysical counterfactual generalizations – or nonstrict "laws" – cannot alone "back" psychophysical causal relations.

Most philosophers accepted the token identity theory as the simplest account that both reconciled materialism with multirealizability and raised no metaphysical issues about mind–body causation. Insofar as the view rests on the hope of finding empirical correlations between types that would inductively support token identities, however, it seems highly speculative. Some philosophers adopted an even more liberal materialism. They held, roughly, that although an instance of a mental event kind may not be an instance of a physical natural kind, they are always *constituted* of events that are instances of physical natural kinds.[52]

In any case, materialism in one form or another has widespread support among North American philosophers, largely on grounds of its supposed virtues in interpreting causation between mental and physical events. There is a vague sense abroad that alternatives amount to superstition. One common idea is that there is some intrinsic mystery in seeing mental events, imagined as nonphysical, as interacting with physical events. Descartes thought this too; and perhaps there was some plausibility to it, given his conceptions of mental and physical substance. But Cartesian conceptions of substance are not at issue nowadays, and the exact nature of the problem in its modern form needs clearer articulation than it is usually given.

A better-reasoned argument along these lines goes as follows. Macrophysical effects depend on prior macrophysical states or events according to approximately deterministic patterns described by physical laws. Mental causes often give rise to physical movements of human bodies. If such causation did not consist in physical processes, it would yield departures from the approximately deterministic patterns described by physical laws. It would interfere with, disrupt, alter, or otherwise "make a difference" in the physical outcomes. But there is no reason to think that this occurs. Physical antecedent states seem to suffice for the physical effects. Appeal to mentalistic causation that does not consist in physical causation appears, on this reasoning, to invoke physically ungrounded causation that requires us to doubt the adequacy of current forms of physical explanation, even within the physical realm. Not surprisingly, such invocation is widely thought to be unattractive.

This reasoning – and other parallel arguments focusing on the effect of physical processes on mental states – has some force, perhaps enough to nourish materialism indefinitely. But I think that materialism merits more skepticism than it has received in North American philosophy during the last two decades. At any rate, the argument just outlined is not as forceful as it may appear.

Why should mental causes of physical effects interfere with the physical system if they do not *consist in* physical processes? Thinking that they must surely depends heavily on thinking of mental causes on a physical model – as providing an extra "bump" or transfer of energy on the physical effect. In such a context, instances of "overdetermination" – two causes having the same effect – must seem to be aberrations. But whether the physical model of mental causation is appropriate is part of what is at issue. Moreover, the sense in which mental causes must "make a difference" if they do not consist in physical processes is in need of substantial clarification. There are many ways of specifying differences they do make that do not conflict with physical explanations.

It seems to me that we have substantial reason, just from considering mentalistic and physicalistic explanatory goals and practice – before ontology is even considered – to think that mentalistic and physicalistic accounts of causal processes will not interfere with one another. They appeal to common causes (in explaining the physiology and psychology of cognitive processes, for example) and common or at least constitutively related effects (in physiological and psychological explanations of an instance of a man's running to a store, for example). It seems to me perverse, independently of ontological considerations, to assume that these explanations might interfere with one another. They make too few assumptions about one another to allow such an assumption.

There are surely *some* systematic, even necessary, relations between mental events and underlying physical processes. It seems overwhelmingly plausible that mental events depend on physical events in some way or other. But constitution, identity, and physical composition are relations that have specific scientific uses in explaining relations between entities invoked in physical chemistry and biochemistry. These relations so far have no systematic use in nonmetaphysical, scientific theories bridging psychology and neurophysicology. They seem to me to be just one set of possibilities for accounting for relations between entities referred to in these very different explanatory enterprises. Where science does not make clear use of such relations, philosophy should postulate them with some diffidence.

The apparent fact that there are no gaps in physical chains of causation and that mental causes do not disrupt the physical system is perhaps ground for some sort of broad supervenience thesis – no changes in mental states without some sort of change in physical states. But the inference to materialism is, I think, a metaphysical speculation that has come, misleadingly, to seem a relatively obvious scientific-commonsensical bromide.

The issue of mind–body causation is extremely complex and subtle. In recent years, this issue has become an object of intense interest. Much of the discussion concerns "epiphenomenalism."[53] The causal picture that motivates materialism is so firmly entrenched that many philosophers have come to worry that mental "aspects" of events really do not "make a difference": Maybe mental "aspects" or properties are causally inert and just go along for a ride on physical properties of physical events, in something like the way that relations between phenotypal properties of parents and their offspring ride inertly and parasitically on underlying causal relations characterized by the genetic properties of parents and offspring. I think that these worries can be answered, even within a materialist framework. But I think that the very existence of the worries is the main point of philosophical interest. The worry about epiphenomenalism is, in my view, a sign that materialist theories have done a poor job of accounting for the relation between mind–body causal interaction and mentalistic explanation. They have done little to account for the fact that virtually all our knowledge and understanding of the nature and existence of mental causation derives from mentalistic explanations, not from nonintentional functionalist or neurological accounts.[54]

We determine the nature of the causation, and the sort of laws or law-like generalizations that accompany it, by scrutinizing actual explanations in psychology and ordinary discourse. If there turned out to be no clear sense in which mental events fell under predicates that are uncontroversially physical, then it would seem reasonable to count the mental events nonphysical. As far as I can see, there is no reason to be anything but relaxed in the face of this possibility. I see no powerful, clearly articulated reason for worrying about the existence of mind–body causation, or the gaplessness of chains of physical events, if this possibility were realized. What counts in supporting our belief in mind–body causation is the probity of mentalistic explanations. As long as they are informative and fruitful, we can assume that they are relating genuine events, whatever their metaphysical status.

Otherwise put: The theme in naturalism that deserves the status of orthodoxy is not its materialism and not its demand that mentalistic discourse be given some ideologically acceptable underpinning. It is its implicit insitence that one not countenance any form of explanation that will not stand the scrutiny of scientific and other well-established, pragmatically fruitful methods of communal check and testing. (More crudely, it is the opposition to miracles and to postulation of unverified interruptions in chains of causation among physical events.) But the relevant methods are to be drawn from reflection on what works in actual explanantory practice, not from metaphysical or ideological restrictions on these practices. These points are subject to various interpretations. But I think that taking them seriously motivates less confidence in materialist metaphysics than is common in North American philosophy.

I have been discussing ontological responses to Putnam's observation that various kinds of physical state could be, and are, associated with mental states of a given type. The ideological response to Putnam's observation was the development of a new paradigm for indicating how mental states could be given identifications in nonmentalistic terms. Philosophers looked not to neurophysiology but to computer programming as a source of inspiration. Identifying a mental state with some sort of abstract state of a computer appeared to avoid the problems of identifying mental kinds with neural kinds. And unlike the nonreductive forms of token-identity materialism, it promised means of explaining mentalistic notions in other terms, or at least of supplementing and illuminating mentalistic explanation. Most philosophers found the terms of this supplementation compatible with materialism. This new account came to be known as *functionalism*.[55]

The guiding intuition of functionalism was that what entirely determines what kind of state or event a mental state or event is, is its place in a causal or functional network in the mental life of the individual. The original stimulus to this view was a proposed analogy between the mind and a computer program. To specify such a program, one needed to specify possible inputs into the system, the operations that would pass the machine from one state to another, the states that the machine would pass through, and the output of the machine, given each possible input and given the states it was already in. The machine might be either deterministic or probabilistic. On most versions of functionalism, the internal states were to be specified purely in terms of their "place" in the system of input and output – in terms of the possible dependency relations they bore to other states and ultimately to input and output. Input and output were to be specified in nonintentional, nonmentalistic terms. Types of mental state and event were supposed to be determined entirely by the relations of functional dependency within the whole system of input and output.

The notion of determination is subject to three main interpretations. One, the least ambitious and least reductive, claims only that each mental kind supervenes on a place in the functional system, in the sense that the individual would be in a different kind of mental state if and only if he were not in the functional state corresponding to that kind. The other two purport to say what mental kinds "consist in." One version ("analytic functionalism") claims that a functionalist specification of such relations explicates the meaning of mentalistic terms. Another ("scientific functionalism") makes the lesser claim that such a specification gives the true essence of mental kinds, in something like the way that molecular constitution gives the true essence of a natural kind like *water*. Both of these latter two versions claim that functionalist discourse provides the "real explanatory power" latent in mentalistic explanation.[56]

Analytic and scientific functionalism are clearly liberalized heirs to behaviorism. They share with behaviorism the insistence on nonintentional specifications of input (stimulus) and output (response), and the belief that mentalistic explanation is somehow deficient and needs a nonmentalistic underpinning. They also expand on the behaviorist idea that mental states are individuated partly in terms of their relations. Whereas behaviorists focused largely on relations to behavior, functionalists included relations to other mental states, and relations to stimulating input into the system. This is an insight already present in Frege, who claimed that sense is inseparable from a network of inferential capacities.

It has been common to combine functionalism with token-identity materialism. Functionalism was supposed to provide insight into the nature of mental kinds, whereas token-identity materialism provided insight into the nature of mental particulars – into the instantiation of the mental kinds in particular individuals. The computer analogy seemed compelling to many: mentalistic discourse was a sort of gloss on an underlying network functional flowchart, which was ultimately realized in different physical ways in different machines or organisms. Thus neural descriptions were seen as lying at the bottom of a three-level hierarchy of descriptions of the same human subject.

The functionalist position – in its least reductionist garb – was given distinctive form by Fodor. Fodor maintained that the intentional content of propositional attitudes is irreducible via functionalist specifications. But he held that such content is expressed by inner mental representations that have syntactic properties, inner words and sentences that were presumed to be instantiated somehow in the brain. Fodor further claimed that mental representations have their causal roles in virtue of their formal or syntactic properties, and that the input and output of functionalist specifications should be seen as symbols.[57] This picture brought the functionalist tradition into line with a fairly literal interpretation of the computer analogy: psychological explanation was modeled on *proofs* or other types of symbol manipulation by a digital computer. The causal aspects of psychological explanation were to be understood in terms of the physical relations among the particular neural states or events that instantiated the symbolic representations.

Something like this picture had been proposed by Sellars.[58] But Fodor presented his view as an interpretation of work in psycholinguistics and cognitive psychology. To many it gained plausibility because of its appeal to specific scientific practices. The picture and its relation to psychological theory are still very much in dispute.[59] Fodor's work drew attention from linguists, psychologists, and computer scientists. It also benefited from and helped further a significant shift in the degree to which the details of scientific practice were seen to be relevant to philosophical problems about mind.

Until the mid to late 1970s most philosophy in this area was carried on in a relatively a priori analytic spirit. Even those philosophers, such as type–type identity theorists or skeptics about mental states, who purported to take science as a model for philosophy of mind had little to say about the theories of any science. They saw themselves as freeing philosophy from obstacles to scientific progress (whose direction was often predicted with considerable confidence). This was true not only of the philosophy of mind, but of much of the rest of philosophy – even much of the philosophy of natural science, with the exception of historical work in the tradition of Thomas Kuhn.[60] It is an interesting question why such a shift occurred. A similar shift occurred in the philosophies of science and mathematics. Both disciplines undertook much more concentrated discussions of a wider variety of the details of scientific practice, beginning about fifteen years ago.[61] Philosophizing about biology, a science that had not conformed to positivist conceptions of law and explanation, came to prominence in this period.

Perhaps it took two decades for the criticisms of positivism to be digested sufficiently for a more openminded consideration of the actual practice of the sciences to develop. In any case, interest in the details of psychology should be seen in the context of intellectual movements outside the scope of this essay.

The demise of behaviorism might similarly be viewed as requiring a period of assimilation before psychology could be considered a worthwhile object of philosophical reflection. Of course, there was a more positive side to the reconsideration of the practice of psychology. The computer paradigm was a natural object of interest. The continuing success of Chomsky's program in linguistics, coupled as it was with claims that it was a part of a psychology of the mind, made philosophers increasingly interested in mentalistic psychology. And an intellectually substantial cognitive and developmental psychology, and psycholinguistics, offered new forms to questions relevant to traditional philosophical issues: the role of intentional content in explanation, the mind–body problem, differences between the natural and the human sciences, the relation between language and thought, the innateness and universality of various conceptual and linguistic structures, the scope and limits of human rationality.

How much the reflection on psychology will enrich and advance philosophical inquiry remains an open question. Quite a lot of the work in this area seems to me very unreflective. It is at best rare that scientific practice answers philosophical questions in a straightforward way. But philosophy has traditionally given and received aid in the rise of new sciences or new scientific paradigms.

Let us return to functionalism. Although functionalism has enjoyed substantial support – at least among specialists in the philosophy of mind – it has not lacked detractors. The analytic and scientific versions of functionalism have always been afflicted with a programmatic, unspecific character that has seemed to many to render them unilluminating as *accounts* of particular mental kinds.

There are more specific criticisms. Many philosophers find the application of any form of functionalism to sensations like pain or color sensations implausible. For them, the causal relations of the sensations seem less fundamental to their character than their qualitative aspects.[62]

Searle mounted a controversial argument, similar to some of those directed against the applicability of functionalism to qualitative aspects of sensations, to show that functionalism could not account for any propositional attitudes. He postulated a room in which stations are manned by a person who does not understand Chinese, but who memorizes the Chinese words of given instructions. These stations are postulated to correspond to the stages of processing a language. The person is able to produce appropriate Chinese sentences as output, given any Chinese sentence as input. Searle claimed that although the system could be set up to meet the functionalist requirements for understanding Chinese, there is no understanding of Chinese in the room. Most opponents claim that the whole system can be credited with understanding Chinese. Searle finds this reply unconvincing.[63]

A more complex issue concerns the specific formulation of a functionalist account. Clearly, people can share meanings and many beliefs even though they maintain very different theories about the world. Maintaining different theories entails making different inferences, which correspond to different causal relations among the different sets of mental states associated with the theories. So not just any network of causal relations among mental states and events can be relevant to a functional account, on pain of counting no one as sharing any beliefs or meanings. One needs to find a network that is common to all the possible inference networks and theories in which any given belief (or meaning) might be embedded. But it is very difficult to imagine there being such common causal networks for each given belief (or meaning).[64]

Another approach to understanding intentional content and mental kinds developed out of the work on reference. That work showed that proper names and natural kind expressions could succeed in referring even though the speaker's knowledge of the referent was incomplete or defective. Reference depends not just on background descriptions that the speaker associates with the relevant words, but on contextual, not purely cognitive relations that the speaker bears to entities that a term applies to.

The work on reference is relevant to the meaning of terms and to the identity of concepts. For the meaning of a wide range of nonindexical terms and the nature of a wide range of concepts are dependent on the referent or range of application in the sense that if the referent were different, the meaning of the term, and the associated concept, would be different. (Here let us simply take concepts to be elements in the intentional contents of propositional attitudes, elements that have referential aspects.) For example, different meanings or concepts would be expressed by the word-forms "chair" and "arthritis" if the word-forms did not apply exactly to chairs and to instances of arthritis.

The points about reference can be extended to many such terms and concepts. An individual can think of a range of entities via such terms and concepts even though the thinker's knowledge of the entities is not complete enough to pick out that range of entities except through the employment of those terms and concepts. What the individual knows about the range of entities – and hence about those many meanings or concepts whose identities are not independent of their referential range of applications – need not provide a definition that distinguishes them from all other (possible) meanings or concepts. So the meanings of many terms – and the identities of many concepts – are what they are even though what the individual knows about the meaning or concept may be insufficient to determine it uniquely. Their identities are fixed by environmental factors that are not entirely captured in the explicatory or even discriminatory abilities of the individual, unless those discriminatory abilities include application of the concept itself. Since most pro-positional attitudes, like specific beliefs, are the kinds of mental kind that they are because of the meanings, concepts, or intentional contents that are used to specify them, the identities of many mental kinds depend on environmental factors that are not entirely captured in the (nonintentionally specified) discriminatory abilities of the individual. I have just developed one motivation for what is called *"anti-individualism."*

Anti-individualism is the view that not all of an individual's mental states and events can be type-individuated independently of the nature of the entities in the individual's environment. There is, on this view, a deep individuative relation between the individual's being in mental states of certain kinds and the nature of the individual's physical or social environments.

Anti-individualism was supported not only through abstract considerations from the theory of reference, but also through specific thought experiments. For example, one can imagine two individuals who are, for all relevant purposes, identical in the intrinsic physical nature and history of their bodies (described in isolation of their environments). But the two individuals can be imagined to have interacted with different metals (one aluminum, one an aluminum look-alike) in their respective environments. The metals need resemble one another only to the level of detail that the two individuals have noticed. The individuals know about as much about the metals as most ordinary people do, but neither could tell the difference if given the other metal. In such a case, it seems that one individual has thoughts like *aluminum is a light metal*, whereas the other individual (lacking any access to aluminum, even through interlocutors) has analogous thoughts about the other metal. Similar thought experiments appear to show that a person's thoughts can be dependent on relations to a social environment as well as a purely physical one. Some environmental dependence or other can be shown for nearly all empirically applicable terms or concepts.[65]

The thought experiments made trouble for the standard forms of functionalism, which limited specifications of input and output to the surfaces of the individual. They suggested that all an individual's internal functional transactions could remain constant, while his mental states (counterfactually) varied. Some philosophers proposed extending the functional network into the physical or social environments. Such a proposal reduces the reliance on the computer paradigm and requires a vastly more complex account. The main problems for it are those of accounting for (or specifying an illuminating supervenience base for) the notions of meaning, reference, and social dependence, in nonintentional terms. These are tasks commonly underestimated, in my view, because of the programmatic nature of the functionalist proposals.

Most philosophers seem to have accepted the thought experiments. But there remains disagreement about how they bear on mentalistic explanation, especially in psychology.

Some have held that no notion of intentional content that is as dependent for its individuation on matters external to the individual could serve in explaining the individual's behavior. Many of these philosophers have tried to fashion surrogate notions of content or of "mental" states to serve explanatory purposes. Others have maintained that such positions are based on mistakes and that the ordinary notions of intentional content and mental state can and do play a role in ordinary explanation and explanation in psychology. The debate concerns the interpretation of actual psychological practice and the relation between psychological explanation and explanation in other sciences.[66]

In my view, however, the main interest of the thought experiments lies in their giving new forms to many old issues. The arguments for anti-individualism are new. But the broad outline of the conclusion that they support is not. It is clearly maintained by Aristotle, Hegel, and Wittgenstein, and arguably present in Descartes and Kant.[67] Emergence of an old doctrine in a new form is a source of vitality in philosophy. Issues about self-knowledge, skepticism, a priori knowledge, personhood, the nature of meaning, the mind–body problem, are all deeply affected by considerations about necessary, individuative relations between an individual's mind and his environment. The line of development from the anti-descriptivist theories of reference to anti-individualist accounts of mind promises, I think, to entrich traditional philosophy.

I want to close by summarizing some of the main changes in these central areas of philosophy during the last 40 years. Three major, possibly durable contributions in these areas during the period are the criticism of the positivist theory of meaning; the development of a vastly more sophisticated sense of logical form, as applied to natural language; and the fashioning of the nondescriptivist account of reference, with the extension of the line of thought associated with this account into the philosophy of mind. Different philosophers would, of course, provide different lists of achievements, given their own sense of what is true and important.

The dominant currents during the period are more easily agreed upon. The central event is the downfall of positivism and the reopening for discussion of virtually all the traditional problems in philosophy. This event was accompanied by the rediscovery of Frege, the application of logical theory to language, and the rise of the philosophy of language both as a preliminary to reflection on other subjects, and as a more nearly autonomous discipline. The computer paradigm and complex outgrowths of the philosophy of language have brought the philosophy of mind to dominance in the last decade.

Positivism left behind a strong orientation toward the methods of science. This orientation has fueled the acceptance of materialism in the philosophy of mind and, somewhat belatedly, the development of areas of philosophy (philosophy of physics, mathematics, biology, psychology, linguistics, social science) that take the specifics of scientific theories and practices into account.

For all this, the main direction of philosophy during the period has been toward a broader-based, more eclectic, less ideological approach to philosophical problems – and a greater receptivity to interplay between modern philosophy and the history of philosophy. Philosophy of mind emerged as an area of intense ferment not simply as a product of interaction between philosophy and such disciplines as psychology and linguistics. That ferment also represents a greater interest in traditional questions, questions about what is morally and intellectually distinctive about being human. It is hard to overemphasize the degree to which leading North American philosophers have since the 1950s broadened their sympathies toward traditional questions that still help frame what it is to lead a reflective life.

This broadening seems not to have seriously undermined the standards of rigor, clarity, and openness to communal check bequeathed by such figures as Frege, Russell, Carnap, Hempel, Gödel, Church, and Quine. Partly because of its close connection with the development of mathematical logic in this century, the standards of argument in philosophy have certainly been raised.

A corollary of this change, and of the personal example of the positivists in carrying on open, dispassionate discussion, has been the emergence of philosophical community. One of the glories of English-speaking philosophy in the last 40 years has been the fruitful participation of many philosophers in the same discussions. Unlike much traditional philosophy and much philosophy in other parts of the world, English-speaking philosophy has been an open, public forum. The journals of the field, including notably this one, bear witness to a sharing of philosophical concerns, vocabularies, and methods of dispute. We now take this sharing for granted. But in historical perspective, it is remarkable. Although I think that philosophy is not and never will be a science, it has taken on this much of the spirit of science. That is, to my mind, the more important achievement.

This overview has provided at best a blurred glimpse of the enormous complexity and variety of discussion in philosophy of language and mind during the last four decades. It is deficient as a picture not only in its oversimplifications and limited scope, but also in its failure to convey the life and nature of the animal. Philosophy is not primarily a body of doctrine, a series of conclusions or systems or movements. Philosophy, both as product and as activity, lies in the detailed posing of questions, the clarification of meaning, the development and criticism of argument, the working out of ideas and points of view. It resides in the angles, nuances, styles, struggles, and revisions of individual authors. In an overview of this sort, almost all the real philosophy must be omitted. For those not initiated into these issues, the foregoing is an invitation. For those who are initiated, it is a reminder – a reminder of the grandeur, richness, and intellectual substance of our subject.

NOTES

1   What follows is a historical overview pitched to nonspecialists. I have concentrated on English-speaking philosophy, which in these areas has been dominantly North American since the 1960s. The scope of the article has, of course, forced me to omit many topics that are of great importance. I will mention a few of these: intensional contexts, quantifying in and *de re* attitudes, the concept of truth, the relation between theories of meaning and metaphysical issues like realism, the semantical and epistemic paradoxes, speech-act theory and other topics in pragmatics, the subject matter of linguistics, consciousness, and issues about qualia, personal identity, action theory, the innateness of mental structures, knowledge of language, the nature of psychological explanation, the legacy of Wittgenstein. I think that in some loose sense, however, I have caught some of what would be widely counted "the mainstream" of philosophical discussion. I am grateful to Jay Atlas, Ned Block, Susan Carey, Warren Goldfarb, and the editors for good advice.

2   Rudolf Carnap, *The Logical Syntax of Language* (London: Routledge and Kegan Paul, 1937); "Empiricism, Semantics, and Ontology" (1950), reprinted in *Meaning and Necessity* (Chicago: Chicago University Press, 1964), appendix A.

3   Carl Hempel, "Empiricist Criteria of Cognitive Significance: Problems and Changes" (1950), in *Aspects of Scientific Explanation* (New York: Free Press, 1965).

4   W. V. Quine, "Two Dogmas of Empiricism," *Philosophical Review* 60 (1951): 20–43; reprinted in Quine's *From a Logical Point of View* (New York: Harper, 1961); cf. also *Word and Object* (Cambridge, MA: MIT Press, 1960), ch. 1. Similar points were made by Hempel at about the

same time. Cf. "Empiricist Criteria of Cognitive Significance," 112–13, 117. But Quine's work had greater impact, perhaps because of his colorful and forceful exposition and because he attacked the analytic–synthetic distinction as well.

5 W. V. Quine, "Carnap on Logical Truth" (1954), in *The Ways of Paradox* (New York: Random House, 1966); cf. also "On Carnap's Views on Ontology" (1951) in the same collection.

6 *The Philosophy of Rudolf Carnap*, ed. Paul Arthur Schillp (La Salle, IL: Open Court, 1963), pp. 917ff.

7 W. V. Quine, "Truth By Convention" (1936), in *The Ways of Paradox*. The point goes back to Lewis Carroll.

8 Gottlob Frege, *The Foundations of Arithmetic* (1884), trans. J. L. Austin (Evanston, IL: Northwestern University Press, 1968); *The Basic Laws of Arithmetic* (1893–1903), ed. M. Furth (Berkeley: University of California Press, 1967). For an exposition of a positivist interpretation of the logicist program, see Carl Hempel, "On the Nature of Mathematical Truth" (1945), in *The Philosophy of Mathematics*, 2nd edn, eds Paul Benacerraf and Hilary Putnam (Cambridge: Cambridge University Press, 1986).

9 Cf. "Carnap on Logical Truth" and "Two Dogmas of Empiricism"; Hilary Putnam, "The Analytic and the Synthetic" (1962), in *Philosophical Papers*, vol. 2 (Cambridge: Cambridge University Press, 1985).

10 Cf. "Meaning and Synonymy in Natural Languages," *Philosophical Studies* 6 (1955): 337, reprinted in *Meaning and Necessity*, appendix D.

11 Quine, "Two Dogmas of Empiricism." Quine says little about analyticity as opposed to analyticity-2 in "Two Dogmas." Since this article has unfortunately received vastly more attention than "Carnap on Logical Truth," and since much of the attack on analyticity-2 in "Two Dogmas," taken by itself, is not very persuasive, many philosophers are even now baffled about why Quine's criticism of "analyticity" is important. I might note that there is a third conception of "analyticity": roughly, a truth is "analytic" (in this note, "*analytic-3*") if it states a containment relation between concepts or meanings. This conception is not, I think, equivalent to either of the other two. It differs from analyticity-2 in that it need not (should not) count at least some logical truths as "analytic-3." It differs from analyticity in that it need not (should not) count analytic-3 truths vacuous, or independent for their truth of a subject matter. Locke thought of analyticity-3 as equivalent to analyticity. Leibniz held analyticity-2 and analyticity-3 to be equivalent. Kant seems to have thought of all three conceptions as equivalent. In my view, analyticity-3 has not played an important role in the period I am discussing.

12 Frege saw logic as the discipline that applied to all subject matters, and held in particular that it was committed to the existence of an infinity of extensions (including numbers) and functions (*Foundations of Arithmetic* – e.g., sec. 14 and *passim* – or "Thoughts," in *Collected Papers on Mathematics, Logic and Philosophy* [Oxford: Basil Blackwell, 1984].) Russell's logicism is substantially similar to Frege's in holding logic to be about abstract entities that are structures in all domains of the world: "Logic . . . is concerned with the real world just as truly as zoology though with its more abstract and general features" (*Introduction to Mathematical Philosophy* [1919; reprint, New York: Simon and Schuster, 1971], ch. 16). Aristotle thought that definitions stated essences, and that logic uncovered fundamental structures in the world. Cf. *Posterior Analytics* I 1–4; II 10, 19; *Metaphysics* IV 4. Leibniz thought that all knowledge of the world could be derived, at least by God, from logical principles by analysis of concepts. Cf., for example, "Primary Truths"; "Discourse on Metaphysics," sec. 8; and "Monadology," sec. 31; all in *Philosophical Essays*, trans. Ariew and Garber (Indianapolis: Hackett, 1989). More broadly, the idea that, by understanding conceptual relations, one could gain deep and fundamental knowledge of the world is a characteristic tenet of rationalism.

13 H. P. Grice and P. F. Strawson, "In Defense of a Dogma," *Philosophical Review* 65 (1956): 141–58; Putnam, "The Analytic and the Synthetic."

14 Cf., for example, Quine, *Word and Object*, p. 67.

15 For a remarkable collection of methodologically oriented articles from this period, see Richard

Rorty, ed., *The Linguistic Turn* (Chicago: University of Chicago Press, 1967).

16   Ludwig Wittgenstein, *Philosophical Investigations*, trans. E. Anscombe (New York: Macmillan, 1953), and J. L. Austin, "Other Minds" (1946), in *Philosophical Papers* (Oxford: Oxford University Press/Clarendon Press, 1961), are perhaps the outstanding examples of attempts to apply observations about ordinary linguistic use to traditional philosophical problems.

17   The most sophisticated and fascinating example of this dispute occurs in a famous exchange between Carnap and Strawson. Cf. P. F. Strawson, "Carnap's View on Constructed Systems versus Natural languages in Analytic Philosophy", and Carnap's "P. F. Strawson on Linguistic Naturalism," both in Schillp, *The Philosophy of Rudolf Carnap*. Cf., also, Stanley Cavell, "Must We Mean What We Say?" (1958), in *Must We Mean What We Say?* (Cambridge: Cambridge University Press, 1976).

18   The discussion of the paradigm–case argument marks, I think, the downfall of the method. Cf. J. W. N. Watkins, "Farewell to the Paradigm Case Argument," *Analysis* 18 (1957): 25–33; Keith S. Donnellan, "The Paradigm–Case Argument," in *The Encyclopedia of Philosophy*, ed. P. Edwards (New York: Macmillan/Free Press, 1967).

19   J. L. Austin, *How to Do Things with Words* (New York: Oxford University Press, 1965); P. F. Strawson, "On Referring," *Mind* 59 (1950): 320–44; P. F. Strawson, *Introduction to Logical Theory* (London: Methuen, 1952). For more recent work in this tradition, see John Searle, "A Taxonomy of Illocutionary Acts" (1975) and "Indirect Speech Acts" (1975), reprinted in his *Expression and Meaning* (Cambridge: Cambridge University Press, 1979); Jay Atlas, *Philosophy without Ambiguity* (Oxford: Oxford University Press/Clarendon Press, 1989).

20   Rudolf Carnap, "Modalities and Quantification," *Journal of Symbolic Logic* 11 (1946): 33–64; Ruth Barcan Marcus, "A Functional Calculus of First-Order Based on Strict Implication," *Journal of Symbolic Logic* 11 (1946): 1–16; A. N. Prior, *Time and Modality* (Oxford: Oxford University Press, 1957); Saul Kripke, "Semantical Analysis of Modal Logic 1," *Zeitschrift fur Mathematische Logik* 9 (1963): 67–96; Alonzo Church, "A Formulation of the Logic of Sense and Denotation," in *Essays in Honor of Henry Sheffer*, ed. P. Henle (New York: Humanities Press, 1951).

21   Gottlob Frege, *Translations of the Philosophical Writings of Gottlob Frege*, eds P. Geach and M. Black (Oxford: Blackwell, 1952).

22   For a fine statement of this view, see Michael Dummett, "Frege," in Edwards, *The Encyclopedia of Philosophy*.

23   The best systematic discussion of almost all of Frege's work in philosophy of language is Michael Dummett, *Frege: Philosophy of Language* (London: Duckworth, 1973) and *The Interpretation of Frege's Philosophy* (Cambridge, MA: Harvard University Press, 1981).

24   P. F. Strawson, *Logico-Linguistic Papers* (Bungay, Suffolk: Methuen, 1971).

25   See especially chs 3–6.

26   W. V. Quine, "On What There Is," *Review of Metaphysics* 2 (1948): 21–38, reprinted in *From a Logical Point of View*.

27   Donald Davidson, *Inquiries into Truth and Interpretation* (Oxford: Oxford University Press/Clarendon Press, 1984), especially "Truth and Meaning" [reproduced as part of ch. 1 in this volume], "Theories of Meaning and Learnable Languages," "Quotation," "On Saying That"; *Essays on Actions and Events* (Oxford: Oxford University Press/Clarendon Press, 1980), especially "The Logical Form of Action Sentences"; Tyler Burge, "Reference and Proper Names," *Journal of Philosophy* 70 (1973): 425–39; "Truth and Singular Terms," *Nous* 8 (1974): 309–25; James Higginbotham, "The Logical Form of Perceptual Reports," *Journal of Philosophy* 80 (1983): 100–27; W. V. Quine, "Quantifiers and Propositional Attitudes" (1953), in *The Ways of Paradox*; David Kaplan, "Quantifying In," in *Words and Objections: Essays on the Work of W. V. Quine*, ed. D. Davidson and J. Hintikka (Dordrecht, The Netherlands: Reidel, 1969); Scott Soames, "Lost Innocence," *Linguistics and Philosophy* 8 (1985): 59–71.

28   Robert Stalnaker, "A Theory of Conditionals," in *Studies in Logical Theory, American Philosophical Quarterly* monograph series no. 2, ed. N. Rescher (Oxford: Blackwell, 1968); Bas van Fraassen,

"Presuppositions, Supervaluations, and Free Logic," in *The Logical Way of Doing Things*, ed. K. Lambert (New Haven: Yale University Press, 1969); David Lewis, "General Semantics" (1970), in his *Philosophical Papers*, vol. I (Oxford: Oxford University Press, 1983), and *Counterfactuals* (Oxford: Blackwell, 1973); Alonzo Church, "Outline of a Revised Formulation of the Logic of Sense and Denotation, Part I," *Nous* 7 (1973): 24–33, and "Outline of a Revised Formulation of the Logic of Sense and Denotation, Part II," *Nous* 8 (1973): 135–56; Richard Montague, *Formal Philosophy*, ed. R. H. Thomason (New Haven: Yale University Press, 1974); Kit Fine, "Vagueness, Truth, and Logic," *Synthese* 30 (1975): 265–300; David Kaplan, "On the Logic of Demonstratives," in *Contemporary Perspectives in the Philosophy of Language*, eds P. A. French, T. E. Uehling, and H. K. Wettstein (Minneapolis: University of Minnesota Press, 1979); Jon Barwise and John Perry, *Situations and Attitudes* (Cambridge, MA: MIT Press, 1983).

29   Noam Chomsky, *Syntactic Structures* (The Hague: Mouton, 1957); *Aspects of the Theory of Syntax* (Cambridge, MA: MIT Press, 1965).

30   Quine, *Word and Object*, chs 1 and 2; *Ontological Relativity* (New York: Columbia University Press, 1969).

31   Noam Chomsky, "Quine's Empirical Assumptions," in Davidson and Hinlikka, *Words and Objections*.

32   Donald Davidson, "Truth and Meaning," *Synthese* 17 (1967): 304–23, reprinted in *Inquiries into Truth and Interpretation* [reproduced as part of ch. 1 of this volume]. Cf. also, John McDowell "Truth Conditions, Bivalence, and Verificationism," in *Truth and Meaning*, eds G. Evans and J. McDowell (Oxford: Oxford University Press/Clarendon Press, 1976).

33   Michael Dummett, "The Philosophical Basis of Intuitionistic Logic" (1973), in *Truth and Other Enigmas* (Cambridge, MA: Harvard University Press, 1978); "What is a Theory of Meaning?," in *Mind and Language*, ed. S. Guttenplan (Oxford: Oxford University Press/Clarendon Press, 1975); "What is a Theory of Meaning? (II)," in Evans and McDowell, *Truth and Meaning*.

34   Paul Grice, "Meaning," *Philosophical Review* 66 (1957): 377–88 [reproduced as part of ch. 2 in this volume]; Utteret's Meaning, Sentence-Meaning, and Word-Meaning," *Foundations of Language* 4 (1968): 225–42; "Utterer's Meaning and Intentions," *Philosophical Review* 78 (1969): 147–77; all reprinted in *Studies in the Way of Words* (Cambridge, MA: Harvard University Press, 1989). Cf. also Stephen Schiffer, *Meaning* (Oxford: Oxford University Press/Clarendon Press, 1972).

35   Paul Grice, *Studies in the Way of Words*, part 1, given as lectures in 1967 but influential, through his teaching, on Strawson's work as far back as the early 1950s.

36   Cf. Gottlob Frege, "Thoughts," in *Collected Papers on Mathematics, Logic, and Philosophy* (Oxford: Blackwell, 1984); Bertrand Russell, "The Philosophy of Logical Atomism," in *Logic and Knowledge*, ed. R. C. Marsh (London: George Allen and Unwin, 1956).

37   Ludwig Wittgenstein, *Philosophical Investigations*, secs 79, 87; John Searle, "Proper Names," *Mind* 67 (1958): 166–73; P. F. Strawson, *Individuals: An Essay in Descriptive Metaphysics* (London: Methuen, 1959), ch. 6.

38   Keith Donnellan, "Reference and Definite Descriptions," *Philosophical Review* 75 (1966): 281–304. See, also, Leonard Linsky, "Reference and Referents," in *Philosophy and Ordinary Language*, ed. Charles Caton (Urbana: University of Illinois Press, 1963).

39   Saul Kripke, *Naming and Necessity* (Cambridge, MA: Harvard Universty Press, 1972); Keith Donnellan, "Proper Names and Identifying Descriptions," in *Semantics of Natural Language*, eds D. Davidson and G. Harman (Dordrecht, The Netherlands: Reidel, 1972).

40   Cf. Gareth Evans, "The Causal Theory of Names," *Proceedings of the Aristotelian Society* 47 (suppl.) (1973): 187–208; Michael Devitt, *Designation* (New York: Columbia University Press, 1981).

41   Kripke, *Naming and Necessity*; Hilary Putnam, "Is Semantics Possible?" (1970), in *Philosophical Papers*, vol. 2.

42   The "direct reference" view is at least suggested by Kripke. But its main proponent has been David Kaplan, "Demonstratives," in *Themes from Kaplan*, eds J. Almog, J. Perry, and H. Wettstein (New York: Oxford University Press, 1989). Cf., also, various articles in *Propositions*

and Attitudes, eds S. Salmon and S. Soames (Oxford: Oxford University Press, 1988). A neo-Fregean view is developed in John McDowell, "On the Sense and Reference of a Proper Name," *Mind* 86 (1977): 159–85; in Gareth Evans, *The Varieties of Reference* (Oxford: Oxford University Press/ Clarendon Press, 1982); and in Diana Ackerman, "Proper Names, Propositional Attitudes, and Non-Descriptive Connotations," *Philosophical Studies* 35 (1979): 559. Two significantly different intermediate views may be found in John Searle, *Intentionality* (Cambridge: Cambridge University Press, 1983); and in Tyler Burge, "Belief De Re," *Journal of Philosophy* 74 (1977): 338–63, and "Russell's Problem and Intentional Identity," in *Agent, Language and the Structure of the World*, ed. James Tomberlin (Indianapolis: Hackett, 1983).

43   Gilbert Ryle, *The Concept of Mind* (London: Hutchison, 1949); Norman Malcolm, *Dreaming* (London: Routledge and Kegan Paul, 1959); Quine, *Word and Object*.

44   Roderick Chisholm, *Perceiving* (Ithaca, NY: Cornell University Press, 1957), ch 11; Peter Geach, *Mental Acts* (London: Routledge, 1957), ch. 1; Noam Chomsky, review of *Verbal Behavior* by B. F. Skinner, *Language* 35 (1959): 26–58, reprinted in *The Structure of Language*, eds J. Fodor and J. Katz (Englewood Cliffs, NJ: Prentice Hall, 1964) [reproduced as part of ch. 8 in this volume]; Hilary Putnam, "Brains and Behavior" (1963), in *Philosophical Papers*, vol. 2; Jerry Fodor, *Psychological Explanation* (New York: Random House, 1968).

45   In psychology: George Miller, "The Magic Number 7 Plus or Minus Two: Some Limits on Our Capacity for Processing Information," *Psychological Review* 63 (1956): 81–97; J. Brunner, J. Goodnow, and G. Austin, *A Study of Thinking* (New York: John Wiley, 1956); G. Miller, E. Galanter, and K. Pribram, *Plans and the Structure of Behavior* (New York: Holt, Rinehart & Winston, 1960); G. Sperling, "The Information Available in Brief Visual Presentations," *Psychological Monographs* 24 (1960); Ulrich Neisser, "The Multiplicity of Thought," *British Journal of Psychology* 54 (1963): 1–14; M. I. Posner, "Immediate Memory in Sequential Tasks," *Psychology Bulletin* 60 (1963): 333–49; S. Sternberg, "High-Speed Scanning in Human Memory," *Science* 153 (1966): 652–4. In linguistics: Chomsky, *Syntactic Structures*. In computer science: A. Newell, G. L. Shaw, and H. Simon, "Elements of a Theory of Human Problem Solving," *Psychological Review* 65 (1958): 151–66.

46   W. V. Quine, "On Mental Entities" (1952), in *The Ways of Paradox*; U. T. Place, "Is Consciousness a Brian Process?," *British Journal of Psychology* 47 (1956): 44–50; J. J. C. Smart, "Sensations and Brain Processes," *Philosophical Review* 68 (1959): 141–56.

47   J. Y. Lettvin, H. R. Maturana, W. S. McCulloch, and W. H. Pitts, "What the Frog's Eye Tells the Frog's Brain," *Proceedings of the Institute of Radio Engineers* 47 (1959); D. H. Hubel and T. N. Wiesel, "Receptive Fields of Single Neurones in the Cat's Striate Cortex," *Journal of Physiology* 148 (1959): 574–91, and "Receptive Fields, Binocular Interaction, and Functional Architecture in the Cat's Visual Cortex," *Journal of Physiology* (London) 160 (1962): 106–54.

48   The central state identity theory is defended in D. M. Armstrong, *A Materialist Theory of the Mind* (New York: Humanities Press, 1968); David Lewis, "An Argument for the Identity Theory," *Journal of Philosophy* 63 (1966): 17–25. Eliminative materialism, which derives from Quine, is defended in Paul Feyerabend, "Materialism and the Mind–Body Problem," *Review of Metaphysics* 17 (1963): 49–66; Richard Rorty, "Mind–Body Identity, Privacy, and Categories," *Review of Metaphysics* 19 (1965): 24–54; and Daniel Dennett, *Content and Consciousness* (New York: Routledge and Kegan Paul, 1969). Many of these works, and several other significant ones, are collected in *Modern Materialism: Readings on Mind–Body Identity*, ed. J. O'Connor (New York: Harcourt, Brace, and World, 1969).

49   In Wilfrid Sellars, *Science, Perception, and Reality* (London: Routledge and Kegan Paul, 1963).

50   Hilary Putnam, "The Nature of Mental States" (1967), in *Philosophical Papers*, vol. 2; Ned Block and Jerry Fodor, "What Psychological States Are Not," *Philosophical Review* 81 (1972): 159–81.

51   Donald Davidson, "Mental Events" (1970), in *Essays on Actions and Events*.

52   Geoffrey Hellman and Frank Wilson Thompson, "Physicalist Materialism," *Nous* 11 (1977): 309–45; Richard Boyd, "Materialism without Reductionism: What Physicalism Does Not Entail," in *Readings in Philosophy of Psychology*, vol. 1, ed. N. Block (Cambridge, MA: Harvard

University Press, 1980). Another source of reformulations of materialism has been the discussion of supervenience principles. Cf. Jaegwon Kim, "Causality, Identity, and Supervenience in the Mind–Body Problem," *Midwest Studies in Philosophy* 4 (1979): 31–50. It is worth noting, however, that supervenience of the mental on the physical does not entail materialism.

53 Cf., for example, Jaegwon Kim, "Epiphenomenal and Supervenient Causation," *Midwest Studies in Philosophy* 9 (1984): 257–70; Ernest Sosa, "Mind–Body Interaction and Supervenient Causation," *Midwest Studies in Philosophy* 9 (1984): 271–82; Ned Block, "Can the Mind Change the World?," in *Meaning and Method: Essays in Honor of Hilary Putnam*, ed. G. Boolos (Cambridge: Cambridge University Press, 1990).

54 The lack of attention to our source of knowledge of mental causation is one reason why there has recently been a small outpouring of worries among materialists that a form of epiphenomenalism – the view that mentalistic properties or descriptions are causally irrelevant – must be taken seriously.

55 Cf. A. M. Turing, "Computing Machinery and Intelligence," *Mind* 59 (1950) [reproduced as part of ch. 5 in this volume]. Turing's article provided an impetus and a vivid illustration of the computer paradigm, but it was itself an expression of behaviorism about the mind. The papers that inspired machine functionalism were Hilary Putnam's, "Minds and Machines" (1960), "Robots: Machines or Artificially Created Life?" (1964), and "The Mental Life of Some Machines" (1967), in *Philosophical Papers*, vol. 2. Putnam states an explicitly functionalist view in "The Nature of Mental States" (1967), but the idea is not far from the surface of his earlier papers. A type of functionalism less tied to computers was proposed in Lewis, "An Argument for the Identity Theory" 1966, and Armstrong, *A Materialist Theory of the Mind* (1968).

56 The nonreductive version is the least common. It is expressed in the introduction of Jerry Fodor's *RePresentations* (Cambridge, MA: MIT Press, 1981), but he maintains it neither very long before nor very long after. The analytic version may be found in Armstrong, *A Materialist Theory of Mind*; David Lewis, "Psychophysical and Theoretical Identification," *Australasian Journal of Philosophy* 50 (1972): 249–58; Sydney Shoemaker, "Functionalism and Qualia" (1975), in his *Identity, Cause and Mind* (Cambridge: Cambridge University Press, 1984). Putnam proposed the scientific version in "The Nature of Mental States." A view more instrumentalist than functionalist but which bears broad comparison appears in Daniel Dennett, "Intentional Systems," *Journal of Philosophy* 68 (1971): 87–106.

57 Jerry A. Fodor, *The Language of Thought* (Cambridge, MA: Harvard University Press, 1975) and *RePresentations*. Cf., also, Hartry Field, "Mental Representation," *Erkenntnis* 13 (1978): 91.

58 Wilfrid Sellars, "Some Reflections on Language Games" (1954), in *Science, Perception, and Reality*. Cf., also Gilbert Harman, *Thought* (Princeton, NJ: Princeton University Press, 1973).

59 For opposition from different angles to the computer analogy or to other aspects of the language-of-thought hypothesis, see Paul M. Churchland, *Scientific Realism and the Plasticity of Mind* (Cambridge: Cambridge University Press, 1979); Christopher Peacocke, *Sense and Content* (Oxford: Oxford University Press/Clarendon Press, 1983); Stephen Stich, *From Folk Psychology to Cognitive Science* (Cambridge, MA: MIT Press, 1983); Robert Stalnaker, *Inquiry* (Cambridge, MA: MIT Press 1984); Daniel Dennett, *The Intentional Stance* (Cambridge, MA: MIT Press, 1987); Paul Smolensky, "On the Proper Treatment of Connectionism," *Journal of Behavioral and Brain Sciences* 11 (1988): 1–74.

60 T. S. Kuhn, *The Structure of Scientific Revolutions* (Chicago: University of Chicago Press, 1962).

61 The change in the philosophy of physics was foreshadowed by early articles of Hilary Putnam's – for example, "An Examination of Grunbaum's Philosophy of Geometry" (1963), "A Philosopher Looks at Quantum Mechanics" (1965), both in *Philosophical Papers*, vol. I (Cambridge: Cambridge University Press, 1975). But it caught on and received new impetus with the articles of John Earman – for example, "Who's Afraid of Absolute Space?," *Australasian Journal of Philosophy* 48 (1970): 287–319. For an overview of broadly analogous changes in the philosophy of mathematics, see Thomas Tymoczko, ed., *New Directions in the Philosophy of Mathematics* (Boston: Birkhauser, 1985).

62   Criticism of this aspect of functionalism may be found in Ned Block, "Troubles with Function-
     alism," in *Minnesota Studies in the Philosophy of Science*, vol. 9, ed. C. W. Savage (Minneapolis:
     University of Minnesota Press, 1978), and "Are Absent Qualia Impossible?," *Philosophical Review*
     89 (1980): 257–74. An influential article with a different, but related, point is Thomas Nagel,
     "What is it Like to Be a Bat?," *Philosophical Review* 83 (1974): 435–50. Cf., also, Frank Jackson,
     "Epiphenomenal Qualia," *Philosophical Quarterly* 32 (1982): 127–36. The numerous defenses of
     functionalism on this score include: Sydney Shoemaker, "Functionalism and Qualia," and "Ab-
     sent Qualia are Impossible – A Reply to Block," in *Identity, Cause and Mind*; and David Lewis,
     "Mad Pain and Martian Pain" (1980), in his *Philosophical Papers*, vol. I (New York: Oxford
     University Press, 1983).

63   John Searle, "Minds, Brains, and Programs," *The Behavioral and Brain Sciences* 3 (1980): 417–24.
     Searle's argument is anticipated in Ned Block, "Troubles with Functionalism."

64   These problems have long been recognized. But as with some of the fundamental difficulties with
     positivism, such recognition does not always convince proponents of a program to give it up. For
     a summary of some of these problems, see Hilary Putnam, *Representation and Reality* (Cambridge,
     MA: MIT Press, 1988).

65   Tyler Burge, "Individualism and the Mental," *Midwest Studies in Philosophy* 4 (1979): 73–121;
     "Other Bodies," in *Thought and Object*, ed. A. Woodfield (London: Oxford University Press,
     1982); "Intellectual Norms and Foundations of Mind," *Journal of Philosophy* 83 (1986): 697–720;
     "Cartesian Error and the Objectivity of Perception," in *Contents of Thought*, eds R. H. Grimm and
     D. D. Merrill (Tucson: University of Arizona Press, 1988); "Wherein is Language Social?," in
     Reflections on Chomsky, ed. A. George (Oxford: Blackwell, 1989). The thought experiments use
     the methodology set out in Hilary Putnam, "The Meaning of 'Meaning'" (1975), in *Philosophical
     Papers*, vol. 2 [reproduced as ch. 3 in this volume]. Putnam's argument, however, was not applied
     to intentional elements in mind or meaning. In fact, it contained remarks that are incompatible
     with anti-individualism about mental states. Much in subsequent papers is, however, anti-
     individualistic. Cf. "Computational Psychology and Interpretation Theory," in *Philosophical
     Papers*, vol. 3 (Cambridge: Cambridge University Press, 1983); *Representation and Reality*, ch. 5.
     But ambivalences remain. Cf. ibid., pp. 19–22.

66   For versions of the former approach, see Stephen White, "Partial Character and the Language of
     Thought," *Pacific Philosophical Quarterly* 63 (1982): 347–65; Stephen Stich, "On the Ascription
     of Content," in Woodfield, *Thought and Object*; Jerry Fodor, *Psychosemantics* (Cambridge, MA:
     MIT Press, 1987); Brian Loar, "Social Content and Psychological Content," in Grimm and
     Merrill, *Contents of Thoguht*. For defenses of anti-individualistic conceptions of psychology, see
     Fred Dretske, *Knowledge and the Flow of Information* (Cambridge, MA: MIT Press, 1981); Tyler
     Burge, "Individualism and Psychology," *Philosophical Review* 95 (1986): 3–45 [reproduced as
     part of ch. 7 in this volume], and "Causation and Individuation in Psychology," *Pacific Philosophi-
     cal Quarterly* 70 (1989): 303–22; Lynne Rudder Baker, *Saving Belief* (Princeton, NJ: Princeton
     University Press, 1987); and Robert Stalnaker, "What's in the Head," *Philosophical Perspectives* 8
     (1989): 287–316.

67   Descartes's Demon hypothesis is paradigmatically individualistic. But Descartes thought that the
     hypothesis was incoherent. His causal argument for the existence of the physical world (in
     Meditation 6) and his principle that the reality of ideas cannot exceed the reality of their objects
     are anti-individualistic in spirit. The question of whether Descartes was an individualist is very
     complex and entangled wiht his views about God. As regards Kant, the Refutation of Idealism
     (*Critique of Pure Reason*, B 274ff) contains a fundamentally anti-individualistic strategy. But the
     overall question of how to interpret Kant with regard to anti-individualism is, again, very
     complex, since it is bound up with the interpretation of his transcendental idealism.

Part I

The Meaning of Language

1

Natural and Formal Languages

Introduction

The study of language in the twentieth century has important roots in the study of artificial languages tailored for formal systems such as mathematics or logic. These formal languages were built in such a way that they would only permit truth-preserving inferences, that is, true sentences would only lead to true sentences and never false ones. Consequently, it was important to have a rigorous understanding of the concept of truth. Developing a definition of truth that was satisfactory for doing formal work was the lasting achievement of the Polish logician, mathematician, and philosopher Alfred Tarski.

What makes the concept of truth especially troublesome for rigorous formal work is that truth appears to be the source of paradoxes. This was already noticed by the ancient Greeks, who were struck by the paradoxical nature of someone saying of herself that she is lying. Tarski, who formulates an especially clear version of this paradox, solves it for formal languages by banishing from them predicates like "is true" that can apply to themselves. If we want to talk about the truth of a language L, we need to have a language M that is distinct from L but in which we can refer to L. M would be a metalanguage for L and it can contain a truth predicate that applies to L, but not to itself.

Once we have a metalanguage for L, truth can be defined for L by a finite set of rules that generate for every sentence of L a sentence in M that has the following form or schema, which Tarski calls "T":

"s" is true in L if and only if s

where "s" is a name of a sentence of L. One instance of the schema is

"Snow is white" is true in L if and only if snow is white

which gives the necessary and sufficient conditions for the truth of the sentence "Snow is white." On Tarski's account, in a satisfactory theory of truth this sentence stating the truth condition for "Snow is white" would follow from rules about the denotation of "snow" and "is white."

Tarski's definition suggests a very general and powerful way of treating infinitely large languages. Tarski defined truth for a language by giving a finite set of rules that, when repeatedly applied, can generate an infinite number of sentences that have the form of T. This approach was used extensively for formal languages, but it took a leap of imagination to apply it to ordinary natural languages like English and in effect treat natural languages like formal systems. Noam Chomsky made this leap in linguistics in his treatment of syntax in *Syntactic Structures* (1957), and the philosophers Donald Davidson and Richard Montague did the same for the meaning of language. In "Truth and Meaning" Davidson argues that we can extend Tarski's account of truth to account for the meaning of natural languages. Davidson thinks that once we have provided the truth conditions for language, then we have said all we fundamentally need to say about the meaning of language. Davidson furthermore believes that such an account would explain how we understand language. As Davidson puts it, "To know the semantic concept of truth for a language is to know what it is for a sentence – any sentence – to be true, and this amounts, in one good sense we can give to the phrase, to understanding the language."

Can a Tarski-style truth definition provide us with meaning in the way Davidson thinks it can? That is something we leave to the reader to decide. Let us point out, though, that what we are concerned with when we are dealing with meaning is what propositions sentences express. A monolingual German who sincerely assents to "Schnee ist weiss" and a monolingual Englishman who sincerely assents to "Snow is white" believe the same thing, for the German sentence and the English sentence express the same proposition. But Tarski's truth definition doesn't apply to propositions; it applies to sentences in an object language.

A closely related approach to natural languages is to apply the formal techniques of model theory to natural languages. This approach was pioneered by Richard Montague, whose work has been influential in linguistics. A brief and general outline of this approach can be found in the essays by Barbara Partee and Robert Stalnaker. The basic idea is to treat the actual world and its objects as only one member of a model that contains other possible worlds distinct from the actual one. Truth and meaning are now characterized in terms of possible worlds. For example, the predicates of a language, such as "is brown" in English, are assigned rules that pick out the sets of brown objects in each possible world, and sentences are assigned rules that determine whether or not they are true in each possible world. In effect, every sentence of a language given such a formal treatment will have a rule that picks out the set of possible worlds in which it is true and the set of possible worlds in which it is false. We can call this rule, or function, the intension or proposition that is expressed by the sentence.

An area that appears to resist this formal approach to natural languages is pragmatics. While syntax is concerned with the form of language and semantics with its meaning, pragmatics is concerned with the diverse ways in which people use language in different contexts. Stalnaker's essay "Pragmatics" is devoted to showing how to give a formal treatment of the pragmatic features of language. The basic scheme Stalnaker proposes is as follows. Syntactical and semantical rules for a language determine the interpretation for a sentence. An interpreted sentence, together with some features of the context of use, determines a proposition. So in order to assign a proposition to a sentence, we need not only an interpretation, but a context of use.

These formal treatments of natural languages might succeed in giving us the formal rules that can generate the syntax, semantics and pragmatics of a language, but are these rules psychologically realistic? Can we suppose that these rules in fact play a role in the psychology of language or are they just nifty formal devices that are irrelevant to psychology? In "Semantics – Mathematics or Psychology?" Partee argues that the speaker's psychology matters as well. What may seem to be an adequate "mathematical" or formal treatment of natural languages might be inadequate from a psychological perspective. For instance, consider these two logically equivalent sentences:

> If the ball is round, then it has a shape.
> Either it is not the case that the ball is round or it has a shape.

Because they are logically equivalent, a formal treatment of language such as Montague's would require that the following two sentences are also logically equivalent:

> Irene believes that if the ball is round, then it has a shape.
> Irene believes that either it is not the case that the ball is round or it has a shape.

But this seems wrong. Our knowledge of logic can be limited, and thus a person can believe a proposition while disbelieving a logically equivalent proposition.

Partee uses this case to show that the semantic meaning of the logically equivalent sentences is different from their psychological meaning. Thus a proper treatment of language must consider psychology, although it is not altogether clear to Partee how this can be done properly from a formal point of view because psychological factors vary so much from person to person and moment to moment.

The points Stalnaker and Partee make raise interesting issues. It appears that we cannot look at a natural language as an object of investigation in isolation from its speakers. The language and its speakers are constantly interacting and the interaction has to be taken into account in any attempt to formalize natural languages. Furthermore, the speakers might be working with psychological meanings that cannot be captured in a formal system. An already challenging task suddenly became a lot more challenging! Can the interactive and subjective or psychological aspects of natural languages be treated formally so that we can simulate all of these natural features in the formal and artificial languages that computers have to use?

With this last question we return to where we started with Tarski, namely with artificial and formal languages, but now the tables are turned. We started with using results from work on artificial languages in the study of natural languages, but now results in the study of natural languages suggest new tasks for workers studying and developing artificial languages. It is this lively interaction and cross-fertilization between different fields and projects that is characteristic of the cognitive sciences.

FURTHER READING

Chierchia, G. and McConnell-Ginet, S. (1990). *Meaning and Grammar: An Introduction to Semantics.* Cambridge, MA: MIT Press.

Church, A. (1951). The Need for Abstract Entities. *American Academy of Arts and Science Proceedings* 80: 101–13.

Davidson, D. and Harman, G. (eds) (1975). *The Semantics of Natural Language.* Dordrecht: Reidel.

Dowty, D. R., Wall, R. E., and Peters, S. (1981). *Introduction to Montague Semantics.* Dordrecht: Reidel.

Field, H. (1972). Tarski's Theory of Truth. *Journal of Philosophy* 79: 347–75.

Frege, G. (1967). The Thought: A Logical Inquiry. In *Philosophical Logic*. Ed. P. F. Strawson. Oxford: Oxford University Press.

Frege, G. (1970). *The Philosophical Writings of Gottlob Frege*. Eds P. Geach and M. Black. Oxford: Blackwell.

LePore, E. (1986). *Truth and Interpretation: Perspectives on the Philosophy of Donald Davidson*. Oxford: Blackwell.

Lewis, D. (1975). General Semantics. In Davidson and Harman 1975.

Montague, R. (1974). *Formal Philosophy: Selected Papers of Richard Montague*. Ed. R. H. Thomason. New Haven: Yale University Press.

The Semantic Conception of Truth and the Foundations of Semantics

ALFRED TARSKI

This paper consists of two parts; the first has an expository character, and the second is rather polemical.

In the first part I want to summarize in an informal way the main results of my investigations concerning the definition of truth and the more general problem of the foundations of semantics. These results have been embodied in a work which appeared in print several years ago.[1] Although my investigations concern concepts dealt with in classical philosophy, they happen to be comparatively little known in philosophical circles, perhaps because of their strictly technical character. For this reason I hope I shall be excused for taking up the matter once again.[2]

Since my work was published, various objections, of unequal value, have been raised to my investigations; some of these appeared in print, and others were made in public and private discussions in which I took part.[3] In the second part of the paper I should like to express my views regarding these objections. I hope that the remarks which will be made in this context will not be considered as purely polemical in character, but will be found to contain some constructive contributions to the subject.

In the second part of the paper I have made extensive use of material graciously put at my disposal by Dr Marja Kokoszyńska (University of Lwów). I am especially indebted and grateful to Professors Ernest Nagel (Columbia University) and David Rynin (University of California, Berkeley) for their help in preparing the final text and for various critical remarks.

I Exposition

1 The main problem – a satisfactory definition of truth

Our discussion will be centered on the notion[4] of *truth*. The main problem is that of giving a *satisfactory definition* of this notion, i.e., a definition which is *materially adequate* and *formally correct*. But such a formulation of the problem, because of its generality, cannot be considered unequivocal, and requires some further comments.

In order to avoid any ambiguity, we must first specify the conditions under which the definition of truth will be considered adequate from the material point of view. The desired definition does not aim to specify the meaning of a familiar word used to denote a novel notion; on the contrary, it aims to catch hold of the actual meaning of an old notion. We must then characterize this notion precisely enough to enable anyone to determine whether the definition actually fulfills its task.

Secondly, we must determine on what the formal correctness of the definition depends. Thus, we must specify the words or concepts which we wish to use in defining the notion of truth; and we must also give the formal rules to which the definition should conform. Speaking more generally, we must describe the formal structure of the language in which the definition will be given.

The discussion of these points will occupy a considerable portion of the first part of the paper.

2   The extension of the term "true"

We begin with some remarks regarding the extension of the concept of truth which we have in mind here.

The predicate "*true*" is sometimes used to refer to psychological phenomena such as judgments or beliefs, sometimes to certain physical objects, namely, linguistic expressions and specifically sentences, and sometimes to certain ideal entities called "propositions." By "sentence" we understand here what is usually meant in grammar by "declarative sentence"; as regards the term "proposition," its meaning is notoriously a subject of lengthy disputations by various philosophers and logicians, and it seems never to have been made quite clear and unambiguous. For several reasons it appears most convenient to *apply the term "true" to sentences*, and we shall follow this course.[5]

Consequently, we must always relate the notion of truth, like that of a sentence, to a specific language; for it is obvious that the same expression which is a true sentence in one language can be false or meaningless in another.

Of course, the fact that we are interested here primarily in the notion of truth for sentences does not exclude the possibility of a subsequent extension of this notion to other kinds of object.

3   The meaning of the term "true"

Much more serious difficulties are connected with the problem of the meaning (or the intension) of the concept of truth.

The word "*true*," like other words from our everyday language, is certainly not unambiguous. And it does not seem to me that the philosophers who have discussed this concept have helped to diminish its ambiguity. In works and discussions of philosophers we meet many different conceptions of truth and falsity, and we must indicate which conception will be the basis of our discussion.

We should like our definition to do justice to the intuitions which adhere to the *classical Aristotelian conception of truth* – intuitions which find their expression in the well-known words of Aristotle's *Metaphysics*:

> *To say of what is that it is not, or of what is not that it is, is false, while to say of what is that it is, or of what is not that it is not, is true.*

If we wished to adapt ourselves to modern philosophical terminology, we could perhaps express this conception by means of the familiar formula:

> *The truth of a sentence consists in its agreement with (or correspondence to) reality.*

(For a theory of truth which is to be based upon the latter formulation the term "correspondence theory" has been suggested.)

If, on the other hand, we should decide to extend the popular usage of the term "*designate*" by applying it not only to names, but also to sentences, and if we agreed to speak of the designata of sentences as "states of affairs," we could possibly use for the same purpose the following phrase:

> *A sentence is true if it designates an existing state of affairs.*[6]

However, all these formulations can lead to various misunderstandings, for none of them is sufficiently precise and clear (though this applies much less to the original Aristotelian formulation than to either of the others); at any rate, none of them can be considered a satisfactory definition of truth. It is up to us to look for a more precise expression of our intuitions.

4   *A criterion for the material adequacy of the definition*[7]

Let us start with a concrete example. Consider the sentence "*snow is white.*" We ask the question under what conditions this sentence is true or false. It seems clear that if we base ourselves on the classical conception of truth, we shall say that the sentence is true if snow is white, and that it is false if snow is not white. Thus, if the definition of truth is to conform to our conception, it must imply the following equivalence:

> *The sentence "snow is white" is true if, and only if, snow is white.*

Let me point out that the phrase "*snow is white*" occurs on the left side of this equivalence in quotation marks, and on the right without quotation marks. On the right side we have the sentence itself, and on the left the name of the sentence. Employing the medieval logical terminology we could also say that on the right side the words "*snow is white*" occur in *suppositio formalis*, and on the left in *suppositio materialis*. It is hardly necessary to explain why we must have the name of the sentence, and not the sentence itself, on the left side of the equivalence. For, in the first place, from the point of view of the grammar of our language, an expression of the form "*X is true*" will not become a meaningful sentence if we replace in it "*X*" by a sentence or by anything other than a name, since the subject of a sentence may be only a noun or an expression functioning like a noun. And, in the second place, the fundamental conventions regarding the use of any language require that in any utterance we make about an object it is the name of the object which must be employed, and not the object itself. In consequence, if we wish to say something about a sentence – for example, that it is true – we must use the name of this sentence, and not the sentence itself.[8]

It may be added that enclosing a sentence in quotation marks is by no means the only way of forming its name. For instance, by assuming the usual order of letters in our alphabet, we can use the following expression as the name (the description) of the sentence "*snow is white*":

the sentence constituted by three words, the first of which consists of the 19th, 14th, 15th, and 23rd letters, the second of 9th and 19th letters, and the third of the 23rd, 8th, 9th, 20th, and 5th letters of the English alphabet.

We shall now generalize the procedure which we have applied above. Let us consider an arbitrary sentence; we shall replace it by the letter "*p*." We form the name of this sentence and we replace it by another letter, say "*X*." We ask now what is the logical relation between the two sentences "*X is true*" and "*p*." It is clear that from the point of view of our basic conception of truth these sentences are equivalent. In other words, the following equivalence holds:

(T)   *X is true if, and only if, p.*

We shall call any such equivalence (with "*p*" replaced by any sentence of the language to which the word "*true*" refers, and "*X*" replaced by a name of this sentence) "*an equivalence of the form (T)*."

Now at last we are able to put into a precise form the conditions under which we will consider the usage and the definition of the term "*true*" as adequate from the material point of view; we wish to use the term "*true*" in such a way that all equivalences of the form (T) can be asserted, and *we shall call a definition of truth "adequate" if all these equivalences follow from it.*

It should be emphasized that neither the expression (T) itself (which is not a sentence, but only a schema of a sentence) nor any particular instance of the form (T) can be regarded as a definition of truth. We can only say that every equivalence of the form (T) obtained by replacing "*p*" by a particular sentence, and "*X*" by a name of this sentence, may be considered a partial definition of truth, which explains wherein the truth of this one individual sentence consists. The general definition has to be, in a certain sense, a logical conjunction of all these partial definitions.

(The last remark calls for some comments. A language may admit the construction of infinitely many sentences; and thus the number of partial definitions of truth referring to sentences of such a language will also be infinite. Hence to give our remark a precise sense we should have to explain what is meant by a "logical conjunction of infinitely many sentences"; but this would lead us too far into technical problems of modern logic.)

5   *Truth as a semantic concept*

I should like to propose the name "*the semantic conception of truth*" for the conception of truth which has just been discussed.

Semantics is a discipline which, speaking loosely, *deals with certain relations between expressions of a language and the objects* (or "states of affairs") *"referred to" by those expressions.* As typical examples of semantic concepts we may mention the concepts of *designation*, *satisfaction*, and *definition* as these occur in the following examples:

the expression "the father of his country" designates (denotes) George Washington;

snow satisfies the sentential function (the condition) "x is white";

the equation "2x = 1" defines (uniquely determines) the number ¹/₂.

While the words *"designates," "satisfies,"* and *"defines"* express relations (between certain expressions and the objects "referred to" by these expressions), the word *"true"* is of a different logical nature. It expresses a property (or denotes a class) of certain expressions, viz., of sentences. However, it is easily seen that all the formulations which were given earlier and which aimed to explain the meaning of this word (cf. sections 3 and 4) referred not only to sentences themselves, but also to objects "talked about" by these sentences, or possibly to "states of affairs" described by them. And, moreover, it turns out that the simplest and the most natural way of obtaining an exact definition of truth is one which involves the use of other semantic notions, e.g., the notion of satisfaction. It is for these reasons that we count the concept of truth which is discussed here among the concepts of semantics, and the problem of defining truth proves to be closely related to the more general problem of setting up the foundations of theoretical semantics.

It is perhaps worth while saying that semantics as it is conceived in this paper (and in former papers of the author) is a sober and modest discipline which has no pretensions of being a universal patent medicine for all the ills and diseases of mankind, whether imaginary or real. You will not find in semantics any remedy for decayed teeth or illusions of grandeur or class conflicts. Nor is semantics a device for establishing that everyone except the speaker and his friends is speaking nonsense.

From antiquity to the present day the concepts of semantics have played an important role in the discussions of philosophers, logicians, and philologists. Nevertheless, these concepts have been treated for a long time with a certain amount of suspicion. From a historical standpoint, this suspicion is to be regarded as completely justified. For although the meaning of semantic concepts as they are used in everyday language seems to be rather clear and understandable, still all attempts to characterize this meaning in a general and exact way miscarried. And what is worse, various arguments in which these concepts were involved, and which seemed otherwise quite correct and based upon apparently obvious premises, led frequently to paradoxes and antinomies. It is sufficient to mention here the *antinomy of the liar*, Richard's *antinomy of definability* (by means of a finite number of words), and Grelling and Nelson's *antinomy of heterological terms.*[9]

I believe that the method which is outlined in this paper helps to overcome these difficulties and assures the possibility of consistent use of semantic concepts.

6 Languages with a specified structure

Because of the possible occurrence of antinomies, the problem of specifying the formal structure and the vocabulary of a language in which definitions of semantic concepts are to be given becomes especially acute; and we turn now to this problem.

There are certain general conditions under which the structure of a language is regarded as *exactly specified*. Thus, to specify the structure of a language, we must characterize unambiguously the class of those words and expressions which are to be considered *meaningful*. In particular, we must indicate all words which we decide to use without defining them, and which are called *"undefined* (or *primitive) terms"*; and we must give the so-called *rules of definition* for introducing new or *defined terms*. Furthermore, we must set up criteria for distinguishing within the class of expressions those which we call *"sentences."* Finally, we must formulate the conditions under which a sentence of the language can be *asserted*. In particular, we must indicate all *axioms* (or *primitive sentences*), i.e., those sentences which we decide to assert without proof; and we must give the so-called *rules of inference* (or *rules of proof*) by means of which we can deduce new asserted sentences from other sentences which have been previously asserted. Axioms, as well as sentences deduced from them by means of rules of inference, are referred to as "*theorems*" or "*provable sentences.*"

If in specifying the structure of a language we refer exclusively to the form of the expressions involved, the language is said to be *formalized*. In such a language theorems are the only sentences which can be asserted.

At the present time the only languages with a specified structure are the formalized languages of various systems of deductive logic, possibly enriched by the introduction of certain nonlogical terms. However, the field of application of these languages is rather comprehensive; we are able, theoretically, to develop in them various branches of science, for instance, mathematics and theoretical physics.

(On the other hand, we can imagine the construction of languages which have an exactly specified structure without being formalized. In such a language the assertability of sentences, for instance, may depend not always on their form, but sometimes on other, nonlinguistic factors. It would be interesting and important actually to construct a language of this type, and specifically one which would prove to be sufficient for the development of a comprehensive branch of empirical science; for this would justify the hope that languages with specified structure could finally replace everyday language in scientific discourse.)

The problem of the definition of truth obtains a precise meaning and can be solved in a rigorous way only for those languages whose structure has been exactly specified. For other languages – thus, for all natural, "spoken" languages – the meaning of the problem is more or less vague, and its solution can have only an approximate character. Roughly speaking, the approximation consists in replacing a natural language (or a portion of it in which we are interested) by one whose structure is exactly specified, and which diverges from the given language "as little as possible."

7   The antinomy of the liar

In order to discover some of the more specific conditions which must be satisfied by languages in which (or for which) the definition of truth is to be given, it will be advisable to begin with a discussion of that antinomy which directly involves the notion of truth, namely, the antinomy of the liar.

To obtain this antinomy in a perspicuous form,[10] consider the following sentence:

The sentence printed in this paper on p. 41, l. 32, is not true.

For brevity we shall replace the sentence just stated by the letter "s."

According to our convention concerning the adequate usage of the term "*true*," we assert the following equivalence of the form (T):

(1)   *"s" is true if, and only if, the sentence printed in this paper on p. 41, l. 32, is not true.*

On the other hand, keeping in mind the meaning of the symbol "s," we establish empirically the following fact:

(2)   *"s" is identical with the sentence printed in this paper on p. 41, l. 32.*

Now, by a familiar law from the theory of identity (Leibniz's law), it follows from (2) that we may replace in (1) the expression "*the sentence printed in this paper on p. 41, l. 32*" by the symbol "*s*." We thus obtain what follows:

(3)　"*s*" is true if, and only if, "*s*" is not true.

In this way we have arrived at an obvious contradiction.

In my judgment, it would be quite wrong and dangerous from the standpoint of scientific progress to depreciate the importance of this and other antinomies, and to treat them as jokes or sophistries. It is a fact that we are here in the presence of an absurdity, that we have been compelled to assert a false sentence (since (3), as an equivalence between two contradictory sentences, is necessarily false). If we take our work seriously, we cannot be reconciled with this fact. We must discover its cause, that is to say, we must analyze premises upon which the antinomy is based; we must then reject at least one of these premises, and we must investigate the consequences which this has for the whole domain of our research.

It should be emphasized that antinomies have played a pre-eminent role in establishing the foundations of modern deductive sciences. And just as class-theoretical antinomies, and in particular Russell's antinomy (of the class of all classes that are not members of themselves), were the starting point for the successful attempts at a consistent formalization of logic and mathematics, so the antinomy of the liar and other semantic antinomies give rise to the construction of theoretical semantics.

8　The inconsistency of semantically closed languages

If we now analyze the assumptions which lead to the antinomy of the liar, we notice the following:

I　We have implicitly assumed that the language in which the antinomy is constructed contains, in addition to its expressions, also the names of these expressions, as well as semantic terms such as the term "*true*" referring to sentences of this language; we have also assumed that all sentences which determine the adequate usage of this term can be asserted in the language. A language with these properties will be called "*semantically closed*."

II　We have assumed that in this language the ordinary laws of logic hold.

III　We have assumed that we can formulate and assert in our language an empirical premise such as the statement (2) which has occurred in our argument.

It turns out that the assumption (III) is not essential, for it is possible to reconstruct the antinomy of the liar without its help.[11] But the assumptions (I) and (II) prove essential. Since every language which satisfies both of these assumptions is inconsistent, we must reject at least one of them.

It would be superfluous to stress here the consequences of rejecting the assumption (II), that is, of changing our logic (supposing this were possible) even in its more elementary and fundamental parts. We thus consider only the possibility of rejecting the assumption (I). Accordingly, we decide *not to use any language which is semantically closed* in the sense given.

This restriction would of course be unacceptable for those who, for reasons which are not clear to me, believe that there is only one "genuine" language (or, at least, that all "genuine" languages are mutually translatable). However, this restriction does not affect the needs or interests of science in any essential way. The languages (either the formalized languages or – what is more frequently the case – the portions of everyday language) which are used in scientific discourse do not have to be semantically closed. This is obvious in case linguistic phenomena and, in particular, semantic notions do not enter in any way into the subject matter of a science; for in such a case the language of this science does not have to be provided with any semantic terms at all. However, we shall see in the next section how semantically closed languages can be dispensed with even in those scientific discussions in which semantic notions are essentially involved.

The problem arises as to the position of everyday language with regard to this point. At first blush it would seem that this language satisfies both assumptions (I) and (II), and that therefore it must be inconsistent. But actually the case is not so simple. Our everyday language is certainly not one with an exactly specified structure. We do not know precisely which expressions are sentences, and we know even to a smaller degree which sentences are to be taken as assertible. Thus the problem of consistency has no exact meaning with respect to this language. We may at best only risk the guess that a language whose structure has been exactly specified and which resembles our everyday language as closely as possible would be inconsistent.

9 Object–language and metalanguage

Since we have agreed not to employ semantically closed languages, we have to use two different languages in discussing the problem of the definition of truth and, more generally, any problems in the field of semantics. The first of these languages is the language which is "talked about" and which is the subject matter of the whole discussion; the definition of truth which we are seeking applies to the sentences of this language. The second is the language in which we "talk about" the first language, and in terms of which we wish, in particular, to construct the definition of truth for the first language. We shall refer to the first language as "*the object-language*," and to the second as "*the metalanguage*."

It should be noticed that these terms "object-language" and "metalanguage" have only a relative sense. If, for instance, we become interested in the notion of truth applying to sentences, not of our original object-language, but of its metalanguage, the latter becomes automatically the object-language of our discussion; and in order to define truth for this language, we have to go to a new metalanguage – so to speak, to a metalanguage of a higher level. In this way we arrive at a whole hierarchy of languages.

The vocabulary of the metalanguage is to a large extent determined by previously stated conditions under which a definition of truth will be considered materially adequate. This definition, as we recall, has to imply all equivalences of the form (T):

(T) *X is true if, and only if, p.*

The definition itself and all the equivalences implied by it are to be formulated in the metalanguage. On the other hand, the symbol "*p*" in (T) stands for an arbitrary sentence of our object-language. Hence it follows that every sentence which occurs in the object-language must also occur in the metalanguage; in other words, the metalanguage must contain the object-language as a part. This is at any rate necessary for the proof of the adequacy of the definition – even though the definition itself can sometimes be formulated in a less comprehensive metalanguage which does not satisfy this requirement.

(The requirement in question can be somewhat modified, for it suffices to assume that the object-language can be translated into the metalanguage; this necessitates a certain change in the interpretation of the symbol "*p*" in (T). In all that follows we shall ignore the possibility of this modification.)

Furthermore, the symbol "*X*" in (T) represents the name of the sentence which "*p*" stands for. We see therefore that the metalanguage must be rich enough to provide possibilities of constructing a name for every sentence of the object-language.

In addition, the metalanguage must obviously contain terms of a general logical character, such as the expression "if, and only if."[12]

It is desirable for the metalanguage not to contain any undefined terms except such as are involved explicitly or implicitly in the remarks above, i.e.: terms of the object-language; terms referring to the form of the expressions of the object-language, and used in building names for these expressions; and terms of logic. In particular, we desire *semantic terms* (referring to the object-language) to *be introduced into the metalanguage only by definition*. For, if this postulate is satisfied, the definition of truth, or of any other semantic concept, will fulfill what we intuitively expect from every definition; that is, it will explain the meaning of the term being defined in terms whose meaning appears to be completely clear and un-equivocal. And, moreover, we have then a kind of guarantee that the use of semantic concepts will not involve us in any contradictions.

We have no further requirements as to the formal structure of the object-language and the metalanguage; we assume that it is similar to that of other formalized languages known at the present time. In particular, we assume that the usual formal rules of definition are observed in the metalanguage.

10   Conditions for a positive solution of the main problem

Now, we have already a clear idea both of the conditions of material adequacy to which the definition of truth is subjected, and of the formal structure of the language in which this definition is to be constructed. Under these circumstances the problem of the definition of truth acquires the character of a definite problem of a purely deductive nature.

The solution of the problem, however, is by no means obvious, and I would not attempt to give it in detail without using the whole machinery of contemporary logic. Here I shall confine myself to a rough outline of the solution and to the discussion of certain points of a more general interest which are involved in it.

The solution turns out to be sometimes positive, sometimes negative. This depends upon some formal relations between the object-language and its metalanguage; or, more spe-cifically, upon the fact whether the metalanguage in its logical part is "*essentially richer*" than the object-language or not. It is not easy to give a general and precise definition of this notion of "essential richness." If we restrict ourselves to languages based on the logical theory of types, the condition for the metalanguage to be "essentially richer" than the object-language is that it contain variables of a higher logical type than those of the object-language.

If the condition of "essential richness" is not satisfied, it can usually be shown that an interpretation of the metalanguage in the object-language is possible; that is to say, with any given term of the metalanguage a well-determined term of the object-language can be correlated in such a way that the assertible sentences of the one language turn out to be correlated with assertible sentences of the other. As a result of this interpretation, the hypothesis that a satisfactory definition of truth has been formulated in the metalanguage turns out to imply the possibility of reconstructing in that language the antinomy of the liar; and this in turn forces us to reject the hypothesis in question.

(The fact that the metalanguage, in its nonlogical part, is ordinarily more comprehensive than the object-language does not affect the possibility of interpreting the former in the latter. For example, the names of expressions of the object-language occur in the metalanguage, though for the most part they do not occur in the object-language itself; but, nevertheless, it may be possible to interpret these names in terms of the object-language.)

Thus we see that the condition of "essential richness" is necessary for the possibility of a satisfactory definition of truth in the metalanguage. If we want to develop the theory of truth in a metalanguage which does not satisfy this condition, we must give up the idea of defining truth with the exclusive help of those terms which were indicated above (in section 8). We have then to include the term "*true*," or some other semantic term, in the list of undefined terms of the metalanguage, and to express fundamental properties of the notion of truth in a series of axioms. There is nothing essentially wrong in such an axiomatic procedure, and it may prove useful for various purposes.[13]

It turns out, however, that this procedure can be avoided. For *the condition of the "essential richness" of the metalanguage proves to be, not only necessary, but also sufficient for the construction of a satisfactory definition of truth;* i.e., if the metalanguage satisfies this condition, the notion of truth can be defined in it. We shall now indicate in general terms how this construction can be carried through.

11   The construction (in outline) of the definition[14]

A definition of truth can be obtained in a very simple way from that of another semantic notion, namely, of the notion of *satisfaction.*

Satisfaction is a relation between arbitrary objects and certain expressions called "*sentential functions.*" These are expressions like "*x is white,*" "*x is greater than y,*" etc. Their formal structure is analogous to that of sentences; however, they may contain the so-called free variables (like "*x*" and "*y*" in "*x is greater than y*") which cannot occur in sentences.

In defining the notion of a sentential function in formalized languages, we usually apply what is called a "recursive procedure"; i.e., we first describe sentential functions of the simplest structure (which ordinarily presents no difficulty), and then we indicate the operations by means of which compound functions can be constructed from simpler ones. Such an operation may consist, for instance, in forming the logical disjunction or conjunction of two given functions, i.e., by combining them by the word "*or*" or "*and.*" A sentence can now be defined simply as a sentential function which contains no free variables.

As regards the notion of satisfaction, we might try to define it by saying that given objects satisfy a given function if the latter becomes a true sentence when we replace in it free variables by names of given objects. In this sense, for example, snow satisfies the sentential function "*x is white*" since the sentence "*snow is white*" is true. However, apart from other difficulties, this method is not available to us, for we want to use the notion of satisfaction in defining truth.

To obtain a definition of satisfaction we have rather to apply again a recursive procedure. We indicate which objects satisfy the simplest sentential functions; and then we state the conditions under which given objects satisfy a compound function – assuming that we know which objects satisfy the simpler functions from which the compound one has been constructed. Thus, for instance, we say that given numbers satisfy the logical disjunction "*x is greater than y or x is equal to y*" if they satisfy at least one of the functions "*x is greater than y*" or "*x is equal to y.*"

Once the general definition of satisfaction is obtained, we notice that it applies automatically also to those special sentential functions which contain no free variables, i.e., to sentences. It turns out that for a sentence only two cases are possible: a sentence is either satisfied by all objects, or by no objects. Hence we arrive at a definition of truth and falsehood simply by saying that *a sentence is true if it is satisfied by all objects, and false otherwise.*[15]

(It may seem strange that we have chosen a roundabout way of defining the truth of a sentence, instead of trying to apply, for instance, a direct recursive procedure. The reason is that compound sentences are constructed from simpler sentential functions, but not always from simpler sentences; hence no general recursive method is known which applies specifically to sentences.)

From this rough outline it is not clear where and how the assumption of the "essential richness" of the metalanguage is involved in the discussion; this becomes clear only when the construction is carried through in a detailed and formal way.[16]

12   Consequences of the definition

The definition of truth which was outlined above has many interesting consequences.

In the first place, the definition proves to be not only formally correct, but also materially adequate (in the sense established in section 4); in other words, it implies all equivalences of the form (T). In this connection it is important to notice that the conditions for the material adequacy of the definition determine uniquely the extension of the term "*true.*" Therefore, every definition of truth which is materially adequate would necessarily be equivalent to that actually constructed. The semantic conception of truth gives us, so to speak, no possibility of choice between various nonequivalent definitions of this notion.

Moreover, we can deduce from our definition various laws of a general nature. In particular, we can prove with its help the *laws of contradiction and of excluded middle*, which are so characteristic of the Aristotelian conception of truth; i.e., we can show that one and only one of any two contradictory sentences is true. These semantic laws should not be identified with the related logical laws of contradiction and excluded middle; the latter belong to the sentential calculus, i.e., to the most elementary part of logic, and do not involve the term "*true*" at all.

Further important results can be obtained by applying the theory of truth to formalized languages of a certain very comprehensive class of mathematical disciplines; only disciplines of an elementary character and a very elementary logical structure are excluded from this class. It turns out that for a discipline of this class *the notion of truth never coincides with that of provability*; for all provable sentences are true, but there are true sentences which are not provable.[17] Hence it follows further that every such discipline is consistent, but incomplete; that is to say, of any two contradictory sentences at most one is provable, and – what is more – there exists a pair of contradictory sentences neither of which is provable.[18]

13   Extension of the results to other semantic notions

Most of the results at which we arrived in the preceding sections in discussing the notion of truth can be extended with appropriate changes to other semantic notions, for instance, to the notion of satisfaction (involved in our previous discussion), and to those of *designation* and *definition*.

Each of these notions can be analyzed along the lines followed in the analysis of truth. Thus, criteria for an adequate usage of these notions can be established; it can be shown that each of these notions, when used in a semantically closed language according to those criteria, leads necessarily to a contradiction;[19] a distinction between the object-language and the metalanguage becomes again indispensable; and the "essential richness" of the metalanguage proves in each case to be a necessary and sufficient condition for a satisfactory definition of the notion involved. Hence the results obtained in discussing one particular semantic notion apply to the general problem of the foundations of theoretical semantics.

Within theoretical semantics we can define and study some further notions, whose intuitive content is more involved and whose semantic origin is less obvious; we have in mind, for instance, the important notions of *consequence, synonymity*, and *meaning*.[20]

We have concerned ourselves here with the theory of semantic notions related to an individual object-language (although no specific properties of this language have been involved in our arguments). However, we could also consider the problem of developing *general semantics* which applies to a comprehensive class of object-languages. A considerable part of our previous remarks can be extended to this general problem; however, certain new difficulties arise in this connection, which will not be discussed here. I shall merely observe that the axiomatic method (mentioned in section 10) may prove the most appropriate for the treatment of the problem.[21]

II Polemical Remarks

14 Is the semantic conception of truth the right one?

I should like to begin the polemical part of the paper with some general remarks.

I hope nothing which is said here will be interpreted as a claim that the semantic conception of truth is the "right" or indeed the "only possible" one. I do not have the slightest intention to contribute in any way to those endless, often violent discussions on the subject: "What is the right conception of truth?"[22] I must confess I do not understand what is at stake in such disputes; for the problem itself is so vague that no definite solution is possible. In fact, it seems to me that the sense in which the phrase "the right conception" is used has never been made clear. In most cases one gets the impression that the phrase is used in an almost mystical sense based upon the belief that every word has only one "real" meaning (a kind of Platonic or Aristotelian idea), and that all the competing conceptions really attempt to catch hold of this one meaning; since, however, they contradict each other, only one attempt can be successful, and hence only one conception is the "right" one.

Disputes of this type are by no means restricted to the notion of truth. They occur in all domains where – instead of an exact, scientific terminology – common language with its vagueness and ambiguity is used; and they are always meaningless, and therefore in vain.

It seems to me obvious that the only rational approach to such problems would be the following: We should reconcile ourselves with the fact that we are confronted, not with one concept, but with several different concepts which are denoted by one word; we should try to make these concepts as clear as possible (by means of definition, or of an axiomatic procedure, or in some other way); to avoid further confusions, we should agree to use different terms for different concepts; and then we may proceed to a quiet and systematic study of all concepts involved, which will exhibit their main properties and mutual relations.

Referring specifically to the notion of truth, it is undoubtedly the case that in philosophical discussions – and perhaps also in everyday usage – some incipient conceptions of this notion can be found that differ essentially from the classical one (of which the semantic conception is but a modernized form). In fact, various conceptions of this sort have been discussed in the literature, for instance, the pragmatic conception, the coherence theory, etc.

It seems to me that none of these conceptions has been put so far in an intelligible and unequivocal form. This may change, however; a time may come when we find ourselves confronted with several incompatible, but equally clear and precise, conceptions of truth. It will then become necessary to abandon the ambiguous usage of the word "*true*," and to introduce several terms instead, each to denote a different notion. Personally, I should not feel hurt if a future world congress of the "theoreticians of truth" should decide – by a majority of votes – to reserve the word "*true*" for one of the nonclassical conceptions, and should suggest another word, say, "*frue*," for the conception considered here. But I cannot imagine that anybody could present cogent arguments to the effect that the semantic conception is "wrong" and should be entirely abandoned.

15   Formal correctness of the suggested definition of truth

The specific objections which have been raised to my investigations can be divided into several groups; each of these will be discussed separately.

I think that practically all these objections apply, not to the special definition I have given, but to the semantic conception of truth in general. Even those which were leveled against the definition actually constructed could be related to any other definition which conforms to this conception.

This holds, in particular, for those objections which concern the formal correctness of the definition. I have heard a few objections of this kind; however, I doubt very much whether any one of them can be treated seriously.

As a typical example let me quote in substance such an objection.[23] In formulating the definition we use necessarily sentential connectives, i.e., expressions like "*if . . . , then*," "*or*," etc. They occur in the definiens; and one of them, namely, the phrase "*if, and only if,*" is usually employed to combine the definiendum with the definiens. However, it is well known that the meaning of sentential connectives is explained in logic with the help of the words "*true*" and "*false*"; for instance, we say that an equivalence, i.e., a sentence of the form "*p if, and only if, q,*" is true if either or both of its members, i.e., the sentences represented by "*p*" and "*q*," are true or both are false. Hence the definition of truth involves a vicious circle.

If this objection were valid, no formally correct definition of truth would be possible; for we are unable to formulate any compound sentence without using sentential connectives, or other logical terms defined with their help. Fortunately, the situation is not so bad.

It is undoubtedly the case that a strictly deductive development of logic is often preceded by certain statements explaining the conditions under which sentences of the form "*if p, then q,*" etc., are considered true or false. (Such explanations are often given schematically, by means of the so-called truth tables.) However, these statements are outside of the system of logic, and should not be regarded as definitions of the terms involved. They are not formulated in the language of the system, but constitute rather special consequences of the definition of truth given in the metalanguage. Moreover, these statements do not influence the deductive development of logic in any way. For in such a development we do not discuss the question whether a given sentence is true, we are only interested in the problem whether it is provable.[24]

On the other hand, the moment we find ourselves within the deductive system of logic – or of any discipline based upon logic, e.g., of semantics – we either treat sentential connectives as undefined terms, or else we define them by means of other sentential connectives, but never by means of semantic terms like "*true*" or "*false*." For instance, if we agree to regard the expressions "*not*" and "*if . . . , then*" (and possibly also "*if, and only if*") as undefined terms, we can define the term "*or*" by stating that a sentence of the form "*p or q*" is equivalent to the corresponding sentence of the form "*if not p, then q*." The definition can be formulated, e.g., in the following way:

(p or q) if, and only if, (if not p, then q).

This definition obviously contains no semantic terms.

However, a vicious circle in definition arises only when the definiens contains either the term to be defined itself, or other terms defined with its help. Thus we clearly see that the use of sentential connectives in defining the semantic term "*true*" does not involve any circle.

I should like to mention a further objection which I have found in the literature and which seems also to concern the formal correctness, if not of the definition of truth itself, then at least of the arguments which lead to this definition.[25]

The author of this objection mistakenly regards scheme (T) (from section 4) as a definition of truth. He charges this alleged definition with "inadmissible brevity, i.e., incompleteness," which "does not give us the means of deciding whether by 'equivalence' is meant a logical-formal, or a non-logical and also structurally non-describable relation." To remove this "defect" he suggests supplementing (T) in one of the two following ways:

(T')   *X is true if, and only if, p is true,*

or

(T")   *X is true if, and only if, p is the case (i.e., if what p states is the case).*

Then he discusses these two new "definitions," which are supposedly free from the old, formal "defect," but which turn out to be unsatisfactory for other, nonformal reasons.

This new objection seems to arise from a misunderstanding concerning the nature of sentential connectives (and thus to be somehow related to that previously discussed). The author of the objection does not seem to realize that the phrase "*if, and only if*" (in opposition to such phrases as "*are equivalent*" or "*is equivalent to*") expresses no relation between sentences at all since it does not combine names of sentences.

In general, the whole argument is based upon an obvious confusion between sentences and their names. It suffices to point out that – in contradistinction to (T) – schemata (T') and (T") do not give any meaningful expressions if we replace in them "*p*" by a sentence; for the phrases "*p is true*" and "*p is the case*" (i.e., "*what p states is the case*") become meaningless if "*p*" is replaced by a sentence, and not by the name of a sentence (cf. section 4).[26]

While the author of the objection considers schema (T) "inadmissibly brief," I am inclined, on my part, to regard schemata (T') and (T") as "inadmissibly long." And I think even that I can rigorously prove this statement on the basis of the following definition: An expression is said to be "inadmissibly long" if (1) it is meaningless, and (2) it has been obtained from a meaningful expression by inserting superfluous words.

16   Redundancy of semantic terms – their possible elimination

The objection I am going to discuss now no longer concerns the formal correctness of the definition, but is still concerned with certain formal features of the semantic conception of truth.

We have seen that this conception essentially consists in regarding the sentence "*X is true*" as equivalent to the sentence denoted by "*X*" (where "*X*" stands for a name of a sentence of the object-language). Consequently, the term "*true*" when occurring in a simple sentence of the form "*X is true*" can easily be eliminated, and the sentence itself, which belongs to the metalanguage, can be replaced by an equivalent sentence of the object-language; and the same applies to compound sentences provided the term "*true*" occurs in them exclusively as a part of the expressions of the form "*X is true.*"

Some people have therefore urged that the term "*true*" in the semantic sense can always be eliminated, and that for this reason the semantic conception of truth is altogether sterile and useless. And since the same considerations apply to other semantic notions, the conclusion has been drawn that semantics as a whole is a purely verbal game and at best only a harmless hobby.

But the matter is not quite so simple.[27] The sort of elimination here discussed cannot always be made. It cannot be done in the case of universal statements which express the fact that all sentences of a certain type are true, or that all true sentences have a certain property. For instance, we can prove in the theory of truth the following statement:

   All consequences of true sentences are true.

However, we cannot get rid here of the word "*true*" in the simple manner contemplated.

Again, even in the case of particular sentences having the form "*X is true*" such a simple elimination cannot always be made. In fact, the elimination is possible only in those cases in which the name of the sentence which is said to be true occurs in a form that enables us to reconstruct the sentence itself. For example, our present historical knowledge does not give us any possibility of eliminating the word "*true*" from the following sentence:

   The first sentence written by Plato is true.

Of course, since we have a definition for truth and since every definition enables us to replace the definiendum by its definiens, an elimination of the term "*true*" in its semantic sense is always theoretically possible. But this would not be the kind of simple elimination discussed above, and it would not result in the replacement of a sentence in the metalanguage by a sentence in the object-language.

If, however, anyone continues to urge that – because of the theoretical possibility of eliminating the word "*true*" on the basis of its definition – the concept of truth is sterile, he must accept the further conclusion that all defined notions are sterile. But this outcome is so absurd and so unsound historically that any comment on it is unnecessary. In fact, I am rather inclined to agree with those who maintain that the moments of greatest creative advancement in science frequently coincide with the introduction of new notions by means of definition.

17   Conformity of the semantic conception of truth with philosophical and commonsense usage

The question has been raised whether the semantic conception of truth can indeed be regarded as a precise form of the old, classical conception of this notion.

Various formulations of the classical conception were quoted in the early part of this paper (section 3). I must repeat that in my judgment none of them is quite precise and clear. Accordingly, the only sure way of settling the question would be to confront the authors of those statements with our new formulation, and to ask them whether it agrees with their intentions. Unfortunately, this method is impractical since they died quite some time ago.

As far as my own opinion is concerned, I do not have any doubts that our formulation does conform to the intuitive content of that of Aristotle. I am less certain regarding the later formulations of the classical conception, for they are very vague indeed.[28]

Furthermore, some doubts have been expressed whether the semantic conception does reflect the notion of truth in its commonsense and everyday usage. I clearly realize (as I already indicated) that the common meaning of the word "*true*" – as that of any other word of everyday language – is to some extent vague, and that its usage more or less fluctuates. Hence the problem of assigning to this word a fixed and exact meaning is relatively unspecified, and every solution of this problem implies necessarily a certain deviation from the practice of everyday language.

In spite of all this, I happen to believe that the semantic conception does conform to a very considerable extent with the commonsense usage – although I readily admit I may be mistaken. What is more to the point, however, I believe that the issue raised can be settled scientifically, though of course not by a deductive procedure, but with the help of the statistical questionnaire method. As a matter of fact, such research has been carried on, and some of the results have been reported at congresses and in part published.[29]

I should like to emphasize that in my opinion such investigations must be conducted with the utmost care. Thus, if we ask a highschool boy, or even an adult intelligent man having no special philosophical training, whether he regards a sentence to be true if it agrees with reality, or if it designates an existing state of affairs, it may simply turn out that he does not understand the question; in consequence his response, whatever it may be, will be of no value for us. But his answer to the question whether he would admit that the sentence "*it is snowing*" could be true although it is not snowing, or could be false although it is snowing, would naturally be very significant for our problem.

Therefore, I was by no means surprised to learn (in a discussion devoted to these problems) that in a group of people who were questioned only 15 percent agreed that "*true*" means for them "*agreeing with reality*," while 90 percent agreed that a sentence such as "*it is snowing*" is true if, and only if, it is snowing. Thus, a great majority of these people seemed to reject the classical conception of truth in its "philosophical" formulation, while accepting the same conception when formulated in plain words (waiving the question whether the use of the phrase "the same conception" is here justified).

18   The definition in its relation to the philosophical problem of truth and to various epistemological trends

I have heard it remarked that the formal definition of truth has nothing to do with "the philosophical problem of truth."[30] However, nobody has ever pointed out to me in an intelligible way just what this problem is. I have been informed in this connection that my definition, though it states necessary and sufficient conditions for a sentence to be true, does not really grasp the "essence" of this concept. Since I have never been able to understand what the "essence" of a concept is, I must be excused from discussing this point any longer.

In general, I do not believe that there is such a thing as "the philosophical problem of truth." I do believe that there are various intelligible and interesting (but not necessarily philosophical) problems concerning the notion of truth, but I also believe that they can be exactly formulated and possibly solved only on the basis of a precise conception of this notion.

While on the one hand the definition of truth has been blamed for not being philosophical enough, on the other a series of objections has been raised charging this definition with serious philosophical implications, always of a very undesirable nature. I shall discuss now one special objection of this type; another group of such objections will be dealt with in the next section.

It has been claimed that – due to the fact that a sentence like "snow is white" is taken to be semantically true if snow is *in fact* white (italics by the critic) – logic finds itself involved in a most uncritical realism.[31]

If there were an opportunity to discuss the objection with its author, I should raise two points. First, I should ask him to drop the words *"in fact,"* which do not occur in the original formulation and which are misleading, even if they do not affect the content. For these words convey the impression that the semantic conception of truth is intended to establish the conditions under which we are warranted in asserting any given sentence, and in particular any empirical sentence. However, a moment's reflection shows that this impression is merely an illusion; and I think that the author of the objection falls victim to the illusion which he himself created.

In fact, the semantic definition of truth implies nothing regarding the conditions under which a sentence like (1):

(1)   *snow is white*

can be asserted. It implies only that, whenever we assert or reject this sentence, we must be ready to assert or reject the correlated sentence (2):

(2)   *the sentence "snow is white" is true.*

Thus, we may accept the semantic conception of truth without giving up any epistemological attitude we may have had; we may remain naive realists, critical realists or idealists, empiricists, or metaphysicians – whatever we were before. The semantic conception is completely neutral toward all these issues.

In the second place, I should try to get some information regarding the conception of truth which (in the opinion of the author of the objection) does not involve logic in a most naive realism. I would gather that this conception must be incompatible with the semantic one. Thus, there must be sentences which are true in one of these conceptions without being true in the other. Assume, e.g., the sentence (1) to be of this kind. The truth of this sentence in the semantic conception is determined by an equivalence of the form (T):

The sentence "snow is white" is true if, and only if, snow is white.

Hence in the new conception we must reject this equivalence, and consequently we must assume its denial:

> *The sentence "snow is white" is true if, and only if, snow is not white* (or perhaps: *snow, in fact, is not white*).

This sounds somewhat paradoxical. I do not regard such a consequence of the new conception as absurd; but I am a little fearful that someone in the future may charge this conception with involving logic in a "most sophisticated kind of irrealism." At any rate, it seems to me important to realize that every conception of truth which is incompatible with the semantic one carries with it consequences of this type.

I have dwelt a little on this whole question, not because the objection discussed seems to me very significant, but because certain points which have arisen in the discussion should be taken into account by all those who for various epistemological reasons are inclined to reject the semantic conception of truth.

19 *Alleged metaphysical elements in semantics*

The semantic conception of truth has been charged several times with involving certain metaphysical elements. Objections of this sort have been made to apply not only to the theory of truth, but to the whole domain of theoretical semantics.[32]

I do not intend to discuss the general problem whether the introduction of a metaphysical element into a science is at all objectionable. The only point which will interest me here is whether and in what sense metaphysics is involved in the subject of our present discussion.

The whole question obviously depends upon what one understands by "metaphysics." Unfortunately, this notion is extremely vague and equivocal. When listening to discussions in this subject, sometimes one gets the impression that the term "metaphysical" has lost any objective meaning, and is merely used as a kind of professional philosophical invective.

For some people metaphysics is a general theory of objects (ontology) – a discipline which is to be developed in a purely empirical way, and which differs from other empirical sciences only by its generality. I do not know whether such a discipline actually exists (some cynics claim that it is customary in philosophy to baptize unborn children); but I think that in any case metaphysics in this conception is not objectionable to anybody, and has hardly any connections with semantics.

For the most part, however, the term "metaphysical" is used as directly opposed – in one sense or another – to the term "empirical"; at any rate, it is used in this way by those people who are distressed by the thought that any metaphysical elements might have managed to creep into science. This general conception of metaphysics assumes several more specfic forms.

Thus, some people take it to be symptomatic of a metaphysical element in a science when methods of inquiry are employed which are neither deductive nor empirical. However, no trace of this symptom can be found in the development of semantics (unless some metaphysical elements are involved in the object-language to which the semantic notions refer). In particular, the semantics of formalized languages is constructed in a purely deductive way.

Others maintain that the metaphysical character of a science depends mainly on its vocabulary and, more specifically, on its primitive terms. Thus, a term is said to be meta-physical if it is neither logical nor mathematical, and if it is not associated with an empirical procedure which enables us to decide whether a thing is denoted by this term or not. With respect to such a view of metaphysics it is sufficient to recall that a metalanguage includes only three kinds of undefined terms: (1) terms taken from logic, (2) terms of the correspond-ing object-language, and (3) names of expressions in the object-language. It is thus obvious that no metaphysical undefined terms occur in the metalanguage (again, unless such terms appear in the object-language itself).

There are, however, some who believe that, even if no metaphysical terms occur among the primitive terms of a language, they may be introduced by definitions; namely, by those definitions which fail to provide us with general criteria for deciding whether an object falls under the defined concept. It is argued that the term "*true*" is of this kind, since no universal criterion of truth follows immediately from the definition of this term, and since it is generally believed (and in a certain sense can even be proved) that such a criterion will never be found. This comment on the actual character of the notion of truth seems to be perfectly just. However, it should be noticed that the notion of truth does not differ in this respect from many notions in logic, mathematics, and theoretical parts of various empirical sciences, e.g., in theoretical physics.

In general, it must be said that if the term "metaphysical" is employed in so wide a sense as to embrace certain notions (or methods) of logic, mathematics, or empirical sciences, it will apply a fortiori to those of semantics. In fact, as we know from part I of the paper, in developing the semantics of a language we use all the notions of this language, and we apply even a stronger logical apparatus than that which is used in the language itself. On the other hand, however, I can summarize the arguments given above by stating that in no interpre-tation of the term "metaphysical" which is familiar and more or less intelligible to me does semantics involve any metaphysical elements peculiar to itself.

I should like to make one final remark in connection with this group of objections. The history of science shows many instances of concepts which were judged metaphysical (in a loose, but in any case derogatory, sense of this term) before their meaning was made precise; however, once they received a rigorous, formal definition, the distrust in them evaporated. As typical examples we may mention the concepts of negative and imaginary numbers in mathematics. I hope a similar fate awaits the concept of truth and other semantic concepts and it seems to me, therefore, that those who have distrusted them because of their alleged metaphysical implications should welcome the fact that precise definitions of these concepts are now available. If in consequence semantic concepts lose philosophical interest, they will only share the fate of many other concepts of science, and this need give rise to no regret.

20   *Applicability of semantics to special empirical sciences*

We come to the last and perhaps the most important group of objections. Some strong doubts have been expressed whether semantic notions find or can find applications in various domains of intellectual activity. For the most part such doubts have concerned the applica-bility of semantics to the field of empirical science, either to special sciences or to the general methodology of this field; although similar skepticism has been expressed regarding possible applications of semantics to mathematical sciences and their methodology.

I believe that it is possible to allay these doubts to a certain extent, and that some optimism with respect to the potential value of semantics for various domains of thought is not without ground.

To justify this optimism, it suffices I think to stress two rather obvious points. First, the development of a theory which formulates a precise definition of a notion and establishes its general properties provides *eo ipso* a firmer basis for all discussions in which this notion is involved; and, therefore, it cannot be irrelevant for anyone who uses this notion, and desires to do so in a conscious and consistent way. Secondly, semantic notions are actually involved in various branches of science, and in particular of empirical science.

The fact that in empirical research we are concerned only with natural languages, and that theoretical semantics applies to these languages only with certain approximation, does not affect the problem essentially. However, it has undoubtedly this effect that progress in semantics will have but a delayed and somewhat limited influence in this field. The situation with which we are confronted here does not differ essentially from that which arises when we apply laws of logic to arguments in everyday life or, generally, when we attempt to apply a theoretical science to empirical problems.

Semantic notions are undoubtedly involved, to a larger or smaller degree, in psychology, sociology, and practically all the humanities. Thus, a psychologist defines the so-called intelligence quotient in terms of the numbers of *true* (right) and *false* (wrong) answers given by a person to certain questions; for a historian of culture the range of objects for which a human race in successive stages of its development possesses adequate *designations* may be a topic of great significance; a student of literature may be strongly interested in the problem whether a given author always uses two given words with the same *meaning*. Examples of this kind can be multiplied indefinitely.

The most natural and promising domain for the applications of theoretical semantics is clearly linguistics – the empirical study of natural languages. Certain parts of this science are even referred to as "semantics," sometimes with an additional qualification. Thus, this name is occasionally given to that portion of grammar which attempts to classify all words of a language into parts of speech, according to what the words mean or designate. The study of the evolution of meanings in the historical development of a language is sometimes called "historical semantics." In general, the totality of investigations on semantic relations which occur in a natural language is referred to as "descriptive semantics." The relation between theoretical and descriptive semantics is analogous to that between pure and applied mathematics, or perhaps to that between theoretical and empirical physics; the role of formalized languages in semantics can be roughly compared to that of isolated systems in physics.

It is perhaps unnecessary to say that semantics cannot find any direct applications in natural sciences such as physics, biology, etc.; for in none of these sciences are we concerned with linguistic phenomena, and even less with semantic relations between linguistic expressions and objects to which these expressions refer. We shall see, however, in the next section that semantics may have a kind of indirect influence even on those sciences in which semantic notions are not directly involved.

21 *Applicability of semantics to the methodology of empirical science*

Besides linguistics, another important domain for possible applications of semantics is the methodology of science; this term is used here in a broad sense so as to embrace the theory of science in general. Independent of whether a science is conceived merely as a system of statements or as a totality of certain statements and human activities, the study of scientific language constitutes an essential part of the methodological discussion of a science. And it seems to me clear that any tendency to eliminate semantic notions (like those of truth and designation) from this discussion would make it fragmentary and inadequate.[33] Moreover, there is no reason for such a tendency today, once the main difficulties in using semantic terms have been overcome. The semantics of scientific language should be simply included as a part in the methodology of science.

I am by no means inclined to charge methodology and, in particular, semantics – whether theoretical or descriptive – with the task of clarifying the meanings of all scientific terms. This task is left to those sciences in which the terms are used, and is actually fulfilled by them (in the same way in which, e.g., the task of clarifying the meaning of the term "*true*" is left to, and fulfilled by, semantics). There may be, however, certain special problems of this sort in which a methodological approach is desirable or indeed necessary (perhaps, the problem of the notion of causality is a good example here); and in a methodological discussion of such problems semantic notions may play an essential role. Thus, semantics may have some bearing on any science whatsoever.

The question arises whether semantics can be helpful in solving general and, so to speak, classical problems of methodology. I should like to discuss here with some detail a special, though very important, aspect of this question.

One of the main problems of the methodology of empirical science consists in establishing conditions under which an empirical theory or hypothesis should be regarded as acceptable. This notion of acceptability must be relativized to a given stage of the development of a science (or to a given amount of presupposed knowledge). In other words, we may consider it as provided with a time coefficient; for a theory which is acceptable today may become untenable tomorrow as a result of new scientific discoveries.

It seems a priori very plausible that the acceptability of a theory somehow depends on the truth of its sentences, and that consequently a methodologist in his (so far rather unsuccessful) attempts at making the notion of acceptability precise can expect some help from the semantic theory of truth. Hence we ask the question: Are there any postulates which can be reasonably imposed on acceptable theories and which involve the notion of truth? And, in particular, we ask whether the following postulate is a reasonable one:

An accepable theory cannot contain (or imply) any false sentences.

The answer to the last question is clearly negative. For, first of all, we are practically sure, on the basis of our historical experience, that every empirical theory which is accepted today will sooner or later be rejected and replaced by another theory. It is also very probable that the new theory will be incompatible with the old one; i.e., will imply a sentence which is contradictory to one of the sentences contained in the old theory. Hence, at least one of the two theories must include false sentences, in spite of the fact that each of them is accepted at a certain time. Secondly, the postulate in question could hardly ever be satisfied in practice; for we do not know, and are very unlikely to find, any criteria of truth which enable us to show that no sentence of an empirical theory is false.

The postulate in question could be at most regarded as the expression of an ideal limit for successively more adequate theories in a given field of research; but this hardly can be given any precise meaning.

Nevertheless, it seems to me that there is an important postulate which can be reasonably imposed on acceptable empirical theories and which involves the notion of truth. It is closely related to the one just discussed, but is essentially weaker. Remembering that the notion of acceptability is provided with a time coefficient, we can give this postulate the following form:

As soon as we succeed in showing that an empirical theory contains (or implies) false sentences, it cannot be any longer considered acceptable.

In support of this postulate, I should like to make the following remarks.

I believe everybody agrees that one of the reasons which may compel us to reject an empirical theory is the proof of its inconsistency: a theory becomes untenable if we succeed in deriving from it two contradictory sentences. Now we can ask what are the usual motives for rejecting a theory on such grounds. Persons who are acquainted with modern logic are inclined to answer this question in the following way: A well-known logical law shows that a theory which enables us to derive two contradictory sentences enables us also to derive every sentence; therefore, such a theory is trivial and deprived of any scientific interest.

I have some doubts whether this answer contains an adequate analysis of the situation. I think that people who do not know modern logic are as little inclined to accept an inconsistent theory as those who are thoroughly familiar with it; and probably this applies even to those who regard (as some still do) the logical law on which the argument is based as a highly controversial issue, and almost as a paradox. I do not think that our attitude toward an inconsistent theory would change even if we decided for some reasons to weaken our system of logic so as to deprive ourselves of the possibility of deriving every sentence from any two contradictory sentences.

It seems to me that the real reason for our attitude is a different one: We know (if only intuitively) that an inconsistent theory must contain false sentences; and we are not inclined to regard as acceptable any theory which has been shown to contain such sentences.

There are various methods of showing that a given theory includes false sentences. Some of them are based upon purely logical properties of the theory involved; the method just discussed (i.e., the proof of inconsistency) is not the sole method of this type, but is the simplest one, and the one which is most frequently applied in practice. With the help of certain assumptions regarding the truth of empirical sentences, we can obtain methods to the same effect which are no longer of a purely logical nature. If we decide to accept the general postulate suggested above, then a successful application of any such method will make the theory untenable.

22   *Applications of semantics to deductive science*

As regards the applicability of semantics to mathematical sciences and their methodology, i.e., to metamathematics, we are in a much more favorable position than in the case of empirical sciences. For, instead of advancing reasons which justify some hopes for the future (and thus making a kind of pro-semantics propaganda) we are able to point out concrete results already achieved.

Doubts continue to be expressed whether the notion of a true sentence – as distinct from that of a provable sentence – can have any significance for mathematical disciplines and play any part in a methodological discussion of mathematics. It seems to me, however, that just this notion of a true sentence constitutes a most valuable contribution to metamathematics by semantics. We already possess a series of interesting metamathematical results gained with the help of the theory of truth. These results concern the mutual relations between the notion of truth and that of provability; establish new properties of the latter notion (which, as well known, is one of the basic notions of metamathematics); and throw some light on the fundamental problems of consistency and completeness. The most significant among these results have been briefly discussed in section 12.[34]

Furthermore, by applying the method of semantics we can adequately define several important metamathematical notions which have been used so far only in an intuitive way – such as, e.g., the notion of definability or that of a model of an axiom system; and thus we can undertake a systematic study of these notions. In particular, the investigations of definability have already brought some interesting results, and promise even more in the future.[35]

We have discussed the applications of semantics only to metamathematics, and not to mathematics proper. However, this distinction between mathematics and metamathematics is rather unimportant. For metamathematics is itself a deductive discipline and hence, from a certain point of view, a part of mathematics; and it is well known that – due to the formal character of deductive method – the results obtained in one deductive discipline can be automatically extended to any other discipline in which the given one finds an interpretation. Thus, for example, all metamathematical results can be interpreted as results of number theory. Also from a practical point of view there is no clear-cut line between meta-mathematics and mathematics proper; for instance, the investigations on definability could be included in either of these domains.

23   Final remarks

I should like to conclude this discussion with some general and rather loose remarks concerning the whole question of the evaluation of scientific achievements in terms of their applicability. I must confess I have various doubts in this connection.

Being a mathematician (as well as a logician, and perhaps a philosopher of a sort), I have had the opportunity to attend many discussions between specialists in mathematics, where the problem of applications is especially acute, and I have noticed on several occasions the following phenomenon: If a mathematician wishes to disparage the work of one of his colleagues, say, A, the most effective method he finds for doing this is to ask where the results can be applied. The hard-pressed man, with his back against the wall, finally unearths the researches of another mathematician B as the locus of the application of his own results. If next B is plagued with a similar question, he will refer to another mathematician C. After a few steps of this kind we find ourselves referred back to the researches of A, and in this way the chain closes.

Speaking more seriously, I do not wish to deny that the value of a man's work may be increased by its implications for the research of others and for practice. But I believe, nevertheless, that it is inimical to the progress of science to measure the importance of any research exclusively or chiefly in terms of its usefulness and applicability. We know from the history of science that many important results and discoveries have had to wait centuries before they were applied in any field. And, in my opinion, there are also other important factors which cannot be disregarded in determining the value of a scientific work. It seems to me that there is a special domain of very profound and strong human needs related to scientific research, which are similar in many ways to aesthetic and perhaps religious needs. And it also seems to me that the satisfaction of these needs should be considered an important task of research. Hence, I believe, the question of the value of any research cannot be adequately answered without taking into account the intellectual satisfaction which the results of that research bring to those who understand it and care for it. It may be unpopular and out-of-date to say it – but I do not think that a scientific result which gives us a better understanding of the world and makes it more harmonious in our eyes should be held in lower esteem than, say, an invention which reduces the cost of paving roads, or improves household plumbing.

It is clear that the remarks just made become pointless if the word "application" is used in a very wide and liberal sense. It is perhaps not less obvious that nothing follows from these general remarks concerning the specific topics which have been discussed in this paper; and I really do not know whether research in semantics stands to gain or lose by introducing the standard of value I have suggested.

NOTES

1 Compare Tarski, "Der Wahrheitsbegriff in den formalisierten Sprachen" (see references at the end of the paper). This work may be consulted for a more detailed and formal presentation of the subject of the paper, especially of the material included in sections 6 and 9–13. It contains also references to my earlier publications on the problems of semantics (a communication in Polish, 1930; the article "Sur les ensembles définissables de nombres réels" in French, 1931; a communication in German, 1932; and a book in Polish, 1933). The expository part of the present paper is related in its character to Tarski, "Grundlegung der Wissenschaftlichen Semantik." My investigations on the notion of truth and on theoretical semantics have been reviewed or discussed in Hofstadter, "On Semantic Problems"; Juhos, "The Truth of Empirical Statements"; Kokoszyńka, "Über den absoluten Wahrheitsbegriff und einige andere semantische Begriffe" and "Syntase, Semantik und Wissenschaftslogik"; Kotarbiński, *Elementy teorji poznania*; Scholz, review of *Studia Philosophica*, vol. I; Weinberg, review of *Studia Philosophica*, vol. I; et al.

2 It may be hoped that the interest in theoretical semantics will now increase, as a result of the recent publication of the important work Carnap, *Introduction to Semantic*.

3 This applies, in particular, to public discussions during the First International Congress for the Unity of Science (Paris, 1935) and the Conference of International Congresses for the Unity of Science (Paris, 1937); cf., e.g., Neurath, "Erster Internationaler Kongress für Einheit der Wissenschaft in Paris 1935," and Gonseth, "Le Congrès Descartes."

4 The words "notion" and "concept" are used in this paper with all of the vagueness and ambiguity with which they occur in philosophical literature. Thus, sometimes they refer simply to a term, sometimes to what is meant by a term, and in other cases to what is denoted by a term. Sometimes it is irrelevant which of these interpretations is meant; and in certain cases perhaps none of them applies adequately. While on principle I share the tendency to avoid these words in any exact discussion, I did not consider it necessary to do so in this informal presentation.

5 For our present purposes it is somewhat more convenient to understand by "expressions," "sentences," etc., not individual inscriptions, but classes of inscriptions of similar form (thus, not individual physical things, but classes of such things).

6 For the Aristotelian formulation see Aristotle, *Metaphysica*, Γ, 7, 27. The other two formulations are very common in the literature, but I do not know with whom they originate. A critical discussion of various conceptions of truth can be found, e.g., in Kotarbiński, *Elementy teorji poznania* (so far available only in Polish), pp. 123ff, and Russell, *An Inquiry into Meaning and Truth*, pp. 362ff.

7 For most of the remarks contained in sections 4 and 8, I am indebted to the late S. Leśniewski, who developed them in his unpublished lectures in the University of Warsaw (in 1919 and later). However, Leśniewski did not anticipate the possibility of a rigorous development of the theory of

truth, and still less of a definition of this notion; hence, while indicating equivalences of the form (T) as premises in the antinomy of the liar, he did not conceive them as any sufficient conditions for an adequate usage (or definition) of the notion of truth. Also the remarks in section 8 regarding the occurrence of an empirical premiss in the antinomy of the liar, and the possibility of eliminating this premiss, do not originate with him.

8　In connection with various logical and methodological problems involved in this paper the reader may consult Tarski, *Introduction to Logic*.

9　The antinomy of the liar (ascribed to Eubulides or Epimenides) is discussed here in sections 7 and 8. For the antinomy of definability (due to J. Richard) see, e.g., Hilbert and Bernays, *Grundlagen der Mathematik*, vol. 2, pp. 263ff; for the antinomy of heterological terms see Grelling and Nelson, "Bemerkungen zu den Paradoxien von Russell und Burali-Forti," p. 307.

10　Due to Professor J. Łukasiewicz (University of Warsaw).

11　This can roughly be done in the following way. Let *S* be any sentence beginning with the words "*Every sentence*." We correlate with *S* a new sentence *S** by subjecting *S* to the following two modifications: we replace in *S* the first word, "*Every*," by "*The*" and we insert after the second word, "*sentence*," the whole sentence *S* enclosed in quotation marks. Let us agree to call the sentence *S* "(self-)applicable" or "non-(self-)applicable" dependent on whether the correlated sentence *S** is true or false. Now consider the following sentence:

Every sentence is non-applicable.

It can easily be shown that the sentence just stated must be both applicable and non-applicable; hence a contradiction. It may not be quite clear in what sense this formulation of the antinomy does not involve an empirical premiss; however, I shall not elaborate on this point.

12　The terms "logic" and "logical" are used in this paper in a broad sense, which has become almost traditional in the last decades; logic is assumed here to comprehend the whole theory of classes and relations (i.e., the mathematical theory of sets). For many different reasons I am personally inclined to use the term "logic" in a much narrower sense, so as to apply it only to what is sometimes called "elementary logic," i.e., to the sentential calculus and the (restricted) predicate calculus.

13　Cf. here, however, Tarski, "Grundlegung der Wissenschaftlichen Semantik," pp. 5ff.

14　The method of construction we are going to outline can be applied – with appropriate changes – to all formalized languages that are known at the present time; although it does not follow that a language could not be constructed to which this method would not apply.

15　In carrying through this idea a certain technical difficulty arises. A sentential function may contain an arbitrary number of free variables; and the logical nature of the notion of satisfaction varies with this number. Thus, the notion in question when applied to functions with one variable is a binary relation between these functions and single objects; when applied to functions with two variables it becomes a ternary relation between functions and couples of objects; and so on. Hence, strictly speaking, we are confronted, not with one notion of satisfaction, but with infinitely many notions; and it turns out that these notions cannot be defined independently of each other, but must all be introduced simultaneously.

　　To overcome this difficulty, we employ the mathematical notion of an infinite sequence (or, possibly, of a finite sequence with an arbitrary number of terms). We agree to regard satisfaction, not as a many-termed relation between sentential functions and an indefinite number of objects, but as a binary relation between functions and sequences of objects. Under this assumption the formulation of a general and precise definition of satisfaction no longer presents any difficulty; and a true sentence can now be defined as one which is satisfied by every sequence.

16　To define recursively the notion of satisfaction, we have to apply a certain form of recursive definition which is not admitted in the object-language. Hence the "essential richness" of the metalanguage may simply consist in admitting this type of definition. On the other hand, a general method is known which makes it possible to eliminate all recursive definitions and to replace them by normal, explicit ones. If we try to apply this method to the definition of satisfaction, we see that we have either to introduce into the metalanguage variables of a higher logical type than those which occur in the object-language; or else to assume axiomatically in the metalanguage the existence of classes that are more comprehensise than all those whose existence can be established in the object-language. See here Tarski, "Der Wahrheitsbegriff in den formalisierten Sprachen," pp. 393ff, and "On Undecidable Statements," p. 110.

17 Due to the development of modern logic, the notion of mathematical proof has undergone a far-reaching simplification. A sentence of a given formalized discipline is provable if it can be obtained from the axioms of this discipline by applying certain simple and purely formal rules of inference, such as those of detachment and substitution. Hence to show that all provable sentences are true, it suffices to prove that all the sentences accepted as axioms are true, and that the rules of inference when applied to true sentences yield new true sentences; and this usually presents no difficulty.

On the other hand, in view of the elementary nature of the notion of provability, a precise definition of this notion requires only rather simple logical devices. In most cases, those logical devices which are available in the formalized discipline itself (to which the notion of provability is related) are more than sufficient for this purpose. We know, however, that as regards the definition of truth just the opposite holds. Hence, as a rule, the notions of truth and provability cannot coincide; and since every provable sentence is true, there must be true sentences which are not provable.

18 Thus the theory of truth provides us with a general method for consistency proofs for formalized mathematical disciplines. It can be easily realized, however, that a consistency proof obtained by this method may possess some intuitive value – i.e., may convince us or strengthen our belief that the discipline under consideration is actually consistent – only in case we succeed in defining truth in terms of a metalanguage which does not contain the object-language as a part (cf. here a remark in section 9). For only in this case the deductive assumptions of the metalanguage may be intuitively simpler and more obvious than those of the object-language – even though the condition of "essential richness" will be formally satisfied. Cf. here also Tarski, "Grundlegung der Wissenschaftlichen Semantik," p. 7.

The incompleteness of a comprehensive class of formalized disciplines constitutes the essential content of a fundamental theorem of K. Gödel; cf. Gödel, "Über formal unentscheidbare Sätze," pp. 187ff. The explanation of the fact that the theory of truth leads so directly to Gödel's theorem is rather simple. In deriving Gödel's result from the theory of truth we make an essential use of the fact that the definition of truth cannot be given in a metalanguage which is only as "rich" as the object-language (cf. n. 17); however, in establishing this fact, a method of reasoning has been applied which is very closely related to that used (for the first time) by Gödel. It may be added that Gödel was clearly guided in his proof by certain intuitive considerations regarding the notion of truth, although this notion does not occur in the proof explicitly; cf. Gödel, "Über formal unentscheidbare Sätze," pp. 174ff.

19 The notions of designation and definition lead respectively to the antinomies of Grelling and Nelson and of Richard (cf. n. 9). To obtain an antinomy for the notion of satisfaction, we construct the following expression:

The sentential function X does not satisfy X.

A contradiction arises when we consider the question whether this expression, which is clearly a sentential function, satisfies itself or not.

20 All notions mentioned in this section can be defined in terms of satisfaction. We can say, e.g., that a given term designates a given object if this object satisfies the sentential function "*x is identical with T*" where "*T*" stands for the given term. Similarly, a sentential function is said to define a given object if the latter is the only object which satisfies this function. For a definition of

consequence see Tarski, "Über den Begriff der logischen Folgerung," and for that of synonymity, see to Carnap, *Introduction to Semantics*.

21   General semantics is the subject of Carnap, *Introduction to Semantics*. Cf. here also remarks in Tarski, "Der Wahrheitsbegriff in den formalisierten Sprachen," pp. 388ff.

22   Cf. various quotations in Ness, "Truth as Conceived by Those who Are Not Professional Philosophers," pp. 13ff.

23   The names of persons who have raised objections will not be quoted here, unless their objections have appeared in print.

24   It should be emphasized, however, that as regards the question of an alleged vicious circle the situation would not change even if we took a different point of view, represented, e.g., in Carnap, *Introduction to Semantics*; i.e., if we regarded the specification of conditions under which sentences of a language are true as an essential part of the description of this language. On the other hand, it may be noticed that the point of view represented in the text does not exclude the possibility of using truth tables in a deductive development of logic. However, these tables are to be regarded then merely as a formal instrument for checking the provability of certain sentences; and the symbols "*T*" and "*F*" which occur in them and which are usually considered abbreviations of "*true*" and "*false*" should not be interpreted in any intuitive way.

25   Cf. Juhos, "The Truth of Empirical Statements." I must admit that I do not clearly understand von Juhos' objections and do not know how to classify them; therefore, I confine myself here to certain points of a formal character. Von Juhos does not seem to know my definition of truth; he refers only to an informal presentation in Tarski, "Grundlegung der Wissenschaftliken Semantik," where the definition has not been given at all. If he knew the actual definition, he would have to change his argument. However, I have no doubt that he would discover in this definition some "defects" as well. For he believes he has proved that "on ground of principle it is impossible to give such a definition at all."

26   The phrases "*p is true*" and "*p is the case*" (or better "*it is true that p*"and "*it is the case that p*") are sonletimes used in informal discussions, mainly for stylistic reasons; but they are considered then as synonymous with the sentence represented by "*p*." On the other hand, as far as I understand the situation, the phrases in question cannot be used by von Juhos synonymously with "*p*"; for otherwise the replacement of (T) by (T′) or (T″) would not constitute an "improvement."

27   Cf. the discussion of this problem in Kokoszyńska, "Über den absoluten Wahheitsbegriff und Leinige andere semantische Begriffe," pp. 161ff.

28   Most authors who have discussed my work on the notion of truth are of the opinion that my definition does conform with the classical conception of this notion; see, e.g., Kotarbiński, *Elementy teorji poznania*, and Scholz, review of *Studia Philosophica*, vol. I.

29   Cf. Ness, "Truth as Conceived by Those who Are Not Professional Philosophers." Unfortunately, the results of that part of Ness's research which is especially relevant for our problem are not discussed in his book; compare p. 148, fn. 1.

30   Though I have heard this opinion several times, I have seen it in print only once and, curiously enough, in a work which does not have a philosophical character – in fact, in Hilbert and Bernays, *Grundlagen der Mathematik*, vol. II, p. 269 (where, by the way, it is not expressed as any kind of objection). On the other hand, I have not found any remark to this effect in discussions of my work by professional philosophers (cf. n. 1).

31   Cf. Gonseth, "Le Congrès Descartes,", pp. 187ff.

32   See Nagel, review of Hofstadten, "On Semantic Problems," and review of Carnap, *Introduction to Semantics*, pp. 471 ff. A remark which goes, perhaps, in the same direction is also to be found in Weinberg, review of *Studia Philosophica*, vol. I, p. 77; cf., however, his earlier remarks, pp. 75ff.

33   Such a tendency, was evident in earlier works of Carnap (see, e.g., Carnap, *Logical Syntax of Language*, especially part V) and in writings of other members of the Vienna Circle. Cf. here Kokoszyńska, "Syntax, Semantik und Wissenschaftslogik," and Weinberg, review of *Studia Philosophica*, vol. I.

34 For other results obtained with the help of the theory of truth see Gödel, "Über die Länge von Beweisen"; Tarski, "Der Wahrheitsbegriff in den formalisierten Sprachen," pp. 401ff; and Tarski, "On Undecidable Statements," pp. 111ff.

35 An object – e.g., a number or a set of numbers – is said to be definable (in a given formalism) if there is a sentential function which defines it; cf. n. 20. Thus, the term "definable," though of a metamathematical (semantic) origin, is purely mathematical as to its extension, for it expresses a property (denotes a class) of mathematical objects. In consequence, the notion of definability can be redefined in purely mathematical terms, though not within the formalized discipline to which this notion refers; however, the fundamental idea of the definition remains unchanged. Cf. here also for further bibliographic references Tarski, "Sur les ensembles définissables de nombres réels"; various other results concerning definability can also be found in the literature, e.g., in Hilbert and Bernays, *Grundlagen der Mathematik*, vol. I, pp. 354ff, 369ff, 456ff, etc., and in Lindenbaum and Tarski, "Über die Beschänktheit der Ausdrucksmittel deduktiver Theorien." It may be noticed that the term "definable" is sometimes used in another, metamathematical (but not semantic), sense; this occurs, for instance, when we say that a term is definable in other terms (on the basis of a given axiom system). For a definition of a model of an axiom system see Tarski, "Über den Begriff den logischen Folgerung."

REFERENCES

Aristotle. *Metaphysica*. (*Works*, vol. VIII.) English trans. W. D. Ross. Oxford, 1908.

Carnap, R. *Logical Syntax of Language*. London and New York, 1937.

Carnap, R. *Introduction to Semantics*. Cambridge, 1942.

Gödel, K. "Über formal unentscheidbare Sätze der *Principia Mathematica* und verwandter Systeme, I." *Monatshefte für Mathematik und Physik*, vol. XXXIII, 1931, pp. 173–98.

Gödel, K. "Über die Länge von Beweisen." *Ergebnisse eines mathematischen Kolloquiums*, vol. VII, 1936, pp. 23–4.

Gonseth, F. "Le Congrès Descartes. Questions de Philosophie scientifique." *Revue thomiste*, vol. XLIV, 1938, pp. 183–93.

Grelling, K., and Nelson, L. "Bemerkungen zu den Paradoxien von Russell und Burali-Forti." *Abhandlungen der Fries'schen Schule*, vol. II (new series), 1908, pp. 301–34.

Hilbert, D., and Bernays, P. *Grundlagen der Mathematik*. 2 vols. Berlin, 1934–9.

Hofstadter, A. "On Semantic Problems." *Journal of Philosophy*, vol. XXXV, 1938, pp. 225–32.

Juhos, B. von. "The Truth of Empirical Statements." *Analysis*, vol. IV, 1937, pp. 65–70.

Kokoszyńska, M. "Über den absoluten Wahrheitsbegriff und einige andere semantische Begriffe." *Erkenntnis*, vol. VI, 1936, pp. 143–65.

Kokoszyńska, M. "Syntax, Semantik und Wissenschaftslogik." *Actes du Congrès International de Philosophie Scientifique*, vol. III, Paris, 1936, pp. 9–14.

Kotarbiński, T. *Elementy teorji poznania, logiki formalnej i metodologji nauk*. (*Elements of Epistemology, Formal Logic, and the Methodology of Sciences*, in Polish.) Lwów, 1929.

Kotarbiński, T. "W sprawie pojecia prawdy." ("Concerning the Concept of Truth," in Polish.) *Przeglad filozoficzny*, vol. XXXVII, 1935, pp. 85–91.

Lindenbaum, A., and Tarski, A. "Über die Beschränktheit der Ausdrucksmittel deduktiver Theorien." *Ergebnisse eines mathematischen Kolloquiums*, vol. VII, 1936, pp. 15–23.

Nagel, E. Review of Hofstadter, "On Semantic Problems." *Journal of Symbolic Logic*, vol. III, 1938, p. 90.

Nagel, E. Review of Carnap, *Introduction & Semantics*. *Journal of Philosophy*, vol. XXXIX, 1942, pp. 468–73.

Ness, A. " 'Truth' as Conceived by Those who Are Not Professional Philosophers." *Skrifter utgitt av Det Norske Videnskaps-Akademi i Oslo, II. Historisk-Filosofisk Klasse*, vol. IV, Oslo, 1938.

Neurath, O. "Erster Internationaler Kongress für Einheit der Wissenschaft in Paris 1935." *Erkenntnis*, vol. V, 1935, pp. 377–406.

Russell, B. *An Inquiry into Meaning and Truth*. New York, 1940.

Scholz, H. Review of *Studia Philosophica*, vol. I. *Deutsche Literaturzeitung*, vol. LVIII, 1937, pp. 1914–17.

Tarski, A. "Sur les ensembles définissables de nombres réels. I." *Fundamenta mathematicae*, vol. XVII, 1931, pp. 210–39.

Tarski, A. "Der Wahrheitsbegriff in den formalisierten Sprachen." (German translation of a book in Polish, 1933.) *Studia Philosophica*, vol. I, 1935, pp. 261–405.

Tarski, A. "Grundlegung der Wissenschaftlichen Semantik." *Actes du Congrès International de Philosophie Scientifique*, vol. III, Paris, 1936, pp. 1–8.

Tarski, A. "Über den Begriff der logischen Folgerung." *Actes du Congrès International de Philosophie Scientifique*, vol. VII, Paris, 1937, pp. 1–11.

Tarski, A. "On Undecidable Statements in Enlarged Systems of Logic and the Concept of Truth." *Journal of Symbolic Logic*, vol. IV, 1939, pp. 105–12.

Tarski, A. *Introduction to Logic*. New York, 1941.

Weinberg, J. Review of *Studia Philosophica*, vol. I. *Philosophical Review*, vol. XLVII, 1939, pp. 70–7.

Truth and Meaning

DONALD DAVIDSON

It is conceded by most philosophers of language, and recently even by some linguists, that a satisfactory theory of meaning must give an account of how the meanings of sentences depend upon the meanings of words. Unless such an account could be supplied for a particular language, it is argued, there would be no explaining the fact that we can learn the language: no explaining the fact that, on mastering a finite vocabulary and a finitely stated set of rules, we are prepared to produce and to understand any of a potential infinitude of sentences. I do not dispute these vague claims, in which I sense more than a kernel of truth.[1] Instead I want to ask what it is for a theory to give an account of the kind adumbrated.

One proposal is to begin by assigning some entity as meaning to each word (or other significant syntactical feature) of the sentence; thus we might assign Theaetetus to "Theaetetus" and the property of flying to "flies" in the sentence "Theaetetus flies." The problem then arises how the meaning of the sentence is generated from these meanings. Viewing concatenation as a significant piece of syntax, we may assign to it the relation of participating in or instantiating; however, it is obvious that we have here the start of an infinite regress. Frege sought to avoid the regress by saying that the entities corresponding to predicates (for example) are "unsaturated" or "incomplete" in contrast to the entities that correspond to names, but this doctrine seems to label a difficulty rather than solve it.

The point will emerge if we think for a moment of complex singular terms, to which Frege's theory applies along with sentences. Consider the expression "the father of Annette"; how does the meaning of the whole depend on the meaning of the parts? The answer would seem to be that the meaning of "the father of" is such that when this expression is prefixed to a singular term the result refers to the father of the person to whom the singular term refers. What part is played, in this account, by the unsaturated or incomplete entity for which "the father of" stands? All we can think to say is that this entity "yields" or "gives" the father of x as value when the argument is x, or perhaps that this entity maps people onto their fathers. It may not be clear whether the entity for which "the father of" is said to stand performs any genuine explanatory function as long as we stick to individual expressions; so think instead of the infinite class of expressions formed by writing "the father of" zero or more times in front of "Annette." It is easy to supply a theory that tells, for an arbitrary one of these singular terms, what it refers to: if the term is "Annette" it refers to Annette, while if the term is complex, consisting of "the father of" prefixed to a singular term t, then it refers to the father of the person to whom t refers. It is obvious that no entity corresponding to "the father of" is, or needs to be, mentioned in stating this theory.

It would be inappropriate to complain that this little theory *uses* the words "the father of" in giving the reference of expressions containing those words. For the task was to give the meaning of all expressions in a certain infinite set on the basis of the meaning of the parts; it was not in the bargain also to give the meanings of the atomic parts. On the other hand, it is now evident that a satisfactory theory of the meanings of complex expressions may not require entities as meanings of all the parts. It behooves us then to rephrase our demand on a satisfactory theory of meaning so as not to suggest that individual words must have meanings at all, in any sense that transcends the fact that they have a systematic effect on the meanings of the sentences in which they occur. Actually, for the case at hand we can do better still in stating the criterion of success: what we wanted, and what we got, is a theory that entails every sentence of the form "t refers to x" where "t" is replaced by a structural description[2] of a singular term, and "x" is replaced by that term itself. Further, our theory accomplishes this without appeal to any semantical concepts beyond the basic "refers to." Finally, the theory clearly suggests an effective procedure for determining, for any singular term in its universe, what that term refers to.

A theory with such evident merits deserves wider application. The device proposed by Frege to this end has a brilliant simplicity: count predicates as a special case of functional expressions, and sentences as a special case of complex singular terms. Now, however, a difficulty looms if we want to continue in our present (implicit) course of identifying the meaning of a singular term with its reference. The difficulty follows upon making two reasonable assumptions: that logically equivalent singular terms have the same reference; and that a singular term does not change its reference if a contained singular term is replaced by another with the same reference. But now suppose that "R" and "S" abbreviate any two sentences alike in truth value. Then the following four sentences have the same reference:

(1) R

(2) $\hat{x}(x = x \cdot R) = \hat{x}(x = x)$

(3) $\hat{x}(x = x \cdot S) = \hat{x}(x = x)$

(4) S

For (1) and (2) are logically equivalent, as are (3) and (4), while (3) differs from (2) only in containing the singular term "$\hat{x}(x = x \cdot S)$" where (2) contains "$\hat{x}(x = x \cdot R)$", and these refer to the same thing if S and R are alike in truth value. Hence any two sentences have the same reference if they have the same truth value.[3] And if the meaning of a sentence is what it refers to, all sentences alike in truth value must be synonymous – an intolerable result.

Apparently we must abandon the present approach as leading to a theory of meaning. This is the natural point at which to turn for help to the distinction between meaning and reference. The trouble, we are told, is that questions of reference are, in general, settled by extralinguistic facts, questions of meaning not, and the facts can conflate the references of expressions that are not synonymous. If we want a theory that gives the meaning (as distinct from reference) of each sentence, we must start with the meaning (as distinct from reference) of the parts.

Up to here we have been following in Frege's footsteps; thanks to him, the path is well known and even well worn. But now, I would like to suggest, we have reached an impasse: the switch from reference to meaning leads to no useful account of how the meanings of sentences depend upon the meanings of the words (or other structural features) that compose them. Ask, for example, for the meaning of "Theaetetus flies." A Fregean answer might go something like this: given the meaning of "Theaetetus" as argument, the meaning of "flies" yields the meaning of "Theaetetus flies" as value. The vacuity of this answer is obvious. We wanted to know what the meaning of "Theaetetus flies" is; it is no progress to be told that it is the meaning of "Theaetetus flies." This much we knew before any theory was in sight. In the bogus account just given, talk of the structure of the sentence and of the meanings of words was idle, for it played no role in producing the given description of the meaning of the sentence.

The contrast here between a real and pretended account will be plainer still if we ask for a theory, analogous to the miniature theory of reference of singular terms just sketched, but different in dealing with meanings in place of references. What analogy demands is a theory that has as consequences all sentences of the form "*s* means *m*" where "*s*" is replaced by a structural description of a sentence and "*m*" is replaced by a singular term that refers to the meaning of that sentence; a theory, moreover, that provides an effective method for arriving at the meaning of an arbitrary sentence structurally described. Clearly some more articulate way of referring to meanings than any we have seen is essential if these criteria are to be met.[4] Meanings as entities, or the related concept of synonymy, allow us to formulate the following rule relating sentences and their parts: sentences are synonymous whose corresponding parts are synonymous ("corresponding" here needs spelling out, of course). And meanings as entities may, in theories such as Frege's, do duty, on occasion, as references, thus losing their status as entities distinct from references. Paradoxically, the one thing meanings do not seem to do is oil the wheels of a theory of meaning – at least as long as we require of such a theory that it nontrivially give the meaning of every sentence in the language. My objection to meanings in the theory of meaning is not that they are abstract or that their identity conditions are obscure, but that they have no demonstrated use.

This is the place to scotch another hopeful thought. Suppose we have a satisfactory theory of syntax for our language, consisting of an effective method of telling, for an arbitrary expression, whether or not it is independently meaningful (i.e., a sentence), and assume as usual that this involves viewing each sentence as composed, in allowable ways, out of elements drawn from a fixed finite stock of atomic syntactical elements (roughly, words). The hopeful thought is that syntax, so conceived, will yield semantics when a dictionary giving the meaning of each syntactic atom is added. Hopes will be dashed, however, if semantics is to comprise a theory of meaning in our sense, for knowledge of the structural characteristics that make for meaningfulness in a sentence, plus knowledge of the meanings of the ultimate parts, does not add up to knowledge of what a sentence means. The point is easily illustrated by belief sentences. Their syntax is relatively unproblematic. Yet adding a dictionary does not touch the standard semantic problem, which is that we cannot account for even as much as the truth conditions of such sentences on the basis of what we know of the meanings of the words in them. The situation is not radically altered by refining the dictionary to indicate which meaning or meanings an ambiguous expression bears in each of its possible contexts; the problem of belief sentences persists after ambiguities are resolved.

The fact that recursive syntax with dictionary added is not necessarily recursive semantics has been obscured in some recent writing on linguistics by the intrusion of semantic criteria into the discussion of purportedly syntactic theories. The matter would boil down to a harmless difference over terminology if the semantic criteria were clear; but they are not. While there is agreement that it is the central task of semantics to give the semantic interpretation (the meaning) of every sentence in the language, nowhere in the linguistic literature will one find, so far as I know, a straightforward account of how a theory performs this task, or how to tell when it has been accomplished. The contrast with syntax is striking. The main job of a modest syntax is to characterize *meaningfulness* (or, sentencehood). We may have as much confidence in the correctness of such a characterization as we have in the representativeness of our sample and our ability to say when particular expressions are meaningful (sentences). What clear and analogous task and test exist for semantics?[5]

We decided a while back not to assume that parts of sentences have meanings except in the ontologically neutral sense of making a systematic contribution to the meaning of the sentences in which they occur. Since postulating meanings has netted nothing, let us return to that insight. One direction in which it points is a certain holistic view of meaning. If sentences depend for their meaning on their structure, and we understand the meaning of each item in the structure only as an abstraction from the totality of sentences in which it features, then we can give the meaning of any sentence (or word) only by giving the meaning of every sentence (and word) in the language. Frege said that only in the context of a sentence does a word have meaning; in the same vein he might have added that only in the context of the language does a sentence (and therefore a word) have meaning.

This degree of holism was already implicit in the suggestion that an adequate theory of meaning must entail *all* sentences of the form "*s* means *m*." But now, having found no more help in meanings of sentences than in meanings of words, let us ask whether we can get rid of the troublesome singular terms supposed to replace "*m*" and to refer to meanings. In a way, nothing could be easier: just write "*s* means that *p*," and imagine "*p*" replaced by a sentence. Sentences, as we have seen, cannot name meanings, and sentences with "that" prefixed are not names at all, unless we decide so. It looks as though we are in trouble on another count, however, for it is reasonable to expect that in wrestling with the logic of the apparently nonextensional "means that" we will encounter problems as hard as, or perhaps identical with, the problems our theory is out to solve.

The only way I know to deal with this difficulty is simple, and radical. Anxiety that we are enmeshed in the intensional springs from using the words "means that" as filling between description of sentence and sentence, but it may be that the success of our venture depends not on the filling but on what it fills. The theory will have done its work if it provides, for every sentence *s* in the language under study, a matching sentence (to replace "*p*") that, in some way yet to be made clear, "gives the meaning" of *s*. One obvious candidate for matching sentence is just *s* itself, if the object-language is contained in the metalanguage; otherwise a translation of *s* in the metalanguage. As a final bold step, let us try treating the position occupied by "*p*" extensionally: to implement this, sweep away the obscure "means that," provide the sentence that replaces "p" with a proper sentential connective, and supply the description that replaces "s" with its own predicate. The plausible result is

(T) s is T if and only if p.

What we require of a theory of meaning for a language L is that without appeal to any (further) semantical notions it place enough restrictions on the predicate "is T" to entail all sentences got from schema T when "s" is replaced by a structural description of a sentence of L, and "p" by that sentence.

Any two predicates satisfying this condition have the same extension,[6] so if the metalanguage is rich enough, nothing stands in the way of putting what I am calling a theory of meaning into the form of an explicit definition of a predicate "is T." But whether explicitly defined or recursively characterized, it is clear that the sentences to which the predicate "is T" applies will be just the true sentences of L, for the condition we have placed on satisfactory theories of meaning is in essence Tarski's Convention T that tests the adequacy of a formal semantical definition of truth.[7]

The path to this point has been tortuous, but the conclusion may be stated simply: a theory of meaning for a language L shows "how the meanings of sentences depend upon the meanings of words" if it contains a (recursive) definition of truth-in-L. And, so far at least, we have no other idea how to turn the trick. It is worth emphasizing that the concept of truth played no ostensible role in stating our original problem. That problem, upon refinement, led to the view that an adequate theory of meaning must characterize a predicate meeting certain conditions. It was in the nature of a discovery that such a predicate would apply exactly to the true sentences. I hope that what I am doing may be described in part as defending the philosophical importance of Tarski's semantical concept of truth. But my defense is only distantly related, if at all, to the question whether the concept Tarski has shown how to define is the (or a) philosophically interesting conception of truth, or the question whether Tarski has cast any light on the ordinary use of such words as "true" and "truth." It is a misfortune that dust from futile and confused battles over these questions has prevented those with a theoretical interest in language – philosophers, logicians, psychologists, and linguists alike – from recognizing in the semantical concept of truth (under whatever name) the sophisticated and powerful foundation of a competent theory of meaning.

There is no need to suppress, of course, the obvious connection between a definition of truth of the kind Tarski has shown how to construct, and the concept of meaning. It is this: the definition works by giving necessary and sufficient conditions for the truth of every sentence, and to give truth conditions is a way of giving the meaning of a sentence. To know the semantic concept of truth for a language is to know what it is for a sentence – any sentence – to be true, and this amounts, in one good sense we can give to the phrase, to understanding the language. This at any rate is my excuse for a feature of the present discussion that is apt to shock old hands: my freewheeling use of the word "meaning," for what I call a theory of meaning has after all turned out to make no use of meanings, whether of sentences or of words. Indeed since a Tarski-type truth definition supplies all we have asked so far of a theory of meaning, it is clear that such a theory falls comfortably within what Quine terms the "theory of reference" as distinguished from what he terms the "theory of meaning." So much to the good for what I call a theory of meaning, and so much, perhaps, against my so calling it.[8]

A theory of meaning (in my mildly perverse sense) is an empirical theory, and its ambition is to account for the workings of a natural language. Like any theory, it may be tested by comparing some of its consequences with the facts. In the present case this is easy, for the theory has been characterized as issuing in an infinite flood of sentences each giving the truth conditions of a sentence; we only need to ask, in selected cases, whether what the theory avers to be the truth conditions for a sentence really are. A typical test case might involve deciding whether the sentence "Snow is white" is true if and only if snow is white. Not all cases will be so simple (for reasons to be sketched), but it is evident that this sort of test does not invite counting noses. A sharp conception of what constitutes a theory in this domain furnishes an exciting context for raising deep questions about when a theory of language is correct and how it is to be tried. But the difficulties are theoretical, not practical. In application, the trouble is to get a theory that comes close to working; anyone can tell whether it is right.[9] One can see why this is so. The theory reveals nothing new about the conditions under which an individual sentence is true; it does not make those conditions any clearer than the sentence itself does. The work of the theory is in relating the known truth conditions of each sentence to those aspects ("words") of the sentence that recur in other sentences, and can be assigned identical roles in other sentences. Empirical power in such a theory depends on success in recovering the structure of a very complicated ability – the ability to speak and understand a language. We can tell easily enough when particular pronouncements of the theory comport with our understanding of the language; this is consistent with a feeble insight into the design of the machinery of our linguistic accomplishments.

The remarks of the last paragraph apply directly only to the special case where it is assumed that the language for which truth is being characterized is part of the language used and understood by the characterizer. Under these circumstances, the framer of a theory will as a matter of course avail himself when he can of the built-in convenience of a metalanguage with a sentence guaranteed equivalent to each sentence in the object-language. Still, this fact ought not to con us into thinking a theory any more correct that entails "'Snow is white' is true if and only if snow is white" than one that entails instead:

(*S*) "Snow is white" is true if and only if grass is green,

provided, of course, we are as sure of the truth of (*S*) as we are of that of its more celebrated predecessor. Yet (*S*) may not encourage the same confidence that a theory that entails it deserves to be called a theory of meaning.

The threatened failure of nerve may be counteracted as follows. The grotesqueness of (*S*) is in itself nothing against a theory of which it is a consequence, provided the theory gives the correct results for every sentence (on the basis of its structure, there being no other way). It is not easy to see how (*S*) could be party to such an enterprise, but if it were – if, that is, (*S*) followed from a characterization of the predicate "is true" that led to the invariable pairing of truths with truths and falsehoods with falsehoods – then there would not, I think, be anything essential to the idea of meaning that remained to be captured.

What appears to the right of the biconditional in sentences of the form "*s* is true if and only if *p*," when such sentences are consequences of a theory of truth, plays its role in determining the meaning of *s* not by pretending synonymy but by adding one more brushstroke to the picture which, taken as a whole, tells what there is to know of the meaning of *s*; this stroke is added by virtue of the fact that the sentence that replaces "*p*" is true if and only if *s* is.

It may help to reflect that (*S*) is acceptable, if it is, because we are independently sure of the truth of "snow is white" and "grass is green"; but in cases where we are unsure of the truth of a sentence, we can have confidence in a characterization of the truth predicate only if it pairs that sentence with one we have good reason to believe equivalent. It would be ill advised for someone who had any doubts about the color of snow or grass to accept a theory that yielded (*S*), even if his doubts were of equal degree, unless he thought the color of the one was tied to the color of the other. Omniscience can obviously afford more bizarre theories of meaning than ignorance; but then, omniscience has less need of communication.

It must be possible, of course, for the speaker of one language to construct a theory of meaning for the speaker of another, though in this case the empirical test of the correctness of the theory will no longer be trivial. As before, the aim of theory will be an infinite correlation of sentences alike in truth. But this time the theory-builder must not be assumed to have direct insight into likely equivalences between his own tongue and the alien. What he must do is find out, however he can, what sentences the alien holds true in his own tongue (or better, to what degree he holds them true). The linguist then will attempt to construct a characterization of truth-for-the-alien which yields, so far as possible, a mapping of sentences held true (or false) by the alien onto sentences held true (or false) by the linguist. Supposing no perfect fit is found, the residue of sentences held true translated by sentences held false (and vice versa) is the margin for error (foreign or domestic). Charity in interpreting the words and thoughts of others is unavoidable in another direction as well: just as we must maximize agreement, or risk not making sense of what the alien is talking about, so we must maximize the self-consistency we attribute to him, on pain of not understanding *him*. No single principle of optimum charity emerges; the constraints therefore determine no single theory. In a theory of radical translation (as Quine calls it) there is no completely disentangling questions of what the alien means from questions of what he believes. We do not know what someone means unless we know what he believes; we do not know what someone believes unless we know what he means. In radical translation we are able to break into this circle, if only incompletely, because we can sometimes tell that a person accedes to a sentence we do not understand.[10]

In the past few pages I have been asking how a theory of meaning that takes the form of a truth definition can be empirically tested, and have blithely ignored the prior question whether there is any serious chance such a theory can be given for a natural language. What are the prospects for a formal semantical theory of a natural language? Very poor, according to Tarski; and I believe most logicians, philosophers of language, and linguists agree.[11] Let me do what I can to dispel the pessimism. What I can in a general and programmatic way, of course; for here the proof of the pudding will certainly be in the proof of the right theorems.

Tarski concludes the first section of his classic essay on the concept of truth in formalized languages with the following remarks, which he italicizes:

> *The very possibility of a consistent use of the expression "true sentence" which is in harmony with the laws of logic and the spirit of everyday language seems to be very questionable, and consequently the same doubt attaches to the possibility of constructing a correct definition of this expression.*[12]

Later in the same essay, he returns to the subject:

> the concept of truth (as well as other semantical concepts) when applied to colloquial language in conjunction with the normal laws of logic leads inevitably to confusions and contradictions.

Whoever wishes, in spite of all difficulties, to pursue the semantics of colloquial language with the help of exact methods will be driven first to undertake the thankless task of a reform of this language. He will find it necessary to define its structure, to overcome the ambiguity of the terms which occur in it, and finally to split the language into a series of languages of greater and greater extent, each of which stands in the same relation to the next in which a formalized language stands to its metalanguage. It may, however be doubted whether the language of everyday life, after being "rationalized" in this way, would still preserve its naturalness and whether it would not rather take on the characteristic features of the formalized languages.[13]

Two themes emerge: that the universal character of natural languages leads to contradiction (the semantic paradoxes), and that natural languages are too confused and amorphous to permit the direct application of formal methods. The first point deserves a serious answer, and I wish I had one. As it is, I will say only why I think we are justified in carrying on without having disinfected this particular source of conceptual anxiety. The semantic paradoxes arise when the range of the quantifiers in the object language is too generous in certain ways. But it is not really clear how unfair to Urdu or to Hindi it would be to view the range of their quantifiers as insufficient to yield an explicit definition of "true-in-Urdu" or "true-in-Hindi." Or, to put the matter in another, if not more serious way, there may in the nature of the case always be something we grasp in understanding the language of another (the concept of truth) that we cannot communicate to him. In any case, most of the problems of general philosophical interest arise within a fragment of the relevant natural language that may be conceived as containing very little set theory. Of course these comments do not meet the claim that natural languages are universal. But it seems to me this claim, now that we know such universality leads to paradox, is suspect.

Tarski's second point is that we would have to reform a natural language out of all recognition before we could apply formal semantical methods. If this is true, it is fatal to my project, for the task of a theory of meaning as I conceive it is not to change, improve, or reform a language, but to describe and understand it. Let us look at the positive side. Tarski has shown the way to giving a theory for interpreted formal languages of various kinds; pick one as much like English as possible. Since this new language has been explained in English and contains much English we not only may, but I think must, view it as part of English for those who understand it. For this fragment of English we have, *ex hypothesi*, a theory of the required sort. Not only that, but in interpreting this adjunct of English in old English we necessarily gave hints connecting old and new. Wherever there are sentences of old English with the same truth conditions as sentences in the adjunct we may extend the theory to cover them. Much of what is called for is just to mechanize as far as possible what we now do by art when we put ordinary English into one or another canonical notation. The point is not that canonical notation is better than the rough original idiom, but rather that if we know what idiom the canonical notation is canonical *for*, we have as good a theory for the idiom as for its kept companion.

Philosophers have long been at the hard work of applying theory to ordinary language by the device of matching sentences in the vernacular with sentences for which they have a theory. Frege's massive contribution was to show how "all," "some," "every," "each," "none," and associated pronouns, in some of their uses, could be tamed; for the first time, it was possible to dream of a formal semantics for a significant part of a natural language. This dream came true in a sharp way with the work of Tarski. It would be a shame to miss the fact that as a result of these two magnificent achievements, Frege's and Tarski's, we have gained a deep insight into the structure of our mother tongues. Philosophers of a logical bent have tended to start where the theory was and work out toward the complications of natural language. Contemporary linguists, with an aim that cannot easily be seen to be different, start with the ordinary and work toward a general theory. If either party is successful, there must be a meeting. Recent work by Chomsky and others is doing much to bring the complexities of natural languages within the scope of serious semantic theory. To give an example: suppose success in giving the truth conditions for some significant range of sentences in the active voice. Then with a formal procedure for transforming each such sentence into a corresponding sentence in the passive voice, the theory of truth could be extended in an obvious way to this new set of sentences.[14]

One problem touched on in passing by Tarski does not, at least in all its manifestations, have to be solved to get ahead with theory: the existence in natural languages of "ambiguous terms." As long as ambiguity does not affect grammatical form, and can be translated, ambiguity for ambiguity, into the metalanguage, a truth definition will not tell us any lies. The trouble, for systematic semantics, with the phrase "believes that" in English is not its vagueness, ambiguity, or unsuitability for incorporation in a serious science: let our metalanguage be English, and all *these* problems will be translated without loss or gain into the metalanguage. But the central problem of the logical grammar of "believes that" will remain to haunt us.

The example is suited to illustrating another, and related, point, for the discussion of belief sentences has been plagued by failure to observe a fundamental distinction between tasks: uncovering the logical grammar or form of sentences (which is in the province of a theory of meaning as I construe it), and the analysis of individual words or expressions (which are treated as primitive by the theory). Thus Carnap, in the first edition of *Meaning and Necessity*, suggested we render "John believes that the earth is round" as "John responds affirmatively to 'the earth is round' as an English sentence." He gave this up when Mates pointed out that John might respond affirmatively to one sentence and not to another no matter how close in meaning.[15] But there is a confusion here from the start. The semantic structure of a belief sentence, according to this idea of Carnap's, is given by a three-place predicate with places reserved for expressions referring to a person, a sentence, and a language. It is a different sort of problem entirely to attempt an analysis of this predicate, perhaps along behavioristic lines. Not least among the merits of Tarski's conception of a theory of truth is that the purity of method it demands of us follows from the formulation of the problem itself, not from the self-imposed restraint of some adventitious philosophical puritanism.

I think it is hard to exaggerate the advantages to philosophy of language of bearing in mind this distinction between questions of logical form or grammar, and the analysis of individual concepts. Another example may help advertise the point.

If we suppose questions of logical grammar settled, sentences like "Bardot is good" raise no special problems for a truth definition. The deep differences between descriptive and evaluative (emotive, expressive, etc.) terms do not show here. Even if we hold there is some important sense in which moral or evaluative sentences do not have a truth value (for example, because they cannot be "verified"), we ought not to boggle at " 'Bardot is good' is true if and only if Bardot is good"; in a theory of truth, this consequence should follow with the rest, keeping track, as must be done, of the semantic location of such sentences in the language as a whole – of their relation to generalizations, their role in such compound sentences as "Bardot is good and Bardot is foolish," and so on. What is special to evaluative words is simply not touched: the mystery is transferred from the word "good" in the object-language to its translation in the metalanguage.

But "good" as it features in "Bardot is a good actress" is another matter. The problem is not that the translation of this sentence is not in the metalanguage – let us suppose it is. The problem is to frame a truth definition such that " 'Bardot is a good actress' is true if and only if Bardot is a good actress" – and all other sentences like it – are consequences. Obviously "good actress" does not mean "good and an actress." We might think of taking "is a good actress" as an unanalyzed predicate. This would obliterate all connection between "is a good actress" and "is a good mother," and it would give us no excuse to think of "good," in these uses, as a word or semantic element. But worse, it would bar us from framing a truth definition at all, for there is no end to the predicates we would have to treat as logically simple (and hence accommodate in separate clauses in the definition of satisfaction): "is a good companion to dogs," "is a good 28-year-old conversationalist," and so forth. The problem is not peculiar to the case: it is the problem of attributive adjectives generally.

It is consistent with the attitude taken here to deem it usually a strategic error to undertake philosophical analysis of words or expressions which is not preceded by or at any rate accompanied by the attempt to get the logical grammar straight. For how can we have any confidence in our analyses of words like "right," "ought," "can," and "obliged," or the phrases we use to talk of actions, events, and causes, when we do not know what (logical, semantical) parts of speech we have to deal with? I would say much the same about studies of the "logic" of these and other words, and the sentences containing them. Whether the effort and ingenuity that has gone into the study of deontic logics, modal logics, imperative and erotetic logics has been largely futile or not cannot be known until we have acceptable semantic analyses of the sentences such systems purport to treat. Philosophers and logicians sometimes talk or work as if they were free to choose between, say, the truth-functional conditional and others, or free to introduce non-truth-functional sentential operators like "Let it be the case that" or "It ought to be the case that." But in fact the decision is crucial. When we depart from idioms we can accommodate in a truth definition, we lapse into (or create) language for which we have no coherent semantical account – that is, no account at all of how such talk can be integrated into the language as a whole.

To return to our main theme: we have recognized that a theory of the kind proposed leaves the whole matter of what individual words mean exactly where it was. Even when the metalanguage is different from the object-language, the theory exerts no pressure for improvement, clarification, or analysis of individual words, except when, by accident of vocabulary, straightforward translation fails. Just as synonymy, as between expressions, goes generally untreated, so also synonymy of sentences, and analyticity. Even such sentences as "A vixen is a female fox" bear no special tag unless it is our pleasure to provide it. A truth definition does not distinguish between analytic sentences and others, except for sentences that owe their truth to the presence alone of the constants that give the theory its grip on structure: the theory entails not only that these sentences are true but that they will remain true under all significant rewritings of their nonlogical parts. A notion of logical truth thus given limited application, related notions of logical equivalence and entailment will tag along. It is hard to imagine how a theory of meaning could fail to read a logic into its object-language to this degree; and to the extent that it does, our intuitions of logical truth, equivalence, and entailment may be called upon in constructing and testing the theory.

I turn now to one more, and very large, fly in the ointment: the fact that the same sentence may at one time or in one mouth be true and at another time or in another mouth be false. Both logicians and those critical of formal methods here seem largely (though by no means

universally) agreed that formal semantics and logic are incompetent to deal with the distur-
bances caused by demonstratives. Logicians have often reacted by downgrading natural
language and trying to show how to get along without demonstratives; their critics react by
downgrading logic and formal semantics. None of this can make me happy: clearly,
demonstratives cannot be eliminated from a natural language without loss or radical change,
so there is no choice but to accommodate theory to them.

No logical errors result if we simply treat demonstratives as constants;[16] neither do any
problems arise for giving a semantic truth definition. "'I am wise' is true if and only if I am
wise," with its bland ignoring of the demonstrative element in "I," comes off the assembly
line along with "'Socrates is wise' is true if and only if Socrates is wise," with its bland
indifference to the demonstrative element in "is wise" (the tense).

What suffers in this treatment of demonstratives is not the definition of a truth predicate,
but the plausibility of the claim that what has been defined is truth. For this claim is
acceptable only if the speaker and circumstances of utterance of each sentence mentioned
in the definition are matched by the speaker and circumstances of utterance of the truth
definition itself. It could also be fairly pointed out that part of understanding demonstratives is knowing the rules by which they adjust their reference to circumstance;
assimilating demonstratives to constant terms obliterates this feature. These complaints
can be met, I think, though only by a fairly far-reaching revision in the theory of truth. I
shall barely suggest how this could be done, but bare suggestion is all that is needed: the
idea is technically trivial, and quite in line with work being done on the logic of the
tenses.[17]

We could take truth to be a property, not of sentences, but of utterances, or speech acts,
or ordered triples of sentences, times, and persons; but it is simplest just to view truth as a
relation between a sentence, a person, and a time. Under such treatment, ordinary logic as
now read applies as usual, but only to sets of sentences relativized to the same speaker and
time; further logical relations between sentences spoken at different times and by different
speakers may be articulated by new axioms. Such is not my concern. The theory of meaning
undergoes a systematic but not puzzling change: corresponding to each expression with a
demonstrative element there must in the theory be a phrase that relates the truth conditions
of sentences in which the expression occurs to changing times and speakers. Thus the theory
will entail sentences like the following:

> "I am tired" is true as (potentially) spoken by p at t if and only if p is tired at t.

> "That book was stolen" is true as (potentially) spoken by p at t if and only if the book
> demonstrated by p at t is stolen prior to t.[18]

Plainly, this course does not show how to eliminate demonstratives; for example, there is
no suggestion that "the book demonstrated by the speaker" can be substituted ubiquitously
for "that book" *salva veritate*. The fact that demonstratives are amenable to formal treatment ought greatly to improve hopes for a serious semantics of natural language, for it is
likely that many outstanding puzzles, such as the analysis of quotations or sentences about
propositional attitudes, can be solved if we recognize a concealed demonstrative
construction.

Now that we have relativized truth to times and speakers, it is appropriate to glance back
at the problem of empirically testing a theory of meaning for an alien tongue. The essence of
the method was, it will be remembered, to correlate held-true sentences with held-true

sentences by way of a truth definition, and within the bounds of intelligible error. Now the picture must be elaborated to allow for the fact that sentences are true, and held true, only relative to a speaker and a time. The real task is therefore to translate each sentence by another that is true for the same speakers at the same times. Sentences with demonstratives obviously yield a very sensitive test of the correctness of a theory of meaning, and constitute the most direct link between language and the recurrent macroscopic objects of human interest and attention.[19]

In this paper I have assumed that the speakers of a language can effectively determine the meaning or meanings of an arbitrary expression (if it has a meaning), and that it is the central task of a theory of meaning to show how this is possible. I have argued that a characterization of a truth predicate describes the required kind of structure, and provides a clear and testable criterion of an adequate semantics for a natural language. No doubt there are other reasonable demands that may be put on a theory of meaning. But a theory that does no more than define truth for language comes far closer to constituting a complete theory of meaning than superficial analysis might suggest; so, at least, I have urged.

Since I think there is no alternative, I have taken an optimistic and programmatic view of the possibilities for a formal characterization of a truth predicate for a natural language. But it must be allowed that a staggering list of difficulties and conundrums remains. To name a few: we do not know the logical form of counterfactual or subjunctive sentences, nor of sentences about probabilities and about causal relations; we have no good idea what the logical role of adverbs is, nor the role of attributive adjectives; we have no theory for mass terms like "fire," "water," and "snow," nor for sentences about belief, perception, and intention, nor for verbs of action that imply purpose. And finally, there are all the sentences that seem not to have truth values at all: the imperatives, optatives, interrogatives, and a host more. A comprehensive theory of meaning for a natural language must cope successfully with each of these problems

NOTES

An earlier version or this paper was read at the Eastern Division meeting of the American Philosophical Association in December, 1966; the main theme traces back to an unpublished paper delivered to the Pacific Division of the American Philosophical Association in 1953. Present formulations owe much to John Wallace, with whom I have discussed these matters since 1962. My research was supported by the National Science Foundation.

1 Elsewhere I have urged that it is a necessary condition, if a language is to be learnable, that it have only a finite number or semantical primitives: see "Theories or Meaning and Learnable Languages," in *Proceedings of the 1964 International Congress for Logic, Methodology and Philosophy of Science* (North-Holland, Amsterdam: 1965), pp. 383–94.

2 A "structural description" or an expression describes the expression as a concatenation of elements drawn from a fixed finite list (for example of words or letters).

3 The argument is essentially Frege's. See A. Church, *Introduction to Mathematical Logic*, vol. I (Princeton University Press, Princeton, NJ: 1956), pp. 24–5. It is perhaps worth mentioning that the argument does not depend on any particular identification of the entities to which sentences are supposed to refer.

4 It may be thought that Church, in "A Formulation of the Logic of Sense and Denotation," in *Structure, Method and Meaning: Essays in Honor of H. M. Sheffer*, P. Henle, H. M. Kallen, and S. K. Langer, eds (Liberal Arts Press, New York: 1951), pp. 3–24, has given a theory of meaning that makes essential use of meanings as entities. But this is not the case: Church's logics of sense and

denotation are interpreted as being about meanings, but they do not mention expressions and so cannot of course be theories of meaning in the sense now under discussion.

5   For a recent and instructive statement of the role of semantics in linguistics, see Noam Chomsky, "Topics in the Theory of Generative Grammar," in *Current Trends in Linguistics*, Thomas A. Sebeok, ed. vol. III (Mouton, The Hague: 1966). In this article, Chomsky (1) emphasizes the central importance of semantics in linguistic theory, (2) argues for the superiority of transformational grammars over phrase-structure grammars largely on the grounds that, although phrase-structure grammars may be adequate to define sentencehood for (at least) some natural languages, they are inadequate as a foundation for semantics, and (3) comments repeatedly on the "rather primitive state" of the concepts of semantics and remarks that the notion of semantic interpretation "still resists any deep analysis."

6   Assuming, of course, that the extension of these predicates is limited to the sentences of *L*.

7   Alfred Tarski, "The Concept of Truth in Formalized Languages," in *Logic, Semantics, Metamathematics* (Oxford, Clarendon Press: 1956), pp. 152–278.

8   But Quine may be quoted in support of my usage: "in point of *meaning* . . . a word may be said to be determined to whatever extent the truth or falsehood of its contexts is determined." "Truth by Convention," first published in 1936; now in *The Ways of Paradox* (Harvard University Press, New York: 1966), p. 82. Since a truth definition determines the truth value of every sentence in the object-language (relative to a sentence in the metalanguage), it determines the meaning of every word and sentence. This would seem to justify the title "theory of meaning."

9   To give a single example: it is clearly a count in favor of a theory that it entails " 'Snow is white' is true if and only if snow is white." But to contrive a theory that entails this (and works for all related sentences) is not trivial. I do not know a theory that succeeds with this very case (the problem of "mass terms").

10 This sketch of how a theory of meaning for an alien tongue can be tested obviously owes its inspiration to Quine's account of radical translation in ch. II of *Word and Object* (MIT Press, New York: 1960). In suggesting that an acceptable theory of radical translation take the form of a recursive characterization or truth, I go beyond anything explicit in Quine. Toward the end of this paper, in the discussion of demonstratives, another strong point of agreement will turn up.

11 So far as I am aware, there has been very little discussion of whether a formal truth definition can be given for a natural language. But in a more general vein, several people have urged that the concepts of formal semantics be applied to natural language. See, for example, the contributions of Yehoshua Bar-Hillel and Evert Beth to *The Philosophy of Rudolph Carnap*, Paul A. Schilpp, ed. (Open Count, La Salle, IL: 1963), and Bar-Hillel's "Logical Syntax and Semantics," *Language* 30, 230–7.

12 Tarski, "Concept of Truth," p. 165.

13 Ibid., p. 267.

14 The rapprochement I prospectively imagine between transformational grammar and a sound theory of meaning has been much advanced by a recent change in the conception of transformational grammar described by Chomsky in the article referred to above (n. 5). The structures generated by the phrase-structure part of the grammar, it has been realized for some time, are those suited to semantic interpretation; but this view is inconsistent with the idea, held by Chomsky until recently, that recursive operations are introduced only by the transformation rules. Chomsky now believes the phrase-structure rules are recursive. Since languages to which normal semantic methods directly and naturally apply are ones for which a (recursive) phrase-structure grammar is appropriate, it is clear that Chomsky's present picture of the relation between the structures generated by the phrase-structure part of the grammar, and the sentences of the language, is very much like the picture many logicians and philosophers have had of the relation between the richer formalized languages and ordinary language. (In these remarks I am indebted to Bruce Vermazen.)

15 B. Mates, "Synonymity," in *Semantics and the Philosophy of Language*, L. Linsky, ed. (University of Illinois Press, Urbana: 1952).

16 Quine has good things to say about this in *Methods of Logic* (Holt, New York: 1950). See n. 8.

17 For an up-to-date bibliography, and discussion, see A. N. Prior, *Past, Present, and Future* (Clarendon Press, Oxford: 1967).
18 There is more than an intimation of this approach to demonstratives and truth in Austin's 1950 article "Truth," reprinted in *Philosophical Papers* (Clarendon Press, Oxford: 1961). See pp. 89–90.
19 These remarks clearly derive from Quine's idea that "occasion sentences" (those with a demonstrative element) must play a central role in constructing a translation manual.

Pragmatics

ROBERT C. STALNAKER

Until recently, pragmatics – the study of language in relation to the users of language – has been the neglected member of the traditional three-part division of the study of signs; syntax, semantics, pragmatics. The problems of pragmatics have been treated informally by philosophers in the ordinary-language tradition, and by some linguists, but logicians and philosophers of a formalistic frame of mind have generally ignored pragmatic problems, or else pushed them into semantics and syntax. My project in this paper is to carve out a subject matter that might plausibly be called pragmatics and which is in the tradition of recent work in formal semantics. The discussion will be programmatic. My aim is not to solve the problems I shall touch on, but to persuade you that the theory I sketch has promise. Although this paper gives an informal presentation, the subject can be developed in a relatively straightforward way as a *formal pragmatics* no less rigorous than present-day logical syntax and semantics. The subject is worth developing, I think, first to provide a framework for treating some philosophical problems that cannot be adequately handled within traditional formal semantics, and second to clarify the relation between logic and formal semantics and the study of natural language.

I shall begin with the second member of the triad, semantics. The boundaries of this subject are not so clear as is sometimes supposed, and since pragmatics borders on semantics, these boundaries will determine where our subject begins. After staking out a claim for pragmatics, I shall describe some of the tasks that fall within its range and try to defend a crucial distinction on which the division between semantics and pragmatics is based.

1 Semantics

If we look at the general characterizations of semantics offered by Morris and Carnap, it will seem an elusive object. Semantics, according to them, concerns the relationship between signs and their *designata*. The *designatum* of a sign, Morris writes, is what is "taken account of in virtue of the presence of the sign." He also says "a *designatum* is not a thing, but a kind of object, or a class of objects."[1] Carnap is equally vague in giving a general characterization. The designatum of an expression, he says, is what he who uses it intends to refer to by it, "e.g., to an object or a property or a state of affairs. . . . (For the moment, no exact definition for 'designatum' is intended; this word is merely to serve as a convenient common term for different cases – object, properties, etc., whose fundamental differences in other respects are not hereby denied.)"[2]

Though a clear general definition is hard to come by, the historical development of formal semantics is well delineated. The central problems in semantics have concerned the definition of truth, or truth conditions, for the sentences of certain languages. Formal semantics abstracts the problem of giving truth conditions for sentences away from problems concerning the purposes for which those sentences are uttered. People do many things with language, one of which is to express *propositions* for one reason or another, propositions being abstract objects representing truth conditions. Semantics has studied that aspect of language use in isolation from others. Hence I shall consider semantics to be the study of propositions.

The explication of *proposition* given in formal semantics is based on a very homely intuition: when a statement is made, two things go into determining whether it is true or false. First, what did the statement say: what proposition was asserted? Second, what is the world like: does what was said correspond to it? What, we may ask, must a proposition be in order that this simple account be correct? It must be a rule, or a function, taking us from the way the world is into a truth value. But since our ideas about how the world is change, and since we may wish to consider the statement relative to hypothetical and imaginary situations, we want a function taking not just the actual state of the world, but various possible states of the world into truth values. Since there are two truth values, a proposition will be a way – any way – of dividing a set of possible states of the world into two parts: the ones that are ruled out by the truth of the proposition, and the ones that are not.[3]

Those who find the notion of a *possible world* obscure may feel that this explication of proposition is unhelpful, since formal semantics generally takes that notion, like the notion of an individual, as primitive.[4] Some explanation is perhaps needed, but I am not sure what kind. Even without explanation, the notion has, I think, enough intuitive content to make it fruitful in semantics. I shall say only that one requirement for identifying a possible world is to specify a domain of individuals said to exist in that world.[5]

If we explain propositions as functions from possible worlds into truth values, they will have the properties that have traditionally been ascribed to them. Propositions are things that may be considered in abstraction on the one hand from particular languages and linguistic formulations (the sentences that express them), and on the other hand from the kinds of linguistic act in which they figure (for example the assertions and commands in which a proposition is asserted or commanded). Thus once the homely intuition mentioned above has done its work, we may forget about assertions and consider propositions themselves, along with similar things such as functions taking individuals into propositions, and functions taking propositions into propositions.

Generally, the study of formal semantics has proceeded by first setting up a language, and then laying down rules for matching up the sentences of that language with propositions or truth values. But the languages are set up usually for no other purpose than to represent the propositions, or at least this is how formalized languages have been used by philosophers. Regimentation or formalization is simply a way to make clearer what the truth conditions are – what proposition is expressed by what is regimented or formalized. But with an adequate theory of propositions themselves, such philosophical analyses can proceed without the mediation of a regimented or formalized object-language. Rather than translate a problematic locution into an object-language in which it is clear what propositions are expressed by the sentences, one can simply state what proposition is expressed by that locution. The effect is the same. Unless one is concerned with proof theory, he may drop the language out altogether with no loss.

According to this characterization of semantics, then, the subject has no essential connection with languages at all, either natural or artificial. (Of course semantical theories are expressed *in* language, but so are theories about rocks.) This is not to deny the possibility of a *causal* relationship between language and our conception of a proposition. It may be, for example, that the fact that we think of a possible world as a domain of individuals together with the ascription of properties to them is a result of the fact that our language has a subject – predicate structure. It is also not to deny that the study of the grammar of natural language may be a rich source of insight into the nature of propositions and a source of evidence for distinctions among propositions. If we find in grammar a device for marking a distinction of content, we may presume that there is a distinction of content to be marked. But whatever the causal or evidential story, we may still abstract the study of propositions from the study of language. By doing so, I think we get a clearer conception of a relation between them.

Though one may study propositions apart from language, accounting for the relation between language and propositions still falls partly within the domain of semantics. One of the jobs of natural language is to express propositions, and it is a semantical problem to specify the rules for matching up sentences of a natural language with the propositions that they express. In most cases, however, the rules will not match sentences directly with propositions, but will match sentences with propositions relative to features of the context in which the sentence is used. These contextual features are a part of the subject matter of pragmatics, to which I shall now turn.

2 Pragmatics

Syntax studies sentences, semantics studies propositions. Pragmatics is the study of linguistic acts and the contexts in which they are performed. There are two major types of problem to be solved within pragmatics: first, to define interesting types of speech act and speech product; second, to characterize the features of the speech context which help determine which proposition is expressed by a given sentence. The analysis of illocutionary acts is an example of a problem of the first kind; the study of indexical expressions is an example of the second. My primary concern will be with problems of the second kind, but I shall say a few general things about the first before I go on to that.

Assertions, commands, counterfactuals, claims, conjectures and refutations, requests, rebuttals, predictions, promises, pleas, speculations, explanations, insults, inferences, guesses, generalizations, answers, and lies are all kinds of linguistic act. The problem of analysis in each case is to find necessary and sufficient conditions for the successful (or perhaps in some cases normal) performance of the act. The problem is a pragmatic one since these necessary and sufficient conditions will ordinarily involve the presence or absence of various properties of the context in which the act is performed,[6] for example, the intentions of the speaker, the knowledge, beliefs, expectations, or interests of the speaker and his audience, other speech acts that have been performed in the same context, the time of utterance, the effects of the utterance, the truth value of the proposition expressed, the semantic relations between the proposition expressed and some others involved in some way.

Almost all of the speech act types mentioned above involve the expression of a proposition, and in the first type of pragmatic problem, the identity of that proposition is taken to be unproblematic. In most cases, however, the context of utterance affects not only the force with which the proposition is expressed, but also the proposition itself. It may be that the semantical rules determine the proposition expressed by a sentence or clause only relative to some feature of the situation in which the sentence is used.

Consider a statement "everybody is having a good time." I assume that you understand the *sentence* well enough. Now assume also that you are omniscient with respect to people having a good time: you know for each person that ever lived and for each time up to now whether or not that person was having a good time at that time. Under these conditions, you may still be in doubt about the truth of the statement for at least two reasons: first, you do not know when it was made; second, you do not know what class of people it was made about. It is unlikely that the speaker meant everybody in the universe. He may have meant everybody at some party, or everyone listening to some philosophical lecture, and if so, then we have to know what party, or what lecture before we know even what was said, much less whether what was said is true.

Statements involving personal pronouns and demonstratives furnish the most striking examples of this kind. When you say "We shall overcome," I need to know who you are, and for whom you are speaking. If you say "that is a great painting," I need to know what you are looking at, or pointing to, or perhaps what you referred to in your previous utterance. Modal terms also are notoriously dependent on context for their interpretation. For a sentence using *can*, *may*, *might*, *must*, or *ought*, to determine a proposition unambiguously, a domain of "all possible worlds" must be specified or intended. It need not be *all* conceivable worlds in any absolute sense, if there is such a sense. Sentences involving modals are usually to be construed relative to all possible worlds consistent with the speaker's knowledge, or with some set of presuppositions, or with what is morally right, or legally right, or normal, or what is within someone's power. Unless the relevant domain of possible worlds is clear in the context, the proposition expressed is undetermined.

The formal *semantic* analysis of such concepts as universality and necessity isolates the relevant contextual or pragmatic parameters of an interpretation (as, for example, a domain of discourse in classical first-order logic, a set of possible worlds and a relation of relative possibility on them in Kripke's semantics for modal logic), and defines truth conditions relative to these parameters. The second kind of pragmatic problem is to explicate the relation of these parameters to each other and to more readily identifiable features of linguistic contexts.

The scheme I am proposing looks roughly like this: the syntactical and semantic rules for a language determine an interpreted sentence or clause; this, together with some features of the context of use of the sentence or clause determines a proposition; this in turn, together with a possible world, determines a truth value. An interpreted sentence, then, corresponds to a function from contexts into propositions, and a proposition is a function from possible worlds into truth values.

According to this scheme, both contexts and possible worlds are partial determinants of the truth value of what is expressed by a given sentence. One might merge them together, considering a proposition to be a function from context-possible worlds (call them points of reference) into truth values. Pragmatics–semantics could then be treated as the study of the way in which, not propositions, but truth values are dependent on context, and part of the context would be the possible world in which the sentence is uttered. This is, I think, the kind of analysis of pragmatics proposed and developed by Richard Montague.[7] It is a simpler analysis than the one I am sketching; I need some argument for the necessity or desirability of the extra step on the road from sentences to truth values. The step is justified only if the middlemen – the propositions – are of some independent interest, and only if there is some functional difference between contexts and possible worlds.

   The independent interest in propositions comes from the fact that they are the objects of illocutionary acts and propositional attitudes. A proposition is supposed to be the common content of statements, judgments, promises, wishes and wants, questions and answers, things that are possible or probable. The meanings of sentences, or rules determining truth values directly from contexts, cannot plausibly represent these objects.

   If O'Leary says "Are you going to the party?" and you answer, "Yes, I'm going," your answer is appropriate because the proposition you affirm is the only one expressed in his question. On the simpler analysis, there is nothing to be the common content of question and answer except a truth value. The propositions are expressed from different points of reference, and according to the simpler analysis, they are different propositions. A truth value, of course, is not enough to be the common content. If O'Leary asks "Are you going to the party?" it would be inappropriate for you to answer, "Yes, snow is white."

   When O'Leary says at the party, "I didn't have to be here you know," he means something like this: it was not necessary that O'Leary be at that party. The words *I* and *here* contribute to the determination of a proposition, and this proposition is what O'Leary declares to be not necessary. Provided he was under no obligation or compulsion to be there, what he says is correct. But if the proposition declared to be not necessary were something like the meaning of the sentence, then O'Leary would be mistaken, since the sentence "I am here" is true from all points of reference, and hence necessarily true on the simpler analysis.

   Suppose you say "He is a fool" looking in the direction of Daniels and O'Leary. Suppose it is clear to me that O'Leary is a fool and that Daniels is not, but I am not sure whom you are talking about. Compare this with a situation in which you say "He is a fool" pointing unambiguously at O'Leary, but I am in doubt about whether he is one or not. In both cases, I am unsure about the truth of what you say, but the source of the uncertainty seems radically different. In the first example, the doubt is about what proposition was expressed, while in the second there is an uncertainty about the facts.

   These examples do not provide any criteria for distinguishing the determinants of truth which are part of the context from those which are part of the possible world, but they do support the claims that there is a point to the distinction, and that we have intuitions about the matter. I certainly do not want to suggest that the distinction is unproblematic, or that it is not sometimes difficult or arbitrary to characterize certain truth determinants as semantic or pragmatic.[8] I want to suggest only that there are clear cases on which to rest the distinction between context and possible world, and differences in language use which depend on how it is made. To lend more detailed support to the suggestion, I shall first discuss a concept of *pragmatic presupposition* which is central to the characterization of contexts, as opposed to possible worlds, and second describe a kind of *pragmatic ambiguity* which depends on the distinction.

3   Presuppositions

The notion of presupposition that I shall try to explicate is a pragmatic concept, and must be distinguished from the semantic notion of presupposition analyzed by van Fraassen.[9] According to the *semantic* concept, a proposition P presupposes a proposition Q if and only if Q is necessitated both by P and by *not-P*. That is, in every model in which P is either true or false, Q is true. According to the *pragmatic* conception, presupposition is a propositional attitude, not a semantic relation. People, rather than sentences or propositions, are said to have, or make, presuppositions in this sense. More generally, any participant in a linguistic content (a person, a group, an institution, perhaps a machine) may be the subject of a presupposition. Any proposition may be the object, or context of one.

There is no conflict between the semantic and pragmatic concepts of presupposition: they are explications of related but different ideas. In general, any semantic presupposition of a proposition expressed in a given context will be a pragmatic presupposition of the people in that context, but the converse clearly does not hold.

To presuppose a proposition in the pragmatic sense is to take its truth for granted, and to assume that others involved in the context do the same. This does not imply that the person need have any particular mental attitude toward the proposition, or that he need assume anything about the mental attitudes of others in the context. Presuppositions are probably best viewed as complex dispositions which are manifested in linguistic behavior. One has presuppositions in virtue of the statements he makes, the questions he asks, the commands he issues. Presuppositions are propositions implicitly *supposed* before the relevant linguistic business is transacted.

The set of all the presuppositions made by a person in a given context determines a class of possible worlds, the ones consistent with all the presuppositions. This class sets the boundaries of the linguistic situation. Thus, for example, if the situation is an inquiry, the question will be, which of the possible worlds consistent with the presuppositions is the actual world? If it is a deliberation then the question is, which of *those* worlds shall we make actual? If it is a lecture, then the point is to inform the audience more specifically about the location of the actual world within that class of possible worlds. Commands and promises are expected to be obeyed and kept within the bounds of the presuppositions. Since the presuppositions play such a large part in determining what is going on in a linguistic situation, it is important that the participants in a single context have the same set of presuppositions if misunderstanding is to be avoided. This is why presupposition involves not only taking the truth of something for granted, but also assuming that others do the same.

The boundaries determined by presuppositions have two sides. One cannot normally assert, command, promise, or even conjecture what is inconsistent with what is presupposed. Neither can one assert, command, promise, or conjecture what is itself presupposed. There is no point in expressing a presupposition unless it distinguishes among the possible worlds which are considered live options in the context.

Presuppositions, of course, need not be true. Where they turn out false, sometimes the whole point of the inquiry, deliberation, lecture, debate, command, or promise is destroyed, but at other times it does not matter much at all. Suppose, for example, we are discussing whether we ought to vote for Daniels or O'Leary for president, presupposing that they are the Democratic and Republican candidates, respectively. If our real interest is in coming to a decision about whom to vote for in the presidential election, then the debate will seem a waste of time when we discover that, in reality, the candidates are Nixon and Muskie. However, if our real concern is with the relative merits of the character and executive ability of Daniels and O'Leary, then our false presupposition makes little difference. Minor revisions might bring our debate in line with new presuppositions. The same contrast applies to a scientific experiment performed against the background of a presupposed theoretical framework. It may lose its point when the old theory is rejected, or it may easily be accommodated to the new theory. Sometimes, in fact, puzzlement is resolved and anomalies are explained by the discovery that a presupposition is false, or that a falsehood was presupposed. An experimental result may be more easily accommodated to the new presuppositions than to the old ones.

Normally, presuppositions are at least *believed* to be true. That is one reason that we can often infer more about a person's beliefs from his assertions than he says in them. But in some cases, presuppositions may be things we are unsure about, or even propositions believed or known to be untrue. This may happen in cases of deception: the speaker presupposes things that his audience believes but that he knows to be false in order to get them to believe further false things. More innocently, a speaker may presuppose what is untrue to facilitate communication, as when an anthropologist adopts the presuppositions of his primitive informant in questioning him. Most innocent of all are cases of fiction and pretending: speaker and audience may conspire together in presupposing things untrue, as when the author of a novel presupposes some of what was narrated in earlier chapters. In some contexts, the truth is beside the point. The actual world is, after all, only one possible world among many.

The shared presuppositions of the participants in a linguistic situation are perhaps the most important constituent of a context. The concept of pragmatic presupposition should play a role, both in the definition of various speech acts such as assertion, prediction, or counterfactual statement, and also in specifying semantic rules relating sentences to propositions relative to contexts.

4 Pragmatic Ambiguity

The best example of the kind of ambiguity that I shall describe is given in Keith Donnellan's distinction between referential and attributive uses of definite descriptions.[10] After sketching an account of his distinction within the theory of pragmatics, I shall give some examples of other pragmatic ambiguities which have similar explanations.

Consider the following three statements, together with parenthetical comments on the contexts in which they were made:

(1) Charles Daniels is bald (said about a philosopher named Charles Daniels by one of his friends).

(2) I am bald (said by Charles Daniels, the man mentioned above).

(3) The man in the purple turtleneck shirt is bald (said by someone in a room containing one and only one man in a purple turtleneck shirt, that man being Charles Daniels).

The question is, what proposition was expressed in each of these three cases? In the first case, since "Charles Daniels" is a proper name, and since the speaker knows the intended referent well, there is no problem: the proposition is the one that says that *that* man has the property of being bald. In possible worlds in which that same man, Charles Daniels, is bald, the statement is true; in possible worlds in which he is not bald, the statement is false. What is the truth value in possible worlds where he does not exist? Perhaps the function is undefined for those arguments. We need not worry about it though, since the existence of Charles Daniels will be presupposed in any context in which that presupposition is expressed.

The second statement expresses exactly the same proposition as the first since it is true in possible worlds where the referent of the pronoun, *I*, Charles Daniels, is bald, and false when he is not. To believe what is expressed in the one statement is to believe what is expressed in the other; the second might be made as a report of what was said in the first. To interpret the second *sentence*, one needs to know different things about the context than one needs to know to interpret the first, but once both statements are understood, there is no difference between them.

In both cases, there is a pragmatic problem of determining from the context which individual is denoted by the similar term. The answer to this question fixes the proposition – the content of what is said. In case (1), a relatively unsystematic convention, the convention of matching proper names to individuals, is involved. In case (2), there is a systematic rule matching a feature of the context (the speaker) with the singular term *I*. Different rules applied to different sentences in different contexts determine the same proposition.

What about the third case? Here there are two ways to analyze the situation corresponding to the referential and attributive uses of definite descriptions distinguished by Donnellan. We might say that the relation between the singular term "the man in the purple turtleneck shirt" and the referent, Charles Daniels, is determined by the context, and so the proposition expressed is the same as that expressed by statements (1) and (2). As with the term *I*, there are relatively systematic rules for matching up definite descriptions with their denotations in a context: the referent is the one and only one member of the appropriate domain who is *presupposed* to have the property expressed in the description. The rule cannot always be applied, but in the case described, it can be.

Alternatively, we might understand the rule picking out the denotation of the singular term to be itself a part of the proposition. This means that the relation between the definite description and its denotation is a function, not of the context, but of the possible world. In different possible worlds the truth value of the proposition may depend on different individuals. It also means that we may understand the proposition – the content of the statement – without knowing who the man in the purple turtleneck shirt is, although we may have to know who he is in order to know that it is true.

The simpler account of pragmatics which merges possible worlds with contexts cannot account for Donnellan's distinction. If one goes directly from sentence (together with context) to truth value, one misses the ambiguity, since the truth conditions for the sentence in a fixed context (in normal cases at least) coincide for the two readings. If one goes from the sentence together with context to proposition, and proposition together with possible world to truth value, however, the ambiguity comes out in the intermediate step. There are at least three important differences between the referential and attributive uses of descriptions. These differences provide further argument for a theory which allows the distinction to be made and which gives some account of it.

First, in modal contexts and contexts involving propositional attitudes, the distinction makes a difference even for the *truth value* of statements in which descriptions occur. Compare

(4)   The man in the purple turtleneck shirt might have been someone else.

(5)   The man in the purple turtleneck shirt might have worn white tie and tails.

Both statements say approximately that a certain proposition was possibly true. But in each case there are two propositions that can be intended, and which one is chosen may make a difference in the truth value of the ascription of possibility to the proposition. If the first means, roughly, that Daniels might have been someone else, it is false, perhaps contradictory. On the other hand, if it means that someone else might have been the one wearing the turtleneck shirt (perhaps he almost lent it to me), then it may be true. The second statement can mean either that Daniels might have worn white tie and tails, or that it might have been the case that whoever was wearing the purple turtleneck shirt was *also* wearing white tie and tails. Clearly, the truth conditions are different for these two readings.

In a formal language containing modal or epistemic operators and descriptions, the distinction can he interpreted as a *syntactical* distinction. That is, statements (4) and (5) could each be formalized in two syntactically different ways with the description falling inside of the scope of the modal operator in one and outside the scope in the other.[11] But this procedure has two limitations: (a) it would be highly implausible to suggest that the *English* sentences (4) and (5) are syntactically ambiguous. There are no natural syntactical transformations of (4) and (5) which remove the ambiguity. (b) Modal and propositional attitude concepts may be involved, not only as parts of statements, but as comments on them and attitudes toward them. The content of statement (3) above, which cannot be treated as syntactically ambiguous even in a formalized language, may be doubted, affirmed, believed, or lamented. What one is doing in taking these attitudes or actions depends on which of the two readings is given to the statement.

Second, as Donnellan noted, the distinction makes a difference for the presuppositions required by the context in which the statement is made. In general, we may say that when a simple subject–predicate statement is made, the existence of the subject is normally presupposed. When you say "the man in the purple turtleneck shirt is bald," you presuppose that the man in the purple turtleneck shirt exists. But of course the same ambiguity infects that statement of presupposition; how it is to be taken depends on what reading is given to the original statement. If the statement is given the referential reading, then so must be the presupposition. What is presupposed is that Daniels exists. If the statement is given the attributive reading, then the presupposition is that there is one and only one man (in the appropriate domain) wearing a purple turtleneck shirt. This is exactly the presupposition difference pointed out by Donnellan. Within the framework I am using, the different presuppositions can be seen to be instances of a single principle.

Third, the distinction is important if one considers what happens when the description fails to apply uniquely in the context. In *both* referential and attributive uses of descriptions, it is a presupposition of the context that the description applies uniquely, but if this presupposition is false, the consequences are different. In the case of referential uses, Donnellan has noted, the fact that the presupposition fails may have little effect on the statement. The speaker may still have successfully referred to someone, and successfully said something about him. When the presupposition fails in the attributive sense, however, that normally means that nothing true or false has been said at all. This difference has a natural explanation within our framework.

Where the rules determining the denotation of the singular term are considered as part of the context, what is relevant is not what is true, but what is presupposed. The definite description in statement (3) above, on the referential reading, denotes the person who is *presupposed* to be the one and only one man in a purple turtleneck shirt (in the appropriate domain). If there is no one person who is presupposed to fit the description, then reference fails (even if some person does *in fact* fit the description uniquely). But if there is one, then it makes no difference whether that presupposition is true or false. The presupposition helps to determine the proposition expressed, but once that proposition is determined, it can stand alone. The fact that Daniels is bald in no way depends on the color of his shirt.

On the attributive reading, however, the rule determining the denotation of the description is a part of the proposition, so it is what is true that counts, not what is presupposed. The proposition is about whoever uniquely fits the description, so if no one does, no truth value is determined.

The points made in distinguishing these two uses of definite descriptions can be generalized to apply to other singular terms. Proper names, for example, are normally used to refer, but can be used in a way resembling the attributive use of definite descriptions. When you ask, "Which one is Daniels?" you are not *referring* to Daniels, since you do not presuppose of any one person that he is Daniels. When I answer "Daniels is the bald one," I am using "the bald one" referentially, and the name Daniels attributively. I am telling you not that Daniels is bald, but that he is Daniels. Using this distinction, we can explain how identity statements can be informative, even when two proper names flank the identity sign.

It has been emphasized by many philosophers that referring is something done by people with terms, and not by terms themselves. That is why reference is a problem of pragmatics, and it is why the role of a singular term depends less on the syntactic or semantic category of the term (proper name, definite description, pronoun) than it does on the speaker, the context, and the presuppositions of the speaker in that context.

The notion of pragmatic ambiguity can be extended to apply to other kinds of case. In general, a sentence has the potential for pragmatic ambiguity if some rule involved in the interpretation of that sentence may be applied either to the context or to the possible world. Applied to the context, the rule will either contribute to the determination of the proposition (as in the case of the referential use of definite descriptions) or it will contribute to the force with which the proposition is expressed. Applied to the possible world, the rule is incorporated into the proposition itself, contributing to the determination of a truth value. Conditional sentences, sentences containing certain modal terms, and sentences containing what have been called parenthetical verbs are other examples of sentences which have this potential.

If a person says something of the form "If A then B" this may be interpreted either as the categorical assertion of a conditional proposition or as the assertion of the consequent made conditionally on the truth of the antecedent. In the former case, a proposition is determined on the level of semantics as a function of the propositions expressed by antecedent and consequence. In the latter case, the antecedent is an additional presupposition made temporarily, either because the speaker wishes to commit himself to the consequent only should the antecedent be true, or because the assertion of the consequent would not be relevant unless the antecedent is true (as in, for example, "there are cookies in the cupboard if you want some").[12]

A sentence of the form "It may be that P" can be interpreted as expressing a modal proposition, that proposition being a function of P, or it may be interpreted as making explicit that the negation of P is not presupposed in the context. In the latter case, P is the only *proposition* involved. The modal word indicates the force with which it is expressed.

A sentence of the form "I suppose that P" may be meant as a report about a supposition of the speaker, or as a rather tentative assertion of P. To read it the second way is to treat *I suppose* as a *parenthetical verb*, since on this reading, the sentence is synonomous with "P, I suppose." The differences between these two readings are explored in Urmson's famous article on parenthetical verbs.[13]

Each of these examples has its own special features and problems. I do not want to suggest that they are instances of a common form. But the ambiguity, in each case, rests on the distinction between context and possible world.

5 Conclusion

Let me summarize the main points that I have tried to make. In section 1 I claimed that semantics is best viewed as the study of propositions, and argued that propositions may be studied independently of language. In section 2 I defined pragmatics as the study of linguistic acts and the contexts in which they are performed. Two kinds of pragmatic problem were considered; first, the definition of speech acts – the problem of giving necessary and sufficient conditions, not for the truth of a proposition expressed in the act, but for the act being performed; second, the study of the ways in which the linguistic context determines the proposition expressed by a given sentence in that context. The formulation of problems of the second kind depends on a basic distinction between contextual determinants of propositions and propositional determinants of truth. I argued that the distinction has an intuitive basis and is useful in analyzing linguistic situations. In the final two sections, I tried to support this distinction, first by characterizing a pragmatic notion of presupposition that is a central feature of contexts as opposed to possible worlds, and second by describing a kind of pragmatic ambiguity which rests on the distinction.

In this sketch of a theory of pragmatics, I have relied on some undefined and problematic concepts, for example, possible worlds, contexts, and presuppositions. I have given some heuristic account of these concepts, or relied on the heuristic accounts of others, but I have made no attempt to reduce them to each other, or to anything else. It may be charged that these concepts are too unclear to be the basis concepts of a theory, but I think that this objection mistakes the role of basic concepts. It is not assumed that these notions are clear. In fact, one of the points of the theory is to clarify them. So long as certain concepts all have *some* intuitive content, then we can help to explicate them all by relating them to each other. The success of the theory should depend not on whether the concepts can be defined, but on whether or not it provides the machinery to define linguistic acts that seem interesting and to make conceptual distinctions that seem important. With philosophical as well as scientific theories, one may explain one's theoretical concepts, not by defining them, but by using them to account for the phenomena.

NOTES

The research for and preparation of this paper was supported by the National Science Foundation, grant number GS-2574. I would like to thank Professors David Shwayder and Richmond Thomason for their helpful comments on a draft of this paper.

1   Charles W. Morris, *Foundations of the Theory of Signs* (Chicago: 1938), pp. 4–5.
2   Rudolf Carnap, *Foundations of Logic and Mathematics* (Chicago: 1939), p. 4.
3   See Dana Scott, "Advice on Modal Logic," in *Philosophical Problbems in Logic: Recent Developments*, ed. Karel Lambert (Dordrecht: Reidel, 1970), pp. 143–73.
4   This is not an inevitable strategy. Instead of taking individuals and possible worlds as primitive, defining properties and relations as functions from one to the other, one might take individuals, properties, and relations as primitive and define possible worlds in terms of these.
5   A theory of possible worlds and propositions defined in terms of them is not committed to any absolute notion of synonymy or analyticity. Since propositions are functions taking possible worlds as arguments, a domain of possible worlds must be specified as the domain of the function. But the domain need not be *all* possible worlds in any absolute or metaphysical sense. We may leave open the possibility that the domain may be extended as our imaginations develop, or as

discoveries are made, or as our interests change. Propositional identity is, of course, relative to the specification of a domain of possible worlds.

6   This is not necessarily so, however. Since speech act types can be *any* way of picking out a class of particular speech acts, one might define one in such a way that the context was irrelevant, and the problem of analysis reduced to a problem of syntax or semantics, as for example the speech act of uttering a grammatical sentence of English, or the speech act of expressing the proposition *X*.

7   R. Montague, "Pragmatics," in *Contemporary Philosophie – La philosophie contemporaine*, ed. R. Klibansky (Florence: 1968), vol. 1. pp. 102–22. Montague uses the phrase "point of reference" as does Dana Scott in the paper mentioned in n. 3.

8   Tenses and times, for example, are an interesting case. Does a tensed sentence determine a proposition which is sometimes true, sometimes false, or does it express different timeless propositions at different times? I doubt that a single general answer can be given, but I suspect that one's philosophical views about time may be colored by his tendency to think in one of these ways or the other.

9   Bas C. van Fraassen, "Singular Terms, Truth Value Gaps, and Free Logic," *Journal of Philosophy*, 63 (1966), 481–95, and "Presupposition, Implication, and Self Reference," *Journal of Philosophy* 65 (1968), 136–51.

10 Keith Donnellan, "Reference and Definite Descriptions," *Philosophical Review*, 75 (1966), 281–304.

11 See R. Thomason and R. Stalnaker, "Modality and Reference," *Nous* 2 (1968): 359–72; and R. Stalnaker and R. Thomason, "Abstraction in First Order Modal Logic," *Theoria*, 34 (1968), 203–7.

12 See R. Stalnaker, "A Theory of Conditionals," in *Studies in Logical Theory*, ed. Nicholas Rescher (Oxford: 1968), pp. 98–112, for a semantical theory of conditional propositions. Nuel Belnap has developed a theory of conditional assertion in "Conditional Assertion and Restricted Quantification," *Nous* 4 (1970): 1–12.

13 J. O. Urmson, "Parenthetical Verbs, *Mind*, 61 (1952), 192–212.

Semantics – Mathematics or Psychology?

BARBARA PARTEE

1   Introduction

My goal in this paper is to argue that the question in the title is one that urgently needs attention from both linguists and philosophers, although I do not have an answer for it. I believe that we will not be able to find an adequate account of the semantics of propositional attitudes without a theory which reconciles the conflicting demands of the two kinds of view of what semantics is.

Where do these two views come from? The view that semantics is a branch of psychology is a part of the Chomskyan view that linguistics as a whole is a branch of psychology. This view, which is shared by many linguists, derives from taking the central goal of linguistic theory to be an account of what the native speaker of a language knows when he or she knows a language, and of how such knowledge is acquired. Most linguists take it for granted that people know their language; within the Chomskyan view, it is the knowledge of the individual language user that is criterial for determining what his or her language *is*.

The contrasting view is ascribed to Richard Montague (and endorsed) by Thomason in his introduction to *Formal Philosophy: Selected Papers of Richard Montague*: "Many linguists may not realize at first glance how fundamentally Montague's approach differs from current linguistic conceptions. . . . According to Montague the syntax, semantics, and pragmatics of natural languages are branches of mathematics, not of psychology" (p. 2). (Thomason holds that lexicography is an empirical science that demands considerable knowledge of the world, but is not part of semantics proper. I will return to that issue below.) The view that semantics is not psychology can also be reasonably ascribed to Frege ("Der Gedanke") and seems to be either implicit or explicit in the work of many logicians and philosophers.

It might seem from the recent growth of cooperation among linguists, philosophers, and logicians that the question really doesn't matter. And for many purposes I believe it doesn't. To put some perspective on what I take to be the real problem, let me list some respects in which the question is *not* a problem.

1   There is no reason why a psychological theory can't be expressed in mathematical terms. In fact on a Chomskyan view it should be, since we are trying to discover something about the structure of a certain mental faculty, and mathematics is the best available tool for describing structure. So I am not suggesting that there is any incompatibility between mathematics in general and psychology in general.

2   The fact that some logician is not interested in psychology does not preclude the possibility that he or she may develop a theory which can be taken as a serious candidate for a psychological theory. This was an argument that can be used in urging linguists to take Montague's theory seriously (Partee, "Montague Grammar and Transformational Grammar"); it may be hoped that one might turn Montague's general theory of language (Montague, "Universal Grammar") into a theory of possible human languages simply by adding additional constraints, constraints designed to reflect human linguistic capacities. I still have hopes that such a program can be carried out for a theory bearing some resemblance to Montague's, since the progress that has been made in syntax and semantics working in constrained versions of that theory and similar ones seems too great to be an artifactual illusion. But I now believe that Montague's theory (and relevantly similar ones) cannot be the basis of a linguistic theory without some radical revisions in the foundations of the semantics.[1]

3   As far as I can see, there are no problems with logicians' treatment of syntax analogous to the problems in the semantics. But I can't say any more about the difference until I have described the semantic problems. I will return to this later.

Having said what I think the problems are not, let me turn to the discussion of what they are.

2   Idealizations

Idealizations are of course indispensable for making headway in any science. Linguists are accustomed to making a distinction between competence and performance, and Cresswell ("Semantic Competence") shows that the same distinction can be used to argue for the reasonableness of truth-conditional semantics as an account of semantic competence. But the arguments of Putnam ("The Meaning of 'Meaning'" and "Language and Reality"), Chomsky (*Reflections on Language*), and Linsky ("Believing and Necessity") can be used to show that some of Montague's idealizations are incompatable with the view of semantics as psychology. In "Montague Grammar, Mental Representations, and Reality," I discussed the Putnam arguments and concluded that speakers of a language do not in fact know their language; but Linsky's arguments and further reflection on the semantics of propositional attitudes have convinced me that even if this is so, some of Montague's idealizations must be given up.

The crucial idealizations that Montague makes are the following:

1   The objects of propositional attitudes are propositions.
2   The intensions of sentences are propositions.
3   The intensions of sentences are compositionally determined, i.e., recursively built up from the intensions of their parts.
4   Intensions are functions from possible worlds to extensions.
5   Words have intensions.

The crucial linguistic assumptions which I believe are incompatible with those are the following:

6   People know their language.
7   The brain is finite.

A typical Putnam example is the intension of natural kind terms such as *gold*, *water*, or *tiger*. Putnam has shown that a speaker can, by all reasonable standards, be in command of a word like *water* without being able to command the intension that would represent the word in possible worlds semantics.

We might attribute this difficulty to the more general impossibility of fitting a Montague model into a speaker's head, since by any reasonable assumptions there must be nondenumerably many possibly worlds, and hence the possible worlds could not all be represented distinctly within a finite brain. I don't think this is the source of the problem, however. For one thing, you don't need to represent all of the possible worlds distinctly in order to know a function which has them as domain. We know the function for adding arbitrary real numbers without being able to represent all the real numbers distinctly.[2] For another thing, it makes sense independently to assume that our knowledge of meanings of lexical items should be represented by partial functions rather than total functions from possible worlds to extensions. The finite brain could be just a special sort of "performance" limitation, just as finite memory span is often assumed to be in syntax.

Kasher ("Logical Rationalism") focuses on similar problems with a similar goal in mind, which he characterizes as the goal of achieving a "logical rationalism" in semantics. Accepting the linguists' assumptions, (6) and (7) above, he makes finite representability a condition of elementary adequacy on a semantic theory, and explores the kinds of restriction and modification that would be required to make Montague grammar finitely representable. He suggests as one major modification that the possible worlds not be viewed as atomic but as constructs from a finitely and uniformly representable (conceptual) "logical space." He also proposes the quite reasonable restriction that the interpretation of all operators (functions from functions to functions) be required to be computable.

If we didn't worry about propositional attitudes, I think we might be able to achieve a reconciliation of psychological semantics with the possible worlds approach in another way, along the following lines. Take the Fregean or Montague semantics as representing a kind of super-competence: what we would be like if not limited by finite brains and finite experience (e.g., if we were God). Finiteness restricts us to constructing partial models, and in place of complete intensions of words we construct imperfect algorithms which yield partial functions on these partial models.[3] Different individuals will have different partial models and different algorithms, since our brains and our real-world experience are not identical. Communication will be possible as long as there is sufficient similarity in our partial models and our imperfect semantics. Viewed in this way, there may be no problem in principle in regarding a theory like Montague's as a kind of competence model. It could be telling correctly how we can determine the meaning of a sentence from the meanings of its parts, with "performance" factors like finite brains explaining why we don't have complete meanings of lexical items to begin with and why we sometimes make logical mistakes along the way.

But such a story remains plausible only so long as we ignore the propositional attitudes.

3   Propositional Attitudes

The trouble is that we know that we have these limitations, and this knowledge is reflected in propositional attitude sentences. The difficulty of formulating an appropriate semantics for belief sentences and other sentences about propositional attitudes is well known, and I would certainly not want to suggest abandoning any semantic theory out of hand simply because that theory did not so far seem to allow any adequate treatment of the propositional attitudes. But I believe that some of the idealizations that we take as fundamental in possible worlds semantics are the source of some of the problems we have in dealing with the propositional attitudes, and that an attempt to make our theories more psychologically realistic may be essential for solving those problems.

Among the problems associated with propositional attitude sentences, I believe that possible worlds semantics works relatively well for the problem of "quantifying in" and the problems associated with demonstratives and other indexical words inside propositional attitude contexts. More "quotational" or "linguistic" approaches have serious difficulties with those problems. A quotational analysis of a sentence such as:

(1)   Smith believes that the earth is flat

on its natural opaque reading, will treat *believes* as a relation between Smith and something like the *sentence* "the earth is flat," with perhaps the suggestion that (1) is true if Smith is in a certain mental state that involves something like a semantic representation of the sentence "the earth is flat." The sorts of difficulty I am referring to can be illustrated by the following sentence:

(2)   Smith believes that *that* door is locked, but she doesn't believe that *that* door is locked.

Sentence (2) can be used to make a noncontradictory statement, so long as the two occurrences of the demonstrative expression "that door" are used to refer to different doors. So the relation of believing here cannot be a relation simply between Smith and the sentence type "that door is locked." So one may try something like saying that Smith stands in the opaque believing relation to *some* sentence of the form "α is locked" where α represents or denotes that (first) door for Smith, and doesn't stand in that relation to some other sentence "β is locked," where β represents that other door for Smith. The problem here, as Burge ("Belief *De Re*") clearly points out, is that in many typical cases of *de re* beliefs, it is implausible to assume that the believer's internal name or description (the α or β above) is one which will individuate the object in question in a context-independent manner. And if it does not, it is not reducible to a purely *de dicto* belief or to a relation between a person and a sentence type.

This kind of problem arises for any sentence containing indexical elements: demonstratives, deictic pronouns, tenses, *here*, *now*, etc. It is a problem for any theory that identifies propositions with sentence types or with meanings of sentence types, taking these to be characterizable purely in terms of internal mental states of language users independently of the real-world environment or context in which the sentence tokens occur. Fodor ("Methodological Solipsism") provides a clear example of such a theory with what he calls "the computational theory of the mind." He requires that "two thoughts can be distinct in content only if they can be identified with relations to formally distinct representations" (p. 4). "If mental processes are formal, then they have access only to the formal properties of such representations of the environment as the senses provide. Hence they have no access to the *semantic* properties of such representations, including the property of being true, of having referents" (p. 9). (I should say that Fodor does acknowledge that demonstratives are so far an unsolved problem for his approach.)

But there are two major problems that are not dealt with at all in Montague's sort of theory.

3.1   The logical equivalence problem

The first is the well-known nonsubstitutivity of logical equivalents in propositional attitudes. If *P* and *Q* are logically equivalent, we cannot validly make an inference from (3) to (4).

(3)   Irene believes that *P*.

(4)   Irene believes that *Q*.

This problem is widely admitted, but seldom confronted within Montague semantics, since it results directly from the assumption that propositions are the intensions of sentences and are functions from possible worlds to truth values.[4] Montague's semantics requires that logical equivalents be intersubstitutable everywhere, and it will take a major modification to remove that requirement. To describe what I see as the source of the problem, let me refer informally to a language with no propositional attitude expressions as a level 0 language, one with a single layer of propositional attitudes as a level 1 language, and so on. (This is an informal borrowing from Russell's theory of ramified types.) And suppose we were to accept something like the view of Montague's theory as a theory of competence for speakers of a level 0 language, as I sketched in the previous section. Then we could express the argument of Linsky ("Believing and Necessity") by saying that the performance limitations of speakers of a level 0 language must be acknowledged at the competence level of speakers of a level 1 language, and in general the level *i* performance limitations must be acknowledged at the level $i + 1$ competence level. That is, as Linsky argues, even if an idealized speaker will always recognize the logical equivalence of P and Q, he or she should not make the inference from (3) to (4), since part of his or her competence would be the knowledge that holders of propositional attitudes can make logical mistakes. I see this as one deep-rooted connection between the demands of a psychological theory of semantics and the demands of an adequate account of the semantics of propositional attitudes.

Another way of putting the point is this. Suppose we view Montague's semantics as a super-competence model: a semantics for English as spoken by God. Then the semantics works perfectly well for the level 0 parts of the language, but it still fails for the propositional attitudes, since God would not make the inference from (3) to (4).

Note that we cannot get around this problem by assigning the objects of propositional attitudes to some other semantic type within a Montague-like system that retains his intensional logic, since substitution of logical equivalents is valid in such a system for *every* semantic type. Nor can we solve it by allowing nonstandard interpretations for the logical connectives if, as I believe, the typical case of failure of the inference from (3) to (4) arises simply because holders of propositional attitudes don't always recognize logical equivalence, independently of what logic they are using.[5]

3.2   The rigid designator problem

The second major inadequacy of Montague's treatment of propositional attitudes has to do with the nature of lexical meaning. Let me add some background before stating it. Within the nonpsychological semantic tradition, there are excellent arguments for why certain words such as proper names and perhaps natural kind terms should be viewed as rigid designators, that is, intensions which pick out the same extension in every possible world. As Putnam and others have persuasively argued, *such* intensions cannot be identified with psychological states narrowly defined. The mystery of how people can *use* such words at all can be solved by the causal chain story (see Kripke, "Naming and Necessity"; Donnellan, "Speaking of Nothing"; Evans, "The Causal Theory of Names"). On such a story, a person who knows nothing about Frege can use the name "Frege" to refer to Frege, for instance in asking the question "Who is Frege?," simply by intending to use the name in the way that others before him have used it, so long as there is an appropriate causal chain tracing back to a situation that makes an appropriate connection to the individual Frege himself. Similar remarks apply to certain words that designate natural kind terms such as names of species, chemical elements, etc.

In these cases the gap between the "mathematical" view and the psychological view seems much wider, perhaps unbridgeable. What is in a speaker's head in association with a proper name bears almost no resemblance to the intension.[6] The intension is a rigid designator, while the psychological representation is probably more like an incomplete and possibly incorrect definite description, or a partial algorithm for picking out the referent across times and worlds by qualitative characteristics. One complicating factor is that if the rigid designator theory is correct, then people in effect intend to use proper names as rigid designators, and therefore do not regard their associated descriptions and identifying procedures as constituting the meaning or intension of the name. Thus on a kind of metalevel (all this is unconscious, of course), our psychological states may be quite compatible with the rigid designator analysis, but on the ground level the individual speaker's psychological state will not in general determine a rigid designator.

As Mondadori ("Interpreting Modal Semantics") says, the intension in the modal semantics sense is a function from *really* possible worlds to extensions therein, whereas the kind of concept that can be "grasped" (by us) is a function from *epistemically* possible worlds to extensions therein, and these are likely to diverge in the case of proper names and other rigid designators.[7]

With this background, we can state the second problem, which is that rigid designators do not remain rigid designators in propositional attitude contexts. Almost everyone agrees that sentence (5) does not entail sentence (6) and that (7) does not entail (8).[8]

(5)   The ancients did not know that Hesperus was Phosphorus.

(6)   The ancients did not know that Hesperus was Hesperus.

(7)   John wonders whether woodchucks are groundhogs.

(8)   John wonders whether woodchucks are woodchucks.

The standard treatment in intensional logic works well enough where either or both of the terms are non-rigid descriptions, but it seems to fail in cases like these where the two terms are rigid designators which rigidly designate the same entity or species. The failure seems to me to be directly attributable to the fact that the rigid designators are not "in our heads." The identity statement (9)

(9)   Hesperus is Phosphorus.

is necessarily true but not known a priori; the ancients may have used "Hesperus" and "Phosphorus" as rigid designators for the same planet, but they didn't know it. The two names were not psychologically equivalent for them (nor are they for us). Sentence (5) can have a different truth value from sentence (6) *because* it involves a psychological modality, and not a metaphysical modality, applied to a sentence which is (psychologically) informative although metaphysically necessary. Therefore I believe that this is another case where even a super-competence model (the "God's language" model) cannot ignore the psychological view of semantics.

There are at least two other approaches to diagnosing the problem. One is to say that these cases are peculiarly metalinguistic, and should perhaps not be treated quite literally, since they are really statements about their subjects' lack of knowledge of the language. In favor of this view[9] is the fact that these sentences are not as readily translatable into other languages as are most propositional attitude sentences. And such sentences seem to make no sense at all when their subjects are dogs, pre-linguistic children, etc., to whom many propositional attitudes can reasonably be attributed.

Yet I think one would be hard pressed to find criteria for dividing propositional attitude sentences into two classes, one metalinguistic in this sense and the other not. When we judge the truth of a propositional attitude sentence we often take into consideration *both* the subject's dispositions to assent and his or her dispositions to act. When we attribute beliefs to dogs we are generally judging by their actions, and when we utter (5) we are generally judging by the ancients' assertions, or by actions which essentially include linguistic acts. But this is not enough to show that there is an ambiguity, either lexical (in the attitude verbs) or structural (e.g., true that-clause vs. quotation.) Perhaps there is, but it remains to be shown.

Another approach which has been suggested recently involves ideas of Stalnaker's and

Kaplan's about the role of context in determining the content of an utterance.[10] Stalnaker ("Assertion") includes the possible world in which an utterance occurs as part of the context, which lets us bring into play the fact that it is contingent that the expressions in the utterance mean what they do and refer to what they refer to. It is contingent that "Hesperus" and "Phosphorus" are names of the same planet. What Stalnaker calls the *propositional concept* associated with the linguistic form "Hesperus is Phosphorus" is a function from contexts of use, including a possible world, to propositions (functions from possible worlds to truth values.) (I believe this is very close to what David Kaplan, "Demonstratives," calls *character*.) In the context of the actual world, that propositional concept picks out the necessary proposition, but in a world compatible with the beliefs of someone who thinks the names are names of distinct planets, it picks out the necessarily false proposition.

This sounds like it has the ingredients we need, but I am still quite uncertain about how to incorporate it into a compositional semantics of *belief* sentences. The appeal to the context can explain why an assertion of "Hesperus is Phosphorus" in isolation is informative; but when a sentence like (5) or (7) is uttered, the world of the context of the utterance is (loosely speaking) the speaker's world, not the subject's world. To somehow invoke the context of the ancients (for (5)) or of John (for (7)), contexts must be recursively manipulated. And it seems to be still an open question within this approach[11] whether it is character or content that is the object of the attitudes. At any rate, this seems to me potentially a very promising approach to this problem (although I do not so far see that it would bear on the first problem, the problem of logical equivalence).

There is an additional example that I will mention here because I think it is closely related to the rigid designator problem, although I am not certain. Piaget (*The Child's Conception of the World*) observes that many children go through a stage of believing that clouds are alive. On first encounter, we may be quite unsure what that means, since it may seem to us analytic that clouds are not alive. We can be sure that the children have some belief that differs from some belief of ours, but without further investigation we don't know whether it's a belief about what "clouds" means, or about the nature of clouds, or about what "alive" means, or about the nature of life, or something else. (The explanations the children give when queried further tend to rest on the auxiliary beliefs that clouds move by themselves, cause wind, manage not to "sink," etc.)

Perhaps such examples should be dismissed. We might justify dismissing them on the grounds that if someone's whole belief structure, including beliefs about what many words mean, differs very radically from mine, I cannot hope to describe his or her belief in my language. A compositional semantics may be impossible without the assumption of a homogeneous interpretation system (both the model theory and the interpretation into it).

Yet I am uneasy about dismissing them, because it seems to me that the difference between the children's language and ours is greater in degree but not in kind than the differences between any two of us, and that we often use belief sentences to report beliefs that differ from our own in cases where we really don't know how much of the difference is "linguistic" and how much is "factual." Assuming homogeneous interpretation may be a necessary idealization for getting started, but it carries the danger of making us all seem egocentrically dogmatic when we attribute beliefs to others.

Let me summarize the two problems that I have been discussing. The first is the nonsubstitutability of logical equivalents in propositional attitude contexts. My claim is that this problem arises in formal semantics because of the idealization away from psychological limitations on our capacity to do logic; but propositional attitudes *are* psychological, and it is just these psychological limitations that make substitutions of logical equivalents fail in such contexts. The second problem is that rigid designators are not always rigid in propositional attitude contexts and, more generally, that words do not appear always to have their usual intensions in propositional attitude contexts. I believe this problem to have a similar source: the psychological semantic representation of a word is often very different from its intension, and properties of the psychological representation are often the crucial factor in propositional attitude contexts.

4   Is Semantics Possible?

My general theme so far has been that the view of natural-language semantics as psychology is not just a reflection of a Chomskyan approach to what linguistics is all about. We can start from the logician's goal of giving a correct account of the entailment relations among sentences of a natural language, even with the idealization to a super-ideal speaker who is omniscient about all possible worlds and who never makes logical mistakes. Montague's semantics, and any other semantics that has a similar treatment of intensions, will make false predictions about entailment relations among the propositional attitude sentences for such a speaker.

So I don't see how we can get a correct account of propositional attitudes without bringing psychology into the picture, but I don't see how can get along *with* it. The relevant psychological factors are ones which vary from speaker to speaker and moment to moment. No one can infallibly recognize logical equivalence, but there is no general way of determining who will recognize which equivalence when. The psychological correlates of word intensions are similarly variable across speakers and times. These were the very reasons why Frege suggested that if we want propositions to stand in a close relation both to language and to truth, we must not equate them with ideas.

At this point, I think it can be made clear why I think syntax does not face the same difficulty as semantics does. In syntax, we can safely use the notion of an idiolect of a single speaker, determined completely by what's in his or her head. At no point do the syntactic rules of one speaker have to be sensitive to the syntactic rules of any other speaker, or to nonlinguistic context. There are no syntactic analogues to the propositional attitude problems. (It might be thought that direct quotation could present a similar problem, but I argue in "The Syntax and Semantics of Quotation" that quotations should not be regarded as linguistic parts of the sentences that contain them.)

The problem we are faced with in trying to give a semantics for propositional attitudes is twofold: first, to determine what kind of semantic entity the objects of the propositional attitudes are, and second, to determine the compositional rules that will assign the appropriate entities to the syntactic objects of the propositional attitude verbs. For the first problem, I have no solution; my arguments have been mainly negative, to the effect that there is no semantic type of the right sort available within Montague's intensional logic.

The second problem cannot be solved before the first has been, but we can make some tentative claims about some of the factors that need to be involved:

1   The structure of the embedded sentence matters. We lose too much information if we just compute out intensions as we proceed up the analysis tree of the embedded sentence. This factor is related to the notion of intensional isomorphism in Camap, *Meaning and Necessity*, and to what Lewis calls "meanings" in "General Semantics."[12]

2   Context clearly matters, not only for indexicals, but also in the broader senses discussed above in connection with Stalnaker's and Kaplan's suggestions.
3   The believer's interpretation of lexical items matters for the rigid designator problems, and the believer's "logical performance factors" matter for the logical equivalence problems. Neither of these can be determined compositionally, since the speaker of the sentence may not know what they are. But perhaps there is a way of introducing variables for such factors, and introducing existential quantifiers connect those variables to the subject of the propositional attitude predicate.

One conclusion we may be forced to is that there are virtually no valid inferences from the propositional part of propositional attitude sentences except via additional premises. Within an approach like Montague's, this would make it much harder to see what the adequacy criteria for a correct account of propositional attitudes would be.[13]

5   Conclusion

I certainly have not answered the question whether semantics is mathematics or psychology. There are undoubtedly too many different kinds of mathematics and psychology for a general answer to be possible. What I have tried to suggest is that the linguist's concern for psychological representation may be relevant to every semanticist's concern for an account of the semantics of propositional attitudes. So far I don't see how to achieve either goal; my only positive suggestion is that a good theory might be expected to achieve both at once.

NOTES

I received many helpful criticisms and suggestions from the participants in the Konstanz colloquium for which this paper was prepared, and also from the audiences at the 1978 Chapel Hill Philosophy Colloquium and at MIT, where slightly revised versions of the first draft were read. Many people read the first draft and gave me useful suggestions; I would particularly like to thank Emmon Bach, Tyler Burge, Greg Carlson, David Dowty, Elisabet Engdahl, Janet Fodor, Jerry Fodor, Frank Heny, Stephen Isard, Hans Kamp, David Kaplan, Asa Kasher, David Lewis, John McCarthy, Julius Moravcsik, Robert Stalnaker, Richmond Thomason, and Bas van Fraassen. I am also grateful to Noam Chomsky for his comments on an earlier paper which led to some changes in my thinking that are reflected in this one.

1   Dowty, *Word Meaning and Montague Grammar* (see references), citing recent arguments of Putnam's, suggests that "possible worlds semantics on the one hand and most linguistic theories of semantics on the other should not be taken as *competing* explanations of the same phenomenon but rather as *complementary* theories of distinct though related phenomena." On this view, Montague's theory is a theory of truth and reference, or correspondence, and what linguists are aiming for is a theory of language understanding, and both kinds of theory will be needed to explain all of what is usually called "meaning."
     I believe that even if this view is correct, Montague's semantics still needs radical revision just to do its own job adequately, and that its inadequacies reflect certain properties of human understanding.
2   Stephen Isard (personal communication) has suggested that we can't really be said to know the function for adding arbitrary real numbers. We don't know it extensionally; that is, we don't have any representation of the entire set of ordered triples (a, b, c) such that a and b are real numbers

and $c = a + b$. And any finitely specifiable algorithm for addition must operate on representations of numbers; e.g. the algorithm for adding fractions is different from the algorithm for adding decimals. Then since we can't have finite representations of all the real numbers which the algorithm is to operate on, we can't have a finite specification of the algorithm itself. (You certainly can't build a Turing machine that will add arbitrary real numbers, even if you let it run forever, since you can't get the inputs onto the tape to begin with.) I'm not sure whether I believe this argument; but I will postpone considering it further to a later occasion. Finite representability of infinite structures seems to me to be a question deserving much more attention in semantics than it has had, and one where we could probably learn a good deal from computer scientists. The work of Friedman et al., "Dynamic Interpretation," is certainly relevant here.

3   I am thinking here of something along the lines of Cresswell's communication class in *Logics and Language*.

4   Katz and Katz, "Is Necessity the Mother of Intension?," make this point forcefully. It should be noted that Montague addressed this problem in at least two places. In "Pragmatics and Intensional Logic," he defends the substitution of logical equivalents in belief contexts as correct, with the remark that "its counterintuitive character can perhaps be traced to the existence of another notion of belief, of which the objects are sentences or, in some cases, complexes consisting in part of open formulas" (Partee, "Montague Grammar, Mental Representations, and Reality," p. 139). In "Universal Grammar," he provides a framework which he says permits "a natural treatment of belief contexts that lacks the controversial property of always permitting interchange on the basis of logical equivalence" (*Formal Philosophy*, p. 231). However, he does not spell that treatment out, since he still prefers to allow substitution of logical equivalents. I believe he had in mind a treatment in which logical words receive nonstandard interpretations at certain "unactualizable" points of reference; as I mention below, I don't believe that solution is on the right track.

5   John McCarthy (personal communication) pointed out that this problem arises as much for machines as for people. His observation suggests that the real tension is not between a mathematical and a psychological view of semantics but between a purely Platonistic semantics (which Montague's is) and an operational (his term) semantics.

   Hintikka solves this problem by analyzing *belief* sentences in terms of epistemically possible worlds which are not all logically possible worlds. His notions of surface and depth information are directly related to the problem of logical non-omniscience, and Rantala, "Urn Models," and Hintikka, "Impossible Possible Worlds Vindicated," offer an interesting non-standard model theory ("urn models") to provide a semantic backing to the notion of "impossible possible worlds." I do not understand the system well enough to know how difficult it would be to incorporate into a system like Montague's.

   For examples of some very interesting psychological work on people's performance on various kinds of inference tasks, see Wason and Johnson-Laird, *Psychology of Reasoning*.

6   Moravcsik, "Singular Terms, Belief and Reality," argues in this connection that Frege's and Kripke's differing theories of proper names are really theories of very different things, built from different conception of "mastery of a language." Frege was concerned with *informativeness* of identity statements involving proper names, Kripke with their necessary truth. In the terms of n. 1, Frege was after a theory of understanding and Kripke a theory of correspondence. Moravscik doubts that a single theory can or should achieve both.

7   This is clearly a central and pervasive problem, not just for proper names. Mondadori, "Interpreting Modal Semantics," and Moravscik, "Singular Terms, Belief and Reality," use it to argue against the likely fruitfulness of an attempt to construct a unitary theory of meaning; Kasher, "Logical Rationalism," like me, sees it as a place where the foundations of Montague's semantics need to be changed, the open question being whether they can be changed without sacrificing the logicians' goals.

8   We are concerned here with the readings on which the terms in subordinate clause are entirely within the scope of *know* or *wonder*, i.e., the "opaque" readings. The trouble is that (at least in Montague's system) the rigid designator treatment of proper names makes all the *readings* of (5)

come out equivalent, and likewise for (6); the same would be true of (7) and (8) if either (a) *woodchuck* and *groundhog* are given the same intension, or (b) *woodchucks* and *groundhogs* are treated as rigid designator names of species.

9 Greg Carlson kindly brought this point (back) to my attention.

10 This approach was not mentioned in the first draft of this paper, and I am grateful to David Lewis, David Kaplan, and Bas Van Fraasen for suggesting it and to Robert Stalnaker for a helpful and stimulating conversation about it. Their suggestions did not all agree, and none of them thinks the problems have all been solved. None of them is responsible for my description of this approach.

11 This is a point on which there was not agreement among those mentioned in n. 10. I won't say who thinks what because some of them were expressly tentative.

12 Thomason, "A Model Theory for Propositional Attitudes," proposes a method for achieving this effect in a system which takes propositions as a primitive semantic type. Parsons suggests something similar in *Nonexistent Objects*.

13 Tyler Burge (personal communication) suggests that this conclusion is not grounds for the pessimism of my earlier draft. Compositional semantics can provide an important part of the basis on which we make practical or probabilistic inferences, even if there are no valid entailments to be gotten. It may be that the seeming impossibility of giving a semantics for propositional attitudes is partly the result of Montague's narrow focus on capturing valid entailments as virtually the sole criterion for the adequacy of semantics – indeed, as *the* job of a semantic theory.

REFERENCES

Tyler Burge: "Belief *De Re*," *Journal of Philosophy* 74 (1977), 338–62.

Rudolf Carnap: *Meaning and Necessity: A Study in Semantics and Modal Logic*, University of Chicago Press, Chicago, enlarged edition (1956).

Noam Chomsky: *Reflections on Language*, Pantheon Books, New York (1975).

M. J. Cresswell: *Logics and Language*, Methuen, London (1973).

M. J. Cresswell: "Semantic Competence," in M. Guenthner-Reutter and F. Guenthner, eds, *Meaning and Translation: Philosophical and Linguistic Approaches*, Duckworth, London (1978).

Keith Donnellan: "Speaking of Nothing," *Philosophical Review* 83, 3–32, reprinted in Stephen R. Schwartz, ed., *Naming, Necessity, and Natural Kinds*, Cornell University Press, Ithaca, NY (1977).

David Dowty: *Word Meaning and Montague Grammar*, Synthese Language Library, Reidel, Dordrecht (forthcoming) [1979].

Gareth Evans: "The Causal Theory of Names," *Aristotelian Society Supplementary Volume* 47, 187–208, reprinted in Stephen R. Schwartz, ed., *Naming, Necessity and Natural Kinds*, Cornell University Press, Ithaca, NY (1977).

J. A. Fodor: "Methodological Solipsism Considered as a Research Strategy in Cognitive Psychology," MIT, Cambridge, MA (unpublished) [reproduced as part of ch. 7 in this volume].

G. Frege: "Der Gedanke," *Beiträge zur Philosophie des deutschen Idealismus*, vol. 1 (1919); trans. A. Quinton and M. Quinton as "The Thought: A Logical Inquiry," *Mind* 65 (1956), 289–311.

Joyce Friedman, Douglas Moran, and David Warren: "Dynamic Interpretation," N-16, Department of Computer and Communication Sciences, University of Michigan, Ann Arbor (unpublished).

Jaakko Hintikka: "Impossible Possible Worlds Vindicated," *Journal of Philosophical Logic* 4 (1975), 475–84.

David Kaplan: "Demonstratives: An Essay on the Semantics, Logic, Metaphysics and Epistemology of Demonstratives and Other Indexicals," read in part at the March, 1977, meeting of the Pacific Division of the American Philosophical Association, "Draft #2," manuscript, UCLA (1977).

Asa Kasher: "Logical Rationalism: On Degrees of Adequacy for Semantics of Natural Languages," *Philosophica* 18 (1976), 139–57.

Fred M. Katz and Jerrold J. Katz: "Is Necessity the Mother of Intension?," *Philosophical Review* 86 (1977), 70–96.

Saul Kripke, "Naming and Necessity," in D. Davidson and G. Harman, eds, *Semantics of Natural Language*, Reidel, Dordrecht (1972).

David Lewis: "General Semantics," *Synthese* 21 (1970), 18–67.

L. Linsky: "Believing and Necessity," *Proceedings and Addresses of the American Philosophical Association* 50 (1977), 526–30.

F. Mondadori: "Interpreting Modal Semantics," in F. Guenthner and C. Rohrer, eds, *Studies in Formal Semantics*, North-Holland, Amsterdam (1978).

Richard Montague: "Pragmatics and Intensional Logic," *Synthese* 22, 68–94, reprinted in *Formal Philosophy: Selected Papers of Richard Montague*, ed. and intro. Richmond Thomason, Yale University Press, New Haven (1974).

Richard Montague: "Universal Grammar," *Theoria* 36, 373–98, reprinted in *Formal Philosophy: Selected Papers of Richard Montague*, ed. and intro. Richmond Thomason, Yale University Press, New Haven (1974).

Richard Montague: *Formal Philosophy: Selected Papers of Richard Montague*, ed. and intro. Richmond Thomason, Yale University Press, New Haven (1974).

J. M. E. Moravcsik: "Singular Terms, Belief, and Reality," *Dialectica* 31 (1977), 259–72.

Terence Parsons: *Nonexistent Objects*. Yale University Press, New Haven (forthcoming) [1980].

B. H. Partee: "The Syntax and Semantics of Quotation," in S. R. Anderson and P. Kisarsky, eds, *A Festschrift for Morris Halle*, Holt, Rinehart, and Winston, New York (1973).

B. H. Partee: "Montague Grammar and Transformational Grammar," *Linguistic Inquiry* 6 (1975), 203–300.

B. H. Partee: "Montague Grammar, Mental Representations, and Reality," to be published in proceedings of the symposium "Philosophy and Grammar," Uppsala University, June, 1977, Stig Kanger and Sven Ohman, eds (forthcoming). [Reidel, Dordrecht (1981).]

Jean Piaget: *The Child's Conception of the World*, trans. J. and A. Tomlinson, 1972 edn, Littlefield, Adams & Co., Totowa, NJ (1929).

Hilary Putnam: "The Meaning of 'Meaning,'" in K. Gunderson, ed., *Language, Mind and Knowledge*, Minnesota Studies in the Philosophy of Science VII, University of Minnesota Press, Minneapolis, reprinted in *Mind, Language and Reality: Philosophical Papers*, vol. 2, Cambridge University Press, Cambridge (1975) [reproduced as ch. 3 in this volume].

Hilary Putnam: "Language and Reality," in *Mind, Language and Reality: Philosophical Papers*, vol. 2, Cambridge University Press, Cambridge (1975).

Hilary Putnam: *Mind, Language and Reality: Philosophical Papers*, vol. 2, Cambridge University Press, Cambridge (1975).

Veikko Rantala: "Urn Models: A New Kind of Nonstandard Model for First Order Logic," *Journal of Philosophical Logic* 4 (1975), 455–74.

Stephen R. Schwartz, ed.: *Naming, Necessity, and Natural Kinds*, Cornell University Press, Ithaca, NY (1977).

Robert Stalnaker: "Assertion," in Peter Cole, ed., *Syntax and Semantics, vol. 9: Pragmatics*, Academic Press, NY (1978).

Richmond Thomason: "A Model Theory for Propositional Attitudes," ms. 1977, University of Pittsburgh (unpublished).

P. C. Wason and P. N. Johnson-Laird: *Psychology of Reasoning: Structure and Content*, Harvard University Press, Cambridge, MA (1972).

2

Language and Communication

Introduction

In the last section we saw attempts to formalize natural languages and how those attempts need to take into account the way people use language. The current section focuses in more detail on the complex uses of natural languages. Grice's paper, "Meaning," started the kind of analysis of meaning that was carried on for the next 25 years and that has influenced philosophy of language to this day. "Meaning" contains Grice's first attempt to connect semantic notions, such as linguistic meaning, with what people intend to do with language.

At the basis of Grice's analysis of meaning is what he calls nonnatural meaning, or meaning$_{NN}$. Grice's analysis of meaning$_{NN}$ is fairly complex (and later became much more complex), but it includes at least the following elements:

1 The speaker intends to produce in the audience some specific effect or response.
2 The speaker intends that the audience recognize her intention.
3 The speaker intends that the audience's recognition of her intention leads to the intended response or effect.

If this account is to succeed, it must make sure that the psychological notion of an intention is legitimate, and this is something Grice worries about in the last few paragraphs of this paper. He is writing during the heyday of behaviorism, which was suspicious about mental states such as intentions.

Grice's account was not satisfactory and had to be modified. For example, some philosophers argued that communication requires that not only does the speaker intend the audience to recognize her intention to produce an effect in the audience, but the speaker also intends the audience to recognize that she intends the audience to recognize this intention. The speaker wants the audience to know that she is trying to produce an effect in the audience.

Still other modifications to Grice's account rest on a distinction made by John L. Austin and discussed by John Searle. Austin observed that one can perform a number of distinguishable acts with an utterance. First there is the locutionary act of using an utterance with more or less definite meaning and reference. The illocutionary act is getting the audience to interpret or understand the locutionary act in a certain way, for instance as a warning, assertion, command, promise, or hint. Finally, the perlocutionary act is getting the audience to do something or be in a certain state by means of the illocutionary act. For example, suppose I issue a warning that it is raining with the intention of getting you to wear a raincoat. In this case I have performed the locutionary act of saying "It is raining" and expressing the proposition that it is raining, I have performed the illocutionary act of issuing a warning with this locution, and I have also performed a perlocutionary act of getting you to heed my warning.

In "What Is a Speech Act?" Searle argues that Grice is too generous in his account of meaning. Searle give an example of an American soldier in the Second World War who is captured by Italian troops. Trying to get the Italian soldiers to believe that he is a German officer, the soldier addresses the Italians with the only German sentence he remembers, "Kennst du das Land, wo die Zitronen blühen?" As Searle points out, it seems plainly false to claim that the soldier means "I am a German officer" when he utters the German sentence. What is needed, says Searle, is an account of meaning which captures both the intentional and the conventional aspects of the illocutionary act. For this purpose Searle gives us an account of both rules and propositions, and employs those when giving us a precise account of the illocutionary act of promising.

One feature Searle uses in his account of promising is what he calls function-indicating devices. Function-indicating devices in English include word order, stress, intonation, punctuation and the mood of the verb. Sometimes, in actual speech situations, the context will make clear the illocutionary force of an utterance, but on other occasions it might be necessary to invoke various function-indicating devices to make clear the illocutionary force of the utterance.

Given the highly social character of language emphasized by philosophers such as Austin, Grice, and Searle, one wonders how attempts to formalize languages can succeed. David Lewis, in "Languages and Language," makes an attempt to combine a formal system that correlates sentences with meanings in a systematic way with the social character of language. The formal part of a language is represented by ordered pairs consisting of sentences and meanings (sets of possible worlds). The social character of a language allows us to communicate, initiate actions, and understand behaviors, feeling and desires of others. According to Lewis it is possible to synthesize the two because of two conventions shared in the community where the language is spoken; the conventions of truthfulness and trust. These two conventions provide the link between a formalized language and a language-using population. If Lewis is right, then he has taken a big step in the direction of reconciling the formal approach to language and the approach that emphasizes the pragmatics of communication.

Further Reading

Alston, W. P. (1964). *Philosophy of Language*. Englewood Cliffs, NJ: Prentice Hall.

Austin, J. L. (1975). *How to Do Things with Words*. 2nd edn. Cambridge, MA: Harvard University Press.

Bach, K. (1994). Conversational Implicature. *Mind and Language* 9: 124–62.

Grice, H. P. (1978). Further Notes on Logic and Conversation. In *Syntax and Semantics: Pragmatics*. Vol. 7. Ed. P. Cole. New York: Academic Press.

Grice, H. P. (1989). *Studies in the Way of Words*. Cambridge, MA: Harvard University Press.

Lewis, D. (1969). *Convention: A Philosophical Study*. Cambridge, MA: Harvard University Press.

Recanati, F. (1989). The Pragmatics of What is Said. *Mind and Language* 4: 294–328.

Schiffer, S. (1972). *Meaning*. Oxford: Oxford University Press.
Searle, J. R. (1969). *Speech Acts*. Cambridge: Cambridge University Press.
Searle, J. R. (1989). How Performatives Work. *Linguistics and Philosophy* 12: 535–58.
Strawson, P. F. (1964). Intention and Convention in Speech Acts. *Philosophical Review* 73: 439–60.
Strawson, P. F. (1970). *Meaning and Truth*. Oxford: Oxford University Press.

Meaning

H. P. GRICE

Consider the following sentences:

"Those spots mean (meant) measles."

"Those spots didn't mean anything to me, but to the doctor they meant measles."

"The recent budget means that we shall have a hard year."

1   I cannot say, "Those spots meant measles, but he hadn't got measles," and I cannot say, "The recent budget means that we shall have a hard year, but we shan't have." That is to say, in cases like the above, *x meant that p and x means that p* entail *p*.

2   I cannot argue from "Those spots mean (meant) measles" to any conclusion about "what is (was) meant by those spots"; for example, I am not entitled to say, "What was meant by those spots was that he had measles." Equally I cannot draw from the statement about the recent budget the conclusion "What is meant by the recent budget is that we shall have a hard year."

3   I cannot argue from "Those spots meant measles" to any conclusion to the effect that somebody or other meant by those spots so–and–so. *Mutatis mutandis*, the same is true of the sentence about the recent budget.

4   For none of the above examples can a restatement be found in which the verb "mean" is followed by a sentence or phrase in inverted commas. Thus "Those spots meant measles" cannot be reformulated as "Those spots meant 'measles'" or as "Those spots meant 'he has measles.'"

5   On the other hand, for all these examples an approximate restatement can be found beginning with the phrase "The fact that . . ."; for example, "The fact that he had those spots meant that he had measles" and "The fact that the recent budget was as it was means that we shall have a hard year."

Now contrast the above sentences with the following:

"Those three rings on the bell (of the bus) mean that the 'bus is full.'"

"That remark, 'Smith couldn't get on without his trouble and strife,' meant that Smith found his wife indispensable."

1   I can use the first of these and go on to say, "But it isn't in fact full – the conductor has made a mistake"; and I can use the second and go on, "But in fact Smith deserted her seven years ago." That is to say, here *x means that p* and *x meant that p* do not entail *p*.

2   I can argue from the first to some statement about "what is (was) meant" by the rings on the bell and from the second to some statement about "what is (was) meant" by the quoted remark.

3   I can argue from the first sentence to the conclusion that somebody (viz., the conductor) meant, or at any rate should have meant, by the rings that the bus is full, and I can argue analogously for the second sentence.

4   The first sentence can be restated in a form in which the verb "mean" is followed by a phrase in inverted commas, that is, "Those three rings on the bell mean 'the bus is full.'" So also can the second sentence.

5   Such a sentence as "The fact that the bell has been rung three times means that the bus is full" is not a restatement of the meaning of the first sentence. Both may be true, but they do not have, even approximately, the same meaning.

When the expressions "means," "means something," "means that" are used in the kind of way in which they are used in the first set of sentences, I shall speak of the sense, or senses, in which they are used as the *natural* sense, or senses, of the expressions in question. When the expressions are used in the kind of way in which they are used in the second set of sentences, I shall speak of the sense, or senses, in which they are used, as the *nonnatural* sense, or senses, of the expressions in question. I shall use the abbreviation "means$_{NN}$" to distinguish the nonnatural sense or senses.

I propose, for convenience, also to include under the head of natural senses of "mean" such senses of "mean" as may be exemplified in sentences of the pattern "A means (meant) *to do* so-and-so (by x)," where A is a human agent. By contrast, as the previous examples show, I include under the head of nonnatural senses of "mean" any senses of "mean" found in sentences of the patterns "A means (meant) something by x" or "A means (meant) by x that. . . ." (This is overrigid; but it will serve as an indication.)

I do not want to maintain that *all* our uses of "mean" fall easily, obviously, and tidily into one of the two groups I have distinguished; but I think that in most cases we should be at least fairly strongly inclined to assimilate a use of "mean" to one group rather than to the other. The question which now arises is this: "What more can be said about the distinction between the cases where we should say that the word is applied in a natural sense and the cases where we should say that the word is applied in a nonnatural sense?" Asking this question will not of course prohibit us from trying to give an explanation of "meaning$_{NN}$" in terms of one or another natural sense of "mean."

The question about the distinction between natural and nonnatural meaning is, I think, what people are getting at when they display an interest in a distinction between "natural" and "conventional" signs. But I think my formulation is better. For some things which can mean$_{NN}$ something are not signs (e.g., words are not), and some are not conventional in any ordinary sense (e.g., certain gestures); while some things which mean naturally are not signs of what they mean (cf. the recent budget example).

I want first to consider briefly, and reject, what I might term a causal type of answer to the question, "What is meaning$_{NN}$?" We might try to say, for instance, more or less with C. L. Stevenson,[1] that for x to mean$_{NN}$ something, x must have (roughly) a tendency to produce in an audience some attitude (cognitive or otherwise) and a tendency, in the case of a speaker, to be produced by that attitude, these tendencies being dependent on "an elaborate process of conditioning attending the use of the sign in communication."[2] This clearly will not do.

1   Let us consider a case where an utterance, if it qualifies at all as meaning$_{NN}$ something, will be of a descriptive or informative kind and the relevant attitude, therefore, will be a cognitive one, for example, a belief. (I use "utterance" as a neutral word to apply to any candidate for meaning$_{NN}$; it has a convenient act–object ambiguity.) It is no doubt the case that many people have a tendency to put on a tail coat when they think they are about to go to a dance, and it is no doubt also the case that many people, on seeing someone put on a tail coat, would conclude that the person in question was about to go to a dance. Does this satisfy us that putting on a tail coat means$_{NN}$ that one is about to go to a dance (or indeed means$_{NN}$ anything at all)? Obviously not. It is no help to refer to the qualifying phrase "dependent on an elaborate process of conditioning. . . ." For if all this means is that the response to the sight of a tail coat being put on is in some way learned or acquired, it will not exclude the present case from being one of meaning$_{NN}$. But if we have to take seriously the second part of the qualifying phrase ("attending the use of the sign in communication"), then the account of meaning$_{NN}$ is obviously circular. We might just as well say, "X has meaning$_{NN}$ if it is used in communication," which, though true, is not helpful.

2   If this is not enough, there is a difficulty – really the same difficulty, I think – which Stevenson recognizes: how we are to avoid saying, for example, that "Jones is tall" is part of what is meant by "Jones is an athlete," since to tell someone that Jones is an athlete would tend to make him believe that Jones is tall. Stevenson here resorts to invoking linguistic rules, namely, a permissive rule of language that "athletes may be nontall." This amounts to saying that we are not prohibited by rule from speaking of "nontall athletes." But why are we not prohibited? Not because it is not bad grammar, or is not impolite, and so on, but presumably because it is not meaningless (or, if this is too strong, does not in any way violate the rules of meaning for the expressions concerned). But this seems to involve us in another circle. Moreover, one wants to ask why, if it is legitimate to appeal here to rules to distinguish what is meant from what is suggested, this appeal was not made earlier, in the case of groans, for example, to deal with which Stevenson originally introduced the qualifying phrase about dependence on conditioning.

A further deficiency in a causal theory of the type just expounded seems to be that, even if we accept it as it stands, we are furnished with an analysis only of statements about the *standard* meaning, or the meaning in general, of a "sign." No provision is made for dealing with statements about what a particular speaker or writer means by a sign on a particular occasion (which may well diverge from the standard meaning of the sign); nor is it obvious how the theory could be adapted to make such provision. One might even go further in criticism and maintain that the causal theory ignores the fact that the meaning (in general) of a sign needs to be explained in terms of what users of the sign do (or should) mean by it on particular occasions; and so the latter notion, which is unexplained by the causal theory, is in fact the fundamental one. I am sympathetic to this more radical criticism, though I am aware that the point is controversial.

I do not propose to consider any further theories of the "causal tendency" type. I suspect no such theory could avoid difficulties analogous to those I have outlined without utterly losing its claim to rank as a theory of this type.

I will now try a different and, I hope, more promising line. If we can elucidate the meaning of

"x meant$_{NN}$ something (on a particular occasion)" and

"x meant$_{NN}$ that so-and-so (on a particular occasion)"

and of

"A meant$_{NN}$ something by x (on a particular occasion)" and

"A meant$_{NN}$ by x that so-and-so (on a particular occasion),"

this might reasonably be expected to help us with

"x means$_{NN}$ (timeless) something (that so-and-so),"

"A means$_{NN}$ (timeless) by x something (that so-and-so),"

and with the explication of "means the same as," "understands," "entails," and so on. Let us for the moment pretend that we have to deal only with utterances which might be informative or descriptive.

A first shot would be to suggest that "x meant$_{NN}$ something" would be true if x was intended by its utterer to induce a belief in some "audience" and that to say what the belief was would be to say what x meant$_{NN}$. This will not do. I might leave B's handkerchief near the scene of a murder in order to induce the detective to believe that B was the murderer; but we should not want to say that the handkerchief (or my leaving it there) meant$_{NN}$ anything or that I had meant$_{NN}$ by leaving it that B was the murderer. Clearly we must at least add that, for x to have meant$_{NN}$ anything, not merely must it have been "uttered" with the intention of inducing a certain belief but also the utterer must have intended an "audience" to recognize the intention behind the utterance.

This, though perhaps better, is not good enough. Consider the following cases:

(1)   Herod presents Salome with the head of St John the Baptist on a charger.

(2)   Feeling faint, a child lets its mother see how pale it is (hoping that she may draw her own conclusions and help).

(3)   I leave the china my daughter has broken lying around for my wife to see.

Here we seem to have cases which satisfy the conditions so far given for meaning$_{NN}$. For example, Herod intended to make Salome believe that St John the Baptist was dead and no doubt also intended Salome to recognize that he intended her to believe that St John the Baptist was dead. Similarly for the other cases. Yet I certainly do not think that we should want to say that we have here cases of meaning$_{NN}$.

What we want to find is the difference between, for example, "deliberately and openly letting someone know" and "telling" and between "getting someone to think" and "telling."

The way out is perhaps as follows. Compare the following two:

(1)   I show Mr X a photograph of Mr Y displaying undue familiarity to Mrs X.

(2)   I draw a picture of Mr Y behaving in this manner and show it to Mr X.

I find that I want to deny that in (1) the photograph (or my showing it to Mr X) meant$_{NN}$ anything at all; while I want to assert that in (2) the picture (or my drawing and showing it) meant$_{NN}$ something (that Mr Y had been unduly unfamiliar), or at least that I had meant$_{NN}$

by it that Mr *Y* had been unduly familiar. What is the difference between the two cases? Surely in case (1) Mr *X*'s recognition of my intention to make him believe that there is something between Mr *Y* and Mrs *X* is (more or less) irrelevant to the production of this effect by the photograph. Mr *X* would be led by the photograph at least to suspect Mrs *X* even if instead of showing it to him I had left it his room by accident; and I (the photograph shower) would not be unaware of this. But it will make a difference to the effect of my picture on Mr *X* whether or not he takes me to be intending to inform him (make him believe something) about Mrs *X*, and not to be just doodling or trying to produce a work of art.

But now we seem to be landed in a further difficulty if we accept this account. For consider now, say, frowning. If I frown spontaneously, in the ordinary course of events, someone looking at me may well treat the frown as a natural sign of displeasure. But if I frown deliberately (to convey my displeasure), an onlooker may be expected, provided he recognizes my intention, *still* to conclude that I am displeased. Ought we not then to say, since it could not be expected to make any difference to the onlooker's reaction whether he regards my frown as spontaneous or as intended to be informative, that my frown (deliberate) does *not* mean$_{NN}$ anything? I think this difficulty can be met; for though in general a deliberate frown may have the same effect (as regards inducing belief in my displeasure) as a spontaneous frown, it can be expected to have the same effect only *provided* the audience takes it as intended to convey displeasure. That is, if we take away the recognition of intention, leaving the other circumstances (including the recognition of the frown as deliberate), the belief-producing tendency of the frown must be regarded as being impaired or destroyed.

Perhaps we may sum up what is necessary for *A* to mean something by *x* as follows. *A* must intend to induce by *x* a belief in an audience, and he must also intend his utterance to be recognized as so intended. But these intentions are not independent; the recognition is intended by *A* to play its part in inducing the belief, and if it does not do so something will have gone wrong with the fulfillment of *A*'s intentions. Moreover, *A*'s intending that the recognition should play this part implies, I think, that he assumes that there is some chance that it will in fact play this part, that he does not regard it as a foregone conclusion that the belief will be induced in the audience whether or not the intention behind the utterance is recognized. Shortly, perhaps, we may say that "*A* meant$_{NN}$ something by *x*" is roughly equivalent to "*A* uttered *x* with the intention of inducing a belief by means of the recognition of this intention." (This seems to involve a reflexive paradox, but it does not really do so.)

Now perhaps it is time to drop the pretense that we have to deal only with "informative" cases. Let us start with some examples of imperatives or quasi-imperatives. I have a very avaricious man in my room, and I want him to go; so I throw a pound note out of the window. Is there here any utterance with a meaning$_{NN}$? No, because in behaving as I did, I did not intend his recognition of my purpose to be in any way effective in getting him to go. This is parallel to the photograph case. If on the other hand I had pointed to the door or given him a little push, then my behavior might well be held to constitute a meaningful$_{NN}$ utterance, just because the recognition of my intention would be intended by me to be effective in speeding his departure. Another pair of cases would be (1) a policeman who stops a car by standing in its way and (2) a policeman who stops a car by waving.

Or, to turn briefly to another type of case, if as an examiner I fail a man, I may well cause him distress or indignation or humiliation; and if I am vindictive, I may intend this effect and even intend him to recognize my intention. But I should not be inclined to say that my failing him meant$_{NN}$ anything. On the other hand, if I cut someone in the street I do feel inclined to assimilate this to the cases of meaning$_{NN}$, and this inclination seems to me dependent on the fact that I could not reasonably expect him to be distressed (indignant, humiliated) unless he recognized my intention to affect him in this way. (Cf., if my college stopped my salary altogether I should accuse them of ruining me; if they cut it by 2/6d I might accuse them of insulting me; with some intermediate amounts I might not know quite what to say.)

Perhaps then we may make the following generalizations:

1   "*A* meant$_{NN}$ something by *x*" is (roughly) equivalent to "*A* intended the utterance of *x* to produce some effect in an audience by means of the recognition of this intention"; and we may add that to ask what *A* meant is to ask for a specification of the intended effect (though, of course, it may not always be possible to get a straight answer involving a "that" clause, for example, "a belief that . . .").

2   "*x* meant something" is (roughly) equivalent to "Somebody meant$_{NN}$ something by *x*." Here again there will be cases; where this will not quite work. I feel inclined to say that (as regards traffic lights) the change to red meant$_{NN}$ that the traffic was to stop; but it would be very unnatural to say, "Somebody (e.g., the Corporation) meant$_{NN}$ by the red-light change that the traffic was to stop." Nevertheless, there seems to be *some* sort of reference to somebodys intentions.

3   "*x* means$_{NN}$ (timeless) that so-and-so" might as a first shot be equated with some statement or disjunction of statements about what "people" (vague) intend (with qualifications about "recognition") to effect by *x*. I shall have a word to say about this.

Will any kind of intended effect do, or may there be cases where an effect is intended (with the required qualifications) and yet we should not want to talk of meaning$_{NN}$? Suppose I discovered some person so constituted that, when I told him that whenever I grunted in a special way I wanted him to blush or to incur some physical malady, thereafter whenever he recognized the grunt (and with it my intention), he did blush or incur the malady. Should we then want to say that the grunt meant$_{NN}$ something? I do not think so. This points to the fact that for *x* to have meaning$_{NN}$, the intended effect must be something which in some sense is within the control of the audience, or that in some sense of "reason" the recognition of the intention behind *x* is for the audience a reason and not merely a cause. It might look as if there is a sort of pun here ("reason for believing" and "reason for doing"), but I do not think this is serious. For though no doubt from one point of view questions about reasons for believing are questions about evidence and so quite different from questions about reasons for doing, nevertheless to recognize an utterer's intention in uttering *x* (descriptive utterance), to have a reason for believing that so-and-so, is at least quite like "having a motive for" accepting so-and-so. Decisions "that" seem to involve decisions "to" (and this is why we can "refuse to believe" and also be "compelled to believe"). (The "cutting" case needs slightly different treatment, for one cannot in any straightforward sense "decide" to be offended; but one can refuse to be offended.) It looks then as if the intended effect must be something within the control of the audience, or at least the *sort* of thing which is within its control.

One point before passing to an objection or two. I think it follows that from what I have said about the connection between meaning$_{NN}$ and recognition of intention that (insofar as I am right) only what I may call the primary intention of an utterer is relevant to the meaning of an utterance. For if I utter *x*, intending (with the aid of the recognition of this intention) to induce an effect *E*, and intend this effect *E* to lead to a further effect, then insofar as the occurrence of *F* is thought to be dependent solely on *E*, I cannot regard *F* as in the least dependent on recognition of my intention to induce E. That is, if (say) I intend to get a man to do something by giving him some information, it cannot be regarded as relevant to the meaning$_{NN}$ of my utterance to describe what I intend him to do.

Now some question may be raised about my use, fairly free, of such words as "intention" and "recognition." I must disclaim any intention of peopling all our talking life with armies of complicated psychological occurrences. I do not hope to solve any philosophical puzzles about intending, but I do want briefly to argue that no special difficulties are raised by my use of the word "intention" in connection with meaning. First, there will be cases where an utterance is accompanied or preceded by a conscious "plan," or explicit formulation of intention (e.g., I declare how I am going to use x, or ask myself how to "get something across"). The presence of such an explicit "plan" obviously counts fairly heavily in favor of the utterer's intention (meaning) being as "planned"; though it is not, I think, conclusive; for example, a speaker who has declared an intention to use a familiar expression in an unfamiliar way may slip into the familiar use. Similarly in nonlinguistic cases: if we are asking about an agent's intention, a previous expression counts heavily; nevertheless, a man might plan to throw a letter in the dustbin and yet take it to the post; when lifting his hand he might "come to" and say *either* "I didn't intend to do this at all" *or* "I suppose I must have been intending to put it in."

Explicitly formulated linguistic (or quasi-linguistic) intentions are no doubt comparatively rare. In their absence we would seem to rely on very much the same kinds of criterion as we do in the case of nonlinguistic intentions where there is a general usage. An utterer is held to intend to convey what is normally conveyed (or normally intended to be conveyed), and we require a good reason for accepting that a particular use diverges from the general usage (e.g., he never knew or had forgotten the general usage). Similarly in nonlinguistic cases: we are presumed to intend the normal consequences of our actions.

Again, in cases where there is doubt, say, about which of two or more things an utterer intends to convey, we tend to refer to the context (linguistic or otherwise) of the utterance and ask which of the alternatives would be relevant to other things he is saying or doing, or which intention in a particular situation would fit in with some purpose he obviously has (e.g., a man who calls for a "pump" at a fire would not want a bicycle pump). Nonlinguistic parallels are obvious: context is a criterion in settling the question of why a man who has just put a cigarette in his mouth has put his hand in his pocket; relevance to an obvious end is a criterion in settling why a man is running away from a bull.

In certain linguistic cases we ask the utterer afterward about his intention, and in a few of these cases (the very difficult ones, like a philosopher asked to explain the meaning of an unclear passage in one of his works), the answer is not based on what he remembers but is more like a decision, a decision about how what he said is to be taken. I cannot find a nonlinguistic parallel here; but the case is so special as not to seem to contribute a vital difference.

All this is very obvious; but surely to show that the criteria for judging linguistic intentions are very like the criteria for judging nonlinguistic intentions is to show that linguistic intentions are very like nonlinguistic intentions.

NOTES

1   *Ethics and Language* (New Haven, 1944), ch. 3.
2   Ibid., p. 57.

What Is a Speech Act?

JOHN R. SEARLE

1   Introduction

In a typical speech situation involving a speaker, a hearer, and an utterance by the speaker, there are many kinds of act associated with the speaker's utterance. The speaker will characteristically have moved his jaw and tongue and made noises. In addition, he will characteristically have performed some acts within the class which includes informing or irritating or boring his hearers; he will further characteristically have performed acts within the class which includes referring to Kennedy or Khrushchev or the North Pole; and he will also have performed acts within the class which includes making statements, asking questions, issuing commands, giving reports, greeting, and warning. The members of this last class are what Austin[1] called illocutionary acts and it is with this class that I shall be concerned in this paper, so the paper might have been called "What Is an Illocutionary Act?" I do not attempt to define the expression "illocutionary act," although if my analysis of a particular illocutionary act succeeds it may provide the basis for a definition. Some of the English verbs and verb phrases associated with illocutionary acts are: state, assert, describe, warn, remark, comment, command, order, request, criticize, apologize, censure, approve, welcome, promise, express approval, and express regret. Austin claimed that there were over a thousand such expressions in English.

By way of introduction, perhaps I can say why I think it is of interest and importance in the philosophy of language to study speech acts, or, as they are sometimes called, language acts or linguistic acts. I think it is essential to any specimen of linguistic communication that it involve a linguistic act. It is not, as has generally been supposed, the symbol or word or sentence, or even the token of the symbol or word or sentence, which is the unit of linguistic communication, but rather it is the *production* of the token in the performance of the speech act that constitutes the basic unit of linguistic communication. To put this point more precisely, the production of the sentence token under certain conditions is the illocutionary act, and the illocutionary act is the minimal unit of linguistic communication.

I do not know how to *prove* that linguistic communication essentially involves acts but I can think of arguments with which one might attempt to convince someone who was skeptical. One argument would be to call the skeptic's attention to the fact that when he takes a noise or a mark on paper to be an instance of linguistic communication, as a message, one of the things that is involved in his so taking that noise or mark is that he should regard it as having been produced by a being with certain intentions. He cannot just regard it as a natural phenomenon, like a stone, a waterfall, or a tree. In order to regard it as an instance of linguistic communication one must suppose that its production is what I am calling a speech act. It is a logical presupposition, for example, of current attempts to decipher the Mayan hieroglyphs that we at least hypothesize that the marks we see on the stones were produced by beings more or less like ourselves and produced with certain kinds of intention. If we were certain the marks were a consequence of, say, water erosion, then the question of deciphering them or even calling them hieroglyphs could not arise. To construe them under the category of linguistic communication necessarily involves construing their production as speech acts.

To perform illocutionary acts is to engage in a rule-governed form of behavior. I shall argue that such things as asking questions or making statements are rule-governed in ways quite similar to those in which getting a base hit in baseball or moving a knight in chess are rule-governed forms of acts. I intend therefore to explicate the notion of an illocutionary act by stating a set of necessary and sufficient conditions for the performance of a particular kind of illocutionary act, and extracting from it a set of semantical rules for the use of the expression (or syntactic device) which marks the utterance as an illocutionary act of that kind. If I am successful in stating the conditions and the corresponding rules for even one kind of illocutionary act, that will provide us with a pattern for analyzing other kinds of act and consequently for explicating the notion in general. But in order to set the stage for actually stating conditions and extracting rules for performing an illocutionary act I have to discuss three other preliminary notions: *rules*, *propositions*, and *meaning*. I shall confine my discussion of these notions to those aspects which are essential to my main purposes in this paper, but, even so, what I wish to say concerning each of these notions, if it were to be at all complete, would require a paper for each; however, sometimes it may be worth sacrificing thoroughness for the sake of scope and I shall therefore be very brief.

2 Rules

In recent years there has been in the philosophy of language considerable discussion involving the notion of rules for the use of expressions. Some philosophers have even said that knowing the meaning of a word is simply a matter of knowing the rules for its use or employment. One disquieting feature of such discussions is that no philosopher, to my knowledge at least, has ever given anything like an adequate formulation of the rules for the use of even one expression. If meaning is a matter of rules of use, surely we ought to be able to state the rules for the use of expressions in a way which would explicate the meaning of those expressions. Certain other philosophers, dismayed perhaps by the failure of their colleagues to produce any rules, have denied the fashionable view that meaning is a matter of rules and have asserted that there are no semantical rules of the proposed kind at all. I am inclined to think that this skepticism is premature and stems from a failure to distinguish different sorts of rule, in a way which I shall now attempt to explain.

I distinguish between two sorts of rule: Some regulate antecedently existing forms of behavior; for example, the rules of etiquette regulate interpersonal relationships, but these relationships exist independently of the rules of etiquette. Some rules on the other hand do not merely regulate but create or define new forms of behavior. The rules of football, for example, do not merely regulate the game of football but as it were create the possibility of or define that activity. The activity of playing football is constituted by acting in accordance with these rules; football has no existence apart from these rules. I call the latter kind of rule constitutive rule and the former kind regulative rules. Regulative rules regulate a pre-existing activity, an activity whose existence is logically independent of the existence of the rules. Constitutive rules constitute (and also regulate) an activity the existence of which is logically dependent on the rules.[2]

Regulative rules characteristically take the form of or can be paraphrased as imperatives, e.g., "When cutting food hold the knife in the right hand," or "Officers are to wear ties at dinner." Some constitutive rules take quite a different form, e.g., a checkmate is made if the king is attacked in such a way that no move will leave it unattacked; a touchdown is scored when a player crosses the opponents' goal line in possession of the ball while a play is in progress. If our paradigms of rules are imperative regulative rules, such nonimperative constitutive rules are likely to strike us as extremely curious and hardly even as rules at all. Notice that they are almost tautological in character, for what the "rule" seems to offer is a partial definition of "checkmate" or "touchdown." But, of course, this quasi-tautological character is a necessary consequence of their being constitutive rules: the rules concerning touchdowns must define the notion of "touchdown" in the same way as the rules concerning football define "football." That, for example, a touchdown can be scored in such and such ways and counts six points can appear sometimes as a rule, sometimes as an analytic truth; and that it can be construed as a tautology is a clue to the fact that the rule in question is a constitutive one. Regulative rules generally have the form "Do X" or "If Y do X." Some members of the set of constitutive rules have this form but some also have the form "X counts as Y."[3]

The failure to perceive this is of some importance in philosophy. Thus, e.g., some philosophers ask "How can a promise create an obligation?" A similar question would be "How can a touchdown create six points?" And as they stand both questions can only be answered by stating a rule of the form "X counts as Y."

I am inclined to think that both the failure of some philosophers to state rules for the use of expressions and the skepticism of other philosophers concerning the existence of any such rules stem at least in part from a failure to recognize the distinctions between constitutive and regulative rules. The model or paradigm of a rule which most philosophers have is that of a regulative rule, and if one looks in semantics for purely regulative rules one is not likely to find anything interesting from the point of view of logical analysis. There are no doubt social rules of the form "One ought not to utter obscenities at formal gatherings," but that hardly seems a rule of the sort that is crucial in explicating the semantics of a language. The hypothesis that lies behind the present paper is that the semantics of a language can be regarded as a series of systems of constitutive rules and that illocutionary acts are acts performed in accordance with these sets of constitutive rules. One of the aims of this paper is to formulate a set of constitutive rules for a certain kind of speech act. And if what I have said concerning constitutive rules is correct, we should not be surprised if not all these rules take the form of imperative rules. Indeed we shall see that the rules fall into several different categories, none of which is quite like the rules of etiquette. The effort to state the rules for an illocutionary act can also be regarded as a kind of test of the hypothesis that there are constitutive rules underlying speech acts. If we are unable to give any satisfactory rule formulations, our failure could be construed as partially disconfirming evidence against the hypothesis.

3   Propositions

Different illocutionary acts often have features in common with each other. Consider utterances of the following sentences:

(1)   Will John leave the room?

(2)   John will leave the room.

(3)   John, leave the room!

(4)   Would that John left the room.

(5)   If John will leave the room, I will leave also.

Utterances of each of these on a given occasion would characteristically be performances of different illocutionary acts. The first would, characteristically, be a question, the second an assertion about the future, that is, a prediction, the third a request or order, the fourth an expression of a wish, and the fifth a hypothetical expression of intention. Yet in the performance of each the speaker would characteristically perform some subsidiary acts which are common to all five illocutionary acts. In the utterance of each the speaker *refers* to a particular person John and *predicates* the act of leaving the room of that person. In no case is that all he does, but in every case it is a part of what he does. I shall say, therefore, that in each of these cases, although the illocutionary acts are different, at least some of the nonillocutionary acts of reference and predication are the same.

The reference to some person John and predication of the same thing of him in each of these illocutionary acts inclines me to say that there is a common *content* in each of them. Something expressible by the clause "that John will leave the room" seems to be a common feature of all. We could, with not too much distortion, write each of these sentences in a way which would isolate this common feature: "I assert that John will leave the room," "I ask whether John will leave the room," etc.

For lack of a better word I propose to call this common content a proposition, and I shall describe this feature of these illocutionary acts by saying that in the utterance of each of (1)–(5) the speaker expresses the proposition that John will leave the room. Notice that I do not say that the sentence expresses the proposition; I do not know how sentences could perform acts of that kind. But I shall say that in the utterance of the sentence the speaker expresses a proposition. Notice also that I am distinguishing between a proposition and an assertion or statement of that proposition. The proposition that John will leave the room is expressed in the utterance of all of (1)–(5), but only in (2) is that proposition asserted. An assertion is an illocutionary act, but a proposition is not an act at all, although the act of expressing a proposition is a part of performing certain illocutionary acts.

I might summarize this by saying that I am distinguishing between the illocutionary act and the propositional content of an illocutionary act. Of course, not all illocutionary acts have a propositional content, for example, an utterance of "Hurrah!" or "Ouch!" does not. In one version or another this distinction is an old one and has been marked in different ways by authors as diverse as Frege, Sheffer, Lewis, Reichenbach, and Hare, to mention only a few.

From a semantical point of view we can distinguish between the propositional indicator in the sentence and the indicator of illocutionary force. That is, for a large class of sentences used to perform illocutionary acts, we can say for the purpose of our analysis that the sentence has two (not necessarily separate) parts, the proposition-indicating element and the function-indicating device.[4] The function-indicating device shows how the proposition is to be taken, or, to put it in another way, what illocutionary force the utterance is to have, that is, what illocutionary act the speaker is performing in the utterance of the sentence. Function-indicating devices in English include word order, stress, intonation contour, punctuation, the mood of the verb, and finally a set of so-called performative verbs: I may indicate the kind of illocutionary act I am performing by beginning the sentence with "I apologize," "I warn," "I state," etc. Often in actual speech situations the context will make it clear what the illocutionary force of the utterance is, without its being necessary to invoke the appropriate function-indicating device.

If this semantical distinction is of any real importance, it seems likely that it should have some syntactical analogue, and certain recent developments in transformational grammar tend to support the view that it does. In the underlying phrase marker of a sentence there is a distinction between those elements which correspond to the function-indicating device and those which correspond to the propositional content.

The distinction between the function-indicating device and the proposition-indicating device will prove very useful to us in giving an analysis of an illocutionary act. Since the same proposition can be common to all sorts of illocutionary act, we can separate our analysis of the proposition from our analysis of kinds of illocutionary act. I think there are rules for expressing propositions, rules for such things as reference and predication, but those rules can be discussed independently of the rules for function indicating. In this paper I shall not attempt to discuss propositional rules but shall concentrate on rules for using certain kinds of function-indicating device.

4   Meaning

Speech acts are characteristically performed in the utterance of sounds or the making or marks. What is the difference between *just* uttering sounds or making marks and performing a speech act? One difference is that the sounds or marks one makes in the performance of a speech act are characteristically said to *have meaning*, and a second related difference is that one is characteristically said to *mean something* by those sounds or marks. Characteristically when one speaks one means something by what one says, and what one says, the string of morphemes that one emits, is characteristically said to have a meaning. Here, incidentally, is another point at which our analogy between performing speech acts and playing games breaks down. The pieces in a game like chess are not characteristically said to have a meaning, and furthermore when one makes a move one is not characteristically said to mean anything by that move.

But what is it for one to mean something by what one says, and what is it for something to have a meaning? To answer the first of these questions I propose to borrow and revise some ideas of Paul Grice. In an article entitled "Meaning,"[5] Grice gives the following analysis of one sense of the notion of "meaning." To say that *A* meant something by *x* is to say that *A* intended the utterance of *x* to produce some effect in an audience by means of the recognition of this intention. This seems to me a useful start on an analysis of meaning, first because it shows the close relationship between the notion of meaning and the notion of intention, and secondly because it captures something which is, I think, essential to speaking a language: In speaking a language I attempt to communicate things to my hearer by means of getting him to recognize my intention to communicate just those things. For example, characteristically, when I make an assertion, I attempt to communicate to and convince my hearer of the truth of a certain proposition; and the means I employ to do this are to utter certain sounds, which utterance I intend to produce in him the desired effect by means of his recognition of my intention to produce just that effect. I shall illustrate this with an example. I might on the one hand attempt to get you to believe that I am French by speaking French all the time, dressing in the French manner, showing wild enthusiasm for de Gaulle, and cultivating French acquaintances. But I might on the other hand attempt to get you to believe that I am French by simply telling you that I am French. Now, what is the difference between these two ways of my attempting to get you to believe that I am French? One crucial difference is that in the second case I attempt to get you to believe that I am French by getting you to recognize that it is my purported intention to get you to believe just that. That is one of the things involved in telling you that I am French. But of course if I try to get you to believe that I am French by putting on the act I described, then your recognition of my intention to produce in you the belief that I am French is not the means I am employing. Indeed in this case you would, I think, become rather suspicious if you recognized my intention.

However valuable this analysis of meaning is, it seems to me to be in certain respects defective. First of all, it fails to distinguish the different kinds of effects – perlocutionary versus illocutionary – that one may intend to produce in one's hearers, and it further fails to show the way in which these different kinds of effects are related to the notion of meaning. A second defect is that it fails to account for the extent to which meaning is a matter of rules or conventions. That is, this account of meaning does not show the connection between one's meaning something by what one says and what that which one says actually means in the language. In order to illustrate this point I now wish to present a counterexample to this analysis of meaning. The point of the counterexample will be to illustrate the connection between what a speaker means and what the words he utters mean.

Suppose that I am an American soldier in the Second World War and that I am captured by Italian troops. And suppose also that I wish to get these troops to believe that I am a German officer in order to get them to release me. What I would like to do is to tell them in German or Italian that I am a German officer. But let us suppose I don't know enough German or Italian to do that. So I, as it were, attempt to put on a show of telling them that I am a German officer by reciting those few bits of German that I know, trusting that they don't know enough German to see through my plan. Let us suppose I know only one line of German, which I remember from a poem I had to memorize in a highschool German course. Therefore I, a captured American, address my Italian captors with the following sentence: "Kennst du das Land, wo die Zitronen blühen?" Now, let us describe the situation in Gricean terms. I intend to produce a certain effect in them, namely, the effect of believing that I am a German officer; and I intend to produce this effect by means of their recognition of my intention. I intend that they should think that I am trying to tell them is that I am a German officer. But does it follow from this account that when I say "Kennst du das Land . . . ," etc., what I mean is, "I am a German officer"? Not only does it not follow, but in this case it seems plainly false that when I utter the German sentence what I mean is "I am a German officer," or even "Ich bin ein deutscher Offizier," because what the words mean is, "Knowest thou the land where the lemon trees bloom?" Of course, I want my captors to be deceived into thinking that what I mean is "I am a German officer," but part of what is involved in the deception is getting them to think that that is what the words which I utter mean in German. At one point in the *Philosophical Investigations* Wittgenstein says "Say 'it's cold here' and mean its warm here.' "[6] The reason we are unable to do this is that what we can mean is a function of what we are saying. Meaning is more than a matter of intention, it is also a matter of convention.

Grice's account can be amended to deal with counterexamples of this kind. We have here a case where I am trying to produce a certain effect by means of the recognition of my intention to produce that effect, but the device I use to produce this effect is one which is conventionally, by the rules governing the use of that device, used as a means of producing quite different illocutionary effects. We must therefore reformulate the Gricean account of meaning in such a way as to make it clear that one's meaning something when one says something is more than just contingently related to what the sentence means in the language one is speaking. In our analysis of illocutionary acts, we must capture both the intentional and the conventional aspects and especially the relationship between them. In the performance of an illocutionary act the speaker intends to produce a certain effect by means of getting the hearer to recognize his intention to produce that effect, and furthermore, if he is using words literally, he intends this recognition to be achieved in virtue of the fact that the rules for using the expressions he utters associate the expressions with the production of that effect. It is this *combination* of elements which we shall need to express in our analysis of the illocutionary act.

5   How to Promise

I shall now attempt to give an analysis of the illocutionary act of promising. In order to do this I shall ask what conditions are necessary and sufficient for the act of promising to have been performed in the utterance of a given sentence. I shall attempt to answer this question by stating these conditions as a set of propositions such that the conjunction of the members of the set entails the proposition that a speaker made a promise, and the proposition that the speaker made a promise entails this conjunction. Thus each condition will be a necessary condition for the performance of the act of promising, and taken collectively the set of conditions will be a sufficient condition for the act to have been performed.

If we get such a set of conditions we can extract from them a set of rules for the use of the function-indicating device. The method here is analogous to discovering the rules of chess by asking oneself what are the necessary and sufficient conditions under which one can be said to have correctly moved a knight or castled or checkmated a player, etc. We are in the position of someone who has learned to play chess without ever having the rules formulated and who wants such a formulation. We learned how to play the game of illocutionary acts, but in general it was done without an explicit formulation of the rules, and the first step in getting such a formulation is to set out the conditions for the performance of a particular illocutionary act. Our inquiry will therefore serve a double philosophical purpose. By stating a set of conditions for the performance of a particular illocutionary act we shall have offered a partial explication of that notion and shall also have paved the way for the second step, the formulation of the rules.

I find the statement of the conditions very difficult to do and I am not entirely satisfied with the list I am about to present. One reason for the difficulty is that the notion of a promise, like most notions in ordinary language, does not have absolutely strict rules. There are all sorts of odd, deviant, and borderline promises; and counterexamples, more or less bizarre, can be produced against my analysis. I am inclined to think we shall not be able to get a set of knockdown necessary and sufficient conditions that will exactly mirror the ordinary use of the word "promise." I am confining my discussion, therefore, to the center of the concept of promising and ignoring the fringe, borderline, and partially defective cases. I also confine my discussion to fullblown explicit promises and ignore promises made by elliptical turns of phrase, hints, metaphors, etc.

Another difficulty arises from my desire to state the conditions without certain forms of circularity. I want to give a list of conditions for the performance of a certain illocutionary act, which do not themselves mention the performance of any illocutionary acts. I need to satisfy this condition in order to offer an explication of the notion of an illocutionary act in general, otherwise I should simply be showing the relation between different illocutionary acts. However, although there will be no reference to illocutionary *acts*, certain illocutionary *concepts* will appear in the analysans as well as in the analysandum; and I think this form of circularity is unavoidable because of the nature of constitutive rules.

In the presentation of the conditions I shall first consider the case of a sincere promise and then show how to modify the conditions to allow for insincere promises. As our inquiry is semantical rather than syntactical, I shall simply assume the existence of grammatically well-formed sentences.

Given that a speaker *S* utters a sentence *T* in the presence of a hearer *H*, then, in the utterance of *T*, *S* sincerely (and nondefectively) promises that *p* to *H* if and only if:

1 *Normal input and output conditions obtain.* I use the terms "input" and "output" to cover the large and indefinite range of conditions under which any kind of serious linguistic communication is possible. "Output" covers the conditions for intelligible speaking and "input" covers the conditions for understanding. Together they include such things as that the speaker and hearer both know how to speak the language; both are conscious of what they are doing; the speaker is not acting under duress or threats; they have no physical impediments to communication, such as deafness, aphasia, or laryngitis; they are not acting in a play or telling jokes, etc.

2 *S expresses that p in the utterance of T.* This condition isolates the propositional content from the rest of the speech act and enables us to concentrate on the peculiarities of promising in the rest of the analysis.

3 *In expressing that p, S predicates a future act A of S.* In the case of promising, the function-indicating device is an expression whose scope includes certain features of the proposition. In a promise an act must be predicated of the speaker and it cannot be a past act. I cannot promise to have done something, and I cannot promise that someone else will do something. (Although I can promise to see that he will do it.) The notion of an act, as I am construing it for present purposes, includes refraining from acts, and performing series of acts, and may also include states and conditions: I may promise not to do something, I may promise to do something repeatedly, and I may promise to be or remain in a certain state or condition. I call conditions (2) and (3) the *propositional content conditions.*

4 *H would prefer S's doing A to his not doing A, and S believes H would prefer his doing A to his not doing A.* One crucial distinction between promises on the one hand and threats on the other is that a promise is a pledge to do something for you, not to you, but a threat is a pledge to do something to you, not for you. A promise is defective if the thing promised is something the promisee does not want done; and it is further defective if the promisor does not believe the promisee wants it done, since a nondefective promise must be intended as a promise and not as a threat or warning. I think both halves of this double condition are necessary in order to avoid fairly obvious counterexamples.

One can, however, think of apparent counterexamples to this condition as stated. Suppose I say to a lazy student "If you don't hand in your paper on time I promise you I will give you a failing grade in the course." Is this utterance a promise? I am inclined to think not; we would more naturally describe it as a warning or possibly even a threat. But why then is it possible to use the locution "I promise" in such a case? I think we use it here because "I promise" and "I hereby promise" are among the strongest function-indicating devices for *commitment* provided by the English language. For that reason we often use these expressions in the performance of speech acts which are not strictly speaking promises but in which we wish to emphasize our commitment. To illustrate this, consider another apparent counterexample to the analysis along different lines. Sometimes, more commonly I think in the United States than in Britain, one hears people say "I promise" when making an emphatic assertion. Suppose, for example, I accuse you of having stolen the money. I say, "You stole that money, didn't you?" You reply "No, I didn't, I promise you I didn't." Did you make a promise in this case? I find it very unnatural to describe your utterance as a promise. This utterance would be more aptly described as an emphatic denial, and we can explain the occurrence of the function-indicating device "I promise" as derivative from genuine promises and serving here as an expression adding emphasis to your denial.

In general the point stated in condition (4) is that if a purported promise is to be nondefective the thing promised must be something the hearer wants done, or considers to be in his interest, or would prefer being done to not being done, etc.; and the speaker must be aware of or believe or know, etc., that this is the case. I think a more elegant and exact formulation of this condition would require the introduction of technical terminology.

5   *It is not obvious to both S and H that S will do A in the normal course of events.* This condition is an instance of a general condition on many different kinds of illocutionary acts to the effect that the act must have a point. For example, if I make a request to someone to do something which it is obvious that he is already doing or is about to do, then my request is pointless and to that extent defective. In an actual speech situation, listeners, knowing the rules for performing illocutionary acts, will assume that this condition is satisfied. Suppose, for example, that in the course of a public speech I say to a member of my audience "Look here, Smith, pay attention to what I am saying." In order to make sense of this utterance the audience will have to assume that Smith has not been paying attention or at any rate that it is not obvious that he has been paying attention, that the question of his paying attention has arisen in some way; because a condition for making a request is that it is not obvious that the hearer is doing or about to do the thing requested.

Similarly with promises. It is out of order for me to promise to do something that it is obvious I am going to do anyhow. If I do seem to be making such a promise, the only way my audience can make sense of my utterance is to assume that I believe that it is not obvious that I am going to do the thing promised. A happily married man who promises his wife he will not desert her in the next week is likely to provide more anxiety than comfort.

Parenthetically I think this condition is an instance of the sort of phenomenon stated in Zipf's law. I think there is operating in our language, as in most forms of human behavior, a principle of least effort, in this case a principle of maximum illocutionary ends with minimum phonetic effort; and I think condition (5) is an instance of it.

I call conditions such as (4) and (5) *preparatory conditions.* They are *sine quibus non* of happy promising, but they do not yet state the essential feature.

6   *S intends to do A.* The most important distinction between sincere and insincere promises is that in the case of the sincere promise the speaker intends to do the act promised, in the case of the insincere promise he does not intend to do the act. Also in sincere promises the speaker believes it is possible for him to do the act (or to refrain from doing it), but I think the proposition that he intends to do it entails that he thinks it is possible to do (or refrain from doing) it, so I am not stating that as an extra condition. I call this condition the *sincerity condition.*

7   *S intends that the utterance of T will place him under an obligation to do A.* The essential feature of a promise is that it is the undertaking of an obligation to perform a certain act. I think that this condition distinguishes promises (and other members of the same family such as vows) from other kinds of speech act. Notice that in the statement of the condition we only specify the speaker's intention; further conditions will make clear how that intention is realized. It is clear, however, that having this intention is a necessary condition of making a promise; for if a speaker can demonstrate that he did not have this intention in a given utterance, he can prove that the utterance was not a promise. We know, for example, that Mr

Pickwick did not promise to marry the woman because we know he did not have the appropriate intention.

I call this the *essential condition*.

8   *S intends that the utterance of T will produce in H a belief that conditions (6) and (7) obtain by means of the recognition of the intention to produce that belief, and he intends this recognition to be achieved by means of the recognition of the sentence as one conventionally used to produce such beliefs.* This captures our amended Gricean analysis of what it is for the speaker to mean to make a promise. The speaker intends to produce a certain illocutionary effect by means of getting the hearer to recognize his intention to produce that effect, and he also intends this recognition to be achieved in virtue of the fact that the lexical and syntactical character of the item he utters conventionally associates it with producing that effect.

Strictly speaking this condition could be formulated as part of condition (1), but it is of enough philosophical interest to be worth stating separately. I find it troublesome for the following reason. If my original objection to Grice is really valid, then surely, one might say, all these iterated intentions are superfluous; all that is necessary is that the speaker should seriously utter a sentence. The production of all these effects is simply a consequence of the hearer's knowledge of what the sentence means, which in turn is a consequence of his knowledge of the language, which is assumed by the speaker at the outset. I think the correct reply to this objection is that condition (8) explicates what it is for the speaker to "seriously" utter the sentence, i.e., to utter it and mean it, but I am not completely confident about the force either of the objection or of the reply.

9   *The semantical rules of the dialect spoken by S and are such that T is correctly and sincerely uttered if and only if conditions (1)–(8) obtain.* This condition is intended to make clear that the sentence uttered is one which by the semantical rules of the language are used to make a promise. Taken together with condition (8), it eliminates counterexamples like the captured soldier example considered earlier. Exactly what the formulation of the rules is, we shall soon see.

So far we have considered only the case of a sincere promise. But insincere promises are promises nonetheless, and we now need to show how to modify the conditions to allow for them. In making an insincere promise the speaker does not have all the intentions and beliefs he has when making a sincere promise. However, he purports to have them. Indeed it is because he purports to have intentions and beliefs which he does not have that we describe his act as insincere. So to allow for insincere promises we need only to revise our conditions to state that the speaker takes responsibility for having the beliefs and intentions rather than stating that he actually has them. A clue that the speaker does take such responsibility is the fact that he could not say without absurdity, e.g., "I promise to do A but I do not intend to do A." To say "I promise to do A" is to take responsibility for intending to do A, and this condition holds whether the utterance was sincere or insincere. To allow for the possibility of an insincere promise then we have only to revise condition (6) so that it states not that the speaker intends to do A, but that he takes responsibility for intending to do A, and to avoid the charge of circularity I shall phrase this as follows:

(6*)   *S intends that the utterance of T will make him responsible for intending to do A.*

Thus amended (and with "sincerely" dropped from our analysandum and from condition (9)), our analysis is neutral on the question whether the promise was sincere or insincere.

6   Rules for the Use of the Function-indicating Device

Our next task is to extract from our set of conditions a set of rules for the use of the function-indicating device. Obviously not all of our conditions are equally relevant to this task. Condition (1) and conditions of the forms (8) and (9) apply generally to all kinds of normal illocutionary act and are not peculiar to promising. Rules for the function-indicating device for promising are to be found corresponding to conditions (2)–(7).

The semantical rules for the use of any function-indicating device P for promising are:

Rule 1 P is to be uttered only in the context of a sentence (or larger stretch of discourse) the utterance of which predicates some future act A of the speaker S. I call this the *propositional content rule*. It is derived from the propositional content conditions (2) and (3).

Rule 2 P is to be uttered only if the hearer H would prefer S's doing A to his not doing A, and S believes H would prefer S's doing A to his not doing A.

Rule 3 P is to be uttered only if it is not obvious to both S and H that S will do A in the normal course of events. I call rules (2) and (3) *preparatory rules*. They are derived from the preparatory conditions (4) and (5).

Rule 4 P is to be uttered only if S intends to do A. I call this the *sincerity rule*. It is derived from the sincerity condition (6).

Rule 5   The utterance of P counts as the undertaking of an obligation to do A. I call this the *essential rule*.

These rules are ordered: Rules 2–5 apply only if rule 1 is satisfied, and rule 5 applies only if rules 2 and 3 are satisfied as well.

Notice that whereas rules 1–4 take the form of quasi-imperatives, i.e., they are of the form: utter P only if x, rule 5 is of the form: the utterance of P counts as Y. Thus rule 5 is of the kind peculiar to systems of constitutive rules, which I discussed in section 2.

Notice also that the rather tiresome analogy with games is holding up remarkably well. If we ask ourselves under what conditions a player could be said to move a knight correctly, we would find preparatory conditions, such as that it must be his turn to move, as well as the essential condition stating the actual positions the knight can move to. I think that there is even a sincerity rule for competitive games, the rule that each side tries to win. I suggest that the team which "throws" the game is behaving in a way closely analogous to the speaker who lies or makes false promises. Of course, there usually are no propositional content rules for games, because games do not, by and large, represent states of affairs. If this analysis is of any general interest beyond the case of promising then it would seem that these distinctions should carry over into other types of speech act, and I think a little reflection will show that they do. Consider, e.g., giving an order. The preparatory conditions include that the speaker should be in a position of authority over the hearer, the sincerity condition is that the speaker wants the ordered act done, and the essential condition has to do with the fact that the utterance is an attempt to get the hearer to do it. For assertions the preparatory conditions include the fact that the hearer must have some basis for supposing the asserted proposition is true, the sincerity condition is that he must believe it to be true, and the essential condition has to do with the fact that the utterance is an attempt to inform the hearer and convince him of its truth. Greetings are a much simpler kind of speech act, but even here some of the distinctions apply. In the utterance of "Hello" there is no propositional content and no sincerity condition. The preparatory condition is that the speaker must have just encountered the hearer, and the essential rule is that the utterance indicates courteous recognition of the hearer.

A proposal for further research then is to carry out a similar analysis of other types of speech act. Not only would this give us an analysis of concepts interesting in themselves, but the comparison of different analyses would deepen our understanding of the whole subject and incidentally provide a basis for a more serious taxonomy than any of the usual facile categories such as evaluative versus descriptive, or cognitive versus emotive.

NOTES

1 Austin, J. L., *How to Do Things with Words* (Oxford: 1962).
2 This distinction occurs in J. Rawls, "Two Concepts of Rules," *Philosophical Review*, 1955, and J. R. Searle, "How to Derive 'Ought' from 'Is'," *Philosophical Review*, 1964.
3 The formulation "*X* counts as *Y*" was originally suggested to me by Max Black.
4 In the sentence "I promise that I will come" the function-indicating device and the propositional element are separate. In the sentence "I promise to come," which means the same as the first and is derived from it by certain transformations, the two elements are not separate.
5 *Philosophical Review*, 1957.
6 *Philosophical Investigations* (Oxford: 1953), para. 510.

Logic and Conversation

H. P. GRICE

It is a commonplace of philosophical logic that there are, or appear to be, divergences in meaning between, on the one hand, at least some of what I shall call the formal devices – $\sim$, $\wedge$, $\vee$, $\supset$, (x), (ιx), $\exists(x)$ (when these are given a standard two-valued interpretation) – and, on the other, what are taken to be their analogues or counterparts in natural language–such expressions as *not, and, or, if, all, some* (or *at least one*), *the*. Some logicians may at some time have wanted to claim that there are in fact no such divergences; but such claims, if made at all, have been somewhat rashly made, and those suspected of making them have been subjected to some pretty rough handling.

Those who concede that such divergences exist adhere, in the main, to one or the other of two rival groups, which for the purposes of this article I shall call the formalist and the informalist groups. An outline of a not uncharacteristic formalist position may be given as follows: Insofar as logicians are concerned with the formulation of very general patterns of valid inference, the formal devices possess a decisive advantage over their natural counterparts. For it will be possible to construct in terms of the formal devices a system of very general formulas, a considerable number of which can be regarded as, or are closely related to, patterns of inferences the expression of which involves some or all of the devices: Such a system may consist of a certain set of simple formulas that must be acceptable if the devices have the meaning that has been assigned to them, and an indefinite number of further formulas, many of them less obviously acceptable, each of which can be shown to be acceptable if the members of the original set are acceptable. We have, thus, a way of handling dubiously acceptable patterns of inference, and if, as is sometimes possible, we can apply a decision procedure, we have an even better way. Furthermore, from a philo-sophical point of view, the possession by the natural counterparts of those elements in their meaning, which they do not share with the corresponding formal devices, is to be regarded as an imperfection of natural languages; the elements in question are undesirable excrescences. For the presence of these elements has the result that the concepts within which they appear cannot be precisely/clearly defined, and that at least some statements involving them cannot, in some circumstances, be assigned a definite truth value; and the indefiniteness of these concepts is not only objectionable in itself but leaves open the way to metaphysics—we cannot be certain that none of these natural-language expressions is meta-physically "loaded." For these reasons, the expressions, as used in natural speech, cannot be regarded as finally acceptable, and may turn out to be, finally, not fully intelligible. The proper course is to conceive and begin to construct an ideal language, incorporating the formal devices, the sentences of which will be clear, determinate in truth value, and certifi-ably free from metaphysical implications; the foundations of science will now be philosophi-cally secure, since the statements of the scientist will be expressible (though not necessarily actually expressed) within this ideal language. (I do not wish to suggest that all formalists would accept the whole of this outline, but I think that all would accept at least some part of it.)

To this, an informalist might reply in the following vein. The philosophical demand for an ideal language rests on certain assumptions that should not be conceded; these are, that the primary yardstick by which to judge the adequacy of a language is its ability to serve the needs of science, that an expression cannot be guaranteed as fully intelligible unless an explication or analysis of its meaning has been provided, and that every explication or analysis must take the form of a precise definition that is the expression/assertion of a logical equivalence. Language serves many important purposes besides those of scientific inquiry; we can know perfectly well what an expression means (and so a fortiori that it is intelligible) without knowing its analysis, and the provision of an analysis may (and usually does) consist in the specification, as generalized as possible, of the conditions that count for or against the applicability of the expression being analyzed. Moreover, while it is no doubt true that the formal devices are especially amenable to systematic treatment by the logician, it remains the case that there are very many inferences and arguments, expressed in natural language and not in terms of these devices, that are nevertheless recognizably valid. So there must be a place for an unsimplified, and so more or less unsystematic, logic of the natural counter-parts of these devices; this logic may be aided and guided by the simplified logic of the formal devices but cannot be supplanted by it; indeed, not only do the two logics differ, but sometimes they come into conflict; rules that hold for a formal device may not hold for its natural counterpart.

Now, on the general question of the place in philosophy of the reformation of natural language, I shall, in this article, have nothing to say. I shall confine myself to the dispute in its relation to the alleged divergences mentioned at the outset. I have, moreover, no intention of entering the fray on behalf of either contestant. I wish, rather, to maintain that the common assumption of the contestants that the divergences do in fact exist is (broadly speaking) a common mistake, and that the mistake arises from an inadequate attention to the nature and importance of the conditions governing conversation. I shall, therefore, proceed at once to inquire into the general conditions that, in one way or another, apply to conver-sation as such, irrespective of its subject matter.

Implicature

Suppose that A and B are talking about a mutual friend, C, who is now working in a bank. A asks B how C is getting on in his job, and B replies, "Oh quite well, I think; he likes his colleagues, and he hasn't been to prison yet." At this point, A might well inquire what B was implying, what he was suggesting, or even what he meant by saying that C had not yet been to prison. The answer might be any one of such things as that C is the sort of person likely to yield to the temptation provided by his occupation, that C's colleagues are really very unpleasant and treacherous people, and so forth. It might, of course, be quite unnecessary for A to make such an inquiry of B, the answer to it being, in the context, clear in advance. I think it is clear that whatever B implied, suggested, meant, etc., in this example, is distinct from what B said, which was simply that C had not been to prison yet. I wish to introduce, as terms of art, the verb "*implicate*" and the related nouns "implicature" (cf. implying) and "implicatum" (cf. what is implied). The point of this maneuver is to avoid having, on each occasion, to choose between this or that member of the family of verbs for which "implicate" is to do general duty. I shall, for the time being at least, have to assume to a considerable extent an intuitive understanding of the meaning of "say" in such contexts, and an ability to recognize particular verbs as members of the family with which "implicate" is associated. I can, however, make one or two remarks that may help to clarify the more problematic of these assumptions, namely, that connected with the meaning of the word "say."

In the sense in which I am using the word "say," I intend what someone has said to be closely related to the conventional meaning of the words (the sentence) he has uttered. Suppose someone to have uttered the sentence "He is in the grip of a vice." Given a knowledge of the English language, but no knowledge of the circumstances of the utterance, one would know something about what the speaker had said, on the assumption that he was speaking standard English, and speaking literally. One would know that he had said, about some particular male person or animal , that at the time of the utterance (whatever that was), either (1) x was unable to rid himself of a certain kind of bad character trait or (2) some part of x's person was caught in a certain kind of tool or instrument (approximate account, of course). But for a full identification of what the speaker had said, one would need to know (a) the identity of x, (b) the time of utterance, and (c) the meaning, on the particular occasion of utterance, of the phrase "in the grip of a vice" (a decision between (1) and (2)). This brief indication of my use of "say" leaves it open whether a man who says (today) "Harold Wilson is a great man" and another who says (also today) "The British Prime Minister is a great man" would, if each knew that the two singular terms had the same reference, have said the same thing. But whatever decision is made about this question, the apparatus that I am about to provide will be capable of accounting for any implicatures that might depend on the presence of one rather than another of these singular terms in the sentence uttered. Such implicatures would merely be related to different maxims.

In some cases the conventional meaning of the words used will determine what is implicated, besides helping to determine what is said. If I say (smugly), "He is an Englishman; he is, therefore, brave," I have certainly committed myself, by virtue of the meaning of my words, to its being the case that his being brave is a consequence of (follows from) his being an Englishman. But while I have said that he is an Englishman, and said that he is brave, I do not want to say that I have *said* (in the favored sense) that it follows from his being an Englishman that he is brave, though I have certainly indicated, and so implicated, that this is so. I do not want to say that my utterance of this sentence would be, *strictly speaking*, false should the consequence in question fail to hold. So *some* implicatures are conventional, unlike the one with which I introduced this discussion of implicature.

I wish to represent a certain subclass of nonconventional implicatures, which I shall call *conversational* implicatures, as being essentially connected with certain general features of discourse; so my next step is to try to say what these features are.

The following may provide a first approximation to a general principle. Our talk exchanges do not normally consist of a succession of disconnected remarks, and would not be rational if they did. They are characteristically, to some degree at least, cooperative efforts; and each participant recognizes in them, to some extent, a common purpose or set of purposes, or at least a mutually accepted direction. This purpose or direction may be fixed from the start (e.g., by an initial proposal of a question for discussion), or it may evolve during the exchange; it may be fairly definite, or it may be so indefinite as to leave very considerable latitude to the participants (as in a casual conversation). But at each stage, *some* possible conversational moves would be excluded as conversationally unsuitable. We might then formulate a rough general principle which participants will be expected (*ceteris paribus*) to observe, namely: Make your conversational contribution such as is required, at the stage at which it occurs, by the accepted purpose or direction of the talk exchange in which you are engaged. One might label this the *Cooperative Principle*.

On the assumption that some such general principle as this is acceptable, one may perhaps distinguish four categories under one or another of which will fall certain more specific maxims and submaxims, the following of which will, in general, yield results in accordance with the Cooperative Principle. Echoing Kant, I call these categories Quantity, Quality, Relation, and Manner. The category of *Quantity* relates to the quantity of information to be provided, and under it fall the following maxims: (1) Make your contribution as informative as is required (for the current purposes of the exchange). (2) Do not make your contribution more informative than is required. (The second maxim is disputable; it might be said that to be overinformative is not a transgression of the Cooperative Principle but merely a waste of time. However, it might be answered that such overinformativeness may be confusing in that it is liable to raise side issues; and there may also be an indirect effect, in that the hearers may be misled as a result of thinking that there is some particular *point* in the provision of the excess of information. However this may be, there is perhaps a different reason for doubt about the admission of this second maxim, namely, that its effect will be secured by a later maxim, which concerns relevance.)

Under the category of *Quality* falls a supermaxim – "Try to make your contribution one that is true" – and two more specific maxims:

1   Do not say what you believe to be false.
2   Do not say that for which you lack adequate evidence.

Under the category of *Relation* I place a single maxim, namely, "Be relevant." Though the maxim itself is terse, its formulation conceals a number of problems that exercise me a good deal: questions about what different kinds and focuses of relevance there may be, how these shift in the course of a talk exchange, how to allow for the fact that subjects of conversation are legitimately changed, and so on. I find the treatment of such questions exceedingly difficult, and I hope to revert to them in a later work.

Finally, under the category of *Manner*, which I understand as relating not (like the previous categories) to what is said but, rather, to *how* what is said is to be said, I include the supermaxim – "Be perspicuous" – and various maxims such as:

1   Avoid obscurity of expression.
2   Avoid ambiguity.
3   Be brief (avoid unnecessary prolixity).
4   Be orderly.

And one might need others.

It is obvious that the observance of some of these maxims is a matter of less urgency than is the observance of others; a man who has expressed himself with undue prolixity would, in general, be open to milder comment than would a man who has said something he believes to be false. Indeed, it might be felt that the importance of at least the first maxim of Quality is such that it should not be included in a scheme of the kind I am constructing; other maxims come into operation only on the assumption that this maxim of Quality is satisfied. While this may be correct, so far as the generation of implicatures is concerned it seems to play a role not totally different from the other maxims, and it will be convenient, for the present at least, to treat it as a member of the list of maxims.

There are, of course, all sorts of other maxim (aesthetic, social, or moral in character), such as "Be polite," that are also normally observed by participants in talk exchanges, and these may also generate nonconventional implicatures. The conversational maxims, however, and the conversational implicatures connected with them, are specially connected (I hope) with the particular purposes that talk (and so, talk exchange) is adapted to serve and is primarily employed to serve. I have stated my maxims as if this purpose were a maximally effective exchange of information; this specification is, of course, too narrow, and the scheme needs to be generalized to allow for such general purposes as influencing or directing the actions of others.

As one of my avowed aims is to see talking as a special case or variety of purposive, indeed rational, behavior, it may be worth noting that the specific expectations or presumptions connected with at least some of the foregoing maxims have their analogues in the sphere of transactions that are not talk exchanges. I list briefly one such analogue for each conversational category.

1   *Quantity.* If you are assisting me to mend a car, I expect your contribution to be neither more nor less than is required; if, for example, at a particular stage I need four screws, I expect you to hand me four, rather than two or six.
2   *Quality.* I expect your contributions to be genuine and not spurious. If I need sugar as an ingredient in the cake you are assisting me to make, I do not expect you to hand me salt; if I need a spoon, I do not expect a trick spoon made of rubber.
3   *Relation.* I expect a partner's contribution to be appropriate to immediate needs at each stage of the transaction; if I am mixing ingredients for a cake, I do not expect to be handed a good book, or even an oven cloth (though this might be an appropriate contribution at a later stage).
4   *Manner.* I expect a partner to make it clear what contribution he is making, and to execute his performance with reasonable dispatch.

These analogies are relevant to what I regard as a fundamental question about the Cooperative Principle and its attendant maxims, namely, what the basis is for the assumption which we seem to make, and on which (I hope) it will appear that a great range of implicatures depends, that talkers will in general (*ceteris paribus* and in the absence of indications to the contrary) proceed in the manner that these principles prescribe. A dull but, no doubt at a certain level, adequate answer is that it is just a well-recognized empirical fact that people *do* behave in these ways; they have learned to do so in childhood and not lost the habit of doing so; and, indeed, it would involve a good deal of effort to make a radical departure from the habit. It is much easier, for example, to tell the truth than to invent lies.

I am, however, enough of a rationalist to want to find a basis that underlies these facts, undeniable though they may be; I would like to be able to think of the standard type of conversational practice not merely as something that all or most do *in fact* follow but as something that it is *reasonable* for us to follow, that we *should not* abandon. For a time, I was attracted by the idea that observance of the Cooperative Principle and the maxims, in a talk exchange, could be thought of as a quasi-contractual matter, with parallels outside the realm of discourse. If you pass by when I am struggling with my stranded car, I no doubt have some degree of expectation that you will offer help, but once you join me in tinkering under the hood, my expectations become stronger and take more specific forms (in the absence of indications that you are merely an incompetent meddler); and talk exchanges seemed to me to exhibit, characteristically, certain features that jointly distinguish cooperative transactions:

1   The participants have some common immediate aim, like getting a car mended; their ultimate aims may, of course, be independent and even in conflict–each may want to get the car mended in order to drive off, leaving the other stranded. In characteristic talk exchanges, there is a common aim even if, as in an over-the-wall chat, it is a second-order one, namely, that each party should, for the time being, identify himself with the transitory conversational interests of the other.
2   The contributions of the participants should be dovetailed, mutually dependent.
3   There is some sort of understanding (which may be explicit but which is often tacit) that, other things being equal, the transaction should continue in appropriate style unless both parties are agreeable that it should terminate. You do not just shove off or start doing something else.

But while some such quasi-contractual basis as this may apply to some cases, there are too many types of exchange, like quarreling and letter writing, that it fails to fit comfortably. In any case, one feels that the talker who is irrelevant or obscure has primarily let down not his audience but himself. So I would like to be able to show that observance of the Cooperative Principle and maxims is reasonable (rational) along the following lines: that any one who cares about the goals that are central to conversation/communication (e.g., giving and receiving information, influencing and being influenced by others) must be expected to have an interest, given suitable circumstances, in participating in talk exchanges that will be profitable only on the assumption that they are conducted in general accordance with the Cooperative Principle and the maxims. Whether any such conclusion can be reached, I am uncertain; in any case, I am fairly sure that I cannot reach it until I am a good deal clearer about the nature of relevance and of the circumstances in which it is required.

It is now time to show the connection between the Cooperative Principle and maxims, on the one hand, and conversational implicature on the other.

A participant in a talk exchange may fail to fulfill a maxim in various ways, which include the following:

1   He may quietly and unostentatiously *violate* a maxim; if so, in some cases he will be liable to mislead.

2   He may *opt out* from the operation both of the maxim and of the Cooperative Principle; he may say, indicate, or allow it to become plain that he is unwilling to cooperate in the way the maxim requires. He may say, for example, "I cannot say more; my lips are sealed."

3   He may be faced by a *clash*: He may be unable, for example, to fulfill the first maxim of Quantity (Be as informative as is required) without violating the second maxim of Quality (Have adequate evidence for what you say).

4   He may *flout* a maxim; that is, he may *blatantly* fail to fulfill it. On the assumption that the speaker is able to fulfill the maxim and to do so without violating another maxim (because of a clash), is not opting out, and is not, in view of the blatancy of his performance, trying to mislead, the hearer is faced with a minor problem: How can his saying what he did say be reconciled with the supposition that he is observing the overall Cooperative Principle? This situation is one that characteristically gives rise to a conversational implicature; and when a conversational implicature is generated in this way, I shall say that a maxim is being *exploited*.

I am now in a position to characterize the notion of conversational implicature. A man who, by (in, when) saying (or making as if to say) that *p* has implicated that *q*, may be said to have conversationally implicated that *q*, *provided that* (1) he is to be presumed to be observing the conversational maxims, or at least the cooperative principle; (2) the supposition that he is aware that, or thinks that, *q* is required in order to make his saying or making as if to say *p* (or doing so in those terms) consistent with this presumption; and (3) the speaker thinks (and would expect the hearer to think that the speaker thinks) that it is within the competence of the hearer to work out, or grasp intuitively, that the supposition mentioned in (2) is required. Apply this to my initial example, to B's remark that C has not yet been to prison. In a suitable setting A might reason as follows: "(1) B has apparently violated the maxim 'Be relevant' and so may be regarded as having flouted one of the maxims conjoining perspicuity, yet I have no reason to suppose that he is opting out from the operation of the Cooperative Principle; (2) given the circumstances, I can regard his irrelevance as only apparent if, and only if, I suppose him to think that C is potentially dishonest; (3) B knows that I am capable of working out step (2). So B implicates that C is potentially dishonest."

The presence of a conversational implicature must be capable of being worked out; for even if it can in fact be intuitively grasped, unless the intuition is replaceable by an argument, the implicature (if present at all) will not count as a *conversational* implicature; it will be a *conventional* implicature. To work out that a particular conversational implicature is present, the hearer will rely on the following data: (1) the conventional meaning of the words used, together with the identity of any references that may be involved; (2) the Cooperative Principle and its maxims; (3) the context, linguistic or otherwise, of the utterance; (4) other items of background knowledge; and (5) the fact (or supposed fact) that all relevant items falling under the previous headings are available to both participants and both participants know or assume this to be the case. A general pattern for the working out of a conversational implicature might be given as follows: "He has said that *p*; there is no reason to suppose that he is not observing the maxims, or at least the Cooperative Principle; he could not be doing this unless he thought that *q*; he knows (and knows that I know that he knows) that I can see that the supposition that he thinks that *q* is required; he has done nothing to stop me thinking that *q*; he intends me to think, or is at least willing to allow me to think, that *q*; and so he has implicated that *q*."

Examples

I shall now offer a number of examples, which I shall divide into three groups.

Group A: Examples in which no maxim is violated, or at least in which it is not clear that any maxim is violated:

1   A is standing by an obviously immobilized car and is approached by B, the following exchange takes place:
    A: I am out of petrol.
    B: There is a garage round the corner.
(Gloss: B would be infringing the maxim "Be relevant" unless he thinks, or thinks it possible, that the garage is open, and has petrol to sell; so he implicates that the garage is, or at least may be open, etc.)
   In this example, unlike the case of the remark "He hasn't been to prison yet," the unstated connection between B's remark and A's remark is so obvious that, even if one interprets the supermaxim of Manner, "Be perspicuous," as applying not only to the expression of what is said but also to the connection of what is said with adjacent remarks, there seems to be no case for regarding that supermaxim as infringed in this example.

2   The next example is perhaps a little less clear in this respect:
    A: Smith doesn't seem to have a girlfriend these days.
    B: He has been paying a lot of visits to New York lately.
B implicates that Smith has, or may have, a girlfriend in New York. (A gloss is unnecessary in view of that given for the previous example.)

   In both examples, the speaker implicates that which he must be assumed to believe in order to preserve the assumption that he is observing the maxim of relation.

Group B: An example in which a maxim is violated, but its violation is to be explained by the supposition of a clash with another maxim:

3   A is planning with B an itinerary for a holiday in France. Both know that A wants to see his friend C, if to do so would not involve too great a prolongation of his journey:
    A: Where does C live?
    B: Somewhere in the South of France.
(Gloss: There is no reason to suppose that B is opting out; his answer is, as he well knows, less informative than is required to meet A's needs. This infringement of the first maxim of Quantity can be explained only by the supposition that B is aware that to be more informative would be to say something that infringed the maxim of Quality, "Don't say what you lack adequate evidence for," so B implicates that he does not know in which town C lives.)

Group C: Examples that involve exploitation, that is, a procedure by which a maxim is flouted for the purpose of getting in a conversational implicature by means of something of the nature of a figure of speech.

In these examples, though some maxim is violated at the level of what is said, the hearer is entitled to assume that that maxim, or at least the overall Cooperative Principle, is observed at the level of what is implicated.

1a   A flouting of the first maxim of Quantity.

A is writing a testimonial about a pupil who is a candidate for a philosophy job, and his letter reads as follows: "Dear Sir, Mr X's command of English is excellent, and his attendance at tutorials has been regular. Yours, etc." (Gloss: A cannot be opting out, since if he wished to be uncooperative, why write at all? He cannot be unable, through ignorance, to say more, since the man is his pupil; moreover, he knows that more information than this is wanted. He must, therefore, be wishing to impart information that he is reluctant to write down. This supposition is tenable only on the assumption that he thinks Mr X is no good at philosophy. This, then, is what he is implicating.)

Extreme examples of a flouting of the first maxim of Quantity are provided by utterances of patent tautologies like "Women are women" and "War is war." I would wish to maintain that at the level of what is said, in my favored sense, such remarks are totally noninformative and so, at that level, cannot but infringe the first maxim of Quantity in any conversational context. They are, of course, informative at the level of what is implicated, and the hearer's identification of their informative content at this level is dependent on his ability to explain the speaker's selection of this *particular* patent tautology.

1b   An infringement of the second maxim of Quantity, "Do not give more information than is required," on the assumption that the existence of such a maxim should be admitted.

A wants to know whether p, and B volunteers not only the information that p, but information to the effect that it is certain that p, and that the evidence for its being the case that p is so-and-so and such-and-such.

B's volubility may be undesigned, and if it is so regarded by A it may raise in A's mind a doubt as to whether B is as certain as he says he is ("Methinks the lady doth protest too much"). But if it is thought of as designed, it would be an oblique way of conveying that it is to some degree controversial whether or not p. It is, however, arguable that such an implicature could be explained by reference to the maxim of Relation without invoking an alleged second maxim of Quantity.

2a   Examples in which the first maxim of Quality is flouted.

    (i)   Irony: X, with whom A has been on close terms until now, has betrayed a secret of A's to a business rival. A and his audience both know this. A says "X is a fine friend." (Gloss: It is perfectly obvious to A and his audience that what A has said or has made as if to say is something he does not believe, and the audience knows that A knows that this is obvious to the audience. So, unless A's utterance is entirely pointless, A must be trying to get across some other proposition than the one he purports to be putting forward. This must be some obviously related proposition; the most obviously related proposition is the contradictory of the one he purports to be putting forward.)

    (ii)   Metaphor: Examples like "You are the cream in my coffee" characteristically involve categorial falsity, so the contradictory of what the speaker has made as if to say will, strictly speaking, be a truism; so it cannot be that that such a speaker is trying to get across. The most likely supposition is that the speaker is attributing to his audience some feature or features in respect of which the audience resembles (more or less fancifully) the mentioned substance.

It is possible to combine metaphor and irony by imposing on the hearer two stages of interpretation. I say "You are the cream in my coffee," intending the hearer to reach first the metaphor interpretant "You are my pride and joy" and then the irony interpretant "You are my bane."

(iii)   Meiosis: Of a man known to have broken up all the furniture, one says "He was a little intoxicated."

(iv)   Hyperbole: Every nice girl loves a sailor.

2b   Examples in which the second maxim of Quality, "Do not say that for which you lack adequate evidence," is flouted are perhaps not easy to find, but the following seems to be a specimen.

I say of X's wife, "She is probably deceiving him this evening." In a suitable context, or with a suitable gesture or tone of voice, it may be clear that I have no adequate reason for supposing this to be the case. My partner, to preserve the assumption that the conversational game is still being played, assumes that I am getting at some related proposition for the acceptance of which I *do* have a reasonable basis. The related proposition might well be that she is given to deceiving her husband, or possibly that she is the sort of person who would not stop short of such conduct.

3   Examples in which an implicature is achieved by real, as distinct from apparent, violation of the maxim of Relation are perhaps rare, but the following seems to be a good candidate.

At a genteel tea party, A says "Mrs X is an old bag." There is a moment of appalled silence, and then B says "The weather has been quite delightful this summer, hasn't it?" B has blatantly refused to make what *he* says relevant to A's preceding remark. He thereby implicates that A's remark should not be discussed and, perhaps more specifically, that A has committed a social gaffe.

4   Examples in which various maxims falling under the supermaxim "Be perspicuous" are flouted.

(i)   Ambiguity. We must remember that we are concerned only with ambiguity that is deliberate, and that the speaker intends or expects to be recognized by his hearer. The problem the hearer has to solve is why a speaker should, when still playing the conversational game, go out of his way to choose an ambiguous utterance. There are two types of case:

(a)   Examples in which there is no difference, or no striking difference, between two interpretations of an utterance with respect to straightforwardness; neither interpretation is notably more sophisticated, less standard, more recondite or more far-fetched than the other. We might consider Blake's lines: "Never seek to tell thy love, Love that never told can be." To avoid the complications introduced by the presence of the imperative mood, I shall consider the related sentence, "I sought to tell my love, love that never told can be." There may be a double ambiguity here. "My love" may refer to either a state of emotion or an object of emotion, and "love that never told can be" may mean either "Love that cannot be told" or "love that if told cannot continue to exist." Partly because of the sophistication of the poet and partly because of internal evidence (that the ambiguity is kept up), there seems to be no alternative to supposing that the ambiguities are deliberate and that the poet is conveying both what he would be saying if one interpretation were intended rather than the other, and vice versa; though no doubt the poet is not explicitly *saying* any one of these things but only conveying or suggesting them (cf. "Since she [nature] pricked thee out for women's pleasure, Mine be thy love, and thy love's use their treasure.")

(b)   Examples in which one interpretation is notably less straightforward than another. Take the complex example of the British general who captured the town of Sind and sent back the message *Peccavi*. The ambiguity involved ("I have Sind"/"I have sinned") is phonemic, not morphemic; and the expression actually used is unambiguous, but since it is in a language foreign to speaker and hearer, translation is called for, and the ambiguity resides in the standard translation into native English.

   Whether or not the straightforward interpretant ("I have sinned") is being conveyed, it seems that the nonstraightforward must be. There might be stylistic reasons for conveying by a sentence merely its nonstraightforward interpretant, but it would be pointless, and perhaps also stylistically objectionable, to go to the trouble of finding an expression that nonstraightforwardly conveys that p, thus imposing on an audience the effort involved in finding this interpretant, if this interpretant were otiose so far as communication was concerned. Whether the straightforward interpretant is also being conveyed seems to depend on whether such a supposition would conflict with other conversational requirements, for example, would it be relevant, would it be something the speaker could be supposed to accept, and so on. If such requirements are not satisfied, then the straightforward interpretant is not being conveyed. If they are, it is. If the author of *Peccavi* could naturally be supposed to think that he had committed some kind of transgression, for example, had disobeyed his orders in capturing Sind, and if reference to such a transgression would be relevant to the presumed interests of the audience, then he would have been conveying both interpretants; otherwise he would be conveying only the nonstraightforward one.

(ii) Obscurity. How do I exploit, for the purposes of communication, a deliberate and overt violation of the requirement that I should avoid obscurity? Obviously, if the Cooperative Principle is to operate, I must intend my partner to understand what I am saying despite the obscurity I import into my utterance. Suppose that A and B are having a conversation in the presence of a third party, for example, a child, then A might be deliberately obscure, though not too obscure, in the hope that B would understand and the third party not. Furthermore, if A expects B to see that A is being deliberately obscure, it seems reasonable to suppose that, in making his conversational contribution in this way, A is implicating that the contents of his communication should not be imparted to the third party.

(iii)   Failure to be brief or succinct. Compare the remarks:
(a)   Miss X sang "Home sweet home."
(b)   Miss X produced a series of sounds that corresponded closely with the score of "Home sweet home."

Suppose that a reviewer has chosen to utter (b) rather than (a). (Gloss: Why has he selected that rigmarole in place of the concise and nearly synonymous "sang"? Presumably, to indicate some striking difference between Miss X's performance and those to which the word "singing" is usually applied. The most obvious supposition is that Miss X's performance suffered from some hideous defect. The reviewer knows that this supposition is what is likely to spring to mind, so that is what he is implicating.)

I have so far considered only cases of what I might call particularized conversational implicature – that is to say, cases in which an implicature is carried by saying that *p* on a particular occasion in virtue of special features of the context, cases in which there is no room for the idea that an implicature of this sort is *normally* carried by saying that *p*. But there are cases of generalized conversational implicature. Sometimes one can say that the use of a certain form of words in an utterance would normally (in the *absence* of special circumstances) carry such-and-such an implicature or type of implicature. Noncontroversial examples are perhaps hard to find, since it is all too easy to treat a generalized conversational implicature as if it were a conventional implicature. I offer an example that I hope may be fairly noncontroversial.

Anyone who uses a sentence of the form "X is meeting a woman this evening" would normally implicate that the person to be met was someone other than X's wife, mother, sister, or perhaps even close Platonic friend. Similarly, if I were to say "X went into a house yesterday and found a tortoise inside the front door," my hearer would normally be surprised if some time later I revealed that the house was X's own. I could produce similar linguistic phenomena involving the expressions "*a garden*," "*a car*," "*a college*," and so on. Sometimes, however, there would normally be no such implicature ("I have been sitting in a car all morning"), and sometimes a reverse implicature ("I broke a finger yesterday"). I am inclined to think that one would not lend a sympathetic ear to a philosopher who suggested that there are three senses of the form of expression "an X": one in which it means roughly "something that satisfies the conditions defining the word X," another in which it means approximately "an X (in the first sense) that is only remotely related in a certain way to some person indicated by the context," and yet another in which it means "an X (in the first sense) that is closely related in a certain way to some person indicated by the context." Would we not much prefer an account on the following lines (which, of course, may be incorrect in detail): When someone, by using the form of expression "an X," implicates that the X does not belong to or is not otherwise closely connected with some identifiable person, the implicature is present because the speaker has failed to be specific in a way in which he might have been expected to be specific, with the consequence that it is likely to be assumed that he is not in a position to be specific. This is a familiar implicature situation and is classifiable as a failure, for one reason or another, to fulfill the first maxim of Quantity. The only difficult question is why it should, in certain cases, be presumed, independently of information about particular contexts of utterance, that specification of the closeness or remoteness of the connection between a particular person or object and a further person who is mentioned or indicated by the utterance should be likely to be of interest. The answer must lie in the following region: Transactions between a person and other persons or things closely connected with him are liable to be very different as regards their concomitants and results from the same sorts of transaction involving only remotely connected persons or things; the concomitants and results, for instance, of my finding a hole in *my* roof are likely to be very different from the concomitants and results of my finding a hole in someone else's roof. Information, like money, is often given without the giver's knowing to just what use the recipient will want to put it. If someone to whom a transaction is mentioned gives it further consideration he is likely to find himself wanting the answers to further questions that the speaker may not be able to identify in advance; if the appropriate specification will be likely to enable the hearer to answer a considerable variety of such questions for himself then there is a presumption that the speaker should include it in his remark; if not, then there is no such presumption.

Finally, we can now show that, conversational implicature being what it is, it must possess certain features.

1   Since, to assume the presence of a conversational implicature, we have to assume that at least the Cooperative Principle is being observed, and since it is possible to opt out of the observation of this principle, it follows that a generalized conversational implicature can be canceled in a particular case. It may be explicitly canceled, by the addition of a clause that states or implies that the speaker has opted out, or it may be contextually canceled, if the form of utterance that usually carries it is used in a context that makes it clear that the speaker *is* opting out.

2   Insofar as the calculation that a particular conversational implicature is present requires, besides contextual and background information, only a knowledge of what has been said (or of the conventional commitment of the utterance), and insofar as the manner of expression plays no role in the calculation, it will not be possible to find another way of saying the same thing, which simply lacks the implicature in question, except where some special feature of the substituted version is itself relevant to the determination of an implicature (in virtue of one of the maxims of Manner). If we call this feature *nondetachability*, one may expect a generalized conversational implicature that is carried by a familiar, nonspecial locution to have a high degree of nondetachability.

3   To speak approximately, since the calculation of the presence of a conversational implicature presupposes an initial knowledge of the conventional force of the expression the utterance of which carries the implicature, a conversational implicatum will be a condition that is not included in the original specification of the expression's conventional force. Though it may not be impossible for what starts life, so to speak, as a conversational implicature to become conventionalized, to suppose that this is so in a given case would require special justification. So, initially at least, conversational implicata are not part of the meaning of the expressions to the employment of which they attach.

4   Since the truth of a conversational implicatum is not required by the truth of what is said (what is said may be true what is implicated may be false), the implicature is not carried by what is said, but only by the saying of what is said, or by "putting it that way."

5   Since to calculate a conversational implicature is to calculate what has to be supposed in order to preserve the supposition that the Cooperative Principle is being observed, and since there may be various possible specific explanations, a list of which may be open, the conversational implicatum in such cases will be disjunction of such specific explanations; and if the list of these is open, the implicatum will have just the kind of indeterminacy that many actual implicata do in fact seem to possess.

Languages and Language
DAVID LEWIS

1   Thesis

What is a language? Something which assigns meanings to certain strings of types of sound or of mark. It could therefore be a function, a set of ordered pairs of strings and meanings. The entities in the domain of the function are certain finite sequences of types of vocal sounds, or of types of inscribable marks; if σ is in the domain of a language $\pounds$, let us call σ a *sentence of $\pounds$*. The entities in the range of the function are meanings; if σ is a sentence of $\pounds$, let us call $\pounds(\sigma)$ *the meaning of σ in $\pounds$*. What could a meaning of a sentence be? Something which, when combined with factual information about the world – or factual information about *any* possible world – yields a truth value. It could therefore be a function from worlds to truth values – or more simply, a set of worlds. We can say that a sentence σ is true in a language $\pounds$ at a world w if and only if w belongs to the set of worlds $\pounds(\sigma)$. We can say that σ is true in $\pounds$ (without mentioning a world) if and only if our actual world belongs to $\pounds(\sigma)$. We can say that σ is analytic in $\pounds$ if and only if every possible world belongs to $\pounds(\sigma)$. And so on, in the obvious way.

2   Antithesis

What is language? A social phenomenon which is part of the natural history of human beings; a sphere of human action, wherein people utter strings of vocal sounds, or inscribe strings of marks, and wherein people respond by thought or action to the sounds or marks which they observe to have been so produced.

This verbal activity is, for the most part, rational. He who produces certain sounds or marks does so for a reason. He knows that someone else, upon hearing his sounds or seeing his marks, is apt to form a certain belief or act in a certain way. He wants, for some reason, to bring about that belief or action. Thus his beliefs and desires give him a reason to produce the sounds or marks, and he does. He who responds to the sounds or marks in a certain way also does so for a reason. He knows how the production of sounds or marks depends upon the producer's state of mind. When he observes the sounds or marks, he is therefore in a position to infer something about the producer's state of mind. He can probably also infer something about the conditions which caused that state of mind. He may merely come to believe these conclusions, or he may act upon them in accordance with his other beliefs and his desires.

Not only do both have reasons for thinking and acting as they do; they know something about each other, so each is in a position to replicate the other's reasons. Each one's replication of the other's reasons forms part of his own reason for thinking and acting as he does; and each is in a position to replicate the other's replication of his own reasons. Therefore the Gricean mechanism[1] operates: X intends to bring about a response on the part of Y by getting Y to recognize that X intends to bring about that response; Y does recognize X's intention, and is thereby given some sort of reason to respond just as X intended him to.

Within any suitable population, various regularities can be found in this rational verbal activity. There are regularities whereby the production of sounds or marks depends upon various aspects of the state of mind of the producer. There are regularities whereby various aspects of responses to sounds or marks depend upon the sounds or marks to which one is responding. Some of these regularities are accidental. Others can be explained, and different ones can be explained in very different ways.

Some of them can be explained as conventions of the population in which they prevail. Conventions are regularities in action, or in action and belief, which are arbitrary but perpetuate themselves because they serve some sort of common interest. Past conformity breeds future conformity because it gives one a reason to go on conforming; but there is some alternative regularity which could have served instead, and would have perpetuated itself in the same way if only it had got started.

More precisely: a regularity R, in action or in action and belief, is a *convention* in a population P if and only if, within P, the following six conditions hold. (Or at least they almost hold. A few exceptions to the "everyone"s can be tolerated.)

1   Everyone conforms to R.
2   Everyone believes that the others conform to R.
3   This belief that the others conform to R gives everyone a good and decisive reason to conform to R himself. His reason may be that, in particular, those of the others he is now dealing with conform to R; or his reason may be that there is general or widespread conformity, or that there has been, or that there will be. His reason may be a practical reason, if conforming to R is a matter of acting in a certain way; or it may be an epistemic reason, if conforming to R is a matter of believing in a certain way. First case: according to his beliefs, some desired end may be reached by means of some sort of action in conformity to R, provided that the others (all or some of them) also conform to R; therefore he wants to conform to R if they do. Second case: his beliefs, together with the premiss that others conform to R, deductively imply or inductively support some conclusion; and in believing this conclusion, he would thereby conform to R. Thus reasons for conforming to a convention by believing something – like reasons for belief in general – are believed premises tending to confirm the truth of the belief in question. Note that I am *not* speaking here of practical reasons for acting so as to somehow produce in oneself a certain desired belief.
4   There is a general preference for general conformity to R rather than slightly-less-than-general-conformity – in particular, rather than conformity by all but any one. (This is not to deny that some state of *widespread* nonconformity to R might be even more preferred.) Thus everyone who believes that at least almost everyone conforms to R will want the others, as well as himself, to conform. This condition serves to distinguish cases of convention, in which there is a predominant coincidence of interest, from cases of deadlocked conflict. In the latter cases, it may be that each is doing the best he can by conforming to R, given that the others do so; but each wishes the others did not conform to R, since he could then gain at their expense.
5   R is not the only possible regularity meeting the last two conditions. There is at least one alternative R' such that the belief that the others conformed to R' would give everyone a good and decisive practical or epistemic reason to conform to R' likewise; such that there is a general preference for general conformity to R' rather than slightly-less-than-general conformity to R'; and such that there is normally no way of conforming to R and R' both. Thus the alternative R' could have perpetuated itself as a

convention instead of R; this condition provides for the characteristic arbitrariness of conventions.

6 Finally, the various facts listed in conditions (1) to (5) are matters of *common* (or *mutual*) knowledge: they are known to everyone, it is known to everyone that they are known to everyone, and so on. The knowledge mentioned here may be merely potential: knowledge that would be available if one bothered to think hard enough. Everyone must potentially know that (1) to (5) hold; potentially know that the others potentially know it; and so on. This condition ensures stability. If anyone tries to replicate another's reasoning, perhaps including the other's replication of his own reasoning, . . . , the result will reinforce rather than subvert his expectation of conformity to R. Perhaps a negative version of (6) would do the job: no one disbelieves that (1) to (5) hold, no one believes that others disbelieve this, and so on.

This definition can be tried out on all manner of regularities which we would be inclined to call conventions. It is a convention to drive on the right. It is a convention to mark poisons with skull and crossbones. It is a convention to dress as we do. It is a convention to train beasts to turn right on "gee" and left on "haw". It is a convention to give goods and services in return for certain pieces of paper or metal. And so on.

The common interests which sustain conventions are as varied as the conventions themselves. Our convention to drive on the right is sustained by our interest in not colliding. Our convention for marking poisons is sustained by our interest in making it easy for everyone to recognize poisons. Our conventions of dress might be sustained by a common aesthetic preference for somewhat uniform dress, or by the low cost of mass-produced clothes, or by a fear on everyone's part that peculiar dress might be thought to manifest a peculiar character, or by a desire on everyone's part not to be too conspicuous, or – most likely – by a mixture of these and many other interests.

It is a platitude – something only a philosopher would dream of denying – that there are conventions of language, although we do not find it easy to say what those conventions are. If we look for the fundamental difference in verbal behavior between members of two linguistic communities, we can be sure of finding something which is arbitrary but perpetuates itself because of a common interest in coordination. In the case of conventions of language, that common interest derives from our common interest in taking advantage of, and in preserving, our ability to control other's beliefs and actions to some extent by means of sounds and marks. That interest in turn derives from many miscellaneous desires we have; to list them, list the ways you would be worse off in Babel.

3 Synthesis

What have languages to do with language? What is the connection between what I have called *languages*, functions from strings of sounds or of marks to sets of possible worlds, semantic systems discussed in complete abstraction from human affairs, and what I have called *language*, a form of rational, convention-governed human social activity? We know what to *call* this connection we are after: we can say that a given language $\mathcal{L}$ is *used by*, or is a (or the) language *of*, a given population P. We know also that this connection holds by virtue of the conventions of language prevailing in P. Under suitably different conventions, a different language would be used by P. There is some sort of convention whereby P uses

£ – but what is it? It is worthless to call it a convention to use £, even if it can correctly be so described, for we want to know what it is to use £.

My proposal[2] is that the convention whereby a population P uses a language £ is a convention of *truthfulness* and *trust* in £. To be truthful in £ is to act in a certain way: to try never to utter any sentence of £ that are not true in £. Thus it is to avoid uttering any sentence of £ unless one believes it to be true in £. To be trusting in £ is to form beliefs in a certain way: to impute truthfulness in £ to others, and thus to tend to respond to another's utterance of any sentence of £ by coming to believe that the uttered sentence is true in £.

Suppose that a certain language £ is used by a certain population P. Let this be a perfect case of normal language use. Imagine what would go on; and review the definition of a convention to verify that there does prevail in P a convention of truthfulness and trust in £.

(1)   There prevails in P at least a regularity of truthfulness and trust in £. The members of P frequently speak (or write) sentences of £ to one another. When they do, ordinarily the speaker (or writer) utters one of the sentences he believes to be true in £; and the hearer (or reader) responds by coming to share that belief of the speaker's (unless he already had it), and adjusting his other beliefs accordingly.

(2)   The members of P believe that this regularity of truthfulness and trust in £ prevails among them. Each believes this because of his experience of others' past truthfulness and trust in £.

(3)   The expectation of conformity ordinarily gives everyone a good reason why he himself should conform. If he is a speaker, he expects his hearer to be trusting in £; wherefore he has reason to expect that by uttering certain sentences that are true in £ according to his beliefs – by being truthful in £ in a certain way – he can impart certain beliefs that he takes to be correct. Commonly, a speaker has some reason or other for wanting to impart some or other correct beliefs. Therefore his beliefs and desires constitute a practical reason for acting in the way he does: for uttering some sentence truthfully in £.

As for the hearer: he expects the speaker to be truthful in £, wherefore he has good reason to infer that the speaker's sentence is true in £ according to the speaker's beliefs. Commonly, a hearer also has some or other reason to believe that the speaker's beliefs are correct (by and large, and perhaps with exceptions for certain topics); so it is reasonable for him to infer that the sentence he has heard is probably true in £. Thus his beliefs about the speaker give him an epistemic reason to respond trustingly in £.

We have coordination between truthful speaker and trusting hearer. Each conforms as he does to the prevailing regularity of truthfulness and trust in £ because he expects complementary conformity on the part of the other.

But there is also a more diffuse and indirect sort of coordination. In coordinating with his present partner, a speaker or hearer also is coordinating with all those whose past truthfulness and trust in £ have contributed to his partner's present expectations. This indirect coordination is a four-way affair: between present speakers and past speakers, present speakers and past hearers, present hearers and past speakers, and present hearers and past hearers. And whereas the direct coordination between a speaker and his hearer is a coordination of truthfulness with trust for a single sentence of £, the indirect coordination with one's partner's previous partners (and with *their* previous partners, etc.) may involve various sentences of £. It may happen that a hearer, say, has never before encountered the sentence now addressed to him; but he forms the appropriate belief on hearing it – one such that he has responded trustingly in $\mathcal{L}$ – because his past experience with truthfulness in $\mathcal{L}$ has involved many sentences grammatically related to this one.

(4)   There is in P a general preference for general conformity to the regularity of truthfulness and trust in $\mathcal{L}$. Given that most conform, the members of P want all to conform. They desire truthfulness and trust in $\mathcal{L}$ from each other, as well as from themselves. This general preference is sustained by a common interest in communication. Everyone wants occasionally to impart correct beliefs and bring about appropriate actions in others by means of sounds and marks. Everyone wants to preserve his ability to do so at will. Everyone wants to be able to learn about the parts of the world that he cannot observe for himself by observing instead the sounds and marks of his fellows who have been there.

(5)   The regularity of truthfulness and trust in $\mathcal{L}$ has alternatives. Let $\mathcal{L}'$ be any language that does not overlap $\mathcal{L}$ in such a way that it is possible to be truthful and trusting simultaneously in $\mathcal{L}$ and in $\mathcal{L}'$, and that is rich and convenient enough to meet the needs of P for communication. Then the regularity of truthfulness and trust in $\mathcal{L}'$ is an alternative to the prevailing regularity of truthfulness and trust in $\mathcal{L}$. For the alternative regularity, as for the actual one, general conformity by the others would give one a reason to conform; and general conformity would be generally preferred over slightly-less-than-general conformity.

(6)   Finally, all these facts are common knowledge in P. Everyone knows them, everyone knows that everyone knows them, and so on. Or at any rate none believes that another doubts them, none believes that another believes that another doubts them, and so on.

In any case in which a language $\mathcal{L}$ clearly is used by a population P, then, it seems that there prevails in P a convention of truthfulness and trust in $\mathcal{L}$, sustained by an interest in communication. The converse is supported by an unsuccessful search for counterexamples: I have not been able to think of any case in which there is such a convention and yet the language $\mathcal{L}$ is clearly not used in the population P. Therefore I adopt this definition, claiming that it agrees with ordinary usage in the cases in which ordinary usage is fully determinate:

> a language $\mathcal{L}$ is *used by* a population P if and only if there prevails in P a convention of truthfulness and trust in $\mathcal{L}$, sustained by an interest in communication.

Such conventions, I claim, provide the desired connection between languages and language-using populations.

Once we understand how languages are connected to populations, whether by conventions of truthfulness and trust for the sake of communication or in some other way, we can proceed to redefine relative to a population all those semantic concepts that we previously defined relative to a language. A string of sounds or of marks is a sentence of P if and only if it is a sentence of some language $\mathcal{L}$ which is used in P. It has a certain meaning in P if and only if it has that meaning in some language $\mathcal{L}$ which is used in P. It is true in P at a world w if and only if it is true at w in some language $\mathcal{L}$ which is used in P. It is true in P if and only if it is true in some language $\mathcal{L}$ which is used in P.

The account just given of conventions in general, and of conventions of language in particular, differs in one important respect from the account given in my book *Convention*.[3]

Formerly, the crucial clause in the definition of convention was stated in terms of a conditional preference for conformity: each prefers to conform if the others do, and it would be the same for the alternatives to the actual convention. (In some versions of the definition, this condition was subsumed under a broader requirement of general preference for general conformity.) The point of this was to explain why the belief that others conform would give everyone a reason for conforming likewise, and so to explain the rational self-perpetuation of conventions. But a reason involving preference in this way must be a practical reason for acting, not an epistemic reason for believing. Therefore I said that conventions were regularities in action alone. It made no sense to speak of believing something in conformity to convention. (Except in the peculiar case that other's conformity to the convention gives one a practical reason to conform by acting to somehow produce a belief in oneself; but I knew that this case was irrelevant to ordinary language use.) Thus I was cut off from what I now take to be the primary sort of conventional coordination in language use: that between the action of the truthful speaker and the responsive believing of his trusting hearer. I resorted to two different substitutes.

Sometimes it is common knowledge how the hearer will want to act if he forms various beliefs, and we can think of the speaker not only as trying to impart beliefs but also as trying thereby to get the hearer to act in a way that speaker and hearer alike deem appropriate under the circumstances that the speaker believes to obtain. Then we have speaker–hearer coordination of action. Both conform to a convention of truthfulness for the speaker plus appropriate responsive action by the hearer. The hearer's trustful believing need not be part of the content of the convention, though it must be mentioned to explain why the hearer acts in conformity. In this way we reach the account of "signaling" in *Convention*, chapter IV.

But signaling was all too obviously a special case. There may be no appropriate responsive action for the hearer to perform when the speaker imparts a belief to him. Or the speaker and hearer may disagree about how the hearer ought to act under the supposed circumstances. Or the speaker may not know how the hearer will decide to act; or the hearer may not know that he knows; and so on. The proper hearer's response to consider is *believing*, but that is not ordinarily an action. So in considering language use in general, in *Convention*, chapter V, I was forced to give up on speaker–hearer coordination. I took instead the diffuse coordination between the present speaker and the past speakers who trained the present hearer. Accordingly, I proposed that the convention whereby a population *P* used a language $\mathcal{L}$ was simply a convention of truthfulness in $\mathcal{L}$. Speakers conform; hearers do not, until they become speakers in their turn, if they ever do.

I think now that I went wrong when I went beyond the special case of signaling. I should have kept my original emphasis on speaker–hearer coordination, broadening the definition of convention to fit. It was Jonathan Bennett[4] who showed me how that could be done: by restating the crucial defining clause not in terms of preference for conformity but rather in terms of reasons for conformity – practical or *epistemic* reasons. The original conditional preference requirement gives way now to clause (3): the belief that others conform gives everyone a reason to conform likewise, and it would be the same for the alternatives to the actual convention. Once this change is made, there is no longer any obstacle to including the hearer's trust as part of the content of a convention.

(The old conditional preference requirement is retained, however, in consequence of the less important clause (4). Clause (3) as applied to practical reasons, but not as applied to epistemic reasons, may be subsumed under (4).)

Bennett pointed out one advantage of the change: suppose there is only one speaker of an idiolect, but several hearers who can understand him. Shouldn't he and his hearers comprise a population that uses his idiolect? More generally, what is the difference between (a) someone who does not utter sentences of a language because he does not belong to any population that uses it, and (b) someone who does not utter sentences of the language although he does belong to such a population because at present – or always, perhaps – he has nothing to say? Both are alike, so far as action in conformity to a convention of truthfulness goes. Both are vacuously truthful. In *Convention*, I made it a condition of truthfulness in £ that one sometimes does utter sentences of £, though not that one speaks up on any particular occasion. But that is unsatisfactory: what degree of truthful talkativeness does it take to keep up one's active membership in a language-using population? What if someone just never thought of anything worth saying?

(There is a less important difference between my former account and the present one. Then and now, I wanted to insist that cases of convention are cases of predominant coincidence of interest. I formerly provided for this by a defining clause that seems now unduly restrictive: in any instance of the situation to which the convention applies, everyone has approximately the same preferences regarding all possible combinations of actions. Why *all*? It may be enough that they agree in preferences to the extent specified in my present clause (4). Thus I have left out the further agreement-in-preferences clause.)

4   Objections and Replies

Objection: Many things which meet the definition of a language given in the thesis – many functions from strings of sounds or of marks to sets of possible worlds – are not really possible languages. They could not possibly be adopted by any human population. There may be too few sentences, or too few meanings, to make as many discriminations as language-users need to communicate. The meanings may not be anything language-users would wish to communicate about. The sentences may be very long, impossible to pronounce, or otherwise clumsy. The language may be humanly unlearnable because it has no grammar, or a grammar of the wrong kind.

Reply: Granted. The so-called languages of the thesis are merely an easily specified superset of the languages we are really interested in. A language in a narrower and more natural sense is any one of these entities that could possibly – possibly in some appropriately strict sense – be used by a human population.

Objection: The so-called languages discussed in the thesis are excessively simplified. There is no provision for indexical sentences, dependent on features of the context of their utterance: for instance, tensed sentences, sentences with personal pronouns or demonstratives, or anaphoric sentences. There is no provision for ambiguous sentences. There is no provision for nonindicative sentences: imperatives, questions, promises and threats, permissions, and so on.

Reply: Granted. I have this excuse: the phenomenon of language would be not too different if these complications did not exist, so we cannot go too far wrong by ignoring them. Nevertheless, let us sketch what could be done to provide for indexicality, ambiguity, or nonindicatives. In order not to pile complication on complication we shall take only one at a time.

We may define an *indexical language* £ as a function that assigns sets of possible worlds not to its sentences themselves, but rather to sentences paired with possible occasions of their utterance. We can say that σ is true in £ at a world w on a possible occasion o of the utterance of σ if and only if w belongs to £(σ, o). We can say that σ is true in £ on o (without mentioning a world) if and only if the world in which o is located – our actual world if o is an actual occasion of utterance of σ, or some other world if not – belongs to £(σ, o). We can say that a speaker is truthful in $\mathcal{L}$ if he tries not to utter any sentence σ of $\mathcal{L}$ unless σ would be true in $\mathcal{L}$ on the occasion of his utterance of σ. We can say that a hearer is trusting in $\mathcal{L}$ if he believes an uttered sentence of $\mathcal{L}$ to be true in $\mathcal{L}$ on its occasion of utterance.

We may define an *ambiguous language* $\mathcal{L}$ as a function that assigns to its sentences not single meanings, but finite sets of alternative meanings. (We might or might not want to stipulate that these sets are nonempty.) We can say that a sentence σ is true in $\mathcal{L}$ at w under some meaning if and only if w belongs to some member of $\mathcal{L}(\sigma)$. We can say that σ is true in $\mathcal{L}$ under some meaning if and only if our actual world belongs to some member of $\mathcal{L}(\sigma)$. We can say that someone is (minimally) truthful in $\mathcal{L}$ if he tries not to utter any sentence σ of $\mathcal{L}$ unless σ is true in $\mathcal{L}$ under some meaning. He is trusting if he believes an uttered sentence of $\mathcal{L}$ to be true in $\mathcal{L}$ under some meaning.

We may define a *polymodal language* $\mathcal{L}$ as a function which assigns to its sentences meanings containing two components: a set of worlds, as before; and something we can call a *mood*: indicative, imperative, etc. (It makes no difference what things these are – they might, for instance, be taken as code numbers.) We can say that a sentence σ is indicative, imperative, etc., in $\mathcal{L}$ according as the mood component of the meaning $\mathcal{L}(\sigma)$ is indicative, imperative, etc. We can say that a sentence σ is true in $\mathcal{L}$, regardless of its mood in $\mathcal{L}$, if and only if our actual world belongs to the set-of-worlds-component of the meaning $\mathcal{L}(\sigma)$. We can say that someone is truthful in $\mathcal{L}$ with respect to indicatives if he tries not to utter any indicative sentence of $\mathcal{L}$ which is not true in $\mathcal{L}$; truthful in $\mathcal{L}$ with respect to imperatives if he tries to act in such a way as to make true in $\mathcal{L}$ any imperative sentence of $\mathcal{L}$ that is addressed to him by someone in a relation of authority to him; and so on for other moods. He is trusting in $\mathcal{L}$ with respect to indicatives if he believes uttered indicative sentences of $\mathcal{L}$ to be true in $\mathcal{L}$; trusting in $\mathcal{L}$ with respect to imperatives if he expects his utterance of an imperative sentence of $\mathcal{L}$ to result in the addressee's acting in such a way as to make that sentence true in $\mathcal{L}$, provided he is in a relation of authority to the addressee; and so on. We can say simply that he is truthful and trusting in $\mathcal{L}$ if he is so with respect to all moods that occur in $\mathcal{L}$. It is by virtue of the various ways in which the various moods enter into the definition of truthfulness and of trust that they deserve the familiar names we have given them. (I am deliberating stretching the ordinary usage of "true", "truthfulness", and "trust' in extending them to nonindicatives. For instance, truthfulness with respect to imperatives is roughly what we might call *obedience* in $\mathcal{L}$.)

Any natural language is simultaneously indexical, ambiguous, and polymodal; I leave the combination of complications as an exercise. Henceforth, for the most part, I shall lapse into ignoring indexicality, ambiguity, and nonindicatives.

Objection: We cannot always discover the meaning of a sentence in a population just by looking into the minds of the members of the population, no matter what we look for there. We may also need some information about the causal origin of what we find in their minds. So, in particular, we cannot always discover the meaning of a sentence in a population just by looking at the conventions prevailing therein. Consider an example: What is the meaning of the sentence Mik Karthee was wise in the language of our 137th-century descendants, if all we can find in any of their minds is the inadequate dictionary entry: Mik Karthee: controversial American politician of the early atomic age? It depends, we might think, partly on which man stands at the beginning of the long causal chain ending in that inadequate dictionary entry.

Reply: If this doctrine is correct, I can treat it as a subtle sort of indexicality. The set of worlds in which a sentence σ is true in a language $\mathcal{L}$ may depend on features of possible occasions of utterance of σ. One feature of a possible occasion of utterance – admittedly a more recondite feature than the time, place, or speaker – is the causal history of a dictionary entry in a speaker's mind.

As with other kinds of indexicality, we face a problem of nomenclature. Let a *meaning*$_1$ be that which an indexical language $\mathcal{L}$ assigns to a sentence σ on a possible occasion o of its utterance: $\mathcal{L}(\sigma, o)$, a set of worlds on our account. Let a meaning be that fixed function whereby the meaning$_1$ in $\mathcal{L}$ of a sentence σ varies with its occasions of utterance. Which one is a *meaning*$_2$? That is unclear – and it is no clearer which one is a sense, intension, interpretation, truth condition, or proposition.

The objection says that we sometimes cannot find the meaning$_1$ of σ on o in P by looking into the minds of members of P. Granted. But what prevents it is that the minds do not contain enough information about o: in particular, not enough information about its causal history. We have been given no reason to doubt that we can find the meaning$_2$ of σ in P by looking into minds; and that is all we need do to identify the indexical language used by P.

An exactly similar situation arises with more familiar kinds of indexicality. We may be unable to discover the time of an utterance of a tensed sentence by looking into minds, so we may know the meaning$_2$ of the sentence uttered in the speaker's indexical language without knowing its meaning$_1$ on the occasion in question.

Objection: It makes no sense to say that a mere string of sounds or of marks can bear a meaning or a truth value. The proper bearers of meanings and truth values are particular speech acts.

Reply: I do not say that a string of types of sound or of mark, by itself, can bear a meaning or truth value. I say it bears a meaning and truth value relative to a language, or relative to a population. A particular speech act by itself, on the other hand, can bear a meaning and truth value, since in most cases it uniquely determines the language that was in use on the occasion of its performance. So can a particular uttered string of vocal sounds, or a particular inscribed string of marks, since in most cases that uniquely determines the particular speech act in which it was produced, which in turn uniquely determines the language.

Objection: It is circular to give an account of meanings in terms of possible worlds. The notion of a possible world must itself be explained in semantic terms. Possible worlds are models of the analytic sentences of some language, or they are the diagrams or theories of such models.[5]

Reply: I do not agree that the notion of a possible world ought to be explained in semantic terms, or that possible worlds ought to be eliminated from our ontology and replaced by their linguistic representatives – models or whatever.

For one thing, the replacement does not work properly. Two worlds indistinguishable in the representing language will receive one and the same representative.

But more important, the replacement is gratuitous. The notion of a possible world is familiar in its own right, philosophically fruitful, and tolerably clear. Possible worlds are deemed mysterious and objectionable because they raise questions we may never know how to answer: Are any possible worlds five–dimensional? We seem to think that we do not understand possible worlds at all unless we are capable of omniscience about them – but why should we think that? Sets also raise unanswerable questions, yet most of us do not repudiate sets.

But if you insist on repudiating possible worlds, much of my theory can be adapted to meet your needs. We must suppose that you have already defined truth and analyticity in some base language – that is the price you pay for repudiating possible worlds – and you want to define them in general, for the language of an arbitrary population P. Pick your favorite base language, with any convenient special properties you like: Latin, Esperanto,

Begriffsschrift, Semantic Markerese, or what have you. Let's say you pick Latin. Then you may redefine a language as any function from certain strings of sound or of marks to sentences of Latin. A sentence σ of a language $\pounds$ (in your sense) is true, analytic, etc., if and only if $\pounds(\sigma)$ is true, analytic, etc., in Latin.

You cannot believe in languages in my sense, since they involve possible worlds. But I can believe in languages in your sense. And I can map your languages onto mine by means of a fixed function from sentences of Latin to sets of worlds. This function is just the language Latin, in my sense. My language $\pounds$ is the composition of two functions: your language $\pounds$, and my language Latin. Thus I can accept your approach as part of mine.

Objection: Why all this needless and outmoded hypostasis of meanings? Our ordinary talk about meaning does not commit us to believing in any such entities as meanings, any more than our ordinary talk about actions for the sake of ends commits us to believing in any such entities as sakes.

Reply: Perhaps there are some who hypostatize meanings compulsively, imagining that they could not possibly make sense of our ordinary talk about meaning if they did not. Not I. I hypostatize meanings because I find it convenient to do so, and I have no good reason not to. There is no point in being a part-time nominalist. I am persuaded on independent grounds that I ought to believe in possible worlds and possible beings therein, and that I ought to believe in sets of things I believe in. Once I have these, I have all the entities I could ever want.

Objection: A language consists not only of sentences with their meanings, but also of constituents of sentences – things sentences are made of – with their meanings. And if any language is to be learnable without being finite, it must somehow be determined by finitely many of its constituents and finitely many operations on constituents.

Reply: We may define a class of objects called *grammars*. A grammar γ is a triple comprising (1) a large finite *lexicon of elementary constituents* paired with meanings; (2) a finite set of *combining operations* which build larger constituents by combining smaller constituents, and derive a meaning for the new constituent out of the meanings of the old ones; and (3) a *representing operation* which effectively maps certain constituents onto strings of sounds or of marks. A grammar Γ generates a function which assigns meanings to certain constituents, called *constituents in* Γ. It generates another function which assigns meanings to certain strings of sounds or of marks. Part of this latter function is what we have hitherto called a language. A grammar uniquely determines the language it generates. But a language does not uniquely determine the grammar that generates it, not even when we disregard superficial differences between grammars.

I have spoken of meanings for constituents in a grammar, but what sort of thing are these? Referential semantics tried to answer that question. It was a near miss, failing because contingent facts got mixed up with the meanings. The cure, discovered by Carnap,[6] is to do referential semantics not just in our actual world but in every possible world. A meaning for a name can be a function from worlds to possible individuals; for a common noun, a function from worlds to sets; for a sentence, a function from worlds to truth values (or more simply, the set of worlds where that function takes the value truth). Other derived categories may be defined by their characteristic modes of combination. For instance, an adjective combines with a common noun to make a compound common noun; so its meaning may be a function from common-noun meanings to common-noun meanings, such that the meaning of an adjective-plus-common-noun compound is the value of this function when given as argument the meaning of the common noun being modified. Likewise a verb phrase takes a name to make a sentence; so its meaning may be a function that takes the meaning of the name as argument to give the meaning of the sentence as value. An adverb (of one sort) takes a verb phrase to make a verb phrase, so its meaning may be a function from verb-phrase meanings to verb-phrase meanings. And so on, as far as need be, to more and more complicated derived categories.[7]

If you repudiate possible worlds, an alternative course is open to you: let the meanings for constituents in a grammar be phrases of Latin, or whatever your favorite base language may be.

A grammar, for us, is a semantically interpreted grammar – just as a language is a semantically interpreted language. We shall not be concerned with what are called grammars or languages in a purely syntactic sense. My definition of a grammar is meant to be general enough to encompass transformational or phrase-structure grammars for natural language[8] (when provided with semantic interpretations) as well as systems of formation and valuation rules for formalized languages. Like my previous definition of a language, my definition of a grammar is too general: it gives a large superset of the interesting grammars.

A grammar, like a language, is a set-theoretical entity which can be discussed in complete abstraction from human affairs. Since a grammar generates a unique language, all the semantic concepts we earlier defined relative to a language $\mathcal{L}$ – sentencehood, truth, analyticity, etc. – could just as well have been defined relative to a grammar Γ. We can also handle other semantic concepts pertaining to constituents, or to the constituent structure of sentences.

We can define the meaning in Γ, denotation in Γ, etc., of a subsentential constituent in Γ. We can define the meaning in Γ, denotation in Γ, etc., of a *phrase*: a string of sounds or of marks representing a subsentential constituent in Γ via the representing operation of Γ. We can define something we may call the *fine structure of meaning* in Γ of a sentence or phrase: the manner in which the meaning of the sentence or phrase is derived from the meanings of its constituents and the way it is built out of them. Thus we can take account of the sense in which, for instance, different analytic sentences are said to differ in meaning.

Now the objection can be restated: what ought to be called a language is what I have hitherto called a grammar, not what I have hitherto called a language. Different grammar, different language – at least if we ignore superficial differences between grammars. Verbal disagreement aside, the place I gave to my so-called languages ought to have been given instead to my so-called grammars. Why not begin by saying what it is for a grammar Γ to be used by a population P? Then we could go on to define sentencehood, truth, analyticity, etc., in P as sentencehood, truth, analyticity, etc., in whatever grammar is used by P. This approach would have the advantage that we could handle the semantics of constituents in a population in an exactly similar way. We could say that a constituent or phrase has a certain meaning, denotation, etc., in P if it has that meaning, denotation, etc., in whatever grammar is used by P. We could say that a sentence or phrase has a certain fine structure of meaning in P if it has it in whatever grammar is used by P.

Unfortunately, I know of no promising way to make objective sense of the assertion that a grammar Γ is used by a population P whereas another grammar, Γ', which generates the same language as Γ, is not. I have tried to say how there are facts about P which objectively select the languages used by P. I am not sure there are facts about P which objectively select privileged grammars for those languages. It is easy enough to define truthfulness and trust in a grammar, but that will not help: a convention of truthfulness and trust in Γ will also be a convention of truthfulness and trust in Γ' whenever Γ and Γ' generate the same language.

I do not propose to discard the notion of the meaning in P of a constituent or phrase, or the fine structure of meaning in P of a sentence. To propose that would be absurd. But I hold that these notions depend on our methods of evaluating grammars, and therefore are no clearer and no more objective than our notion of a *best* grammar for a given language. For I would say that a grammar Γ is used by P if and only if Γ is a best grammar for a language $\pounds$ that is used by P in virtue of a convention in P of truthfulness and trust in $\pounds$; and I would define the meaning in P of a constituent or phrase, and the fine structure of meaning in P of a sentence, accordingly.

The notions of a language used by P, of a meaning of a sentence in P, and so on, are independent of our evaluation of grammars. Therefore I take these as primary. The point is not to refrain from ever saying anything that depends on the evaluation of grammars. The point is to do so only when we must, and that is why I have concentrated on languages rather than grammars.

We may meet little practical difficulty with the semantics of constituents in populations, even if its foundations are as infirm as I fear. It may often happen that all the grammars anyone might call best for a given language will agree on the meaning of a given constituent. Yet there is trouble to be found: Quine's examples of indeterminacy of reference[9] seem to be disagreements in constituent semantics between alternative good grammars for one language. We should regard with suspicion any method that purports to settle objectively whether, in some tribe, "gavagai" is true of temporally continuant rabbits or timeslices thereof. You can give their language a good grammar of either kind – and that's that.

It is useful to divide the claimed indeterminacy of constituent semantics into three separate indeterminacies. We begin with undoubted objective fact: the dependence of the subject's behavioral output on his input of sensory stimulation (both as it actually is and as it might have been) together with all the physical laws and anatomical facts that explain it. (a) This information either determines or underdetermines the subject's system of propositional attitudes: in particular, his beliefs and desires. (b) These propositional attitudes either determine or underdetermine the truth conditions of full sentences – what I have here called his language. (c) The truth conditions of full sentences either determine or undetermine the meanings of subsentential constituents – what I have here called his grammar.

My present discussion has been directed at the middle step, from beliefs and desires to truth conditions for full sentences. I have said that the former determine the latter – provided (what need not be the case) that the beliefs and desires of the subject and his fellows are such as to comprise a fully determinate convention of truthfulness and trust in some definite language. I have said nothing here about the determinacy of the first step; and I am inclined to share in Quine's doubts about the determinacy of the third step.

Objection: Suppose that whenever anyone is party to a convention of truthfulness and trust in any language $\pounds$, his competence to be party to that convention – to conform, to expect conformity, etc. – is due to his possession of some sort of unconscious internal representation of a grammar for $\pounds$. That is a likely hypothesis, since it best explains what we know about linguistic competence. In particular, it explains why experience with some sentences leads spontaneously to expectations involving others. But on that hypothesis, we might as well bypass the conventions of language and say that $\pounds$ is used by P if and only if everyone in P possesses an internal representation of a grammar for $\pounds$.

Reply: In the first place, the hypothesis of internally represented grammars is not an explanation – best or otherwise – of anything. Perhaps it is *part* of some theory that best explains what we know about linguistic competence; we can't judge until we hear something about what the rest of the theory is like.

Nonetheless, I am ready enough to believe in internally represented grammars. But I am much less certain that there are internally represented grammars than I am that languages are used by populations; and I think it makes sense to say that languages might be used by populations even if there were no internally represented by grammars. I can tentatively agree that $\mathcal{L}$ is used by P if and only if everyone in P possesses an internal representation of a grammar for $\mathcal{L}$, if that is offered as a scientific hypothesis. But I cannot accept it as any sort of analysis of "$\mathcal{L}$ is used by P," since the analysandum clearly could be true although the analysans was false.

Objection: The notion of a convention of truthfulness and trust in $\mathcal{L}$ is a needless complication. Why not say, straightforwardly, that $\mathcal{L}$ is used by P if and only if there prevails in P a convention to bestow upon each sentence of $\mathcal{L}$ the meaning that $\mathcal{L}$ assigns to it? Or, indeed, that a grammar Γ of $\mathcal{L}$ is used by P if and only if there prevails in P a convention to bestow upon each constituent in Γ the meaning that Γ assigns to it?

Reply: A convention, as I have defined it, is a regularity in action, or in action and belief. If that feature of the definition were given up, I do not see how to salvage any part of my theory of conventions. It is essential that a convention is a regularity such that conformity by others gives one a reason to conform; and such a reason must either be a practical reason for acting or an epistemic reason for believing. What other kind of reason is there?

Yet there is no such thing as an action of bestowing a meaning (except for an irrelevant sort of action that is performed not by language-users but by creators of language), so we cannot suppose that language-using populations have conventions to perform such actions. Neither does bestowal of meaning consist in forming some belief. Granted, bestowal of meaning is conventional in the sense that it depends on convention: the meanings would have been different if the conventions of truthfulness and trust had been different. But bestowal of meaning is not an action done in conformity to a convention, since it is not an action, and it is not a belief formation in conformity to a convention, since it is not a belief formation.

Objection: The beliefs and desires that constitute a convention are inaccessible mental entities, just as much as hypothetical internal representations of grammars are. It would be best if we could say in purely behavioristic terms what it is for a language $\mathcal{L}$ to be used by a population P. We might be able to do this by referring to the way in which members of P would answer counterfactual questionnaires; or by referring to the way in which they would or would not assent to sentences under deceptive sensory stimulation; or by referring to the way in which they would intuitively group sentences into similarity classes; or in some other way.

Reply: Suppose we succeeded in giving a behavioristic operational definition of the relation "$\mathcal{L}$ is used by P." This would not help us to understand what it is for $\mathcal{L}$ to be used by P; for we would have to understand that already, and also know a good deal of commonsense psychology, in order to check that the operational definition was a definition of what it is supposed to be a definition of. If we did not know what it meant for $\mathcal{L}$ to be used by P, we would not know what sort of behavior on the part of members of P would indicate that $\mathcal{L}$ was used by P.

Objection: The conventions of language are nothing more nor less than our famously obscure old friends, the rules of language, renamed.

Reply: A convention of truthfulness and trust in $\mathcal{L}$ might well be called a rule, though it lacks many features that have sometimes been thought to belong to the essence of rules. It is not promulgated by any authority. It is not enforced by means of sanctions except to the extent that, because one has some sort of reason to conform, something bad may happen if one does not. It is nowhere codified and therefore is not "laid down in the course of teaching the language" or "appealed to in the course of criticizing a person's linguistic performance."[10] Yet it is more than a mere regularity holding "as a rule"; it is a regularity accompanied and sustained by a special kind of system of beliefs and desires.

A convention of truthfulness and trust in $\pounds$ might have as consequences other regularities which were conventions of language in their own right: specializations of the convention to certain special situations. (For instance, a convention of truthfulness in $\pounds$ on weekdays.) Such derivative conventions of language might also be called rules; some of them might stand a better chance of being codified than the overall convention which subsumes them.

However, there are other so-called rules of language which are not conventions of language and are not in the least like conventions of language: for instance, "rules" of syntax and semantics. They are not even regularities and cannot be formulated as imperatives. They might better be described not as rules, but as clauses in the definitions of entities which are to be mentioned in rules: clauses in the definition of a language $\pounds$, of the act of being truthful in $\pounds$, of the act of stating that the moon is blue, etc.

Thus the conventions of language might properly be called rules, but it is more informative and less confusing to call them conventions.

Objection: Language is not conventional. We have found that human capacities for language acquisition are highly specific and dictate the form of any language that humans can learn and use.

Reply: It may be that there is less conventionality than we used to think: fewer features of language which depend on convention, more which are determined by our innate capacities and therefore are common to all languages which are genuine alternatives to our actual language. But there are still conventions of language; and there are still convention-dependent features of language, differing from one alternative possible convention of language to another. That is established by the diversity of actual languages. There are conventions of language so long as the regularity of truthfulness in a given language has even a single alternative.

Objection: Unless a language-user is also a set-theorist, he cannot expect his fellows to conform to a regularity of truthfulness and trust in a certain language $\pounds$. For to conform to this regularity is to bear a relation to a certain esoteric entity: a set of ordered pairs of sequences of sound types or of mark types and sets of possible worlds (or something more complicated still, if $\pounds$ is a natural language with indexicality, ambiguity, and nonindicatives). The common man has no concept of any such entity. Hence he can have no expectations regarding such an entity.

Reply: The common man need not have any concept of $\pounds$ in order to expect his fellows to be truthful and trusting in $\pounds$. He need only have suitable particular expectations about how they might act, and how they might form beliefs, in various situations. He can tell whether any actual or hypothetical particular action or belief formation on their part is compatible with his expectations. He expects them to conform to a regularity of truthfulness and trust in $\pounds$ if any particular activity or belief formation that would fit his expectations would fall under what we – but not *he* – could describe as conformity to that regularity.

It may well be that his elaborate, infinite system of potential particular expectations can only be explained on the hypothesis that he has some unconscious mental entity somehow analogous to a general concept of $\pounds$ – say, an internally represented grammar. But it does not matter whether this is so or not. We are concerned only to say what system of expectations a normal member of a language-using population must have. We need not engage in psychological speculation about how those expectations are generated.

Objection: If there are conventions of language, those who are party to them should know what they are. Yet no one can fully describe the conventions of language to which he is supposedly a party.

Reply: He may nevertheless know what they are. It is enough to be able to recognize conformity and nonconformity to his convention, and to be able to try to conform to it. We know ever so many things we cannot put into words.

Objection: Use of language is almost never a rational activity. We produce and respond to utterances by habit, not as the result of any sort of reasoning or deliberation.

Reply: An action might be rational, and might be explained by the agent's beliefs and desires, even though that action was done by habit, and the agent gave no thought to the beliefs or desires which were his reason for acting. A habit may be under the agent's rational control in this sense: if that habit ever ceased to serve the agent's desires according to his beliefs, it would at once be overridden and corrected by conscious reasoning. Action done by a habit of this sort is both habitual and rational. Likewise for habits of believing. Our normal use of language is rational, since it is under rational control.

Perhaps use of language by young children is not a rational activity. Perhaps it results from habits which would not be overridden if they ceased to serve the agent's desires according to his beliefs. If that is so, I would deny that these children have yet become party to conventions of language, and I would deny that they have yet become normal members of a language-using population. Perhaps language is first acquired and afterward becomes conventional. That would not conflict with anything I have said. I am not concerned with the way in which language is acquired, only with the condition of a normal member of a language-using population when he is done acquiring language.

Objection: Language could not have originated by convention. There could not have been an agreement to begin being truthful and trusting in a certain chosen language, unless some previous language had already been available for use in making the agreement.

Reply: The first language could not have originated by an agreement, for the reason given. But that is not to say that language cannot be conventional. A convention is so-called because of the way it persists, not because of the way it originated. A convention need not originate by convention – that is, by agreement – though many conventions do originate by agreement, and others could originate by agreement even if they actually do not. In saying that language is convention-governed, I say nothing whatever about the origins of language.

Objection: A man isolated all his life from others might begin – through genius or a miracle – to use language, say to keep a diary. (This would be an accidentally private language, not the necessarily private language Wittgenstein is said to have proved to be impossible.) In this case, at least, there would be no convention involved.

Reply: Taking the definition literally, there would be no convention. But there would be something very similar. The isolated man conforms to a certain regularity at many different times. He knows at each of these times that he has conformed to that regularity in the past, and he has an interest in uniformity over time, so he continues to conform to that regularity instead of to any of various alternative regularities that would have done about as well if he had started out using them. He knows at all times that this is so, knows that he knows at all times that this is so, and so on. We might think of the situation as one in which a convention prevails in the population of different time-slices of the same man.

Objection: It is circular to define the meaning in P of sentences in terms of the beliefs held by members of P. For presumably the members of P think in their language. For instance, they hold beliefs by accepting suitable sentences of their language. If we do not already know the meaning in P of a sentence, we do not know what belief a member of P would hold by accepting that sentence.

Reply: It may be true that men think in language, and that to hold a belief is to accept a sentence of one's language. But it does not follow that belief should be analyzed as acceptance of sentences. It should not be. Even if men do in fact think in language, they might not. It is at least possible that men – like beasts – might hold beliefs otherwise than by accepting sentences. (I shall not say here how I think belief should be analyzed.) No circle arises from the contingent truth that a member of P holds beliefs by accepting sentences, so long as we can specify his beliefs without mentioning the sentences he accepts. We can do this for men, as we can for beasts.

Objection: Suppose a language $\mathcal{L}$ is used by a population of inveterate liars, who are untruthful in $\mathcal{L}$ more often than not. There would not be even a regularity – still less a convention, which implies a regularity – of truthfulness and trust in $\mathcal{L}$.

Reply: I deny that $\mathcal{L}$ is used by the population of liars. I have undertaken to follow ordinary usage only where it is determinate; and, once it is appreciated just how extraordinary the situation would have to be, I do not believe that ordinary usage is determinate in this case. There are many similarities to clear cases in which a language is used by a population, and it is understandable that we should feel some inclination to classify this case along with them. But there are many important differences as well.

Although I deny that the population of liars *collectively* uses $\mathcal{L}$, I am willing to say that each liar *individually* may use $\mathcal{L}$, provided that he falsely believes that he is a member – albeit an exceptional, untruthful member – of a population wherein there prevails a convention of truthfulness and trust in $\mathcal{L}$. He is in a position like that of a madman who thinks he belongs to a population which uses $\mathcal{L}$, and behaves accordingly, and so can be said to use $\mathcal{L}$, although in reality all the other members of this $\mathcal{L}$-using population are figments of his imagination.

Objection: Suppose the members of a population are untruthful in their language $\mathcal{L}$ more often than not, not because they lie, but because they go in heavily for irony, metaphor, hyperbole, and such. It is hard to deny that the language $\mathcal{L}$ is used by such a population.

Reply: I claim that these people *are* truthful in their language $\mathcal{L}$, though they are not *literally truthful* in $\mathcal{L}$. To be literally truthful in $\mathcal{L}$ is to be truthful in another language related to $\mathcal{L}$, a language we can call literal-$\mathcal{L}$. The relation between $\mathcal{L}$ and literal-$\mathcal{L}$ is as follows: a good way to describe $\mathcal{L}$ is to start by specifying literal-$\mathcal{L}$ and then to describe $\mathcal{L}$ as obtained by certain systematic departures from literal-$\mathcal{L}$. This two-stage specification of $\mathcal{L}$ by way of literal-$\mathcal{L}$ may turn out to be much simpler than any direct specification of $\mathcal{L}$.

Objection: Suppose they are often untruthful in $\mathcal{L}$ because they are not communicating at all. They are joking, or telling tall tales, or telling white lies as a matter of social ritual. In these situations, there is neither truthfulness nor trust in $\mathcal{L}$. Indeed, it is common knowledge that there is not.

Reply: Perhaps I can say the same sort of thing about this nonserious language use as I did about nonliteral language use. That is: Their seeming untruthfulness in nonserious situations is untruthfulness not in the language $\mathcal{L}$ that they actually use, but only in a simplified approximation to $\mathcal{L}$. We may specify $\mathcal{L}$ by first specifying the approximation language, then listing the signs and features of context by which nonserious language use can be recognized, then specifying that when these signs or features are present, what would count as untruths in the approximation language do not count as such in $\mathcal{L}$ itself. Perhaps they are automatically true in $\mathcal{L}$, regardless of the facts; perhaps they cease to count as indicative.

Example: What would otherwise be an untruth may not be one if said by a child with crossed fingers. Unfortunately, the signs and features of context by which we recognize nonserious language use are seldom as simple, standardized, and conventional as that. While they must find a place somewhere in a full account of the phenomenon of language, it may be inexpedient to burden the specification of $\pounds$ with them.

Perhaps it may be enough to note that these situations of nonserious language use must be at least somewhat exceptional if we are to have anything like a clear case of use of $\pounds$; and to recall that the definition of a convention was loose enough to tolerate some exceptions. We could take the nonserious cases simply as violations – explicable and harmless ones – of the conventions of language.

There is a third alternative, requiring a modification in my theory. We may say that a *serious communication situation* exists with respect to a sentence a of $\pounds$ whenever it is true, and common knowledge between a speaker and a hearer, that (a) the speaker does, and the hearer does not, know whether σ is true in $\pounds$; (b) the hearer wants to know; (c) the speaker wants the hearer to know; and (d) neither the speaker nor the hearer has other (comparably strong) desires as to whether or not the speaker utters σ. (Note that when there is a serious communication situation with respect to σ, there is one also with respect to synonyms or contradictories in $\pounds$ of σ, and probably also with respect to other logical relatives in $\pounds$ of σ.) Then we may say that the convention whereby P uses $\pounds$ is a convention of truthfulness and trust in $\pounds$ in serious communication situations. That is: When a serious communication situation exists with respect to σ, then the speaker tries not to utter σ unless it is true in $\pounds$, and the hearer responds, if σ is uttered, by coming to believe that σ is true in $\pounds$. If that much is a convention in P, it does not matter what goes on in other situations: they use $\pounds$.

The definition here given of a serious communication resembles that of a signaling problem in *Convention*, chapter IV, the difference being that the hearer may respond by belief formation only, rather than by what speaker and hearer alike take to be appropriate action. If this modification were adopted, it would bring my general account of language even closer to my account in *Convention* of the special case of signaling.

Objection: Truthfulness and trust cannot be a convention. What could be the alternative to uniform truthfulness – uniform untruthfulness, perhaps? But it seems that if such untruthfulness were not intended to deceive, and did not deceive, then it too would be truthfulness.

Reply: The convention is not the regularity of truthfulness and trust *simpliciter*. It is the regularity of truthfulness and trust in some particular language $\pounds$. Its alternatives are possible regularities of truthfulness and trust in other languages. A regularity of uniform untruthfulness and nontrust in a language $\pounds$ can be redescribed as a regularity of truthfulness and trust in a different language anti-$\pounds$ complementary to $\pounds$. Anti-$\pounds$ has exactly the same sentences as $\pounds$, but with opposite truth conditions. Hence the true sentences of anti-$\pounds$ are all and only the untrue sentences of $\pounds$.

There is a different regularity that we may call a regularity of truthfulness and trust *simpliciter*. That is the regularity of being truthful and trusting in whichever language is used by one's fellows. This regularity neither is a convention nor depends on convention. If any language whatever is used by a population P, then a regularity (perhaps with exceptions) of truthfulness and trust *simpliciter* prevails in P.

Objection: Even truthfulness and trust in $\pounds$ cannot be a convention. One conforms to a convention, on my account, because doing so answers to some sort of interest. But a decent man is truthful in $\pounds$ if his fellows are, whether or not it is in his interest. For he recognizes that he is under a moral obligation to be truthful in $\pounds$: an obligation to reciprocate the benefits he has derived from others' truthfulness in $\mathcal{L}$, or something of that sort. Truthfulness in $\mathcal{L}$ may bind the decent man against his own interest. It is more like a social contract than a convention.

Reply: The objection plays on a narrow sense of "interest" in which only selfish interests count. We commonly adopt a wider sense. We count also altruistic interests and interests springing from one's recognition of obligations. It is this wider sense that should be understood in the definition of convention. In this wider sense, it is nonsense to think of an obligation as outweighing one's interests. Rather, the obligation provides one interest which may outweigh the other interests.

A convention of truthfulness and trust in $\mathcal{L}$ is sustained by a mixture of selfish interests, altruistic interests, and interests derived from obligation. Usually all are present in strength; perhaps any one would be enough to sustain the convention. But occasionally truthfulness in $\mathcal{L}$ answers only to interests derived from obligation and goes against one's selfish or even altruistic interests. In such a case, only a decent man will have an interest in remaining truthful in $\mathcal{L}$. But I dare say such cases are not as common as moralists might imagine. A convention of truthfulness and trust among scoundrels might well be sustained – with occasional lapses – by selfish interests alone.

A convention persists because everyone has reason to conform if others do. If the convention is a regularity in action, this is to say that it persists because everyone prefers general conformity rather than almost-general conformity with himself as the exception. A (demythologized) social contract may also be described as a regularity sustained by a general preference for general conformity, but the second term of the preference is different. Everyone prefers general conformity over a certain state of general nonconformity called the state of nature. This general preference sets up an obligation to reciprocate the benefits derived from other's conformity, and that obligation creates an interest in conforming which sustains the social contract. The objection suggests that, among decent men, truthfulness in $\mathcal{L}$ is a social contract. I agree; but there is no reason why it cannot be a social contract and a convention as well, and I think it is.

Objection: Communication cannot be explained by conventions of truthfulness alone. If I utter a sentence σ of our language $\mathcal{L}$, you – expecting me to be truthful in $\mathcal{L}$ – will conclude that I take σ to be true in $\mathcal{L}$. If you think I am well informed, you will also conclude that probably σ is true in $\mathcal{L}$. But you will draw other conclusions as well, based on your legitimate assumption that it is for some good reason that I chose to utter σ rather than remain silent, and rather than utter any of the other sentences of $\mathcal{L}$ that I also take to be true in $\mathcal{L}$. I can communicate all sorts of misinformation by exploiting your beliefs about my conversational purposes, without ever being untruthful in $\mathcal{L}$. Communication depends on principles of helpfulness and relevance as well as truthfulness.

Reply: All this does not conflict with anything I have said. We do conform to conversational regularities of helpfulness and relevance. But these regularities are not independent conventions of language; they result from our convention of truthfulness and trust in $\mathcal{L}$ together with certain general facts – not dependent on any convention – about our conversational purposes and our beliefs about one another. Since they are byproducts of a convention of truthfulness and trust, it is unnecessary to mention them separately in specifying the conditions under which a language is used by a population.

Objection: Let $\mathcal{L}$ be the language used in P, and let $\mathcal{L}-$ be some fairly rich fragment of $\mathcal{L}$. That is, the sentences of $\mathcal{L}-$ are many but not all of the sentences of $\mathcal{L}$ (in an appropriate special sense if $\mathcal{L}$ is infinite); and any sentence of both has the same meaning in both. Then $\mathcal{L}-$ also turns out to be a language used by P; for by my definition there prevails in P a convention of truthfulness and trust in $\mathcal{L}-$, sustained by an interest in communication. Not one but many – perhaps infinitely many – languages are used by P.

Reply: That is so, but it is no problem. Why not say that any rich fragment of a language used by P is itself a used language?

Indeed, we will need to say such things when P is linguistically inhomogeneous. Suppose, for instance, that P divides into two classes: the learned and the vulgar. Among the learned there prevails a convention of truthfulness and trust in a language $\mathcal{L}$; among P as a whole there does not, but there does prevail a convention of truthfulness and trust in a rich fragment $\mathcal{L}-$ of $\mathcal{L}$. We wish to say that the learned have a common language with the vulgar, but that is so only if $\mathcal{L}-$, as well as $\mathcal{L}$, counts as a language used by the learned.

Another case: the learned use $\mathcal{L}_1$, the vulgar use $\mathcal{L}_2$, neither is included in the other, but there is extensive overlap. Here $\mathcal{L}_1$ and $\mathcal{L}_2$ are to be the most inclusive languages used by the respective classes. Again we wish to say that the learned and the vulgar have a common language: in particular, the largest fragment common to $\mathcal{L}_1$ and $\mathcal{L}_2$. That can be so only if this largest common fragment counts as a language used by the vulgar, by the learned, and by the whole population.

I agree that we often do not count the fragments; we can speak of *the* language of P, meaning by this not the one and only thing that is a language used by P, but rather the most inclusive language used by P. Or we could mean something else: the union of all the languages used by substantial subpopulations of P, provided that some quite large fragment of this union is used by (more or less) all of P. Note that the union as a whole need not be used at all, in my primary sense, either by P or by any subpopulation of P. Thus in my example of the last paragraph, the language of P might be taken either as the largest common fragment of $\mathcal{L}_1$ and $\mathcal{L}_2$ or as the union of $\mathcal{L}_1$ and $\mathcal{L}_2$.

Further complications arise. Suppose that half of the population of a certain town uses English, and also uses basic Welsh; while the other half uses Welsh, and also uses basic English. The most inclusive language used by the entire population is the union of basic Welsh and basic English. The union of languages used by substantial subpopulations is the union of English and Welsh, and the proviso is satisfied that some quite large fragment of this union is used by the whole population. Yet we would be reluctant to say that either of these unions is the language of the population of the town. We might say that Welsh and English are the two languages of the town, or that basic English and basic Welsh are. It is odd to call either of the two language unions a language; though once they are called that, it is no further oddity to say that one or the other of them is the language of the town. There are two considerations. First: English, or Welsh, or basic English, or basic Welsh, can be given a satisfactory unified grammar; whereas the language unions cannot. Second: English, or Welsh, or basic Welsh, or basic English, is (in either of the senses I have explained) the language of a large population outside the town; whereas the language unions are not. I am not sure which of the two considerations should be emphasized in saying when a language is the language of a population.

Objection: Let $\mathcal{L}$ be the language of P; that is, the language that ought to count as the most inclusive language used by P. (Assume that P is linguistically homogeneous.) Let $\mathcal{L}+$ be obtained by adding garbage to $\mathcal{L}$: some extra sentences, very long and difficult to pronounce, and hence never uttered in P, with arbitrary chosen meanings in $\mathcal{L}+$. Then it seems that $\mathcal{L}+$ is a language used by P, which is absurd.

A sentence never uttered at all is a fortiori never uttered untruthfully. So truthfulness-as-usual in $\mathcal{L}$ plus truthfulness-by-silence on the garbage sentences constitutes a kind of truthfulness in $\mathcal{L}+$; and the expectation thereof constitutes trust in $\mathcal{L}+$. Therefore we have a prevailing regularity of truthfulness and trust in $\mathcal{L}+$. This regularity qualifies as a convention in P sustained by an interest in communication.

Reply: Truthfulness-by-silence is truthfulness, and expectation thereof is expectation of truthfulness; but expectation of truthfulness-by-silence is not yet trust. Expectation of (successful) truthfulness – expectation that a given sentence will not be uttered falsely – is a necessary but not sufficient condition for trust. There is no regularity of trust in $\mathcal{L}+$, so far as the garbage sentences are concerned. Hence there is no convention of truthfulness and trust in $\mathcal{L}+$, and $\mathcal{L}+$ is not used by P.

For trust, one must be able to take an utterance of a sentence as evidence that the sentence is true. That is so only if one's degree of belief that the sentence will be uttered falsely is low, not only absolutely, but as a fraction of one's degree of belief – perhaps already very low – that the sentence will be uttered at all. Further, this must be so not merely because one believes in advance that the sentence is probably true: one's degree of belief that the sentence will be uttered falsely must be substantially lower than the product of one's degree of belief that the sentence will be uttered times one's prior degree of belief that it is false. A garbage sentence of $\mathcal{L}+$ will not meet this last requirement, not even if one believes to high degrees both that it is true in $\mathcal{L}+$ and that it never will be uttered.

This objection was originally made, by Stephen Schiffer, against my former view that conventions of language are conventions of truthfulness. I am inclined to think that it succeeds as a counterexample to that view. I agree that $\mathcal{L}+$ is not used by P, in any reasonable sense, but I have not seen any way to avoid conceding that $\mathcal{L}+$ is a possible language it might *really* be used – and that there does prevail in P a convention of truthfulness in $\mathcal{L}+$, sustained by an interest in communication. Here we have another advantage of the present account over my original one.

Objection: A sentence either is or isn't analytic in a given language, and a language either is or isn't conventionally adopted by a given population. Hence there is no way for the analytic–synthetic distinction to be unsharp. But not only can it be unsharp; it usually is, at least in cases of interest to philosophers. A sharp analytic–synthetic distinction is available only relative to particular rational reconstructions of ordinary language.

Reply: One might try to explain unsharp analyticity by a theory of degrees of convention. Conventions do admit of degree in a great many ways: by the strengths of the beliefs and desires involved, and by the fraction of exceptions to the many almost universal quantifications in the definition of convention. But this will not help much. It is easy to imagine unsharp analyticity even in a population whose conventions of language are conventions to the highest degree in every way.

One might try to explain unsharp analyticity by recalling that we may not know whether some worlds are really possible. If a sentence is true in our language in all worlds except some worlds of doubtful possibility, then that sentence will be of doubtful analyticity. But this will not help much either. Unsharp analyticity usually seems to arise because we cannot decide whether a sentence would be true in some bizarre but clearly possible world.

A better explanation would be that our convention of language is not exactly a convention of truthfulness and trust in a single language, as I have said so far. Rather it is a convention of truthfulness and trust in whichever we please of some cluster of similar languages: languages with more or less the same sentences, and more or less the same truth values for the sentences in worlds close to our actual world, but with increasing divergence in truth values as we go to increasingly remote, bizarre worlds. The convention confines us to the cluster, but leaves us with indeterminacies whenever the languages of the cluster disagree. We are free to settle these indeterminacies however we like. Thus an ordinary, open-textured, imprecise language is a sort of blur of precise languages – a region, not a point, in the space of languages. Analyticity is sharp in each language of our cluster. But when different languages of our cluster disagree on the analyticity of a sentence, then that sentence is unsharply analytic among us.

Rational reconstructions have been said to be irrelevant to philosophical problems arising in ordinary, unreconstructed language. My hypothesis of conventions of truthfulness and trust in language clusters provides a defense against this accusation. Reconstruction is not – or not always – departure from ordinary language. Rather it is selection from ordinary language: isolation of one precise language, or of a subcluster, out of the language cluster wherein we have a convention of truthfulness and trust.

Objection: The thesis and the antithesis pertain to different subjects. The thesis, in which languages are regarded as semantic systems, belongs to the philosophy of artificial languages. The antithesis, in which language is regarded as part of human natural history, belongs to the philosophy of natural language.

Reply: Not so. *Both* accounts – just like almost any account of almost anything – can most easily be applied to simple, artificial, imaginary examples. Language games are just as artificial as formalized calculi.

According to the theory I have presented, philosophy of language is a single subject. The thesis and antithesis have been the property of rival schools; but in fact they are complementary essential ingredients in any adequate account either of languages or of language.

NOTES

1   H. P. Grice, "Meaning," *Philosophical Review*, 66 (1957): 377–88 [reproduced as part of ch. 2 in this volume].
2   This proposal is adapted from the theory given in Erik Stenius, "Mood and Language-Game," *Synthese*, 17 (1967): 254–74.
3   (Harvard University Press, Cambridge, MA: 1969). A similar account was given in the original version of this paper, written in 1968.
4   Personal communication, 1971. Bennett himself uses the broadened concept of convention differently, wishing to exhibit conventional meaning as a special case of Gricean meaning. See his "The Meaning–Nominalist Strategy," *Foundations of Language*, 10 (1973): 141–68.
5   Possible worlds are taken as models in S. Kripke, "A Completeness Theorem in Modal Logic," *Journal of Symbolic Logic*, 24 (1959): 1–15; in Carnap's recent work on semantics and inductive logic, discussed briefly in sections 9, 10, and 25 of "Replies and Systematic Expositions," *The Philosophy of Rudolf Carnap*, ed. P. Schilpp (Open Court, La Salle, IL: 1963); and elsewhere. Worlds are taken as state descriptions – diagrams of models – in Carnap's earlier work: For instance, section 18 of *Introduction to Semantics* (Harvard University Press, Cambridge, MA: 1942). Worlds are taken as complete, consistent novel – theories of models – in R. Jeffrey, *The Logic of Decision* (McGraw-Hill, New York, 1965), section 12.8.
6   "Replies and Systematic Expositions," section 9.v. A better-known presentation of essentially the same idea is in S. Kripke, "Semantical Considerations on Modal Logic," *Acta Philosophica Fennica*, 16 (1963): 83–94.
7   See my "General Semantics," *Synthese*, 22 (1970): 18–67.
8   For a description of the sort of grammars I have in mind (minus the semantic interpretation) see N. Chomsky, *Aspects of the Theory of Syntax* (MIT Press, Cambridge, MA: 1965), and G. Harman, "Generative Grammars without Transformational Rules," *Language*, 37 (1963): 597–

616. My constituents correspond to semantically interpreted deep phrasemarkers, or subtrees thereof, in a transformational grammar. My "representing operation" may work in several steps and thus subsumes both the transformational

9   W. V. Quine, "Ontological Relativity," *Journal of Philosophy*, 65 (1968): 185–212; *Word and Object* (MIT Press, Cambridge, MA: 1960), pp. 68–79.

10 P. Ziff, *Semantic Analysis* (Cornell University Press, Ithaca, NY: 1960), pp. 34–5.

3

Language and Environment

Introduction

Philosophers' approach to linguistic meaning changed dramatically in the seventies. To understand the significance of this shift, it is helpful to go back to Gottlob Frege, a logician, mathematician and philosopher who is rightfully considered the founder of the philosophy of language in the twentieth century. According to Frege, the meaning of a name determined its reference, and knowing the meaning of a word was a matter of being in a certain psychological state. Subsequent theories of meaning accepted these assumptions, but it is precisely these assumptions that Hilary Putnam challenges in "The Meaning of 'Meaning'."

Putnam asks us to imagine a world, W_2, which is just like the world we inhabit, W_1, except for the fact that what looks, behaves, and tastes like water at W_2 is not H_2O, but a different compound, XYZ. Suppose now that an Earthling travels to W_2 and discovers that when the inhabitants of W_2 talk about water they mean, not H_2O, but rather XYZ. In that situation, Putnam says, the Earthlings would correctly report back to earth that at W_2 "water" means XYZ. The extension or reference of "water" is different at the two worlds.

Now imagine we go back in time a few hundred years. Chemistry had not been developed and the chemical composition of H_2O and XYZ was not known. In spite of that, the extension of "water" remained different at the two worlds. My duplicate at W_2 is, of course, in exactly the same psychological state as I when we entertain the term "water." Still, when entertaining the term "water," my duplicate and I are thinking about different things. Thus, the extension of a term is not a function of the psychological state one is in. So, there is a sense in which knowing the meaning of a term is not a matter of being in a given psychological state.

The extension of a term, Putnam argues, is in many cases socially determined. A speaker of a language is said to have acquired the term if her use of the term is appropriate, and the term has in her idiolect the same extension as it has in her linguistic community. This means, e.g., that if the extension of "tiger" differs in the two worlds, then my duplicate at W_2 has not acquired our word "tiger" even though the verbal behavior of his community in no way differs from ours. The reason for this difference is that. My duplicate and I are in the same psychological states and make the same sounds when we say "Tigers are carnivorous," but, still, because the extension of "tiger" differs in our societies, we mean different things by what we say. We are seeing here the first argument developed for anti-individualism, an issue that is dealt with in the section "Mind and Environment."

Once we drop the assumption that what a name refers to is determined by what the person using the name has in mind, we need an alternative account of meaning and reference. Putnam suggests that instead of looking into the head for meanings we should look at causal connections between human beings and the objects in their environment. Causal connections could explain the differences between the meanings of "water" and "tiger" here on Earth and their meanings in W_2. The reference of "water" in W_1 and W_2 differ because here "water" is causally connected to H_2O, while at W_2 "water" is connected by a causal chain to XYZ.

Other pioneers of the direct designation theory of names are Saul Kripke and Keith Donnellan. Kripke argued that a speaker's beliefs about the object are neither necessary nor sufficient for a proper name to refer to that object. Our beliefs can fail to identify anybody, as in the case of our beliefs about Jonah, the one who was swallowed by a whale, or Feynman, the physicist who played bongos, and nevertheless we can succeed in referring to an object in virtue of a causal chain that connects us to the object. Donnellan argued that sometimes we can use definite descriptions to refer to a particular individual even if it does not match the description. For example, I might say that the man with a martini is a famous philosopher and succeed in referring to a particular man even though he does not have a martini in his glass but water.

All these views have been very influential, but we include only Putnam's essay, which is rich in content and played an important role not only in the philosophy of language, but also in the philosophy of mind and psychology. The discussion of whether psychology and cognitive science has to be individualistic owes much to Putnam's discussion. Also note Putnam's critique of the Davidsonian approach to semantics.

FURTHER READING

Devitt, M. (1980). *Designation*. New York: Columbia University Press.
Donnellan, K. (1966). Reference and Definite Descriptions. *Philosophical Review* 75: 281–304.
Evans, G. (1982). *The Varieties of Reference*. Oxford: Clarendon Press.
Kaplan, D. (1989). Demonstratives. In *Themes from Kaplan*. Eds J. Almog, J. Perry, and H. Wettstein. Oxford: Oxford University Press.
Kripke, S. (1972). *Naming and Necessity*. Cambridge, MA: Harvard University Press.
Recanati, F. (1993). *Direct Reference: From Language to Thought*. Oxford: Blackwell.
Russell, B. (1919). Descriptions. In *Introduction to Mathematical Philosophy*. London: George Allen and Unwin.
Salmon, N. (1981). *Reference and Essence*. Princeton, NJ: Princeton University Press.
Searle, J. (1957). Proper Names. *Mind* 67: 166–73.
Searle, J. (1983). Proper Names and Intentionality. In *Intentionality*. Cambridge: Cambridge University Press.

The Meaning of "Meaning"

HILARY PUTNAM

Language is the first broad area of human cognitive capacity for which we are beginning to obtain a description which is not exaggeratedly oversimplified. Thanks to the work of contemporary transformational linguists,[1] a very subtle description of at least some human languages is in the process of being constructed. Some features of these languages appear to be *universal*. Where such features turn out to be "species- specific" – "not explicable on some general grounds of functional utility or simplicity that would apply to arbitrary systems that serve the functions of language" – they may shed some light on the structure of mind. While it is extremely difficult to say to what extent the structure so illuminated will turn out to be a universal structure of *language*, as opposed to a universal structure of innate general learning strategies,[2] the very fact that this discussion can take place is testimony to the richness and generality of the descriptive material that linguists are beginning to provide, and also testimony to the depth of the analysis, insofar as the features that appear to be candidates for "species-specific" features of language are in no sense surface or phenomenological features of language, but lie at the level of deep structure.

The most serious drawback to all of this analysis, as far as a philosopher is concerned, is that it does not concern the meaning of words. Analysis of the deep structure of linguistic forms gives us an incomparably more powerful description of the *syntax* of natural languages than we have ever had before. But the dimension of language associated with the word "meaning" is, in spite of the usual spate of heroic if misguided attempts, as much in the dark as it ever was.

In this essay, I want to explore why this should be so. In my opinion, the reason that so-called semantics is in so much worse condition than syntactic theory is that the *prescientific* concept on which semantics is based – the prescientific concept of *meaning* – is itself in much worse shape than the prescientific concept of syntax. As usual in philosophy, skeptical doubts about the concept do not at all help one in clarifying or improving the situation any more than dogmatic assertions by conservative philosophers that all's really well in this best of all possible worlds. The reason that the prescientific concept of meaning is in bad shape is not clarified by some general skeptical or nominalistic argument to the effect that meanings don't exist. Indeed, the upshot of our discussion will be that meanings don't exist in quite the way we tend to think they do. But electrons don't exist in quite the way Bohr thought they did, either. There is all the distance in the world between this assertion and the assertion that meanings (or electrons) "don't exist."

I am going to talk almost entirely about the meaning of words rather than about the meaning of sentences because I feel that our concept of word-meaning is more defective than our concept of sentence-meaning. But I will comment briefly on the arguments of philosophers such as Donald Davidson who insist that the concept of word-meaning *must* be secondary and that study of sentence-meaning must be primary. Since I regard the traditional theories about meaning as myth-eaten (notice that the topic of "meaning" is the one topic discussed in philosophy in which there is literally nothing but "theory" – literally nothing that can be labelled or even ridiculed as the "commonsense view"), it will be necessary for me to discuss and try to disentangle a number of topics concerning which the received view is, in my opinion, wrong. The reader will give me the greatest aid in the task of trying to make these matters clear if he will kindly assume that *nothing* is clear in advance.

1   Meaning and Extension

Since the Middle Ages at least, writers on the theory of meaning have purported to discover an ambiguity in the ordinary concept of meaning, and have introduced a pair of terms –

extension and *intension*, or *Sinn* and *Bedeutung*, or whatever – to disambiguate the notion. The *extension* of a term, in customary logical parlance, is simply the set of things the term is true of. Thus, "rabbit," in its most common English sense, is true of all and only rabbits, so the extension of "rabbit" is precisely the set of rabbits. Even this notion – and it is the *least* problematical notion in this cloudy subject – has its problems, however. Apart from problems it inherits from its parent notion of *truth*, the foregoing example of "rabbit" *in its most common English sense* illustrates one such problem: strictly speaking, it is not a term, but an ordered pair consisting of a term and a "sense" (or an occasion of use, or something else that distinguishes a term in one sense from the same term used in a different sense) that has an extension. Another problem is this: a "set," in the mathematical sense, is a "yes–no" object; any given object either definitely belongs to S or definitely does not belong to S, if S is a set. But words in a natural language are not generally "yes–no": there are things of which the description "tree" is clearly true and things of which the description "tree" is clearly false, to be sure, but there are a host of borderline cases. Worse, the line between the clear cases and the borderline cases is itself fuzzy. Thus the idealization involved in the notion of *extension* – the idealization involved in supposing that there is such a thing as the set of things of which the term "tree" is true – is actually very severe.

Recently some mathematicians have investigated the notion of *fuzzy set* – that is, of an object to which other things belong or do not belong with a given probability or to a given degree, rather than belong "yes–no." If one really wanted to formalize the notion of extension as applied to terms in a natural language, it would be necessary to employ "fuzzy sets" or something similar rather than sets in the classical sense.

The problem of a word's having more than one sense is standardly handled by treating each of the senses as a different word (or rather, by treating the word as if it carried invisible subscripts, thus: "rabbit$_1$" – animal of a certain kind; "rabbit$_2$," – coward; and as if "rabbit$_1$," and " rabbit$_2$," or whatever were different words entirely). This again involves two very severe idealizations (at least two, that is): supposing that words have discretely many senses, and supposing that the entire repertoire of senses is fixed once and for all. Paul Ziff has recently investigated the extent to which both of these suppositions distort the actual situation in natural language;[3] nevertheless, we will continue to make these idealizations here.

Now consider the compound terms "creature with a heart" and "creature with a kidney." Assuming that every creature with a heart possesses a kidney and vice versa, the extension of these two terms is exactly the same. But they obviously differ in meaning. Supposing that there is a sense of " meaning" in which meaning = extension, there must be another sense of "meaning" in which the meaning of a term is not its extension but something else, say the "concept" associated with the term. Let us call this "something else" the *intension* of the term. The concept of a creature with a heart is clearly a different concept from the concept of a creature with a kidney. Thus the two terms have different intension. When we say they have different "meaning," meaning = intension.

2 Intension and Extension

Something like the preceding paragraph appears in every standard exposition of the notions "intension" and "extension." But it is not at all satisfactory. Why it is not satisfactory is, in a sense, the burden of this entire essay. But some points can be made at the very outset:

first of all, what evidence is there that "extension" is a sense of the word "meaning"? The canonical explanation of the notions "intension" and "extension" is very much like "in one sense 'meaning' means *extension* and in the other sense 'meaning' means *meaning*." The fact is that while the notion of "extension" is made quite precise, relative to the fundamental logical notion of *truth* (and under the severe idealizations remarked above), the notion of intension is made no more precise than the vague (and, as we shall see, misleading) notion "concept." It is as if someone explained the notion "probability" by saying: "in one sense 'probability' means frequency, and in the other sense it means *propensity*." "Probability" never means "frequency," and "propensity" is at least as unclear as "probability."

Unclear as it is, the traditional doctrine that the notion "meaning" possesses the extension/intension ambiguity has certain typical consequences. Most traditional philosophers thought of concepts as something *mental*. Thus the doctrine that the meaning of a term (the meaning "in the sense of intension," that is) is a concept carried the implication that meanings are mental entities. Frege and more recently Carnap and his followers, however, rebelled against this "psychologism," as they termed it. Feeling that meanings are *public* property – that the *same* meaning can be "grasped" by more than one person and by persons at different times – they identified concepts (and hence "intensions" or meanings) with abstract entities rather than mental entities. However, "grasping" these abstract entities was still an individual psychological act. None of these philosophers doubted that understanding a word (knowing its intension) was just a matter of being in a certain psychological state (somewhat in the way in which knowing how to factor numbers in one's head is just a matter of being in a certain very complex psychological state).

Secondly, the timeworn example of the two terms "creature with a kidney" and "creature with a heart" does show that two terms can have the same extension and yet differ in intension. But it was taken to be obvious that the reverse is impossible: two terms cannot differ in extension and have the same intension. Interestingly, no argument for this impossibility was ever offered. Probably it reflects the tradition of the ancient and medieval philosophers who assumed that the concept corresponding to a term was just a conjunction of predicates, and hence that the concept corresponding to a term must always provide a necessary and sufficient condition for falling into the extension of the term.[4] For philosophers like Carnap, who accepted the verifiability theory of meaning, the concept corresponding to a term provided (in the ideal case, where the term had "complete meaning") a *criterion* for belonging to the extension (not just in the sense of "necessary and sufficient condition," but in the strong sense of *way of recognizing* if a given thing falls into the extension or not). Thus these positivistic philosophers were perfectly happy to retain the traditional view on this point. So theory of meaning came to rest on two unchallenged assumptions:

1   That knowing the meaning of a term is just a matter of being in a certain psychological state (in the sense of "psychological state," in which states of memory and psychological dispositions are "psychological states"; no one thought that knowing the meaning of a word was a continuous state of consciousness, of course).
2   That the meaning of a term (in the sense of intension) determines its extension (in the sense that sameness of intension entails sameness of extension).

I shall argue that these two assumptions are not jointly satisfied by any notion, let alone any notion of meaning. The traditional concept of meaning is a concept which rests on a false theory.

3 "Psychological State" and Methodological Solipsism

In order to show this, we need first to clarify the traditional notion of a psychological state. In one sense a state is simply a two-place predicate whose arguments are an individual and a time. In this sense, *being five feet tall*, *being in pain*, *knowing the alphabet*, and even *being a thousand miles from Paris* are all states. (Note that the *time* is usually left implicit or "contextual"; the full form of an atomic sentence of these predicates would be "*x is five feet tall at time t*," "*x is in pain at time t*," etc.) In science, however, it is customary to restrict the term state to properties which are defined in terms of the parameters of the individual which are fundamental from the point of view of the given science. Thus, being five feet tall is a state (from the point of view of physics); being in pain is a state (from the point of view of mentalistic psychology, at least); knowing the alphabet might be a state (from the point of view of cognitive psychology), although it is hard to say; but being a thousand miles from Paris would *not* naturally be called a *state*. In one sense, a psychological state is simply a state which is studied or described by psychology. In this sense it may be trivially true that, say *knowing the meaning of the word "water"* is a "psychological state" (viewed from the standpoint of cognitive psychology). But this is not the sense of psychological state that is at issue in the above assumption (1).

When traditional philosophers talked about psychological states (or "mental" states), they made an assumption which we may call the assumption of methodological solipsism. This assumption is the assumption that no psychological state, properly so called, presupposes the existence of any individual other than the subject to whom that state is ascribed. (In fact, the assumption was that no psychological state presupposes the existence of the subject's *body* even: if *P* is a psychological state, properly so called, then it must be logically possible for a "disembodied mind" to be in *P*.) This assumption is pretty explicit in Descartes, but it is implicit in just about the whole of traditional philosophical psychology. Making this assumption is, of course, adopting a *restrictive program* – a program which deliberately limits the scope and nature of psychology to fit certain mentalistic preconceptions or, in some cases, to fit an idealistic reconstruction of knowledge and the world. Just how restrictive the program is, however, often goes unnoticed. Such common or garden variety psychological states as *being jealous* have to be reconstructed, for example, if the assumption of methodological solipsism is retained. For, in its ordinary use, *x is jealous of y* entails that *y* exists, and *x is jealous of y's regard for z* entails that both *y* and *z* exist (as well as *x*, of course). Thus *being jealous* and *being jealous of someone's regard for someone else* are not psychological states permitted by the assumption of methodological solipsism. (We shall call them "psychological states in the wide sense" and refer to the states which are permitted by methodological solipsism as "psychological states in the narrow sense.") The reconstruction required by methodological solipsism would be to reconstrue *jealousy* so that I can be jealous of my own hallucinations, or of figments of my imagination, etc. Only if we assume that psychological states in the narrow sense have a significant degree of causal closure (so that restricting ourselves to psychological states in the narrow sense will facilitate the statement of psychological laws) is there any point in engaging in this reconstruction, or in making the assumption of methodological solipsism. But the three centuries of failure of mentalistic psychology is tremendous evidence against this procedure, in my opinion.

Be that as it may, we can now state more precisely what we claimed at the end of the preceding section. Let *A* and *B* be any two terms which differ in extension. By assumption (2) they must differ in meaning (in the sense of "intension"). By assumption (1), *knowing the meaning of A* and *knowing the meaning of B* are psychological states *in the narrow sense* – for this is how we shall construe assumption (1). *But these psychological states must determine the extension of the terms A and B just as much as the meanings ("intensions") do.*

To see this, let us try assuming the opposite. Of course, there cannot be two terms *A* and *B* such that *knowing the meaning of A* is the same state as *knowing the meaning of B* even though *A* and *B* have different extensions. For *knowing the meaning of A* isn't just "grasping the intension" of *A*, whatever that may come to; it is also knowing that the intension "that one has" grasped' *is* the intension of *A*. (Thus, someone who knows the meaning of "wheel" presumably "grasps the intension" of its German synonym *Rad*; but if he doesn't know that the "intension" in question is the intension of *Rad* he isn't said to "know the meaning of *Rad*.") If *A* and *B* are different terms, then *knowing the meaning of A* is a different state from *knowing the meaning of B* whether the meanings of *A* and *B* be themselves the same or different. But by the same argument, if I_1 and I_2 are different intensions and *A* is a term, then *knowing that I_1 is the meaning of A* is a different psychological state from *knowing that I_2 is the meaning of A*. Thus, there cannot be two different logically possible worlds L_1 and L_2 such that, say, Oscar is in the *same* psychological state (in the narrow sense) in L_1 and in L_2 (in all respects), but in L_1 Oscar understands *A* as having the meaning I_1 and in L_2 Oscar understands *A* as having the meaning I_2. (For, if there were, then in L_1 Oscar would be in the psychological state *knowing that I_1 is the meaning of A* and in L_2 Oscar would be in the psychological state *knowing that I_2 is the meaning of A*, and these are different and even – assuming that *A* has just one meaning for Oscar in each world – incompatible psychological states in the narrow sense.)

In short, if *S* is the sort of psychological state we have been discussing – a psychological state of the form *knowing that I is the meaning of A*, where I is an "intension" and *A* is a term – then the *same* necessary and sufficient condition for falling into the extension of *A* "works" in every logically possible world in which the speaker is in the psychological state *S*. For the state *S determines* the intension *I*, and by assumption (2) the intension amounts to a necessary and sufficient condition for membership in the *extension*.

If our interpretation of the traditional doctrine of intension and extension is fair to Frege and Carnap, then the whole psychologism/platonism issue appears somewhat a tempest in a teapot, as far as meaning-theory is concerned. (Of course, it is a very important issue as far as general philosophy of mathematics is concerned.) For even if meanings are "Platonic" entities rather than "mental" entities on the Frege–Carnap view, "grasping" those entities is presumably a psychological state (in the narrow sense). Moreover, the psychological state uniquely determines the "Platonic" entity. So whether one takes the "Platonic" entity or the psychological state as the "meaning" would appear to be somewhat a matter of convention. And taking the psychological state to be the meaning would hardly have the consequence that Frege feared, that meanings would cease to be public. For psychological states are "public" in the sense that different people (and even people in different epochs) can be in the *same* psychological state. Indeed, Frege's argument against psychologism is only an argument against identifying concepts with mental particulars, not with mental entities in general.

The "public" character of psychological states entails, in particular, that if Oscar and Elmer understand a word *A* differently, then they must be in *different* psychological states. For the state of *knowing the intension of A to be, say, I* is the same state whether Oscar or Elmer be in it. Thus two speakers cannot be in the same psychological state in all respects and understand the term *A* differently; the psychological state of the speaker determines the intension (and hence, by assumption (2), the extension) of *A*.

It is this last consequence of the joint assumptions (1), (2) that we claim to be false. We claim that it is possible for two speakers to be in exactly the *same* psychological state (in the narrow sense), even though the extension of the term A in the idiolect of the one is different from the extension of the term A in the idiolect of the other. Extension is *not* determined by psychological state.

This will be shown in detail in later sections. If this is right, then there are two courses open to one who wants to rescue at least one of the traditional assumptions; to give up the idea that psychological state (in the narrow sense) determines *intension*, or to give up the idea that intension determines extension. We shall consider these alternatives later.

4 Are Meanings in the Head?

That psychological state does not determine extension will now be shown with the aid of a little science-fiction. For the purpose of the following science-fiction examples, we shall suppose that somewhere in the galaxy there is a planet we shall call Twin Earth. Twin Earth is very much like Earth; in fact, people on Twin Earth even speak *English*. In fact, apart from the differences we shall specify in our science-fiction examples, the reader may suppose that Twin Earth is exactly like Earth. He may even suppose that he has a *Doppelgänger* – an identical copy – on Twin Earth, if he wishes, although my stories will not depend on this.

Although some of the people on Twin Earth (say, the ones who call themselves "Americans" and the ones who call themselves "Canadians" and the ones who call themselves "Englishmen," etc.) speak English, there are, not surprisingly, a few tiny differences which we will now describe between the dialects of English spoken on Twin Earth and Standard English. These differences themselves depend on some of the peculiarities of Twin Earth.

One of the peculiarities of Twin Earth is that the liquid called "water" is not H_2O but a different liquid whose chemical formula is very long and complicated. I shall abbreviate this chemical formula simply as XYZ. I shall suppose that XYZ is indistinguishable from water at normal temperatures and pressures. In particular, it tastes like water and it quenches thirst like water. Also, I shall suppose that the oceans and lakes and seas of Twin Earth contain XYZ and not water, that it rains XYZ on Twin Earth and not water, etc.

If a spaceship from Earth ever visits Twin Earth, then the supposition at first will be that "water" has the same meaning on Earth and on Twin Earth. This supposition will be corrected when it is discovered that "water" on Twin Earth is XYZ, and the Earthian spaceship will report somewhat as follows:

"On Twin Earth the word 'water' means XYZ"

(It is this sort of use of the word "means" which accounts for the doctrine that extension is one sense of "meaning," by the way. But note that although "means" does mean something like "has as extension" in this example, one would *not* say

"On Twin Earth the meaning of the word 'water' is XYZ."

unless, possibly, the fact that "water is XYZ" was known to every adult speaker of English on Twin Earth. We can account for this in terms of the theory of meaning we develop below; for the moment we just remark that although the verb "means" sometimes means "has as extension," the nominalization "meaning" *never* means "extension.")

Symmetrically, if a spaceship from Twin Earth ever visits Earth, then the supposition at first will be that the word "water" has the same meaning on Twin Earth and on Earth. This supposition will be corrected when it is discovered that "water" on Earth is H_2O, and the Twin Earthian spaceship will report:

"On Earth[5] the word 'water' means H_2O."

Note that there is no problem about the extension of the term "water." The word simply has two different meanings (as we say): in the sense in which it is used on Twin Earth, the sense of water$_{TE}$, what *we* call "water" simply isn't water; while in the sense in which it is used on Earth, the sense of water$_E$, what the Twin Earthians call "water" simply isn't water. The extension of "water" in the sense of water$_E$ is the set of all wholes consisting of H_2O molecules, or something like that; the extension of water in the sense of water$_{TE}$ is the set of all wholes consisting of XYZ molecules, or something like that.

Now let us roll the time back to about 1750. At that time chemistry was not developed on either Earth or Twin Earth. The typical Earthian speaker of English did not know water consisted of hydrogen and oxygen, and the typical Twin Earthian speaker of English did not know "water" consisted of XYZ. Let Oscar$_1$ be such a typical Earthian English speaker, and let Oscar$_2$ be his counterpart on Twin Earth. You may suppose that there is no belief that Oscar$_1$ had about water that Oscar$_2$ did not have about "water." If you like, you may even suppose that Oscar$_1$ and Oscar$_2$ were exact duplicates in appearance, feelings, thoughts, interior monologue, etc. Yet the extension of the term "water" was just as much H_2O on Earth in 1750 as in 1950; and the extension of the term "water" was just as much XYZ on Twin Earth in 1750 as in 1950. Oscar$_1$ and Oscar$_2$ understood the term "water" differently in 1750 *although they were in the same psychological state*, and although, given the state of science at the time, it would have taken their scientific communities about fifty years to discover that they understood the term "water" differently. Thus the extension of the term "water" (and, in fact, its "meaning" in the intuitive preanalytical usage of that term) is *not* a function of the psychological state of the speaker by itself.

But, it might be objected, why should we accept it that the term "water" has the same extension in 1750 and in 1950 (on both Earths)? The logic of natural-kind terms like "water" is a complicated matter, but the following is a sketch of an answer. Suppose I point to a glass of water and say "this liquid is called water" (or "this is called water," if the marker "liquid" is clear from the context). My "ostensive definition" of water has the following empirical presupposition: that the body of liquid I am pointing to bears a certain sameness relation (say, *x is the same liquid as y, or x is the same$_L$ as y*) to most of the stuff I and other speakers in my linguistic community have on other occasions called "water." If this presupposition is false because, say, I am without knowing it pointing to a glass of gin and not a glass of water, then I do not intend my ostensive definition to be accepted. Thus the ostensive definition conveys what might be called a defeasible necessary and sufficient condition: the necessary and sufficient condition for being water is bearing the relation same$_L$ to the stuff in the glass; but this is the necessary and sufficient condition only if the empirical presupposition is satisfied. If it is not satisfied, then one of a series of, so to speak, "fallback" conditions becomes activated.

The key point is that the relation same$_L$ is a *theoretical* relation: whether something is or is not the same liquid as this may take an indeterminate amount of scientific investigation to determine. Moreover, even if a "definite" answer has been obtained either through scientific investigation or through the application of some "commonsense" test, the answer is *defeasible*: future investigation might reverse even the most "certain" example. Thus, the fact that an English speaker in 1750 might have called XYZ "water," while he or his successors would not have called XYZ water in 1800 or 1850, does not mean that the "meaning" of "water" changed for the average speaker in the interval. In 1750 or in 1850 or in 1950 one might have pointed to, say, the liquid in Lake Michigan as an example of "water." What changed was that in 1750 we would have mistakenly thought that XYZ bore the relation same$_L$ to the liquid in Lake Michigan, while in 1800 or 1850 we would have known that it did not (I am ignoring the fact that the liquid in Lake Michigan was only dubiously water in 1950, of course).

Let us now modify our science-fiction story. I do not know whether one can make pots and pans out of molybdenum; and if one can make them out of molybdenum, I don't know whether they could be distinguished easily from aluminum pots and pans. (I don't know any of this even though I have acquired the word "molybdenum.") So I shall suppose that molybdenum pots and pans can't be distinguished from aluminum pots and pans save by an expert. (To emphasize the point, I repeat that this could be true for all I know, and a fortiori it could be true for all I know by virtue of "knowing the meaning" of the words *aluminum* and *molybdenum*.) We will now suppose that molybdenum is as common on Twin Earth as aluminum is on Earth, and that aluminum is as rare on Twin Earth as molybdenum is on Earth. In particular, we shall assume that "aluminum" pots and pans are made of molybdenum on Twin Earth. Finally, we shall assume that the words "aluminum" and "molybdenum" are *switched* on Twin Earth: "aluminum" is the name of *molybdenum* and "molybdenum" is the name of *aluminum*.

This example shares some features with the previous one. If a spaceship from Earth visited Twin Earth, the visitors from Earth probably would not suspect that the "aluminum" pots and pans on Twin Earth were not made of aluminum, especially when the Twin Earthians *said* they were. But there is one important difference between the two cases. An Earthian metallurgist could tell very easily that "aluminum" was molybdenum, and a Twin Earthian metallurgist could tell equally easily that aluminum was "molybdenum." (The shudder quotes in the preceding sentence indicate Twin earthian usages.) Whereas in 1750 no one on either Earth or Twin Earth could have distinguished water from "water," the confusion of aluminum with "aluminum" involves only a part of the linguistic communities involved.

The example makes the same point as the preceding one. If Oscar$_1$ and Oscar$_2$ are standard speakers of Earthian English and Twin Earthian English respectively, and neither is chemically or metallurgically sophisticated, then there may be no difference at all in their psychological state when they use the word "aluminum"; nevertheless we have to say that "aluminum" has the extension *aluminum* in the idiolect of Oscar$_1$ and the extension *molybdenum* in the idiolect of Oscar$_2$. (Also we have to say that Oscar$_1$ and Oscar$_2$ mean different things by "aluminum," that "aluminum" has a different meaning on Earth than it does on Twin Earth, etc.) Again we see that the psychological state of the speaker does *not* determine the extension (*or* the "meaning," speaking preanalytically) of the word.

Before discussing this example further, let me introduce a *non*-science-fiction example. Suppose you are like me and cannot tell an elm from a beech tree. We still say that the extension of "elm" in my idiolect is the same as the extension of "elm" in anyone else's, viz., the set of all elm trees, and that the set of all beech trees is the extension of "beech" in *both* of our idiolects. Thus "elm" in my idiolect has a different extension from "beech" in your idiolect (as it should). Is it really credible that this difference in extension is brought about by some difference in our *concepts*? My concept of an elm tree is exactly the same as my concept of a beech tree (I blush to confess). (This shows that the identification of meaning "in the sense of intension" with *concept* cannot be correct, by the way.) If someone heroically attempts to maintain that the difference between the extension of "elm" and the extension of "beech" in *my* idiolect is explained by a difference in my psychological state, then we can always refute him by constructing a "Twin Earth" example – just let the words "elm" and "beech" be switched on Twin Earth (the way "aluminum" and "molybdenum" were in the previous example). Moreover, I suppose I have a *Doppelgänger* on Twin Earth who is molecule for molecule "identical" with me (in the sense in which two neckties can be "identical"). If you are a dualist, then also suppose my *Doppelgänger* thinks the same verbalized thoughts I do, has the same sense data, the same dispositions, etc. It is absurd to think *his* psychological state is one bit different from mine: yet he "means" *beech* when he says "elm" and *I* "mean" *elm* when I say "elm." Cut the pie any way you like, meanings just ain't in the *head*!

5   A Sociolinguistic Hypothesis

The last two examples depend upon a fact about language that seems, surprisingly, never to have been pointed out: that there is *division of linguistic labor*. We could hardly use such words as "elm" and "aluminum" if no one possessed a way of recognizing elm trees and aluminum metal; but not everyone to whom the distinction is important has to be able to make the distinction. Let us shift the example: consider *gold*. Gold is important for many reasons: it is a precious metal, it is a monetary metal, it has symbolic value (it is important to most people that the "gold" wedding ring they wear *really* consist of gold and not just *look* gold), etc. Consider our community as a "factory": in this "factory" some people have the "job" of *wearing gold wedding rings*, other people have the "job" of *selling gold wedding rings*, still other people have the "job" of *telling whether or not something is really gold*. It is not at all necessary or efficient that everyone who wears a gold ring (or a gold cufflink, etc.), or discusses the "gold standard," etc., engage in buying and selling gold. Nor is it necessary or efficient that everyone who buys and sells gold be able to tell whether or not something is really gold in a society where this form of dishonesty is uncommon (selling fake gold) and in which one can easily consult an expert in case of doubt. And it is *certainly* not necessary or efficient that everyone who has occasion to buy or wear gold be able to tell with any reliability whether or not something is really gold.

The foregoing facts are just examples of mundane division of labor (in a wide sense). But they engender a division of linguistic labor: everyone to whom gold is important for any reason has to *acquire* the word "gold"; but he does not have to acquire the *method of recognizing* if something is or is not gold. He can rely on a special subclass of speakers. The features that are generally thought to be present in connection with a general name – necessary and sufficient conditions for membership in the extension, ways of recognizing if something is in the extension ("criteria"), etc. – are all present in the linguistic community *considered as a collective body*; but that collective body divides the "labor" of knowing and employing these various parts of the "meaning" of "gold."

This division of linguistic labor rests upon and presupposes the division of *non*linguistic labor, of course. If only the people who know how to tell if some metal is really gold or not have any reason to have the word "gold" in their vocabulary, then the word "gold" will be as the word "water" was in 1750 with respect to that subclass of speakers, and the other speakers just won't acquire it at all. And some words do not exhibit any division of linguistic labor: "chair," for example. But with the increase of division of labor in the society and the rise of science, more and more words begin to exhibit this kind of division of labor. "Water," for example, did not exhibit it at all prior to the rise of chemistry. Today it is obviously necessary for every speaker to be able to recognize water (reliably under normal conditions), and probably every adult speaker even knows the necessary and sufficient condition "water is H_2O," but only a few adult speakers could distinguish water from liquids which superficially resembled water. In case of doubt, other speakers would rely on the judgement of these "expert" speakers. Thus the way of recognizing possessed by these "expert" speakers is also, through them, possessed by the collective linguistic body, even though it is not possessed by each individual member of the body, and in this way the most recherché fact about water may become part of the *social* meaning of the word while being unknown to almost all speakers who acquire the word.

It seems to me that this phenomenon of division of linguistic labor is one which it will be very important for sociolinguistics to investigate. In connection with it, I should like to propose the following hypothesis:

> HYPOTHESIS OF THE UNIVERSALITY OF THE DIVISION OF LINGUISTIC LABOR: Every linguistic community exemplifies the sort of division of linguistic labor just described: that is, possesses at least some terms whose associated "criteria" are known only to a subset of the speakers who acquire the terms, and whose use by the other speakers depends upon a structured cooperation between them and the speakers in the relevant subsets

It would be of interest, in particular, to discover if extremely primitive peoples were sometimes exceptions to this hypothesis (which would indicate that the division of linguistic labor is a product of social evolution), or if even they exhibit it. In the latter case, one might conjecture that division of labor, including linguistic labor, is a fundamental trait of our species.

It is easy to see how this phenomenon accounts for some of the examples given above of the failure of the assumptions (1), (2). Whenever a term is subject to the division of linguistic labor, the "average" speaker who acquires it does not acquire anything that fixes its extension. In particular, his individual psychological state *certainly* does not fix its extension; it is only the sociolinguistic state of the collective linguistic body to which the speaker belongs that fixes the extension.

We may summarize this discussion by pointing out that there are two sorts of tool in the world: there are tools like a hammer or a screwdriver which can be used by one person; and there are tools like a steamship which require the cooperative activity of a number of persons to use. Words have been thought of too much on the model of the first sort of tool.

6   Indexicality and Rigidity[6]

The first of our science-fiction examples – "water" on Earth and on Twin Earth in 1750 – does not involve division of linguistic labor, or at least does not involve it in the same way the examples of "aluminum" and "elm" do. There were not (in our story, anyway) any "experts" on water on Earth in 1750, nor any experts on "water" on Twin Earth. (The example *can* be construed as involving division of labor *across time*, however. I shall not develop this method of treating the example here.) The example *does* involve things which are of fundamental importance to the theory of reference and also to the theory of necessary truth, which we shall now discuss.

There are two obvious ways of telling someone what one means by a natural-kind term such as "water" or "tiger" or "lemon." One can give him a so-called ostensive definition – "this (liquid) is water"; "this (animal) is a tiger"; "this (fruit) is a lemon"; where the parentheses are meant to indicate that the "markers" *liquid, animal, fruit,* may be either explicit or implicit. Or one can give him a *description*. In the latter case the description one gives typically consists of one or more markers together with a *stereotype*[7] – a standardized description of features of the kind that are typical, or "normal," or at any rate stereotypical. The central features of the stereotype generally are *criteria* – features which in normal situations constitute ways of recognizing if a thing belongs to the kind or, at least, necessary conditions (or probabilistic necessary conditions) for membership in the kind. Not all criteria used by the linguistic community as a collective body are included in the stereotype, and in some cases the stereotypes may be quite weak. Thus (unless I am a very atypical speaker), the stereotype of an elm is just that of a common deciduous tree. These features are indeed necessary conditions for membership in the kind (I mean "necessary" in a loose sense; I don't think "elm trees are deciduous" is *analytic*), but they fall far short of constituting a way of recognizing elms. On the other hand, the stereotype of a tiger does enable one to recognize tigers (unless they are albino, or some other atypical circumstance is present), and the stereotype of a lemon generally enables one to recognize lemons. In the extreme case, the stereotype may be *just* the marker: the stereotype of molybdenum might be *just* that molybdenum is a *metal*. Let us consider both of these ways of introducing a term into someone's vocabulary.

Suppose I point to a glass of liquid and say "*this* is water," in order to teach someone the word "water." We have already described some of the empirical presuppositions of this act, and the way in which this kind of meaning-explanation is defeasible. Let us now try to clarify further how it is supposed to be taken.

In what follows, we shall take the notion of "possible world" as primitive. We do this because we feel that in several senses the notion makes sense and is scientifically important even if it needs to be made more precise. We shall assume further that in at least some cases it is possible to speak of the same individual as existing in more than one possible world.[8] Our discussion leans heavily on the work of Saul Kripke, although the conclusions were obtained independently.

Let W_1 and W_2 be two possible worlds in which I exist and in which this glass exists and in which I am giving a meaning explanation by pointing to this glass and saying "this is water." (We do *not* assume that the *liquid* in the glass is the same in both worlds.) Let us suppose that in W_1 the glass is full of H_2O and in W_2 the glass is full of XYZ. We shall also suppose that W_1 is the actual world and that XYZ is the stuff typically called "water" in the world W_2 (so that the relation between English speakers in W_1 and English speakers in W_2 is exactly the same as the relation between English speakers on Earth and English speakers on Twin Earth). Then there are two theories one might have concerning the meaning of "water."

1   One might hold that "water" was *world-relative* but *constant* in meaning (i.e., the word has a *constant relative meaning*). In this theory, "water" *means the same* in W_1 and W_2; it's just that water is H_2O in W_1 and water is XYZ in W_2.
2   One might hold that water is H_2O in all worlds (the stuff called "water" in W_2 isn't water), but "water" doesn't have the same meaning in W_1 and W_2.

If what was said before about the Twin Earth case was correct, then (2) is clearly the correct theory. When I say "*this* (liquid) is water," the "this" is, so to speak, a *de re* "this" –

i.e., the force of my explanation is that "water" is whatever bears a certain equivalence relation (the relation we called "same$_L$" above) to the piece of liquid referred to as "this" *in the actual world*.

We might symbolize the difference between the two theories as a "scope" difference in the following way. In theory (1), the following is true:

(1′)   (For every world W) (For every x in W) (x is water $\equiv$ x bears same$_L$ to the entity referred to as "this" in W)

while on theory (2):

(2′)   (For every world W) (For every x in W) (x is water $\equiv$ x bears same$_L$ to the entity referred to as "this" *in the actual world W_1*).

(I call this a "scope" difference because in (1′) "the entity referred to as 'this'" is within the scope of "For every world W" – as the qualifying phrase "in W" makes explicit, whereas in (2′) "the entity referred to as 'this'" means "the entity referred to as 'this' *in the actual world*," and has thus a reference *independent* of the bound variable "W.")

Kripke calls a designator "rigid" (in a given sentence) if (in that sentence) it refers to the same individual in every possible world in which the designator designates. If we extend the notion of rigidity to substance names, then we may express Kripke's theory and mine by saying that the term "water" is *rigid*.

The rigidity of the term "water" follows from the fact that when I give the ostensive definition "*this* (liquid) is water" I intend (2′) and not (1′).

We may also say, following Kripke, that when I give the ostensive definition "this (liquid) is water," the demonstrative "this" is *rigid*.

What Kripke was the first to observe is that this theory of the meaning (or "use," or whatever) of the word "water" (and other natural-kind terms as well) has startling consequences for the theory of necessary truth.

To explain this, let me introduce the notion of a *cross-world relation*. A two-term relation R will be called *cross-world* when it is understood in such a way that its extension is a set of ordered pairs of individuals *not all in the same possible world*. For example, it is easy to understand the relation *same height as* as a cross-world relation: just understand it so that, e.g., if x is an individual in a world W_1 who is five feet tall (in W_1) and y is an individual in W_2 who is five feet tall (in W_2), then the ordered pair x, y belongs to the extension of *same height as*. (Since an individual may have different heights in different possible worlds in which that same individual exists, strictly speaking it is not the ordered pair x, y that constitutes an element of the extension of *same height as*, but rather the ordered pair x-in-world-W_1, y-in-world-W_2.)

Similarly, we can understand the relation *same$_L$* (same liquid as) as a cross-world relation by understanding it so that a liquid in world W_1 which has the same important physical properties (in W_1) that a liquid in W_2 possesses (in W_2) bears *same$_L$* to the latter liquid.

Then the theory we have been presenting may be summarized by saying that an entity x, in an arbitrary possible world, is *water* if and only if it bears the relation *same$_L$* (construed as a cross-world relation) to the stuff *we* call "water" in the *actual* world.

Suppose, now, that I have not yet discovered what the important physical properties of water are (in the actual world) – i.e., I don't yet know that water is H_2O. I may have ways of *recognizing* water that are successful (of course, I may make a small number of mistakes that I won't be able to detect until a later stage in our scientific development) but not know the microstructure of water. If I agree that a liquid with the superficial properties of "water" but a different microstructure *isn't really water*, then my ways of recognizing water (my "operational definition," so to speak) cannot be regarded as an analytical specification of *what it is to be water*. Rather, the operational definition, like the ostensive one, is simply a way of pointing out a standard – pointing out the stuff *in the actual world* such that for x to be water, in *any* world, is for x to bear the relation $same_L$ to the *normal* members of the class of *local* entities that satisfy the operational definition. "Water" on Twin Earth is not water, even if it satisfies the operational definition, because it doesn't bear $same_L$ to the local stuff that satisfies the operational definition, and local stuff that satisfies the operational definition but has a microstructure different from rest of the local stuff that satisfies the operational definition isn't water either, because it doesn't bear $same_L$ to the *normal* examples of the local "water."

Suppose, now, that I discover the microstructure of water – that water is H_2O. At this point I will be able to say that the stuff on Twin Earth that I earlier *mistook* for water isn't really water. In the same way, if you describe not another planet in the actual universe, but another possible universe in which there is stuff with the chemical formula XYZ which passes the "operational test" for *water*, we shall have to say that that stuff isn't water but merely XYZ. You will not have described a possible world in which "water is XYZ," but merely a possible world in which there are lakes of XYZ, people drink XYZ (and not water), or whatever. In fact, once we have discovered the nature of water, nothing counts as a possible world in which water doesn't have that nature. Once we have discovered that water (in the actual world) is H_2O, *nothing counts as a possible world in which water isn't H_2O.* In particular, if a "logically possible" statement is one that holds in some "logically possible world," *it isn't logically possible that water isn't H_2O.*

On the other hand, we can perfectly well imagine having experiences that would convince us (and that would make it rational to believe that) water *isn't* H_2O. In that sense, it is conceivable that water isn't H_2O. It is conceivable but it isn't logically possible! Conceivability is no proof of logical possibility.

Kripke refers to statements which are rationally unrevisable (assuming there are such) as *epistemically necessary*. Statements which are true in all possible worlds he refers to simply as necessary (or sometimes as "metaphysically necessary"). In this terminology, the point just made can be restated as: a statement can be (metaphysically) necessary and epistemically contingent. Human intuition has no privileged access to metaphysical necessity.

Since Kant there has been a big split between philosophers who thought that all necessary truths were analytic and philosophers who thought that some necessary truths were synthetic a priori. But none of these philosophers thought that a (metaphysically) necessary truth could fail to be a priori: the Kantian tradition was as guilty as the empiricist tradition of equating metaphysical and epistemic necessity. In this sense Kripke's challenge to received doctrine goes far beyond the usual empiricism/Kantianism oscillation.

In this paper our interest is in theory of meaning, however, and not in theory of necessary truth. Points closely related to Kripke's have been made in terms of the notion of *indexicality*.[9] Words like "now," "this," "here," have long been recognized to be *indexical*, or *token-reflexive* – i.e., to have an extension which varied from context to context or token to token. For these words no one has ever suggested the traditional theory that "intension determines extension." To take our Twin Earth example: if I have a *Doppelgänger* on Twin Earth, then when I think "I have a headache," *he* thinks "I have a headache." But the extension of the particular token of "I" in his verbalized thought is himself (or his unit class, to be precise), while the extension of the token of "I" in my verbalized thought is *me* (or my unit class, to be precise). So the same word, "I," has two different extensions in two different idiolects; but it does not follow that the concept I have of myself is in any way different from the concept my *Doppelgänger* has of himself.

Now then, we have maintained that indexicality extends beyond the *obviously* indexical words and morphemes (e.g., the tenses of verbs). Our theory can be summarized as saying that words like "water" have an unnoticed indexical component: "water" is stuff that bears a certain similarity relation to the water *around here*. Water at another time or in another place or even in another possible world has to bear the relation $same_L$ to our *"water" in order to be water*. Thus the theory that (1) words have "intensions," which are something like concepts associated with the words by speakers; and that (2) intension determines extension, cannot be true of natural-kind words like "water" for the same reason the theory cannot be true of obviously indexical words like "I."

The theory that natural-kind words like "water" are indexical leaves it open, however, whether to say that "water" in the Twin Earth dialect of English has the same *meaning* as "water" in the Earth dialect and a different extension (which is what we normally say about "I" in different idiolects), thereby giving up the doctrine that "meaning (intension) determines extension"; or to say, as we have chosen to do, that difference is extension is ipso facto a difference in meaning for natural-kind words, thereby giving up the doctrine that meanings are concepts, or, indeed, mental entities of *any* kind.

It should be clear, however, that Kripke's doctrine that natural-kind words are rigid designators and our doctrine that they are indexical are but two ways of making the same point. We heartily endorse what Kripke says when he writes:

> Let us suppose that we do fix the reference of a name by a description. Even if we do so, we do not then make the name synonymous with the description, but instead we use the name rigidly to refer to the object so named, even in talking about counterfactual situations where the thing named would not satisfy the description in question. Now, this is what I think is in fact true for those cases of naming where the reference is fixed by description. But, in fact, I also think, contrary to most recent theorists, that the reference of names is rarely or almost never fixed by means of description. And by this I do not just mean what Searle says: "It's not a single description, but rather a cluster, a family of properties that fixes the reference." I mean that properties in this sense are not used at all.[10]

7   Let's Be Realistic

I wish now to contrast my view with one which is popular, at least among students (it appears to arise spontaneously). For this discussion, let us take as our example of a natural-kind word the word *gold*. We will not distinguish between "gold" and the cognate words in Greek, Latin, etc. And we will focus on "gold" in the sense of gold in the solid state. With this understood, we maintain: "gold" has not changed its *extension* (or not changed it significantly) in two thousand years. Our methods of *identifying* gold have grown incredibly sophisticated. But the extension of χρυσος in Archimedes' dialect of Greek is the same as the extension of *gold* in my dialect of English.

It is possible (and let us suppose it to be the case) that just as there were pieces of metal which could *not* have been determined not to be gold prior to Archimedes, so there were or are pieces of metal which could not have been determined *not* to be gold in Archimedes' day, but which we can distinguish from gold quite easily with modern techniques. Let X be such a piece of metal. Clearly X does not lie in the extension of "gold" in standard English; my view is that it did not lie in the extension of "χρυος" in Attic Greek, either, although an ancient Greek would have *mistaken X* for gold (or, rather, χρυος).

The alternative view is that "gold" *means* whatever satisfies the contemporary "operational definition" of *gold*. "Gold" a hundred years ago meant whatever satisfied the "operational definition" of *gold* in use a hundred years ago; "gold" now means whatever satisfies the operational definition of *gold* in use in 1973; and "χρυος" meant whatever satisfied the operational definition of χρυος in use *then*.

One common motive for adopting this point of view is a certain skepticism about *truth*. In the view I am advocating, when Archimedes asserted that something was gold (χρυος) he was not just saying that it had the superficial characteristics of gold (in exceptional cases, something may belong to a natural kind and *not* have the superficial characteristics of a member of that natural kind, in fact); he was saying that it had the same general *hidden structure* (the same "essence," so to speak) as any normal piece of local gold. Archimedes would have said that our hypothetical piece of metal *X* was gold, but he would have been *wrong*. But *who's to say* he would have been wrong?

The obvious answer is: *we are* (using the best theory available today). For most people either the question (*who's to say?*) has bite, and our answer has no bite, or our answer has bite and the question has no bite. Why is this?

The reason, I believe, is that people tend either to be strongly anti-realistic or strongly realistic in their intuitions. To a strongly anti-realistic intuition it makes little sense to say that what is in the extension of Archimedes' term "χρυος" is to be determined using *our* theory. For the anti-realist does not see our theory and Archimedes" theory as two approximately correct descriptions of some fixed realm of theory-independent entities, and he tends to be skeptical about the idea of "convergence" in science – he does not think our theory is a *better* description of the *same* entities that Archimedes was describing. But if our theory is just our theory, then to use it in deciding whether or not *X* lies in the extension of "χρυος" is just as arbitrary as using Neanderthal theory to decide whether or not *X* lies in the extension of "χρυος." The only theory that it is *not* arbitrary to use is the one the speaker himself subscribes to.

The trouble is that for a strong anti-realist *truth* makes no sense except as an intratheoretic notion.[11] The anti-realist can use truth intratheoretically in the sense of a "redundancy theory"; but he does not have the notions of truth and reference available *extratheoretically*. But *extension is tied to the notion of truth*. The extension of a term is just what the term is *true of*. Rather than try to retain the notion of extension via an awkward operationalism, the anti-realist should reject the notion of extension as he does the notion of truth (in any extratheoretic sense). Like Dewey, for example, he can fall back on a notion of "warranted assertibility" instead of truth (relativized to the scientific method, if he thinks there is a *fixed* scientific method, or to the best methods available at the time, if he agrees with Dewey that the scientific method itself evolves). Then he can say that "*X* is gold (χρυος)" was warrantedly assertible in Archimedes" time and is not warrantedly assertible today (indeed, this is a *minimal* claim, in the sense that it represents the minimum that the realist and the anti-realist can agree on); but the assertion that *X* was in the extension of "χρυος" will be rejected as meaningless, like the assertion that "*X* is gold (χρυος)" was *true*.

It is well known that narrow operationalism cannot successfully account for the actual use of scientific or commonsense terms. Loosened versions of operationalism, like Carnap's version of Ramsey's theory, agree with, if they do not account for, actual scientific use (mainly because the loosened versions agree with any possible use!), but at the expense of making the communicability of scientific results a *miracle*. It is beyond question that scientists use terms as if the associated criteria were not *necessary and sufficient conditions*, but rather *approximately* correct characterizations of some world of theory-independent entities, and that they talk as if later theories in a mature science were, in general, *better* descriptions of the *same* entities that earlier theories referred to. In my opinion the hypothesis that this is *right* is the only hypothesis that can account for the communicability of scientific results, the closure of acceptable scientific theories under first-order logic, and many other features of the scientific method.[12] But it is not my task to argue this here. My point is that if we are to use the notions of truth and extension in an extratheoretic way (i.e., to regard those notions as defined for statements couched in the languages of theories other than our own), then we should accept the realist perspective to which those notions belong. The doubt about whether *we* can say that X does not lie in the extension of "gold" as *Jones* used it is the *same* doubt as the doubt whether it makes sense to think of Jones's statement that "X is gold" as *true or false* (and not just "warrantedly assertible for Jones and not warrantedly assertible for us"). To square the notion of truth, which is essentially a realist notion, with one's anti-realist prejudices by adopting an untenable theory of meaning is no progress.

A second motive for adopting an extreme operationalist account is a dislike of unverifiable hypotheses. At first blush it may seem as if we are saying that "X is gold (χρυος)" was false in Archimedes' time although Archimedes could not *in principle* have known that it was false. But this is not exactly the situation. The fact is that there is a host of situations that *we* can describe (using the very theory that tells us that X isn't gold) in which X would have behaved quite unlike the rest of the stuff Archimedes classified as gold. Perhaps X would have separated into two different metals when melted, or would have had different conductivity properties, or would have vaporized at a different temperature, or whatever. If we had performed the experiments with Archimedes watching, he might not have known the theory, but he would have been able to check the empirical regularity that "X behaves differently from the rest of the stuff I classify as χρυος in several respects." Eventually he would have concluded that "X may not be gold."

The point is that even if something satisfies the criteria used at a given time to identify gold (i.e., to recognize if something is gold), it may behave differently in one or more situations from the rest of the stuff that satisfies the criteria. This may not *prove* that it isn't gold, but it puts the hypothesis that it may not be gold in the running, even in the absence of theory. If, now, we had gone on to inform Archimedes that gold had such and such a molecular structure (except for X), and that X behaved differently because it had a different molecular structure, is there any doubt that he would have agreed with us that X isn't gold? In any case, to worry because things may be *true* (at a given time) that can't be *verified* (at that time) seems to me ridiculous. In any reasonable view there are surely things that are true and can't be verified at *any* time. For example, suppose there are infinitely many binary stars. Must we be able to verify this, even *in principle*?[13]

So far we have dealt with *metaphysical* reasons for rejecting our account. But someone might disagree with us about the empirical facts concerning the intentions of speakers. This would be the case if, for instance, someone thought that Archimedes (in the *Gedankenexperiment* described above) would have said: "it doesn't matter if X does act differently from other pieces of gold; X is a piece of gold, because X has such-and-such properties and that's all it takes to be gold." While, indeed, we cannot be certain that natural-kind words in ancient Greek had the properties of the corresponding words in present-day English, there cannot be any serious doubt concerning the properties of the latter. If we put philosophical prejudices aside, then I believe that we know perfectly well that no operational definition does provide a necessary and sufficient condition for the application of any such word. We may give an "operational definition," or a cluster of properties, or whatever, but the intention is never to "make the name *synonymous* with the description." Rather "we use the name *rigidly*" to refer to whatever things share the *nature* that things satisfying the description normally possess.

8 Other Senses

What we have analyzed so far is the predominant sense of natural-kind words (or, rather, the predominant *extension*). But natural-kind words typically possess a number of senses. (Ziff has even suggested that they possess a *continuum* of senses.)

Part of this can be explained on the basis of our theory. To be water, for example, is to bear the relation $same_L$ to certain things. But what is the relation $same_L$?

x bears the relation $same_L$ to y just in case (1) x and y are both liquids, and (2) x and y agree in important physical properties. The term "liquid" is itself a natural-kind term that I shall not try to analyze here. The term "property" is a broad-spectrum term that we have analyzed in previous papers. What I want to focus on now is the notion of *importance*. Importance is an interest-relative notion. Normally the "important" properties of a liquid or solid, etc., are the ones that are *structurally* important: the ones that specify what the liquid or solid, etc., is ultimately made out of – elementary particles, or hydrogen and oxygen, or earth, air, fire, water, or whatever – and how they are arranged or combined to produce the superficial characteristics. From this point of view the characteristic of a typical bit of water is consisting of H_2O. But it may or may not be important that there are impurities; thus, in one context "water" may mean *chemically pure water*, while in another it may mean the stuff in Lake Michigan. And a speaker may sometimes refer to XYZ as water if one is *using* it as water. Again, normally it is important that water is in the liquid state; but sometimes it is unimportant, and one may refer to a single H_2O molecule as water, or to water vapor as water ("water in the air").

Even senses that are so far out that they have to be regarded as a bit "deviant" may bear a definite relation to the core sense. For example, I might say "did you see the lemon," meaning the *plastic* lemon. A less deviant case is this: we discover "tigers" on Mars. That is, they look just like tigers, but they have a silicon-based chemistry instead of a carbon-based chemistry. (A remarkable example of parallel evolution!) Are Martian "tigers" tigers? It depends on the context.

In the case of this theory, as in the case of any theory that is orthogonal to the way people have thought about something previously, misunderstandings are certain to arise. One which has already arisen is the following: a critic has maintained that the *predominant* sense of, say, "lemon" is the one in which anything with (a sufficient number of) the superficial characteristics of a lemon is a lemon. The same critic has suggested that having the hidden structure – the genetic code – of a lemon is necessary to being a lemon only when "lemon" is used as a term of *science*. Both of these contentions seem to me to rest on a misunderstanding, or, perhaps, a pair of complementary misunderstandings. The sense in which literally anything with the superficial characteristics of a lemon is necessarily a lemon, far from being the dominant one, is extremely deviant. In that sense something would be a lemon if it looked and tasted like a lemon, even if it had a silicon-based chemistry, for example, or even if an electron-microscope revealed it to be a machine. (Even if we include growing "like a lemon" in the superficial characteristics, this does not exclude the silicon lemon, if there are "lemon" trees on Mars. It doesn't even exclude the machine-lemon; maybe the tree is a machine too!)

At the same time the sense in which to be a lemon something has to have the genetic code of a lemon is *not* the same as the technical sense (if there is one, which I doubt). The technical sense, I take it, would be one in which "lemon" was *synonymous* with a description which *specified* the genetic code. But when we said (to change the example) that to be *water* something has to be H_2O we did not mean, as we made clear, that the *speaker* has to *know* this. It is only by confusing *metaphysical* necessity with *epistemological* necessity that one can conclude that, if the (metaphysically necessary) truth condition for being water is being H_2O, then "water" must be synonymous with H_2O – in which case it is certainly a term of science. And similarly, even though the predominant sense of "lemon" is one in which to be a lemon something has to have the genetic code of a lemon (I believe), it does not follow that "lemon" is synonymous with a description which specifies the genetic code explicitly or otherwise.

The mistake of thinking that there is an important sense of "lemon" (perhaps the predominant one) in which to have the superficial characteristics of a lemon is at least *sufficient* for being a lemon is more plausible if among the superficial characteristics one includes *being cross-fertile with lemons*. But the characteristic of being cross-fertile with lemons presupposes the notion of being a lemon. Thus, even if one can obtain a sufficient condition in *this* way, to take this as inconsistent with the characterization offered here is question-begging. Moreover, the characterization in terms of *lemon*, presupposing "superficial characteristics" (like being cross-fertile with *lemons*), gives no truth condition which would enable us to decide which objects in other possible worlds (or which objects a million years ago, or which objects a million light years from here) are lemons. (In addition, I don't think this characterization, question-begging as it is, is *correct*, even as a sufficient condition. I think one could invent cases in which something which was not a lemon was cross-fertile with lemons and looked like a lemon, etc.)

Again, one might try to rule out the case of the machine-lemon (lemon-machine?) which "grows" on a machine-tree (tree-machine?) by saying that "growing" is not really *growing*. That is right; but it's right because *grow* is a natural-kind *verb*, and precisely the sort of account we have been presenting applies to *it*.

Another misunderstanding that should be avoided is the following: to take the account we have developed as implying that the members of the extension of a natural-kind word necessarily *have* a common hidden structure. It could have turned out that the bits of liquid we call "water" had *no* important common physical characteristics *except* the superficial ones. In that case the necessary and sufficient condition for being "water" would have been possession of sufficiently many of the superficial characteristics.

Incidentally, the last statement does not imply that water could have failed to have a hidden structure (or that water could have been anything but H_2O). When we say that it could have *turned out* that water had no hidden structure what we mean is that a liquid with no hidden structure (i.e., many bits of different liquids, with nothing in common *except* superficial characteristics) could have looked like water, tasted like water, and have filled the lakes, etc., that are actually full of water. In short, we could have been in the same epistemological situation with respect to a liquid with no hidden structure as we were actually with respect to water at one time. Compare Kripke on the "lectern made of ice."[14]

There are, in fact, almost continuously many cases. Some diseases, for example, have turned out to have no hidden structure (the only thing the paradigm cases have in common is a cluster of symptoms), while others have turned out to have a common hidden structure in the sense of an etiology (e.g., tuberculosis). Sometimes we still don't know; there is a controversy still raging about the case of multiple sclerosis.

An interesting case is the case of *jade*. Although the Chinese do not recognize a difference, the term "jade" applies to two minerals: jadeite and nephrite. Chemically, there is a marked difference. Jadeite is a combination of sodium and aluminum. Nephrite is made of calcium, magnesium, and iron. These two quite different microstructures produce the same unique textural qualities!

Coming back to the Twin Earth example, for a moment; if H_2O and XYZ had both been plentiful on Earth, then we would have had a case similar to the jadeite/nephrite case: it would have been correct to say that there were *two kinds of "water."* And instead of saying that "the stuff on Twin Earth turned out not to really be water," we would have to say "it turned out to be the *XYZ kind of water.*"

To sum up: if there is a hidden structure, then generally it determines what it is to be a member of the natural kind, not only in the actual world, but in all possible worlds. Put another way, it determines what we can and cannot counterfactually suppose about the natural kind ("water could have all been vapor?" yes/"water could have been XYZ" no). But the local water, or whatever, may have two or more hidden structures – or so many that "hidden structure" becomes irrelevant, and superficial characteristics become the decisive ones.

9   Other Words

So far we have only used natural-kind words as examples; but the points we have made apply to many other kinds of words as well. They apply to the great majority of all nouns, and to other parts of speech as well.

Let us consider for a moment the names of artifacts – words like "pencil," "chair," "bottle," etc. The traditional view is that these words are certainly defined by conjunctions, or possibly clusters, of properties. Anything with all of the properties in the conjunction (or sufficiently many of the properties in the cluster, on the cluster model) is necessarily a *pencil*, *chair*, *bottle*, or whatever. In addition, some of the properties in the cluster (on the cluster model) are usually held to be *necessary* (on the conjunction-of-properties model, *all* of the properties in the conjunction are necessary*)*. *Being an artifact* is supposedly necessary, and belonging to a kind with a certain standard purpose – e.g., "pencils are artifacts" and "pencils are standardly intended to be written with" are supposed to be necessary. Finally, this sort of necessity is held to be *epistemic* necessity – in fact, analyticity.

Let us once again engage in science-fiction. This time we use an example devised by Rogers Albritton. Imagine that we someday discover that *pencils are organisms*. We cut them open and examine them under the electron microscope, and we see the almost invisible tracery of nerves and other organs. We spy upon them, and we see them spawn, and we see the offspring grow into full-grown pencils. We discover that these organisms are not imitating other (artifactual) pencils – there are not and never were any pencils except these organisms. It is strange, to be sure, that there is *lettering* on many of these organisms – e.g., BONDED *Grants* DELUXE made in USA No. 2 – perhaps they are intelligent organisms, and this is their form of camouflage. (We also have to explain why no one ever attempted to manufacture pencils, etc., but this is clearly a possible world, in some sense.)

If this is conceivable, and I agree with Albritton that it is, then it is epistemically possible that *pencils could turn out to be organisms*. It follows that *pencils are artifacts* is not epistemically necessary in the strongest sense and, a fortiori, not analytic.

Let us be careful, however. Have we shown that there is a possible world in which pencils are organisms? I think not. What we have shown is that there is a possible world in which certain organisms are the *epistemic counterparts* of pencils (the phrase is Kripke's). To return to the device of Twin Earth: imagine this time that pencils on Earth are just what we think they are, artifacts manufactured to be written with, while "pencils" on Twin Earth are organisms à la Albritton. Imagine, further, that this is totally unsuspected by the Twin Earthians – they have exactly the beliefs about "pencils" that we have about pencils. When we discovered this, we would not say: "some pencils are organisms." We would be far more likely to say: "the things on Twin Earth that pass for pencils aren't really pencils. They're really a species of organism."

Suppose now the situation to be as in Albritton's example both on Earth and on Twin Earth. Then we would say "pencils are organisms." Thus, whether the "pencil-organisms" on Twin Earth (or in another possible universe) are really *pencils* or not is a function of whether or not the local pencils are organisms or not. If the local pencils are just what we think they are, then a possible world in which there are pencil-organisms is *not* a possible world in which *pencils are organisms*; there are *no* possible worlds in which pencils are organisms in this case (which is, of course, the actual one). That pencils are artifacts is necessary in the sense of true in all possible worlds – metaphysically necessary. But it doesn't follow that it's epistemically necessary.

It follows that "pencil" is not *synonymous* with any description – not even loosely synonymous with a *loose* description. When we use the word "pencil," we intend to refer to whatever has the same *nature* as the normal examples of the local pencils in the actual world. "Pencil" is just as *indexical* as "water" or "gold."

In a way, the case of pencils turning out to be organisms is complementary to the case we discussed some years ago[15] of cats turning out to be robots (remotely controlled from Mars). In Katz (forthcoming),[16] Katz argues that we misdescribed this case: that the case should rather be described as its *turning out that there are no cats in this world*. Katz admits that we might *say* "Cats have turned out not to be animals, but robots"; but he argues that this is a semantically deviant sentence which is glossed as "the things I am referring to as 'cats' have turned out not to be animals, but robots." Katz's theory is bad linguistics, however. First of all, the explanation of how it is we can *say* "Cats are robots" is simply an all-purpose explanation of how we can say *anything*. More important, Katz's theory predicts that "Cats are robots" is *deviant*, while "There are no cats in the world" is nondeviant, in fact standard, in the case described. Now then, I don't deny that there *is* a case in which "There are not (and never were) any cats in the world" would be standard: we might (speaking epistemically) discover that we have been suffering from a collective hallucination. ("Cats" are like pink elephants.) But in the case I described, "Cats have turned out to be robots remotely controlled from Mars" is surely nondeviant, and "There are no cats in the world" is highly deviant.

Incidentally, Katz's account is not only bad linguistics; it is also bad as a rational reconstruction. The reason we *don't* use "cat" as synonymous with a description is surely that we know enough about cats to know that they do have a hidden structure, and it is good scientific methodology to use the name to refer rigidly to the things that possess that hidden structure, and not to whatever happens to satisfy some description. Of course, if we *knew* the hidden structure we could frame a description in terms of *it*; but we don't at this point. In this sense the use of natural-kind words reflects an important fact about our relation to the world: we know that there are kinds of thing with common hidden structure, but we don't yet have the knowledge to describe all those hidden structures.

Katz's view has more plausibility in the "pencil" case than in the "cat" case, however. We think we *know* a necessary and sufficient condition for being a *pencil*, albeit a vague one. So it is possible to make "pencil" synonymous with a loose description. We *might* say, in the case that "pencils turned out to be organisms" *either* "Pencils have turned out to be organisms" *or* "There are no pencils in the world" – i.e., we might use "pencil" either as a natural-kind word or as a "one-criterion" word.[17]

On the other hand, we might doubt that there *are* any true one-criterion words in natural language, apart from stipulative contexts. Couldn't it turn out that pediatricians aren't doctors but Martian spies? Answer "yes," and you have abandoned the synonymy of "pediatrician" and "doctor specializing in the care of children." It seems that there is a strong tendency for words which are introduced as "one-criterion" words to develop a "natural-kind" sense, with all the concomitant rigidity and indexicality. In the case of artifact names, this natural-kind sense seems to be the predominant one.

(There is a joke about a patient who is on the verge of being discharged from an insane asylum. The doctors have been questioning him for some time, and he has been giving perfectly sane responses. They decide to let him leave, and at the end of the interview one of the doctors inquires casually, "What do you want to be when you get out?" "A teakettle." The joke would not be intelligible if it were literally inconceivable that a person could be a teakettle.)

There are, however, words which retain an almost pure one-criterion character. These are words whose meaning derives from a transformation: *hunter = one who hunts.*

Not only does the account given here apply to most nouns, but it also applies to other parts of speech. Verbs like "grow," adjectives like "red," etc., all have indexical features. On the other hand, some syncategorematic words seem to have more of a one-criterion character. "Whole," for example, can be explained thus: *The army surrounded the town* could be true even if the *A* division did not take part. *The whole army surrounded the town* means every part of the army (of the relevant kind, e.g., the *A* division) took part in the action signified by the verb.[18]

10   Meaning

Let us now see where we are with respect to the notion of meaning. We have now seen that the extension of a term is not fixed by a concept that the individual speaker has in his head, and this is true both because extension is, in general, determined *socially* – there is division of linguistic labor as much as of "real" labor – and because extension is, in part, determined *indexically*. The extension of our terms depends upon the actual nature of the particular things that serve as paradigms,[19] and this actual nature is not, in general, fully known to the speaker. Traditional semantic theory leaves out only two contributions to the determination of extension – the contribution of society and the contribution of the real world!

We saw at the outset that meaning cannot be identified with extension. Yet it cannot be identified with "intension" either, if intension is something like an individual speaker's *concept*. What are we to do?

There are two plausible routes that we might take. One route would be to retain the identification of meaning with concept and pay the price of giving up the idea that meaning determines extension. If we followed this route, we might say that "water" has the same *meaning* on Earth and on Twin Earth, but a different *extension*. (Not just a different *local* extension but a different *global* extension. The *XYZ* on Twin Earth isn't in the extension of the tokens of "water" that I utter, but it is in the extension of the tokens of "water" that my

Doppelgänger utters, and this isn't just because Twin Earth is far away from me, since molecules of H_2O are in the extension of the tokens of "water" that I utter no matter how far away from me they are in space and time. Also, what I can counterfactually suppose water to be is different from what my *Doppelgänger* can counterfactually suppose "water" to be.) While this is the correct route to take for an *absolutely* indexical word like "I," it seems incorrect for the words we have been discussing. Consider "elm" and "beech," for example. If these are "switched" on Twin Earth, then surely we would *not* say that "elm" has the same meaning on Earth and Twin Earth, even if my *Doppelgänger*'s stereotype of a beech (or an "elm," as he calls it) is identical with my stereotype of an elm. Rather, we would say that "elm" in my *Doppelgänger*'s idiolect means *beech*. For this reason, it seems preferable to take a different route and identify "meaning" with an ordered pair (or possibly an ordered *n*-tuple) of entities, *one of which is the extension*. (The other components of the, so to speak, "meaning vector" will be specified later). Doing this makes it trivially true that *meaning determines extension* (i.e., difference in extension is ipso facto difference in meaning), but totally abandons the idea that if there is a difference in the meaning my *Doppelgänger* and I assign to a word, then there *must* be some difference in our concepts (or in our psychological state). Following this route, we can say that my *Doppelgänger* and I *mean something different* when we say "elm," but this will not be an assertion about our psychological states. All this means is that the tokens of the word he utters have a different extension than the tokens of the word I utter; but this difference in extension is not a reflection of any difference in our individual linguistic competence considered in isolation.

If this is correct, and I think it is, then the traditional problem of meaning splits into two problems. The first problem is to account for the *determination of extension*. Since, in many cases, extension is determined socially and not individually, owing to the division of linguistic labor, I believe that this problem is properly a problem for sociolinguistics. Solving it would involve spelling out in detail exactly how the division of linguistic labor works. The so-called "causal theory of reference," introduced by Kripke for proper names and extended by us to natural-kind words and physical-magnitude terms,[20] falls into this province. For the fact that, in many contexts, we assign to the tokens of a name that I utter whatever referent we assign to the tokens of the same name uttered by the person from whom I acquired the name (so that the reference is transmitted from speaker to speaker, starting from the speakers who were present at the "naming ceremony," even though no fixed *description* is transmitted) is simply a special case of social cooperation in the determination of reference.

The other problem is to describe *individual competence*. Extension may be determined socially, in many cases, but we don't assign the standard extension to the tokens of a word W uttered by Jones *no matter* how Jones uses W. Jones has to have some particular ideas and skills in connection with W in order to play his part in the linguistic division of labor. Once we give up the idea that individual competence has to be so strong as to actually determine extension, we can begin to study it in a fresh frame of mind.

In this connection it is instructive to observe that nouns like "tiger" or "water" are very different from proper names. One can use the proper name "Sanders" correctly without knowing anything about the referent except that he is called "Sanders" – and even that may not be correct. ("Once upon a time, a very long time ago now, about last Friday, Winnie-the-Pooh lived in a forest all by himself under the name of 'Sanders'.") But one cannot use the word tiger correctly, save *per accidens*, without knowing a good deal about tigers, or at least about a certain conception of tigers. In this sense concepts *do* have a lot to do with meaning.

Just as the study of the first problem is properly a topic in sociolinguistics, so the study of the second problem is properly a topic in psycholinguistics. To this topic we now turn.

11   Stereotypes and Communication

Suppose a speaker knows that "tiger" has a set of physical objects as its extension, but no more. If he possesses normal linguistic competence in other respects, then he could use "tiger" in *some* sentences: for example, "tigers have mass," "tigers take up space," "give me a tiger," "is that a tiger?," etc. Moreover, the *socially determined* extension of "tiger" in these sentences would be the standard one, i.e., the set of tigers. Yet we would not count such a speaker as "knowing the meaning" of the word *tiger*. Why not?

Before attempting to answer this question, let us reformulate it a bit. We shall speak of someone as having *acquired* the word "tiger" if he is able to use it in such a way that (1) his use passes muster (i.e., people don't say of him such things as "he doesn't know what a tiger *is*," "he doesn't know the meaning of the word 'tiger'," etc.); and (2) his total way of being situated in the world and in his linguistic community is such that the socially determined extension of the word "tiger" in his idiolect is the set of tigers. Clause (1) means, roughly, that speakers like the one hypothesized in the preceding paragraph don't count as having acquired the word "tiger" (or whichever). We might speak of them, in some cases, as having *partially acquired* the word; but let us defer this for the moment. Clause (2) means that speakers on Twin Earth who have the same linguistic habits as we do, count as having acquired the word "tiger" only if the extension of "tiger" in their idiolect is the set of tigers. The burden of the preceding sections of this paper is that it does *not* follow that the extension of "tiger" in Twin Earth dialect (or idiolects) is the set of tigers merely because their linguistic habits are the same as ours: the nature of Twin Earth "tigers" is also relevant. (If Twin Earth organisms have a silicon chemistry, for example, then their "tigers" aren't really tigers, even if they look like tigers, although the linguistic habits of the lay Twin Earth speaker exactly correspond to those of Earth speakers.) Thus clause (2) means that in this case we have decided to say that Twin Earth speakers have not acquired our word "tiger" (although they have acquired another word with the same spelling and pronunciation).

Our reason for introducing this way of speaking is that the question "does he know the meaning of the word 'tiger'?" is biased in favor of the theory that acquiring a word is coming to possess a thing called its "meaning." Identify this thing with a concept, and we are back at the theory that a sufficient condition for acquiring a word is associating it with the right concept (or, more generally, being in the right psychological state with respect to it) – the very theory we have spent all this time refuting. So, henceforth, we will "acquire" words, rather than "learn their meaning."

We can now reformulate the question with which this section began. The use of the speaker we described does not pass muster, although it is not such as to cause us to assign a nonstandard extension to the word "tiger" in his idiolect. Why doesn't it pass muster?

Suppose our hypothetical speaker points to a snowball and asks, "is that a tiger?" Clearly there isn't much point in talking tigers with *him*. Significant communication requires that people know something of what they are talking about. To be sure, we hear people "communicating" every day who clearly know nothing of what they are talking about; but the sense in which the man who points to a snowball and asks "is that a tiger?" doesn't know anything about tigers is so far beyond the sense in which the man who thinks that Vancouver is going to win the Stanley Cup, or that the Vietnam War was fought to help the South Vietnamese, doesn't know what he is talking about as to boggle the mind. The problem of people who think that Vancouver is going to win the Stanley Cup, or that the Vietnam war was fought to help the South Vietnamese, is one that obviously cannot be remedied by the adoption of linguistic conventions; but not knowing what one is talking about in the second, mind-boggling sense can be and is prevented, near enough, by our conventions of language. What I contend is that speakers are *required* to know something about (stereotypical) tigers in order to count as having acquired the word "tiger"; something about elm trees (or anyway, about the stereotype thereof) to count as having acquired the word "elm"; etc.

This idea should not seem too surprising. After all, we do not permit people to drive on the highways without first passing some tests to determine that they have a *minimum* level of competence; and we do not dine with people who have not learned to use a knife and fork. The linguistic community too has its minimum standards, with respect both to syntax and to "semantics." The nature of the required minimum level of competence depends heavily upon both the culture and the topic, however. In our culture speakers are required to know what tigers look like (if they acquire the word "tiger," and this is virtually obligatory); they are not required to know the fine details (such as leaf shape) of what an elm tree looks like. English speakers are *required by their linguistic community* to be able to tell tigers from leopards; they are not required to be able to tell elm trees from beech trees.

This could easily have been different. Imagine an Indian tribe, call it the Cheroquoi, who have words, say *uhaba'* and *wa'arabi* for elm trees and beech trees respectively, and who make it *obligatory* to know the difference. A Cheroquoi who could not recognize an elm would be said not to know what an *uhaba'* is, not to know the meaning of the word "*uhaba'*" (perhaps, not to know the word, or not to *have* the word); just as an English speaker who had no idea that tigers are striped would be said not to know what a tiger is, not to know the meaning of the word "tiger" (of course, if he at least knows that tigers are large felines we might say he knows part of the meaning, or partially knows the meaning), etc. Then the translation of "*uhaba'*" as "elm" and "*wa'arabi*" as "beech" would, in our view, be only *approximately* correct. In this sense there is a real difficulty with radical translation,[21] but this is not the abstract difficulty that Quine is talking about.[22]

12   What Stereotypes Are

I introduced the notion of a "stereotype" in my lectures at the University of Washington and at the Minnesota Center for the Philosophy of Science in 1968. The subsequently published "Is Semantics Possible?" follows up the argumentation, and in the present essay I want to introduce the notion again and to answer some questions that have been asked about it.

In ordinary parlance a "stereotype" is a conventional (frequently malicious) idea (which may be wildly inaccurate) of what an X looks like or acts like or is. Obviously, I am trading on some features of the ordinary parlance. I am not concerned with malicious stereotypes (save where the language itself is malicious); but I am concerned with conventional ideas, which may be inaccurate. I am suggesting that just such a conventional idea is associated with "tiger," with "gold," etc., and, moreover, that this is the sole element of truth in the "concept" theory. In this view someone who knows what "tiger" means (or, as we have decided to say instead, has acquired the word "tiger") is *required* to know that *stereotypical* tigers are striped. More precisely, there is *one* stereotype of tigers (he may have others) which is required by the linguistic community as such; he is required to have this stereotype, and to know (implicitly) that it is obligatory. This stereotype must include the feature of stripes if his acquisition is to count as successful.

The fact that a feature (e.g., stripes) is included in the stereotype associated with a word X does not mean that it is an analytic truth that all Xs have that feature, nor that most Xs have that feature, nor that all normal *X*s have that feature, nor that some *X*s have that feature.[23] Three-legged tigers and albino tigers are not logically contradictory entities. Discovering that our stereotype has been based on nonnormal or unrepresentative members of a natural kind is not discovering a logical contradiction. If tigers lost their stripes they would not thereby cease to be tigers, nor would butterflies necessarily cease to be butterflies if they lost their wings.

(Strictly speaking, the situation is more complicated than this. It is possible to give a word like "butterfly" a sense in which butterflies would cease to be butterflies if they lost their wings – through mutation, say. Thus one can find *a* sense of "butterfly" in which it is analytic that "butterflies have wings." But the most important sense of the term, I believe, is the one in which the wingless butterflies would still be butterflies.)

At this point the reader may wonder what the value to the linguistic community of having stereotypes is, if the "information" contained in the stereotype is not necessarily correct. But this is not really such a mystery. Most stereotypes do in fact capture features possessed by paradigmatic members of the class in question. Even where stereotypes go wrong, the way in which they go wrong sheds light on the contribution normally made by stereotypes to communication. The stereotype of gold, for example, contains the feature *yellow* even though chemically pure gold is nearly white. But the gold we see in jewelry is typically yellow (due to the presence of copper), so the presence of this feature in the stereotype is even useful in lay contexts. The stereotype associated with *witch* is more seriously wrong, at least if taken with existential import. Believing (with existential import) that witches enter into pacts with Satan, that they cause sickness and death, etc., facilitates communication only in the sense of facilitating communication internal to witch-theory. It does not facilitate communication in any situation in which what is needed is more agreement with the world than agreement with the theory of other speakers. (Strictly speaking, I am speaking of the stereotype as it existed in New England three hundred years ago; today that witches aren't *real* is itself part of the stereotype, and the baneful effects of witch-theory are thereby neutralized.) But the fact that our language has *some* stereotypes which impede rather than facilitate our dealings with the world and each other only points to the fact that we aren't infallible beings, and how could we be? The fact is that we could hardly communicate successfully if most of our stereotypes weren't pretty accurate as far as they go.

13   The "Operational Meaning" of Stereotypes

A trickier question is this: how far is the notion of stereotype "operationally definable"? Here it is necessary to be extremely careful. Attempts in the physical sciences to *literally* specify operational definitions for terms have notoriously failed; and there is no reason the attempt should succeed in linguistics when it failed in physics. Sometimes Quine's arguments against the possibility of a theory of meaning seem to reduce to the demand for operational definitions in linguistics; when this is the case the arguments should be ignored. But it frequently happens that terms do have operational definitions not in the actual world but in idealized circumstances. Giving these "operational definitions" has heuristic value, as idealization frequently does. It is only when we mistake operational definition for more than convenient idealization that it becomes harmful. Thus we may ask: what is the "operational meaning" of the statement that a word has such and such a stereotype, without supposing that the answer to this question counts as a theoretical account of what it is to be a stereotype.

The theoretical account of what it is to be a stereotype proceeds in terms of the notion of *linguistic obligation*; a notion which we believe to be fundamental to linguistics and which we shall not attempt to explicate here. What it means to say that being striped is part of the (linguistic) stereotype of "tiger" is that it is *obligatory* to acquire the information that stereotypical tigers are striped if one acquires "tiger," in the same sense of "obligatory" in which it is obligatory to indicate whether one is speaking of lions in the singular or lions in the plural when one speaks of lions in English. To describe an idealized experimental test of this hypothesis is not difficult. Let us introduce a person whom we may call the linguist's *confederate*. The confederate will be (or pretend to be) an adult whose command of English is generally excellent, but who for some reason (raised in an alien culture? brought up in a monastery?) has totally failed to acquire the word "tiger." The confederate will say the word "tiger" or, better yet, point to it (as if he wasn't sure how to pronounce it), and ask "what does this word mean?" or "what is this?" or some such question. Ignoring all the things that go wrong with experiments in practice, what our hypothesis implies is that informants should typically tell the confederate that tigers are, inter alia, striped.

Instead of relying on confederates, one might expect the linguist to study children learning English. But children learning their native language aren't taught it nearly as much as philosophers suppose; they learn it but they aren't taught it, as Chomsky has emphasized. Still, children do sometimes ask such questions as "what is a tiger?" and our hypothesis implies that in these cases too informants should tell them, inter alia, that tigers are striped. But one problem is that the informants are likely to be parents, and there are the vagaries of parental time, temper, and attention to be allowed for.

It would be easy to specify a large number of additional "operational" implications of our hypothesis, but to do so would have no particular value. The fact is that we are fully competent speakers of English ourselves, with a devil of a good sense of what our linguistic obligations are. Pretending that we are in the position of Martians with respect to English is not the route to methodological clarity; it was, after all, only when the operational approach was abandoned that transformational linguistics blossomed into a handsome science.

Thus if anyone were to ask me for the meaning of "tiger," I know perfectly well what I would tell him. I would tell him that tigers were feline, something about their size, that they are yellow with black stripes, that they (sometimes) live in the jungle, and are fierce. Other things I might tell him too, depending on the context and his reason for asking; but the above items, save possibly for the bit about the jungle, I would regard it as obligatory to convey. I don't have to experiment to know that this is what I regard it as *obligatory* to convey, and I am sure that approximately this is what other speakers regard it as obligatory to convey too. Of course, there is some variation from idiolect to idiolect; the feature of having stripes (apart from figure–ground relations, e.g., are they black stripes on a yellow ground, which is the way I see them, or yellow stripes on a black ground?) would be found in all normal idiolects, but some speakers might regard the information that tigers (stereotypically) inhabit jungles as obligatory, while others might not. Alternatively, some features of the stereotype (big-cat-hood, stripes) might be regarded as obligatory, and others as *optional*, on the model of certain syntactical features. But we shall not pursue this possibility here.

14   Quine's "Two Dogmas" Revisited

In "Two Dogmas of Empiricism" Quine launched a powerful and salutory attack on the currently fashionable analytic–synthetic distinction. The distinction had grown to be a veritable philosophical man-eater: analytic *equaling* necessary *equaling* unrevisable in principle *equaling* whatever truth the individual philosopher wished to explain away. But Quine's attack itself went too far in certain respects; some limited class of analytic sentences can be saved, we feel.[24] More importantly, the attack was later construed, both by Quine himself and by others, as implicating the whole notion of meaning in the downfall of the analytic–synthetic distinction. While we have made it clear that we agree that the traditional notion of meaning has serious troubles, our project in this paper is constructive, not destructive. We come to revise the notion of meaning, not to bury it. So it will be useful to see how Quine's arguments fare against our revision.

Quine's arguments against the notion of analyticity can basically be reduced to the following: that no behavioral significance can be attached to the notion. His argument (again simplifying somewhat) was that there were, basically, only two candidates for a behavioral index of analyticity, and both are totally unsatisfactory, although for different reasons. The first behavioral index is *centrality*: many contemporary philosophers call a sentence analytic if, in effect some community (say, Oxford dons) holds it immune from revision. But, Quine persuasively argues, maximum immunity from revision is no exclusive prerogative of analytic sentences. Sentences expressing fundamental laws of physics (e.g., the conservation of energy) may well enjoy maximum behavioral immunity from revision, although it would hardly be customary or plausible to classify them as analytic. Quine does not, however, rely on the mere implausibility of classifying all statements that we are highly reluctant to give up as analytic; he points out that "immunity from revision" is, in the actual history of science, a *matter of degree*. There is no such thing, in the actual practice of rational science, as *absolute* immunity from revision. Thus to identify analyticity with immunity from revision would alter the notion in two fundamental ways: analyticity would become a matter of degree, and there would be no such thing as an absolutely analytic sentence. This would be such a departure from the classical Carnap–Ayer–et al. notion of analyticity that Quine feels that if *this* is what we mean to talk about, then it would be less misleading to introduce a different term altogether, say, *centrality*.

The second behavioral index is *being called "analytic."* In effect, some philosophers take the hallmark of analyticity to be that trained informants (say, Oxford dons) *call* the sentence analytic. Variants of this index are: that the sentence be deducible from the sentences in a finite list at the top of which someone who bears the ancestral of the graduate–student relation to Carnap has printed the words "Meaning Postulate"; that the sentence be obtainable from a theorem of logic by substituting synonyms for synonyms. The last of these variants looks promising, but Quine launches against it the question, "what is the criterion of synonymy?" One possible criterion might be that words W_1 and W_2 are synonymous if and only if the biconditional (x) (x is in the extension of $W_1 \equiv x$ is in the extension of W_2) is *analytic*; but this leads us right back in a circle. Another might be that words W_1 and W_2 are synonymous if and only if trained informants *call* them synonymous; but this is just our second index in a slightly revised form. A promising line is that words W_1 and W_2 are synonymous if and only if W_1 and W_2 are interchangeable (i.e., the words can be switched) *salva veritate* in all contexts of a suitable class. But Quine convincingly shows that this proposal too leads us around in a circle. Thus the second index reduces to this: a sentence is analytic if either it or some expression, or sequence of ordered pairs of expressions, or set of expressions, related to the sentence in certain specified ways, lies in a class to all the members of which trained informants apply a certain *noise*: either the *noise* ANALYTIC, or the *noise* MEANING POSTULATE, or the *noise* SYNONYMOUS. Ultimately, this proposal leaves "analytic," etc., *unexplicated noises.*

Although Quine does not discuss this explicitly, it is clear that taking the intersection of the two unsatisfactory behavioral indexes would be no more satisfactory; explicating the analyticity of a sentence as consisting in centrality *plus* being called ANALYTIC is just saying that the analytic sentences are a subclass of the central sentences without in any way telling us wherein the exceptionality of the subclass consists. In effect, Quine's conclusion is that analyticity is either centrality misconceived or it is nothing.

In spite of Quine's forceful argument, many philosophers have gone on abusing the notion of analyticity, often confusing it with a supposed highest degree of centrality. Confronted with Quine's alternatives, they have elected to identify analyticity with centrality, and to pay the price the price of classifying such obviously synthetic-looking sentences as "space has three dimensions" as analytic, and the price of undertaking to maintain the view that there is, after all, such a thing as absolute unrevisability in science in spite of the impressive evidence to the contrary. But this line can be blasted by coupling Quine's argument with an important argument of Reichenbach's. Reichenbach (Reichenbach, 1965, p. 31)[25] showed that there exists a *set* of principles each of which Kant would have regarded as synthetic a priori, but whose conjunction is incompatible with the principles of special relativity and general covariance. (These include normal induction, the continuity of space, and the Euclidean character of space.) A Kantian can consistently hold on to Euclidean geometry come what may; but then experience may force him to give up normal induction or the continuity of space. Or he may hold on to normal induction and the continuity of space come what may; but then experience may force him to give up Euclidean geometry (this happens in the case that physical space is not even homeomorphic to any Euclidean space). In his article in Schilpp (1951) Reichenbach gives essentially the same argument in a slightly different form.[26]

Applied to our present context, what this shows is that there are principles such that philosophers fond of the overblown notion of analyticity, and in particular philosophers who identify analyticity with (maximum) unrevisability, would classify them as analytic, but whose conjunction has testable empirical consequences. Thus either the identification of analyticity with centrality must be given up once and for all, or one must give up the idea that analyticity is closed under conjunction, or one must swallow the unhappy consequence that an analytic sentence can have testable empirical consequences (and hence that an *analytic* sentence might turn out to be *empirically false*).

It is no accident, by the way, that the sentences that Kant would have classified as synthetic a priori would be classified by these latter-day empiricists as analytic; their purpose in bloating the notion of analyticity was precisely to dissolve Kant's problem by identifying apriority with analyticity and then identifying analyticity in turn with truth by convention. (This last step has also been devastatingly criticized by Quine, but discussion of it would take us away from our topic.)

Other philosophers have tried to answer Quine by distinguishing between *sentences* and *statements*: all *sentences* are revisable, they agree, but some *statements* are not. Revising a sentence is not changing our mind about the statement formerly expressed by that sentence just in case the sentence (meaning the syntactical object together with its meaning) after the revision is, in fact, not synonymous with the sentence prior to the revision, i.e., just in case the revision is a case of meaning change and not change of theory. But (1) this reduces at once to the proposal to explicate analyticity in terms of synonymy; and (2) if there is one thing that Quine has decisively contributed to philosophy, it is the realization that meaning change and theory change cannot be sharply separated. We do not agree with Quine that meaning change cannot be defined at all, but it does not follow that the dichotomy "meaning change *or* theory change" is tenable. Discovering that we live in a non-Euclidean world *might* change the meaning of "straight line" (this would happen in the – somewhat unlikely – event that something like the parallels postulate was part of the stereotype of straightness); but it would not be a *mere* change of meaning. In particular it would not be a change of *extension*: thus it would not be right to say that the parallels postulate was "true in the former sense of the words." From the fact that giving up a sentence *S* would involve meaning change, it does not follow that *S* is *true*. Meanings may not fit the world; and meaning change can be forced by empirical discoveries.

Although we are not, in this paper, trying to explicate a notion of analyticity, we are trying to explicate a notion that might seem closely related, the notion of meaning. Thus it might seem that Quine's arguments would also go against our attempt. Let us check this out.

In our view there is a perfectly good sense in which being striped is part of the meaning of "tiger." But it does not follow, in our view, that "tigers are striped" is analytic. If a mutation occurred, all tigers might be albinos. Communication presupposes that I have a stereotype of tigers which includes stripes, and that you have a stereotype of tigers which includes stripes, and that I know that your stereotype includes stripes, and that you know that my stereotype includes stripes, and that you know that I know . . . (and so on, à la Grice, forever). But it does not presuppose that any particular stereotype be *correct*, or that the majority of our stereotypes remain correct forever. Linguistic obligatoriness is not supposed to be an index of unrevisability or even of truth; thus we can hold that "tigers are striped" is part of the meaning of "tiger" without being trapped in the problems of analyticity.

Thus Quine's arguments against identifying analyticity with centrality are not arguments against identifying a feature's being "part of the meaning" of *X* with its being obligatorily included in the stereotype of *X*. What of Quine's "noise" argument?

Of course, evidence concerning what people *say*, including explicit metalinguistic remarks, is important in "semantics" as it is in syntax. Thus, if a speaker points to a *clam* and asks "is that a tiger?" people are likely to guffaw. (When they stop laughing) they might say "he doesn't know the meaning of 'tiger'," or "he doesn't know what tigers are." Such comments can be helpful to the linguist. But we are not *defining* the stereotype in terms of such comments. To say that being "big-cat-like" is part of the meaning of "tiger" is not merely to say that application of "tiger" to something which is not big-cat-like (and also not a tiger) would provoke certain *noises*. It is to say that speakers acquire the information that "tigers are (stereotypically) big-cat-like" as they acquire the word "tiger" and that they feel an obligation to guarantee that those to whom they teach the use of the word do likewise. Information about the minimum skills required for entry into the linguistic community is significant information; no circularity of the kind Quine criticized appears here.

15   Radical Translation

What our theory does not do, by itself at any rate, is solve Quine's problem of "radical translation" (i.e., translation from an alien language/culture). We cannot translate our hypothetical Cheroquoi into English by matching stereotypes, just because finding out what the stereotype of, say, *wa'arabi* is involves translating Cheroquoi utterances. On the other hand, the constraint that each word in Cheroquoi should match its image in English under the translation function as far as stereotype is concerned (or approximately match, since in many cases exact matching may not be attainable), places a severe *constraint* on the translation function. Once we have succeeded in translating the basic vocabulary of Cheroquoi, we can start to elicit stereotypes, and these will serve both to constrain future translations and to check the internal correctness of the piece of the translation function already constructed.

Even where we can determine stereotypes (relative, say, to a tentative translation of "basic vocabulary"), these do not suffice, in general, to determine a unique translation. Thus the German words *Ulme* and *Buche* have the same stereotype as elm; but *Ulme* means "elm" while *Buche* means "beech." In the case of German, the fact that *Ulme* and "elm" are cognates could point to the correct translation (although this is far from foolproof – in general, cognate words are not synonymous); but in the case of Greek we have no such clue as to which of the two words $o\xi\nu\alpha$ and $\pi\lambda\varepsilon\alpha$ means *elm* and which *beech*; we would just have to find a Greek who could tell elms from beeches (or *oxya* from *ptelea*). What this illustrates is that it may not be the typical speakers" dispositions to assent and dissent that the linguist must seek to discover; because of the division of linguistic labor, it is frequently necessary for the linguist to assess who are the experts with respect to *oxya*, or *wa'arabi*, or *gavagai*, or whatever, before he can make a guess at the socially determined extension of a word. Then this socially determined extension *and* the stereotype of the *typical* speaker, inexpert though he is, will *both* function as constraints upon the translation function. Discovery that the stereotype of *oxya* is wildly different from the stereotype of "elm" would disqualify the translation of *oxya* by "elm" in all save the most extensional contexts; but the discovery that the *extension* of *oxya* is not even approximately the class of elms would wipe out the translation altogether, in all contexts.

It will be noted that we have already enlarged the totality of facts counted as evidence for a translation function beyond the ascetic base that Quine allows in *Word and Object*. For example, the fact that speakers say such-and-such when the linguist's "confederate" points to the word *oxya* and asks "what does this mean?" or "what is this?" or whatever is not allowed by Quine (as something the linguist can "know") on the ground that this sort of "knowledge" presupposes already having translated the query "what does this word mean?" However, if Quine is willing to assume that one can *somehow* guess at the words which signify *assent* and *dissent* in the alien language, it does not seem at all unreasonable to suppose that one can somehow convey to a native speaker that one does not understand a word. It is not necessary that one discover a locution in the alien language which literally means "what does this word mean?" (as opposed to: "I don't understand this word" or "this word is unfamiliar to me" or "I am puzzled by this word," etc.). Perhaps just saying the word *oxya*, or whatever, with a tone of puzzlement would suffice. Why should *puzzlement* be less accessible to the linguist than *assent*?

Also, we are taking advantage of the fact that segmentation into *words* has turned out to be linguistically universal (and there even exist tests for word and morpheme segmentation which are independent of meaning). Clearly, there is no motivated reason for allowing the linguist to utter whole sentences and look for assent and dissent, while refusing to allow him to utter words and morphemes in a tone of puzzlement.

I repeat, the claim is not being advanced that enlarging the evidence base in this way solves the problem of radical translation. What it does is add further constraints on the class of admissible candidates for a correct translation. What I believe is that enlarging the class of constraints can determine a unique translation, or as unique a translation as we are able to get in practice. But constraints that go beyond linguistic theory proper will have to be used, in my opinion; there will also have to be constraints on what sorts of belief (and connection between beliefs, and connection of beliefs to the culture and the world) we can reasonably impute to people. Discussion of these matters will be deferred to another paper.

16   A Critique of Davidsonian Semantic Theory

In a series of publications, Donald Davidson has put forward the interesting suggestion that a semantic theory of a natural language might be modelled on what mathematical logicians call a *truth definition* for a formalized language. Stripped of technicalities, what this suggestion comes down to is that one might have a set of rules specifying (1) for each word, under what conditions that word is true of something (for words for which the concept of an extension makes sense, all other words are to be treated as syncategorematic); (2) for sentences longer than a single word, a rule is given specifying the conditions under which the sentence is true as a function of the way it is built up out of shorter sentences (counting words as if they were one-word sentences, e.g., "snow" as "that's snow"). The choice of one-word sentences as the starting point is my interpretation of what Davidson intends; in any case, he means one to start with a *finite* stock of *short* sentences for which truth conditions are to be laid down *directly*. The intention of (2) is not that there should be a rule for each sentence not handled under (1), since this would require an infinite number of rules, but that there should be a rule for each sentence *type*. For example, in a formalized language one of the rules of kind (2) might be: if S is (S_1 & S_2) for some sentences S_1, S_2, then S is true if and only if S_1, S_2, are both true.

It will be noticed that, in the example just given, the truth condition specified for sentences of the sentence type (S_1 & S_2) performs the job of specifying the meaning of "&." More precisely, it specifies the meaning of the structure (——&——). This is the sense in which a truth definition can be a theory of meaning. Davidson's contention is that the *entire* theory of meaning for a natural language can be given in this form.

There is no doubt that rules of the type illustrated can give the meaning of some words and structures. The question is, what reason is there to think that the meaning of most words can be given in this way, let alone all?

The obvious difficulty is this: For many words, an extensionally correct truth definition can be given which is in no sense a theory of the meaning of the word. For example, consider *"Water" is true of* − *if and only if x is H₂O.* This is an extensionally correct truth definition for "water" (strictly speaking, it is not a truth definition but a "truth of" definition – i.e., a *satisfaction*-in-the-sense-of-Tarski definition – but we will not bother with such niceties here). At least it is extensionally correct if we ignore the problem that water with impurities is also called "water," etc. Now, suppose most speakers don't *know* that water is H_2O. Then this formula in no way tells us anything about the *meaning* of "water." It might be of interest to a chemist, but it doesn't count as a theory of the meaning of the term "water." Or, it counts as a theory of the *extension* of the term "water," but Davidson is promising us more than just that.

Davidson is quite well aware of this difficulty. His answer (in conversation, anyway) is that we need to develop a theory of *translation*. This he, like Quine, considers to be the real problem. Relativized to such a theory (relativitized to what we admittedly don't yet have), the theory comes down to this: we want a system of truth definitions which is simultaneously a system of translations (or approximate translations, if perfect translation is unobtainable). If we had a theory which specified what it is to be a good translation, then we could rule out the above truth definition for "water" as uninteresting on the grounds that *x is H_2O* is not an acceptable translation or even near-translation of *x is water* (in a prescientific community), even if water = H_2O happens to be true.

This comes perilously close to saying that a theory of meaning is a truth definition plus a theory of meaning. (If we had ham and eggs we'd have ham and eggs – *if* we had ham and *if* we had eggs.) But this story suffers from worse than promissoriness, as we shall see.

A second contention of Davidson's is that the theory of translation that we don't yet have is necessarily a theory whose basic units are *sentences* and not *words* on the grounds that our *evidence* in linguistics necessarily consists of assent and dissent from sentences. Words can be handled, Davidson contends, by treating them as sentences ("water" as "that's water," etc.).

How does this ambitious project of constructing a theory of meaning in the form of a truth definition constrained by a theory of translation tested by "the only evidence we have," speakers' dispositions to use sentences, fare according to the view we are putting forward here?

Our answer is that the theory cannot succeed in principle. In special cases, such as the word "and" in its truth functional sense, a truth definition (strictly speaking, a clause in what logicians call a "truth definition" – the sum total of all the clauses is the inductive definition of "truth" for the particular language) can give the meaning of the word or structure because the stereotype associated with the word (if one wants to speak of a stereotype in the case of a word like "and") is so strong as to actually constitute a necessary and sufficient condition. If all words were like "and" and "bachelor" the program could succeed. And Davidson certainly made an important contribution in pointing out that linguistics has to deal with inductively specified truth conditions. But in the great majority of words, the requirements of a theory of truth and the requirements of a theory of meaning are mutuallyincompatible, at least in the English–English case. But the English–English case – the case in which we try to provide a significant theory of the meaning of English words which is itself couched in English – is surely the basic one.

The problem is that in general the only expressions which are both coextensive with X and have roughly the same stereotype as X are expressions containing X itself. If we rule out such truth definitions (strictly speaking, clauses, but I shall continue using "truth definition" both for individual clauses and for the whole system of clauses, for simplicity) as

> *"X is water" is true if and only if X is water*

on the grounds that they don't say anything about the meaning of the word "water," and we rule out such truth definitions as

> *"X is water" is true if and only if X is H_2O*

on the grounds that what they say is wrong as a description of the *meaning* of the word "water," then we shall be left with nothing.

The problem is that we want

> *W is true of X if and only if* ——

to satisfy the conditions that (1) the clause be extensionally correct (where —— is to be thought of as a condition containing "x," e.g., "x is H_2O"); (2) that —— be a *translation* of W – on our theory, this would mean that the stereotype associated with W is approximately the same as the stereotype associated with ——; (3) that —— not contain W itself, or syntactic variants of W. If we take W to be, for example, the word "elm," then there is absolutely no way to fulfill all three conditions simultaneously. Any condition of the above form that does not contain "elm" and that is extensionally correct will contain a —— that is absolutely terrible as a *translation* of "elm."

Even where the language contains two exact synonyms, the situation is little better. Thus

> *"Heather" is true of x if and only if x is gorse*

is true, and so is

> *"Gorse" is true of x if and only if x is heather*

– this is a theory of the meaning of "gorse" and "heather"?

Notice that the condition (3) is precisely what logicians do *not* impose on *their* truth definitions.

> *"Snow is white" is true if and only if snow is white*

is the paradigm of a truth definition in the logician's sense. But logicians are trying to give the extension of "true" with respect to a particular language, not the meaning of "snow is white." Tarski would have gone so far as to claim he was giving the *meaning* (and not just the extension) of "true"; but he would never have claimed he was saying *anything* about the meaning of "snow is white."

It may be that what Davidson really thinks is that theory of meaning, in any serious sense of the term, is impossible, and that all that is possible is to construct translation functions. If so, he might well think that the only "theory of meaning" possible for English is one that says "'elm' is true of x if and only if x is an elm," "'water' is true of x if and only if x is water," etc., and only rarely something enlightening like "S_1 & S_2 is true if and only if S_1, S_2 are both true." But if Davidson's "theory" is just Quinine skepticism under the disguise of a positive contribution to the study of meaning, then it is a bitter pill to swallow.

The contention that the only evidence available to the linguist is speakers' dispositions with respect to whole sentences is, furthermore, vacuous on one interpretation, and plainly false on the interpretation on which it is not vacuous. If dispositions to say certain things *when queried about individual words or morphemes or syntactic structures* are included in the notion of dispositions to use sentences, then the restriction to dispositions to use sentences seems to rule out nothing whatsoever. On the nonvacuous interpretation, what Davidson is saying is that the linguist cannot have access to such data as what informants (including the linguist himself) say when asked the meaning of a word or morpheme or syntactic structure. No reason has ever been given why the linguist cannot have access to such data, and it is plain that actual linguists place heavy reliance on informants' testimony about such matters, in the case of an alien language, and upon their own intuitions as native speakers, when they are studying their native languages. In particular, when we are trying to translate a whole sentence, there is no reason why we should not be guided by our knowledge of the syntactic and semantic properties of the constituents of that sentence, including the deep structure. As we have seen, there are procedures for gaining information about individual constituents. It is noteworthy that the procedure that Quine and Davidson claim is the only *possible* one – going from whole sentences to individual words – is the *opposite* of the procedure upon which every success ever attained in the study of natural language has been based.

17   Critique of California Semantics

I wish now to consider an approach to semantic theory pioneered by the late Rudolf Carnap. Since I do not wish to be embroiled in textual questions, I will not attribute the particular form of the view I am going to describe to any particular philosopher but will simply refer to it as "California semantics."

We assume the notion of a *possible world*. Let f be a function defined on the "space" of all possible worlds whose value $f(x)$ at any possible world x is always a subset of the set of entities in x. Then f is called an intension. A term T has meaning for a speaker X if X associates T with an intension f_T. The term T is *true* of an entity e in a possible world x if and only if e belongs to the set $f(x)$. Instead of using the term "associated," Carnap himself tended to speak of "grasping" intensions; but, clearly, what was intended was not just that X "grasp" the intension f, but that he grasp *that f is the intension of T* – i.e., that he *associate* f with T in some way.

Clearly this picture of what it is to understand a term disagrees with the story we tell in this paper. The reply of a California semanticist would be that California semantics is a description of an *ideal* language; that actual language is *vague*. In other words, a term T in actual language does not have a single precise intension; it has a set – possibly a fuzzy set – of intensions. Nevertheless, the first step in the direction of describing natural language is surely to study the idealization in which each term T has exactly one intension.

(In his book *Meaning and Necessity*, Carnap employs a superficially different formulation: an intension is simply a *property*. An entity e belongs to the extension of a term T just in case e has whichever property is the intension of T. The later formulation in terms of functions f as described above avoids taking the notion of *property* as primitive.)

The first difficulty with this position is the use of the totally unexplained notion of *grasping* an intension (or, in our reformulation of the position, *associating* an intension with a term). Identifying intensions with set-theoretic entities f provides a "concrete" realization of the notion of intension in the current mathematical style (relative to the notions of possible world and set), but at the cost of making it very difficult to see how anyone could have an intension in his mind, or what it is to think about one or "grasp" one or "associate" one with anything. It will not do to say that thinking of an intension is using a word or functional substitute for a word (e.g., the analogue of a word in "brain code," if, as seems likely, the brain "computes" in a "code" that has analogies to and possibly borrowings from language; or a thought form such as a picture or a private symbol, in cases where such are employed in thinking) which *refers* to the intension in question, since *reference* (i.e., being in the extension of a term) has just been defined in terms of intension. Although the characterization of what it is to think of an abstract entity such as a function or a property is certainly correct, in the present context it is patently circular. But no noncircular characterization of this fundamental notion of the theory has ever been provided.

This difficulty is related to a general difficulty in the philosophy of mathematics pointed out by Paul Benacerraf.[27] Benacerraf has remarked that philosophies of mathematics tend to fall between two stools: either they account for what mathematical objects are and for the necessity of mathematical truth and fail to account for the fact that people can *learn* mathematics, can *refer* to mathematical objects, etc., or else they account for the latter facts and fail to account for the former. California semantics accounts for what intensions *are*, but provides no account that is not completely circular of how it is that we can "grasp" them, associate them with terms, think about them, *refer* to them, etc.

Carnap may not have noticed this difficulty because of his verificationism. In his early years Carnap thought of understanding a term as possessing the *ability to verify* whether or not any given entity falls in the extension of the term. In terms of intensions: "grasping" an intension would amount, then, to possessing the ability to verify if an entity *e* in any possible world *x* belongs to $f(x)$ or not. Later Carnap modified this view, recognizing that, as Quine puts it, sentences face the tribunal of experience collectively and not individually. There is no such thing as the way of verifying that a term *T* is true of an entity, in general, independent of the context of a particular set of theories, auxiliary hypotheses, etc. Perhaps Carnap would have maintained that something like the earlier theory was correct for a limited class of terms, the so-called "observation terms." Our own view is that the verifiability theory of meaning is false both in its central idea and for observation terms, but we shall not try to discuss this here. At any rate, if one is *not* a verificationist, then it is hard to see California semantics as a theory at all, since the notion of *grasping* an intension has been left totally unexplained.

Second, if we assume that "grasping an intension" (associating an intension with a term *T*) is supposed to be a *psychological state* (in the narrow sense), then California semantics is committed to both principles (1) and (2) that we criticized in the first part of this paper. It must hold that the psychological state of the speaker determines the intension of his terms which in turn determines the extension of his terms. It would follow that if two human beings are in the same total psychological state, then they necessarily assign the same extension to every term they employ. As we have seen, this is totally wrong for natural language. The reason this is wrong, as we saw above, is in part that extension is determined socially, not by individual competence alone. Thus California semantics is committed to treating language as something private – to totally ignoring the linguistic division of labor. The extension of each term is viewed by this school as totally determined by something in the head of the individual speaker all by himself. A second reason this is wrong, as we also saw, is that most terms are *rigid*. In California semantics every term is treated as, in effect, a *description*. The *indexical* component in meaning – the fact that our terms refer to things which are similar, in certain ways, to things that we designate *rigidly*, to *these* things, to the stuff we call "water," or whatever, *here* – is ignored.

But what of the defense that it is not actual language that the California semanticist is concerned with, but an idealization in which we "ignore vagueness," and that terms in natural language may be thought of as associated with a set of intensions rather than with a single well-defined intension?

The answer is that an *indexical* word cannot be represented as a vague family of non-indexical words. The word "I," to take the extreme case, is *indexical* but not *vague*. "I" is not synonymous with a *description*; neither is it synonymous with a fuzzy set of descriptions. Similarly, if we are right, "water" is synonymous neither with a description nor with a fuzzy set of descriptions (intensions).

Similarly, a word whose extension is fixed socially and not individually is not the same thing as a word whose extension is *vaguely* fixed individually. The reason my individual "grasp" of "elm tree" does not fix the extension of elm is not that the word is vague – if the problem were simple vagueness, then the fact that my concepts do not distinguish elms from beeches would imply that elms are beeches, as I use the term, or, anyway, borderline cases of beeches, and that beeches are elms, or borderline cases of elms. The reason is rather that the extension of "elm tree" in my dialect is not fixed by what the average speaker "grasps" or doesn't "grasp" at all; it is fixed by the community, including the experts, through a complex cooperative process. A language which exemplifies the division of linguistic labor cannot be approximated successfully by a language which has vague terms and no linguistic division of labor. Cooperation isn't vagueness.

But, one might reply, couldn't one replace our actual language by a language in which (1) terms were replaced by coextensive terms which were *not* indexical (e.g., "water" by "H₂O," assuming "H₂O" is not indexical); and (2) we eliminated the division of linguistic labor by making every speaker an expert on every topic?

We shall answer this question in the negative; but suppose, for a moment, the answer were "yes." What significance would this have? The "ideal" language would in no sense be similar to our actual language; nor would the difference be a matter of "the vagueness of natural language."

In fact, however, one can't carry out the replacement, for the very good reason that *all* natural-kind words and physical-magnitude words are indexical in the way we have described, "hydrogen," and hence "H₂O," just as much as "water." Perhaps "sense-data" terms are not indexical (apart from terms for the self), if such there be; but "yellow" as a *thing* predicate is indexical for the same reason as "tiger"; even if something *looks* yellow it may not *be* yellow. And it doesn't help to say that things that look yellow in normal circumstances (to normal perceivers) are yellow; "normal" here has precisely the feature we called indexicality. There is simply no reason to believe that the project of reducing our language to nonindexical language could be carried out in principle.

The elimination of the division of linguistic labor might, I suppose, be carried out "in principle." But, if the division of linguistic labor is, as I conjectured, a linguistic universal, what interest is there in the possible existence of a language which lacks a constitutive feature of *human* language? A world in which every one is an expert on every topic is a world in which social laws are almost unimaginably different from what they now are. What is the *motivation* for taking such a world and such a language as the model for the analysis of *human* language?

Incidentally, philosophers who work in the tradition of California semantics have recently begun to modify the scheme to overcome just these defects. Thus it has been suggested that an intension might be a function whose arguments are not just possible worlds but, perhaps, a possible world, a speaker, and a nonlinguistic context of utterance. This would permit the representation of some kinds of indexicality and some kinds of division of linguistic labor in the model. As David Lewis develops these ideas, "water," for example, would have the same *intension* (same function) on Earth and on Twin Earth, but a different extension. (In effect, Lewis retains assumption (1) from the discussion in the first part of this paper and gives up (2); we chose to give up (1) and retain (2).) There is no reason why the formal models developed by Carnap and his followers should not prove valuable when so modified. Our interest here has been not in the utility of the mathematical formalism but in the philosophy of language underlying the earlier versions of the view.

18   Semantic Markers

If the approach suggested here is correct, then there is a great deal of scientific work to be done in (1) finding out what sorts of item can appear in stereotypes; (2) working out a convenient system for representing stereotypes; etc. This work is not work that can be done by philosophical discussion, however. It is rather the province of linguistics and psycholinguistics. One idea that can, I believe, be of value is the idea of a *semantic marker*. The idea comes from the work of J. Katz and J. A. Fodor; we shall modify it somewhat here.

Consider the stereotype of "tiger" for a moment. This includes such features as being an animal; being big-cat-like; having black stripes on a yellow ground (yellow stripes on a black ground?); etc. Now, there is something very special about the feature *animal*. In terms of Quine's notion of *centrality* or *unrevisability*, it is qualitatively different from the others listed. It is not impossible to imagine that tigers might not be animals (they might be robots). But spelling this out, they must always have been robots; we don't want to tell a story about the tigers being *replaced* by robots, because then the robots wouldn't be tigers. Or, if they weren't always robots, they must have *become* robots, which is even harder to imagine. If tigers are and always were robots, these robots mustn't be too "intelligent," or else we may not have a case in which tigers aren't animals – we may, rather, have described a case in which some robots are animals. Best make them "other-directed" robots – say, have an operator on Mars controlling each motion remotely. Spelling this out, I repeat, is difficult, and it is curiously hard to think of the case to begin with, which is why it is easy to make the mistake of thinking that it is "logically impossible" for a tiger *not* to be an animal. On the other hand, there is no difficulty in imagining an individual tiger that is not striped; it might be an albino. Nor is it difficult to imagine an individual tiger that doesn't look like a big cat: it might be horribly deformed. We can even imagine the whole species losing its stripes or becoming horribly deformed. But tigers ceasing to be animals? Great difficulty again!

Notice that we are not making the mistake that Quine rightly criticized, of attributing an absolute unrevisability to such statements as "tigers are animals," "tigers couldn't change from animals into something else and still be tigers." Indeed, we can describe far-fetched cases in which these statements would be given up. But we maintain that it is *qualitatively* harder to revise "all tigers are animals" than "all tigers have stripes" – indeed, the latter statement is not even true.

Not only do such features as "animal," "living thing," "artifact," "day of the week," "period of time," attach with enormous centrality to the words "tiger," "clam," "chair," "Tuesday," "hour"; but they also form part of a widely used and important *system of classification*. The centrality guarantees that items classified under these headings virtually never have to be *re*classified; thus these headings are the natural ones to use as category indicators in a host of contexts. It seems to me reasonable that, just as in syntax we use such markers as "noun," "adjective," and, more narrowly, "concrete noun," "verb taking a person as subject and an abstract object," etc., to classify words, so in semantics these category indicators should be used as markers.

It is interesting that when Katz and Fodor originally introduced the idea of a semantic marker, they did not propose to exhaust the meaning – what we call the stereotype – by a list of such markers. Rather, the markers were restricted to just the category indicators of high centrality, which is what we propose. The remaining features were simply listed as a "distinguisher." Their scheme is not easily comparable with ours, because they wanted the semantic markers *plus* the distinguisher to always give a necessary and sufficient condition for membership in the extension of the term. Since the whole thing – markers and distinguisher – were supposed to represent what every speaker implicitly knows, they were committed to the idea that every speaker implicitly knows of a necessary and sufficient condition for membership in the extension of "gold," "aluminum," "elm" – which, as we have pointed out, is not the case. Later Katz went further and demanded that all the features constitute an *analytically* necessary and sufficient condition for membership in the extension. At this point he dropped the distinction between markers and distinguishers; if all the features have, so to speak, the infinite degree of centrality, why call some "markers" and some "distinguishers"? From our point of view, their original distinction between "markers" and "distinguisher" was sound – provided one drop the idea that the distinguisher provides (together with the markers) a necessary and sufficient condition, and the idea that any of this is a theory of *analyticity*. We suggest that the idea of a semantic marker is an important contribution, when taken as suggested here.

19   The Meaning of "Meaning"

We may now summarize what has been said in the form of a proposal concerning how one might reconstruct the notion of "meaning." Our proposal is not the only one that might be advanced on the basis of these ideas, but it may serve to encapsulate some of the major points. In addition, I feel that it recovers as much of ordinary usage in commonsense talk and in linguistics as one is likely to be able to conveniently preserve. Since, in my view something like the assumptions (1) and (2) listed in the first part of this paper are deeply embedded in ordinary meaning talk, and these assumptions are jointly inconsistent with the facts, no reconstruction is going to be without some counterintuitive consequences.

Briefly, my proposal is to define "meaning" not by picking out an object which will be identified with the meaning (although that might be done in the usual set-theoretic style if one insists), but by specifying a normal form (or, rather, a *type* of normal form) for the description of meaning. If we know what a "normal form description" of the meaning of a word should be, then, as far as I am concerned, we know what meaning *is* in any scientifically interesting sense.

My proposal is that the normal form description of the meaning of a word should be a finite sequence, or "vector," whose components should certainly include the following (it might be desirable to have other types of component as well): (1) the syntactic markers that apply to the word, e.g., "noun"; (2) the semantic markers that apply to the word, e.g., "animal," "period of time"; (3) a description of the additional features of the stereotype, if any; (4) a description of the extension.

The following convention is a part of this proposal: the components of the vector all represent a hypothesis about the individual speaker's competence, except the extension. Thus the normal form description for "water" might be, in part:

SYNTACTIC MARKERS	SEMANTIC MARKERS	STEREOTYPE	EXTENSION
mass noun;	*natural kind;*	*colorless;*	H_2O
concrete;	*liquid;*	*transparent;*	*(give or take*
		tasteless;	*impurities)*
		thirst-quenching;	
		etc.	

– this does not mean that knowledge of the fact that water is H_2O is being imputed to the individual speaker or even to the society. It means that (*we* say) the extension of the term "water" as *they* (the speakers in question) use it is *in fact* H_2O. The objection "who are *we* to say what the extension of their term is in fact" has been discussed above. Note that this is fundamentally an objection to the notion of tru*t*h, and that extension is a relative of truth and inherits the family problems.

Let us call two descriptions *equivalent* if they are the same except for the description of the extension, and the two descriptions are coextensive. Then, if the set variously described in the two descriptions is, *in fact*, the extension of the word in question, and the other components in the description are correct characterizations of the various aspects of competence they represent, *both* descriptions count as correct. Equivalent descriptions are both correct or both incorrect. This is another way of making the point that, although we have to use a *description* of the extension to *give* the extension, we think of the component in question as being the *extension* (the *set*), not the description of the extension.

In particular the representation of the words "water" in Earth dialect and "water" in Twin Earth dialect would be the same except that in the last column the normal form description of the Twin Earth word "water" would have XYZ and not H_2O. This means, in view of what has just been said, that we are ascribing the *same* linguistic competence to the typical Earthian/Twin Earthian speaker, but a different extension to the word, nonetheless.

This proposal means that we keep assumption (2) of our early discussion. Meaning determines extension – by construction, so to speak. But (1) is given up; the psychological state of the individual speaker does not determine "what he means."

In most contexts this will agree with the way we speak, I believe. But one paradox: suppose Oscar is a German–English bilingual. In our view, in his total collection of dialects, the words "beech" and "*Buche*" are *exact synonyms*. The normal form descriptions of their meanings would be identical. But he might very well not know that they are synonyms! A speaker can have two synonyms in his vocabulary and not know that they are synonyms!

It is instructive to see how the failure of the apparently obvious "if S_1 and S_2 are synonyms and Oscar understands both S_1 and S_2 then Oscar knows that S_1 and S_2 are synonyms" is related to the falsity of (1), in our analysis. Notice that if we had chosen to omit the extension as a component of the "meaning vector," which is David Lewis's proposal as I understand it, then we would have the paradox that "elm" and "beech" have the *same meaning* but different extensions!

On just about any materialist theory, believing a proposition is likely to involve processing some *representation* of that proposition, be it a sentence in a language, a piece of "brain code," a thought form, or whatever. Materialists, and not only materialists, are reluctant to think that one can believe propositions *neat*. But even materialists tend to believe that, if one believes a proposition, *which* representation one employs is (pardon the pun) immaterial. If S_1 and S_2 are both representations that are *available* to me, then if I believe the proposition expressed by S_1 under the representation S_1, I must also believe it under the representation S_2 – at least, I must do this if I have any claim to rationality. But, as we have just seen, this isn't right. Oscar may well believe that *this* is a "beech" (it has a sign on it that says "beech"), but not believe or disbelieve that this is a "*Buche*." It is not just that belief is a process involving representations; he believes the proposition (if one wants to introduce "propositions" at all) under one representation and not under another.

The amazing thing about the theory of meaning is how long the subject has been in the grip of philosophical misconceptions, and how strong these misconceptions are. Meaning has been identified with a necessary and sufficient condition by philosopher after philosopher. In the empiricist tradition, it has been identified with method of verification, again by philosopher after philosopher. Nor have these misconceptions had the virtue of exclusiveness; not a few philosophers have held that meaning = method of verification = necessary and sufficient condition.

On the other side, it is amazing how weak the grip of the facts has been. After all, what have been pointed out in this essay is little more than home truths about the way we use words and how much (or rather, how little) we actually know when we use them. My own reflection on these matters began after I published a paper in which I confidently maintained that the meaning of a word was "a battery of semantical rules,"[28] and then began to wonder how the meaning of the common word "gold" could be accounted for in this way. And it is not that philosophers had never considered such examples: Locke, for example, uses this word as an example and is not troubled by the idea that its meaning is a necessary and sufficient condition!

If there is a reason for both learned and lay opinion having gone so far astray with respect to a topic which deals, after all, with matters which are in everyone's experience, matters concerning which we all have more data than we know what to do with, matters concerning which we have, if we shed preconceptions, pretty clear intuitions, it must be connected to the fact that the grotesquely mistaken views of language which are and always have been current reflect two specific and very central philosophical tendencies: the tendency to treat cognition as a purely *individual* matter and the tendency to ignore the *world*, insofar as it consists of more than the individual's "observations." Ignoring the division of linguistic labor is ignoring the social dimension of cognition; ignoring what we have called the *indexicality* of most words is ignoring the contribution of the environment. Traditional philosophy of language, like much traditional philosophy, leaves out other people and the world; a better philosophy and a better science of language must encompass both.

Notes

1 The contributors to this area are now too numerous to be listed: the pioneers were, of course, Zellig Harris and Noam Chomsky.

2 For a discussion of this question see my "The 'Innateness Hypothesis' and Explanatory Models in Linguistics," *Synthese* 17 (1967), pp. 12–22.

3 This is discussed by Ziff in *Understanding Understanding* (Ithaca, NY: Cornell University Press, 1972), esp. ch. 1.

4 This tradition grew up because *the* term whose analysis provoked all the discussion in medieval philsophy was the term "God," and the term "God" was thought to be defined through the conjunction of the terms "Good," "Powerful," "Omniscient," etc. – the so-called "Perfections." There was a problem, however, because God was supposed to be a Unity, and Unity was thought to exclude His essences being complex in *any* was – i.e., "God" was defined through a conjunction of terms, but God (without quotes) could not be the logical product of properties, nor could He be the unique thing exemplifying the logical product of two or more *distinct* properties, because even this highly abstract kind of "complexity" was held to be incompatible with His perfection of Unity. This is a theological paradox with which Jewish, Arabic, and Christian theologians wrestled for centuries (e.g., the doctrine of the Negation of Privation in Maimonides and Aquinas). It is amusing that theories of contemporary interest, such as conceptualism and nominalism, were first proposed as solutions to the problem of predication in the case of God. It is also amusing that the favorite model of definition in all of this theology – the conjunction of properties model – should survive, at least through its consquences, in philosophy of language until the present day.

5 Or rather, they will report: "On Twin Earth [*the Twin Earthian name for Terra* – H.P.] the word 'water' means H_2O."

6 The substance of this section was presented at a series of lectures I gave at the University of Washington (Summer Institute in Philosophy) in 1968, and at a lecture at the University of Minnesota.

7 See my "Is Semantics Possible?," in H. E. Kiefer and M. K. Munitz, eds, *Language, Belief, and Metaphysics* (Albany, NY: State University of New York Press, 1970).

8 This assumption is not actually needed in what follows. What is needed is that the same *natural kind* can exist in more than one possible world.

9 These points were made in my 1968 lectures at the University of Washington and the University of Minnesota.

10 See Kripke's "Identity and Necessity," in M. Munitz, ed., *Identity and Individuation* (New York: New York University Press, 1972), p. 157.

11 For a discussion of this point, see my "Explanation and Reference," in G. Pearce and P. Maynard, eds, *Conceptual Change* (Dordrecht: Reidel, 1973).

12 For an illuminating discussion of just these points, see R. Boyd's "Realism and Scientific Epistemology" (unpublished: Xerox draft circulated by author, Cornell Department of Philosophy).

13 See my "Logical Positivism and the Philosophy of Mind," in P. Achinstein, ed., *The Legacy of Logical Positivism* (Baltimore: Johns Hopkins Press, 1969); and also my "Degree of Confirmation and Inductive Logic," in P. A. Schilpp, ed., *The Philosophy of Rudolf Carnap* (La Salle, IL: Open Court, 1962), and my "Probability and Confirmation" (broadcast for the Voice of America Philosophy of Science Series, Spring 1963; reprinted in A. Danto and S. Morgenbesser, eds, *Philosophy of Science Today* (New York: Basic Books, 1967)).

14 See Kripke's "Identity and Necessity."

15 See my "It Ain't Necessarily So," *Journal of Philosophy* 59 (1962), pp. 658–71.

16 J. J. Katz, "Logic and Language: An Examination of Recent Criticism of Intensionalism" (forthcoming). [In K. Gunderson, ed., *Language, Mind, and Knowledge*, Minnesota Studies in the Philosophy of Science, VII (Minneapolis: University of Minnesota Press, 1975)].

17 The idea of a "one-criterion" word, and a theory of analyticity based on this notion, appears in my "The Analytic and the Synthetic," in H. Feigl and G. Maxwell, eds, *Minnesota Studies in the Philosophy of Science*, vol. 3 (Minneapolis: University of Minnesota Press, 1962).

18 This example comes from an analysis by Anthony Kroch (in his MIT doctoral dissertation, 1974, Department of Linguistics).

19 I *don't* have in mind the Flewish notion of "paradigm" in which any paradigm of a *K* is *necessarily* a *K* (in reality).

20 In my "Explanation and Reference," in Pearce and Maynard, *Conceptual Change*.

21 The term is due to Quine (in *Word and Object* (Cambridge, MA: MIT Press, 1960)): it signifies translation without clues from either shared culture or cognates.

22 For a discussion of the supposed impossibility of uniquely correct radical translation, see my "The Refutation of Conventionalism" (forthcoming in *Nous* [8 (1974), pp. 25–40] and also, in a longer version, in a collection edited by M. Munitz to be published by New York University Press under the title *Semantics and Philosophy*).

23 This is argued in "Is Semantics Possible?"

24 See "The Analytic and the Synthetic."

25 H. Reichenbach, *The Theory of Relativity and A Priori Knowledge* (Berkeley: University of California Press, 1965).

26 H. Reichenbach, in P. A. Schilpp, ed., *Albert Einstein: Philosopher-Scientist* (Evanston: Library of Living Philosophers, 1951).

27 Paul Benacerraf, "Mathematical Truth," *Journal of Philosophy* 70 (1973), pp. 661–78.

28 "How Not to Talk About Meaning," in R. Cohen and M. Wartofsky, eds, *Boston Studies in the Philosophy of Science*, vol. 2 (New York: Humanities Press, 1965).

Part II

The Meaning of Mind

4

Language and Mind

Introduction

A traditional picture of language and communication goes like this. We have thoughts, and sometimes with varying degrees of success we try to communicate these thoughts. Language is a tool for this purpose. It allows us to express our thoughts, and it allows an audience, who understands our language, to discover what we had in mind when we spoke or wrote. On this view, language is like a code that represents our hidden inner thoughts, which are mostly formed without the aid of language. It is a consequence of this view that thinking cannot be characterized in terms of the things we say or are disposed to say.

This traditional picture is closely allied to the thesis of the primacy of the intentional. This thesis, often associated with the Austrian psychologist Franz Brentano (1838–1917), has two main components. First, psychological phenomena such as believing, desiring, contemplating, and so on have content or meaning, which can be said to be the object of these psychological phenomena. For instance, if I believe that I lost my job, then the content of my belief is the proposition that I lost my job and this proposition is the object of my belief. Notice that I can have nonexistent things as objects of my thought. If I was misled and in fact I was lucky and I did not lose my job, I am still having beliefs about something that did not happen, namely that I lost my job.

Second, according to Brentano, the fact that psychological phenomena such as beliefs and desires have content, or what Brentano calls "intentionality," is a basic or primary fact about the world that cannot be analyzed or characterized in terms of anything that is not intentional. When we draw up a list of the fundamental and simple elements and properties of the world, we will include not only the fundamental physical processes physicists rely on in their explanations, but also the intentional properties and states of psychology.

In recent philosophy, Roderick Chisholm has been the most prominent defender of the primacy of the intentional. According to Chisholm, the meaning of language and the meaning of thought are related as are the light of the sun and the light of the moon. Without the sun, the moon would have no light, although the sun would still emit light without the moon, and in the same way, without thought, language would be meaningless, although without language, thought would still have content. He defends this view in his essay in this section by arguing that our language about intentionality – our reference to beliefs, desires, etc., and their content, as when I say "Mara believes that she lost her job" – cannot be replaced by language that refers only to nonintentional things.

Chisholm was opposed by many naturalist philosophers, that is, philosophers who assign a primary role to the natural sciences. Naturalists think that intentional phenomena ultimately have to be explained in terms of natural and nonintentional phenomena. A popular approach along these lines is to treat thinking as a kind of speech.

Wilfrid Sellars, a philosopher who played an important role in the rise of naturalism in the philosophy of mind and language, defends this approach in his essay in this section. For Sellars, the meaning of language should not be explained in terms of the intentionality of thought. Instead thought and its content should be explained in terms of language. For Sellars, language is not simply a vehicle for expressing our thoughts. Thought occurs in language; language is the very medium of thought. In Sellars' words, language is "the bearer of conceptual activity," that is, we can "think out loud."

Sellars explains beliefs, e.g., the belief that it will snow tomorrow, in terms of dispositions to think that it will snow tomorrow, and he explains such dispositions to think in terms of other dispositions to make certain utterances that conform to linguistic rules. Language is rule-governed behavior, and Sellars understands these rules as norms or standards for what ought to be done (rules of action) as well as what ought to be the case (rules of criticism). Rules of criticism are especially important for Sellars because these rules do not explicitly prescribe an action but only prescribe what should be the case. Sellars believes that rules of criticism do not presuppose any intentionality and thus can be put to use for a naturalistic analysis of intentionality.

Chisholm and Sellars represent two opposing tendencies: one gives thought primacy over language while the other gives primacy to language. Donald Davidson attempts to cut through this dispute by treating both thought and talk as equals. Nevertheless, for Davidson thought and language are intimately connected because something has thoughts only if it interprets the speech of others. Lara believes that the fishnets are mended only if she interprets the speech of others to mean that the fishnets are mended, and she interprets by assigning truth conditions to the sentences of others. Davidson believes that this means she has to determine under what conditions other people assent or dissent from sentences, including the sentence "The fishnets are mended."

It is only through the activity of interpreting the speech of others – determining under what conditions their sentences are true – that Lara acquires a concept of belief. To be an interpreter is to have beliefs about what others believe, and this is the source of our concept of belief. How is this relevant to belief? Because for Davidson you can have a belief only if you have a concept of belief. Lara can be said to have the belief that the fishnets are mended only if she has a concept of belief in addition to the concepts of a net, fish, mending, and so forth. This holds for all thoughts, not just beliefs. In order to have any thought at all, Davidson believes, you need to have a concept of belief, and this in turn requires that you interpret the speech of others. Creatures such as dogs that, strictly speaking, do not understand language do not have thoughts, according to Davidson.

Although Davidson attempts to rise above the dispute between Chisholm and Sellars, in important ways he sides with Sellars against Chisholm. While Chisholm believes thought is autonomous of language, both Sellars and Davidson make thought depend on public language. Not all naturalist philosophers agree that thought depends on public language, but even among those who disagree language can have a central role. For instance, although for Jerry Fodor (see his "Methodological Solipsism" in the Chapter 7 of this volume) public language is parasitic on inner thoughts, the medium of inner thoughts is still a language, albeit a private language of thought or "mentalese," and this to some degree has been accepted by most classical cognitivists, for whom the processing of symbolic information of a classical computer is a good model for human thinking. We turn to this model in the next section.

FURTHER READING

Biro, J. (1979). Intentionalism and the Theory of Meaning. *Monist* 62:238–57.
Chisholm, R. M. (1984). The Primacy of the Intentional. *Synthese* 61: 89–110.
Chisholm, R. M. and Sellars, W. (1958). Chisholm–Sellars Correspondence on Intentionality. In *Minnesota Studies in the Philosophy of Science, vol. 2: Concepts, Theories and the Mind–Body Problem*. Eds H. Feigel, M. Scriven and G. Maxwell. Minneapolis: University of Minnesota Press.
Fish, S. (1980). *Is There a Text in this Class?*. Cambridge, MA: Harvard University Press.
Gauker, C. (1994). *Thinking Out Loud*. Princeton, NJ: Princeton University Press.
Heil, J. (1992). Talk and Thought. In *The Nature of True Minds*. Cambridge: Cambridge University Press.
Sellars, W. (1963). Empiricism and the Philosophy of Mind. In *Science, Perception and Reality*. New York: Humanities Press.

Sentences About Believing

RODERICK M. CHISHOLM

(1) "I can look for him when he is not there, but not hang him when he is not there."[1] The first of these activities, Brentano would have said, is *intentional*; it may take as its object something which does not exist. But the second activity is "merely physical"; it cannot be performed unless its object is there to work with. "Intentionality," he thought, provides us with a mark of what is psychological.

I shall try to reformulate Brentano's suggestion by describing one of the ways in which we need to use language when we talk about certain psychological states and events. I shall refer to this use as the "intentional use" of language. It is a kind of use we can avoid when we talk about nonpsychological states and events.

In the interests of a philosophy contrary to that of Brentano, many philosophers and psychologists have tried to show, in effect, how we can avoid intentional language when we wish to talk about psychology. I shall discuss some of these attempts in so far as they relate to the sorts of thing we wish to be able to say about *believing*. I believe that these attempts have been so far unsuccessful. And I think that this fact may provide some reason for saying, with Brentano, that "intentionality" is a mark of what is psychological.

(2) In order to formulate criteria by means of which we can identify the "intentional" use of language, let us classify sentences as simple and compound. For our purposes I think it will be enough to say that a compound sentence is one compounded from two or more sentences by means of propositional connectives, such as "and," "or," "if-then," "although," and "because." A simple sentence is one which is not compound. Examples of simple sentences are "He is thinking of the Dnieper Dam," "She is looking for a suitable husband for her daughter," "Their car lacks a spare wheel," and "He believes that it will rain." I shall formulate three criteria for saying that simple declarative sentences are intentional, or are used intentionally.

(a) A simple declarative sentence is intentional if it uses a substantival expression – a name or a description – in such a way that neither the sentence nor its contradictory implies either that there is or that there isn't anything to which the substantival expression truly applies. The first two examples above are intentional by this criterion. When we say that a man is thinking of the Dnieper Dam, we do not imply either that there is or that there isn't such a dam; similarly when we deny that he is thinking of it. When we say that a lady is looking for a suitable husband for her daughter, we do not commit ourselves to saying that her daughter will, or that she will not, have a suitable husband; and similarly when we deny that the lady is looking for one. But the next sentence in our list of examples – "Their car lacks a spare wheel" – is not intentional. It is true that, if we affirm this sentence, we do not commit ourselves to saying either that there are or that there are not any spare wheels. But if we deny the sentence, affirming – "Their car does not lack a spare wheel," then we imply that there is a spare wheel somewhere.

(b) We may describe a second type of intentional use by reference to simple sentences the principal verb of which takes as its object a phrase containing a subordinate verb. The subordinate verb may follow immediately upon the principal verb, as in "He is contemplating killing himself"; it may occur in a complete clause, as in "He believes it will rain"; it may occur in an infinitive, as in "He wishes to speak"; or it may occur in participial form, as in "He accused John of stealing the money" and "He asked John's brother to testify against him." I shall say that such a simple declarative sentence is intentional if neither the sentence nor its contradictory implies either that the phrase following the principal verb is true or that it is false.[2] "He is contemplating killing himself" is intentional, according to this second criterion, because neither it nor its denial implies either that he does or that he doesn't kill himself; similarly with our other examples. But "He prevented John from stealing the money" is not intentional, because it implies that John did not steal the money. And "He knows how to swim" is not intentional, because its denial implies that he isn't swimming.

Sometimes people use substantival expressions in place of the kind of phrases I have just been talking about. Instead of saying, "I want the strike to be called off," they may say, "The strike's being called off is what I want." The latter sentence could be said to be intentional according to our first criterion, for neither the sentence nor its contradictory implies either that "there is such a thing as" the strike's being called off, or that there isn't – that is to say, neither implies that the strike will be, or that it will not be, called off.

Many intentional sentences of our first type may be rewritten in such a way that they become instances of our second type. Instead of saying "I would like a glass of water," one may say "I would like to have a glass of water." And instead of saying "He is looking for the Fountain of Youth," one may say "He is trying to find the Fountain of Youth." But some sentences of the first type seem to resist such transformation into the second type; for example, "I was thinking about you yesterday."

(c) If we make use of Frege's concept of "indirect reference," which is, of course, closely related to that of "intentionality," we can add another important class of sentence to our list of those which are intentional.[3] "Indirect reference" may be defined, without using the characteristic terms of Frege's theory of meaning, in the following way: a name (or description) of a certain thing has an indirect reference in a sentence if its replacement by a different name (or description) of that thing results in a sentence whose truth value may differ from that of the original sentence.[4] It is useful to interpret this criterion in such a way that we can say of those names (or descriptions), such as "the Fountain of Youth" and "a building half again as tall as the Empire State," which don't apply to anything, that they are all names of the same thing. Let us add, then, that a simple declarative sentence is intentional if it contains a name (or description) which has an indirect reference in that sentence. We can now say of certain *cognitive* sentences – sentences which use words such as "know," "remember," "see," "perceive," in one familiar way – that they, too, are intentional. I may see that Albert is here and Albert may be the man who will win the prize; but I do not now see that the man who will win the prize is here. And we all remember that although George IV knew that Scott was the author of *Marmion* he did not know that Scott was the author of *Waverley*.

(d) With respect to the intentionality of compound sentences – sentences constructed by means of propositional connectives from two or more sentences – it is enough to say this: a compound declarative sentence is intentional if and only if one or more of its component sentences is intentional. "I will be gratified if I learn that Albert wins the prize" is intentional, because the if-clause is intentional. But "The career of Ponce de Leon would have been most remarkable if he had found the Fountain of Youth" is not intentional, because neither of its components is intentional. (In order that this final criterion be applicable to sentences in the subjunctive, we should, of course, interpret it to mean a compound declarative sentence is intentional if and only if one or more of the component sentences of its indicative version is intentional.)

(3)   We may now formulate a thesis resembling that of Brentano by referring to intentional language. Let us say (1) that we do not need to use intentional language when we describe nonpsychological, or "physical," phenomena; we can express all that we know, or believe, about such phenomena in language which is not intentional.[5] And let us say (2) that, when we wish to describe certain psychological phenomena – in particular, when we wish to describe thinking, believing, perceiving, seeing, knowing, wanting, hoping, and the like – either (a) we must use language which is intentional or (b) we must use a vocabulary which we do not need to use when we describe nonpsychological, or "physical," phenomena.

I shall discuss this linguistic version of Brentano's thesis with reference to sentences about believing. I do not pretend to be able to show that it is true in its application to believing. But I think that there are serious difficulties, underestimated by many philosophers, which stand in the way of showing that it is false.

I wish to emphasize that my question does not concern "subsistence" or "the being of objects which don't exist." Philosophers may ask whether it is possible to think about unicorns if there are no unicorns for us to think about. They may also ask whether you and I can believe "the same thing" if there is no proposition or objective toward which each of our beliefs is directed. But I am not raising these questions. Possibly the feeling that the intentional use of language commits us to the assumption that there are such entities is one motive for seeking to avoid such use. But I wish to ask only whether we can avoid such use and at the same time say all that we want to be able to say about believing.

(4)   The first part of our thesis states that we do not need to use intentional language when we describe nonpsychological, or "physical," phenomena. I do not believe that this statement presents any serious difficulty. It is true that we do sometimes use intentional sentences in nonpsychological contexts. The following sentences, for example, are all intentional, according to our criteria, but none of them describes anything we would want to call "psychological": "The patient will be immune from the effects of any new epidemics" and "It is difficult to assemble a prefabricated house." But these sentences are not examples counter to our thesis. Anyone who understands the language can readily transform them into conditionals which are not intentional. (A compound sentence, it should be recalled, is intentional only if it has a component which is intentional.) Instead of using intentional

sentences, we could have said, "If there should be any new epidemics, the patient would not be affected by them" and "If anyone were to assemble a prefabricated house, he would have difficulties." (Perhaps the last sentence should be rendered as "If anyone were to try to assemble a prefabricated house, he would have difficulties." In this version the sentence is intentional, once again, but since it contains the verb "to try" it can no longer be said to be nonpsychological.)

I believe that any other ostensibly nonpsychological sentence which is intentional can be transformed, in an equally obvious way, into a sentence conforming to our version of Brentano's thesis. That is to say, it will become a sentence of one of two possible types: either (a) it will be no longer intentional or (b) it will be explicitly psychological. Sentences about probability may be intentional, but, depending upon one's conception of probability, they may be transformed either into the first or into the second type. If I say "It is probable that there is life on Venus," neither my sentence nor its denial implies either that there is life on Venus or that there is not. According to one familiar interpretation of probability, my sentence can be transformed into a nonintentional sentence about frequencies – sentences telling about places where there is life and places where there isn't and comparing Venus with such places, etc. According to another interpretation, my sentence can be transformed into a psychological statement about believing – e.g., "It is reasonable for us to believe that there is life on Venus." Intentional sentences about tendencies and purposes in nature may be treated similarly. If we say, nonintentionally, "The purpose of the liver is to secrete bile," we may mean, psychologically, that the Creator made the liver so that it would secrete bile, or we may mean, nonintentionally, that in most live animals having livers the liver does do this work and that when it does not the animal is unhealthy.

There are people who like to ascribe beliefs, perceptions, plans, desires, and the like to robots and computing machinery. A computing machine might be said to believe, truly, that 7 and 5 are 12; when it is out of order, it may be said to make mistakes and possibly to believe, falsely, that 7 and 5 are 11. But such sentences, once again, are readily transformed into other sentences, usually conditionals, which are no longer intentional. If a man says that the machine believes 7 and 5 to be 11, he may mean merely that, if the keys marked "7" and "5" are pressed, the machine will produce a slip on which "11" is marked. Other intentional sentences about the attitudes of machines may be more complex, but I'm sure that, if they have been given any meaning by those who use them, they can be readily transformed into sentences which are not intentional. Indeed the ease with which robot sentences may be made either intentional or nonintentional may be one ground, or cause, for believing that sentences about the attitudes of human beings may readily be transformed in ways counter to our version of Brentano's thesis.

It should be noted, with respect to those universal sentences of physics which have no "existential import," that they are not intentional. It is true that the sentence, "All moving bodies not acted upon by external forces continue in a state of uniform motion in a straight line," does not imply either that there are, or that there are not, such bodies. But its contradictory implies that there are such bodies.

(5)   The second part of our version of Brentano's thesis states that, when we wish to describe anyone's believing, seeing, knowing, wanting, and the like, either (a) we must use language which is intentional or (b) we must use a vocabulary we don't need when we talk about nonpsychological facts.

Perhaps the most instructive way of looking at our thesis is to contrast it with one which is slightly different. It has often been said, in recent years, that "the language of physical things" is adequate for the description of psychological phenomena – this language being any language whose vocabulary and rules are adequate for the description of nonpsychological phenomena. If we do not need intentional language for describing physical things, then this counterthesis – the thesis that the language of physical things is adequate for the description of psychological phenomena – would imply that we do not need intentional language for the description of psychological phenomena.

The easiest way to construct a nonintentional language for psychology is to telescope nouns and verbs. Finding a psychological verb, say "expects," and its grammatical object, say "food," we may manufacture a technical term by combining the two. We may say that the rat is "food-expectant" or that he "has a food-expectancy." Russell once proposed that, instead of saying "I perceive a cat," we say "I am cat-perceptive," and Professor Ryle has described a man seeing a thimble by saying that the man "is having a visual sensation in a thimble-seeing frame of mind."[6] Sentences about thinking, believing, desiring, and the like could readily be transformed in similar ways. But this way of avoiding intentional language has one serious limitation. If we wish to tell anyone what our technical terms mean, we must use intentional language again. Russell did not propose a definition of his technical term "cat-perceptive" in familiar nonintentional terms; he told us, in effect, that we should call a person "cat-perceptive" whenever the person takes something to be a cat. Our version of Brentano's thesis implies that, if we dispense with intentional language in talking about perceiving, believing, and expecting, we must use a vocabulary we don't need to use when we talk about nonpsychological facts. The terms "food-expectancy," "thimble-seeing frame of mind," and "cat-perceptive" illustrate such a vocabulary.

I shall comment upon three general methods philosophers and psychologists have used in their attempts to provide "physical" translations of belief sentences. The first of these methods makes use of the concepts of "specific response" and "appropriate behavior"; references to these concepts appeared in the writings of the American "New Realists" and can still be found in the works of some psychologists. The second method refers to "verbal behavior"; its clearest statement is to be found in Professor Ayer's *Thinking and Meaning*. The third refers to a peculiar type of "fulfillment" or "satisfaction"; its classic statement is William James's so-called pragmatic theory of truth. I shall try to show that, if we interpret these various methods as attempts to show that our version of Brentano's thesis is false, then we can say that they are inadequate. I believe that the last of these methods – the one which refers to "fulfillment" or "satisfaction" – is the one which has the best chance of success.

(6)   When psychologists talk about the behavior of animals, they sometimes find it convenient to describe certain types of response in terms of the stimuli with which such responses are usually associated. A bird's "nesting responses" might be defined by reference to what the bird does in the presence of its nest and on no other occasions. A man's "rain responses," similarly, might be defined in terms of what he does when and only when he is in the rain. I believe we may say that some of the American "New Realists" assumed that, for every object of which a man can be said ever to be conscious, there is some response he makes when and only when he is in the presence of that object – some response which is specific to that object.[7] And they felt that the specific response vocabulary – "rain response," "fire response," "cat response" – provided a way of describing belief and the other types of phenomenon Brentano would have called "intentional." This "specific response theory" is presupposed in some recent accounts of "sign behavior."

I think Brentano would have said that, if smoke is a *sign* to me of fire, then my perception of smoke causes me to *believe* that there is a fire. But if we have a specific response vocabulary available, we might say this: smoke is a sign to me of fire provided smoke calls up my *fire responses*. We might then say, more generally, that *S* is a sign of *E* for *O* provided only *S* calls up *O*'s *E*-responses. But what would *O*'s *E*-responses be?

What would a man's fire responses be? If smoke alone can call up his fire responses – as it may when it serves as a sign of fire – we can no longer say that his fire responses are the ways he behaves when and *only* when he is stimulated by fire. For we want to be able to say that he can make these responses in the presence of smoke and not of fire. Should we modify our conception of "fire response," then, and say that a man's fire responses are responses which are like those – which are *similar* to those – he makes when stimulated by fire? This would be saying too much, for in *some* respects every response he makes is like those he makes in the presence of fire. *All* of his responses, for example, are alike in being the result of neural and physiological events. But we don't want to say that all of the man's responses are fire responses. It is not enough, therefore, to say that a man's fire responses are *similar* to those he makes, or would make, in the presence of fire; we must also specify the *respect* in which they are similar. But no one, I believe, has been able to do this.

The problem isn't altered if we say that a man's fire responses constitute some *part* of those responses he makes in the presence of fire. More generally, the problem isn't altered if we introduce this definition: *S* is a sign of *E* provided only that *S* calls up *part* of the behavior that *E* calls up. It is not enough to say that the sign and the object call up *some* of the same behavior. The books in this room are not a sign to me of the books in that room, but the books in the two rooms call up some of the same behavior. And it is too much to say that *S* calls up *all* of the behavior that *E* calls up – that the sign evokes *all* of the responses that the subject makes to the object. The bell is a sign of food to the dog, but the dog, as we know, needn't eat the bell.

We might try to avoid our difficulties by introducing qualifications of another sort in our definition of *sign*. Charles E. Osgood proposes the following definition in the chapter entitled "Language Behavior," in *Method and Theory in Experimental Psychology* (New York: Oxford University Press, 1953): "A pattern of stimulation which is not the object is a sign of the object if it evokes in an organism a mediating reaction, this (a) being some fractional part of the total behavior elicited by the object and (b) producing distinctive self-stimulation that mediates responses which would not occur without the previous association of nonobject and object patterns of stimulation"(p. 696). The second qualification in this definition – the requirement that there must have been a "previous association of nonobject and object" and hence that the thing signified must at least once have been experienced by the subject – provides a restriction we haven't yet considered. But this restriction introduces a new set of difficulties. I have never seen a tornado, an igloo, or the queen of England. According to the present definition, therefore, nothing can signify to me that a tornado is approaching, that there are igloos somewhere, or that the queen of England is about to arrive. Hence the definition leaves one of the principal functions of signs and language unprovided for.

We may summarize the difficulties such definitions involve by reference to our attempt to define what a man's "fire responses" might be – those responses which, according to the present type of definition, are evoked by anything that serves as a sign of fire, and by reference to which we had hoped to define *beliefs* about fires. No matter how we formulate our definition of "fire responses," we find that our definition has one or another of these three defects: (1) a man's fire responses become responses that *only* fire can call up – in which case the presence of smoke alone will *not* call them up; (2) his fire responses become responses he sometimes makes when he *doesn't* take anything to be a sign of fire, when he *doesn't* believe that anything is on fire; or (3) our definitions will make use of intentional language.[8]

The "appropriate action" terminology is a variant of the "specific response" terminology. Psychologists sometimes say that, if the bell is a sign of food, then the bell calls up responses *appropriate* to food. And one might say, more generally, that a man *believes* a proposition p provided only he behaves, or is disposed to behave, in a way that is "appropriate to p," or "appropriate to p's being true." But unless we can find a way of defining "appropriate," this way of talking is intentional by our criteria. When we affirm, or when we deny, "The knight is acting in a way that is appropriate to the presence of dragons," we do not imply either that there are, or that there are not, any dragons.[9]

(7)   In the second type of definition we refer to the "verbal behavior" which we would ordinarily take to be symptomatic of belief. This time we try to describe a man's belief – his believing – in terms of his actual uses of words or of his dispositions to use words in various ways.

Let us consider a man who believes that the Missouri River has its source in the northern part of Montana. In saying that he believes this, we do not mean to imply that he is actually doing anything; we mean to say that, if the occasion arose, he would do certain things which he would not do if he did not believe that the Missouri had its source in northern Montana. This fact may be put briefly by saying that when we ascribe a belief to a man we are ascribing a certain set of dispositions to him. What, then, are these dispositions? According to the present suggestion, the man is disposed to use language in ways in which he wouldn't use it if he didn't have the belief. In its simplest form, the suggestion is this: if someone were to ask the man "Where is the source of the Missouri River?" the man would reply by uttering the words, "In the Northern part of Montana"; if someone were to ask him to name the rivers having their sources in the northern part of Montana, he would utter, among other things, the word "Missouri"; if someone were to ask "Does the Missouri arise in northern Montana?" he would say "Yes"; and so on.

We should note that this type of definition, unlike the others, is not obviously applicable to the beliefs of animals. Sometimes we like to say such things as "The dog believes he's going to be punished" and "Now the rat thinks he's going to be fed." But if we accept the present type of definition, we cannot say these things (unless we are prepared to countenance such conditions as "If the rat could speak English, he'd now say 'I am about to be fed'"). I do not know whether this limitation – the fact that the definition does not seem to allow us to ascribe beliefs to animals – should be counted as an advantage, or as a disadvantage, of the "verbal behavior" definition. In any case, the definition involves a number of difficulties of detail and a general difficulty of principle.

The if-then sentences I have used as illustrations describe the ways in which our believer would answer certain questions. But surely we must qualify these sentences by adding that the believer has no desire to deceive the man who is questioning him. To the question "Where is the source of the Missouri?" he will reply by saying "In northern Montana" – provided he wants to tell the truth. But this proviso brings us back to statements which are intentional. If we say "The man wants to tell the truth" we do not imply, of course, either that he does or that he does not tell the truth; similarly, if we assert the contradictory. And when we say "He wants to *tell the truth*" – or, what comes to the same thing, "He doesn't want to *lie*" – we mean, I suppose, he doesn't want to say anything he *believes* to be false. Perhaps we should also add that he has no objection to his questioner *knowing* what it is that he believes about the Missouri.

We should also add that the man speaks English and that he does not misunderstand the questions that are put to him. This means, among other things, that he should not take the other man to be saying something other than what he is saying. If he took the other man to be saying "Where is the source of the *Mississippi*?" instead of "Where is the source of the Missouri?" he might reply by saying "In Minnesota" and not by saying "In Montana." It would seem essential to add, then, that he must not *believe* the other man to be asking anything other than "Where is the source of the Missouri?"

Again, if the man does not speak English, it may be that he will not reply by uttering any of the words discussed above. To accommodate this possibility, we might qualify our if-then statements in some such way as this: "If someone were to ask the man a question which, for him, had the same meaning as 'Where is the source of the Missouri?' has for us, then he would reply by uttering an expression which, for him, has the same meaning as 'In the northern part of Montana' has for us."[10] Or we might qualify our original if-then statements by adding this provision to the antecedents: "and if the man speaks English." When this qualification is spelled out, then, like the previous one, it will contain some reference to the meanings of words – some reference to the ways in which the man uses, applies, or interprets words and sentences. These references to the meanings of words and sentences – to their use, application, or interpretation – take us to the difficulty of principle involved in this linguistic interpretation of believing.

The sentences we use to describe the meanings and uses of words are ordinarily intentional. If I say, "The German word *Riese* means giant," I don't mean to imply, of course, either that there are giants or that there aren't any giants; similarly, if I deny the sentence. If we think of a word as a class of sounds or of designs, we may be tempted to say, at first consideration, that intentional sentences about the meanings and uses of words are examples which run counter to our general thesis about intentional sentences. For here we have sentences which seem to be concerned, not with anyone's thoughts, beliefs, or desires, but rather with the properties of certain patterns of marks and noises. But we must remind ourselves that such sentences are elliptical.

If I say, of the noises and marks constituting the German word *Riese*, that they mean giant, I mean something like this: "When people in Germany talk about giants, they use the word *Riese* to stand for giants, or to refer to giants." To avoid talking about things which don't exist, we might use the expression "gigantic" (interpreting it in its literal sense) and say: "People in Germany would call a thing *ein Riese* if and only if the thing were gigantic." And to make sure that the expression "to call a thing *ein Riese*" does not suggest anything mentalistic, we might replace it by a more complex expression about noises and marks. "To say 'A man calls a thing *ein Riese*' is to say that, in the presence of the thing, he would make the noise, or the mark, *ein Riese*."

Let us ignore all of the difficulties of detail listed above and let us assume, for simplicity, that our speakers have a childlike desire to call things as frequently as possible by their conventional names. Let us even assume that everything having a name is at hand waiting to be called. Is it true that people in Germany would call a thing *ein Riese* – in the present sense of "to call" – if and only if the thing were gigantic?

If a German were in the presence of a giant and took it to be something else – say, a tower or a monument – he would not call it *ein Riese*. Hence we cannot say that, if a thing were a giant, he would call it *ein Riese*. If he were in the presence of a tower or a monument and *took* the thing to be a giant, then he would call the tower or the monument *ein Riese*. And therefore we cannot say he would call a thing *ein Riese* only if the thing were a giant.

Our sentence "The German word *Riese* means giant" does not mean merely that people in Germany – however we may qualify them with respect to their desires – would call a thing *ein Riese* if and only if the thing were gigantic. It means at least this much more – that they would call a thing by this name if and only if they *took* the thing to be gigantic or *believed* it to be gigantic or *knew* it to be gigantic. And, in general, when we use the intentional locution, "People use such and such a word to mean so-and-so," part of what we mean to say is that people use that word when they wish to express or convey something they *know* or *believe* – or *perceive* or *take* – with respect to so-and-so.

I think we can say, then, that, even if we can describe a man's believing in terms of language, his actual use of language, or his dispositions to use language in certain ways, we cannot describe his use of language, or his dispositions to use language in those ways, unless we refer to what he believes, or knows, or perceives.

The "verbal behavior" approach, then, involves difficulties essentially like those we encountered with the "specific response" theory. In trying to define "fire response," it will be recalled, we had to choose among definitions having at least one of three possible defects. We now seem to find that, no matter how we try to define that behavior which is to constitute "using the word *Riese* to mean giant," our definition will have one of these three undesirable consequences: (1) we will be unable to say that German-speaking people ever mistake anything for a giant and call something which is *not* a giant *ein Riese*; (2) we will be unable to say that German-speaking people ever mistake a giant for something else and refuse to call a giant *ein Riese*; or (3) our definition will make use of intentional language.

The final approach I shall examine involves similar difficulties.

(8) One of the basic points in the grammar of our talk about states of consciousness, as Professor Findlay has observed, is that such states always stand opposed to other states which will "carry them out" or "fulfill" them.[11] The final approach to belief sentences I would like to discuss is one based upon this conception of *fulfillment*. I believe that, if we are to succeed in showing that Brentano was wrong, our hope lies here.

Let us consider a lady who reaches for the teakettle, *expecting* to find it full. We can say of her that she has a "motor set" which would be *disrupted* or *frustrated* if the teakettle turns out to be empty and which would be *fulfilled* or *satisfied* if the teakettle turns out to be full. In saying that the empty teakettle would disrupt or frustrate a "motor set," I am thinking of the disequilibration which might result from her lifting it; at the very least, she would be startled or surprised. But in saying that her set would be fulfilled or satisfied if the teakettle turns out to be full, I am not thinking of a positive state which serves as the contrary of disruption or frustration. Russell has introduced the terms "yes-feeling" and "quite-so feeling" in this context and would say, I think, that if the teakettle were full the lady would have a quite-so feeling.[12] Perhaps she would have such a feeling if her expectation had just been challenged – if someone had said, just before she lifted the teakettle, "I think you're mistaken in thinking there's water in that thing." And perhaps expectation always involves a kind of tension, which is relieved, or consummated, by the presence of its object. But we will be on surer ground if we describe the requisite fulfillment, or satisfaction, in negative terms. To say that a full teakettle would cause fulfillment, or satisfaction, is merely to say that, unlike an empty teakettle, it would not cause disruption or frustration. The kind of "satisfaction" we can attribute to successful expectation, then, is quite different from the kind we can attribute to successful strivings or "springs of action."

Our example suggests the possibility of this kind of definition: "*S expects* that *E* will occur within a certain period" means that *S* is in a bodily state which would be frustrated, or disrupted, if and only if *E* were not to occur within that period. Or, if we prefer the term "fulfill," we may say that S is in a bodily state which would be fulfilled if and only if E were to occur within that period. And then we could define "believes" in a similar way, or perhaps define "believes" in terms of "being-disposed-to-expect."

I would like to remark, in passing, that in this type of definition we have what I am sure are the essentials of William James's so-called pragmatic theory of truth – a conception which has been seriously misunderstood, both in Great Britain and in America. Although James used the terms "fulfill" and "fulfillment," he preferred "satisfy" and "satisfaction." In his terms, our suggested definition of "believing" would read: "S believes that E will occur within a certain period" means that S is in a bodily state which would be *satisfied* if and only if E were to occur within that period. If we say that S's belief is true, that he is correct in thinking that E will occur within that period, then we imply, as James well knew, that E is going to occur in that period – and hence that S's belief will be satisfied. If we say that S's belief is false, we imply that E is not going to occur – and hence that S's belief will not be satisfied. And all of this implies that the man's belief is true if and only if he is in a state which is going to be satisfied. But unfortunately James's readers interpreted "satisfy" in its more usual sense, in which it is applicable to strivings and desirings rather than to believings.

Our definitions, as they stand, are much too simple; they cannot be applied, in any plausible way, to those situations for which we ordinarily use the words "believe," "take," and "expect." Let us consider, briefly, the difficulties involved in applying our definition of "believe" to one of James' own examples.

How should we re-express the statement "James believes there are tigers in India"? Obviously it would not be enough to say merely, "James is in a state which would be satisfied if and only if there are tigers in India, or which would be disrupted if and only if there are no tigers in India." We should say at least this much more: "James is in a state such that, if he were to go to India, the state would be satisfied if and only if there are tigers there." What if James went to India with no thought of tigers and with no desire to look for any? If his visit were brief and he happened not to run across any tigers, then the satisfaction, or disruption, would not occur in the manner required by the definition. More important, what if he came upon tigers and took them to be lions? Or if he were to go to Africa, *believing* himself to be in India – or to India, *believing* himself to be in Africa?

I think it is apparent that the definition cannot be applied to the example unless we introduce a number of intentional qualifications into the definiens. Comparable difficulties seem to stand in the way of applying the terms of this type of definition in any of those cases we would ordinarily call instances of believing. Yet this type of definition may have an advantage the others do not have. It may be that there are simple situations, ordinarily described as "beliefs" or "expectations," which can be adequately described, nonintentionally, by reference to fulfillment, or satisfaction, and disruption, or surprise. Perhaps the entire meaning of such a statement as "The dog expects to be beaten" or "The baby expects to be fed" can be conveyed in this manner. And perhaps "satisfaction" or "surprise" can be so interpreted that our ordinary beliefs can be defined in terms of "being disposed to have" a kind of expectation which is definable by reference to "satisfaction" or "surprise." And if all of these suppositions are true then we may yet be able to interpret belief sentences in a way which is contrary to the present version of Brentano's thesis. But, I believe, we aren't able to do so now.

(9)   The philosophers and psychologists I have been talking about seem to have felt that they were trying to do something important – that it would be philosophically significant if they could show that belief sentences can be rewritten in an adequate language which is not

intentional, or at least that it would be significant to show that Brentano was wrong. Let us suppose for a moment that we *cannot* rewrite belief sentences in a way which is contrary to our linguistic version of Brentano's thesis. What would be the significance of this fact? I feel that this question is itself philosophically significant, but I am not prepared to answer it. I do want to suggest, however, that the two answers which are most likely to suggest themselves are not satisfactory.

I think that, if our linguistic thesis about intentionality is true, then the followers of Brentano would have a right to take some comfort in this fact. But if someone were to say that this linguistic fact indicates that there is a ghost in the machine I would feel sure that his answer to our question is mistaken. (And it would be important to remind him that belief sentences, as well as other intentional sentences, seem to be applicable to animals.)

What if someone were to tell us, on the other hand, that intentional sentences about believing and the like don't really say anything and that, in consequence, the hypothetical fact we are considering may have no philosophical significance? He might say something like this to us: "The intentional sentences of ordinary language have many important tasks; we may use the ones about believing and the like to give vent to our feelings, to influence the behavior of other people, and to perform many other functions which psychiatrists can tell us about. But such sentences are not factual; they are not descriptive; they don't say things about the world in the way in which certain non-psychological sentences say things about the world." I do not feel that this answer, as it stands, would be very helpful. For we would not be able to evaluate it unless the man also (1) gave some meaning to his technical philosophical expressions, "factual," "descriptive," and "they don't say things about the world," and (2) had some way of showing that, although these expressions can be applied to the use of certain nonpsychological sentences, they cannot be applied to the use of those psychological sentences which are intentional.

Or suppose something like this were suggested: "Intentional sentences do not say of the world what at first thought we tend to think they say of the world. They are, rather, to be grouped with such sentences as 'The average carpenter has 2.7 children,' 'Charity is an essential part of our obligations,' and 'Heaven forbid,' in that their uses, or performances, differ in very fundamental ways from other sentences having the same grammatical form. We need not assume, with respect to the words which make sentences intentional, such words as 'believe,' 'desire,' 'choose,' 'mean,' 'refer,' and 'signify,' that they stand for a peculiar kind of property, characteristic, or relation. For we need not assume that they stand for properties, characteristics, or relations at all." We could ask the philosopher taking such a stand to give us a positive account of the uses of these words which *would* be an adequate account and which would show us that Brentano was mistaken. But I do not believe that anyone has yet been able to provide such an account.

Notes

1   L. Wittgenstein, *Philosophical Investigations* (London and New York: Macmillan, 1953), 133e.

2   This criterion must be so interpreted that it will apply to sentences wherein the verb phrases following the principal verb are infinitive, prepositional, or participial phrases; hence it must make sense to speak of such phrases as being true or false. When I say of the phrase, following the main verb of "He accused John of stealing the money," that it is true, I mean, of course, that John stole the money. More generally, when I say of such a sentence that the phrase following the principal verb is true, or that it is false, my statement may be interpreted as applying to that new sentence which is like the phrase in question, except that the verb appearing in infinitive or participial form

in the phrase is the principal verb of the new sentence. I should add a qualification about tenses, but I do not believe that my failure to do so is serious. It should be noted that, in English, when the subject of an infinitive or of a participle is the same as that of the principal verb, we do not repeat the subject; although we say "I want John to go," we do not say "I want me to go" or "John wants himself to go." When I say, then, that the last two words of "I want to go" are true, my statement should be interpreted as applying to "I shall go."

3   By adopting Frege's theory of meaning – or his terminology – we could make this criterion do the work of our first two. But I have made use of the first two in order that no one will be tempted to confuse what I want to say with what Frege had to say about meaning. The three criteria overlap to a considerable extent.

4   If E is a sentence obtained merely by putting the identity sign between two names or descriptions of the same thing, if A is a sentence using one of these names or descriptions, if B is like A except that where A uses the one name or description B uses the other, then the one name or description may be said to have an *indirect reference* in A provided that the conjunction of A and E does not imply B.

5   Certain sentences describing relations of comparison (e.g., "Some lizards look like dragons") constitute exceptions to (1). Strictly speaking, then, (1) should read: "we do not need any intentional sentences, other than those describing relations of comparison, when we describe nonpsychological phenomena."

6   See Russell's *Inquiry into Meaning and Truth* (New York: Norton, 1940), p. 142, and Ryle's *Concept of Mind* (London: Hutchinson's University Library, 1949), p. 230.

7   See ch. 9 of E. B. Holt, *The Concept of Consciousness* (London: G. Allen, 1914).

8   If we say that smoke signifies fire to O provided only that, as a result of the smoke, "there is a fire in O's behavioral environment," or "there is a fire for O," and if we interpret the words in the quotations in the way in which psychologists have tended to interpret them, our language is intentional.

9   R. B. Braithwaite, in "Belief and Action" (*Proceedings of the Aristotelian Society*, supplementary vol. 20, p. 10), suggests that a man may be said to believe a proposition *p* provided this condition obtains: "If at a time when an occasion arises relevant to *p*, his springs of action are *s*, he will perform an action which is such that, if *p* is true, it will tend to fulfill *s*, and which is such that, if *p* is false, it will not tend to satisfy *s*." But the definition needs qualifications in order to exclude those people who, believing the true proposition *p* that there are people who can reach the summit of Mt Everest, and having the desire *s* to reach the summit themselves, have yet acted in a way which has not tended to satisfy *s*. Moreover, if we are to use such a definition to show that Brentano was wrong, we must provide a nonintentional definition of the present use of "wish," "desire," or "spring of action."

10   See Alonzo Church's "On Carnap's Analysis of Statements of Assertion and Belief," *Analysis* 10 (1950).

11   "The Logic of *Bewusstseinslagen*," *Philosophical Quarterly* 5 (1955).

12   See *Human Knowledge* (New York: Simon and Schuster, 1948), pp. 148 and 125; compare *The Analysis of Matter* (New York: Harcourt, Brace, 1927), p. 184.

Language as Thought and as Communication

WILFRID SELLARS

My aim in this paper is to throw light from several directions on the intimate connections which exist between conceptual thinking and the linguistic behavior which is said to "express" it. The position which I shall ultimately delineate and defend, though behavioristic in its methodological orientation, is not, initial appearances to the contrary, behavioristic in its substantive contentions. It can, nevertheless, be characterized as an attempt to give a naturalistic interpretation of the intentionality of conceptual acts.

The early sections (I–IV) stress the essentially rule-governed character of linguistic behavior. I argue that a proper understanding of the nature and status of linguistic rules is a *sine qua non* of a correct interpretation of the sense in which linguistic behavior can be said to be (and not merely to express) conceptual activity. The second, and larger, part of the paper (sections Vff) is devoted to exploring the sense (or senses) in which language can be said to "express" thought. A distinction is drawn between three different contexts in which the verb occurs. It is argued that they involve radically different meanings which, if confused, blur the distinction between language as conceptual act and language as means of communication, and preclude the possibility of an adequate philosophy of language.

I

There are many interesting questions about the exact meaning or meanings of the term "rule" in nonphilosophical contexts. What, for example, is the difference between a "rule" and a "principle"? Are principles simply "first" rules in that they are not special applications of more general rules? Or is the primary difference that rules can be arbitrary? Or are principles rules for choosing rules? Is the principle of induction, for example, a higher-order rule for choosing law-like statements, themselves construed as extralogical rules of inference? Though these questions are intrinsically interesting and relevant to the general topic of this paper, I shall not discuss them. For however the domain of norms and standards is to be stratified and botanized, the term "rule" has acquired over the years a technical and generic sense in which it applies to general statements concerning that which ought or ought not to be done or to be the case or to be permissible or not permissible – distinctions which can be put in many different ways.

For our purposes, then, a rule is roughly a general "ought" statement. Such statements have been traditionally divided into hypothetical and categorical "oughts," or, as it has often misleadingly been put, "imperatives." The distinction between hypothetical and categorical oughts is an important one, though I believe that they are far more intimately related than is ordinarily taken to be the case.[1]

Hypothetical oughts have the form "if one wants X, one ought to do Y." They transpose a relation of implication between a state of affairs X and a doing of Y into an implication appropriate to practical reasoning. In spite of their crucial importance to a theory of normative discourse, I shall have nothing to say about them, save by implication.

As far as anything I have so far said is concerned, a categorical ought is simply one that is not, in the familiar Kantian sense, a hypothetical ought. I shall continue my division informally by calling attention to the most familiar variety of general categorical oughts, those, namely, of the form

If one is in C, one ought to do A.

Notice that although this proposition is conditional in form, it is not, in the Kantian sense, a hypothetical ought; and it is *as* contrasted with the latter that, even though it is conditional, it is called categorical. By application and the use of *modus ponens* one can derive conclusions of the form

> *S* ought to do *A*

which not only are not hypothetical oughts, but are categorical (non-iffy) statements. Notice, by contrast, that from "If one wants *X*, one ought to do *A*," together with "*S* wants *X*" it is not correct to infer "*S* ought to do *A*."

The important feature, for our purposes, of general categorical oughts of the above form is that for actual existence to conform to these oughts is a matter of the agents to which they apply doing *A* when they are actually in the specified circumstance *C*; and this, in turn, is a matter of their setting about doing *A* when they believe that the circumstances are *C*.

It follows that the "subjects" to which these rules apply must have the concepts of *doing A* and *being in C*. They must have, to use a current turn of phrase, the appropriate "recognitional capacities." Furthermore, for the rule itself to play a role in bringing about the conformity of "is" to "ought," the agents in question must conceive of action *A as* what ought to be done in circumstances *C*. This requires that they have the concept of what it is for an action to be called for by a certain kind of circumstance.

II

Importantly different from rules of the above form – which may be called, in a straightforward sense, *rules of action* – are rules that specify not what someone ought to do, but how something *ought to be*. Of these an important subclass has the form:

> *X*s ought to be in state φ, whenever such and such is the case.

The purpose of such a rule is achieved to the extent that it comes to be the case that *X*s are in state φ when such and such is indeed the case. This time, however, the conformity of actual existence to the ought does not, in general, require that the *X*s which are, in a sense, the subjects of the rule, i.e., that to which it applies, have the concept of what it is to be in state φ or of what it is for such and such to be the case. This is obvious when the *X*s in question are inanimate objects, as in the example:

> Clock chimes ought to strike on the quarter hour.

Now ought-to-bes (or *rules of criticism* as I shall also call them), though categorical in form, point beyond themselves in two ways. In the first place they imply (in some sense of this protean term) a *reason*, a *because* clause. The exploration of this theme would seem to take us back to the excluded topic of hypothetical imperatives. In the second place, though ought-to-bes are carefully to be distinguished from ought-to-dos they have an essential connection with them. The connection is, roughly, that ought-to-bes imply ought-to-dos. Thus the ought-to-be about clock chimes implies, roughly:

> (Other things being equal and where possible) one ought to bring it about that clock chimes strike on the quarter hour.

This rule belongs in our previous category, and is a rule of action. As such it requires that the items to which *it* applies (persons rather than chimes) have the appropriate concepts or recognitional capacities.

The distinction between ought-to-dos (rules of action) and ought-to-bes (rules of criticism) stands out clearly when the examples are suitably chosen. A possibility of confusion arises, however, when the ought-to-bes concern persons rather than inanimate objects. Consider, for example,

One ought to feel sympathy for bereaved people.

This example is interesting for two reasons: (1) It is a rule conformity to which requires that the subjects to which it applies have the concept of what it is to be bereaved. In this respect it is like a rule of action. (2) In the absence of a clear theory of action one might think of *feeling sympathy* as an action. Thus a casual and uninformed look might lead to the subsumption of the example under the form:

One ought to do *A*, if *C*.

It is clear on reflection, however, that feeling sympathy is an action only in that broad sense in which anything expressed by a verb in the active voice is an action.

Nor should it be assumed that all ought-to-bes which apply to persons and concern their being in a certain state whenever a certain circumstance obtains are such that the conformity to them of actual fact requires that the persons in question have the concept of this circumstance. The point is of decisive importance for our problem. To set the stage, consider ought-to-bes pertaining to the training of animals.

These rats ought-to-be in state φ, whenever *C*.

The conformity of the rats in question to this rule does not require that they have a concept of *C*, though it does require that they be able to respond differentially to cues emanating from *C*. Since the term "recognitional capacity" is one of those accordion words which can be used now in one sense and now in another, it is a menace to sound philosophy.

On the other hand, the subjects of the ought-to-dos corresponding to these ought-to-bes, i.e., the trainers, must have the concept both of the desirable state φ and of the circumstances in which the animals are to be in it.

If we now return to the sympathy example, we notice another interesting feature. If we compare the ought-to-be with the corresponding ought-to-do,

(Other things being equal and where possible) one ought to bring it about that people feel sympathy for the bereaved,

we see that the "subjects" of the ought-to-be (i.e., those who ought to feel sympathy) coincide with the "subjects" of the corresponding ought-to-do (i.e., those who ought to bring it about that people feel sympathy for the bereaved). It is the same items (people) who are the *agent*-subjects of the ought-to-do and the *subject-matter* subjects of the ought-to-be.

III

It is obvious, from the above considerations, that if all rules of language were ought-to-dos we would be precluded from explaining what it is to have concepts in terms of rules of language. Now many rules of language are ought-to-dos thus,

(Other things being equal) one ought to say such and such, if in *C*

and as such they can be efficacious in linguistic activity only to the extent that people have the relevant concepts. It is therefore of the utmost importance to note that many of the rules of language which are of special interest to the epistemologist are ought-to-bes rather than ought-to-dos. For only by taking this fact into account is it possible to carry out a program according to which (1) linguistic activity is, in a primary sense, conceptual activity; (2) linguistic activity is through and through rule-governed.

Much attention has been devoted of late to linguistic *actions*,[2] where the term "action" is taken in the strict sense of what an agent does, a piece of conduct, a performance – the practical sense of action, as contrasted with the general metaphysical sense in which action is contrasted with passion. The topic of linguistic actions, whether performatory, locutionary, illocutionary, perlocutionary,[3] or perhaps, elocutionary is an important one. Indeed, it is important not only for a theory of communication, but for epistemology, for there are linguistic *actions* which are of essential interest to the epistemologist: thus asking questions and seeking to answer them. On the other hand it can scarcely be overemphasized that to approach language in terms of the paradigm of *action* is to make a commitment which, if the concept of action is taken seriously, and the concept of rule is taken seriously, leads to (1) the Cartesian idea of linguistic episodes as *essentially* the sort of thing brought about by an agent whose conceptualizing is not linguistic; (2) an inability to understand the rule-governed character of this conceptualizing itself, as contrasted with its overt expression. For if thought is analogous to linguistic activity to the extent implied by Plato's metaphor "dialogue in the soul," the idea that overt speech is *action* and its rules *rules of action* will generate the idea that all inner speech is *action* and *its* rules *rules of action*, which leads to paradox and absurdity without end.

I propose, instead that the epistemologist, while recognizing that language is an instrument of communication, should focus attention on language as the bearer of conceptual activity. This is not to say that the two aspects can be separated as with a knife. Indeed, by pointing out that ought-to-bes imply ought-to-dos we have already recognized that language users exist at the level of agents. Roughly, to be a being capable of conceptual activity is to be a being which acts, which recognizes norms and standards, and which engages in practical reasoning. It is, as Kant pointed out, one and the same reason which is in some of its activities "theoretical," and in some of its activities "practical." Of course, if one gives to "practical" the specific meaning *ethical* then a fairly sharp separation of these activities can be maintained. But if one means by "practical" *pertaining to norms*, then so-called theoretical reason is as larded with the practical as is practical reasoning itself.

IV

Even if it be granted that many of the linguistic oughts which are of special interest to an epistemologist are ought-to-bes, the fact that ought-to-bes and ought-to-dos are conceptually inseparable might be thought to preclude a linguistic approach to conceptual abilities. Clearly primary epistemic ought-to-dos (and by calling them "primary" I mean simply that they are not the unfolding of ought-to-bes, whether as primary they are categorical or hypothetical), pertaining to the systematic use of linguistic abilities and propensities to arrive at correct linguistic representations of the way things are, presuppose the possession of concepts by the agents to which they apply. And since all ought-to-bes unfold into ought-to-dos which, in their turn, presuppose concepts, the outlook for a linguistic theory of concepts would seem to be dark indeed. Yet the fundamental clues for a resolution of the problem have already been given.

To fix our ideas, let us consider an example which, though simplified to its bare bones contain the essence of the matter:

> (*Ceteris paribus*) one ought to respond to red objects in sunlight by uttering or being disposed to utter "this is red."

This ought-to-be rule must not be confused with (fictitious) ought-to-do rule,

> (*Ceteris paribus*) one ought to say "this is red" in the presence of red objects in sunlight.

The latter presupposes that those to whom it applies have the concepts of "red" objects, "sunlight," and, even more important, of what it is to say "this is red." In other words, they must already have the conceptual framework of what it is to do something in a circumstance.

The distinction between *saying* and *uttering*, or being disposed to utter, is diagnostic of the difference between the "ought-to-do" and the "ought to-be." It might be objected that to use language meaningfully is to *say* rather than merely utter. But to merely utter is to parrot, and we need a concept which mediates between merely uttering and saying.

Notice that the ought-to-do which corresponds to the above ought-to-be, namely

> One ought to bring it about (*ceteris paribus*) that people respond to red objects in sunlight by uttering or being disposed to utter "this is red,"

presupposes that *its* agent-subjects have a conceptual framework which includes the concepts of a red object, or sunlight, of uttering "this is red," of what it is to do or bring about something, and of what it is for an action to be called for by a circumstance.

On the other hand, this ought-to-do does *not* presuppose that the subjects in which the disposition to utter "this is red" in the presence of red objects in sunlight *is to be brought about* have any of these concepts.

But what of the objection that the *subject-matter* subjects of the ought-to-be coincide with the agent-subjects of the ought-to-do and hence that they too must have the concepts in question? The answer should be obvious; the members of a linguistic community are first language learners and only potentially "people," but *subsequently* language *teachers*, possessed of the rich conceptual framework this implies. They start out by being the *subject-matter* subjects of the ought-to-bes and graduate to the status of agent-subjects of the ought-to-dos. Linguistic ought-to-bes are translated into *uniformities* by training. As Wittgenstein has stressed, it is the linguistic community as a self-perpetuating whole which is the minimum unit in terms of which conceptual activity can be understood.

Furthermore, there are radically different kinds of linguistic ought-to-bes: not only word–object ought-to-bes (or, as I have called then elsewhere, language entry transitions),[4] but also the ought-to-bes formulated by formation and transformation rules.

The oughts governing utterances as perceptual responses to the environment are not ought-to dos – though, as the pragmatists have emphasized, perception as an element in inquiry occurs in a context of actions, epistemic and otherwise. Similarly the oughts governing inference are not ought-to-dos. Inferring is not a *doing* in the conduct sense – which, however, by no means implies that it is not a *process*. Again, as the pragmatists have stressed, inference as an element in inquiry occurs in the context of action, epistemic and otherwise.

A language is a many-leveled structure. There are not only the ought-to-bes which connect linguistic responses to extralinguistic objects, but also the equally essential ought-to-bes which connect linguistic responses to linguistic objects. There could be no training of language users unless this were the case. Finally, there would be no language training unless there were the uniformities pertaining to the use of practical language, the language of action, intention, of "shall" and "ought," which, as embodying epistemic norms and standards, is but one small (but essential) part of the conceptual structure of human agency.

One isn't a full-fledged member of the linguistic community until one not only *conforms* to linguistic ought-to-bes (and may-bes) by exhibiting the required uniformities, but grasps these ought-to-bes and may-bes themselves (i.e., knows the rules of the language.) One must, therefore, have the concept of oneself as an agent, as not only the *subject-matter* subject of ought-to-bes but the *agent*-subject of ought-to-dos. Thus, even though conceptual activity rests on a foundation of *conforming* to ought-to-bes of *uniformities* in linguistic behavior, these uniformities exists in an ambience of action, epistemic or otherwise. To be a language user is to conceive of oneself as an agent subject to rules. My point has been that one can grant this without holding that all meaningful linguistic episodes are *actions* in the conduct sense, and all linguistic rules, rules for doing.

A living language is a system of elements which play many different types of role, and no one of these types of role make sense apart from the others. Thus, while the mere concept of a kind of vocalizing being a response by a human organism in specified circumstances to a certain kind of object does make sense in isolation, this concept is not as such the concept of the vocalizing as a *linguistic response*. For to classify an item as linguistic involves relating it to just such a system as I have been sketching. "Word" goes not only with "object" but with "person," "ought-to-bes," "ought-to-dos" and much, much more.

V

Within the framework sketched above, I propose to explore the idea that insofar as it has conceptual meaning language is essentially a means whereby one thinker can express his thoughts to others. Now the term "thought" has a wide range of application, including such items as assumptions, the solving of problems, wishes, intentions, and perceptions. It is also ambiguous, sometimes referring to *what* is thought, sometimes to the *thinking* of it. To limit the range of my paper, I shall concentrate on thought as belief, and since the latter term shares the ambiguity indicated above, I note that, for the time being at least, I shall be concerned with believings rather than things believed.

The following characterization of the state of believing something will seem to get the discussion under way:

Jones believes that-p = Jones has a settled disposition to think that-p.

It would be foolhardy – indeed downright mistaken – to claim that this formula captures "the" meaning of "believes," and even more so to put it by saying that "a belief is a settled disposition to think that something is the case." For, as with most, if not all, of the words in which philosophers are interested, we are confronted with a cluster of senses which resemble each other in the family way.

To say that the senses of cognate expressions bear a family resemblance to one another must not be taken to imply that they present themselves as a family, nor even that they constitute a family. Aristotle seems to have thought that philosophically interesting concepts present themselves to us as families in which, with a little effort, we can discern the fathers, mothers, aunts, uncles, and cousins of various degrees. In some cases something like this may be true. But the matter is rarely so simple, and there is more than a little truth to the idea that the families are "created" by reconstruction (hopefully rational) or regimentation rather than found.[5]

If the above account of belief gets us started, it does so by confronting us with the equally problematic concepts of *disposition* and *thinking that-p*. Before stepping into these quick-sands, let us ostensibly make matters worse by turning our attention from *believing* itself to the more complicated concept of the *expression* of belief. For sound philosophical strategy calls for the examination of concepts as they function in larger contexts, rather than subjecting them to scrutiny in splendid isolation. By taking elusive concepts together, one may limit the degrees of freedom which enable them separately to elude our grasp. If beliefs are to be construed as dispositions, this strategy would have us seek to relate the sense in which beliefs are "expressed" to the sense in which the dispositions of things and persons are manifested by what they do. This suggests the schema:

> x expresses Jones's belief that-p = x is a manifestation of Jones's settled disposition to think that-p.

If the right-hand side of this attempted explication were clear cut and unambiguous, substantial progress would have been made. But it isn't; and our only hope is that a spark of clarity may result from rubbing unclarities together.

A first unclarity concerns what it is for a disposition to be "manifested" by a doing, and how the class of doings by which a given disposition is manifested is to be delimited. If the "disposition" is of the familiar kind to which we refer by such expressions as "an angry disposition" or, perhaps, by such a term as "humility," then it would seem that, depending on circumstances, any of a wide range of episodes could be its manifestation. Indeed, there is a sense in which, depending on circumstances, any of a wide range of episodes could count as a "manifestation" of Jones's belief that-p. But to characterize belief that-p as a settled disposition to *think that-p* is, if sound, to narrow things down in an interesting way. For to do so is to introduce a conceptual tie between the designation of the disposition and the kind of episode which can be said, at least in a primary sense, to "manifest" it.

For if we ask what episodes manifest a disposition to V, when "V" represents a verb which stands for a doing (e.g., "laugh"), the answer must be, in the first instance, episodes of V-ing (e.g., laughing). We have consequently committed ourselves to the idea that it is episodes of *thinking that-p* which are, in a primary sense at least, manifestations of Jones's disposition to *think that-p*; and consequently that it is episodes of thinking that-p which are, in a primary sense, manifestations of Jones's belief that-p. This gives us the schema:

> x is a primary manifestation of Jones's belief that-p $\rightarrow$ x is a thinking that-p.

But now our troubles really begin. For there is a prima facie tension between "being a thinking that-p" and being a "manifestation" of anything. The latter term carries with it the implication of "making something manifest," i.e., apparent, (roughly) perceptible, observable. But, we are tempted to expostulate, what need be less "manifest" than an episode of thinking that-*p*.

It might be thought that all we need do is replace "manifestation" by a term which lacks this implication. And there are, indeed, such terms at hand – thus "realization," "actualization." The statements:

> Episodes of thinking that-*p* are *realizations* of the settled disposition to think that-*p*

and:

> Episodes of thinking that-*p* are *actualizations* of the settled disposition to think that-*p*

trip easily off the metaphysically trained tongue. But they are ruled out by our strategy. For the concept with which we are concerned is that of the *expression* of a belief, and "expression" clearly has the same implication of "overtness" or "perceptibility" as does the "manifestation" to which our initial intuitions have led us.

The boulder may have slipped, but perhaps it has not rolled to the bottom. Our task may ultimately prove to be like that of Sisyphus, but perhaps we are not yet forced to make a new beginning. To continue is to look for a way of making coherent the idea that episodes of thinking that-*p* are the primary *expressions* (with all that this implies) of the belief that-*p*.

To do so within the allotted space however, I must abandon the leisurely dialectic which consults intuition at each stage of the argument, and instead must draw upon the familiarity of standard philosophical moves. In terms of this new strategy, the obvious move is to espouse a form of logical behaviorism according to which, in first approximation, "thinking that-*p*" is, in its most episodic sense, to be equated with "candidly and spontaneously uttering '*p*'"[6] where the person, call him Jones, who utters "*p*" is doing so *as one who knows the language to which "p" belongs*. I need not remind you of all the troubles which beset this move. Some of them will be taken into account as the argument moves along. But since, in any case, my strategy remains in a broad sense dialectical, the fact that the above equation suffers from serious inadequacies need not prevent it from playing an essential role in the argument.

The phrase "candidly and spontaneously" is intended to sum up an openended set of conditions without which the suggestion can't get off the ground. Jones's thinking that-*p* obviously cannot be a quoting of *p* or uttering it on the stage in the course of acting. The qualifying phrase also clearly rules out the case where Jones is lying, i.e., using words to deceive. Somewhat less obviously, it is intended to imply that Jones is not choosing his words to express his convictions. He is neither lying nor speaking truthfully. In a sense, as we shall see, he is not *using* the words at all.

According to the behavioristic position we are now considering, thinking that-*p* is, in its *primary episodic* sense, thinking-out-loud that-*p*. As thinking-out-loud, an utterance of "*p*" is not directed to an audience. It is not, as such, a social act. Explicit performatives (e.g., "I promise") are clearly out of place in utterances which are, in the desired sense, to be thinkings-out-loud. Nor is it appropriate to characterize thinkings-out-loud in terms of the categories of illocutionary performance – at least those which require an audience (e.g., "statement," "avowal," "argument")[7] – even though exactly similar utterances would, *in a context of "communication,"* be appropriately so characterized.

VI

It is important to realize that the ways in which we classify linguistic expressions are not only bound up with the jobs they do, but with the purposes for which the classification is made. Since these purposes tend, for obvious reasons, to concern the role of language as a means of communication, i.e., as that by which we give information, warn, make statements, predict, describe, etc., we should not be surprised, our behaviorist will tell us, if expressions which, as candidly uttered in *noncommunicative* contexts, are thinking-out-loud, are classified in a way which is conceptually tied to communication, and, hence, to functions of quite a different order of complexity. One needs only think of the difference between the purely logical characterization of "it is not raining" as the "negation" of "it is raining," and characterizing it as the "denial" of the latter, or note the social implications of classifying a word as a *referring* expression.

Thus the ways in which common sense, and not only common sense, classifies linguistic expressions, and the verbs which it uses to describe what people do with them, are heavily weighted in the direction of linguistic *performances* in a context of *communication*. That it is legitimate to view language in this way is not to be doubted. Indeed, it is philosophically important to be clear about the categories in terms of which the variety of ways in which language functions in interpersonal exchange are to be understood. But there is a danger that exclusive concern with this perspective will obscure those connections between thought and language where the latter is *not* functioning as a means of communication.

The point is not that there are failures of communication, e.g., the supposed hearer may be an inanimate object mistaken for a man or a foreigner. It is not even that there are soliloquies, if by this is meant cases of "talking to oneself." It is the more radical point that thinking-out-loud is a form of meaningful speech which doesn't consist in talking *to* anyone at all, even oneself, and hence is not, in any ordinary sense, *talking*.

VII

But before I develop this point, let me return to the formula we were considering before this digression on the orientation toward contexts of communication of the categories in terms of which common sense, linguistics, and many philosophies of language approach linguistic behavior. The formula was:

x is a primary expression of Jones's belief that-p = x is a primary manifestation of his settled disposition to think that-p (i.e., is a thinking that-p).

The implications of the term "manifestation" (and, for that matter, of "expression") led us in the direction of a logical behaviorism according to which the relevant sense of "thinking that-p" is "thinking-out-loud that-p." Thus reinterpreted, the formula becomes:

x is a primary expression of Jones's belief that-p = x is a primary manifestation of Jones's settled disposition to think-out-loud that-p (i.e., is a thinking-out-loud that-p).

It will be remembered that the point of this behavioristic move was to assimilate the sense in which an episode is a primary *expression* (implying overtness) of a belief to the sense in which an episode of, for example, a piece of litmus paper turning red is a *manifestation* (implying overtones) of its disposition to turn red.

It should be noted in passing that in the case of the litmus paper we seem required to expand the characterization of the disposition into:

> disposition to turn red, *if put in acid*.

This generates the suspicion that if we are to continue with our strategy, we must similarly expand our analysis of "Jones believes that-*p*" into:

> Jones has a settled disposition to think-out-loud that-*p*, if . . .

If what? There many pitfalls here, though we can, perhaps, cover them up temporarily with something like "if the question whether-*p* arises." To do so, however, would immediately confront us with a more serious difficulty. For it simply isn't the case that if a person believes that-*p*, he utters "*p*," let alone thinks-out-loud that-*p*, whenever the question whether-*p* arises.

Confronted by this fact, we are strongly tempted to abandon our strategy and say that if a person believes that-*p*, then (other things being equal) whenever the question whether-*p* arises, he tends to *think* (*not* think-out-loud) that-*p*; to which we might add that if the circumstances are appropriate he may *express* his thought by uttering (saying?) "*p*."

VIII

On the other hand, if, however, we are to continue with our original strategy, we must resolutely put aside the temptation to draw the kind of distinction between *thought* and its *expression* which this formulation implies, and continue with the intriguing idea that an uttering of "*p*" which is a primary expression of a belief that-*p* is not merely an *expression* of a thinking that-*p*, but is itself a *thinking*, i.e., a thinking-out-loud that-*p*.

Yet the preceding remarks do remind us that we must take into account the fact that there is a sense of "express" in which we can be said to express our thoughts by *using* language for this purpose. Thus, we express our thought that-*p* by *saying* "*p*." Can we sophisticate our logical behaviorism to do justice to this fact?

Let us take a closer look at the words "thought" and "express." First the latter: it will be noticed that the reference to observability implied by the term "manifestation" in the context "manifestation of the disposition to think that-*p*" was absorbed by the behaviorist into the phrase which describes the disposition. Thus, "*manifestation* of the disposition to think that-*p*" became, in effect "*actualization* of the disposition to I think-*out-loud* that-*p*."

Thus the behaviorist's formula becomes, in effect,

> *x* is a primary expression of Jones's belief that-*p* = *x* is a manifestation of Jones's settled disposition to think that-*p* = *x* is an actualization of Jones's settled disposition to think-out-loud that-*p* (i.e., *x* is a thinking-out-loud that-*p*).

It is only too clear that by pushing this analysis of the context "expression of belief" in this direction the behaviorist has lost contact with the idea that people *express* their beliefs by *using* language. The point can be put simply – indeed bluntly – by saying that the concept of the *actualization of a disposition* is not, as such, the concept of an *action*, whereas expressing their beliefs is something people do.

The statement:

Jones, by saying "*p*," expressed his belief that-*p*

requires an interpretation of *saying p* as an action which is undertaken by Jones *in order to express (to someone)* his belief that-*p*. If we suspect that Jones is lying, we could equally describe him as saying "*p*," but we would then go on to say something like:

Jones, by saying "*p*," *pretended* to believe that-*p*.

In neither case could Jones's saying "*p*" be construed as a case of *thinking* (even "out loud") that-*p*. Thus were Jones speaking truthfully, the thinking immediately involved, if any, would be of the sort described by such formulas as:

Jones thought that saying ". . ." would express his belief that-*p*
Jones intended to express his belief that-*p* by saying ". . ."

or, in the case of lying:

Jones intended to pretend to believe that-*p* by saying ". . ."

Thus, granted the validity of the concept of thinking-out-loud, the thinking-out-loud which, were it to occur, would be immediately involved in the situation formulated by:

Jones, by uttering ". . . ," expressed his belief that-*p*

would be *not*:

Jones thought-out-loud that-*p*

but rather:

Jones thought-out-loud that saying ". . ." would express his belief that-*p*

or, where Jones is lying,

Jones thought-out-loud that he would pretend to believe that-*p* by saying ". . ."

Needless to say, the latter thinking-out-loud would be self-frustrating in the presence of the audience he intends to deceive.

IX

If we leave behaviorism aside for a moment, we can add a new dimension to the discussion by noting that the term "express" in contexts pertaining to thought has two radically different senses. The difference can be brought out by relating these senses to two different contexts, namely,

(1)   *Jones* expressed his thought (belief) that-*p* by saying . . .

(2)   *Jones's utterance* of "*p*" expressed his thought that-*p*

I shall call the former the "action" sense of express and the latter, for want of a better term, the "causal" sense. Both, as we shall see, are to be distinguished from a third sense illustrated by the context:

Jones's utterance of "*p*" expressed *the* thought that-*p*

where the phrase "*the* thought that-*p*" stands for an abstract entity, a thought in Frege's sense (i.e., in one sense of this term, a "proposition"). I shall call this the logical (or semantical) sense of "express."

Although my ultimate aim is to show how a logical behaviorist might draw these distinctions, my initial move will be to discuss them in more traditional terms. I shall, therefore, construct a regimented (I dare not say idealized) model according to which, in the course of learning to speak a language, a child acquires the capacity to be in mental states which are *counterparts*, in a sense to be analyzed, of the utterances which come to belong to his repertory of linguistic behavior. The idea can be blocked out in two steps:

1   A mental episode which is a thinking that-*p* is correlated, in a certain linguistic community, with a piece of linguistic behavior which stands for (expresses in the logical or semantical sense) the thought (proposition) that-*p*.

2   In the initial stages of the child's mastery of the language, whenever it has a thought that-*p*, this thought is manifested in a purely involuntary way by the corresponding verbal behavior.

As our model for understanding the sense in which the uttering of "*p*" is the involuntary manifestation of a thinking that-*p*, let us take the instinctive connection between a pain and a piece of unlearned pain behavior. The fact that a connection between states *A* and *B* in a child is, in some sense, *learned* rather than *instinctive*, *acquired* rather than *part of its initial equipment*, by no means entails that either *A* or *B* is under the child's voluntary control. Not all learning to do something in a broad sense of "do" consists in the addition of new behaviors to the stock of things that are under one's voluntary control.

The key feature of our model is that the acquired connection between the mental act and the verbal behavior is not to be construed on the action model of "using the behavior to express one's thought." Thus, verbal behavior is not in our child's voluntary control in that, although, *once the language is learned*, a necessary and sufficient condition of the child saying "*p*" is that it thinks that-*p*, the saying is the involuntary manifestation of the thinking.

Notice that the model allows the child a rich vocabulary, including the language of intention and resolve as well as the language in which matters of fact are stated. It also allows that the child learns to verbalize about verbal behavior and even about the mental acts of which its verbal behavior is the involuntary manifestation.

X

We are now in a position to weaken our model and still make our point. We need not suppose that the child remains a chatterbox. We can suppose it acquires the ability to keep its thoughts to itself in the sense that it can effectively tell itself to keep quiet, without ceasing to think. We can grant that to this limited extent its verbal behavior becomes under its voluntary control. When it is thinking without speaking, we shall say that it is in a keeping-its-thoughts-to-itself frame of mind. When not in this frame of mind, it thinks out loud.[8] Thus, "Thinking out loud" remains the primary form in which thinking occurs. The child's keeping its thoughts to itself can be compared to the opening of a general switch which breaks or (to mix metaphors) short circuits the initial acquired connection between thoughts and verbal behavior.

At this stage, the child has no conception of locutionary acts (e.g., predicting, telling) as verbal behavior which can be engaged in whether or not one is thinking the corresponding thoughts. It has no concept of *saying "p" without thinking that-p*.

On the other hand, it is perfectly capable of having concepts of actions involving thinking out loud. Thus, wondering out loud about the weather; "I shall wonder out loud about the likelihood of rain." It is important to see that this by no means entails that there is such a thing as an action of *thinking out loud that-p*. Even in our more sophisticated framework there is no such thing as an *action* of thinking that-p, though there is the action of *deliberating* (i.e., deliberating out loud) what to do. By granting, as we must, that it can conceive of actions consisting of thinkings out loud, we admit a further sense in which its verbal behavior (*as* thinkings out loud) would be under its voluntary control.

The child's verbal behavior would express its thoughts, but, to put it paradoxically, the child could not express them.

Notice, also, that although its linguistic behavior would be meaningful, and we could say of each of its utterances what, specifically it meant, e.g.:

> *Jones's utterance* meant "it is raining."

It would, on our assumptions, be incorrect to say, for example:

> *Jones*, by uttering "...," meant (to convey) ...

For the latter supposes that Jones has the concept of an action, of uttering "..." as a piece of linguistic behavior which could exist independently of its being the 'spontaneous verbal expression" of the corresponding mental act. There being no such action as bringing about a specific mental act, there could be no such thing as bringing about a thinking-out-loud for the purpose of conveying a thought.

In other words, just as our regimenting fiction enables us to draw a distinction between a sense in which a mode of verbal behavior can *express* thoughts without being *used to express* them, so it enables us to distinguish between the context:

> utterance of *E* (in *L*) means ...

and the sense of "means," closely related to "intends," which involves the context:

Jones, by uttering *E*, means (to convey) . . .

The familiar saw that words have meaning only because people mean things by them is harmless if it tells us that words have no meaning in abstraction from their involvement in the verbal behavior of language users. It is downright mistaken if it tells us that for an expression to have a certain sense or reference is for it to be *used* by people *to convey* the corresponding thought. Rather, we should say, it is because the expression has a certain meaning that it can be effectively used to convey the corresponding thought.

XI

Let us now return to the initial accounts we gave of belief and its expression. The first thing to note is that if we were to reformulate them in terms of our model we would get something like the following schema:

> Jones believes that-*p* = Jones has a settled disposition to think that-*p*, if the question occurs to him whether-*p*, and, indeed, to think out loud that-*p*, unless he is in a keeping-his-thoughts-to-himself frame of mind.[9]

We also get the following formulas with respect to "expression of belief":

> *x* is a primary actualization of Jones's belief that-*p* → *x* is a thinking that-*p* (and, indeed, a thinking-out-loud that-*p* unless he is in a keeping-his-thoughts-to himself frame of mind.)

> *x* is a primary expression of Jones's belief that-*p* → *x* is a thinking out loud that-*p*.

Thus, where Jones is in a thinking-out-loud frame of mind, the verbal behavior is both an *actualization of* and, in the "causal" sense, an *expression of* his belief, both a *thinking* and an *expression of thought*.

XII

But what will our logical behaviorist say to all this? Clearly he will be unhappy about our uncritical acceptance of mental acts as covert inner episodes. What moves might he make? He may well accept our initial formula

> Jones believes that-*p* = Jones has a settled disposition to think that-*p*.

But he will emphasize the "settled," which we have not yet done, and will call attention to the fact that it presumably contrasts with something. It is not obvious what the contrasting adjective should be, but it, too, should apply to dispositions. Let us, he suggests, try "proximate," drawing on the contrast between "settled" and "near the surface." Another appropriate contrast would be provided by "short-term."

Objects, as is well known, can have causal properties which are not, so to speak, immediately available. Thus iron attracts filings, *if* it has been treated in a certain way. A *proximate* disposition can roughly be characterized as one which is immediately available.

Our logical behaviorist, consequently, suggests that

> Jones believes that-*p* = Jones has the *settled* disposition to have *short-term*, proximate dispositions to think-out-loud that-*p*, if the question whether-*p* arises, and he is in a thinking out-loud frame of mind.

In other words, our logical behaviorist construes the contrast between fleeting thought episodes and settled beliefs as falling within the broad category of dispositions, and hence construes the "covertness" of thoughts as simply a special case of the covertness of dispositions. Flammability, he reminds us, is not a covert flame.

Many features of our previous discussion can be fitted into this framework, once its distinctive character is understood. Thus, the behaviorist substitutes for the previous account of the child's candid and spontaneous verbal behavior as the expression (in the "causal" sense) of classically conceived *episodes* of thought, an account according to which a:

> thinking-out-loud that-*p*

is simply an "actualization" of a short-term, proximate disposition to think-out-loud that-*p*.

In the nonbehavioristic model we stipulated that the child be unable to verbalize without thinking the appropriate thought, in other words, that only if it has the mental act of thinking that-*p* does it utter "*p*." In the behavioristic reconstruction framework, the corresponding stipulation would be that all utterances of "*p*" be thinking-out-loud that-*p*.

Both stipulations could be formulated in the same words, thus "the child utters '*p*' only in the course of thinking out loud that-*p*." But the two concepts of thinking out loud are radically different. In the nonbehavioristic model, the phrase "thinking-out-loud" referred to thoughts together with their verbal expression. In the behavioristic reconstruction, it is to be taken as an unanalyzed expression which means roughly the same as "candid, spontaneous verbal behavior," but serves, by its hyphenated mode of composition, to emphasize that the basic meaningfulness of candid, spontaneous verbal behavior is not to be construed in terms of its being the reverberation at the tip of the tongue of covert episodes which are thoughts properly speaking, in accordance with the schema:

> *x* is candid, spontaneous verbal behavior = is an expression[10] of thought.

XIII

It is important not to confuse logical behaviorism with what might be called logical physicalism. I mean by the latter the view which denies that, to quote Chisholm, "when we analyze the kind of meaning that is involved in natural language we need some concepts we do not need in physics or behavioristics."[11] Chisholm thinks that to deny the need for such an irreducible concept is tantamount to trying to "analyze the semantics . . . of natural language in a physicalistic vocabulary of a behavioristic psychology with no undefined semantical term and no reference to thoughts."[12]

In the essay which led to the correspondence from which I am quoting, I had argued that the concept of meaning which belongs in the context:

E (in L) means . . .

is not to be analyzed in terms of a reference to "thoughts." Thus I rejected any analysis along *either* of the following lines:

E (in L) means . . . = *candid and spontaneous utterances* of F causally express thoughts pertaining to . . .

E (in L) means . . . = *speakers of L use E to express their thoughts pertaining to* . . .

where "thought" is to be taken as referring to classically conceived inner episodes or mental acts.

On the other hand, though I denied that "means" in the sense appropriate to the context "E (in L) means . . ." is to be analyzed (defined) in terms of a reference to thoughts, I also argued that it cannot be analyzed in physicalistic terms. From Chisholm's point of view this was a blatant attempt to have my cake and eat it. As he saw it, to *admit* that "to analyze the kind of meaning that is involved in natural language" we need a distinctively semantical term ("means") which *cannot* be analyzed in physicalistic terms, but *deny* that the explication of this distinctively semantical term requires a reference to *thoughts*, has all the appearance of paradox.

The correspondence went on at some length, and although some progress was made, the issue was never really joined. As I now diagnose the situation some ten years later, the cause of this failure was my inability to clarify adequately two points:

1   the exact nature of statements of the form "E (in L) means . . .";
2   the exact relation of the concept of *meaning* to that of *thought*.

The space which remains is too short to do anything more than indicate the moves I should have made.

My basic move should have been to clarify along the lines of the present paper the distinction between the contexts:

person expresses

and:

utterance expresses.

My second move should have been to give a more adequate clarification of the concept of meaning as it occurs in the context "expression (in L) means . . ." (as contrasted with the context "person, by uttering E, means . . ."). At the time of the correspondence I was unable to do much more than offer the rather cryptic suggestion that statements of this form (1) are sui generis, and 2 *convey* (rather than *describe*) how the subject expression is used, by exhibiting an expression in the hearer's active vocabulary which has the same job – the idea being that by rehearsing his use of the latter, he will be able to grasp the use of the former. As I have since argued,[13] to say what an expression means is to *classify* it by the use of a sortal predicate the application of which implies that the expression in question does the job in its language which is done in the speaker's language by an expression from which the predicate is formed. Thus, roughly:

"*und*" (in German) means *and*

has the form:

"*und*"s (in German) are *ands*

where ".*and*." is a sortal predicate of the kind in question.

But above all I should have made it clear that in my view the fundamental concept pertaining to thinking is thinking-out-loud as conceived by our logical behaviorist.[14] This is not to say that I agree with him in rejecting the classical conception of thoughts as inner episodes in a nondispositional sense. Rather I accept mental acts in something like the classical sense, but argue that the concept of such acts is, in a sense I have attempted to clarify, a derivative concept.

Finally, I should have emphasized my total commitment to the thesis that the concept of thought essentially involves that of intentionality in the following sense. To say of a piece of verbal behavior that it is a thinking-out-loud is to commit oneself to say of it that it *means something*, while to say of it specifically that it is a thinking-out-loud that-*p* is to commit oneself to say of it that it is a piece of verbal behavior which means *p*.

Thus, at the primary level, instead of analyzing the intentionality or aboutness of verbal behavior in terms of its expressing or being used to express classically conceived thoughts or beliefs, we should recognize that this verbal behavior is already thinking in its own right, and its intentionality or aboutness is simply the appropriateness of classifying it in terms which relate to the linguistic behavior of the group to which one belongs.

NOTES

1   For an exploration of this and related issues, see my *Science and Metaphysics* (London: Routledge and Kegan Paul, 1968), ch. VI (esp. sections xiv–xvii).

2   I have in mind particularly John Austin and his students. The best statement of this approach is to be found in Austin's *How to do Things with Words* (London: Oxford University Press, 1963.)

3   For an explanation and defense of these distinctions see Austin's *How to Do Things with Words*.

4   "Some Reflections on Language Games," *Philosophy of Science*, 21 (1954). (Reprinted as ch. 11 in *Science, Perception and Reality*.) It is important to note that a full discussion would refer to may-be's (or permitteds) as well as ought-to-be's – otherwise the concept of "free" as opposed to "tied" (stimulus-bound) linguistic activity, essential to any account of the functioning of a conceptual system, would be left out of the system.

5   Equally dangerous are such metaphorical contrasts as those between "paradigm" and "border-line," "shadow" and "penumbra." All suggest a sequential strategy according to which, once we find the thread, we know how to begin and what kinds of difficulty to expect.

6   Similarly, "wondering whether-*p*" would be equated with "uttering '*p*?'", "wishing that-*p*" with "uttering 'would (that) *p*'" and "deciding to do *A*" with uttering "I shall do *A*."

7   We can grant that a thinking-out-loud that-*p* might be a constituent of a reasoning-out-loud or a deliberating-out-loud on a certain topic.

8   The concept of "thinking out loud" appropriate to this model should not be equated with thinking-out-loud as construed by the behavioristic position we have been considering. The latter does not recognize "mental episodes" in the sense required by the present model.

9   The "if the question occurs to him whether-*p*" condition can be taken to cover all cases in which, where the alternatives "*p*" and "not *p*" are relevant to his course of thought, he thinks that-*p*, even if the question whether-*p* is not actually raised.

10   "Expression" in the causal sense, i.e., a manifestation at the "surface" of a covert process which is its cause.

11   *Minnesota Studies in the Philosophy of Science*, vol. II (1958), p. 523.
12   Ibid.
13   Most recently in *Science and Metaphysics*, ch. III.
14   The priority in question, to use Aristotle's distinction, is in the order of knowing as contrasted with the order of being. As an analogy, notice that concepts pertaining to things as perceived by the senses are prior in the order of knowing to concepts of microphysical particles, whereas (for the Scientific Realist), microphysical particles are prior in the order of being to objects as perceived by the senses.

Thought and Talk

DONALD DAVIDSON

What is the connection between thought and language? The dependence of speaking on thinking is evident, for to speak is to express thoughts. This dependence is manifest in endless further ways. Someone who utters the sentence "The candle is out" as a sentence of English must intend to utter words that are true if and only if an indicated candle is out at the time of utterance, and he must believe that by making the sounds he does he is uttering words that are true only under those circumstances. These intentions and beliefs are not apt to be dwelt on by the fluent speaker. But though they may not normally command attention, their absence would be enough to show he was not speaking English, and the absence of any analogous thoughts would show he was not speaking at all.

The issue lies on the other side: Can there be thought without speech? A first and natural reaction is that there can be. There is the familiar, irksome experience of not being able to find the words to express one's ideas. On occasion one may decide that the editorial writer has put a point better than one could oneself. And there is Norman Malcolm's dog who, having chased a squirrel into the woods, barks up the wrong tree.[1] It is not hard to credit the dog with the belief that the squirrel is in that tree.

A definite, if feebler, intuition tilts the other way. It is possible to wonder whether the speaker who can't find the right words has a clear idea. Attributions of intentions and beliefs to dogs smack of anthropomorphism. A primitive behaviorism, baffled by the privacy of unspoken thoughts, may take comfort in the view that thinking is really "talking to oneself" – silent speech.

Beneath the surface of these opposed tendencies run strong, if turgid, currents, which may help to explain why philosophers have, for the most part, preferred taking a stand on the issue to producing an argument. Whatever the reason, the question of the relationship between thought and speech seems seldom to have been asked for its own sake. The usual assumption is that one or the other, speech or thought, is by comparison easy to understand, and therefore the more obscure one (whichever that is) may be illuminated by analyzing or explaining it in terms of the other.

The assumption is, I think, false: neither language nor thinking can be fully explained in terms of the other, and neither has conceptual priority. The two are, indeed, linked, in the sense that each requires the other in order to be understood; but the linkage is not so complete that either suffices, even when reasonably reinforced, to explicate the other. To make good this claim, what is chiefly needed is to show how thought depends on speech, and this is the thesis I want to refine, and then to argue for.

We attribute a thought to a creature whenever we assertively employ a positive sentence the main verb of which is psychological – in English, "believes," "knows," "hopes," "desires," "thinks," "fears" are examples – followed by a sentence and preceded by the name or description of the creature. (A "that" may optionally or necessarily follow the verb.) Some such sentences attribute states, others report events or processes: "believes," "thinks," and "wants" report states, while "came to believe," "forgot," "concluded," "noticed," "is proving" report events or processes. Sentences that can be used to attribute a thought exhibit what is often called, or analyzed as, semantic intensionality, which means that the attribution may be changed from true to false, or false to true, by substitutions in the contained sentences that would not alter the truth value of the sentence in isolation.

I do not take for granted that if a creature has a thought, then we can, with resources of the kind just sketched, correctly attribute that thought to him. But thoughts so attributable at least constitute a good sample of the totality.

It is doubtful whether the various sorts of thought can be reduced to one, or even to a few: desire, knowledge, belief, fear, interest, to name some important cases, are probably logically independent to the extent that none can be defined using the others, even along with such further notions as truth and cause. Nevertheless, belief is central to all kinds of thought. If someone is glad that, or notices that, or remembers that, or knows that, the gun is loaded, then he must believe that the gun is loaded. Even to wonder whether the gun is loaded, or to speculate on the possibility that the gun is loaded, requires the belief, for example, that a gun is a weapon, that it is a more or less enduring physical object, and so on. There are good reasons for not insisting on any particular list of beliefs that are needed if a creature is to wonder whether a gun is loaded. Nevertheless, it is necessary that there be endless interlocked beliefs. The system of such beliefs identifies a thought by locating it in a logical and epistemic space.

Having a thought requires that there be a background of beliefs, but having a particular thought does not depend on the state of belief with respect to that very thought. If I consider going to a certain concert, I know I will be put to a degree of trouble and expense, and I have more complicated beliefs about the enjoyment I will experience. I will enjoy hearing Beethoven's "Grosse Fuge," say, but only provided the performance achieves a reasonable standard, and I am able to remain attentive. I have the thought of going to the concert, but until I decide whether to go, I have no fixed belief that I will go; until that time, I merely entertain the thought.

We may say, summarizing the last two paragraphs, that a thought is defined by a system of beliefs, but is itself autonomous with respect to belief.

We usually think that having a language consists largely in being able to speak, but in what follows speaking will play only an indirect part. What is essential to my argument is the idea of an interpreter, someone who understands the utterances of another. The considerations to be put forward imply, I think, that a speaker must himself be an interpreter of others, but I shall not try to demonstrate that an interpreter must be a speaker, though there may be good reason to hold this. Perhaps it is worth pointing out that the notion of a language, or of two people speaking the same language, does not seem to be needed here. Two speakers could interpret each other's utterances without there being, in any ordinary sense, a common language. (I do not want to deny that in other contexts the notion of a shared language may be very important.)

The chief thesis of this paper is that a creature cannot have thoughts unless it is an interpreter of the speech of another. This thesis does not imply the possibility of reduction, behavioristic or otherwise, of thought to speech; indeed the thesis imputes no priority to language, epistemological or conceptual. The claim also falls short of similar claims in that it allows that there may be thoughts for which the speaker cannot find words, or for which there are no words.

Someone who can interpret an utterance of the English sentence "The gun is loaded" must have many beliefs, and these beliefs must be much like the beliefs someone must have if he entertains the thought that the gun is loaded. The interpreter must, we may suppose, believe that a gun is a weapon, and that it is a more or less enduring physical object. There is probably no definite list of things that must be believed by someone who understands the sentence "The gun is loaded," but it is necessary that there be endless interlocked beliefs.

An interpreter knows the conditions under which utterances of sentences are true, and often knows that if certain sentences are true, other must be. For example, an interpreter of English knows that if "The gun is loaded and the door is locked" is true, then "The door is locked" is true. The sentences of a language have a location in the logical space created by the pattern of such relationships. Obviously the pattern of relations between sentences is very much like the pattern of relations between thoughts. This fact has encouraged the view that it is redundant to take both patterns as basic. If thoughts are primary, a language seems to serve no purpose but to express or convey thoughts; while if we take speech as primary, it is tempting to analyze thoughts as speech dispositions: as Sellars puts it, "thinking at the distinctly human level . . . is essentially verbal activity."[2] But clearly the parallel between the structure of thoughts and the structure of sentences provides no argument for the primacy of either, and only a presumption in favor of their interdependence.

We have been talking freely of thoughts, beliefs, meanings, and interpretations; or rather, freely using sentences that contain these words. But of course it is not clear what entities, or sorts of entity, there must be to make systematic sense of such sentences. However, talk apparently of thoughts and sayings does belong to a familiar mode of explanation of human behavior and must be considered an organized department of common sense which may as well be called a theory. One way of examining the relation between thought and language is by inspecting the theory implicit in this sort of explanation.

Part of the theory deals with the teleological explanation of action. We wonder why a man raises his arm; an explanation might be that he wanted to attract the attention of a friend. This explanation would fail if the arm-raiser didn't believe that by raising his arm he would attract the attention of his friend, so the complete explanation of his raising his arm, or at any rate a more complete explanation, is that he wanted to attract the attention of his friend *and* believed that by raising his arm he would attract his friend's attention. Explanation of this familiar kind has some features worth emphasizing. It explains what is relatively apparent – an arm-raising – by appeal to factors that are far more problematical: desires and beliefs. But if we were to ask for evidence that the explanation is correct, this evidence would in the end consist of more data concerning the sort of event being explained, namely further behavior which is explained by the postulated beliefs and desires. Adverting to beliefs and desires to explain action is therefore a way of fitting an action into a pattern of behavior made coherent by the theory. This does not mean, of course, that beliefs are nothing but patterns of behavior, or that the relevant patterns can be defined without using the concepts of belief and desire. Nevertheless, there is a clear sense in which attributions of belief and desire, and hence teleological explanations of belief and desire, are supervenient on behavior more broadly described.

A characteristic of teleological explanation not shared by explanation generally is the way in which it appeals to the concept of *reason*. The belief and desire that explain an action must be such that anyone who had that belief and desire would have a reason to act in that way. What's more, the descriptions we provide of desire and belief must, in teleological explanation, exhibit the rationality of the action in the light of the content of the belief and the object of the desire.

The cogency of a teleological explanation rests, as remarked, on its ability to discover a coherent pattern in the behavior of an agent. Coherence here includes the idea of rationality both in the sense that the action to be explained must be reasonable in the light of the assigned desires and beliefs, and also in the sense that the assigned desires and beliefs must fit with one another. The methodological presumption of rationality does not make it impossible to attribute irrational thoughts and actions to an agent, but it does impose a burden on such attributions. We weaken the intelligibility of attributions of thoughts of any kind to the extent that we fail to uncover a consistent pattern of beliefs and, finally, of actions, for it is only against a background of such a pattern that we can identify thoughts. If we see a man pulling on both ends of a piece of string, we may decide he is fighting against himself, that he wants to move the string in incompatible directions. Such an explanation would require elaborate backing. No problem arises if the explanation is that he wants to break the string.

From the point of view of someone giving teleological explanations of the actions of another, it clearly makes no sense to assign priority either to desires or to beliefs. Both are essential to the explanation of behavior, and neither is more directly open to observation than the other. This creates a problem, for it means that behavior, which is the main evidential basis for attributions of belief and desire, is reckoned the result of two forces less open to public observation. Thus where one constellation of beliefs and desires will rationalize an action, it is always possible to find a quite different constellation that will do as well. Even a generous sample of actions threatens to leave open an unacceptably large number of alternative explanations.

Fortunately a more refined theory is available, one still firmly based on common sense: the theory of preference, or decision making under uncertainty. The theory was first made precise by Frank Ramsey, though he viewed it as a matter of providing a foundation for the concept of probability rather than as a piece of philosophical psychology.[3] Ramsey's theory works by quantifying strength of preference and degree of belief in such a way as to make sense of the natural idea that in choosing a course of action we consider not only how desirable various outcomes are, but also how apt available courses of action are to produce those outcomes. The theory does not assume that we can judge degrees of belief or make numerical comparisons of value directly. Rather it postulates a reasonable pattern of preferences between courses of action, and shows how to construct a system of quantified beliefs and desires to explain the choices. Given the idealized conditions postulated by the theory, Ramsey's method makes it possible to identify the relevant beliefs and desires uniquely. Instead of talking of postulation, we might put the matter this way: to the extent that we can see the actions of an agent as falling into a consistent (rational) pattern of a certain sort, we can explain those actions in terms of a system of quantified beliefs and desires.

We shall come back to decision theory presently; now it is time to turn to the question of how speech is interpreted. The immediate aim of a theory of interpretation is to give the meaning of an arbitrary utterance by a member of a language community. Central to interpretation, I have argued, is a theory of truth that satisfies Tarski's Convention *T* (modified in certain ways to apply to a natural language). Such a theory may be taken as giving an interpretation of each sentence a speaker might utter. To belong to a speech community – to be an interpreter of the speech of others – one needs, in effect, to know such a theory, and to know that it is a theory of the right kind.[4]

A theory of interpretation, like a theory of action, allows us to redescribe certain events in a revealing way. Just as a theory of action can answer the question of what an agent is doing when he has raised his arm by redescribing the act as one of trying to catch his friend's attention, so a method of interpretation can lead to redescribing the utterance of certain sounds as an act of saying that snow is white. At this point, however, the analogy breaks down. For decision theory can also explain actions, while it is not at all clear how a theory of interpretation can explain a speaker's uttering the words "Snow is white." But this is, after all, to be expected, for uttering words is an action, and so must draw for its teleological explanation on beliefs and desires. Interpretation is not irrelevant to the teleological explanation of speech, since to explain why someone said something we need to know, among other things, his own interpretation of what he said, that is, what he believes his words mean in the circumstances under which he speaks. Naturally this will involve some of his beliefs about how others will interpret his words.

The interlocking of the theory of action with interpretation will emerge in another way if we ask how a method of interpretation is tested. In the end, the answer must be that it helps bring order into our understanding of behavior. But at an intermediate stage, we can see that the attitude of *holding true* or *accepting as true*, as directed toward sentences, must play a central role in giving form to a theory. On the one hand, most uses of language tell us directly, or shed light on the question, whether a speaker holds a sentence to be true. If a speaker's purpose is to give information, or to make an honest assertion, then normally the speaker believes he is uttering a sentence true under the circumstances. If he utters a command, we may usually take this as showing that he holds a certain sentence (closely related to the sentence uttered) to be false; similarly for many cases of deceit. When a question is asked, it generally indicates that the questioner does not know whether a certain sentence is true; and so on. In order to infer from such evidence that a speaker holds a sentence true we need to know much about his desires and beliefs, but we do not have to know what his words mean.

On the other hand, knowledge of the circumstances under which someone holds sentences true is central to interpretation. We saw in the case of thoughts that although most thoughts are not beliefs, it is the pattern of belief that allows us to identify any thought; analogously, in the case of language, although most utterances are not concerned with truth, it is the pattern of sentences held true that gives sentences their meaning.

The attitude of holding a sentence to be true (under specified conditions) relates belief and interpretation in a fundamental way. We can know that a speaker holds a sentence to be true without knowing what he means by it or what belief it expresses for him. But if we know he holds the sentence true *and* we know how to interpret it, then we can make a correct attribution of belief. Symmetrically, if we know what belief a sentence held true expresses, we know how to interpret it. The methodological problem of interpretation is to see how, given the sentences a man accepts as true under given circumstances, to work out what his beliefs are and what his words mean. The situation is again similar to the situation in decision theory where, given a man's preferences between alternative courses of action, we can discern both his beliefs and his desires. Of course it should not be thought that a theory of interpretation will stand alone, for as we noticed, there is no chance of telling when a sentence is held true without being able to attribute desires and being able to describe actions as having complex intentions. This observation does not deprive the theory of interpretation of interest, but assigns it a place within a more comprehensive theory of action and thought.[5]

It is still unclear whether interpretation is required for a theory of action, which is the question we set ourselves to answer. What is certain is that all the standard ways of testing theories of decision or preference under uncertainty rely on the use of language. It is relatively simple to eliminate the necessity for verbal responses on the part of the subject: he can be taken to have expressed a preference by taking action, by moving directly to achieve his end, rather than by saying what he wants. But this cannot settle the question of what he has chosen. A man who takes an apple rather than a pear when offered both may be expressing a preference for what is on his left rather than his right, what is red rather than yellow, what is seen first, or judged more expensive. Repeated tests may make some readings of his actions more plausible than others, but the problem will remain how to determine when he judges two objects of choice to be identical. Tests that involve uncertain events – choices between gambles – are even harder to present without using words. The psychologist, skeptical of his ability to be certain how a subject is interpreting his instructions, must add a theory of verbal interpretation to the theory to be tested. If we think of all choices as revealing a preference that one sentence rather than another be true, the resulting total theory should provide an interpretation of sentences, and at the same time assign beliefs and desires, both of the latter conceived as relating the agent to sentences or utterances. This composite theory would explain all behavior, verbal and otherwise.

All this strongly suggests that the attribution of desires and beliefs (and other thoughts) must go hand in hand with the interpretation that of speech, that neither the theory of decision nor that of interpretation can be successfully developed without the other. But it remains to say, in more convincing detail, why the attribution of thought depends on the interpretation of speech. The general, and not very informative, reason is that without speech we cannot make the fine distinctions between thoughts that are essential to the explanations we can sometimes confidently supply. Our manner of attributing attitudes ensures that all the expressive power of language can be used to make such distinctions. One can believe that Scott is not the author of *Waverley* while not doubting that Scott is Scott; one can want to be the discoverer of a creature with a heart without wanting to be the discoverer of a creature with a kidney. One can intend to bite into the apple in the hand without intending to bite into the only apple with a worm in it; and so forth. The intensionality we make so much of in the attribution of thoughts is very hard to make much of when speech is not present. The dog, we say, knows that its master is home. But does it know that Mr Smith (who is his master), or that the president of the bank (who is that same master), is home? We have no real idea how to settle, or make sense of, these questions. It is much harder to say, when speech is not present, how to distinguish universal thoughts from conjunctions of thoughts, or how to attribute conditional thoughts, or thoughts with, so to speak, mixed quantification ("He hopes that everyone is loved by someone").

These considerations will probably be less persuasive to dog lovers than to others, but in any case they do not constitute an argument. At best what we have shown, or claimed, is that unless there is behavior that can be interpreted as speech, the evidence will not be adequate to justify the fine distinctions we are used to making in the attribution of thoughts. If we persist in attributing desires, beliefs, or other attitudes under these conditions, our attributions and consequent explanations of actions will be seriously underdetermined in that many alternative systems of attribution, many alternative explanations, will be equally justified by the available date. Perhaps this is all we can say against the attribution of thoughts to dumb creatures; but I do not think so.

Before going on I want to consider a possible objection to the general line I have been pursuing. Suppose we grant, the objector says, that very complex behavior not observed in infants and elephants is necessary if we are to find application for the full apparatus available for the attribution of thoughts. Still, it may be said, the sketch of how interpretation works does not show that this complexity must be viewed as connected with language. The reason is that the sketch makes too much depend on the special attitude of being thought true. The most direct evidence for the existence of this attitude is honest assertion. But then it would seem that we could treat as speech the behavior of creatures that never did anything with language except make honest assertions. Some philosophers do dream of such dreary tribes; but would we be right to say they had a language? What has been lost to view is what may be called *the autonomy of meaning*. Once a sentence is understood, an utterance of it may be used to serve almost any extralinguistic purpose. An instrument that could be put to only one use would lack autonomy of meaning; this amounts to saying it should not be counted as a language. So the complexity of behavior needed to give full scope to attributions of thought need not, after all, have exactly the same complexity that allows, or requires, interpretation as a language.

I agree with the hypothetical objector that autonomy of meaning is essential to language; indeed it is largely this that explains why linguistic meaning cannot be defined or analyzed on the basis of extra linguistic intentions and beliefs. But the objector fails to distinguish between a language that *could* be used for only one purpose and one that is used for only one purpose. An instrument that could be used for only one purpose would not be language. But honest assertion alone might yield a theory of interpretation, and so a language that, though capable of more, might never be put to further uses. (As a practical matter, the event is unthinkable. Someone who knows under what conditions his sentences are socially true cannot fail to grasp, and avail himself of, the possibilities for dishonest assertion or for joking, story-telling, goading, exaggerating, insulting, and all the rest of the jolly crew.)

A method of interpretation tells us that for speakers of English an utterance of "It is raining" by a speaker x at time t is true if and only if it is raining (near x) at t. To be armed with this information, and to know that others know it, is to know what an utterance means independently of knowing the purposes that prompted it. The autonomy of meaning also helps to explain how it is possible, by the use of language, to attribute thoughts. Suppose someone utters assertively the sentence "Snow is white." Knowing the conditions under which such an utterance is true I can add, if I please, "I believe that too," thus attributing a belief to myself. In this case we may both have asserted that snow is white, but sameness of force is not necessary to the self-attribution. The other may say with a sneer, expressing disbelief, "Snow is white" – and I may again attribute a belief to myself by saying, "But *I* believe that." It can work as well in another way: If I can take advantage of an utterance of someone else's to attribute a belief to myself, I can use an utterance of my own to attribute a belief to someone else. First I utter a sentence, perhaps "Snow is white," and then I add "He believes that." The first utterance may or may not be an assertion; in any case, it does not attribute a belief to anyone (though if it is an assertion, then I do *represent* myself as believing that snow is white). But if my remark "He believes that" is an assertion, I have attributed a belief to someone else. Finally, there is no bar to my attributing a belief to myself by saying first, "Snow is white" and then adding, "I believe that."

In all these examples, I take the word "that" to refer demonstratively to an utterance, whether it is an utterance by the speaker of the "that" or by another speaker. The "that" cannot refer to a sentence, both because, as Church has pointed out in similar cases, the reference would then have to be relativized to a language, since a sentence may have different meanings in different languages;[6] but also, and more obviously, because the same sentence may have different truth values in the same language.

What demonstrative reference to utterances does in the sort of case just considered it can do as well when the surface structure is altered to something like "I believe that snow is white" or "He believes that snow is white." In these instances also I think we should view the "that" as a demonstrative, now referring ahead to an utterance on the verge of production. Thus the logical form of standard attributions of attitude is that of two utterances paratactically joined. There is no connective, though the first utterance contains a reference to the second. (Similar remarks go, of course, for inscriptions of sentences.)

I have discussed this analysis of verbal attributions of attitude elsewhere, and there is no need to repeat the arguments and explanations here.[7] It is an analysis with its own difficulties, especially when it comes to analyzing quantification into the contained sentence, but I think these difficulties can be overcome while preserving the appealing features of the idea. Here I want to stress a point that connects the paratactic analysis of attributions of attitude with our present theme. The proposed analysis directly relates the autonomous feature of meaning with our ability to describe and attribute thoughts, since it is only because the interpretation of a sentence is independent of its use that the utterance of a sentence can serve in the description of the attitudes of others. If my analysis is right, we can dispense with the unlikely (but common) view that a sentence bracketed into a "that"-clause needs an entirely different interpretation from the one that works for it in other contexts. Since sentences are not names or descriptions in ordinary contexts, we can in particular reject the assumption that the attitudes have objects such as propositions which "that"-clauses might be held to name or describe. There should be no temptation to call the utterance to which reference is made according to the paratactic analysis the object of the attributed attitude.

Here a facile solution to our problem about the relation between thoughts and speech suggests itself. One way to view the paratactic analysis, a way proposed by Quine in *Word and Object*, is this: when a speaker attributes an attitude to a person, what he does is ape or mimic an actual or possible speech act of that person.[8] Indirect discourse is the best example, and assertion is another good one. Suppose I say, "Herodotus asserted that the Nile rises in the Mountains of the Moon." My second utterance – my just past utterance of "The Nile rises in the Mountains of the Moon" – must, if my attribution to Herodotus is correct, bear a certain relationship to an utterance of Herodotus': it must, in some appropriate sense, be a translation of it. Since, assuming still that the attribution is correct, Herodotus and I are *samesayers*, my utterance mimicked his. Not with respect to force, of course, since I didnt assert anything about the Nile. The sameness is with respect to the content of our utterances. If we turn to other attitudes, the situation is more complicated, for there is typically no utterance to ape. If I affirm "Jones believes that snow is white," my utterance of "Snow is white" may have no actual utterance of Jones's to imitate. Still, we could take the line that what I affirm is that Jones would be honestly speaking his mind were he to utter a sentence translating mine. Given some delicate assumptions about the conditions under which such a subjunctive conditional is true, we could conclude that only someone with a language could have a thought, since to have a thought would be to have a disposition to utter certain sentences with appropriate force under given circumstances.

We could take this line, but unfortunately there seems no clear reason why we have to.

We set out to find an argument to show that only creatures with speech have thoughts. What has just been outlined is not an argument, but a proposal, and a proposal we need not accept. The paratactic analysis of the logical form of attributions of attitude can get along without the mimic-theory of utterance. When I say, "Jones believes that snow is white" I describe Jones's state of mind directly: it is indeed the state of mind someone is in who could honestly assert "Snow is white" if he spoke English, but that may be a state a languageless creature could also be in.

In order to make my final main point, I must return to an aspect of interpretation so far neglected. I remarked that the attitude of holding true, directed to sentences under specified circumstances, is the basis for interpretation, but I did not say how it can serve this function. The difficulty, it will be remembered, is that a sentence is held true because of two factors: what the holder takes the sentence to mean, and what he believes. In order to sort things out, what is needed is a method for holding one factor steady while the other is studied.

Membership in a language community depends on the ability to interpret the utterances of members of the group, and a method is at hand if one has, and knows one has, a theory which provides truth conditions, more or less in Tarski's style, for all sentences (relativized, as always, to time and speaker). The theory is correct as long as it entails, by finitely stated means, theorems of the familiar form: " 'It is raining' is true for a speaker x at time t if and only if it is raining (near x) at t." The evidential basis for such a theory concerns sentences held true, facts like the following: " 'It is raining' was held true by Smith at 8 a.m. on August 26 and it did rain near Smith at that time." It would be possible to generate a correct theory simply by considering sentences to be true when held true, provided (1) there was a theory which satisfied the formal constraints and was consistent in this way with the evidence, and (2) all speakers held a sentence to be true just when that sentence was true – provided, that is, all beliefs, at least as far as they could be expressed, were correct.

But of course it cannot be assumed that speakers never have false beliefs. Error is what gives belief its point. We can, however, take it as given that *most* beliefs are correct. The reason for this is that a belief is identified by its location in a pattern of beliefs; it is this pattern that determines the subject matter of the belief, what the belief is about. Before some object in, or aspect of, the world can become part of the subject matter of a belief (true or false) there must be endless true beliefs about the subject matter. False beliefs tend to undermine the identification of the subject matter; to undermine, therefore, the validity of a description of the belief as being about that subject. And so, in turn, false beliefs undermine the claim that a connected belief is false. To take an example, how clear are we that the ancients – some ancients – believed that the earth was flat? *This* earth? Well, this earth of ours is part of the solar system, a system partly identified by the fact that it is a gaggle of large, cool, solid bodies circling around a very large, hot star. If someone believes *none* of this about the earth, is it certain that it is the earth that he is thinking about? An answer is not called for. The point is made if this kind of consideration of related beliefs can shake one's confidence that the ancients believed the earth was flat. It isn't that any one false belief necessarily destroys our ability to identify further beliefs, but that the intelligibility of such identifica-tions must depend on a background of largely unmentioned and unquestioned true beliefs. To put it another way: the more things a believer is right about, the sharper his errors are. Too much mistake simply blurs the focus.

What makes interpretation possible, then, is the fact that we can dismiss a priori the chance of massive error. A theory of interpretation cannot be correct that makes a man assent to very many false sentences: it must generally be the case that a sentence is true when a speaker holds it to be. So far as it goes, it is in favor of a method of interpretation that it counts a sentence true just when speakers hold it to be true. But of course, the speaker may be wrong; and so may the interpreter. So in the end what must be counted in favor of a method of interpretation is that it puts the interpreter in general agreement with the speaker: according to the method, the speaker holds a sentence true under specified conditions, and these conditions obtain, in the opinion of the interpreter, just when the speaker holds the sentence to be true.

No simple theory can put a speaker and interpreter in perfect agreement, and so a workable theory must from time to time assume error on the part of one or the other. The basic methodological precept is, therefore, that a good theory of interpretation maximizes agreement. Or, given that sentences are infinite in number, and given further considerations to come, a better word might be *optimize*.

Some disagreements are more destructive of understanding than others, and a sophisticated theory must naturally take this into account. Disagreement about theoretical matters may (in some cases) be more tolerable than disagreement about what is more evident; disagreement about how things look or appear is less tolerable than disagreement about how they are; disagreement about the truth of attributions of certain attitudes to a speaker by that same speaker may not be tolerable at all, or barely. It is impossible to simplify the considerations that are relevant, for everything we know or believe about the way evidence supports belief can be put to work in deciding where the theory can best allow error, and what errors are least destructive of understanding. The methodology of interpretation is, in this respect, nothing but epistemology seen in the mirror of meaning.

The interpreter who assumes his method can be made to work for a language community will strive for a theory that optimizes agreement throughout the community. Since easy communication has survival value, he may expect usage within a community to favor simple common theories of interpretation.

If this account of radical interpretation is right, at least in broad outline, then we should acknowledge that the concepts of objective truth, and of error, necessarily emerge in the context of interpretation. The distinction between a sentence being held true and being in fact true is essential to the existence of an interpersonal system of communication, and when in individual cases there is a difference, it must be counted as error. Since the attitude of holding true is the same, whether the sentence is true or not, it corresponds directly to belief. The concept of belief thus stands ready to take up the slack between objective truth and the held true, and we come to understand it just in this connection.

We have the idea of belief only from the role of belief in the interpretation of language, for as a private attitude it is not intelligible except as an adjustment to the public norm provided by language. It follows that a creature must be a member of a speech community if it is to have the concept of belief. And given the dependence of other attitudes on belief, we can say more generally that only a creature that can interpret speech can have the concept of a thought.

Can a creature have a belief if it does not have the concept of belief? It seems to me it cannot, and for this reason. Someone cannot have a belief unless he understands the possibility of being mistaken, and this requires grasping the contrast between truth and error – true belief and false belief. But this contrast, I have argued, can emerge only in the context of interpretation, which alone forces us to the idea of an objective, public truth.

It is often wrongly thought that the semantical concept of truth is redundant, that there is no difference between asserting that a sentence *s* is true, and using *s* to make an assertion. What may be right is a redundancy theory of belief, that to believe that *p* is not to be distinguished from the belief that *p* is true. This notion of truth is not the semantical notion:

language is not directly in the picture. But it is only just out of the picture; it is part of the frame. For the notion of a true belief depends on the notion of a true utterance, and this in turn there cannot be without shared language. As Shakespeare's Ulysses puts it:

> no man is the lord of anything,
> Though in and of him there be much consisting,
> Till he communicate his parts to others;
> Nor doth he of himself know them for aught
> Till he behold them formed in th'applause
> Where they're extended.
>   (*Troilus and Cressida*, III. iii. 115–20)

NOTES

1 N. Malcolm, "Thoughtless Brutes," *Proceedings and Addresses of the American Philosophical Association* (1972–3).

2 W. Sellars, "Conceptual Change," in G. Pearce and P. Maynard, eds, *Conceptual Change* (Dordrecht: Reidel, 1973), p.82.

3 F. P. Ramsey, "Truth and Probability," reprinted in *Foundations of Mathematics* (New York: Humanities Press, 1950).

4 See my "Radical Interpretation," *Dialectica* 27 (1973), pp. 313–28; and "Belief and the Basis of Meaning," *Synthese* 27 (1974), pp. 309–23.

5 The interlocking of decision theory and radical interpretation is explored also in "Belief and the Basis of Meaning," in Essay 12 of *Essays in Actions and Events* (Oxford: Clarendon Press, 1980), and in "Toward a Unified Theory of Meaning and Action," *Grazer Philosophische Studien* 2 (1980), pp. 1–12.

6 A. Church, "On Carnap's Analysis of Statements of Assertion and Belief," *Analysis* 10 (1950), pp. 97–9.

7 See "On Saying That," *Synthese* 19 (1968–9), pp. 130–46.

8 W. V. Quine, *Word and Object* (Cambridge, MA: MIT Press, 1960), p. 219.

5

Mind and Machine

Introduction

How do we determine whether other beings do or do not possess certain cognitive abilities, such as being able to add or understanding Chinese? One way to determine that is to conduct some sort of a test of the being's abilities. We might, for instance, in conversation solicit information and ask questions that require the being to reveal its command of the relevant subject matter. If we want to determine whether a being knows how to add, we inquire about addition. If we get the appropriate answers to our questions about addition, we conclude that the being knows how to add. If we want to determine whether the being has a command of Chinese, we turn the conversation to Chinese, preferably in Chinese. Again, if we get the appropriate replies, we conclude that the being has a command of the Chinese language. This way of determining whether a being possesses cognitive abilities is known as the Turing Test.

The test is named after Alan M. Turing, a British mathematician and logician. To characterize computation he introduced the idea of a Turing Machine which manipulates uninterpreted symbols according to a finite set of rules. Turing came to believe that in due course such a symbol-manipulating machine or anything equivalent to it would be intelligent in the way we are. That is, he thought that such machines would pass the Turing Test, and he defends this view in his celebrated paper "Computing Machinery and Intelligence" (1950).

Turing asked the question "Can machines think?" Instead of directly attacking the question, he replaced it with another, related one: Can a machine successfully play the imitation game? The original imitation game is played by three people: a male, a female, and an interrogator who cannot see or hear the other two players. The interrogator's task is to find out who is male and who is female on the basis of written questions and answers. What makes the game interesting is that one of the players tries to fool the interrogator about his or her sexual identity while the other player gives honest answers.

The Turing Test replaces the two players of different sexes with a human and a digital computer. The interrogator's objective is to determine which of the two players is human and which is the computer. Turing's question is "Will the interrogator decide wrongly as often when the game is played like this as when it is played with a male and a female?" Turing believed that 50 years from the time he wrote his article a computer would be able to play the imitation game so well that the interrogator had no more than a 70 percent chance of correctly identifying his subjects after five minutes of questioning. He also believed that 50 years from the time he wrote his article the use of words and general educated opinion would have changed such that people would be able to talk meaningfully about machines thinking.

Turing's work suggested that intelligence in general, including human intelligence, should be characterized in terms of the carrying out of a computation over uninterpreted symbols according to a finite set of rules. This has been the cornerstone of classical artificial intelligence. The basic idea is that in some sense our brains implement a set of symbols and rules for manipulating symbols in much the same way that your PC stores symbols and programs.

This basic idea was challenged by John R. Searle in a paper first published in 1980 in *Behavioral and Brain Sciences*, and summarized here in an article published in the *Scientific American*. He asks us to imagine a non-Chinese speaker locked in a room with a rule book in English matching Chinese symbols with other Chinese symbols. The rules identify the symbols entirely by their shapes, not by their meanings. Outside of the room there is a small group of people who understand Chinese and who hand the non-Chinese speaker Chinese symbols to which she is supposed to respond with the help of the rule book. With this help, the non-Chinese speaker is able to respond to the symbols in a way that might be expected of a native Chinese speaker. In other words, she passes the Turing Test. In spite of that, Searle points out, she does not understand Chinese, nor is it plausible to claim that the room understands Chinese.

If we look at the rule book as being a computer program, the non-Chinese speaker as being the processor, those who wrote the rule book as the programmers, the input as data and the output as answers, then we can look at the Chinese room as being a symbol processor, much like computers. Given that, and given that the system (the Chinese room) does not understand Chinese, Searle concludes that no pure syntax processor is capable of thought and understanding. Thought requires mental content, or semantics, and syntax does not yield semantics, Searle argues.

In the same issue of the *Scientific American* two prominent defenders of the view that the mind is like a computer were given an opportunity to reply. Paul Churchland and Patricia Churchland argue that Searle begs the question. Searle, they argue, assumes that syntax by itself does not yield mental content that is constitutive of or sufficient for semantics. This begs the question because classical artificial intelligence is based on the idea that appropriately manipulated symbols can produce understanding.

Of course, this idea does not fit our ordinary, commonsensical or intuitive understanding of what it is to understand something. When you are thinking about dinner, your thoughts do not appear to be anything like symbol manipulation according to rules. But for the Churchlands this is no more a problem than the fact that light does not appear to us to be oscillating electromagnetic forces. The Churchlands advocate a thoroughly scientific treatment of the mind, and modern science has always distinguished appearances of things from their real underlying natures.

Although the Churchlands believe that the brain's mind is a computer, they do not think it is a classical computer that manipulates formal symbols. They claim that the classical artificial intelligence model fails because certain cognitive tasks that humans are able to perform quickly and efficiently, such as seeing and recognizing an object, require too much time and too much stored information when simulated on a digital computer. The Churchlands describe and endorse a kind of computation – parallel distributed processing – that seems to be much closer to the brain's neural networks. An important feature of these computations is that they are not manipulating symbols according to structure-sensitive rules.

Searle's thought experiment was directed against symbol-processing machines, so it might seem that the model the Churchlands describe is not affected by Searle's argument. Searle, however, disagrees, and the reader will have to decide who is right.

Despite the differences between Searle and the Churchlands, it is important to recognize the similarities in their views. Both agree that behavioral tests are not sufficient for picking out intelligence. Intelligence also depends on the right sort of internal structure that produces behavior. Moreover, both move away from the idea that the manipulation of symbols – be it an external public language such as English or some special language internal to the mind (a language of thought, so to speak) – is sufficient for intelligence. Searle requires content in addition to symbol manipulation and the Churchlands require the subsymbolic computations of parallel distributed processors.

FURTHER READING

Block, N. (1978). Troubles with Functionalism. In *Perception and Cognition: Issues in the Foundations of Psychology*. Ed. C. W. Savage. *Minnesota Studies in the Philosophy of Science*, vol. 9. Minneapolis: University of Minnesota Press.
Boden, M. (1977). *Artificial Intelligence and Natural Man*. New York: Basic Books.
Dreyfus, H. (1979). *What Computers Still Can't Do: A Critique of Artificial Reason*. Cambridge, MA: MIT Press.
Haugeland, J. (1985). *Artificial Intelligence: The Very Idea*. Cambridge, MA: MIT Press.
Hofstadter, D. R. (1981). Metamagical Themas: A Coffeehouse Conversation on the Turing Test to Determine if a Machine Can Think. *Scientific American* 245: 15–36.
Lycan, William G. (1981). Toward a Homuncular Theory of Believing. *Cognition and Brain Theory* 4: 139–59.
Putnam, H. (1967). Psychological Predicates. In *Art, Mind and Religion*. Eds W. H. Capitan and D. D. Merrill. Pittsburgh: University of Pittsburgh Press.
Searle, J. (1980). Minds, Brains and Programs. *Behavioral and Brain Sciences* 3: 417–24.
Sterelny, K. (1990). *The Representational Theory of Mind*. Oxford: Blackwell.
Stich, S. (1983). *From Folk Psychology to Cognitive Science*. Cambridge, MA: MIT Press.

Computing Machinery and Intelligence

ALAN M. TURING

1 The Imitation Game

I propose to consider the question, "Can machines think?" This should begin with definitions of the meaning of the terms "machine" and "think." The definitions might be framed so as to reflect so far as possible the normal use of the words, but this attitude is dangerous. If the meaning of the words "machine" and "think" are to be found by examining how they are commonly used it is difficult to escape the conclusion that the meaning and the answer to the question, "Can machines think?" is to be sought in a statistical survey such as a Gallup poll. But this is absurd. Instead of attempting such a definition I shall replace the question by another, which is closely related to it and is expressed in relatively unambiguous words.

The new form of the problem can be described in terms of a game which we call the "imitation game." It is played with three people, a man (A), a woman (B), and an interrogator (C) who may be of either sex. The interrogator stays in a room apart from the other two. The object of the game for the interrogator is to determine which of the other two is the man and which is the woman. He knows them by labels X and Y, and at the end of the game he says either "X is A and Y is B" or "X is B and Y is A." The interrogator is allowed to put questions to A and B thus:

C: Will X please tell me the length of his or her hair?

Now suppose X is actually A, then A must answer. It is A's object in the game to try and cause C to make the wrong identification. His answer might therefore be:

"My hair is shingled, and the longest strands are about nine inches long."

In order that tones of voice may not help the interrogator the answers should be written, or better still, typewritten. The ideal arrangement is to have a teleprinter communicating between the two rooms. Alternatively the question and answers can be repeated by an intermediary. The object of the game for the third player (B) is to help the interrogator. The best strategy for her is probably to give truthful answers. She can add such things as "I am the woman, don't listen to him!" to her answers, but it will avail nothing as the man can make similar remarks.

We now ask the question, "What will happen when a machine takes the part of A in this game? Will the interrogator decide wrongly as often when the game is played like this as he does when the game is played between a man and a woman?" These questions replace our original, "Can machines think?"

2 Critique of the New Problem

As well as asking, "What is the answer to this new form of the question?," one may ask, "Is this new question a worthy one to investigate?" This latter question we investigate without further ado, thereby cutting short an infinite regress

The new problem has the advantage of drawing a fairly sharp line between the physical and the intellectual capacities of a man. No engineer or chemist claims to be able to produce a material which is indistinguishable from the human skin. It is possible that at some time this might be done, but even supposing this invention available we should feel there was little point in trying to make a "thinking machine" more human by dressing it up in such artificial flesh. The form in which we have set the problem reflects this fact in the condition which prevents the interrogator from seeing or touching the other competitors, or hearing their voices. Some other advantages of the proposed criterion may be shown up by specimen questions and answers. Thus:

Q: Please write me a sonnet on the subject of the Forth Bridge.
A: Count me out on this one. I never could write poetry.

Q: Add 34957 to 70764
A: (Pause about 30 seconds and then give as answer) 105621.
Q: Do you play chess?
A: Yes.
Q: I have K at my K1, and no other pieces. You have only K at K6 and R at R1. It is your move. What do you play?
A: (After a pause of 15 seconds) R–R8 mate.

The question and answer method seems to be suitable for introducing almost any one of the fields of human endeavor that we wish to include. We do not wish to penalize the machine for its inability to shine in beauty competitions, nor to penalize a man for losing in a race against an aeroplane. The conditions of our game make these disabilities irrelevant. The "witnesses" can brag, if they consider it advisable, as much as they please about their charms, strength, or heroism, but the interrogator cannot demand practical demonstrations.

The game may perhaps be criticized on the ground that the odds are weighted too heavily against the machine. If the man were to try and pretend to be the machine he would clearly make a very poor showing. He would be given away at once by slowness and inaccuracy in arithmetic. May not machines carry out something which ought to be described as thinking but which is very different from what a man does? This objection is a very strong one, but at least we can say that if, nevertheless, a machine can be constructed to play the imitation game satisfactorily, we need not be troubled by this objection.

It might be urged that when playing the "imitation game" the best strategy for the machine may possibly be something other than imitation of the behavior of a man. This may be, but I think it is unlikely that there is any great effect of this kind. In any case there is no intention to investigate here the theory of the game, and it will be assumed that the best strategy is to try to provide answers that would naturally be given by a man.

3   The Machines concerned in the Game

The question which we put in §1 will not be quite definite until we have specified what we mean by the word "machine." It is natural that we should wish to permit every kind of engineering technique to be used in our machines. We also wish to allow the possibility that an engineer or team of engineers may construct a machine which works, but whose manner of operation cannot be satisfactorily described by its constructors because they have applied a method which is largely experimental. Finally, we wish to exclude from the machines men born in the usual manner. It is difficult to frame the definitions so as to satisfy these three conditions. One might for instance insist that the team of engineers should be all of one sex, but this would not really be satisfactory, for it is probably possible to rear a complete individual from a single cell of the skin (say) of a man. To do so would be a feat of biological technique deserving of the very highest praise, but we would not be inclined to regard it as a case of "constructing a thinking machine." This prompts us to abandon the requirement that every kind of technique should be permitted. We are the more ready to do so in view of the fact that the present interest in "thinking machines" has been aroused by a particular kind of machine, usually called an "electronic computer" or "digital computer." Following this suggestion we only permit digital computers to take part in our game.

This restriction appears at first sight to be a very drastic one. I shall attempt to show that it is not so in reality. To do this necessitates a short account of the nature and properties of these computers.

It may also be said that this identification of machines with digital computers, like our criterion for "thinking," will only be unsatisfactory if (contrary to my belief) it turns out that digital computers are unable to give a good showing in the game. There are already a number of digital computers in working order, and it may be asked, "Why not try the experiment straight away? It would be easy to satisfy the conditions of the game. A number of interrogators could be used, and statistics compiled to show how often the right identification was given." The short answer is that we are not asking whether all digital computers would do well in the game nor whether the computers at present available would do well, but whether there are imaginable computers which would do well. But this is only the short answer. We shall see this question in a different light later.

4   Digital Computers

The idea behind digital computers may be explained by saying that these machines are intended to carry out any operations which could be done by a human computer. The human computer is supposed to be following fixed rules; he has no authority to deviate from them in any detail. We may suppose that these rules are supplied in a book, which is altered whenever he is put on to a new job. He has also an unlimited supply of paper on which he does his calculations. He may also do his multiplications and additions on a "desk machine," but this is not important.

If we use the above explanation as a definition we shall be in danger of circularity of argument. We avoid this by giving an outline of the means by which the desired effect is achieved. A digital computer can usually be regarded as consisting of three parts:

1   store;
2   executive unit;
3   control.

The store is a store of information, and corresponds to the human computer's paper, whether this is the paper on which he does his calculations or that on which his book of rules is printed. In so far as the human computer does calculations in his head a part of the store will correspond to his memory.

The executive unit is the part which carries out the various individual operations involved in a calculation. What these individual operations are will vary from machine to machine. Usually fairly lengthy operations can be done such as "Multiply 3540675445 by 7076345687," but in some machines only very simple ones such as "Write down 0" are possible.

We have mentioned that the "book of rules" supplied to the computer is replaced in the machine by a part of the store. It is then called the "table of instructions." It is the duty of the control to see that these instructions are obeyed correctly and in the right order. The control is so constructed that this necessarily happens.

The information in the store is usually broken up into packets of moderately small size. In one machine, for instance, a packet might consist of ten decimal digits. Numbers are assigned to the parts of the store in which the various packets of information are stored, in some systematic manner. A typical instruction might say:

"Add the number stored in position 6809 to that in 4302 and put the result back into the latter storage position."

Needless to say it would not occur in the machine expressed in English. It would more likely be coded in a form such as 6809430217. Here 17 says which of various possible operations is to be performed on the two numbers. In this case the operation is that described above, viz. "Add the number . . ." It will be noticed that the instruction takes up 10 digits and so forms one packet of information, very conveniently. The control will normally take the instructions to be obeyed in the order of the positions in which they are stored, but occasionally an instruction such as:

"Now obey the instruction stored in position 5606, and continue from there"

may be encountered, or again:

"If position 4505 contains 0 obey next the instruction stored in 6707, otherwise continue straight on."

Instructions of these latter types are very important because they make it possible for a sequence of operations to be repeated over and over again until some condition is fulfilled, but in doing so to obey, not fresh instructions on each repetition, but the same ones over and over again. To take a domestic analogy. Suppose Mother wants Tommy to call at the cobbler's every morning on his way to school to see if her shoes are done, she can ask him afresh every morning. Alternatively she can stick up a notice once and for all in the hall which he will see when he leaves for school and which tells him to call for the shoes, and also to destroy the notice when he comes back if he has the shoes with him.

The reader must accept it as a fact that digital computers can be constructed, and indeed have been constructed, according to the principles we have described, and that they can in fact mimic the actions of a human computer very closely.

The book of rules which we have described our human computer as using is of course a convenient fiction. Actual human computers really remember what they have got to do. If one wants to make a machine mimic the behavior of the human computer in some complex operation one has to ask him how it is done, and then translate the answer into the form of an instruction table. Constructing instruction tables is usually described as "programming." To "program a machine to carry out the operation *A*" means to put the appropriate instruction table into the machine so that it will do *A*.

An interesting variant on the idea of a digital computer is a "digital computer with a random element." These have instructions involving the throwing of a die or some equivalent electronic process; one such instruction might for instance be, "Throw the die and put the resulting number into store 1000." Sometimes such a machine is described as having free will (though I would not use this phrase myself). It is not normally possible to determine from observing a machine whether it has a random element, for a similar effect can be produced by such devices as making the choices depend on the digits of the decimal for π.

Most actual digital computers have only a finite store. There is no theoretical difficulty in the idea of a computer with an unlimited store. Of course only a finite part can have been used at any one time. Likewise only a finite amount can have been constructed, but we can imagine more and more being added as required. Such computers have special theoretical interest and will be called infinitive capacity computers.

The idea of a digital computer is an old one. Charles Babbage, Lucasian Professor of Mathematics at Cambridge from 1828 to 1839, planned such a machine, called the Analytical Engine, but it was never completed. Although Babbage had all the essential ideas, his machine was not at that time such a very attractive prospect. The speed which would have been available would be definitely faster than a human computer but something like 100 times slower than the Manchester machine, itself one of the slower of the modern machines. The storage was to be purely mechanical, using wheels and cards.

The fact that Babbage's Analytical Engine was to be entirely mechanical will help us to rid ourselves of a superstition. Importance is often attached to the fact that modern digital computers are electrical, and that the nervous system also is electrical. Since Babbage's machine was not electrical, and since all digital computers are in a sense equivalent, we see that this use of electricity cannot be of theoretical importance. Of course electricity usually comes in where fast signaling is concerned, so that it is not surprising that we find it in both these connections. In the nervous system chemical phenomena are at least as important as electrical. In certain computers the storage system is mainly acoustic. The feature of using electricity is thus seen to be only a very superficial similarity. If we wish to find such similarities we should look rather for mathematical analogies of function.

5   Universality of Digital Computers

The digital computers considered in the last section may be classified amongst the "discrete-state machines." These are the machines which move by sudden jumps or clicks from one quite definite state to another. These states are sufficiently different for the possibility of confusion between them to be ignored. Strictly speaking there are no such machines. Everything really moves continuously. But there are many kinds of machine which can profitably be *thought of* as being discrete-state machines. For instance in considering the switches for a lighting system it is a convenient fiction that each switch must be definitely on or definitely off. There must be intermediate positions, but for most purposes we can forget about them. As an example of a discrete-state machine we might consider a wheel which clicks round through 120° once a second, but may be stopped by a lever which can be operated from outside; in addition a lamp is to light in one of the positions of the wheel. This machine could be described abstractly as follows. The internal state of the machine (which is described by the position of the wheel) may be q_1, q_2, or q_3. There is an input signal i_o or i_l (position of lever). The internal state at any moment is determined by the last state and input signal according to the table:

	Last State		
	q_1	q_2	q_3
i_o	q_2	q_3	q_1

Input

| i_l | q_1 | q_2 | q_3 |

The output signals, the only externally visible indication of the internal state (the light) are described by the table:

State	q_1	q_2	q_3
Output	o_0	o_0	o_1

This example is typical of discrete-state machines. They can be described by such tables provided they have only a finite number of possible states.

It will seem that given the initial state of the machine and the input signals it is always possible to predict all future states. This is reminiscent of Laplace's view that from the complete state of the universe at one moment of time, as described by the positions and velocities of all particles, it should be possible to predict all future states. The prediction which we are considering is, however, rather nearer to practicability than that considered by Laplace. The system of the "universe as a whole" is such that quite small errors in the initial conditions can have an overwhelming effect at a later time. The displacement of a single electron by a billionth of a centimeter at one moment might make the difference between a man being killed by an avalanche a year later, or escaping. It is an essential property of the mechanical systems which we have called "discrete-state machines" that this phenomenon does not occur. Even when we consider the actual physical machines instead of the idealized machines, reasonably accurate knowledge of the state at one moment yields reasonably accurate knowledge any number of steps later.

As we have mentioned, digital computers fall within the class of discrete-state machines. But the number of states of which such a machine is capable is usually enormously large. For instance, the number for the machine now working at Manchester it about $2^{165,000}$, i.e., about $10^{50,000}$. Compare this with our example of the clicking wheel described above, which had three states. It is not difficult to see why the number of states should be so immense. The computer includes a store corresponding to the paper used by a human computer. It must be possible to write into the store any one of the combinations of symbols which might have been written on the paper. For simplicity suppose that only digits from 0 to 9 are used as symbols. Variations in handwriting are ignored. Suppose the computer is allowed 100 sheets of paper each containing 50 lines each with room for 30 digits. Then the number of states is $10^{100 \times 50 \times 30}$, i.e., $10^{150,000}$. This is about the number of states of three Manchester machines put together. The logarithm to the base two of the number of states is usually called the "storage capacity" of the machine. Thus the Manchester machine has a storage capacity of about 165,000 and the wheel machine of our example about 1.6. If two machines are put together their capacities must be added to obtain the capacity of the resultant machine. This leads to the possibility of statements such as "The Manchester machine contains 64 magnetic tracks each with a capacity of 2560, eight electronic tubes with a capacity of 1280. Miscellaneous storage amounts to about 300 making a total of 174,380."

Given the table corresponding to a discrete-state machine it is possible to predict what it will do. There is no reason why this calculation should not be carried out by means of a digital computer.Provided it could be carried out sufficiently quickly the digital computer could mimic the behavior of any discrete-state machine. The imitation game could then be played with the machine in question (as *B*) and the mimicking digital computer (as *A*) and the interrogator would be unable to distinguish them. Of course the digital computer must have an adequate storage capacity as well as working sufficiently fast. Moreover, it must be programmed afresh for each new machine which it is desired to mimic.

This special property of digital computers, that they can mimic any discrete-state machine, is described by saying that they are *universal* machines. The existence of machines with this property has the important consequence that, considerations of speed apart, it is unnecessary to design various new machines to do various computing processes. They can all be done with one digital computer, suitably programmed for each case. It will be seen that as a consequence of this all digital computers are in a sense equivalent. We may now consider again the point raised at the end of §3. It was suggested tentatively that the question, "Can machines think?" should be replaced by "Are there imaginable digital computers which would do well in the imitation game?" If we wish we can make this superficially more general and ask, "Are there discrete-state machines which would do well?" But in view of the universality property we see that either of these questions is equivalent to this, "Let us fix our attention on one particular digital computer C. Is it true that by modifying this computer to have an adequate storage, suitably increasing its speed of action, and providing it with an appropriate program, C can be made to play satisfactorily the part of A in the imitation game, the part of B being taken by a man?"

6   Contrary Views on the Main Question

We may now consider the ground to have been cleared and we are ready to proceed to the debate on our question, "Can machines think?" and the variant of it quoted at the end of the last section. We cannot altogether abandon the original form of the problem, for opinions will differ as to the appropriateness of the substitution and we must at least listen to what has to be said in this connection.

It will simplify matters for the reader if I explain first my own beliefs in the matter. Consider first the more accurate form of the question. I believe that in about 50 years' time it will be possible to program computers, with a storage capacity of about 10^9, to make them play the imitation game so well that an average interrogator will not have more than a 70 percent chance of making the right identification after five minutes of questioning. The original question, "Can machines think?" I believe to be too meaningless to deserve discussion. Nevertheless I believe that at the end of the century the use of words and general educated opinion will have altered so much that one will be able to speak of machines thinking without expecting to be contradicted. I believe further that no useful purpose is served by concealing these beliefs. The popular view that scientists proceed inexorably from well-established fact to well-established fact, never being influenced by any unproved conjecture, is quite mistaken. Provided it is made clear which are proved facts and which are conjectures, no harm can result. Conjectures are of great importance since they suggest useful lines of research.

I now proceed to consider opinions opposed to my own.

(1)   The theological objection

Thinking is a function of man's immortal soul. God has given an immortal soul to every man and woman, but not to any other animal or to machines. Hence no animal or machine can think.

I am unable to accept any part of this, but will attempt to reply in theological terms. I should find the argument more convincing if animals were classed with men, for there is a greater difference, to my mind, between the typical animate and the inanimate than there is between man and the other animals. The arbitrary character of the orthodox view becomes clearer if we consider how it might appear to a member of some other religious community. How do Christians regard the Moslem view that women have no souls? But let us leave this point aside and return to the main argument. It appears to me that the argument quoted above implies a serious restriction of the omnipotence of the Almighty.[1] It is admitted that there are certain things that He cannot do such as making one equal to two, but should we not believe that He has freedom to confer a soul on an elephant if He sees fit? We might expect that He would only exercise this power in conjunction with a mutation which provided the elephant with an appropriately improved brain to minister to the needs of this soul. An argument of exactly similar form may be made for the case of machines. It may seem different because it is more difficult to "swallow." But this really only means that we think it would be less likely that He would consider the circumstances suitable for conferring a soul. The circumstances in question are discussed in the rest of this paper. In attempting to construct such machines we should not be irreverently usurping His power of creating souls, any more than we are in the procreation of children: rather we are, in either case, instruments of His will providing mansions for the souls that He creates.

However, this is mere speculation. I am not very impressed with theological arguments whatever they may be used to support. Such arguments have often been found unsatisfactory in the past. In the time of Galileo it was argued that the texts, "And the sun stood still . . . and hasted not to go down about a whole day" (Joshua x. 13) and "He laid the foundations of the earth, that it should not move at any time" (Psalm cv. 5) were an adequate refutation of the Copernican theory. With our present knowledge such an argument appears futile. When that knowledge was not available it made a quite different impression.

(2)   The "heads in the sand" objection

"The consequences of machines thinking would be too dreadful. Let us hope and believe that they cannot do so."

This argument is seldom expressed quite so openly as in the form above. But it affects most of us who think about it at all. We like to believe that man is in some subtle way superior to the rest of creation. It is best if he can be shown to be *necessarily* superior, for then there is no danger of him losing his commanding position. The popularity of the theological argument is clearly connected with this feeling. It is likely to be quite strong in intellectual people, since they value the power of thinking more highly than others, and are more inclined to base their belief in the superiority of man on this power.

I do not think that this argument is sufficiently substantial to require refutation. Consolation would be more appropriate: perhaps this should be sought in the transmigration of souls.

(3)   The mathematical objection

There are a number of results of mathematical logic which can be used to show that there are limitations to the powers of discrete-state machines. The best known of these results is known as Gödel's theorem ("Über formal unentscheidbare Sätze der *Principia Mathematica*"), and shows that in any sufficiently powerful logical system statements can be formulated which can neither be proved nor disproved within the system, unless possibly the system itself is inconsistent. There are other, in some respects similar, results due to Church ("An Unsolvable Problem"), Kleene ("General Recursive Functions"), Rosser, and Turing ("On Computable Numbers"). The latter result is the most convenient to consider, since it refers directly to machines, whereas the others can only be used in a comparatively indirect argument: For instance if Gödel's theorem is to be used we need in addition to have some means of describing logical systems in terms of machines, and machines in terms of logical systems. The result in question refers to a type of machine which is essentially a digital computer with an infinite capacity. It states that there are certain things that such a machine cannot do. If it is rigged up to give answers to questions as in the imitation game, there will be some questions to which it will either give a wrong answer, or fail to give an answer at all however much time is allowed for a reply. There may, of course, be many such questions, and questions which cannot be answered by one machine may be satisfactorily answered by another. We are of course supposing for the present that the questions are of the kind to which an answer "Yes" or "No" is appropriate, rather than questions such as, "What do you think of Picasso?" The questions that we know the machines must fail on are of this type, "Consider the machine specified as follows . . . Will this machine ever answer 'Yes' to any question?" The dots are to be replaced by a description of some machine in a standard form, which could be something like that used in §5. When the machine described bears a certain comparatively simple relation to the machine which is under interrogation, it can be shown that the answer is either wrong or not forthcoming. This is the mathematical result: It is argued that it proves a disability of machines to which the human intellect is not subject.

The short answer to this argument is that although it is established that there are limitations to the powers of any particular machine, it has only been stated, without any sort of proof, that no such limitations apply to the human intellect. But I do not think this view can be dismissed quite so lightly. Whenever one of these machines is asked the appropriate critical question, and gives a definite answer, we know that this answer must be wrong, and this gives us a certain feeling of superiority. Is this feeling illusory? It is no doubt quite genuine, but I do not think too much importance should be attached to it. We too often give wrong answers to questions ourselves to be justified in being very pleased at such evidence of fallibility on the part of the machines. Further, our superiority can only be felt on such an occasion in relation to the one machine over which we have scored our petty triumph. There would be no question of triumphing simultaneously over *all* machines. In short, then, there might be men cleverer than any given machine, but then again there might be other machines cleverer again, and so on.

Those who hold to the mathematical argument would, I think, mostly be willing to accept the imitation game as a basis for discussion. Those who believe in the two previous objections would probably not be interested in any criteria.

(4)   *The argument from consciousness*

This argument is very well expressed in Professor Jefferson's Lister Oration for 1949 ("The Mind of Mechanical Man"), from which I quote. "Not until a machine can write a sonnet or compose a concerto because of thoughts and emotions felt, and not by the chance fall of symbols, could we agree that machine equals brain – that is, not only write it but know that it had written it. No mechanism could feel (and not merely artificially signal, an easy contrivance) pleasure at its successes, grief when its valves fuse, be warmed by flattery, be made miserable by its mistakes, be charmed by sex, be angry or depressed when it cannot get what it wants."

This argument appears to be a denial of the validity of our test. According to the most extreme form of this view the only way by which one could be sure that a machine thinks is to be the machine and to feel oneself thinking. One could then describe these feelings to the world, but of course no one would be justified in taking any notice. Likewise according to this view the only way to know that a *man* thinks is to be that particular man. It is in fact the solipsist point of view. It may be the most logical view to hold but it makes communication of ideas difficult. *A* is liable to believe "*A* thinks but *B* does not" whilst *B* believes "*B* thinks but *A* does not." Instead of arguing continually over this point it is usual to have the polite convention that everyone thinks.

I am sure that Professor Jefferson does not wish to adopt the extreme and solipsist point of view. Probably he would be quite willing to accept the imitation game as a test. The game (with the player *B* omitted) is frequently used in practice under the name of *viva voce* to discover whether some one really understands something or has "learnt it parrot fashion." Let us listen in to a part of such a *viva voce*:

Interrogator: In the first line of your sonnet which reads "Shall I compare thee to a summer's day," would not "a spring day" do as well or better?
Witness: It wouldn't scan.
Interrogator: How about "a winter's day"? That would scan all right.
Witness: Yes, but nobody wants to be compared to a winter's day.
Interrogator: Would you say Mr Pickwick reminded you of Christmas?
Witness: In a way.
Interrogator: Yet Christmas is a winter's day, and I do not think Mr Pickwick would mind the comparison.
Witness: I don't think you're serious. By a winter's day one means a typical winter's day, rather than a special one like Christmas.

And so on. What would Professor Jefferson say if the sonnet-writing machine was able to answer like this in the *viva voce*? I do not know whether he would regard the machine as "merely artificially signaling" these answers, but if the answers were as satisfactory and sustained as in the above passage I do not think be would describe it as "an easy contrivance." This phrase is, I think, intended to cover such devices as the inclusion in the machine of a record of someone reading a sonnet, with appropriate switching to turn it on from time to time.

In short then, I think that most of those who support the argument from consciousness could be persuaded to abandon it rather than be forced into the solipsist position. They will then probably be willing to accept our test.

I do not wish to give the impression that I think there is no mystery about consciousness. There is, for instance, something of a paradox connected with any attempt to localize it. But I do not think these mysteries necessarily need to be solved before we can answer the question with which we are concerned in this paper.

(5)   *Arguments from various disabilities*

These arguments take the form, "I grant you that you can make machines do all the things you have mentioned but you will never be able to make one to do *X*." Numerous features *X* are suggested in this connection. I offer a selection: Be kind, resourceful, beautiful, friendly (p. 256), have initiative, have a sense of humor, tell right from wrong, make mistakes (p. 256), fall in love, enjoy strawberries and cream (p. 256), make some one fall in love with it, learn from experience (pp. 261ff), use words properly, be the subject of its own thought (p. 257), have as much diversity of behavior as a man, do something really new (p. 257). (Some of these disabilities are given special consideration as indicated by the page numbers.)

No support is usually offered for these statements. I believe they are mostly founded on the principle of scientific induction. A man has seen thousands of machines in his lifetime. From what he sees of them he draws a number of general conclusions. They are ugly, each is designed for a very limited purpose, when required for a minutely different purpose they are useless, the variety of behavior of any one of them is very small, etc., etc. Naturally he concludes that these are necessary properties of machines in general. Many of these limitations are associated with the very small storage capacity of most machines. (I am assuming that the idea of storage capacity is extended in some way to cover machines other than discrete-state machines. The exact definition does not matter as no mathematical accuracy is claimed in the present discussion.) A few years ago, when very little had been heard of digital computers, it was possible to elicit much incredulity concerning them, if one mentioned their properties without describing their construction. That was presumably due to a similar application of the principle of scientific induction. These applications of the principle are of course largely unconscious. When a burnt child fears the fire and shows that he fears it by avoiding it, I should say that he was applying scientific induction. (I could of course also describe his behavior in many other ways.) The works and customs of mankind do not seem to be very suitable material to which to apply scientific induction. A very large part of space-time must be investigated, if reliable results are to be obtained. Otherwise we may (as most English children do) decide that everybody speaks English, and that it is silly to learn French.

There are, however, special remarks to be made about many of the disabilities that have been mentioned. The inability to enjoy strawberries and cream may have struck the reader as frivolous. Possibly a machine might be made to enjoy this delicious dish, but any attempt to make one do so would be idiotic. What is important about this disability is that it contributes to some of the other disabilities, e.g., to the difficulty of the same kind of friendliness occurring between man and machine as between white man and white man, or between black man and black man.

The claim that "machines cannot make mistakes" seems a curious one. One is tempted to retort, "Are they any the worse for that?" But let us adopt a more sympathetic attitude, and try to see what is really meant. I think this criticism can be explained in terms of the imitation game. It is claimed that the interrogator could distinguish the machine from the man simply by setting them a number of problems in arithmetic. The machine would be unmasked because of its deadly accuracy. The reply to this is simple. The machine (programmed for playing the game) would not attempt to give the *right* answers to the arithmetic problems. It would deliberately introduce mistakes in a manner calculated to confuse the interrogator. A mechanical fault would probably show itself through an unsuitable decision as to what sort of a mistake to make in the arithmetic. Even this interpretation of the criticism is not sufficiently sympathetic. But we cannot afford the space to go into it much further. It seems to me that this criticism depends on a confusion between two kinds of mistake. We may call them "errors of functioning" and "errors of conclusion." Errors of functioning are due to some mechanical or electrical fault which causes the machine to behave otherwise than it was designed to do. In philosophical discussions one likes to ignore the possibility of such errors; one is therefore discussing "abstract machines." These abstract machines are mathematical fictions rather than physical objects. By definition they are incapable of errors of functioning. In this sense we can truly say that "machines can never make mistakes." Errors of conclusion can only arise when some meaning is attached to the output signals from the machine. The machine might, for instance, type out mathematical equations, or sentences in English. When a false proposition is typed we say that the machine has committed an error of conclusion. There is clearly no reason at all for saying that a machine cannot make this kind of mistake. It might do nothing but type out repeatedly "0 = 1." To take a less perverse example, it might have some method for drawing conclusions by scientific induction. We must expect such a method to lead occasionally to erroneous results.

The claim that a machine cannot be the subject of its own thought can of course only be answered if it can be show that the machine has *some* thought with *some* subject matter. Nevertheless, "the subject matter of a machine's operations" does seem to mean something, at least to the people who deal with it. If, for instance, the machine was trying to find a solution of the equation $x^2 - 40x - 11 = 0$ one would be tempted to describe this equation as part of the machine's subject matter at that moment. In this sort of sense a machine undoubtedly can be its own subject matter. It may be used to help in making up its own programs, or to predict the effect of alterations in its own structure. By observing the results of its own behavior it can modify its own programs so as to achieve some purpose more effectively. These are possibilities of the near future, rather than Utopian dreams.

The criticism that a machine cannot have much diversity of behavior is just a way of saying that it cannot have much storage capacity. Until fairly recently a storage capacity of even a thousand digits was very rare.

The criticisms that we are considering here are often disguised forms of the argument from consciousness. Usually if one maintains that a machine can do one of these things, and describes the kind of method that the machine could use, one will not make much of an impression. It is thought that the method (whatever it may be, for it must be mechanical) is really rather base. Compare the parenthesis in Jefferson's statement quoted on p. 254.

(6)   Lady Lovelace's objection

Our most detailed information of Babbage's Analytical Engine comes from a memoir by Lady Lovelace ("Translator's Notes"). In it she states, "The Analytical Engine has no pretensions to originate anything. It can do *whatever we know how to order it* to perform" (her italics). This statement is quoted by Hartree (*Calculating Instruments*, p. 70), who adds: "This does not imply that it may not be possible to construct electronic equipment which will 'think for itself', or in which, in biological terms, one could set up a conditioned reflex, which would serve as a basis for 'learning'. Whether this is possible in principle or not is a stimulating and exciting question, suggested by some of these recent developments. But it did not seem that the machines constructed or projected at the time had this property."

I am in thorough agreement with Hartree over this. It will be noticed that he does not assert that the machines in question had not got the property, but rather that the evidence available to Lady Lovelace did not encourage her to believe that they had it. It is quite possible that the machines in question had in a sense got this property. For suppose that some discrete-state machine has the property. The Analytical Engine was a universal digital computer, so that, if its storage capacity and speed were adequate, it could by suitable programming be made to mimic the machine in question. Probably this argument did not occur to the countess or to Babbage. In any case there was no obligation on them to claim all that could be claimed.

This whole question will be considered again under the heading of learning machines.

A variant of Lady Lovelace's objection states that a machine can "never do anything really new." This may be parried for a moment with the saw, "There is nothing new under the sun." Who can be certain that "original work" that he has done was not simply the growth of the seed planted in him by teaching, or the effect of following well-known general principles? A better variant of the objection says that a machine can never "take us by surprise." This statement is a more direct challenge and can be met directly. Machines take me by surprise with great frequency. This is largely because I do not do sufficient calculation to decide what to expect them to do, or rather because, although I do a calculation, I do it in a hurried, slipshod fashion, taking risks. Perhaps I say to myself, "I suppose the voltage here ought to be the same as there: anyway let's assume it is." Naturally I am often wrong, and the result is a surprise for me for by the time the experiment is done these assumptions have been forgotten. These admissions lay me open to lectures on the subject of my vicious ways, but do not throw any doubt on my credibility when I testify to the surprises I experience.

I do not expect this reply to silence my critic. He will probably say that such surprises are due to some creative mental act on my part, and reflect no credit on the machine. This leads us back to the argument from consciousness, and far from the idea of surprise. It is a line of argument we must consider closed, but it is perhaps worth remarking that the appreciation of something as surprising requires as much of a "creative mental act" whether the surprising event originates from a man, a book, a machine, or anything else.

The view that machines cannot give rise to surprises is due, I believe, to a fallacy to which philosophers and mathematicians are particularly subject. This is the assumption that as soon as a fact is presented to a mind all consequences of that fact spring into the mind simultaneously with it. It is a very useful assumption under many circumstances, but one too easily forgets that it is false. A natural consequence of doing so is that one then assumes that there is no virtue in the mere working out of consequences from data and general principles.

(7)   Argument from continuity in the nervous system

The nervous system is certainly not a discrete-state machine. A small error in the information about the size of a nervous impulse impinging on a neuron may make a large difference to the size of the outgoing impulse. It may be argued that, this being so, one cannot expect to be able to mimic the behavior of the nervous system with a discrete-state system.

It is true that a discrete-state machine must be different from a continuous machine. But if we adhere to the conditions of the imitation game, the interrogator will not be able to take any advantage of this difference. The situation can be made clearer if we consider some other simpler continuous machine. A differential analyzer will do very well. (A differential analyzer is a certain kind of machine not of the discrete-state type used for some kinds of calculation.) Some of these provide their answers in a typed form, and so are suitable for taking part in the game. It would not be possible for a digital computer to predict exactly what answers the differential analyzer would give to a problem, but it would be quite capable of giving the right sort of answer. For instance, if asked to give the value of π (actually about 3.1416) it would be reasonable to choose at random between the values 3.12, 3.13, 3.14, 3.15, 3.16 with the probabilities of 0.05, 0.15, 0.55, 0.19, 0.06 (say). Under these circumstances it would be very difficult for the interrogator to distinguish the differential analyzer from the digital computer.

(8)   The argument from informality of behavior

It is not possible to produce a set of rules purporting to describe what a man should do in every conceivable set of circumstances. One might for instance have a rule that one is to stop when one sees a red traffic light, and to go if one sees a green one, but what if by some fault both appear together? One may perhaps decide that it is safest to stop. But some further difficulty may well arise from this decision later. To attempt to provide rules of conduct to cover every eventuality, even those arising from traffic lights, appears to be impossible. With all this I agree.

From this it is argued that we cannot be machines. I shall try to reproduce the argument, but I fear I shall hardly do it justice. It seems to run something like this. "If each man had a definite set of rules of conduct by which he regulated his life he would be no better than a machine. But there are no such rules, so men cannot be machines." The undistributed middle is glaring. I do not think the argument is ever put quite like this, but I believe this is the argument used nevertheless. There may however be a certain confusion between "rules of conduct" and "laws of behavior" to cloud the issue. By "rules of conduct" I mean precepts such as "Stop if you see red lights," on which one can act, and of which one can be conscious. By "laws of behavior" I mean laws of nature as applied to a man's body such as "if you pinch him he will squeak." If we substitute "laws of behavior which regulate his life" for "laws of conduct by which he regulates his life" in the argument quoted, the undistributed middle is no longer insuperable. For we believe that it is not only true that being regulated by laws of behavior implies being some sort of machine (though not necessarily a discrete-state machine), but that conversely being such a machine implies being regulated by such laws. However, we cannot so easily convince ourselves of the absence of complete laws of behavior as of complete rules of conduct. The only way we know of for finding such laws is scientific observation, and we certainly know of no circumstances under which we could say, "We have searched enough. There are no such laws."

We can demonstrate more forcibly that any such statement would be unjustified. For suppose we could be sure of finding such laws if they existed. Then given a discrete-state machine it should certainly be possible to discover by observation sufficent about it to predict its future behavior, and this within a reasonable time, say a thousand years. But this does not seem to be the case. I have set up on the Manchester computer a small program using only 1,000 units of storage, whereby the machine supplied with one 16-figure number replies with another within two seconds. I would defy anyone to learn from these replies sufficient about the program to be able to predict any replies to untried values.

(9)   The argument from extrasensory perception

I assume that the reader is familiar with the idea of extrasensory perception, and the meaning of the four items of it, viz. telepathy, clairvoyance, precognition, and psychokinesis. These disturbing phenomena seem to deny all our usual scientific ideas. How we should like to discredit them! Unfortunately the statistical evidence, at least for telepathy, is overwhelming. It is very difficult to rearrange one's ideas so as to fit these new facts in. Once one has accepted them it does not seem a very big step to believe in ghosts and bogies. The idea that our bodies move simply according to the known laws of physics, together with some others not yet discovered but somewhat similar, would be one of the first to go.

This argument is to my mind quite a strong one. One can say in reply that many scientific theories seem to remain workable in practice, in spite of clashing with ESP; that in fact one can get along very nicely if one forgets about it. This is rather cold comfort, and one fears that thinking is just the kind of phenomenon where ESP may be especially relevant.

A more specific argument based on ESP might run as follows: "Let us play the imitation game, using as witnesses a man who is good as a telepathic receiver, and a digital computer. The interrogator can ask such questions as 'What suit does the card in my right hand belong to' The man by telepathy or clairvoyance gives the right answer 130 times out of 400 cards. The machine can only guess at random, and perhaps gets 104 right, so the interrogator makes the right identification." There is an interesting possibility which opens here. Suppose the digital computer contains a random number generator. Then it will be natural to use this to decide what answer to give. But then the random number generator will be subject to the psychokinetic powers of the interrogator. Perhaps this psychokinesis might cause the machine to guess right more often than would be expected on a probability calculation, so that the interrogator might still be unable to make the right identification. On the other hand, he might be able to guess right without any questioning, by clairvoyance. With ESP anything may happen.

If telepathy is admitted it will be necessary to tighten our test up. The situation could be regarded as analogous to that which would occur if the interrogator were talking to himself and one of the competitors was listening with his ear to the wall. To put the competitors into a "telepathy-proof room" would satisfy all requirements.

7   Learning Machines

The reader will have anticipated that I have no very convincing arguments of a positive nature to support my views. If I had I should not have taken such pains to point out the fallacies in contrary views. Such evidence as I have I shall now give.

Let us return for a moment to Lady Lovelace's objection, which stated that the machine can only do what we tell it to do. One could say that a man can "inject" an idea into the machine, and that it will respond to a certain extent and then drop into quiescence, like a piano string struck by a hammer. Another simile would be an atomic pile of less than critical size: An injected idea is to correspond to a neutron entering the pile from without. Each such neutron will cause a certain disturbance which eventually dies away. If, however, the size of the pile is sufficiently increased, the disturbance caused by such an incoming neutron will very likely go on and on increasing until the whole pile is destroyed. Is there a corresponding phenomenon for minds, and is there one for machines? There does seem to be one for the human mind. The majority of them seem to be "subcritical," i.e., to correspond in this analogy to piles of subcritical size. An idea presented to such a mind will on average give rise to less than one idea in reply. A smallish proportion are supercritical. An idea presented to such a mind may give rise to a whole "theory" consisting of secondary, tertiary, and more remote ideas. Animals' minds seem to be very definitely subcritical. Adhering to this analogy we ask, "Can a machine be made to be supercritical?"

The "skin of an onion" analogy is also helpful. In considering the functions of the mind or the brain we find certain operations which we can explain in purely mechanical terms. This we say does not correspond to the real mind: it is a sort of skin which we must strip off if we are to find the real mind. But then in what remains we find a further skin to be stripped off, and so on. Proceeding in this way do we ever come to the "real" mind, or do we eventually come to the skin which has nothing in it? In the latter case the whole mind is mechanical. (It would not be a discrete-state machine, however. We have discussed this.)

These last two paragraphs do not claim to be convincing arguments. They should rather be described as "recitations tending to produce belief."

The only really satisfactory support that can be given for the view expressed at the beginning of §6 will be that provided by waiting for the end of the century and then doing the experiment described. But what can we say in the meantime? What steps should be taken now if the experiment is to be successful?

As I have explained, the problem is mainly one of programming. Advances in engineering will have to be made too, but it seems unlikely that these will not be adequate for the requirements. Estimates of the storage capacity of the brain vary from 10^{10} to 10^{15} binary digits. I incline to the lower values and believe that only a very small fraction is used for the higher types of thinking. Most of it is probably used for the retention of visual impressions. I should be surprised if more than 10^9 was required for satisfactory playing of the imitation game, at any rate against a blind man. (Note: the capacity of the *Encyclopedia Britannica*, 11th edition, is 2×10^9.) A storage capacity of 10^7 would be a very practicable possibility even by present techniques. It is probably not necessary to increase the speed of operations of the machines at all. Parts of modern machines which can be regarded as analogues of nerve cells work about a thousand times faster than the latter. This should provide a "margin of safety" which could cover losses of speed arising in many ways. Our problem then is to find out how to program these machines to play the game. At my present rate of working I produce about 1,000 digits of program a day, so that about 60 workers, working steadily through the 50 years, might accomplish the job, if nothing went into the wastepaper basket. Some more expeditious method seems desirable.

In the process of trying to imitate an adult human mind we are bound to think a good deal about the process which has brought it to the state that it is in. We may notice three components:

1 the initial state of the mind, say at birth;
2 the education to which it has been subjected;
3 other experience, not to be described as education, to which it has been subjected.

Instead of trying to produce a program to simulate the adult mind, why not rather try to produce one which simulates the child's? If this were then subjected to an appropriate course of education one would obtain the adult brain. Presumably the child-brain is something like a notebook as one buys it from the stationers: rather little mechanism, and lots of blank sheets. (Mechanism and writing are from our point of view almost synonymous.) Our hope is that there is so little mechanism in the child-brain that something like it can be easily programmed. The amount of work in the education we can assume, as a first approximation, to be much the same as for the human child.

We have thus divided our problem into two parts: the child-program and the education process. These two remain very closely connected. We cannot expect to find a good child-machine at the first attempt. One must experiment with teaching one such machine and see how well it learns. One can then try another and see if it is better or worse. There is an obvious connection between this process and evolution, by the identifications

Structure of the child machine = Hereditary material
Changes of the child machine = Mutations
Natural selection   = Judgment of the experimenter

One may hope, however, that this process will be more expeditious than evolution. The survival of the fittest is a slow method for measuring advantages. The experimenter, by the exercise of intelligence, should be able to speed it up. Equally important is the fact that he is not restricted to random mutations. If he can trace a cause for some weakness he can probably think of the kind of mutation which will improve it.

It will not be possible to apply exactly the same teaching process to the machine as to a normal child. It will not, for instance, be provided with legs, so that it could not be asked to go out and fill the coal scuttle. Possibly it might not have eyes. But however well these deficiencies might be overcome by clever engineering, one could not send the creature to school without the other children making excessive fun of it. It must be given some tuition. We need not be too concerned about the legs, eyes, etc. The example of Miss Helen Keller shows that education can take place provided that communication in both directions between teacher and pupil can take place by some means or other.

We normally associate punishments and rewards with the teaching process. Some simple child–machines can be constructed or programmed on this sort of principle. The machine has to be so constructed that events which shortly preceded the occurrence of a punishment-signal are unlikely to be repeated, whereas a reward-signal increased the probability of repetition of the events which led up to it. These definitions do not presuppose any feelings on the part of the machine. I have done some experiments with one such child–machine, and succeeded in teaching it a few things, but the teaching method was too unorthodox for the experiment to be considered really successful.

The use of punishments and rewards can at best be a part of the teaching process. Roughly speaking, if the teacher has no other means of communicating to the pupil, the amount of information which can reach him does not exceed the total number of rewards and punishments applied. By the time a child has learnt to repeat "Casabianca" he would probably feel very sore indeed, if the text could only be discovered by a "Twenty Questions" technique, every "No" taking the form of a blow. It is necessary therefore to have some other "unemotional" channels of communication. If these are available it is possible to teach a machine by punishments and rewards to obey orders given in some language, e.g., a symbolic language. These orders are to be transmitted through the "unemotional" channels. The use of this language will diminish greatly the number of punishments and rewards required.

Opinions may vary as to the complexity which is suitable in the child–machine. One might try to make it as simple as possible consistently with the general principles. Alternatively one might have a complete system of logical inference "built in."[2] In the latter case the store would be largely occupied with definitions and propositions. The propositions would have various kinds of status, e.g., well-established facts, conjectures, mathematically proved theorems, statements given by an authority, expressions having the logical form of proposition but not belief value. Certain propositions may be described as "imperatives." The machine should be so constructed that as soon as an imperative is classed as "well-established" the appropriate action automatically takes place. To illustrate this, suppose the teacher says to the machine, "Do your homework now." This may cause "Teacher says 'Do your homework now'" to be included among the well-established facts. Another such fact might be, "Everything that teacher says is true." Combining these may eventually lead to the imperative, "Do your homework now" being included among the well-established facts, and this, by the construction of the machine, will mean that the homework actually gets started, but the effect is very satisfactory. The processes of inference used by the machine need not be such as would satisfy the most exacting logicians. There might for instance be no hierarchy of types. But this need not mean that type fallacies will occur, any more than we are bound to fall over unfenced cliffs. Suitable imperatives (expressed *within* the systems, not forming part of the rules *of* the system) such as, "Do not use a class unless it is a subclass of one which has been mentioned by teacher" can have a similar effect to, "Do not go too near the edge."

The imperatives that can be obeyed by a machine that has no limbs are bound to be of a rather intellectual character, as in the example (doing homework) given above. Important among such imperatives will be ones which regulate the order in which the rules of the logical system concerned are to be applied. For at each stage when one is using a logical system, there is a very large number of alternative steps, any of which one is permitted to apply, so far as obedience to the rules of the logical system is concerned. These choices make the difference between a brilliant and a footling reasoner, not the difference between a sound and a fallacious one. Propositions leading to imperatives of this kind might be, "When Socrates is mentioned, use the syllogism in Barbara" or, "If one method has been proved to be quicker than another, do not use the slower method." Some of these may be "given by authority," but others may be produced by the machine itself, e.g., by scientific induction.

The idea of a learning machine may appear paradoxical to some readers. How can the rules of operation of the machine change? They should describe completely how the machine will react whatever its history might be, whatever changes it might undergo. The rules are thus quite time-invariant. This is quite true. The explanation of the paradox is that the rules which get changed in the learning process are of a rather less pretentious kind, claiming only an ephemeral validity. The reader may draw a parallel with the Constitution of the United States.

An important feature of a learning machine is that its teacher will often be very largely ignorant of quite what is going on inside, although he may still be able to some extent to predict his pupil's behavior. This should apply most strongly to the later education of a machine arising from a child-machine of well-tried design (or program). This is in clear contrast with normal procedure when using a machine to do computations: one's object is then to have a clear mental picture of the state of the machine at each moment in the computation. This object can only be achieved with a struggle. The view that "the machine can only do what we know how to order it to do"[3] appears strange in face of this. Most of the programs which we can put into the machine will result in its doing something that we cannot make sense of at all, or which we regard as completely random behavior. Intelligent behavior presumably consists in a departure from the completely disciplined behavior involved in computation, but a rather slight one, which does not give rise to random behavior, or to pointless repetitive loops. Another important result of preparing our machine for its part in the imitation game by a process of teaching and learning is that "human fallibility" is likely to be omitted in a rather natural way, i.e., without special "coaching." (The reader should reconcile this with the point of view on pp. 256–7.) Processes that are learnt do not produce 100 percent certainty of result; if they did they could not be unlearnt.

It is probably wise to include a random element in a learning machine (see p. 249). A random element is rather useful when we are searching for a solution of some problem. Suppose for instance we wanted to find a number between 50 and 200 which was equal to the square of the sum of its digits, we might start at 51 then try 52 and go on until we got a number that worked. Alternatively we might choose numbers at random until we got a good one. This method has the advantage that it is unnecessary to keep track of the values that have been tried, but the disadvantage that one may try the same one twice, but this is not very important if there are several solutions. The systematic method has the disadvantage that there may be an enormous block without any solutions in the region which has to be investigated first. Now the learning process may be regarded as a search for a form of behavior which will satisfy the teacher (or some other criterion). Since there is probably a very large number of satisfactory solutions the random method seems to be better than the systematic. It should be noticed that it is used in the analogous process of evolution. But there the systematic method is not possible. How could one keep track of the different genetical combinations that had been tried, so as to avoid trying them again?

We may hope that machines will eventually compete with men in all purely intellectual fields. But which are the best ones to start with? Even this is a difficult decision. Many people think that a very abstract activity, like the playing of chess, would be best. It can also be maintained that it is best to provide the machine with the best sense organs that money can buy, and then teach it to understand and speak English. This process could follow the normal teaching of a child. Things would be pointed out and named, etc. Again I do not know what the right answer is, but I think both approaches should be tried.

We can only see a short distance ahead, but we can see plenty there that needs to be done.

NOTES

1 Possibly this view is heretical. St Thomas Aquinas (*Summa Theologica*, quoted by Bertrand Russell, *History of Western Philosophy*, p. 480) states that God cannot make a man to have no soul. But this may not be a real restriction on His powers, but only a result of the fact that men's souls are immortal, and therefore indestructible.
2 Or rather "programmed in," for our child-machine will be programmed in a digital computer. But the logical system will not have to be learnt.
3 Compare Lady Lovelace's statement ("Translator's Notes," quoted on p. 257), which does not contain the word "only."

REFERENCES

Samuel Butler, *Erewhon*, London, 1865. Chs 23, 24, 25, *The Book of the Machines*.
Alonzo Church, "An Unsolvable Problem of Elementary Number Theory," *American Journal of Mathematics*, 58 (1936), 345–63.
K. Gödel, "Über formal unentscheidbare Sätze der *Principia Mathematica* und verwandter Systeme, I," *Monatshefte für Mathematik und Physik* (1931), 173–89.
D. R. Hartree, *Calculating Instruments and Machines*, New York, 1949.
S. C. Kleene, "General Recursive Functions of Natural Numbers," *American Journal of Mathematics*, 57 (1935), 153–73 and 219–44.
G. Jefferson, "The Mind of Mechanical Man," Lister Oration for 1949, *British Medical Journal*, i (1949), 1105–21.
Countess of Lovelace, "Translator's Notes to an Article on Babbage's Analytical Engine," *Scientific Memoirs* (ed. R. Taylor), vol. 3 (1842), 691–731.
Bertrand Russell, *History of Western Philosophy*, London, 1940.
A. M. Turing, "On Computable Numbers, with an Application to the Entscheidungsproblem," *Proceedings of the London Mathematics Society* (2), 42 (1937), 230–65.

Is the Brain's Mind a Computer Program?

JOHN R. SEARLE

Can a machine think? Can a machine have conscious thoughts in exactly the same sense that you and I have? If by "machine" one means a physical system capable of performing certain functions (and what else can one mean?), then humans are machines of a special biological kind, and humans can think, and so of course machines can think. And, for all we know, it might be possible to produce a thinking machine out of different materials altogether – say, out of silicon chips or vacuum tubes. Maybe it will turn out to be impossible, but we certainly do not know that yet.

In recent decades, however, the question of whether a machine can think has been given a different interpretation entirely. The question that has been posed in its place is, "Could a machine think just by virtue of implementing a computer program? Is the program by itself constitutive of thinking?" This is a completely different question because it is not about the physical, causal properties of actual or possible physical systems but rather about the abstract, computational properties of formal computer programs that can be implemented in any sort of substance at all, provided only that the substance is able to carry the program.

A fair number of researchers in artificial intelligence (AI) believe the answer to the second question is yes; that is, they believe that by designing the right programs with the right inputs and outputs, they are literally creating minds. They believe furthermore that they have a scientific test for determining success or failure: the Turing Test, devised by Alan M. Turing, the founding father of artificial intelligence. The Turing test, as currently understood, is simply this: If a computer can perform in such a way that an expert cannot distinguish its performance from that of a human who has a certain cognitive ability – say, the ability to do addition or to understand Chinese – then the computer also has that ability. So the goal is to design programs that will simulate human cognition in such a way as to pass the Turing Test. What is more, such a program would not merely be a model of the mind; it would literally be a mind, in the same sense that a human mind is a mind.

By no means does every worker in artificial intelligence accept so extreme a view. A more cautious approach is to think of computer models as being useful in studying the mind in the same way that they are useful in studying the weather, economics, or molecular biology. To distinguish these two approaches, I call the first strong AI and the second weak AI. It is important to see just how bold an approach strong AI is. Strong AI claims that thinking is merely the manipulation of formal symbols, and that is exactly what the computer does: manipulate formal symbols. This view is often summarized by saying, "The mind is to the brain as the program is to the hardware."

Strong AI is unusual among theories of the mind in at least two respects: It can be stated clearly, and it admits of a simple and decisive refutation. The refutation is one that any person can try for himself or herself. Here is how it goes. Consider a language you don't understand. In my case, I do not understand Chinese. To me Chinese writing looks like so many meaningless squiggles. Now suppose I am placed in a room containing baskets full of Chinese symbols. Suppose also that I am given a rule book in English for matching Chinese symbols with other Chinese symbols. The rules identify the symbols entirely by their shapes and do not require that I understand any of them. The rules might say such things as, "Take a squiggle-squiggle sign from basket number one and put it next to a squoggle-squoggle sign from basket number two."

Imagine that people outside the room who understand Chinese hand in small bunches of symbols and that in response I manipulate the symbols according to the rule book and hand back more small bunches of symbols. Now, the rule book is the "computer program." The people who wrote it are "programmers," and I am the "computer." The baskets full of symbols are the "data base," the small bunches that are handed in to me are "questions" and the bunches I then hand out are "answers."

Now suppose that the rule book is written in such a way that my "answers" to the "questions" are indistinguishable from those of a native Chinese speaker. For example, the people outside might hand me some symbols that unknown to me mean, "What's your favorite color?" and I might after going through the rules give back symbols that, also unknown to me, mean, "My favorite is blue, but I also like green a lot." I satisfy the Turing Test for understanding Chinese. All the same, I am totally ignorant of Chinese. And there is no way I could come to understand Chinese in the system as described, since there is no way that I can learn the meanings of any of the symbols. Like a computer, I manipulate symbols, but I attach no meaning to the symbols.

The point of the thought experiment is this: If I do not understand Chinese solely on the basis of running a computer program for understanding Chinese, then neither does any other digital computer solely on that basis. Digital computers merely manipulate formal symbols according to rules in the program.

What goes for Chinese goes for other forms of cognition as well. Just manipulating the symbols is not by itself enough to guarantee cognition, perception, understanding, thinking, and so forth. And since computers, *qua* computers, are symbol-manipulating devices, merely running the computer program is not enough to guarantee cognition.

This simple argument is decisive against the claims of strong AI. The first premise of the argument simply states the formal character of a computer program. Programs are defined in terms of symbol manipulations, and the symbols are purely formal, or "syntactic." The formal character of the program, by the way, is what makes computers so powerful. The same program can be run on an indefinite variety of hardwares, and one hardware system can run an indefinite range of computer programs. Let me abbreviate this "axiom" as:

Axiom 1   *Computer programs are formal (syntactic).*

This point is so crucial that it is worth explaining in more detail. A digital computer processes information by first encoding it in the symbolism that the computer uses and then manipulating the symbols through a set of precisely stated rules. These rules constitute the program. For example, in Turing's early theory of computers, the symbols were simply 0s and 1s, and the rules of the program said such things as, "Print a 0 on the tape, move one square to the left and erase a 1." The astonishing thing about computers is that any information that can be stated in a language can be encoded in such a system, and any information-processing task that can be solved by explicit rules can be programmed.

Two further points are important. First, symbols and programs are purely abstract notions: They have no essential physical properties to define them and can be implemented in any physical medium whatsoever. The 0s and 1s, *qua* symbols, have no essential physical properties and a fortiori have no physical, causal properties. I emphasize this point because it is tempting to identify computers with some specific technology – say, silicon chips – and to think that the issues are about the physics of silicon chips or to think that syntax identifies some physical phenomenon that might have as yet unknown causal powers, in the way that actual physical phenomena such as electromagnetic radiation or hydrogen atoms have physical, causal properties. The second point is that symbols are manipulated without reference to any meanings. The symbols of the program can stand for anything the programmer or user wants. In this sense the program has syntax but no semantics.

The next axiom is just a reminder of the obvious fact that thoughts, perceptions, understandings and so forth have a mental content. By virtue of their content they can be about objects and states of affairs in the world. If the content involves language, there will be syntax in addition to semantics, but linguistic understanding requires at least a semantic framework. If, for example, I am thinking about the last presidential election, certain words will go through my mind, but the words are about the election only because I attach specific meanings to these words, in accordance with my knowledge of English. In this respect they are unlike Chinese symbols for me. Let me abbreviate this axiom as:

Axiom 2   *Human minds have mental contents (semantics).*

Now let me add the point that the Chinese room demonstrated. Having the symbols by themselves – just having the syntax – is not sufficient for having the semantics. Merely manipulating symbols is not enough to guarantee knowledge of what they mean. I shall abbreviate this as:

Axiom 3   *Syntax by itself is neither constitutive of nor sufficient for semantics.*

At one level this principle is true by definition. One might, of course, define the terms "syntax" and "semantics" differently. The point is that there is a distinction between formal elements, which have no intrinsic meaning or content, and those phenomena that have intrinsic content. From these premises it follows that:

Conclusion 1   *Programs are neither constitutive of nor sufficient for minds.*

And that is just another way of saying that strong AI is false.

It is important to see what is proved and not proved by this argument.

First, I have not tried to prove that "a computer cannot think." Since anything that can be simulated computationally can be described as a computer, and since our brains can at some levels be simulated, it follows trivially that our brains are computers and they can certainly think. But from the fact that a system can be simulated by symbol manipulation and the fact that it is thinking, it does not follow that thinking is equivalent to formal symbol manipulation.

Second, I have not tried to show that only biologically based systems like our brains can think. Right now those are the only systems we know for a fact can think, but we might find other systems in the universe that can produce conscious thoughts, and we might even come to be able to create thinking systems artificially. I regard this issue as up for grabs.

Third, strong AI's thesis is not that, for all we know, computers with the right programs might be thinking, that they might have some as yet undetected psychological properties; rather it is that they must be thinking because that is all there is to thinking.

Fourth, I have tried to refute strong AI so defined. I have tried to demonstrate that the program by itself is not constitutive of thinking because the program is purely a matter of formal symbol manipulation – and we know independently that symbol manipulations by themselves are not sufficient to guarantee the presence of meanings. That is the principle on which the Chinese room argument works.

I emphasize these points here partly because it seems to me the Churchlands (see "Could a Machine Think?" [following article]) have not quite understood the issues. They think that strong AI is claiming that computers might turn out to think and that I am denying this possibility on commonsense grounds. But that is not the claim of strong AI, and my argument against it has nothing to do with common sense.

I will have more to say about their objections later. Meanwhile I should point out that, contrary to what the Churchlands suggest, the Chinese room argument also refutes any strong-AI claims made for the new parallel technologies that are inspired by and modeled on neural networks. Unlike the traditional von Neumann computer, which proceeds in a step-by-step fashion, these systems have many computational elements that operate in parallel and interact with one another according to rules inspired by neurobiology. Although the results are still modest, these "parallel distributed processing," or "connectionist," models raise useful questions about how complex, parallel network systems like those in brains might actually function in the production of intelligent behavior.

The parallel, "brainlike" character of the processing, however, is irrelevant to the purely computational aspects of the process. Any function that can be computed on a parallel machine can also be computed on a serial machine. Indeed, because parallel machines are still rare, connectionist programs are usually run on traditional serial machines. Parallel processing, then, does not afford a way around the Chinese room argument.

What is more, the connectionist system is subject even on its own terms to a variant of the objection presented by the original Chinese room argument. Imagine that instead of a Chinese room, I have a Chinese gym: a hall containing many monolingual, English-speaking men. These men would carry out the same operations as the nodes and synapses in a connectionist architecture as described by the Churchlands, and the outcome would be the same as having one man manipulate symbols according to a rule book. No one in the gym speaks a word of Chinese, and there is no way for the system as a whole to learn the meanings of any Chinese words. Yet with appropriate adjustments, the system could give the correct answers to Chinese questions.

There are, as I suggested earlier, interesting properties of connectionist nets that enable them to simulate brain processes more accurately than traditional serial architecture does. But the advantages of parallel architecture for weak AI are quite irrelevant to the issues between the Chinese room argument and strong AI.

The Churchlands miss this point when they say that a big enough Chinese gym might have higher-level mental features that emerge from the size and complexity of the system, just as whole brains have mental features that are not had by individual neurons. That is, of course, a possibility, but it has nothing to do with computation. Computationally, serial and parallel systems are equivalent: any computation that can be done in parallel can be done in serial. If the man in the Chinese room is computationally equivalent to both, then if he does not understand Chinese solely by virtue of doing the computations, neither do they. The Churchlands are correct in saying that the original Chinese room argument was designed with traditional AI in mind but wrong in thinking that connectionism is immune to the argument. It applies to any computational system. You can't get semantically loaded thought contents from formal computations alone, whether they are done in serial or in parallel; that is why the Chinese room argument refutes strong AI in any form.

Many people who are impressed by this argument are nonetheless puzzled about the differences between people and computers. If humans are, at least in a trivial sense, computers, and if humans have a semantics, then why couldn't we give semantics to other computers? Why couldn't we program a Vax or a Cray so that it too would have thoughts and feelings? Or why couldn't some new computer technology overcome the gulf between form and content, between syntax and semantics? What, in fact, are the differences between animal brains and computer systems that enable the Chinese room argument to work against computers but not against brains?

The most obvious difference is that the processes that define something as a computer – computational processes – are completely independent of any reference to a specific type of hardware implementation. One could in principle make a computer out of old beer cans strung together with wires and powered by windmills.

But when it comes to brains, although science is largely ignorant of how brains function to produce mental states, one is struck by the extreme specificity of the anatomy and the physiology. Where some understanding exists of how brain processes produce mental phenomena – for example, pain, thirst, vision, smell – it is clear that specific neurobiological processes are involved. Thirst, at least of certain kinds, is caused by certain types of neuron firings in the hypothalamus, which in turn are caused by the action of a specific peptide, angiotensin II. The causation is from the "bottom up" in the sense that lower-level neuronal processes cause higher-level mental phenomena. Indeed, as far as we know, every "mental" event, ranging from feelings of thirst to thoughts of mathematical theorems and memories of childhood, is caused by specific neurons firing in specific neural architectures.

But why should this specificity matter? After all, neuron firings could be simulated on computers that had a completely different physics and chemistry from that of the brain. The answer is that the brain does not merely instantiate a formal pattern or program (it does that, too), but also causes mental events by virtue of specific neurobiological processes. Brains are specific biological organs, and their specific biochemical properties enable them to cause consciousness and other sorts of mental phenomenon. Computer simulations of brain processes provide models of the formal aspects of these processes. But the simulation should not be confused with duplication. The computational model of mental processes is no more real than the computational model of any other natural phenomenon.

One can imagine a computer simulation of the action of peptides in the hypothalamus that is accurate down to the last synapse. But equally one can imagine a computer simulation of the oxidation of hydrocarbons in a car engine or the action of digestive processes in a stomach when it is digesting pizza. And the simulation is no more the real thing in the case of the brain than it is in the case of the car or the stomach. Barring miracles, you could not run your car by doing a computer simulation of the oxidation of gasoline, and you could not digest pizza by running the program that simulates such digestion. It seems obvious that a simulation of cognition will similarly not produce the effects of the neurobiology of cognition.

All mental phenomena, then, are caused by neurophysiological processes in the brain. Hence,

Axiom 4   *Brains cause minds.*

In conjunction with my earlier derivation, I immediately derive, trivially,

Conclusion 2   *Any other system capable of causing minds would have to have causal powers (at least) equivalent to those of brains.*

This is like saying that if an electrical engine is to be able to run a car as fast as a gas engine, it must have (at least) an equivalent power output. This conclusion says nothing about the mechanisms. As a matter of fact, cognition is a biological phenomenon: mental states and processes are caused by brain processes. This does not imply that only a biological system could think, but it does imply that any alternative system, whether made of silicon, beer cans, or whatever, would have to have the relevant causal capacities equivalent to those of brains. So now I can derive:

Conclusion 3   *Any artifact that produced mental phenomena, any artificial brain, would have to be able to duplicate the specific causal powers of brains, and it could not do that just by running a formal program.*

Furthermore, I can derive an important conclusion about human brains:

Conclusion 4   *The way that human brains actually produce mental phenomena cannot be solely by virtue of running a computer program.*

I first presented the Chinese room parable in the pages of *Behavioral and Brain Sciences* in 1980, where it appeared, as is the practice of the journal, along with peer commentary, in this case, 26 commentaries. Frankly, I think the point it makes is rather obvious, but to my surprise the publication was followed by a further flood of objections that – more surprisingly – continues to the present day. The Chinese room argument clearly touched some sensitive nerve.

The thesis of strong AI is that any system whatsoever – whether it is made of beer cans, silicon chips, or toilet paper – not only might have thoughts and feelings but *must* have thoughts and feelings, provided only that it implements the right program, with the right inputs and outputs. Now, that is a profoundly anti-biological view, and one would think that people in AI would be glad to abandon it. Many of them, especially the younger generation, agree with me, but I am amazed at the number and vehemence of the defenders. Here are some of the common objections.

1   In the Chinese room you really do understand Chinese, even though you don't know it. It is, after all, possible to understand something without knowing that one understands it.
2   You don't understand Chinese, but there is an (unconscious) subsystem in you that does. It is, after all, possible to have unconscious mental states, and there is no reason why your understanding of Chinese should not be wholly unconscious.
3   You don't understand Chinese, but the whole room does. You are like a single neuron in the brain, and just as such a single neuron by itself cannot understand but only contributes to the understanding of the whole system, you don't understand, but the whole system does.
4   Semantics doesn't exist anyway; there is only syntax. It is a kind of prescientific illusion to suppose that there exist in the brain some mysterious "mental contents," "thought processes," or "semantics." All that exists in the brain is the same sort of syntactic symbol manipulation that goes on in computers. Nothing more.
5   You are not really running the computer program – you only think you are. Once you have a conscious agent going through the steps of the program, it ceases to be a case of implementing a program at all.
6   Computers would have semantics and not just syntax if their inputs and outputs were put in appropriate causal relation to the rest of the world. Imagine that we put the computer into a robot, attached television cameras to the robot's head, installed transducers connecting the television messages to the computer, and had the computer output operate the robot's arms and legs. Then the whole system would have a semantics.
7   If the program simulated the operation of the brain of a Chinese speaker, then it would understand Chinese. Suppose that we simulated the brain of a Chinese person at the level of neurons. Then surely such a system would understand Chinese as well as any Chinese person's brain.

And so on.

All of these arguments share a common feature: they are all inadequate because they fail to come to grips with the actual Chinese room argument. That argument rests on the distinction between the formal symbol manipulation that is done by the computer and the mental contents biologically produced by the brain, a distinction I have abbreviated – I hope not misleadingly – as the distinction between syntax and semantics. I will not repeat my answers to all of these objections, but it will help to clarify the issues if I explain the weaknesses of the most widely held objection, argument (3) – what I call the systems reply. (The brain simulator reply, argument (7), is another popular one, but I have already addressed that one in the previous section.)

The systems reply asserts that of course *you* don't understand Chinese but the whole system – you, the room, the rule book, the bushel baskets full of symbols – does. When I first heard this explanation, I asked one of its proponents, "Do you mean the room understands Chinese?" His answer was yes. It is a daring move, but aside from its implausibility, it will not work on purely logical grounds. The point of the original argument was that symbol shuffling by itself does not give any access to the meanings of the symbols. But this is as much true of the whole room as it is of the person inside. One can see this point by extending the thought experiment. Imagine that I memorize the contents of the baskets and the rule book, and I do all the calculations in my head. You can even imagine that I work out in the open. There is nothing in the "system" that is not in me, and since I don't understand Chinese, neither does the system.

The Churchlands in their companion piece produce a variant of the systems reply by imagining an amusing analogy. Suppose that someone said that light could not be electromagnetic because if you shake a bar magnet in a dark room, the system still will not give off visible light. Now, the Churchlands ask, is not the Chinese room argument just like that? Does it not merely say that if you shake Chinese symbols in a semantically dark room, they will not give off the light of Chinese understanding? But just as later investigation showed that light was entirely constituted by electromagnetic radiation, could not later investigation also show that semantics are entirely constituted of syntax? Is this not a question for further scientific investigation?

Arguments from analogy are notoriously weak, because before one can make the argument work, one has to establish that the two cases are truly analogous. And here I think they are not. The account of light in terms of electromagnetic radiation is a causal story right down to the ground. It is a causal account of the physics of electromagnetic radiation. But the analogy with formal symbols fails because formal symbols have no physical, causal powers. The only power that symbols have, *qua* symbols, is the power to cause the next step in the program when the machine is running. And there is no question of waiting on further research to reveal the physical, causal properties of 0s and 1s. The only relevant properties of 0s and 1s are abstract computational properties, and they are already well known.

The Churchlands complain that I am "begging the question" when I say that uninterpreted formal symbols are not identical to mental contents. Well, I certainly did not spend much time arguing for it, because I take it as a logical truth. As with any logical truth, one can quickly see that it is true, because one gets inconsistencies if one tries to imagine the converse. So let us try it. Suppose that in the Chinese room some undetectable Chinese thinking really is going on. What exactly is supposed to make the manipulation of the syntactic elements into specifically Chinese thought contents? Well, after all, I am assuming that the programmers were Chinese speakers, programming the system to process Chinese information.

Fine. But now imagine that as I am sitting in the Chinese room shuffling the Chinese symbols, I get bored with just shuffling the – to me – meaningless symbols. So, suppose that I decide to interpret the symbols as standing for moves in a chess game. Which semantics is the system giving off now? Is it giving off a Chinese semantics or a chess semantics, or both simultaneously? Suppose there is a third person looking in through the window, and she decides that the symbol manipulations can all be interpreted as stock-market predictions. And so on. There is no limit to the number of semantic interpretations that can be assigned to the symbols because, to repeat, the symbols are purely formal. They have no intrinsic semantics.

Is there any way to rescue the Churchlands' analogy from incoherence? I said above that formal symbols do not have causal properties. But of course the program will always be implemented in some hardware or another, and the hardware will have specific physical, causal powers. And any real computer will give off various phenomena. My computers, for example, give off heat, and they make a humming noise and sometimes crunching sounds. So is there some logically compelling reason why they could not also give off consciousness? No. Scientifically, the idea is out of the question, but it is not something the Chinese room argument is supposed to refute, and it is not something that an adherent of strong AI would wish to defend, because any such giving off would have to derive from the physical features of the implementing medium. But the basic premise of strong AI is that the physical features of the implementing medium are totally irrelevant. What matters are programs, and programs are purely formal.

The Churchlands' analogy between syntax and electromagnetism, then, is confronted with a dilemma; either the syntax is construed purely formally in terms of its abstract mathematical properties, or it is not. If it is, then the analogy breaks down, because syntax so construed has no physical powers and hence no physical, causal powers. If, on the other hand, one is supposed to think in terms of the physics of the implementing medium, then there is indeed an analogy, but it is not one that is relevant to strong AI.

Because the points I have been making are rather obvious – syntax is not the same as semantics, brain processes cause mental phenomena – the question arises, How did we get into this mess? How could anyone have supposed that a computer simulation of a mental process must be the real thing? After all, the whole point of models is that they contain only certain features of the modeled domain and leave out the rest. No one expects to get wet in a pool filled with ping-pong-ball models of water molecules. So why would anyone think a computer model of thought processes would actually think?

Part of the answer is that people have inherited a residue of behaviorist psychological theories of the past generation. The Turing Test enshrines the temptation to think that if something behaves as if it had certain mental processes, then it must actually have those mental processes. And this is part of the behaviorists' mistaken assumption that in order to be scientific, psychology must confine its study to externally observable behavior. Paradoxically, this residual behaviorism is tied to a residual dualism. Nobody thinks that a computer simulation of digestion would actually digest anything, but where cognition is concerned, people are willing to believe in such a miracle because they fail to recognize that the mind is just as much a biological phenomenon as digestion. The mind, they suppose, is something formal and abstract, not a part of the wet and slimy stuff in our heads. The polemical literature in AI usually contains attacks on something the authors call dualism, but what they fail to see is that they themselves display dualism in a strong form, for unless one accepts the idea that the mind is completely independent of the brain or of any other physically specific system, one could not possibly hope to create minds just by designing programs.

Historically, scientific developments in the West that have treated humans as just a part of the ordinary physical, biological order have often been opposed by various rearguard actions. Copernicus and Galileo were opposed because they denied that the earth was the center of the universe; Darwin was opposed because he claimed that humans had descended from the lower animals. It is best to see strong AI as one of the last gasps of this anti-scientific tradition, for it denies that there is anything essentially physical and biological about the human mind. The mind according to strong AI is independent of the brain. It is a computer program and as such has no essential connection to any specific hardware.

Many people who have doubts about the psychological significance of AI think that computers might be able to understand Chinese and think about numbers but cannot do the crucially human things, namely – and then follows their favorite human specialty – falling in love, having a sense of humor, feeling the angst of postindustrial society under late capitalism, or whatever. But workers in AI complain – correctly – that this is a case of moving the goalposts. As soon as an AI simulation succeeds, it ceases to be of psychological importance. In this debate both sides fail to see the distinction between simulation and duplication. As far as simulation is concerned, there is no difficulty in programming my computer so that it prints out, "I love you, Suzy"; "Ha ha"; or "I am suffering the angst of postindustrial society under late capitalism." The important point is that simulation is not the same as duplication, and that fact holds as much import for thinking about arithmetic as it does for feeling angst. The point is not that the computer gets only to the 40-yard line and not all the way to the goal line. The computer doesn't even get started. It is not playing that game.

Could a Machine Think?

PAUL M. CHURCHLAND AND PATRICIA S. CHURCHLAND

Artificial-intelligence research is undergoing a revolution. To explain how and why, and to put John R. Searle's argument in perspective, we first need a flashback.

By the early 1950s the old, vague question, "Could a machine think?" had been replaced by the more approachable question, "Could a machine that manipulated physical symbols according to structure-sensitive rules think?" This question was an improvement because formal logic and computational theory had seen major developments in the preceding half-century. Theorists had come to appreciate the enormous power of abstract systems of symbols that undergo rule-governed transformations. If those systems could just be automated, then their abstract computational power, it seemed, would be displayed in a real physical system. This insight spawned a well-defined research program with deep theoretical underpinnings.

Could a machine think? There were many reasons for saying yes. One of the earliest and deepest reasons lay in two important results in computational theory. The first was Church's thesis, which states that every effectively computable function is recursively computable. "Effectively computable" means that there is a "rote" procedure for determining, in finite time, the output of the function for a given input. "Recursively computable" means more specifically that there is a finite set of operations that can be applied to a given input, and then applied again and again to the successive results of such applications, to yield the function's output in finite time. The notion of a rote procedure is nonformal and intuitive; thus, Church's thesis does not admit of a formal proof. But it does go to the heart of what it is to compute, and many lines of evidence converge in supporting it.

The second important result was Alan M. Turing's demonstration that any recursively computable function can be computed in finite time by a maximally simple sort of symbol-manipulating machine that has come to be called a universal Turing Machine. This machine is guided by a set of recursively applicable rules that are sensitive to the identity, order, and arrangement of the elementary symbols it encounters as input.

These two results entail something remarkable, namely that a standard digital computer, given only the right program, a large enough memory, and sufficient time, can compute *any* rule-governed input–output function. That is, it can display any systematic pattern of responses to the environment whatsoever.

More specifically, these results imply that a suitably programmed symbol-manipulating machine (hereafter, SM machine) should be able to pass the Turing Test for conscious intelligence. The Turing Test is a purely behavioral test for conscious intelligence, but it is a very demanding test even so. (Whether it is a fair test will be addressed below, where we shall also encounter a second and quite different "test" for conscious intelligence.) In the original version of the Turing Test, the inputs to the SM machine are conversational questions and remarks typed into a console by you or me, and the outputs are typewritten responses from the SM machine. The machine passes this test for conscious intelligence if its responses cannot be discriminated from the typewritten responses of a real, intelligent person. Of course, at present no one knows the function that would produce the output behavior of a conscious person. But the Church and Turing results assure us that, whatever that (presumably effective) function might be, a suitable SM machine could compute it.

This is a significant conclusion, especially since Turing's portrayal of a purely teletyped interaction is an unnecessary restriction. The same conclusion follows even if the SM machine interacts with the world in more complex ways: by direct vision, real speech, and so forth. After all, a more complex recursive function is still Turing-computable. The only remaining problem is to identify the undoubtedly complex function that governs the human pattern of response to the environment and then write the program (the set of recursively applicable rules) by which the SM machine will compute it. These goals form the fundamental research program of classical AI.

Initial results were positive. SM machines with clever programs performed a variety of ostensibly cognitive activities. They responded to complex instructions, solved complex arithmetic, algebraic, and tactical problems, played checkers and chess, proved theorems, and engaged in simple dialogue. Performance continued to improve with the appearance of larger memories and faster machines and with the use of longer and more cunning programs. Classical, or "program-writing," AI was a vigorous and successful research effort from almost every perspective. The occasional denial that an SM machine might eventually think appeared uninformed and ill motivated. The case for a positive answer to our title question was overwhelming.

There were a few puzzles, of course. For one thing, SM machines were admittedly not very brainlike. Even here, however, the classical approach had a convincing answer. First, the physical material of any SM machine has nothing essential to do with what function it computes. That is fixed by its program. Second, the engineering details of any machine's functional architecture are also irrelevant, since different architectures running quite different programs can still be computing the same input–output function.

Accordingly, AI sought to find the input–output *function* characteristic of intelligence and the most efficient of the many possible programs for computing it. The idiosyncratic way in which the brain computes the function just doesn't matter, it was said. This completes the rationale for classical AI and for a positive answer to our title question.

Could a machine think? There were also some arguments for saying no. Through the 1960s interesting negative arguments were relatively rare. The objection was occasionally made that thinking was a nonphysical process in an immaterial soul. But such dualistic resistance was neither evolutionarily nor explanatorily plausible. It had a negligible impact on AI research.

A quite different line of objection was more successful in gaining the AI community's attention. In 1972 Hubert L. Dreyfus published a book that was highly critical of the parade-case simulations of cognitive activity. He argued for their inadequacy as simulations of genuine cognition, and he pointed to a pattern of failure in these attempts. What they were missing, he suggested, was the vast store of inarticulate background knowledge every person possesses and the commonsense capacity for drawing on relevant aspects of that knowledge as changing circumstance demands. Dreyfus did not deny the possibility that an artificial physical system of some kind might think, but he was highly critical of the idea that this could be achieved solely by symbol manipulation at the hands of recursively applicable rules.

Dreyfus's complaints were broadly perceived within the AI community, and within the discipline of philosophy as well, as shortsighted and unsympathetic, as harping on the inevitable simplifications of a research effort still in its youth. These deficits might be real, but surely they were temporary. Bigger machines and better programs should repair them in due course. Time, it was felt, was on AI's side. Here again the impact on research was negligible.

Time was on Dreyfus's side as well: the rate of cognitive return on increasing speed and memory began to slacken in the late 1970s and early 1980s. The simulation of object recognition in the visual system, for example, proved computationally intensive to an unexpected degree. Realistic results required longer and longer periods of computer time, periods far in excess of what a real visual system requires. This relative slowness of the simulations was darkly curious; signal propagation in a computer is roughly a million times faster than in the brain, and the clock frequency of a computer's central processor is greater than any frequency found in the brain by a similarly dramatic margin. And yet, on realistic problems, the tortoise easily outran the hare.

Furthermore, realistic performance required that the computer program have access to an extremely large knowledge base. Constructing the relevant knowledge base was problem enough, and it was compounded by the problem of how to access just the contextually relevant parts of that knowledge base in real time. As the knowledge base got bigger and better, the access problem got worse. Exhaustive search took too much time, and heuristics for relevance did poorly. Worries of the sort Dreyfus had raised finally began to take hold here and there even among AI researchers.

At about this time (1980) John Searle authored a new and quite different criticism aimed at the most basic assumption of the classical research program: the idea that the appropriate manipulation of structured symbols by the recursive application of structure-sensitive rules could constitute conscious intelligence.

Searle's argument is based on a thought experiment that displays two crucial features. First, he describes a SM machine that realizes, we are to suppose, an input–output function adequate to sustain a successful Turing Test conversation conducted entirely in Chinese. Second, the internal structure of the machine is such that, however it behaves, an observer remains certain that neither the machine nor any part of it understands Chinese. All it contains is a monolingual English speaker following a written set of instructions for manipulating the Chinese symbols that arrive and leave through a mail slot. In short, the system is supposed to pass the Turing Test, while the system itself lacks any genuine understanding of Chinese or real Chinese semantic content (see "Is the Brain's Mind a Computer Program?" by John R. Searle [preceding article]).

The general lesson drawn is that any system that merely manipulates physical symbols in accordance with structure-sensitive rules will be at best a hollow mock-up of real conscious intelligence, because it is impossible to generate "real semantics" merely by cranking away on "empty syntax." Here, we should point out, Searle is imposing a nonbehavioral test for consciousness: the elements of conscious intelligence must possess real semantic content.

One is tempted to complain that Searle's thought experiment is unfair because his Rube Goldberg system will compute with absurd slowness. Searle insists, however, that speed is strictly irrelevant here. A slow thinker should still be a real thinker. Everything essential to the duplication of thought, as per classical AI, is said to be present in the Chinese room.

Searle's paper provoked a lively reaction from AI researchers, psychologists, and philosophers alike. On the whole, however, he was met with an even more hostile reception than Dreyfus had experienced. In his companion piece in this volume ["Is the Brain's Mind a Computer Program?"], Searle forthrightly lists a number of these critical responses. We think many of them are reasonable, especially those that "bite the bullet" by insisting that, although it is appallingly slow, the overall system of the room-plus-contents does understand Chinese.

We think those are good responses, but not because we think that the room understands Chinese. We agree with Searle that it does not. Rather they are good responses because they reflect a refusal to accept the crucial third axiom of Searle's argument: "*Syntax by itself is neither constitutive of nor sufficient for semantics.*" Perhaps this axiom is true, but Searle cannot rightly pretend to know that it is. Moreover, to assume its truth is tantamount to begging the question against the research program of classical AI , for that program is predicated on the very interesting assumption that if one can just set in motion an appropriately structured internal dance of syntactic elements, appropriately connected to inputs and outputs, it can produce the same cognitive states and achievements found in human beings.

The question-begging character of Searle's axiom 3 becomes clear when it is compared directly with his conclusion 1: "*Programs are neither constitutive of nor sufficient for minds.*" Plainly, his third axiom is already carrying 90 percent of the weight of this almost identical conclusion. That is why Searle's thought experiment is devoted to shoring up axiom 3 specifically. That is the point of the Chinese room.

Although the story of the Chinese room makes axiom 3 tempting to the unwary, we do not think it succeeds in establishing axiom 3, and we offer a parallel argument below in illustration of its failure. A single transparently fallacious instance of a disputed argument often provides far more insight than a book full of logic chopping.

Searle's style of skepticism has ample precedent in the history of science. The eighteenth-century Irish bishop George Berkeley found it unintelligible that compression waves in the air, by themselves, could constitute or be sufficient for objective sound. The English poet–artist William Blake and the German poet–naturalist Johann W. von Goethe found it inconceivable that small particles by themselves could constitute or be sufficient for the objective phenomenon of light. Even in this century, there have been people who found it beyond imagining that inanimate matter by itself, and however organized, could ever constitute or be sufficient for life. Plainly, what people can or cannot imagine often has nothing to do with what is or is not the case, even where the people involved are highly intelligent.

To see how this lesson applies to Searle's case, consider a deliberately manufactured parallel to his argument and its supporting thought experiment.

Axiom 1   *Electricity and magnetism are forces.*

Axiom 2   *The essential property of light is luminance.*

Axiom 3   *Forces by themselves are neither constitutive of nor sufficient for luminance.*

Conclusion *Electricity and magnetism are neither constitutive of nor sufficient for light.*

Imagine this argument raised shortly after James Clerk Maxwell's 1864 suggestion that light and electromagnetic waves are identical but before the world's full appreciation of the systematic parallels between the properties of light and the properties of electromagnetic waves. This argument could have served as a compelling objection to Maxwell's imaginative hypothesis, especially if it were accompanied by the following commentary in support of axiom 3:

> Consider a dark room containing a man holding a bar magnet or charged object. If the man pumps the magnet up and down, then, according to Maxwell's theory of artificial luminance (AL), it will initiate a spreading circle of electromagnetic waves and will thus be luminous. But as all of us who have toyed with magnets or charged balls well know, their forces (or any other forces for that matter), even when set in motion, produce no luminance at all. It is inconceivable that you might constitute real luminance just by moving forces around!

How should Maxwell respond to this challenge? He might begin by insisting that the "luminous room" experiment is a misleading display of the phenomenon of luminance because the frequency of oscillation of the magnet is absurdly low, too low by a factor of 10^{15}. This might well elicit the impatient response that frequency has nothing to do with it, that the room with the bobbing magnet already contains everything essential to light, according to Maxwell's own theory.

In response Maxwell might bite the bullet and claim, quite correctly, that the room really is bathed in luminance, albeit of a grade or quality too feeble to appreciate. (Given the low frequency with which the man can oscillate the magnet, the wavelength of the electromagnetic waves produced is far too long and their intensity is much too weak for human retinas to respond to them.) But in the climate of understanding here contemplated – the 1860s – this tactic is likely to elicit laughter and hoots of derision. "Luminous room, my foot, Mr Maxwell. It's pitch-black in there!"

Alas, poor Maxwell has no easy route out of this predicament. All he can do is insist on the following three points. First, axiom 3 of the above argument is false. Indeed, it begs the question despite its intuitive plausibility. Second, the luminous room experiment demonstrates nothing of interest one way or the other about the nature of light. And third, what is needed to settle the problem of light and the possibility of artificial luminance is an ongoing research program to determine whether under the appropriate conditions the behavior of electromagnetic waves does indeed mirror perfectly the behavior of light.

This is also the response that classical AI should give to Searle's argument. Even though Searle's Chinese room may appear to be "semantically dark," he is in no position to insist, on the strength of this appearance, that rule-governed symbol manipulation can never constitute semantic phenomena, especially when people have only an uninformed, commonsense understanding of the semantic and cognitive phenomena that need to be explained. Rather than exploit one's understanding of these things, Searle's argument freely exploits one's ignorance of them.

With these criticisms of Searle's argument in place, we return to the question of whether the research program of classical AI has a realistic chance of solving the problem of conscious intelligence and of producing a machine that thinks. We believe that the prospects are poor, but we rest this opinion on reasons very different from Searle's. Our reasons derive from the specific performance failures of the classical research program in AI and from a variety of lessons learned from the biological brain and a new class of computational models inspired by its structure. We have already indicated some of the failures of classical AI regarding tasks that the brain performs swiftly and efficiently. The emerging consensus on these failures is that the functional architecture of classical SM machines is simply the wrong architecture for the very demanding jobs required.

What we need to know is this: How does the brain achieve cognition? Reverse engineering is a common practice in industry. When a new piece of technology comes on the market, competitors find out how it works by taking it apart and divining its structural rationale. In the case of the brain, this strategy presents an unusually stiff challenge, for the brain is the most complicated and sophisticated thing on the planet. Even so, the neurosciences have revealed much about the brain on a wide variety of structural levels. Three anatomic points will provide a basic contrast with the architecture of conventional electronic computers.

First, nervous systems are parallel machines, in the sense that signals are processed in millions of different pathways simultaneously. The retina, for example, presents its complex input to the brain not in chunks of eight, 16, or 32 elements, as in a desktop computer, but rather in the form of almost a million distinct signal elements arriving simultaneously at the target of the optic nerve (the lateral geniculate nucleus), there to be processed collectively, simultaneously, and in one fell swoop. Second, the brain's basic processing unit, the neuron, is comparatively simple. Furthermore, its response to incoming signals is analog, not digital, inasmuch as its output spiking frequency varies continuously with its input signals. Third, in the brain, axons projecting from one neuronal population to another are often matched by axons returning from their target population. These descending or recurrent projections allow the brain to modulate the character of its sensory processing. More important still, their existence makes the brain a genuine dynamical system whose continuing behavior is both highly complex and to some degree independent of its peripheral stimuli.

Highly simplified model networks have been useful in suggesting how real neural networks might work and in revealing the computational properties of parallel architectures. For example, consider a three-layer model consisting of neuronlike units fully connected by axonlike connections to the units at the next layer. An input stimulus produces some activation level in a given input unit, which conveys a signal of proportional strength along its "axon" to its many "synaptic" connections to the hidden units. The global effect is that a pattern of activations across the set of input units produces a distinct pattern of activations across the set of hidden units.

The same story applies to the output units. As before, an activation pattern across the hidden units produces a distinct activation pattern across the output units. All told, this network is a device for transforming any one of a great many possible input vectors (activation patterns) into a uniquely corresponding output vector. It is a device for computing a specific function. Exactly which function it computes is fixed by the global configuration of its synaptic weights.

There are various procedures for adjusting the weights so as to yield a network that computes almost any function – that is, any vector-to-vector transformation – that one might desire. In fact, one can even impose on it a function one is unable to specify, so long as one can supply a set of examples of the desired input–output pairs. This process, called "training up the network," proceeds by successive adjustment of the network's weights until it performs the input–output transformations desired.

Although this model network vastly oversimplifies the structure of the brain, it does illustrate several important ideas. First, a parallel architecture provides a dramatic speed advantage over a conventional computer, for the many synapses at each level perform many small computations simultaneously instead of in laborious sequence. This advantage gets larger as the number of neurons increases at each layer. Strikingly, the speed of processing is entirely independent of both the number of units involved in each layer and the complexity of the function they are computing. Each layer could have four units or a hundred million; its configuration of synaptic weights could be computing simple one-digit sums or second-order differential equations. It would make no difference. The computation time would be exactly the same.

Second, massive parallelism means that the system is fault-tolerant and functionally persistent; the loss of a few connections, even quite a few, has a negligible effect on the character of the overall transformation performed by the surviving network.

Third, a parallel system stores large amounts of information in a distributed fashion, any part of which can be accessed in milliseconds. That information is stored in the specific configuration of synaptic connection strengths, as shaped by past learning. Relevant information is "released" as the input vector passes through – and is transformed by – that configuration of connections.

Parallel processing is not ideal for all types of computation. On tasks that require only a small input vector, but many millions of swiftly iterated recursive computations, the brain performs very badly, whereas classical SM machines excel. This class of computations is very large and important, so classical machines will always be useful, indeed, vital. There is, however, an equally large class of computations for which the brain's architecture is the superior technology. These are the computations that typically confront living creatures: recognizing a predator's outline in a noisy environment;recalling instantly how to avoid its gaze, flee its approach, or fend off its attack; distinguishing food from nonfood and mates from nonmates; navigating through a complex and ever-changing physical/social environment; and so on.

Finally, it is important to note that the parallel system described is not manipulating symbols according to structure-sensitive rules. Rather, symbol manipulation appears to be just one of many cognitive skills that a network may or may not learn to display. Rule-governed symbol manipulation is not its basic mode of operation. Searle's argument is directed against rule-governed SM machines; vector transformers of the kind we describe are therefore not threatened by his Chinese room argument even if it were sound, which we have found independent reason to doubt.

Searle is aware of parallel processors but thinks they too will be devoid of real semantic content. To illustrate their inevitable failure, he outlines a second thought experiment, the Chinese gym, which has a gymnasium full of people organized into a parallel network. From there his argument proceeds as in the Chinese room.

We find this second story far less responsive or compelling than his first. For one, it is irrelevant that no unit in his system understands Chinese, since the same is true of nervous systems: no neuron in my brain understands English, although my whole brain does. For another, Searle neglects to mention that his simulation (using one person per neuron, plus a fleet-footed child for each synaptic connection) will require at least 10^{14} people, since the human brain has 10^{11} neurons, each of which averages over 10^3 connections. His system will require the entire human populations of over 10,000 earths. One gymnasium will not begin to hold a fair simulation.

On the other hand, if such a system were to be assembled on a suitably cosmic scale, with all its pathways faithfully modeled on the human case, we might then have a large, slow, oddly made, but still functional brain on our hands. In that case the default assumption is surely that, given proper inputs, it would think, not that it couldn't. There is no guarantee that its activity would constitute real thought, because the vector-processing theory sketched above may not be the correct theory of how brains work. But neither is there any a priori guarantee that it could not be thinking. Searle is once more mistaking the limits on his (or the reader's) current imagination for the limits on objective reality.

The brain is a kind of computer, although most of its properties remain to be discovered. Characterizing the brain as a kind of computer is neither trivial nor frivolous. The brain does compute functions, functions of great complexity, but not in the classical AI fashion. When brains are said to be computers, it should not be implied that they are serial, digital computers, that they are programmed, that they exhibit the distinction between hardware and software, or that they must be symbol manipulators or rule followers. Brains are computers in a radically different style.

How the brain manages meaning is still unknown, but it is clear that the problem reaches beyond language use and beyond humans. A small mound of fresh dirt signifies to a person, and also to coyotes, that a gopher is around; an echo with a certain spectral character signifies to a bat the presence of a moth. To develop a theory of meaning, more must be known about how neurons code and transform sensory signals, about the neural basis of memory, learning, and emotion, and about the interaction of these capacities and the motor system. A neurally grounded theory of meaning may require revision of the very intuitions that now seem so secure and that are so freely exploited in Searle's arguments. Such revisions are common in the history of science.

Could science construct an artificial intelligence by exploiting what is known about the nervous system? We see no principled reason why not. Searle appears to agree, although he qualifies his claim by saying that "any other system capable of causing minds would have to have causal powers (at least) equivalent to those of brains." We close by addressing this claim. We presume that Searle is not claiming that a successful artificial mind must have *all* the causal powers of the brain,such as the power to smell bad when rotting, to harbor slow viruses such as kuru, to stain yellow with horseradish peroxidase, and so forth. Requiring perfect parity would be like requiring that an artificial flying device lay eggs.

Presumably he means only to require of an artificial mind all of the causal powers relevant, as he says, to conscious intelligence. But which exactly are they? We are back to quarreling about what is and is not relevant. This is an entirely reasonable place for a disagreement, but it is an empirical matter, to be tried and tested. Because so little is known about what goes into the process of cognition and semantics, it is premature to be very confident about what features are essential. Searle hints at various points that every level, including the biochemical, must be represented in any machine that is a candidate for artificial intelligence. This claim is almost surely too strong. An artificial brain might use something other than biochemicals to achieve the same ends.

This possibility is illustrated by Carver A. Mead's research at the California Institute of Technology. Mead and his colleagues have used analog VLSI techniques to build an artificial retina and an artificial cochlea. (In animals the retina and cochlea are not mere transducers: Both systems embody a complex processing network.) These are not mere simulations in a minicomputer of the kind that Searle derides; they are real information-processing units responding in real time to real light, in the case of the artificial retina, and to real sound, in the case of the artificial cochlea. Their circuitry is based on the known anatomy and physiology of the cat retina and the barn-owl cochlea, and their output is dramatically similar to the known output of the organs at issue.

These chips do not use any neurochemicals, so neurochemicals are clearly not necessary to achieve the evident results. Of course, the artificial retina cannot be said to see anything, because its output does not have an artificial thalamus or cortex to go to. Whether Mead's program could be sustained to build an entire artificial brain remains to be seen, but there is no evidence now that the absence of biochemicals renders it quixotic.

We, and Searle, reject the Turing Test as a sufficient condition for conscious intelligence. At one level our reasons for doing so are similar: We agree that it is also very important how the input–output function is achieved; it is important that the right sorts of thing be going on inside the artificial machine. At another level, our reasons are quite different. Searle bases his position on commonsense intuitions about the presence or absence of semantic content. We base ours on the specific behavioral failures of the classical SM machines, and on the specific virtues of machines with a more brainlike architecture. These contrasts show that certain computational strategies have vast and decisive advantages over others where typical cognitive tasks are concerned, advantages that are empirically inescapable. Clearly, the brain is making systematic use of these computational advantages. But it need not be the only physical system capable of doing so. Artificial intelligence, in a nonbiological but massively parallel machine, remains a compelling and discernible prospect.

6

Mind and Biology

Introduction

In the preceding section we saw examples of how philosophers have argued how minds can or cannot be modeled in machines. Searle and the Churchlands agreed on one issue, namely that if we are going to understand the mind, we need to get much closer to the biology of the brain than classical computational models. In this section we look at some accounts of mind that pay their respects to biology.

It is fairly widely agreed that minds are intentional in the sense that they can represent the world, and it seems that human minds can come to represent the world on their own without the intervention of programmers and interpreters. In other words, while a standard computer program is about chess, payroll deductions, or chemical reactions because we interpret its symbols to be about chess, payrolls, or chemistry, it seems that the brain's mind has content intrinsically and independently of any outside interpreters. How can biological organisms come to have contentful minds?

Fred Dretske, a philosopher who started out as an engineer, has a longstanding interest in natural systems of representation. In "Representational Systems" he attempts to show how natural systems can come to have intrinsic intentionality. He describes three types of representational system. Systems of the first and second type do not represent anything on their own but are given their representational functions by something external to them. Systems of the third type are natural systems of representation that represent on their own.

Two key notions in Dretske's account are those of an indicator and of a function. An indicator is a natural sign; for instance the tree's growth rings indicate the age of the tree. In order for an indicator to become a representation, it also needs to have the job or function of indicating something. A barometer naturally indicates air pressure no matter what anyone thinks, but it represents air pressure only when in addition to naturally indicating air pressure it has the job or function of indicating air pressure. A barometer does not have this job on its own – it is assigned by us, its users – and thus it is not a Type-III system.

In a Type-III system the representational role of an indicator is assigned by the organism of which the indicator is a part. For example, a mental state C of an animal represents something in the world, for instance nectar on a flower (or beer in a refrigerator), because it was a natural indicator of nectar (or beer) and this fact about C caused C to have the job of indicating nectar (or beer). The organism comes to use C as an indicator of nectar (or beer) even when it may turn out that the flowers have all been picked or the beer is all gone.

Ruth Garrett Millikan is also concerned with showing how biological organisms can come to have content without the intervention of outside intelligences. Part of her task in "Thoughts Without Laws: Cognitive Science with Content" is to show how there can be content in biological systems even though it is difficult to come up with any natural laws about content. When explaining the behavior of intelligent creatures we appeal to mental content: we say that Paula went to the refrigerator because she believed that there was a beer in the refrigerator and she desired it. This kind of ordinary psychological explanation in terms of beliefs and desires has been labeled "folk psychology" by some, and it has been argued that such explanations cannot be part of the science of the mind because, among other things, it seems that there are no natural laws about beliefs, desires, and their content.

Millikan accommodates folk psychology within a science of the mind, arguing that representations, beliefs, and desires are inner "impressions," "images," or "pictures" of sorts. "Beliefs are pictures of what is or was or will be" while "desires are pictures of what will be if the desires produce their proper results." The picture need of course not be similar to what it represents, a point in case being a bee dance which provides information about the location of nectar without being in any way "similar" to the nectar or its location. It is because the bee dance serves its proper function in accordance with a Normal explanation that it represents the location of the nectar, where a Normal explanation is an explanation that historically accounts for the evolution of the bee dance. While there is no guarantee that the bee dance will guide the other bees in the right direction, just as there is no guarantee that the swimming mechanism of a given sperm gets it to an ovum, it is nevertheless the proper function of a bee dance to indicate where the nectar is located, just as it is the proper function of the swimming mechanism of a sperm to get it to an ovum. Still, when all goes properly and Normally the bee dance guides the other bees to the nectar.

It must be noted that not everyone agrees that intentional psychology will have a place in a mature science of the mind. For example, the Churchlands, as we saw in their reply to Searle in the last section, are not keen on vindicating folk psychology. They defend the view that our ordinary belief/desire explanations of the mind will go the way of folk medicine and other superstitions. However, they would agree with Dretske and Millikan that we need to find a model of mind that is much closer to the biological properties of the brain than are the models of mind that rely on a classsical computer.

There is one aspect of biological cognitive systems such as human beings and other animals that seem to have been ignored by all the approaches we have considered so far, namely that a system evolves in real time. Tim van Gelder and Robert Port in "It's About Time" offer an introduction to very recent approaches to mind according to which time is of the essence to cognition. These approaches view naturally evolved cognitive systems as dynamical systems, namely systems that evolve over time in such a way that each state of the system at a given time is determined by the forces at work in the system at the immediately preceding time. This evolution over time from state to state is to be described not by algorithms for manipulating symbol structures, but by differential equations.

These equations will describe temporal properties such as rates of change, duration, periods, and synchrony, and consequently temporal properties will be essential to cognition. This is a stark contrast to classical artificial intelligence. A computer computes an equation if it goes through a certain determined sequence of steps no matter how fast or slow it is, and consequently, on the view that the brain's mind is a computer program, time is not essential to the mind's computations. This approach also differs from the approaches outlined by

Dretske and Millikan. Although Dretske and Millikan are concerned with naturally evolved systems and their functions and origins, they are not concerned with the specific evolution of a system from one moment to the next.

However, Dretske, Millikan, and the dynamical approaches outlined by van Gelder and Port have one important feature in common. They all take seriously the environment in which a cognitive system is embedded. For Dretske and Millikan, the function and content of a mindful system is in part determined by its evolutionary history and the environment to which the cognitive system had to adapt. On dynamical approaches, the evolution of the system from moment to moment will include the system's interaction with the environment. Dynamical cognitive systems are continually evolving and mutually influencing complexes that include the nervous system, body, and environment. Whether or not the environment and our interaction with it must play an essential role in determining the nature of mind, and consequently psychology and cognitive science, will be studied more closely in the last section of part II on "Mind and Environment."

FURTHER READING

Churchland, P. M. (1988). *Matter and Consciousness*. Cambridge, MA: MIT Press.
Churchland, P. S. and Sejnowski, T. J. (1992). *The Computational Brain*. Cambridge, MA: MIT Press.
Dretske, F. (1986). Misrepresentation. In *Belief*. Ed. R. Bogdan. Oxford: Oxford University Press.
Edelman, G. M. (1989). *The Remembered Present: A Biological Theory of Consciousness*. New York: Basic Books.
Fodor, J. (1990). *Theory of Content and Other Essays*. Cambridge, MA: MIT Press.
Gazzaniga, M. S. (1992). *Nature's Mind*. New York: Basic Books.
Millikan, R. G. (1984). *Language, Thought and Other Biological Categories*. Cambridge, MA: MIT Press.
Millikan, R. G. (1989). Biosemantics. *Journal of Philosophy* 86: 281–97.
Port, R. and van Gelder, T. (1995). *Mind as Motion: Explorations in the Dynamics of Cognition*. Cambridge, MA: MIT Press.

Representational Systems

FRED DRETSKE

Some behavior is the expression of intelligent thought and purpose. Clyde goes to the kitchen because he wants another beer and thinks there is one left in the refrigerator. Whether or not they are causes of behavior, Clyde's reasons – his desire for a beer and his belief that there is one in the fridge – are certainly thought to *explain* his behavior. They tell us *why* he made the trip to the kitchen.

This is our ordinary way of explaining behavior (at least, those behaviors we think of as purposeful). It is so familiar, so utterly commonplace to all of us, that it is hard to see how there can be a problem with this type of explanation.

There is, nonetheless, a problem in understanding how this familiar pattern of explanation can take – or hold – its place alongside the emerging neuroscientific picture of living organisms. How do, how can, thoughts and purposes determine what we do when what we do, at least what our bodies do, seems so completely dependent on, and therefore determined by, those neuronal processes and mechanisms described, in increasingly rich detail, by neurophysiologists? If the neurophysiologists don't invoke thoughts, purposes, intentions, desires, hopes, and fears to explain the behavior of a person's body, what excuse (besides ignorance) do we have for appealing to such notions to explain the behavior of the person?

We have already taken the first step toward a better understanding of this apparent conflict. The first step is to understand the difference between a person's behavior and whatever bodily movements and changes constitute this behavior. An understanding of the difference between Clyde's going to the kitchen and the movements that get him to the kitchen is essential to an understanding of why an explanation of the one is not an explanation of the other. Knowing why Clyde went to the kitchen isn't the same as knowing why his legs moved so as to bring him into the kitchen; and knowing the causes of limb movement, at whatever level of biological detail, is not the same as knowing why he went to the kitchen. These are different explanatory games. Our familiar way of explaining purposive behavior in terms of an agent's intentions and beliefs does not *compete* with a neurobiological account of muscular activity and, hence, with a mechanistic account of motor output. It is, rather, an attempt to explain something altogether different: *behavior*, not output.

There is, however, a second step that must be taken. As yet we have no idea of how ordinary explanations, explanations couched in terms of an agent's *reasons*, explain. Since behavior has been identified with a process, with one thing's *causing* another, are reasons supposed to be the cause of one thing's causing another? If so, how is this supposed to work, and what is it about reasons that gives them this peculiar efficacy?

In order to answer these questions, in order to take this second step, it will be necessary to spend some time examining the idea of a representation. For beliefs, normally a prominent part of one's reasons for acting (desire being another prominent part), are special kinds of representations. Beliefs are those representations whose causal role in the production of output is determined by their meaning or content – by *the way* they represent what they represent. The general idea of a representational system is examined in this chapter. The special topic of belief is reserved for chapter 4 [not reproduced here].

1 Conventional Systems of Representation: Type I

By a representational system (RS) I shall mean any system whose function it is to indicate how things stand with respect to some other object, condition, or magnitude. If RS's function is to indicate whether O is in condition A or B, for instance, and the way RS performs this function (*when* it performs it) is by occupying one of two possible states, a (indicating that O is A) and b (indicating that O is B), then a and b are the expressive elements of RS and *what they represent* (about O) is *that* it is A (in the case of a) and *that* it is B (in the case of b).

Depending on the kind of function involved, and on the way a system manages to carry out this function (the way it manages to *indicate*), representational systems can be variously classified. What follows is one possible classification. My chief interest is in *natural* representations (systems of Type III), but the special properties of such systems are best understood by comparing and contrasting them with their conventional (to varying degrees) cousins. So I begin with conventional systems of representation.

Let this dime on the table be Oscar Robertson, let this nickel (heads uppermost) be Kareem Abdul-Jabbar, and let this nickel (tails uppermost) be the opposing center. These pieces of popcorn are the other players, and this glass is the basket. With this bit of stage setting I can now, by moving coins and popcorn around on the table, represent the positions and movements of these players. I can use these objects to describe a basketball play I once witnessed.

If memory fails me, I may end up misrepresenting things. I may move pieces of popcorn here when the players went there. The coins and the popcorn have been assigned a temporary function, the function of *indicating* (by *their* positions and movement) the relative positions and movements of certain players during a particular game. But these elements, the coins and the popcorn, obviously enjoy no intrinsic power to do what they have been assigned the function of doing – *indicating* the positions and the movements of various players in a game long since over. Whatever success they enjoy in the performance of their job obviously derives *from me*, from my memory of the game being represented and my skill in translating that knowledge into the chosen idiom. The popcorn and the coins indicate, and in this sense perform their assigned function, only insofar as *I* am a reliable conduit for information about the situation being represented and a reliable and well-intentioned manipulator of the expressive medium.

The coins and the popcorn do their job, then, only insofar as some *other* indicator system is functioning satisfactorily, only insofar as there is something in the manipulator of these symbols (in this case, something *in me*) that indicates how things stood on the basketball court at the time in question. If I am ignorant of what Oscar and Kareem did with the ball, the coins and the popcorn are unable to perform the function they have been assigned – unable to indicate, by their various positions and movements, what took place on the court that day. This is merely to acknowledge that these objects are, considered by themseves, representationally lifeless. They are merely my representational instruments.

The elements of Type I systems have no *intrinsic* powers of representation – no power that is not derived from us, their creators and users.[1] Both their function (what they, when suitably deployed, are *supposed* to indicate) and their power to perform that function (their success in indicating what it is their function to indicate) are derived from another source: human agents with communicative purposes. Many familiar RSs are like this: maps, diagrams, certain road signs (of the informational variety), prearranged signals, musical notation, gestures, codes, and (to some degree, at least) natural language. I call the representational elements of such systems *symbols*. Symbols are, either explicitly or implicitly, *assigned* indicator functions, functions that they have no intrinsic power to perform. *We* give them their functions, and *we* (when it suits our purposes) see to it that they are *used* in accordance with this function. Such representational systems are, in this sense, *doubly* conventional: *We* give them a job to do, and then *we* do it for them.

2   Natural Signs and Information

In contrast with the relationship between popcorn and professional basketball players, we don't have to let tracks in the snow, bird songs, fingerprints, and cloud formations stand for the things we take them to indicate. There is a sense in which, whether we like it or not, these tracks, prints, songs, and formations indicate what they do quite independent of us, of how we exploit them for investigative purposes, and of whether we even recognize their significance at all. These are what are sometimes called *natural signs*: events and conditions that derive their indicative powers, not (as in the case of symbols) from us, from our *use* of them to indicate, but from the way they are objectively related to the conditions they signify.

To understand conventional systems of representation of Type II and the way they differ from RSs of Type I, it is important to understand the difference between symbols and signs. In systems of Type II, natural signs are *used* in a way that exploits their *natural* meaning, their *unconventional* powers of indication, for representational, and partly conventional, purposes. This makes systems of Type II a curious blend of the conventional and the natural. It is the purpose of this section to say something useful about signs and their meaning in preparation for the description of representational systems of Type II. This, in turn, will prepare the way for our discussion of the representational systems that are of real interest to this project: natural systems of representation.

Although a great deal of intelligent thought and purpose went into the design and manufacture of an ordinary bathroom scale, once the scale has been finished and placed into use there is nothing conventional, purposeful, or intelligent about its operation. This device indicates what it does without any cooperation or help from either its maker or its user. All you do is get *on* it. It then gives you the bad news. Somebody put the numbers on the dial, of course, and did so with certain intentions and purposes; but this is merely a convenience, something that (to use fashionable jargon) makes it user-friendly. It has nothing to do with what the instrument indicates. A clock doesn't stop keeping time if the numerals are removed from its face. The symbols on a clock or on a bathroom scale merely make it easier for us to *tell* what the pointer positions *mean*. They do not change what these pointer positions indicate.

The same is true of any measuring instrument. As long as an instrument is connected properly and functioning normally, it behaves in accordance with electrical and mechanical laws whose validity is quite independent of its creator's or its user's purposes or knowledge. Furthermore, these laws, by determining whether and (if so) how the pointer positions are correlated with weights, times, pressures, and speeds, determine what these pointer positions indicate about weights, times, pressures, and speeds.

Some people think that all indication is indication *for* or *to* someone. Gauge readings and naturally occurring signs (e.g., tracks in the snow) do not indicate anything if there is no one *to whom* or *for whom* they do this. Gauge readings are like trees falling in the forest: if no one is around to hear, there is no sound; if no one peeks at the scale, it doesn't indicate anything about anyone's weight. Tracks in the snow, fingerprints on a gun, and melting ice do not indicate anything about the animals in the woods, the person who touched the gun, or the temperature *unless* someone observes the tracks, the prints, or the melting ice and makes an appropriate inference. If no one knows that quail, and *only* quail, make tracks of *that* kind, then, despite this regularity, the tracks do not indicate that there are (or were) quail in the woods.

This view, I submit, is merely a special version of the more general and even more implausible idea that nothing is true unless it is true for someone, unless someone knows (or at least believes) it. I do not intend to quarrel about this matter. I shall simply assume that if one mistakes a perfectly reliable and properly functioning boiler-pressure gauge for something else, thinks it is broken, completely ignores it, or never even sees it – if, in other words, the registration of this gauge does not indicate what the boiler pressure is to *anyone* – it nonetheless still indicates what the boiler pressure is. It just doesn't indicate it *to* anyone. And, for the same reason, if, for superstitious reasons, everyone takes the color of the wooly caterpillar's fur as an indication or sign of a cold winter, everyone is simply wrong. That isn't what it means. Taking something to be so, taking it to be not so, or not taking it to be either does not make it so, does not make it not so, and does not make it neither. And this holds for what things indicate as well as for where things are and what they are doing.

I have occasionally used the verb "mean" as a synonym for "indicate." Let me explain. Paul Grice (1957) distinguished what he called a natural sense from a nonnatural sense of the word "meaning." The natural sense of "meaning" is virtually identical to that of "indicate," and that is how I shall normally use the word. The 24 rings in a tree stump, the so-called growth rings, mean (indicate) that the tree is 24 years old. A ringing bell – a ringing *door*bell – means (indicates) that someone is at the door. A scar on a twig, easily identified as a leaf scar, means, in this natural sense, that a leaf grew there. As Grice observes, nothing can mean that *P* in the *natural* sense of meaning if *P* is not the case. This distinguishes it from nonnatural meaning where something (e.g., a statement) can mean that *P* without *P*'s being the case. A person can *say*, and *mean*, that a quail was here without a quail's having been here. But the tracks in the snow cannot mean (in this natural sense of "meaning") that a quail was here unless, in fact, a quail *was* here. If the tracks were left by a pheasant, then the tracks might, depending on how distinctive they are, mean that a pheasant was here. But they certainly do not mean that a quail was here, and the fact that a Boy Scout *takes* them to mean that cannot *make* them mean that.

Furthermore, even if *P* does obtain, the indicator or sign does not mean (indicate) that *P* is the case unless the requisite *dependency* exists between the sign and *P*. Even if the tracks in the snow *were* left by a quail, the tracks may not mean or indicate that this is so. If pheasants, also in the woods, leave the very same kind of track, then the tracks, though made by a quail, do not indicate that it was a quail that made them. A picture of a person, taken from the back at a great distance, does not indicate *whom* the picture is a picture of if other people look the same from that angle and distance.

If a fuel gauge is broken (stuck, say, at "half full"), it *never* indicates anything about the gasoline in the tank. Even if the tank *is* half full, and even if the driver, unaware of the broken gauge, comes to believe (correctly, as it turns out) that the tank is half full, the reading is not a sign – does not mean or indicate – that the tank is half full. Broken clocks are *never* right, not even twice a day, if being right requires them to *indicate* the correct time of day.

When there is any chance of confusing this use of the word "meaning" with what Grice calls nonnatural meaning – the kind of meaning associated with language, the kind of meaning that is (I shall later argue) closer to what it is the *function* of something to mean (naturally) or indicate – I shall either combine the word "meaning" with the word "natural" or use it together with its synonym "indicate." The word "represent" is sometimes used in a way that I am using "indicate" and "mean" (naturally). Since I wish to reserve the idea of representation for something that is closer to genuine meaning, the kind of meaning (Grice's nonnatural meaning) in which something can mean that *P without P*'s being the case, I will *never* use the words "represent" and "indicate" interchangeably. As I am using these words, there can be no *mis*indication, only misrepresentation.

The power of signs to mean or indicate something derives from the way they are related to what they indicate or mean. The red spots all over Tommy's face mean that he has the measles, not simply because he *has* the measles, but because people without the measles don't have spots of that kind. In most cases the underlying relations are causal or lawful in character. There is, then, a lawful dependency between the indicator and the indicat*ed*, a dependency that we normally express by conditionals in the subjunctive mood: If Tommy didn't have the measles, he wouldn't have those red spots all over his face. Sometimes, however, the dependency between a natural sign and its meaning derives, at least in part, from other sources. It is partly the fact, presumably not itself a physical law, that animals do not regularly depress doorbuttons while foraging for food that makes a ringing doorbell *mean* that some *person* is at the door. If squirrels changed their habits (because, say, doorbuttons were made out of nuts), then a ringing doorbell would no longer mean what it now does. But as things *now* stand, we can say that the bell would not be ringing unless someone was at the door. It therefore indicates or means that someone is at the door. But this subjunctively expressed dependency between the ringing bell and someone's presence at the door, though not a coincidence, is not grounded in natural law either. There are surely no laws of nature that prevent small animals from pressing, or randomly falling meteorites from hitting, doorbuttons. There certainly is nothing in the laws of physics that prevents an occasional short circuit in the electrical wiring, something that might cause the bell to ring when no one was at the door. Normally, though, these things don't happen. At least they have never happened to *me*. And this is no lucky coincidence, no freaky piece of good fortune. It isn't like getting a long run of heads while flipping a (fair) coin. Chance correlations between two variables, no matter how prolonged, are not enough. In order for one thing to indicate something about the another, the dependencies must be genuine. There must actually be some condition, lawful or otherwise, that *explains* the persistence of the correlation. This is the difference between a lucky run of heads obtained with a fair coin and the not-at-all-lucky run of rings when someone has been at my door, a difference that enables my bell (but not coin flips) to indicate something about the correlated condition. This, of course, is a fact about *my* house, *my* neighborhood, and *my* doorbell wiring. If your house or neighborhood is different, maybe the ringing of *your* doorbell means something different.[2]

In many cases of biological interest, a sign – some internal indicator on which an animal relies to locate and identify, say, food – will only have the kind of local validity. It will, that is, be a reliable indicator only in the animal's natural habitat or in conditions that approximate that habitat. Flies, for instance, when given a choice between nutritionally worthless sugar fructose and some nutritive substance like sorbitrol, will invariably choose the nutritionally worthless substance and starve to death. Surprising? Not really. Under *natural* conditions (Grier, 1984, p. 536) the substances that stimulate the receptors *are* nutritional. Under natural conditions, in a fly's normal habitat, then, receptor activity indicates a nutritional substance. Furthermore, the correlation between receptor activity and nutritional value of its activator is no accident. There is something that explains it. Flies would not have developed (or maintained without modification) such a receptor system in environments where such a correlation did not exist. The same is true of me and my doorbell. I would not keep a doorbell system that did not convey the desired information, that did not (because of pesky squirrels, say) indicate what it was installed to indicate. I would, as I assume the flies (over many generations) would, get a more discriminating detector.

I have elsewhere (1981, 1983), under the rubric *information*, tried to say something more systematic about the idea of an objective, mind-independent, indicator relation. Aside from the above brief remarks tracing the idea of natural meaning to the objective relations of dependency between a natural sign and its meaning, between the indicator and what it indicates, I will not here attempt to recapitulate that earlier analysis. Nor will I presuppose the details. Sufficient unto present purposes is the assumption – an altogether plausible assumption, I hope – that there is something *in* nature (not merely in the minds that struggle to comprehend nature), some objective, observer-independent fact or set of facts, that forms the basis of one thing's meaning or indicating something about another.[3] In what follows I shall occasionally, partly as a terminological convenience but also partly to exhibit the deep connections between representational systems and information-processing models of human cognition, advert to the idea of information. Talking about information is yet a third way of talking about the fundamentally important relation of indication or natural meaning. So, for example, if S (sign, signal), by being a, indicates or means that O is A, then S (or, more precisely, *S*'s being *a*) carries the information that *O* is *A*. What an event or condition (whether we think of it as a signal or not is irrelevant) indicates or means about another situation is the information it carries about that other situation.

3 Conventional Systems of Representation: Type II

In systems of Type II, natural signs take the place of symbols as the representational elements. A sign is given the job of doing what it (suitably deployed) can already do.

It should be remembered that what a system *represents* is *not* what its (expressive) elements indicate or mean. It is what these elements have the *function* of indicating or meaning. It is important to keep this point in mind, since the natural signs used in systems of Type II typically indicate a great many things. Normally, though, they are used to represent only *one* of these conditions – a condition which we, for whatever reason, take a special interest in and give the function of indicating. If a full tank of gas means (because of the weight of the gas) that there is a large downward force on the bolts holding the tank to the car's frame, then the fuel gauge indicates a large downward force on these bolts whenever it indicates a full tank of gas. In addition, electrically operated fuel gauges indicate not only the amount of fuel left in the tank but also the amount of electrical current flowing in the wires connecting the gauge to the tank, the amount of torque on the armature to which the pointer is affixed, and the magnitude of the magnetic field surrounding this armature. Given the way these gauges operate, they cannot indicate (i.e., have their behavior depend on) the amount of fuel in the tank without indicating (exhibiting at least the same degree of dependency on) these related conditions.

Nevertheless, we take one of these indicated conditions to be what the gauge *represents*, one of these correlated conditions to define what *kind* of gauge it is. It is, or so we say, a *fuel* gauge, not a galvanometer recording potential differences between points in the automobile's electrical wiring (though that, in a sense, is precisely what it is). Since we are interested in the amount of gasoline in the tank, not (except derivatively) in these correlated conditions, we *assign* the gauge the function of indicating the amount of gasoline in the tank. We *give* it the job of delivering *this* piece of information, calibrate and label it accordingly, and ignore the collateral pieces of information it necessarily supplies in the process. Since what an instrument or gauge represents is what it is *supposed* to indicate, what it has the *function* of indicating, and since *we* determine these functions, *we* determine what the gauge represents. If, by jacking up the fuel tank, I remove the force on the bolts securing the tank to the car frame, the fuel gauge, though still indicating the amount of fuel in the tank, no longer indicates the amount of force on these bolts. But, under these unusual conditions, the gauge does not *misrepresent* the force on these bolts the way it could, and the way gauges sometimes *do*, misrepresent the amount of fuel in the tank. The reason it doesn't is because the gauge, even when things are operating normally, does not represent (though it does *indicate*) the magnitude of this force. Its *representational* efforts – and therefore its representational failures, its *mis*representations – are limited to what it has the *function* of indicating. And since the gauge does not have the function of indicating the force on these bolts, it does not misrepresent this force when it fails to indicate it. Though it is hard to imagine why we would do this, we could *give* the gauge this function. Were we to do so, then, under the unusual conditions described above, when we removed the force on these bolts by jacking up the tank, the gauge would misrepresent the force on the bolts.

It is for this reason that what the gauge represents is *partly* conventional, *partly* a matter of what we say it represents. In contrast with the case of Type I systems, however, this dependence on us, our interests and purposes, is only partial. The reason it is only partial is because the indicator functions assigned an instrument are limited to what the instrument *can* indicate, to what its various states and conditions depend on. You can't assign a rectal thermometer the job of indicating the Dow-Jones Industrial Average.[4] The height of the mercury doesn't depend on these economic conditions. The mercury and the market fluctuate independently. Trying to use a thermometer in this way is like assigning a rock the job of washing dishes.[5] My son can be given this job (even if he never does it) because he, unlike the rock, *can* wash dishes. The functions we assign to instruments are similarly restricted to what the instruments *can* do, or, if Wright (1973) is correct, what (in the case of artifacts) we *think* they can do. This makes the functions of systems of Type II restricted in a way that those of Type I systems are not restricted. It is this fact, together with the fact that once a device has been given such a functon it performs without any help from us, that makes such systems only *partly* conventional.

The conventional, interest-relative, and purpose-dependent character of systems of Type II is especially obvious when our interests and purposes change. An altimeter represents altitude until we remove it from the aircraft for testing on the ground. It then "becomes" an aneroid barometer, representing not altitude but air pressure – something it *always* indicated, of course, but something in which we weren't interested (except insofar as it depended on, and hence served as an accurate indicator of, altitude) when flying the plane. Calibration is a process in which one's interests and purposes undergo a temporary change. *Now*, during calibration, one uses the needle's position as an indicator, not of the quantity the instrument is usually used to measure, but of the instruments own internal condition – whether, for example, its batteries are getting weak, or whether it needs adjustment, repair, or alignment. With RSs of Type II we can, and sometimes do, change the magnitude being represented (not merely the scale for measuring a given magnitude) merely by consulting a different set of numbers on the face of the instrument. A change in the way we *use* the instrument is enough to change its function and, hence, what it represents.

One way of thinking about the difference between Type I and Type II representational systems is that in systems of Type I the function, as it were, comes first. The representational elements are given a function and then, if things go right, are *used* in conformity with this function – *used* to indicate what, relative to this function, they are supposed to indicate. I first give the dime, *its* position and movements, the function of indicating the position and movements of Oscar Robertson. Then I manipulate the dime in accordance with this assigned function. I, in virtue of my knowledge and manipulative skills, see to it that it indicates what I have assigned it the function of indicating. Not only the coin's *job* but also its *performance* of that job derives, therefore, wholly from me, the creator and user of the representational system. RSs of Type I are, then, *manifestations* or *displays* of the representational talents of their users in much the same way that a TV monitor is a *display* of the information-processing capabilities of the machinery lying behind it. With systems of Type II, however, things are different. The power of their elements to indicate comes first; their function comes second. They acquire or are assigned the function of doing one of the things they are already doing or, if not *already* doing, already *capable* of doing once harnessed in the right way. Their ability to perform their function does *not*, as in the case of systems of Type I, depend on us, on a user-system already in possession of the required indicator skills. The status of these elements as indicators is therefore *intrinsic*. What is extrinsic, and therefore still conventional, still relative to the interests and purposes of its users, is the determination of which among the various things they can already do it is their function to do.

4   Natural Systems of Representation

A natural system of representation is not only one in which the elements, like the elements of Type II systems, have a power to indicate that is independent of the interests, purposes, and capacities of any other system, but also one in which, in contrast with systems of Type II, the functions determining what these signs *represent* are also independent of such extrinsic factors. Natural systems of representation, systems of Type III, are ones which have *their own* intrinsic indicator functions, functions that derive from the way the indicators are developed and used *by the system of which they are a part.* In contrast with systems of Type I and II, these functions are not assigned. They do not depend on the way *others* may use or regard the indicator elements.

Whatever one might think about the possibility of intrinsic functions, the type of functions that define Type III systems (a contentious point to which I will return in a moment), it is clear that what I have been calling natural signs – events, conditions, and structures that somehow indicate how things stand elsewhere in the world – are essential to every animal's biological heritage. Without such internal indicators, an organism has no way to negotiate its way through its environment, no way to avoid predators, find food, locate mates, and do the things it has to do to survive and propagate. This, indeed, is what sense perception is all about. An animal's senses (at least the so-called exteroceptors) are merely the diverse ways nature has devised for making what happens inside an animal depend, in some indicator-relevant way, on what happens outside. If the firing of a particular neuron in a female cricket's brain did not indicate the distinctive chirp of a conspecific male, there would be nothing to guide the female in its efforts to find a mate (Huber and Thorson, 1985). The *place, misplace,* and *displace* neural units in the rat's brain (O'Keefe, 1976), units that guide the animal in its movements through its environment, are merely internal indicators of place, of alterations in place, and of movement through a place. Such is the stuff of which cognitive maps are made, part of the normal endowment for even such lowly organisms as ants and wasps (Gallistel, 1980).

The firing of neural cells in the visual cortex, by indicating the presence and orientation of a certain energy gradient on the surface of the photoreceptors, indicates the whereabouts and the orientation of "edges" in the optical input and therefore indicates something about the surfaces in the environment from which light is being reflected. The activity of these cells, not to mention comparable activity by other cells in a wide variety of sensory systems, is as much a natural sign or indicator as are the more familiar events we commonly think of as signs – the autumnal change in maple leaves, growth rings in a tree, and tracks in the snow.

We are accustomed to hearing about biological functions for various bodily organs. The heart, the kidneys, and the pituitary gland, we are told, have functions – things they are, in this sense, *supposed to do.* The fact that these organs are supposed to do these things, the fact that they have these functions, is quite independent of what *we* think they are supposed to do. Biologists *discovered* these functions, they didn't invent or assign them. We cannot, by agreeing among ourselves, *change* the functions of these organs in the way that I can change, merely by making an appropriate announcement, what the coins and the popcorn in my basketball game stand for. The same seems true for sensory systems, those organs by means of which highly sensitive and continuous dependencies are maintained between external, public events and internal, neural processes. Can there be a serious question about whether, in the same sense in which it is the heart's function to pump the blood, it is, say, the task or function of the noctuid moth's auditory system to detect the whereabouts and movements of its archenemy, the bat?

Some marine bacteria have internal magnets, magnetosomes, that function like compass needles, aligning themselves (and, as a result, the bacterium) parallel to the Earth's magnetic field (Blakemore and Frankel, 1981). Since the magnetic lines incline downward (toward geomagnetic north) in the northern hemisphere, bacteria in the northern hemisphere, oriented by their internal magnetosomes, propel themselves toward geomagnetic north. Since these organisms are capable of living only in the absence of oxygen, and since movement toward geomagnetic north will take northern bacteria away from the oxygen-rich and therefore toxic surface water and toward the comparatively oxygen-free sediment at the bottom, it is not unreasonable to speculate, as Blakemore and Frankel do, that *the function* of this primitive sensory system is to indicate the whereabouts of benign (i.e., anaerobic) environments.[6]

Philosophers may disagree about how best to analyze the attribution of function to the organs, processes, and behaviors of animals and plants (see, for example, Nagel, 1961; Wright, 1973; Boorse, 1976; and Cummins, 1975, all conveniently collected in Sober 1984), but that some of these things *have* functions – functions, like those of the bacterium's magnetic sense or the moth's auditory sense, to be *discovered* (not invented or assigned) – seems evident not only from a commonsense standpoint but also from the practice, if not the explicit avowals, of biologists and botanists.

This is, nevertheless, a controversial topic, at least among philosophers (see, e.g., Dennett, 1987), and I do not wish to rest a case for a *philosophical* thesis on what seems evident to common sense or what is taken for granted by biologists. So for the moment I take the biological examples as more or less (depending on your point of view) plausible illustrations of intrinsic functions – plausible examples, therefore, of sensory systems that, by having such functions, qualify as *natural* systems of representation. As we shall see later (chapter 4 [not reproduced here]), the case for representational systems of Type III will rest on quite different sorts of function: those that are derived, not from the evolution of the species, but from the development of the individual. Nevertheless, it is useful to think, if only for illustrative purposes, about the way certain indicator systems developed, in the evolutionary history of a species, to serve the biological needs of its members. It should be understood, though, that my use of such examples is merely an expository convenience. The *argument* that there are functions of the kind required for Type III systems, hence an argument for the *existence* of Type III systems, systems with a natural power of representation, remains to be made.

5   Intentionality: Misrepresentation[7]

Philosophers have long regarded intentionality as a mark of the mental. One important dimension of intentionality is the capacity to misrepresent, the power (in the case of the so-called propositional attitudes) to say or *mean* that P when P is not the case. The purpose of this section is to describe how systems of representation, as these have now been characterized, possess this capacity and, hence, exhibit some marks of the mental. Two other important dimensions of intentionality will be discussed in the following section.

Before we begin, it is perhaps worth noting that, since systems of Types I and II derive their representational powers, including their power to misrepresent, from systems (typically humans) that already have the full range of intentional states and attitudes (knowledge, purpose, desire, etc.), *their* display of intentional characteristics is not surprising. As we shall see, the traces of intentionality exhibited by such systems are merely *reflections* of the minds, *our* minds, that assign them the properties, in particular the functions, from which they derive their status as representations. This is not so, however, for systems of Type III. If there are such systems, *their* intentionality will not be a thing of *our* making. They will have what Haugeland (1981) calls *original* intentionality and Searle (1980) calls *intrinsic* intentionality.

The first aspect of intentionality to be described is the capacity some systems have to represent something as being so when it is not so – the power of *misrepresentation*. It may be thought odd to accent the negative in this way, odd to focus on a system's ability to get things wrong – on its vices, as it were, instead of its virtues. There is, though, nothing backward about this approach. The ability to correctly represent how things stand elsewhere in the world *is* the ability of primary value, of course, but this value adheres to representations only insofar as the representation in question is the sort of thing that *can* get things wrong. In the game of representation, the game of "saying" how things stand elsewhere in the world, telling the truth isn't a virtue if you *cannot* lie. I have already said that indication, as I am using this word, and as Grice used the idea of natural meaning, describes a relation that cannot fail to hold between an indicator and what it indicates. There can be no *mis*indication. If the gas tank is empty, the gauge *cannot*, in this sense of the word, indicate that it is full. This is not to say that someone might not *take* the gauge as indicating a full tank. It is only to say that the gauge does not, in fact, indicate a full tank. Since indicators cannot, in this sense, fail to indicate, they do not possess the capacity of interest the power to get things wrong. *They* don't get things wrong. *We* get things wrong by (sometimes) misreading the signs, by taking them to indicate something they don't. What we are after is the power of a system to say, mean, or represent (or, indeed, *take*) things as *P whether or not P is the case*. That is the power of words, of beliefs, of thought – the power that *minds* have – and that, therefore, is the power we are seeking in representational systems. Whatever *word* we use to describe the relation of interest (representation? meaning?), it is the power to misrepresent, the capacity to get things wrong, to say things that are not true, that helps *define* the relation of interest. *That* is why it is important to stress a system's capacity for misrepresentation. For only if a system has this capacity does it have, in its power to get things right, something approximating *meaning*. That is why the capacity to misrepresent is an important aspect of intentionality and why it figures so large in the philosophy of mind and the philosophy of language.

For this reason it is important to remember that not every indicator, not even those that occur *in* plants and animals, is a representation. It is essential that it be the indicator's *function* – natural (for systems of Type III) or otherwise (for systems of Type II) – to indicate what it indicates. The width of growth rings in trees growing in semi-arid regions is a sensitive rain gauge, an accurate indication of the amount of rainfall in the year corresponding to the ring. This does not mean, however, that these rings *represent* the amount of rainfall in each year. For that to be the case, it would be necessary that it be the function of these rings to indicate, by their width, the amount of rain in the year corresponding to each ring.[8] This, to say the least, is implausible – unless, of course, we start thinking of the rings as an RS of Type II. We, or botanists, might *use* these rings to learn about past climatic conditions. Should this happen in some regular, systematic way, the rings might take on some of the properties of an instrument or gauge (for the people who use them this way). Insofar as these rings start *functioning* in the information-gathering activities of botanists as a sign of past rainfall, they may, over time, and in the botanical community, acquire an indicator function and thereby assume a genuine representational (of Type II) status. At least they might do so *for* the botanists who use them this way. But this is clearly not an RS of Type III. Though there is something in the tree, the width of the fourteenth ring, that indicates the amount of rainfall fourteen years ago, it is implausible to suppose it is the ring's function to indicate this. The variable width of the rings is merely the effect of variable rainfall. The distension of an animal's stomach is, likewise, an indicator of the amount of food the animal has eaten and (for this reason, perhaps) an indicator of the amount of food available in its environment. But this is surely not the function of a distended stomach.

This point is important if we are to understand the way RSs manage to misrepresent things. The capacity for misrepresentation is easy enough to understand in systems of Type I. For here the power of the elements to misrepresent depends on *our* willingness and skill in manipulating them in accordance with the (indicator) functions we have assigned them. Since I am responsible for what the coins and the popcorn in my basketball game stand for, since I assigned them their indicator function, and since I am responsible for manipulating them in accordance with this function, the arrangement of coins and popcorn can be made to misrepresent whatever I, deliberately or out of ignorance, make them misrepresent. Their misrepresentations are really *my* misrepresentations.

Misrepresentation in systems of Type II is not quite so simple an affair, but, once again, its occurrence ultimately traces to whoever or whatever assigns the functions that determine the system's representational efforts. Since there is no such thing as a *mis*indication, no such thing as a natural sign's meaning that something is so when it is not so, the only way a system of natural signs can misrepresent anything is if the signs that serve as its representational elements fail to indicate something they are *supposed* to indicate. And what they are *supposed* to indicate is what *we*, for purposes of our own, and independent of a sign's success in carrying out its mission on particular occasions, *regard* them as having (or give them) the job of doing. Without *us* there are no standards for measuring failure, nothing the system fails to do that it is supposed to do. Although the actual failures aren't *our* failures, the standards (functions) that make them failures are our standards. Putting chilled alcohol in a glass cylinder doesn't generate a misrepresentation unless somebody calibrates the glass, hangs it on the wall, and calls it a thermometer.

Only when we reach RSs of Type III – only when the functions defining what a system is supposed to indicate are intrinsic functions – do we find a source, not merely a reflection, of intentionality. Only here do we have systems sufficiently self-contained in their representational efforts to serve, in this one respect at least, as models of thought, belief, and judgment.

A system could have acquired the *function* of indicating that something was *F* without, in the present circumstances, or any longer, or perhaps ever, being able to indicate that something is *F*. This is obvious in the case of a Type II RS, where, by careless assembly, a device can fail to do what it was designed to do. As we all know, some shiny new appliances don't work the way they are supposed to work. They *never* do what it is their function to do. When what they are supposed to do is indicate, such devices are doomed to a life of misrepresentation. Others leave the factory in good condition but later wear out and no longer retain the power to indicate what it is their function to indicate. Still others, though they don't wear out, are used in circumstances that curtail their ability to indicate what they were designed to indicate. A compass is no good in a mineshaft, and a thermometer isn't much good in the sun. In order to do what they are supposed to do, care has to be taken that such instruments are used when and where they can do their job.

The same is true of RSs of Type III. Suppose a primitive sensory ability evolves in a species because of what it is capable of telling its possessors about some critical environmental condition F. Let us assume, for the sake of the example, that the manner in which this indicator developed, the way it was (because of its critical role in delivering needed information) favored by the forces of selection, allows us to say that this indicator has the function of indicating F. Through some reproductive accident, an individual member of this species (call him Inverto) inherits his F-detector in defective (let us suppose inverted) condition. Poor Inverto has an RS that always misrepresents his surroundings: it represents things as being F when they are not, and vice versa.[9] Unless he is fortunate enough to be preserved in some artificial way – unless, that is, he is removed from a habitat in which the detection of Fs is critical – Inverto will not long survive. He emerged defective from the factory and will soon be discarded. On the other hand, his cousins, though emerging from the factory in good condition, may simply wear out. As old age approaches, their RSs deteriorate, progressively losing their ability to indicate when and where there is an F. They retain their function, of course, but they lose the capacity to perform that function. Misrepresentation becomes more and more frequent until, inevitably, they share Inverto's fate.

And, finally, we have the analogue, in a Type III system, of an instrument used in disabling circumstances – a compass in a mineshaft, for instance. Consider a sensitive biological detector that, upon removal from the habitat in which it developed, flourished, and faithfully serviced its possessor's biological needs, is put into circumstances in which it is no longer capable of indicating what it is supposed to indicate. We earlier considered bacteria that relied on internal detectors (magnetosomes) of magnetic north in order to reach oxygen-free environments. Put a northern bacterium into the southern hemisphere and it will quickly destroy itself by swimming in the wrong direction. If we suppose (we needn't; see note 6) that it is the function of these internal detectors to indicate the whereabouts of anaerobic conditions, then misrepresentation occurs – in this case with fatal consequences.

Put a frog in a laboratory where carefully produced shadows simulate edible bugs. In these unnatural circumstances the frogs neural detectors – those that have, for good reason, been called "bug detectors" – will no longer indicate the presence or the location of bugs. They will no longer indicate this (even when they are, by chance, caused to fire by real edible bugs) because their activity no longer *depends* in the requisite way on the presence of edible bugs. Taking a frog into the laboratory is like taking a compass down a mineshaft: things no longer work the way they are supposed to work. Indicators stop indicating. If we suppose, then, that it is the function of the frogs neural detectors to indicate the presence of edible bugs, then, in the laboratory, shadows are misrepresented *as* edible bugs. The frog has an analogue of a false belief.[10] Occasionally, when an edible bug flies by, the frog will correctly represent it as an edible bug, but this is dumb luck. The frog has the analogue of a true belief, a *correct* representation, but no *knowledge*, no *reliable* representation. Taking a compass down a mineshaft will not change what it "says" (namely, that whichever way the needle points is geomagnetic north), but it will change the reliability, and (often enough) the truth, of what it says. Likewise, taking a frog into the laboratory will not change what it "thinks," but it will change the number of times it *truly* thinks what it thinks.

All this is conditional on assumptions about what it is the function of an indicator to indicate. Upon realizing that a typical fuel gauge in an automobile cannot distinguish between gasoline and water in the tank, one could insist that it is the gauge's function to register not how much gasoline is left in the tank but how much *liquid* is left in the tank. It is our job, the job of those who use the gauge, to see to it that the liquid is gasoline. If this is indeed how the function of the gauge is understood, then, of course, the gauge does *not* misrepresent anything when there is water in the tank. It correctly represents the tank as half full of liquid. And a similar possibility exists for the frog. If the function of the neural detectors on which the frog depends to find food is merely that of informing the frog of the whereabouts of small moving dark spots, then the frog is *not* misrepresenting its surroundings when, in the laboratory, it starves to death while flicking at shadows. For the internal representation triggering this response is perfectly accurate. It indicates what it is supposed to indicate: the presence and whereabouts of small, moving dark spots. The shadows *are* small moving dark spots, so nothing is being misrepresented.

Misrepresentation depends on two things: the *condition* of the world being represented and the *way* that world is represented. The latter, as we have seen, is determined, not by what a system indicates about the world, but by what it has the function of indicating about the world. And as long as there remains this indeterminacy of function, there is no clear sense in which misrepresentation occurs. Without a determinate function, one can, as it were, always exonerate an RS of error, and thus eliminate the occurrence of misrepresentation, by changing what it is *supposed* to be indicating, by changing what it is its *function* to indicate. It is this indeterminacy that Dennett (1987) dramatizes in his arguments against the idea of *original* or *intrinsic* intentionality.

What this shows is that the occurrence of misrepresentation depends on there being some principled, nonarbitrary way of saying what the indicator function of a system is. In systems of Types I and II there is no special problem because *we* are the source of the functions. We can, collectively as it were, eliminate this indeterminacy of function by agreeing among ourselves or by taking the designer's and the manufacturer's word as to what the device is supposed to do. If a watch is really a calendar watch, as advertised, then it is *supposed* to indicate the date. It "says" today is the fourth day of the month. It isn't. So it is misrepresenting the date. Case closed.

The case is not so easily closed in systems of Type III. It can only be successfully closed when internal indicators are harnessed to a control mechanism. Only by *using* an indicator in the production of movements whose successful outcome depends on *what is being indicated* can this functional indeterminacy be overcome.

6 Intentionality: Reference and Sense

If an RS has the function of indicating that s is F, then I shall refer to the proposition expressed by the sentence "s is F" as the *content* of the representation. There are always two questions that one can ask about representational contents. One can ask, first, about its reference – the object, person, or condition the representation is a representation *of*. Second, one can ask about the way what is represented is represented. What does the representation say or indicate (or, when failure occurs, what is it *supposed* to say or indicate) about what it represents? The second question is a question about what I shall call the sense or meaning of the representational content. Every representational content has both a sense and a reference, or, as I shall sometimes put it, a topic and a comment – what it says (the comment) and what it says it about (the topic). These two aspects of representational systems capture two additional strands of intentionality: the *aboutness* or *reference* of an intentional state and (when the intentional state has a propositional content) the *intensionality* (spelled with an "s") of sentential expressions of that content.

Nelson Goodman (1976) distinguished between pictures *of* black horses and what he called black-horse pictures. This is basically my distinction between topic and comment. Black-horse pictures represent the black horses they are pictures of *as* black horses. Imagine a black horse photographed at a great distance in bad light with the camera slightly out of focus. The horse appears as a blurry spot in the distance. This *is* a picture of a black horse, but not what Goodman calls a black-horse picture. When invited to see pictures of your friend's black horse, you expect to see, not only pictures of a black horse, but black-horse pictures – pictures in which the denotation, topic, or reference of the picture is *identifiably* a black horse or, if not a *black* horse, then at least a horse or an animal of some sort.

Not all representations are pictorial. Many representations are not expected, even under optimal conditions, to *resemble* the objects they represent. Language is a case in point, but even in the case of Type II RSs it is clear that ringing doorbells do not resemble depressed doorbuttons (or people at the door) and that fuel gauges (at least the old-fashioned kind) do not resemble tanks full of gasoline. And if, as seems likely, there is in a wolf's skull some neural representation of the wounded caribou it so relentlessly follows (ignoring the hundreds of healthy animals nearby), this representation of the caribou's condition, position, and movements does not actually resemble, in the way a photograph or a documentary film might resemble, a terrified caribou. A picture, though, is only one kind of representation, a representation in which information about the referent is carried by means of elements that visually resemble the items they represent. A nonpictorial representation, however, exhibits the same dimensions. It has a reference and a meaning, a topic and a comment. My fuel gauge is not only a representation *of* an empty gasoline tank; it is also (when things are working right) an empty-tank representation. That the tank is empty is what it indicates, the information it carries, the comment it makes, about that topic. My gas tank is also very rusty, but the gauge does not comment on this feature of its topic.

The wolf's internal representation of a sick caribou may or may not be a sick-and-fleeing-caribou representation, but it certainly is a representation *of* a sick, fleeing caribou. *How* the neural machinery represents *what* it represents is, to some degree, a matter of speculation, a matter of divining what the patterns of neural activity in the wolf's brain indicate about the caribou and (since we are talking about *representations*) what, if anything, it is the function of these sensory-cognitive elements to indicate about prey. Does the wolf really represent caribou *as* caribou? Sick and lame caribou *as* sick and lame? If it turns out (it doesn't) that the wolf cannot distinguish a caribou from a moose, the answer to the first question is surely No. Perhaps the wolf merely represents caribou as large animals of some sort. Or merely as food. But the point is that unless the wolf has some means of representing comparatively defenseless caribou – a way of commenting on these creatures that is, for practical wolfish purposes, extensionally equivalent to *being a (comparatively) defenseless caribou* – its relentless and unerring pursuit of comparatively defenseless caribou is an absolute mystery, like the flawless performance of an automatic door opener that has nothing in it to signal (indicate) the approach of a person or an object. There has to be something in there that "tells" the door opener what it needs to know in order for it to do what it does – to open the door *when* someone approaches. The same is true of the wolf.

Our ordinary descriptions of what animals (including people) see, hear, smell, feel, know, believe, recognize, and remember reflect the distinction between a representation's topic and its comment. This, I think, lends support to the idea that a cognitive system is a representational system of some kind, presumably a system of Type III. We say, for example, that Clyde can see a black horse in the distance without (for various reasons having to do either with the great distance, the camouflage, the lighting, or the fact that Clyde forgot his glasses) its *looking like* a black horse to Clyde, without its presenting (as some philosophers like to put it) a *black-horse appearance*. Clyde doesn't know what it is, but he thinks it might be the brown cow he has been looking for. In talking this way, and it is a common way of talking, we describe what Clyde's representation is a representation *of* (a black horse) and say how he represents it (as a brown cow). In Goodman's language, Clyde has a brown-cow representation of a black horse. At other times perhaps all we can say about how Clyde represents the black horse is as *something* in the distance. This may be the only comment Clyde's representational system is making about that topic. This isn't much different from a cheap scale's representing a 3.17-pound roast as weighing somewhere between 3 and 4 pounds. It is a rough comment on a perfectly determinate topic.

Compare Clyde's perceptual relationship to the black horse with a fuel gauge's relation to a full tank of gasoline. When things are working properly, the gauge carries information about the tank: the information that it is full. Since it is the gauge's assigned function to deliver this information, it represents the tank as full. It does not, however, carry information about *which* tank is full. Normally, of course, an automobile comes equipped with only one gasoline tank. The gauge is connected to *it*. There is no reason to comment on which topic (which tank) the gauge is making a remark about, since there is only one topic on which to comment and everybody knows this. Suppose, however, there were several auxiliary tanks, with some mechanism letting the gauge systematically access different tanks. Or suppose we were to connect (by radio control, say) Clyde's gauge to *my* tank. In this case the representation would have a different referent, a different topic, but the *same* comment. The gauge would "say" not that Clyde's tank was full but that *my* tank was full. The fact that it was saying this, rather than something else, would not be evident from the representation itself, of course. But neither is it evident from Clyde's representation of the black horse that it is, indeed, a representation of a black horse. To know this one needs to know, just as in the case of the gauge, to what Clyde is connected in the appropriate way. Examining the representation itself won't tell you what condition in the world satisfies it, what condition would (were it to obtain) make the representation an accurate representation. For this one has to look at the wiring. In Clyde's case, there being no wires connecting him to the black horse, you have to look at the connections that *do* establish which topic his representation is a representation of. In the case of vision, that connection is pretty clearly, in most normal cases, whatever it is *from which* the light (entering Clyde's eyes) is reflected.[11]

The job of gauges and instruments is to carry information about the items (tanks, circuits, shafts, etc.) to which they are connected, not information about which item it is to which they are connected. So it is with pictures and most other forms of representation. Perceptual beliefs of a certain sort – what philosophers call *de re* beliefs (e.g., *that* is moving) – are often as silent as gauges about what it is they represent, about what topic it is on which they comment, about their *reference*. Clyde can see a black horse in the distance, thereby getting information about a black horse (say, that it is near a barn), without getting the information that it is a black horse – without, in other words, seeing *what* it is. Just as a gauge represents the gas level in my tank without representing it as the amount of gas in *my* tank, Clyde can have a belief about (a representation *of*) my horse without believing that it is (without representing it *as*) my (or even *a*) horse.

A great many representational contents are of this *de re* variety. There is a representation *of* the tank as being half full, *of* an animal as being lame or sick, *of* a doorbutton as being depressed, *of* a cat as being up a tree (or *of* a cat and *of* a tree as the one being up the other). These are called *de re* contents because the thing (*re*) about which a comment is made is determined by nonrepresentational means, by means other than *how* that item is represented. That this is a picture, a photographic representation, *of* Sue Ellen, *not* her twin sister Ellen Sue, is not evident – indeed (given that they are identical twins) not discoverable – from the representation itself, from the *way* she is represented. One has to know who was standing in front of the camera to know whom it is a picture of, and this fact cannot be learned (given the twin sister) from the picture itself. If causal theories are right (see, e.g., Stampe, 1977), the reference of such representations will be determined by causal relations: that object, condition, or situation which is, as Sue Ellen was, causally responsible for the properties possessed by the representation (e.g., the color and distribution of pigment on the photographic paper).

Though most representations of Type II have a *de re* character, there are ready examples of comparatively simple systems having a *de dicto* content, a content whose reference is determined by *how* it is represented. Imagine a detector whose function it is to keep track of things as they pass it on an assembly line and to record each thing's color and ordinal position. At the time it is registering the color (red) and the position (fourth) of *delta*, it can be said that this mechanism provides a *de re* representation *of delta* as red and as the fourth item to pass by. The reference is *delta* because that is the item on the assembly line that the detector is currently monitoring (to which it is causally connected), and the meaning or sense is given by the expression "is red and number four" because that is what the detector indicates, and has the function of indicating, about the items it is presently scanning. At a later time, though, a time when the apparatus is no longer directly recording facts about *delta*, its representation of the fourth item as red changes its character. Its reference to *delta*, its representation *of delta*, now occurs via its description of *delta* as the fourth item. At this later time, *delta*'s color is relevant to the determination of the correctness of the representation *only insofar* as *delta* was the fourth item on the assembly line. If it wasn't, then even if *delta* was the item the detector registered (incorrectly) as the fourth item, *delta*'s color is irrelevant to the correctness of the representation. It is *the fourth item*, not *delta*, that has to be red in order for this (later) representation to be correct. Compare my belief, one day later, that the fourth person to enter the room was wearing a funny hat. If I retain in memory no other description capable of picking out who I believe to have been wearing a funny hat (as is the case with our imagined detector), then this later belief, unlike the original belief, is a belief about *whoever* was the fourth person to enter the room. I may never have seen, never have been causally connected to, the person who makes this belief true.

One can go further in this direction of separating the reference of a representation from the object that is causally responsible for the representation by equipping an RS with projectional resources, with some means of extrapolating or interpolating indicated patterns. Something like this would obviously be useful in a representation-driven control system that had a "need to act" in the absence of firm information. Imagine our detector, once again, given the function of simultaneously monitoring items on *several* assembly lines, recording the color and the ordinal value of each, and, on the basis of this information, making appropriate adjustments in some sorting mechanism. Think of it as an overworked device for weeding out rotten (nonred) apples. Since "attention" paid to one line requires ignoring the others, the device must "guess" about items it fails to "observe," or else a switching mechanism can be introduced that allows the detector to withdraw continuous attention from a line that exhibits a sufficiently long sequence of red apples. A "safe" line will be sampled intermittently, at a frequency of sampling determined by the line's past safety record. The detector "keeps an eye on" the lines that have poor performance records, and "infers" that the apples on good lines are OK. If things are working reasonably well, this device produces a printed record containing representations of apples it has never inspected.

This device has the function of indicating something about objects to which it is *never* causally related.

It is not hard to imagine nature providing animals with similar cognitive resources. Donald Griffin (1984), drawing on the work of J. L. Gould (1979, 1982), describes the way honeybees perform a comparable piece of extrapolation. Honeybees were offered a dish of sugar water at the entrance of their hive. The dish was then moved a short distance away, and the bees managed to find it. This was continued until, when the feeder was more than 100 or 200 meters from the hive, the bees began waiting for the dish beyond the spot where it had last been left, at what would be the next logical stopping place (20 to 30 meters from the last location). The bees, Griffin observes, "seem to have realized that this splendid new food source moves and that to find it again they should fly farther out from home" (pp. 206–7). The benefits of such extrapolative mechanisms are obvious. Aside from the search technique of the bees, an animal without beliefs (whether we call them anticipations, expectations, or fears) about *the next A* will not survive long in an environment where the next *A* can be dangerous.

Much more can, and should, be said about the reference or topic of a representation. But it is time to turn to its sense or meaning, *how* it represents what it represents, the comment it makes on that topic. All systems of representation, whatever type they happen to be, are what I shall call *property specific*. By this I mean that a system can represent something (call it *s*) as having the property *F* without representing it as having the property *G* even though everything having the first property has the second, even though every *F* is *G*. Even if the predicate expressions "*F*" and "*G*" are *coextensional* (correctly apply to exactly the same things), this doesn't guarantee that an RS will represent *s* as *F* just because it represents *s* as *G* (or vice versa). These extensionally equivalent expressions give expression to quite different representational contents. This is a very important fact about representational systems. It gives their content a fine-grainedness that is characteristic of intentional systems. It makes verbal expressions of their content *intensional* rather than *extensional*. It is this feature, together with the system's capacity for misrepresentation and the reference or aboutness of its elements, that many philosophers regard as the essence of the mental.

Representational contents exhibit this peculiar fine-grainedness because even when properties *F* and *G* are so intimately related that nothing can indicate that something is *F* without indicating that it (or some related item) is *G*, it can be the device's *function* to indicate one without its being its function to indicate the other.[12] Nothing can indicate that *x* is red unless it thereby indicates that *x* is colored, but it can be a device's function to indicate the color of objects (e.g., that they are red) without its being its function to indicate that they are colored.

The specificity of functions to particular properties, even when these properties are related in ways (e.g., by logical or nomological relations) that prevent one's being indicated without the other's being indicated, is easy to illustrate with assigned functions, functions *we* give to instruments and detectors. For here the assignment of functions merely reflects *our* special interest in one property rather than the other. If we are, for whatever reason, interested in the number of angles in a polygon and not in the number of sides, then we can give a detector (or a *word*) the function of indicating the one without giving it the function of indicating the other even though the detector (or word) cannot successfully indicate that something is, say, a triangle without thereby indicating that it has three sides. We can make something into a voltmeter (something having the function of indicating voltage differences) without thereby giving it the function of indicating the amount of current flowing even if, because of constant resistance, these two quantities covary in some lawful way.

Though this phenomenon is easier to illustrate for Type I and Type II systems, it can easily occur, or can easily be imagined to occur, in systems of Type III. Dolphins, we are told, can recognize the shapes of objects placed in their pool from a distance of 50 feet. Apparently there is something in the dolphin, no doubt something involving its sensitive sonar apparatus, that indicates the *shapes* of objects in the water. But a dolphin that can infallibly identify, detect, recognize, or discriminate (use whatever cognitive verb you think appropriate here) cylinders from this distance should *not* be credited with the ability to identify, detect, recognize, or discriminate, say, *red* objects from this distance just because all (and only) the cylinders are red. If the fact that all (and only) the cylinders are red is a coincidence, of course, then something can indicate that X is a cylinder without indicating that X is red. This follows from the fact that an indicator could exhibit the requisite *dependence* on the shape of X without exhibiting any dependence on the color of X. But even if we suppose the connection between color and shape to be more intimate, we can, because of the different relevance of these properties to the well-being of an animal, imagine a detector having the function of indicating the shape of things without having the function of indicating their color.[13]

7 Summary

The elements of a representational system, then, have a content or a meaning, a content or meaning defined by what it is their function to indicate. This meaning or content is a species of what Grice called nonnatural meaning. These meanings display many of the intentional properties of genuine thought and belief. If, then, there are systems of Type III, and these are located in the heads of some animals, then there is, in the heads of some animals (1) something that is *about* various parts of this world, even those parts of the world with which the animal has never been in direct perceptual contact; (2) something capable of representing and, just as important, *misrepresenting* those parts of the world it is about; and (3) something that has, thereby, a *content* or *meaning* (not itself in the head, of course) that is individuated in something like the way we individuate thoughts and beliefs.

NOTES

1   That is, no intrinsic power to indicate *what it is their (assigned) function to indicate*. They may, of course, indicate something *else* in a way that is not dependent on us. For instance, the coins, being metal, indicate (by their volume) the temperature. They *could*, therefore, be used as crude thermometers. But, according to the story I am telling, this isn't their (assigned) function. If it was, then we would be talking about an RS of Type II.

2   Fodor (1987b) mentions an interesting illustration of the phenomenon discussed by David Marr and his associates: an algorithm (in the perceptual system) for computing three-dimensional form from two-dimensional rotation. The algorithm is not strictly valid, since there are worlds in which it reaches *false* three-dimensional conclusions from *true* two-dimensional premises – worlds in which spatial rotations are not rigid. Nevertheless, the algorithm is truth-preserving in the circumstances in which it is in fact employed – viz., here, in our world. Add to this the fact that the perceptual mechanisms that exploit this algorithm were evolved *here*, in *this* world, and we have a biological example of a uniformity – not lawful, but not fortuitous either – that enables sensory "premises" about two-dimensional rotations (that is, premises describing the two-

dimensional transformations of the retinal image) to indicate something about the three-dimensional world we live in.

3 This is not to say that descriptions of what something means or indicates are always free of subjective factors. We often describe what something means or indicates in a way that reflects what we already *know* about the possibilities. If there are only two switches controlling a light, the light indicates that one of the two switches is closed. Knowing, however, that *this switch* (one of the two) *isn't* closed, I take the light's being on as an indication that the *other switch* is closed. In this case, the light (is said) to indicate something that it would not indicate unless I, the speaker, *knew* something about other possibilities.

In this sense the meanings we ascribe to signs is relative. It is relative to what the speaker already knows about possible alternatives. This, however, doesn't mean that natural meaning is *subjective*. A person's weight isn't subjective just because it is relative, just because people weigh less on the moon than they do on earth. If nobody knew anything, things would still indicate other things. They just wouldn't indicate the specific sort of thing (e.g., the other switch is closed) we now describe them as indicating.

4 Not, at least, as an RS of Type II. One could, however, use it as an RS of Type I. Just as I used coins and popcorn to represent basketball players, and the positions and movements of these elements the position and movements of the players, there is nothing preventing one from *using* a rectal thermometer in a similar fashion to represent the Dow-Jones average.

5 For those who want to quarrel about this issue, I could, I suppose, assign a rock the job of doing my dishes if I mistook it for my son, just as I could assign a thermometer the job of indicating fluctuations in the stock market if I mistook it for something else. I do not, however, think a rock could actually *have* this function. Nor do I think a simple instrument could *have* the function of indicating something it could not indicate. This is not to say that the thermometer could not be incorporated into a more complex system that *could* indicate, and therefore could have the function of indicating, something about the stock market. But, by the same token, I could also make the rock part of a machine (pulleys, etc.) that *could* do (and, therefore, could have the function of doing) my dishes.

6 There may be some disagreement about how best to describe the function of this primitive sensory system. Does it have the function of indicating the location, direction, or whereabouts of anaerobic conditions? Or does it, perhaps, have the function of indicating the Earth's magnetic polarity (which in turn indicates the direction of anaerobic conditions)? In Dretske (1986) I described this as an "indeterminacy" of function. As long as this indeterminacy exists, there is, of course, an associated indeterminacy in what the system represents. I return to this point later.

7 The material in this section is based on Dretske (1986). That work, and in fact this entire chapter, was heavily influenced by the important work of Stampe (1975, 1977), Millikan (1984, 1986), Enc (1979, 1982), and Fodor (1984, 1987a). Also see Papineau (1984).

8 Fodor (1984) makes this point against Stampe's (1977) idea that the rings in a tree *represent*, in the relevant sense, the tree's age. See Stampe (1986) for a reply.

9 An artificial approximation of this situation occurred when R. W. Sperry (1956) and his associates rotated, by surgical means, the eyeball of a newt by 180°. The vision of the animal was permanently reversed. As Sperry describes it, "When a piece of bait was held above the newt's head it would begin digging into the pebbles and sand on the bottom of the aquarium. When the lure was presented in front of its head, it would turn around and start searching in the rear."

It should be noted that one doesn't disable an indicator *merely* by reversing the code – letting *b* (formerly indicating *B*) indicate *A* and *a* (formerly indicating *A*) indicate *B*. As long as this reversal is systematic, the change is merely a change in the way information is being coded, not a change in the information being coded. But though *A* and *B* are still being indicated (by *b* and *a* respectively), they are, after the inversion, no longer being accurately *represented* unless there is a corresponding change (inversion) in the way the representational elements (*a* and *b*) function in the rest of the system. This is what did not happen with the newt. It still got the information it needed, but as a result of the coding change it misrepresented the conditions in its environment.

10 But not a real false belief, because, as we shall see in the next chapter [not reproduced here], beliefs are more than internal representations. They are internal representations that help explain the behavior of the system of which they are a part.

11 Here I suppress difficult problems in the philosophy of perception, problems about the correct analysis of the perceptual object. Any responsible discussion of these topics would take me too far afield.

12 See Enc (1982) for further illustrations of this. Enc argues, convincingly to my mind, that we can distinguish between the representation of logically *equivalent* situations by appealing to (among other things) the functions of a system.

13 Taylor (1964, p. 150) notes that an experimenter can condition an animal to respond to red objects without conditioning it to respond to objects that differ in color from the experimenter's tie (which is green). He takes this to be a problem for how the property to which behavior is conditoned is selected. It should be clear that I think the answer to Taylor's problem lies, at least in part, in an adequate theory of representation, one that can distinguish between the representation of X as red and X as not green.

REFERENCES

Blakemore, R. P. and Frankel, R.B. (1981). Magnetic Navigation in Bacteria. *Scientific American* 245: 6.

Boorse, C. (1976). Wright on Functions. *Philosophical Review* 85: 70–86.

Cummins, R. (1975). Functional Analysis. *Journal of Philosophy* 72: 741–65.

Dennett, D. (1987). Evolution, Error and Intentionality. In *Intentional Stance*. Cambridge, MA: MIT Press.

Dretske, F. (1981). *Knowledge and the Flow of Information*. Cambridge, MA: MIT Press.

Dretske, F. (1983). Précis of Knowledge and the Flow of Information. *Behavioral and Brain Sciences* 6: 55–63.

Dretske, F. (1986). Misrepresentation. In *Belief*, ed. R. Bogdan. Oxford: Clarendon Press.

Enc, B. (1979). Function Attribution and Functional Explanations. *Philosophy of Science* 46: 343–65.

Enc, B. (1982). Intentional States of Mechanical Devices. *Mind* 91: 161–82.

Fodor, J. (1984). Semantics, Wisconsin Style. *Synthese* 59: 1–20.

Fodor, J. (1987a). *Psychosemantics*. Cambridge, MA: MIT Press.

Fodor, J. (1987b). A Situated Grandmother. *Mind and Language* 2: 64–81.

Gallistel, C. R. (1980). *The Organization of Action: A New Synthesis*. Hillsdale, NJ: Erlbaum.

Goodman, N. (1976). *Languages of Art*. Indianapolis, IN: Hackett.

Gould, J. L. (1979). Do Honeybees Know What They are Doing? *Natural History* 88: 66–75.

Gould, J. L. (1982). *Ethology, The Mechanisms and Evolution of Behavior*. New York: Norton.

Grice, P. (1957). Meaning. *Philosophical Review* 66: 377–88 [reproduced as part of ch. 2 in this volume].

Grier, J. W. (1984). *Biology and Animal Behavior*. St Louis, MO: Mosby.

Griffin, D. R. (1984). *Animal Thinking*. Cambridge, MA: Harvard University Press.

Haugeland, J. (1981). Semantic Engines: An Introduction to Mind Design. In *Mind Design*. Cambridge, MA: MIT Press.

Huber, F. and Thorson, J. (1985). Cricket Auditory Communication. *Scientific American* 253: 60–8.

Millikan, R. G. (1984). *Language, Thought, and Other Biological Categories: New Foundations for Realism*. Cambridge, MA: MIT Press.

Millikan, R. G. (1986). Thoughts Without Laws: Cognitive Science With Content. *Philosophical Review* 95: 47–80 [reproduced as part of ch. 6 in this volume].

Nagel, E. (1961). *The Structure of Science*. Indianapolis, IN: Hackett.

O'Keefe, J. (1976). Place Units in the Hippocampus of the Freely Moving Rat. *Experimental Neurology* 51: 78–109.

Papineau, D. (1984). Representation and Explanation. *Philosophy of Science* 51: 550–72.

Searle, J. (1980). Minds, Brains and Programs. *Behavioral and Brain Sciences* 3: 417–57.

Sober, E. (1984). *Conceptual Issues in Evolutionary Biology*. Cambridge, MA: MIT Press.

Sperry, R. W. (1956). The Eye and the Brain. In *Perception: Mechanisms and Models*. San Francisco, CA: Freeman.

Stampe, D. (1975). Show and Tell. In B. Freed, A. Marras, and P. Maynard, eds, *Forms of Representation*. Amsterdam: North-Holland.

Stampe, D. (1977). Toward a Causal Theory of Linguistic Representation. In P. French, T. Uehling and H. Wettstein, eds, *Midwest Studies in Philosophy*, vol. 2. Minneapolis, MA: University of Minnesota Press.

Stampe, D. (1986). Verification and a Causal Account of Meaning. *Synthese* 69: 107–37.

Taylor, C. (1964). *The Explanation of Behavior*. London: Routledge and Kegan Paul.

Wright, L. (1973). Functions. *Philosophical Review* 82: 139–68.

Thoughts Without Laws: Cognitive Science with Content

RUTH GARRETT MILLIKAN

Thirty years ago, Wilfrid Sellars introduced the thesis that our ordinary talk about thoughts and other "private episodes" is not in the first instance[1] inner observation talk (nor logical construct talk) but *theory* talk (Sellars, 1956). At that time his position was unintuitive, hard to understand, highly controversial – and wonderfully refreshing. One effect was to cast new light upon the weaknesses and strengths of both introspective psychology and traditional behaviorisms in such a way as to give "aid and comfort" (as Sellars likes to say) to a newly emerging psychology – a psychology that wished to explain behavior by postulating inner episodes of a sort that might eventually be described physiologically. It is marvelous how wanting to think a thesis true can lift it straight from the nether region of the unintuitive, difficult, and problematic to the heights of the clear, distinct, and obvious. At the present time, a premiss shared by many who agree on little else is that ordinary talk about thoughts and other "private episodes" constitutes a sort of folk theory, a primitive science of psychology, the purpose of which is to predict and explain behavior. To attack this premiss (for example, Stich, 1983) is definitely to swim upstream.

Of course to say that folk psychology is a primitive theory designed to explain behavior does not tell us very much that is positive unless accompanied by suitable remarks about what theories are. Sellars did accompany his thesis with such remarks – with an explicit endorsement of a dominant sort of theory of theories current in the 1950s and still current, in the relevant respects, today. This theory of theories has taken various forms, but its core is always the same: theoretical terms are defined by the place they have in a system of postulated *laws* connecting the entities and properties for which they stand with other entities and properties postulated by the theory and with happenings among items outside the domain of the theory proper; the purpose of the theory is to explain and regularize patterns in phenomena outside of the domain of the theory proper by reference to the postulated entities, properties, and laws. In the case of folk psychology, the theoretical items would be mental properties and states, the phenomena to be explained and regularized would be behaviors given the external situations in which they occur. Given this theory of theories, to say that folk psychology was a theory was to say that the items to which folk psychology refers – beliefs, desires, visual images, etc. – are essentially law-governed items, that is, they are law-governed items if they exist at all, if the folk theory is true. To say *that* was indeed to say something positive, even something cheerful. For it was to suggest that a genuine nomological science of psychology might be built from the materials of folk psychology suitably trimmed and trained.[2]

Now the idiom of folk psychology is shot through with references to items that are, in Brentanos sense, "intentional" items that are "about" other things or "of" other things beliefs about whales, fears of falling, recognitions of faces, etc. Putting this another way, these items have "semantic content" or just content. Granted that having content is an essential character of many folk-psychological entities, these entities being, indeed, differentiated or individuated in part in accordance with content, it seemed to be implied that both the intentionality and the specific contents of these intentional items must correspond to the kinds of lawful causal interaction these had with one another, with the environment, and with behavior. This view meshed nicely with popular views derived from the sprawling tradition of philosophical analysis (for example, verificationism) about the nature of meaning, hence, spilling over, of the content of mental terms. According to these views (I am putting things very crudely here) meaning is given by showing what a term implies and/or what implies it and, ultimately, what its proper connections are with sensory data. All that was needed now, it seemed, was to map logical implications onto causal interactions among the contentful entities of folk psychology, thus exposing the *way* in which these entities "meant" things – were intentional, had content.

But in the last ten years or so various arguments have accumulated to the effect that the content of an inner intentional item, say, a belief, is not a direct function of its causal role (for example, Putnam, 1975b; Burge, 1979, 1982; Stich, 1983). This is the same as to say that doubt has been cast on the thesis that folk psychology is a "theory" in the sense described by Sellars, or at least upon the thesis that it might be a *true* theory of this kind. I will not rehearse these arguments here for it is not my purpose to evaluate them. Instead I wish to examine the relevance of the suspicion that folk psychology is not a theory in Sellars's sense to the question of the relation between folk psychology and a mature scientific psychology or "cognitive science."

It seems to be widely assumed that if folk psychology is not a true theory of the kind Sellars described, then folk psychology cannot be used as a footing for construction of cognitive science. Putting this differently, it is assumed that either ascribing semantic content to inner states of people is, implicitly, claiming and claiming truly that people have items or states in them that obey specified kinds of nomological laws, *or* that ascription of content to inner states has no role of importance at all to play in a mature cognitive science. For example, Stich (1983) and the Churchlands (P. M., 1979, 1981; P. S., 1980) deny the first half of this disjunct, hence embrace the second; Burge (1984) has recently denied the second half, hence attempted to reclaim the first.[3] My claim will be that folk psychology is not a rudimentary nomological theory but that it need not be to play a crucial role in the development of cognitive science. Folk-psychological items or states are not defined by reference to laws, not even to rough statistical laws.[4] Similarly, ascribing content to inner psychological states does not involve postulating any laws.

Yet cognitive science could not possibly get on with its tasks without ascribing content to inner psychological states. At the same time I will explain how folk psychology, despite the fact that it postulates no laws, and despite the fact that we seldom know very many *details* about the intentional states of other people, still enables us to do a great deal of explaining and a certain amount of fallible predicting of human behavior.[5]

1 Biological Categories, Proper Functions and Normal Conditions

Psychology, no matter how it is done, necessarily *is* a branch of physiology, hence biology. Human physiology is the study of how the various parts and systems that make up a human work, that is, of what they do and of how they go about doing it. Psychology studies what mental tasks are and how they are performed, on the assumption, of course, that there *are* some special systems (material or nonmaterial) that work in accordance with special principles and do special kinds of task that fall, sensibly, into a distinguishable field for study – study of the "mental."

Now consider: how does physiology differ from, say, organic chemistry? Of course these disciplines study different kinds of body or system. Physiology studies whole human bodies and middle-sized parts and even extremely small parts of bodies; organic chemistry studies systems that are incredibly small – the systems that are organic molecules. But the fundamental difference is that the organic chemist and the physiologist wish to understand how the systems they study work in rather different senses of "work."

To know how an organic molecule "works" is to understand how the system it comprises holds itself together as a system, what kinds of force will destroy it and why, what the products of such destruction or decomposition will be, and what kinds of larger system it can become a part of, when and why. In this sense of "works" there is no such thing as *not* working, or as not working well or not working right; whatever the organic molecule does is part of its "working". For example, if the system flies apart the result is not a molecule that is failing to work but some other molecule, molecules or particles. The human body on the other hand is a kind of system that does not necessarily work, or work right or well. Correlatively, failure to work or to work right or well does not automatically transform a human body into something else (mummies are human bodies too). The objects that physiologists study – human bodies, circulatory systems, red blood cells, etc. – fall into a different kind of ontological category than do organic molecules. Call these categories "biological categories."

Biological categories are carved out not by looking at the actual structure, actual dispositions, or actual functions of the organ or system that falls within the category, but by looking at (or speculating about) its history.[6] A heart, for example, may be large or small (elephant or mouse), three-chambered or four-chambered etc., and it may *also* be diseased or malformed or excised from the body that once contained it, hence unable to pump blood. It falls into the category *heart*, first, because it was produced by mechanisms that have proliferated during their evolutionary history in part because they were producing items that managed to circulate blood efficiently in the species that contained them, thus aiding the proliferation of that species. It is a *heart*, second, because it was produced by such mechanisms in accordance with an explanation that approximated, to some undefined degree, a Normal explanation for production of such items in that species and bears, as a result, some resemblance to Normal hearts of that species. By a "Normal explanation" I mean the sort of explanation that historically accounted for production of the majority of Normal hearts of that species. And by a "Normal heart," I mean a heart that matches, in relevant respects, the majority of hearts that, during the history of that species, managed to pump blood efficiently enough to aid survival and reproduction. In like manner, every body organ or system falls into the biological or physiological categories it does due to its historical connections with prior examples of kinds that have served certain functions or, typically, sets of functions. So whether or not it is itself capable of serving any of these functions, every organ or system is associated with a set of functions that are biologically "proper to it" to it – functions that have helped account for the survival and proliferation of its ancestors. I call these functions "proper functions" of the organ or system.[7]

Associated with each of the proper functions that an organ or system has is a Normal explanation for performance of this function which tells how that organ or system, in that species, has historically managed to perform that function. For example, there are a number of proper functions that *can* be performed by certain systems of the human body given the appropriate lithium compounds in the bloodstream but that were *historically* performed using calcium. The Normal explanations for how these functions are performed make reference to the presence of calcium in the blood rather than lithium. Similarly, the heart of a person who wears a pacemaker to assure that the electrical signals sent to the heart muscle are properly timed does not pump the blood in accordance with a fully Normal explanation. (I am capitalizing "Normal" so that it cannot be read to mean, merely, average. As we will soon see, what is Normal is not always statistically average, indeed, sometimes it is quite unusual.)

Not only body organs and systems but also various states and activities of these organs and systems have proper functions. Consider a chameleon. Its skin contains a system whose job is to arrange pigmented matter in such a way that the chameleon will match whatever it is sitting on at the moment. Obvious further proper functions of this system are to arrange that the chameleon will be invisible to predators, hence will avoid being eaten. If we look at any particular color pattern that characterizes any particular chameleon at a particular time, we can say what the proper functions of this pattern are, even though it is possible (though unlikely) that no chameleon has ever displayed just this particular kind of pattern before. The proper functions of the pattern are to make the chameleon invisible and to prevent it from being eaten – functions that it derives from the proper functions of the mechanism that produced it. The Normal explanation for performance of this function is that some predator comes by, glances toward the chameleon but does not see it because it matches what it sits on, hence goes past without eating the chameleon.

Of course if no predator comes by, this color state of the chameleon cannot perform its proper function – or not in accordance with a Normal explanation. Lots of states (tokens) have proper functions they never get a chance to perform. Also, just as body organs and systems are sometimes diseased or malformed, hence unable to perform their proper functions, so aberrant states and activities of a body or system can have proper functions that they would not be able to perform even under Normal conditions. Consider a chameleon that does *not* match what it sits on. This might have come about because the pigment-arranging system of the chameleon was out of order. Or it might be because, although its pigment-arranging system was perfectly healthy, the chameleon was in an environment that did not provide Normal conditions for operation of this system. (I don't know on what principles this system operates, but suppose that radiant energy in unusual wavelengths could confuse the system.) In either case, just as a thing that has been produced by mechanisms designed to make hearts is a heart with the proper function of pumping blood so long as it bears resemblance to Normal hearts and was produced in accordance with an explanation that approximated a Normal explanation for production of hearts, so the chameleon's wrong color pattern (token) is a protective device or state with the proper function of preventing the chameleon from being eaten. And there is still a Normal explanation associated with this function, though it is very unlikely to be realized. Chameleons' color patterns have historically prevented chameleons from being eaten because what the chameleon sat on matched the chameleons. So a Normal condition for proper performance of the color pattern is that there be something that the chameleon is sitting on that matches it. If this condition held, the color pattern could prevent the chameleon from being eaten in accordance with a Normal explanation. Suppose, for example, that some sympathetic soul places the sick chameleon on something it *does* match. The color pattern still has the same proper function, and *now* it might be performed in accordance with a Normal explanation. The entire history of this proper performance would not have been Normal of course, but from now on, things could proceed Normally.

Consider also a more complex case. There is a mechanism in worker honey bees that has as proper functions to produce, after the bee has spotted a new supply of nectar, a bee dance (a certain activity) that bears a certain mapping relation to the position of the nectar, hence to produce the flying of fellow worker bees in a certain direction, hence to get these bees to nectar, hence to get nectar into the hive. Each particular bee dance has as proper functions, derived from the proper functions of this mechanism, to cause worker bees to fly in a certain direction, hence to find nectar, etc. Now consider a particular bee dance, *Sacre du Sucre*, danced by a particular bee at a particular time. In what direction is it the proper function of *Sacre du Sucre* (the token) to propel the watching bees? First, toward nectar. But equally cogently, in the direction indicated by *Sacre du Sucre*, for the mechanism by which bee dances have historically performed their proper functions is by propelling worker bees in a direction determined by a certain definite function (mathematical sense) of the orientation of the dance. Now suppose that something has gone wrong; *Sacre du Sucre* was danced by mistake and does not in fact indicate the direction of any nectar. *Sacre du Sucre* then has conflicting proper functions: (1) to send the workers toward nectar and (2) to send the workers where the dance says to go, for instance, north-northwest; but there is no honey north-northwest. So not only can states and activities have proper functions without performing them and without even being capable of performing them, they can also have proper functions that, even if performed, would not contribute to performance of certain of their own *further* proper functions (or not, at least, in accordance with an uninterrupted Normal explanation. Someone might, of course, be kind enough to place some nectar where the bees that complied with the incorrect dance were aiming).[8]

2   Psychology as a Branch of Biology

Now it seems reasonable that various states of the systems psychologists study have proper functions (which they may or may not get a chance to perform, or even be capable of performing, indeed, which it might sometimes even be pointless or opposed to their own more ultimate purposes for them to perform) that are derived from the proper functions of the mechanisms that produce them, and that there are Normal explanations for performance of these functions. Thus, although it might be that a certain facet or state of one's cognitive system was unique in history – say, one had a unique belief or a unique desire – still this state has a proper function or set of proper functions and these functions are associated with Normal explanations for their proper performance. There must, after all, be a finite number of general principles that govern the activities of our various cognitive-state-making and cognitive-state-using mechanisms and there must be explanations of why these principles have historically worked to aid our survival. To suppose otherwise is to suppose that our cognitive life is an accidental epiphenomenal cloud hovering over mechanisms that evolution devised with other things in mind.

Now to study how an entity as falling within a biological category "works" involves (1) understanding what functions are proper to it and to its constitutive systems, parts, and states, and (2) understanding how these functions are Normally performed. It does not involve studying just anything at all that the entity might be disposed to do and any old way that one might induce it to do this. For example, the physiologist is not interested in such exotica as why the Normal heart makes just those peculiar sounds that it makes (nor in how one might induce it to make other sounds), for presumably these sounds have no proper functions.[9] But he *is* interested in how the body manages to maintain just that peculiar temperature that it maintains, this maintenance having, it seems, numerous proper functions. True, one thing that physiologists study is diseases. But no parallel to such studies exists within the field of organic chemistry precisely because "disease" is defined with reference to – by *contrast* with – that which is functioning properly or that which is Normally constituted.

Imagine a physiologist trying to study the liver or the eye without having any idea what its proper functions are – what it is supposed to do. Clearly his first job will be to try to find out what it is supposed to do, what it is for it to "work." Until he has formed some kind of hypothesis about this there is no way of proceeding to a study of *how* it works. There is no way of knowing, even, *when* it is working, let alone working right or well, and no way of distinguishing the Normally constituted and properly functioning samples of its kind from those that are malformed, diseased, or malfunctioning. Nor is there any way of proceeding to a study of how it works without knowing something about the surrounding conditions upon which it Normally relies.

Similarly, it seems reasonable that the psychologist would need to begin with some understanding of what the proper functions of the systems he studies are, his concern being to understand the mechanisms whereby and the conditions under which these functions are Normally realized. The systems the psychologist studies differ from many of those the physiologist studies in that they are much more malleable. They are supposed to mold themselves over time and even to adapt themselves moment by moment in time so as to take account of the peculiar environment of the individual organism and its temporary position within that environment. They are designed to change their states or to produce new states with extraordinary frequency, even continually. But these states must still have proper functions and there must be Normal vs. abNormal ways in which they fulfill these functions if and when they do fulfill them. Only by beginning with some hypotheses about the functions of these systems and of their various states could a neurologist begin the work of searching for these systems and states in the brain and of describing *how* these systems and their various states Normally perform their respective functions. Surely there are an infinite number of ways that brain states might be classified or described if one did not care whether or not one was describing state types that had proper functions. But if one does care about this, the only way to begin is by having some hypothesis about what these functions are.

Now suppose that folk psychology were a theory in *this* sense: it postulates that there exist certain entities or states within the body – beliefs, desires, intentions, fears, etc. – that have certain proper functions. (What the defining functions of these states might be can be left open for the moment.) Then if folk psychology were *right* it would surely be necessary for any developed scientific psychology to take account of these entities or states *as* folk psychology understands them, that is, as aspects of the body having certain proper functions. If I can make it plausible that the entities that folk psychology postulates are indeed defined by their proper functions, and make plausible that the proper functions with which folk psychology endows these entities very likely *are* had by some special parts or states of the body, that should be enough to show that cognitive science can probably use folk psychology as a starting point. The job of cognitive science would then be, in part, to explain what the Normal constitution of these psychological entities is and *how* they Normally perform their defining proper functions.

But I said I would argue that folk psychology is not a theory in the sense that Sellars defined – that it does not make reference to nomological laws – even to rough statistical laws in defining the entities that it postulates. What then is the relation between having a certain proper function or proper functions and falling under laws?

3 Proper Functions vs. Laws

Once the physiologist has in his hand a hypothesis about what the proper functions of a body part or system are he can tackle the task of finding out *how* it performs these functions. His eventual aim is to describe the Normal constitution of the simplest component parts of the system in terms such that how the system functions can be understood by principles of physics, organic chemistry, etc. Along the way (and it's a very long way) he uses "functional analyses" in something like Cummins's (1975, 1983) sense.[10] That is, he divides the part or system into smaller and smaller parts and systems, describing the proper functions of each and how these combine to effect the proper function of the whole. At the same time (especially if he is interested in pathology) he examines what the Normal explanations and Normal conditions for performance of these functions are.

Now for the most part it is a proper function of some other parts or systems in the body to produce or to maintain the Normal conditions that a body part or system relies upon for performance of is functions. For example, very many body functions have as a Normal condition for performance that the body be at approximately 98.6° Fahrenheit, and there are several organs or systems within the body whose job it is to see that this condition is maintained. For this reason it can often be assumed that insofar as a body part or system is itself healthy or Normally constituted and insofar as it is operating within a body the rest of which is passably healthy, it *will* perform its proper functions. So although physiology does not uncover universal laws applying to *all* examples of the systems that it studies, it can make some generalizations that hold for all healthy examples of such systems.

However, as we move from the body's interior to its periphery we find exceptions to the rule that healthy parts of healthy bodies invariably perform their proper functions. At the periphery of the body, Normal conditions for proper performance of functions are often external conditions over which other body systems have no control. For example, one proper function of the sweat glands is to cool the body by evaporation of the water that they secrete. This proper function will fail to be performed through no fault of the body's if the humidity is too high. The proper function of the eyeblink reflex is to prevent approaching objects from entering the eye. But it may be that this function usually fails to be performed, not because the reflex is not swift enough but because what triggered it was not in fact something that otherwise would actually have entered the eye. A proper function of the swimming mechanism in a human sperm is to get the sperm to an ovum. But only a minute proportion of these mechanisms actually perform this function – because of the paucity of human ova. Sometimes, then, devices have proper functions that have no tendency to correspond to laws or uniformities even when the constitution of these devices is perfectly Normal. This is because the Normal conditions for performance of a devices proper functions are sometimes optimal conditions rather than statistically average conditions or conditions the device is usually in.

Many biological devices have survived because a critical yet small proportion of their number has performed useful functions or because a critical yet small proportion of their issue has done so.

Now the contentful entities or states that folk psychology postulates – those that exhibit intentionality – would seem to be *par excellence* things that ultimately serve us only via happenings at our peripheries and beyond – as our behaviors impinge on the world, the results effect more happenings in the world, and these return to impinge upon our bodies again. So it would not be surprising if some or all of the proper functions of these contentful entities or states – functions derived from the proper functions of the mechanisms that produced them – often failed to be performed. Then these proper functions would not correspond to laws or even, perhaps, to high probabilities and folk psychology, if it postulated these entities *as* things having certain proper functions, would not be a theory in anything like the sense described by Sellars.

Of course folk psychology might still be used to do quite a lot of explaining and a certain amount of very fallible predicting. Consider an analogy: "I wouldn't light my pipe over there; that's a smoke detector over your head." Smoke detectors can be out of order. Moreover, not all conditions are conditions under which they are designed to operate. (Perhaps they can be too cold, too wet, or too close to a magnet.) But one still knows that they are *liable* to go off when they encounter smoke – that they are more likely to do this than are other gadgets chosen at random. Even if smoke detectors were extremely fallible devices, requiring quite special conditions in order to work, still it would be reasonable to offer as an explanation of why one was beeping simply that it was a smoke detector in the presence of smoke. And it would be reasonable to take the precaution of not lighting one's pipe under smoke detectors.

Yet the relevance of folk psychology to cognitive science would not rest on its feeble ability to predict and explain. If the contentful entities of folk psychology have proper functions, and if these functions are correctly understood by folk psychology, then folk psychology describes the "competence" (in one of Chomsky's senses) of certain devices inside us. It is then up to the neuropsychologist to look for devices that have this kind of competence, and to describe the processes by which, *under the right circumstances*, actual performances of these functions are effected.

4 Motions, Behaviors, and Actions

My job now is to make it plausible that folk psychology is a theory that attempts to explain actions by positing inner things or states having certain proper functions rather than things that obey certain laws. But first we must be clearer about what "actions" are – about *which* phenomena it is appropriate to ask a psychology, whether "folk" or "scientific," to explain (this section). And we must also be clearer about what can and what cannot be predicted or explained about the workings of a thing by knowing only that it has a certain proper function (section 5).

The happenings that either folk psychology or a developed scientific psychology could be expected to explain are strictly limited to those that occur in accordance with proper functions of the body's systems (or that occur as common aberrations of these functions – abnormal psychology). The systems that the psychologist studies are systems that produce, among other things, bodily movements and then effects beyond the body. So the psychologist interests himself in the etiologies of bodily motions and effects. But, just as the physiologist does not care why the heart says "pit-a-pat," the psychologist does not interest himself in just any of these motions and effects. He is interested only in ones it is appropriate to describe as "behaviors" or as "actions." For how an animal's movements, and their effects must be described so as correctly to fall under the heading "behaviors" or "actions" depends upon the proper functions of the mechanisms that produce them.

For example, an ethologist may study certain of a fish's movements under the heading "moving the tail from side to side" but not under the heading "moving the tail from north to south" or "undulating in front of a famous ethologist." This will be because he takes it that the side-to-side movement accords with a proper function – a competence – of certain mechanisms within the fish, whereas the north-to-south direction of the movement and the fact that it occurs in front of a famous ethologist are accidental. Moving the tail from side to side is a genuine behavior of the fish; moving the tail from north to south and undulating in front of a famous ethologist are not behaviors of the fish.[11] The ethologist may also study these movements under the heading "swimming" because a proper function of these movements is to propel the fish through the water, and he may study other movements of the fish under the heading "mating display" because these movements are supposed to attract mates. He will not study either of these movements under the heading "predator display" although these movements may regularly attract predators, for attracting predators is not a proper function of either. Displaying itself to predators is not a behavior of the fish.

Similarly, the psychologist will not be concerned to explain how it happens that I flatten the forest-floor plants and scare the mice away as I pass through the woods unless he supposes that it is a proper function of my system, in its current state and environment, to produce these results (say, I am leaving a trail on purpose and I am afraid of mice). If it is not a proper function of my system to produce these results, these happenings correspond neither to genuine actions nor to genuine behaviors of mine. Also, although "moving my right hand toward you," "handing you a dollar bill," and "paying back what I owe you" (all pointing to the same movement) may describe behaviors or actions of mine, "moving my right hand 20 inches northwest" and "handing you a picture of Washington (still pointing to the same movement) are not likely to describe behaviors or actions of mine (compare Burge 1984; Dretske 1984). Hence it is not likely to be the business either of folk psychology or of scientific psychology to attempt to explain why I move my right hand 20 inches northwest or why I hand you a picture of Washington.

5   What Knowing about a Proper Function Does Not Tell Us

We have noted that knowledge of the main proper function or functions of a thing does not automatically yield knowledge of its inner workings. More interesting, it does not necessarily yield knowledge even of its grossest outer workings. To know that it is the job of a large unenclosed piece of machinery to ingest loose hay and disgorge neatly wired square bales of hay does not necessarily enable one to predict the motions even of its grossest parts as it performs this function. Similarly, turning an example of Daniel Dennett's on its head (Dennett, 1978), knowing only that a chess-playing computer is designed to win chess games, I may guess that it will make allowable chess moves and also beat me at chess. But, *contra* Dennett, this does not tell me *how* it will go about the business of beating me. For this I would need, minimally, a more detailed functional analysis of the computer's capacities, perhaps a look at its program. Of course I may be able to predict some of its moves just by seeing what it would have to do to beat me or probably would *have* to do to beat me – like interposing a bishop as the only possible means of getting out of check or of avoiding getting into an obvious trap.But (unless I have watched it for a while and discerned that it relies on such-and-such simplistic strategies, that is, guessed what some of its subsidiary proper functions are) for the most part I will have no idea exactly what move it will make next.

Summarizing, if folk psychology were to attempt to explain actions by postulating that people contain inner items or states that have certain proper functions, then:

1 Folk psychology would not explain motions of people under random descriptions but would explain only genuine behaviors or actions of people (section 1 above).
2 Especially if the actions to be explained were at a remove from the body (for example, shooting rabbits) or fell under abstract descriptions (for example, paying you back what I owe you), folk psychology might explain these without at the same time explaining or predicting the exact "moves" that effected these actions (section 4).
3 It might be that the proper functions of the inner items or states that folk psychology posits very often failed to be performed, making retrospective explanation rather than prediction the major contribution of folk psychology to folk understanding (section 3).

6   Desires

"Desire" suggests a yearning. It suggests, even, that what is desired is not overlikely to come about. But focus instead upon the wider, more philosophical sense of "desire" – that in which "belief" and "desire" correspond to the traditional categories "cognition" and "volition," these two exhausting the realm of propositional attitudes. For example, in this sense of "desire" I desire whatever I intend even though I may not yearn for but dread going through with this thing, and I desire whatever I adopt as an explicit goal.

Given this overall notion of desire, the most obvious proper function of every desire, it is reasonable to suppose, is to help cause its own fulfillment. For it is reasonable that *the mechanisms in us that manufacture desires* (not, of course, any specific desires) have proliferated because the desires they produce are sometimes (by no means always) relevant to our flourishing and eventually reproducing, and because relevant desires have sometimes participated in processes that ultimately effected their fulfillment. (Reminder: Very many biological devices seem to have survived because *sometimes* they were effective, because they performed well under optimal conditions.) If so, a proper function of the desire to eat is to bring it about that one eats; a proper function of the desire to win the local democratic nomination for first selectman is to bring it about that one wins the local democratic nomination for first selectman. That is, the descriptions that we give of desires are descriptions of their most obvious proper functions.[12] Hence, that desires (types) are distinguished or individuated (named) in accordance with content is as ordinary a fact as, say, that the categories "heart," "kidney," and "eye," as naming parts of both crayfish and people, are carved out by reference to *their* most obvious proper functions. A description of *all* of the proper functions of a human desire, like a description of all of the proper functions of a human heart, would have, of course, to say much more. It would contain a full functional analysis telling exactly how the desire was supposed to effect its fulfillment. Or, more likely, it would tell how human desires in general Normally (not on the average) effect their fulfillments – the mechanisms and principles involved. (These mechanisms may be different for chimpanzees, if chimpanzees have desires. But possibly they are the same for all humans.)

Very often the proper functions in accordance with which desires are named are not performed. Indeed, perhaps most desires, like sperm, are born into a world in which conditions, outer and/or inner, are not Normal for their fulfillment. For example, like baby fishes that run into bigger fishes before practically any of their proper functions have been performed, many desires run into bigger opposing desires before they can even get underway, or they run into beliefs that imply the impossibility of their fulfillment. Still, to know that a person has a certain desire (especially if it is a goal or intention) is to have *some* hold on what he *may* in fact do.

Exactly *how* he will do it, if he does in fact do it, is of course another matter. *Do* we predict one another's exact moves? Or do we predict only that certain of one another's desires (for example, goals, intentions) are likely to be fulfilled – say, getting dinner inside one, getting a dozen eggs home, getting to class, getting the floor washed and the laundry done. What desires (goals, intentions) a person has we guess because they tell us ("I'll bring home some eggs"; "I want to get to Boston this summer") or by generalizing from their past behavior (she almost never misses class) or by generalizing from the behavior of other people or of other similar people, or by *verstehen* – by knowing what goals we would have if we were in the other's shoes. How likely a person is actually to fulfill a certain desire of theirs we guess in the same sort of way. (This likelihood roughly accords with the yearning-desire vs. goal vs. intention series.) When we do expect people to do things but then they don't in fact do them, often this can be explained by reference either to unexpected circumstances or to unexpected beliefs or counterdesires. But this kind of explanation does not fit the covering-law model of explanation. Like historical explanation, it is retrospective. It proceeds not by reference to initial conditions and laws but by telling what happened in sequence – telling that first this factor entered the scene, then that factor, so we can understand how it was that this happened.

Jerry Fodor (1980) has been considerably exercised (as he likes to say) by the (undoubted) fact that, knowing only that it is true *of* the girl next door that John wants to meet her, we cannot predict that John will exhibit next-door-directed behavior. For John may believe that this girl whom he wishes to meet languishes in Latvia. Fodor, following a long tradition, realizes that determinate prediction of a person's behavior starting with knowledge of only certain of their beliefs and desires is blocked by the fact that this behavior may always depend crucially upon some other beliefs and desires about which one does not know. And, supposing the girl who lives next door to be Jane, of course it is true that the exact moves John makes in his attempt to meet Jane – indeed, whether he makes any such moves at all – will depend upon his other beliefs and desires. But a very straight forward (though extremely fallible) surmise still follows immediately from the fact that John desires to meet Jane (especially if this desire is a goal or an intention) and from this fact *alone*. Namely, eventually John *will* meet Jane (say, after he gets back from Latvia). For example, it is a lot more likely, given that he desires to meet *Jane*, that he will meet Jane at some point in his career than it is that he will meet any other girl randomly selected from the world's population. For functional devices (as a class) are more likely to perform their proper functions than to cause any other effects chosen at random. The intentional characterization of John, "He wants to meet . . ." where the blank space is filled in and read fully transparently, *does* give us a handle on what John might well do, and certainly a handle by which we may later be able to explain why John did what he did do, though not a handle that fits into a deductive or nomological scheme.

Further, from the fact that John desires to meet Jane we can say something about *how* John's desire will probably get fulfilled, *if* it gets fulfilled. Folk psychology not only understands the understands main proper functions of desires, but something about the functional analysis of the mechanisms that produce their fulfillment, that is, about the subsidiary proper functions of desires. John will gather relevant information and, using his desire as premiss, make practical inferences on the basis of which he will act – that's how his desire will get fulfilled, if it gets fulfilled Normally.

Exactly *what* information might be used and *what* inferences might be made is not of course specified in saying what desires John has. For example, if both John and Bill want to meet Jane, the identity conditions in accordance with which they have the same desire make no reference to what information each has or might gather or to what inferences each might make. For them to have the same desire it is enough that each be in a state proper functions of which are (1) to meet Jane and (2) to accomplish this by use of appropriate information and inference. Hence an analysis of John's and Bill's concepts of Jane is of no interest here; no reference is made to how each thinks of Jane or how each would recognize Jane if he met her. The networks of inference dispositions that fill out John's and Bill's concepts, their internal wiring, their specific "input–output dispositions," are all irrelevant to whether or not they have the same desire.

But it is tempting to think that if only we did know all of John's beliefs and desires we would be able to predict his moment-by-moment behavior – that, barring breakdowns of the cognitive systems, folk psychology does contain an implicit nomological theory after all. This theory, it is traditionally thought, is obtained by mapping the logical connections among John's beliefs and desires and between these and sensory data onto inference dispositions and "input–output" dispositions. Putting aside current arguments to the effect that the input–output-plus-inference dispositions that characterize a person's brain could not in fact determine the semantic contents of his beliefs or vice versa (for example, Putnam, 1975b; Burge, 1979, 1982; Stich, 1983), there is a quicker reason to reject this traditional view. It has long been recognized that strict mapping of logical implications onto inference dispositions is not possible since people do not always believe the logical consequences of their own beliefs. More recently it has been noticed (for example, Minsky, 1981; Bach, 1984; Dennett, 1984) that if people did believe (in a nondispositional sense of "believe," that is, if they "core-believed," stored or ground out) all of the consequences of their beliefs, their heads would soon be filled with trash to the overflow mark and they would grind to a halt trying to make the simplest practical decisions. Clearly the failure to make all of the inferences that one's beliefs entail is not just a result of malfunction or faulty design. If it is a subsidiary proper function of our beliefs and desires to participate in processes of inference, there must also be mechanisms in us that tell them when to engage in this pastime that tell us when to run our inference-making systems and with which beliefs and desires. Just as logic tells us nothing about how to construct proofs, but only how to check them for validity, so it tells us nothing about these mechanisms, hence nothing about any actual inference dispositions. In no sense then is folk psychology a Sellarsian theory.[13]

7   Beliefs

If that is the sort of postulated thing that the folk call a desire, what sort of thing is a belief? One of its proper functions is to participate in inferences in such a manner as to help produce fulfillment of desires. That much is obvious if our claim was correct that desires have as a subsidiary proper function to participate in practical inferences along with beliefs. But that much, taken alone, yields no information about how beliefs are named – about their type-identity conditions – hence no clue about what gives them specific semantic content. Beliefs are not typed (named) by telling which desires they are supposed to sponsor, nor, it seems plausible, do belief tokens have as proper functions to help fulfill one desire more than another. For similar reasons, although another proper function of beliefs is surely to participate in inferences to yield other beliefs – true ones – this proper function also yields no identity conditions for beliefs. What I will argue is that beliefs are typed not (as beliefs that *p* vs. beliefs that *q*) in accordance with any particular proper functions that they have but in accordance with certain of the conditions that must obtain it they are to fulfill their proper functions (for example, helping to fulfill some desires or other) *in accordance with a Normal explanation.*

A clue that suggests this thesis lies with the labels "true" and "false" with which the folk evaluate beliefs. Notice that these labels are not applied to desires or intentions. Philosophers seeking symmetries have espied one between "true" vs. "false" applied to beliefs and "fulfilled" vs. "unfulfilled" applied to desires, and they have invented the neutral "satisfied" vs. "unsatisfied" to cover both these contrasts. Certainly there is a symmetry between true beliefs and fulfilled desires – one that I will discuss in section 9 below. But there is also an important asymmetry: false beliefs are *defective* whereas unfulfilled desires are not. There is nothing wrong with me or my desire if I desire to visit China yet circumstances prevent my ever getting there or I decide I want to do something else more. But there is something wrong with me or with my belief if I believe that China is west of Europe. "True" and "false" are normative terms; "fulfilled" and "unfulfilled" are merely descriptive.

If a false belief were one that was defective in the same sense in which we speak of other things within the body as being defective, then a false belief would be one that was not likely to serve all of its proper functions. And, indeed, according to folk psychology, though false beliefs may participate in inferences in a Normal way, they *are* unlikely to end up helping one to produce any new beliefs that are true or helping one to fulfill any of one's desires. Or if they do do this, this will not happen *in accordance with any Normal explanation.* For example, if John falsely believes that Jane languishes in Latvia, his resulting trip to Latvia may help him to fulfill some desire or other, perhaps even his burning desire to find the love of his life – say, Lara or Aino. Maybe he will even meet someone in Latvia who knows where *Jane* is. But this will be an accident, not, presumably, a result of the elegant self-programming of his well-designed nervous system. More explicitly, it will not be the result of his nervous system's operating in accordance with general principles that also explained how his ancestor's nervous systems programmed themselves and used these programs so as to help them to proliferate.

Yet surely his belief that Jane languishes in Latvia might help John to arrive at some new true belief or to fulfill some desires or other in accordance with a Normal explanation *if only Jane languished in Latvia.* This suggests that the truth condition of a belief is a *Normal condition* for fulfillment of proper functions that lie beyond simply participating in inferences. That is, the truth condition of a belief is one of the conditions that must obtain if the belief is to fulfill any such functions in accordance with a Normal explanation. Turning this another way, apparently beliefs are named or described (typed) in accordance with certain of their Normal conditions for functioning properly. For example, if both John and Bill believe that Jane languishes in Latvia, the identity conditions in accordance with which they have the same belief make no reference to John's or Bill's *concepts* of Jane or of Latvia – no reference to how each would describe or recognize Jane or Latvia, or to any specific kinds of inference they are disposed to make using their respective beliefs. What John and Bill have in common is only that each harbors in him something that is supposed to participate in inferences so as to help produce new true beliefs and help fulfill desires but that cannot perform these latter functions Normally – that is, in accordance with principles relied upon during evolutionary design of the cognitive systems unless Jane does languish in Latvia.

Now a Normal condition for sweating to cause cooling of the body is that the humidity is less than 100 percent. But that the body sweats when the humidity is not less than 100 percent does not entail that the sweating itself is abNormal or that something is wrong with the body. So why should the absence of a Normal condition for proper performance of a belief imply that the belief is defective? Consider this analogy. If we say, using slightly more precision, that a proper function of the sweating is to help return the body to its Normal temperature, then we see that the body's being overheated is another Normal condition for the sweating's serving its function. And absence of *this* Normal condition when the body is sweating does suggest that something is wrong with the body. For though it is a proper function of the sweat glands to secrete sweat, this is so only if and when the body is overheated. Similarly, presumably it is a proper function of the belief-manufacturing mechanisms in John to produce beliefs-that-*p* only if and when *p*, for example, beliefs that Jane is in Latvia only if and when Jane is in Latvia and beliefs that it is raining only if and when it is raining. Turning this around, a belief that Jane is in Latvia is, and is *essentially*, a thing that is not Normally in John unless Jane is indeed in Latvia.

Notice, however, that if the body sweats when not overheated it does not follow that the sweat glands themselves are defective. More likely, they are working under abNormal conditions, say, stimulated by substances that are not Normally in the blood stream or that are not Normally here unless the body is overheated. Similarly, that John has a false belief need not indicate that his belief-manufacturing mechanisms are faulty. Indeed, it need not indicate that anything in him is abNormal (except the belief). Perhaps his belief-making mechanisms have been laboring under *external* conditions not Normal for performance of their proper functions. For example, perhaps Bill told John that Jane was in Latvia and John's experience has been that Bill is a very reliable person. Normally functioning belief-making mechanisms must often rely on the principle that past regularities can be projected into the future. But of course such mechanisms will then perform properly and Normally only under the condition that this principle holds in the particular case, and it doesn't always hold. John's belief-making mechanisms are no more infallible than are his sweat glands, even when nothing is wrong with either. Similarly, when John perceives things wrong this is not always the fault of his perceptual systems. Sometimes Normal conditions for proper functioning of these systems are not met, as when the train on the track next the Latvian express leaves the station but Johns perception is that it is his train that is leaving instead. The Normal condition that is not met here – a condition that his perceptual systems were built to rely upon or that he has learned, in a Normal way, to rely upon is that the moving object move relative to a background visible to John. Clearly this is a condition that is not inside John.

Because our belief-making systems are dependent for their proper operation upon numerous conditions for which the bodys systems are not responsible, it is not surprising if many of the beliefs of perfectly healthy people are false. Possibly the systems that it is psychology's job to investigate are unique with regard to the high incidence of abNormal or malformed states or parts that they contain. And perhaps because false beliefs are not abnormal states – not states that are unusual – it has been easy to overlook the fact that false beliefs are abNormal states. The search has been for a functional description applying to "the belief that *p*" where "*p*" describes some given content, it being supposed to be quite irrelevant whether the belief that p is true or false. But to expect to find no fundamental difference between descriptions of what true beliefs do and descriptions of what false beliefs do is as absurd as to expect to find no fundamental difference between what healthy livers do and what jaundiced livers do.

8   Independence of Beliefs and Desires: Rational Animals

I have argued that folk psychology postulates inner items (for example, structures or events or states or entities) that have certain proper functions and Normal conditions for proper performance of these functions rather than postulating items that have certain dispositions, that obey certain laws or that are *defined*, say, by reference to certain computational programs. I have promised to argue that folk psychology is probably right – that likely there are inner items that have the functions and depend on the conditions that folk psychology postulates. In order to do this it will be necessary to fill in more details than folk psychology offers about the nature of these inner items. First, however, let us milk folk psychology as dry as possible.

According to the folk, *human* beliefs and desires interact with one another during processes called "inferences," but it is not clear that animal beliefs and desires must do this. For example, consider a toad that is swallowing lead pellets as fast as you toss them at him. It is natural to say (whether literally or by extension is not relevant here) that the toad thinks the pellets are bugs. It is natural to say this even after one understands that this behavior is really the expression of a simple tropism or reflex over which no Normally malleable part of the toad has control, that there is no division of toad-aspects or toad-modes to correspond to the division between believing the pellets are bugs and wanting to eat bugs, in short, that nothing like practical inference is going on in the toad. We say that the toad thinks the pellets are bugs merely because we take it that the toad's behavior would fulfill its proper functions (its "purposes") Normally only if these were bugs *and* that this behavior occurs Normally (not necessarily normally) only upon encounter with bugs. Similarly, we may say of a lobster held firmly by the thorax that it is trying to, that it wants to, pinch us but can't reach, and we say of the toad that what it really wants is to eat bugs. That is, we attribute a desire to a primitive animal whenever it exhibits behavior that we take to have a certain proper function even though we may be certain that the animal is incapable of making inferences or uncertain whether it is capable of this.

But when we (the folk) turn to humans or to animals we take to be more like humans, say, dogs and cats, we are not so indiscriminate. For example, we do not attribute a desire to prevent a foreign object from entering the eye either to you or to your dog just because the eyeblink reflex is triggered. What more, exactly, do we require for belief and desire in the case of humans? Folk theory is not precise on this matter but at least these two theses can be mined from it.

1   In the human case, beliefs are separate entities from desires and nothing is both a belief and a desire. Contrast the belief of the toad swallowing lead pellets. His inner activity does not include separable states or features, one to correspond to his belief that the pellets are bugs, another to his desire to eat bugs. Or consider a bee doing a bee dance. The bee dance might be said to express either a belief that there is nectar at a certain location or a desire that fellow worker bees should go to that location or both. But it is unlikely that there is any distinction *within* the performing bee to correspond to the

distinction between belief and desire – unlikely that the bee either believes or desires anything in the human way.

2   In the human case, beliefs and desires are things that can interact with other beliefs and desires to form new beliefs and desires. That is, beliefs and desires can participate in inference processes. Further, no strictures beyond relevance (some semblance of logic) determine which beliefs and desires may interact with which to form new beliefs and desires or help to produce actions; beliefs are not hooked to certain uses and unavailable for others. Contrast the toad's belief that these are bugs, which is fixedly hooked to its desire to eat bugs. If I believe that something is a beefsteak, I may well use this belief for some purpose other than to fulfill a desire to eat beefsteak, but the toad's belief has no such independence. Also contrast any behavior that is merely a response conditioned to a stimulus. The rat that has been conditioned to press a bar for food when the little green light goes on may be said to believe, when the light goes on, that if he presses the bar food will appear. But only if this belief could be unhooked from his desire to eat food and turned to other purposes (perhaps it could be) would it be like a human belief.

In short, according to folk theory, humans can collect information without having any particular uses for that information in mind and they can have desires without knowing how to fulfill them. Surely there is no reason to challenge the folk on this point. Indeed, this sort of independence between beliefs and desires coupled with the ability to combine beliefs and desires in novel ways is surely the essence of rationality. Thus, not only are human beliefs and desires entities the identity conditions for which make no reference to specific uses or to specific means of fulfillment (beyond that these means include inference), they are free-floating entities the actual mechanics of which must be free from such specifics too. What kind of mechanics might accord with such a description of human beliefs and desires?

9   Inner Maps

On this matter, folk theory offers no guidance. But the philosophical tradition, reaching back at least as far as the wax impressions in Plato's *Theaetetus*, offers a theory that, though currently out of favor, does describe human beliefs and desires as quite independent things. The doctrine of modern computationalism that inner representations are representations in part because they are "calculated over" – because they do something like participating in inferences – is, I believe, peculiar to our times. The classical position was that inner representations are representations because they are *like* what they are *about*. According to this view, beliefs and desires are inner "impressions" or "images" or "pictures" of sorts: Beliefs are pictures of what is or was or will be; desires are pictures of what will be if the desires produce their proper results. Thus beliefs and desires could be stored quite independently of one another, then brought out to interact during processes of inference.

This classical theory is easily parodied. Imagine blue and triangular brain states standing for blue and triangular things, beautiful brain states standing for beautiful things, etc. And imagine a little man inside the brain looking at these colorful brain states and interpreting them. For why would it matter whether or not the states were like what they represented unless someone needed to understand them? At one time Wittgenstein (1922) thought that the first part of this parody could be averted by thinking of the likeness between a thought and the "fact" it represented as a very abstract formal likeness – likeness in "logical form." Roughly, the idea was that something like mathematical mapping relations correlated the domain of thought with the world. But unfortunately (for example, Wittgenstein, 1953; Quine, 1960; Putnam, 1977), mathematical mapping relations are embarrassingly legion. An indefinite number of them can be defined that will correlate, in one way or another, any two domains of entities having much size or complexity. Which of these – which sort of abstract "similarity" – is the kind, then, that makes inner representations represent?

Suppose we begin by considering a very familiar and nonmysterious example of a biological device that works by "picturing" something else: a bee dance. The bee dance represents the location of nectar that has been spotted by the dancing bee; it is "about" the location of nectar. At least it is natural to say this. Bee dances seem to be like inner representations conceived on the classical model though not on the contemporary model that requires inner representations to be "calculated over." Let us try to spell out exactly what is involved in this case of "representing."[14]

Assume that proper functions of a bee dance are causing watching bees to fly toward nectar, causing watching bees to find nectar, causing nectar to be gathered into the hive, etc. Then any bee dance *that serves its proper functions in accordance with a Normal explanation* (that part is important) is related in this way to other bee dances that do the same: Transformations of the dance (say, rotate the axis of the dance 20° clockwise) correspond one-to-one to transformations of the location of nectar relative to hive and sun (say, shift the nectar 20° further west off a direct line between sun and hive). Thus, although the bee dance is not what one would ordinarily call "similar" to what it represents, it is a kind of map or picture *when all goes Normally*.

Now notice these things. First, which mapping rule (which transformation correlation) is the relevant one to mention – which rule determines what the dance represents – is quite obvious. This rule is determined by the evolutionary history of the bee. It is that in accordance with which the dance must map onto the world in order to function properly in accordance with a Normal explanation or, what is the same, in order that the mechanisms within watching bees that translate (physicist's sense) the dance pattern into a direction of flight should perform all of their proper functions (including getting the bees to nectar) in accordance with a Normal explanation. Second, although the dance can serve its proper functions only because it is a sort of map or abstract likeness of where the nectar is, there is no need for any little man inside the interpreting bee to know about this likeness. Interpreting bees just react to the dance appropriately, allowing it to guide them. Third, bee dances have the characteristic feature that Brentano associated with intentionality: unlike natural signs and natural information carriers, say, photographs, they can be of or about something that does not exist. For when a bee dance is wrongly executed and does not map the location of any actual nectar according to B-mese rules, as long as it is still a B-mese well-formed formula, one can still say where there would have had to have been nectar for it to serve its proper functions Normally. One can say what its "truth conditions" are.

When all goes properly and Normally, the bee dance also maps onto the resulting direction of flight of watching bees and onto the place they end up after flight. It is not merely an "indicative" representation but also an "imperative" one. As an imperative representation it has fulfillment conditions, these being different from its truth conditions in that they correspond to proper functions of the dance rather than to Normal conditions for performance of its functions. Like the toad's belief that these are bugs and his desire to eat bugs, these two aspects of the dance – the indicative and the imperative – cannot be torn apart. Bee dances express beliefs and desires in the sense in which toads have beliefs and desires. But it is pretty certain that they do not express beliefs and desires in the sense in which humans have these. Bees, as Bennett (1964) has observed, are not rational.

Now try this. Call the actual condition or state of affairs in the world that makes a human belief that is true to be true or that makes a fulfilled desire to be fulfilled its "real value" (this not to be confused with its truth condition or with its meaning: only beliefs and desires that are satisfied have real values). Then, adding what we have learned from folk psychology, having a real value is one condition that is needed in order that a human belief should help to fulfill desires or to help produce more true beliefs in accordance with a Normal explanation. And a real value to correspond to is one thing that it is a proper function of a desire to produce – to cause to be. Now postulate that the real value of a human belief or desire has a second characteristic: there are transformations (notice, not "aspects" or "parts") of the belief or desire that correspond one-to-one to transformations of its real value so as to produce other thought/real-value pairs in a systematic way. Notice how such transformations differ from the kind described by transformational grammars: they turn representations into other representations having different subject matter. For example, a transformation performed on the belief that x loves y might produce the belief that y loves x, the same transformation applied twice returning us to the original. The corresponding transformation on real value would operate on the state of affairs that is x's loving y to produce y's loving x. Possibly most of the transformations in accordance with which beliefs and desires map are substitution transformations, that is, they have the form, *substitute such-and-such into the what's-it-called place*. (In Millikan 1984 I argued that this is the most common kind of transformation in accordance with which language maps onto the world.) For example, the belief that John loves Aino may be a transformation of the belief that John loves Jane by the transformation rule *substitute the such-and-such mental structure* (the one naming Aino) *into the such-and-such* (direct object?) *place*. Perhaps this transformation corresponds to the transformation upon real value, *substitute Aino into the patient role*. In this way, we suppose, when all goes properly and Normally, beliefs and desires map onto real values in accordance with determinate rules.[15] And when a belief is not true or a desire is not fulfilled, still we can say what its real value would have had to have been for all to go properly and Normally what its satisfaction conditions are – for these are determined by the same rules.

Thus folk psychology, embellished with something akin to the traditional notion that thoughts are like impressions or pictures, might be placed in the context of modern physiology to yield a theory of content for beliefs and desires – a naturalist theory of intentionality.[16] Such a theory would place few restrictions on or, turning things around, would give little guidance to the physiological psychologist speculating a priori about what beliefs and desires are like physically. Structures, states, entities and events are all things to which mathematical transformations can apply and transformations are of many kinds (the most flexible being substitution transformations). So beliefs and desires might be "pictures" in a very abstract sense indeed. Still, to tell the scientist that he should search for some kind of picturing system in the brain, for mechanisms that can produce pictures of actual states of affairs (belief-producing mechanisms), for other mechanisms that can use pictures to produce corresponding states of affairs (desire-fulfilling mechanisms), and for mechanisms that allow these various pictures to interact with one another roughly as folk psychology says they do – that is to tell him what *problem* he is trying to solve. Obviously there is no way to begin an empirical investigation without some such guidance. One has to know what one is investigating!

10   Some Implications

Given this embellished folk theory it would be easy enough to see how the human brain *qua* manipulator of symbols in accordance with their "forms" or "shapes" is the same as the brain *qua* "semantic engine" – as appraiser of meanings and author of truths.[17] Representations that the brain manipulates or calculates over are symbols at all – are things having a *significant* "shape" or "form" – only insofar as they are, first, semantic items – items that map onto the world when they succeed in performing their full proper functions Normally. Compare Dretske's concern (1983, p. 88): "I wonder what makes a structure's role a *conceptual/inferential* role . . . It presupposes that the structures over which computations are being performed already have semantic content. Where did they get it?" But for beliefs and desires to function properly and Normally they must participate in inference processes, that is, they must be calculated over or manipulated. And the *way* they are Normally manipulated must be sensitive to all the differences between them that are *significant* differences in "shape" or "form" – that accord with differences in semantic content. Indeed, *that* these differences correspond to genuine differences in semantic content *depends* upon the fact that these symbols are Normally manipulated differently, that is, upon the fact that different manipulations accord with their subsidiary proper functions. How else could their more removed proper functions (re: desires) or Normal conditions for proper performance (re: beliefs) be different? Thus there is no distinction between the brain as symbol manipulator and as semantic engine.

Similarly, if beliefs and desires are maps of the sort I have described, the distinction that some have wished to draw between an inner representation and a propositional attitude, the latter construed as a relation to the representation of the person or system that has or processes the representation, is at best moot. Suppose that an inner representation were the sort of item that could be removed with tweezers and set under a microscope. Just as a beef heart that lies in the market is still a heart, the representation would still be a belief, desire, visual image or whatever it had been. Not that you could tell, just by inspecting it and seeing what it could do, that it was this. You would have to know or guess its history – that it came out of a body and that it was designed by evolution, or by learning systems that evolution had designed, to serve a certain kind of function. For example, an extracted belief would remain a belief because it would still be the sort of biological item that, in order to function properly and Normally, needed to be embedded in a system that used it in a very specific way – a way that required that it map *so* onto the world.

NOTES

I am much indebted to Stephen Crain for a very careful and constructive reading of the first draft of this essay. Comments on a later draft by Alexander Rosenberg, Barry Loewer, Adam Morton and an unknown referee for *The Philosophical Review* were also helpful.

1   Sellars held that in the second instance private episodes are observed entities. They can be directly observed by those who have them. But observation terms, for Sellars, are merely terms applied without inference, and do not necessarily denote anything real.
2   I am going to argue that Sellars was wrong in thinking that folk psychology is a theory *in this particular sense*. But the basic thesis of "Empiricism and the Philosophy of Mind" is in no way affected by this. The article is a landmark in twentieth-century philosophy.
3   Burge (1984) suggests that it is only "individualistic" interpretations of intentional state attributions that fail to explain behavior nomologically.

4   More accurately, the only plausible *reconstruction* that I can see of folk psychology makes no
    reference to laws. For example, I will try to show that the categories of folk psychology correspond
    to categories that are best explained in terms of evolutionary theory. But of course folk psychology
    makes no explicit reference to evolutionary theory.

5   Many details supporting the position for which I will argue are given in Millikan (1984). The
    emphasis there was on language. Here I will focus more sharply on thought, painting in the
    necessary background with broad intuitive strokes.

6   How biological categories are carved out is described much more exactly in Millikan (1984, chs 1
    and 2).

7   The notions "proper function," "normal constitutions," "Normal explanation for proper per-
    formance" and "Normal conditions for proper performance" are given explicit definitions in
    Millikan (1984, chs 1 and 2).

8   For more details about the derivation of the proper functions of states and about the Normal
    explanations for performance of these functions, see Millikan (1984, chs 2 and 6–8).

9   Should current speculations that a mother's heart-sounds help to synchronize her baby's body
    rhythms turn out to be correct, I would, of course, have to change the example.

10 It should be borne in mind, however, that I have described proper functions in a way that, for
    certain purposes, differs significantly from Cummins's description of functions.

11 I realize that I am forcing the notion "behavior" in this passage – forcing it to do some *work*. In
    the mouths of many students of behavior the notion "behavior" is quite empty, meaning, just, a
    motion or some effect of the motion of an organism.

12 One reader asked concerning the desire that many have not to have children whether a malfunc-
    tion in motivational psychology is always responsible for such a desire. The answer depends
    on what you mean by "malfunction." If external conditions are not optimal, perfectly healthy
    systems sometimes produce states that have proper functions that are not in accord with their own
    ultimate purposes (see section 1). Do they then "malfunction"? Also, there is no reason to suppose
    that the design of our desire-making systems is itself optimal. Even under optimal conditions
    these systems work inefficiently, directly aiming, as it were, at recognizable ends that are merely
    roughly correlated with the biological end that is reproduction. For example, mammals do not, in
    general, cease efforts at individual survival after their fertile life is over, nor is it reasonable to
    suppose that this is only because of the invaluable services they offer to their grandchildren.

13 It is true that folk psychology attributes to people belief in the straightforward logical conse-
    quences of their beliefs. But this is because the folk count mere propensities to core-believe as
    beliefs. The point is that these propensities are not laws. Compare: "Dogs bite" attributes a
    propensity to dogs but not a law or a disposition – at least not if "disposition" makes reference to
    there being some definite conditions under which dogs always bite.

14 I am using the term "representation" in the usual way here, not in the technical sense used in
    Millikan (1984), where full-fledged "representations" are contrasted with mere "intentional
    icons."

15 Notice that this is not a traditional way to describe the mapping of intentional items onto the
    world. It correlates *whole* beliefs with *whole* conditions or affairs in the world and correlates
    transformations of these with *transformations* of world affairs rather than beginning by correlating
    mental "terms" with their referents, then building up to mental "sentences." The reasons for
    describing the mapping functions that correlate intentional items with their real values in this way
    are discussed in Millikan (1984, ch. 6).

16 As for the prospect that contemporary functionalism will eventually explain intentionality (this
    to be carefully distinguished from explaining intelligence or smartness – see Fodor 1980 and
    Cummins 1983), one of the most clearheaded champions of this approach has recently said of it,
    "hard to swallow . . . Yet I think we had better try hard to swallow it, and digest it too, because,
    to echo Fodor, there just isn't any other definite proposal in the offing" (Cummins, 1983, p. 90).
    This is followed by discussion of five unsuccessful functionalist recipes for intentionality and a
    rough suggestion for further culinary experiments. Surely it would be indelicate for an unbeliever

to interrupt this preparation for a last supper. Better just to place another definite proposal in the offing – as I have tried to do here and in Millikan (1984).

17 The "shapes" metaphor is Jerry Fodor's (1980). The term "semantic engine" is Daniel Dennett's (1981).

REFERENCES

Bach, K. (1984). Default Reasoning: Jumping to Conclusions and Knowing when to Think Twice. *Pacific Philosophical Quarterly* 65: 37–58.

Bennett, J. (1964). *Rationality*. London: Routledge and Kegan Paul.

Block, N. (1980). *Readings in the Philosophy of Psychology*, vol. I. Cambridge, MA: Bradford Books/ MIT Press.

Burge, T. (1979). Individualism and the Mental. *Midwest Studies in Philosophy* 4: 73–121.

Burge, T. (1982). Other Bodies. In *Thought and Object*, ed. A. Woodfield. Oxford: Oxford University Press.

Burge, T. (1984). Individualism and Psychology. Delivered at the Sloan Conference, MIT, May 18, 1984 [reproduced as part of ch. 7 in this volume].

Churchland, P. M. (1979). *Scientific Realism and the Plasticity of Mind*. Cambridge: Cambridge University Press.

Churchland, P. M. (1981). Eliminative Materialism and Propositional Attitudes. *Journal of Philosophy* 78: 67–90.

Churchland, P. S. (1980). A Perspective on Mind – Brain Research. *Journal of Philosophy* 77: 185–207.

Cummins, R. (1975). Functional Analysis. *Journal of Philosophy* 72: 741–60. Also in Block (1980).

Cummins, R. (1983). *The Nature of Psychological Explanation*. Cambridge, MA: Bradford Books/MIT Press.

Dennett, D. C. (1978). *Brainstorms*. Montgomery, VT: Bradford Books.

Dennett, D. C. (1981). Three Kinds of Intentional Psychology. In *Reduction, Time and Reality*, ed. R. Healey. Cambridge: Cambridge University Press.

Dennett, D. C. (1984). Cognitive Wheels: The Frame Problem of AI. In *Minds, Machines, and Evolution*, ed. C. Hookway. Cambridge: Cambridge University Press.

Dretske, F. (1983). Author's Response to Commentaries on his "Précis of Knowledge and the Flow of Information." *Behavioral and Brain Sciences* 6: 82–9.

Dretske, F. (1984). Burge on Content. Delivered at the Sloan Conference, MIT, May 18, 1984.

Fodor, J. (1980). Methodological Solipsism Considered as a Research Strategy in Cognitive Psychology. *Behavioral and Brain Sciences* 3: 63–73 [reproduced as part of ch. 7 in this volume].

Fodor, J. (1981). *RePresentations*. Cambridge, MA: Bradford Books/MIT Press.

Millikan, R. G. (1984). *Language, Thought, and Other Biological Categories*. Cambridge, MA: Bradford Books/MIT Press.

Minsky, M. (1981). A Framework for Representing Knowledge. In *Mind Design*, ed. J. Haugland. Cambridge, MA: Bradford Books/MIT Press.

Putnam, H. (1975a). *Mind, Language and Reality*. Cambridge: Cambridge University Press.

Putnam, H. (1975b). The Meaning of "Meaning". *Minnesota Studies in the Philosophy of Science* 7: 131–193 [reproduced as ch. 3 in this volume].

Putnam, H. (1977). Realism and Reason. In *Meaning and the Moral Sciences*. London: Routledge and Kegan Paul.

Quine, W. V. (1960). *Word and Object*. Cambridge, MA: MIT Press.

Sellars, W. (1956). Empiricism and the Philosophy of Mind. *Minnesota Studies in the Philosophy of Science* 1: 253–329. Also in Sellars (1963).

Sellars, W. (1963). *Science, Perception and Reality*. New York: Humanities Press.

Stich, S. (1983). *From Folk Psychology to Cognitive Science*. Cambridge, MA: Bradford Books/MIT Press.

Wittgenstein, L. (1922). *Tractatus Logico-Philosophicus*. London: Routledge and Kegan Paul.
Wittgenstein, L. (1953). *Philosophical Investigations*. New York: Macmillan.

It's About Time: An Overview of the Dynamical Approach to Cognition

TIM VAN GELDER AND ROBERT S. PORT

1 Introduction

How do we do what we do? How do we play tennis, have conversations, or go shopping? At a finer grain, how do we recognize familiar objects such as bouncing balls, words, smiles, faces, jokes? Carry out actions such as returning a serve, pronouncing a word, selecting a book off the shelf? Cognitive scientists are interested in explaining how these kinds of extraordinarily sophisticated behavior come about. They aim to describe cognition: the underlying mechanisms, states, and processes.

For decades, cognitive science has been dominated by one broad approach. That approach takes cognition to be the operation of a special mental *computer*, located in the brain. Sensory organs deliver up to the mental computer representations of the state of its environment. The system computes a specification of an appropriate action. The body carries this action out.

According to this approach, when I return a serve in tennis, what happens is roughly as follows. Light from the approaching ball strikes my retina and my brain's visual mechanisms quickly compute what is being seen (a ball) and its direction and rate of approach. This information is fed to a planning system which holds representations of my current goals (win the game, return the serve, etc.) and other background knowledge (court conditions, weaknesses of the other player, etc.). The planning system is then able to infer what I must do: hit the ball deep into my opponent's backhand. This command is issued to the motor system. My arms and legs move as required.

In its most familiar and successful applications, the computational approach makes a series of further assumptions. Representations are static structures of discrete symbols. Cognitive operations are transformations from one static symbol structure to the next. These transformations are discrete, effectively instantaneous, and sequential. The mental computer is broken down into a number of modules responsible for different symbol-processing tasks. A module takes symbolic representations as inputs and computes symbolic representations as outputs. At the periphery of the system are input and output transducers: systems which transform sensory stimulation into input representations, and output representations into physical movements. The whole system, and each of its modules, operates cyclically: input, internal manipulation, output.

The computational approach provides a very powerful framework for developing theories and models of cognitive processes. The classic work of pioneers such as Newell, Simon, and Minsky was carried out within it. Literally thousands of models conforming to the above picture have been produced. Any given model may diverge from it in one respect or another, but they retain most of its deepest assumptions. The computational approach is nothing less than a research paradigm in Kuhn's sense. It defines a range of questions and the form of answers to those questions (i.e., computational models). It provides an array of exemplars – classic pieces of research which define how cognition is to be thought about and what counts as a successful model. Philosophical tomes have been devoted to its articulation and defense. Unfortunately, it has a major problem.

Natural cognitive systems, such as people, aren't computers.

This need not be very surprising. The history of science is full of episodes in which good theories were developed within bad frameworks. The Ptolemaic Earth-centered conception of the solar system spawned a succession of increasingly sophisticated theories of planetary motion, theories with remarkably good descriptive and predictive capabilities. Yet we now know that the whole framework was structurally misconceived, and that any theory developed within it would always contain anomalies and reach explanatory impasses. Mainstream cognitive science is in a similar situation. Many impressive models of cognitive processes have been developed within the computational framework, yet none of these models is wholly successful even in its own terms,and they completely sidestep numerous critical issues. Just as in the long run astronomy could only make progress by displacing the Earth from the center of the universe, so cognitive science has to displace the inner computer from the center of cognitive performance.

The heart of the problem is *time. Cognitive processes and their context unfold continuously and simultaneously in real time.* Computational models specify a discrete sequence of static internal states in arbitrary "step" time (t_1, t_2, etc.). Imposing the latter onto the former is like wearing shoes on your hands. You can do it, but gloves fit a whole lot better.

This deep problem manifests itself in a host of difficulties confronting particular computational models throughout cognitive science. For just one example, consider how you come to a difficult decision. You have a range of options, and consider first one, then another. There is hesitation, vacillation, anxiety. Eventually you might come to prefer one choice, but the attraction of the others remains. Now, how are decision-making processes conceptualized in the computational worldview? The system begins with symbolic representations of a range of choices and their possible outcomes, with associated likelihoods and values. In a sequence of symbol manipulations, the system calculates the overall expected value for each choice, and determines the choice with the highest expected value. The system adopts that choice. End of decision. There are many variations on this basic "expected utility" structure. Different models propose different rules for calculating the choice the system adopts. But none of these models accounts perfectly for all the data on the choices that humans actually make. Like Ptolemaic theories of the planets, they become increasingly complex in attempting to account for residual anomalies, but for every anomaly dealt with another crops up elsewhere. Further, they say nothing at all about the temporal course of deliberation: how long it takes to reach a decision, how the decision one reaches depends on deliberation time, how a choice can appear more attractive at one time, less attractive at another, etc. They are intrinsically incapable of such predictions, because *they leave time out of the picture*, replacing it only with ersatz "time": a bare, abstract sequence of symbolic states.

What is the alternative to the computational approach? In recent years, many people have touted PDP [parallel distributed processing]-style *connectionism* – the modeling of cognitive processes using networks of neural units – as a candidate. But such proposals generally underestimate the depth and pervasiveness of computationalist assumptions. Much standard connectionist work (e.g., modeling with layered backprop networks) is just a variation on computationalism, substituting activation patterns for symbols. This kind of connectionism took some steps in right directions, but mostly failed to take the needed leap *out* of the computational mindset and *into* time.

The alternative must be an approach to the study of cognition which *begins* from the assumption that cognitive processes happen in time. *Real* time. Conveniently, there already is a mathematical framework for describing how processes in natural systems unfold in real time. It is *dynamics*. It just happens to be the single most widely used, most powerful, most successful, most thoroughly developed and understood descriptive framework in all of natural science. It is used to explain and predict the behavior of everything from subatomic particles to solar systems, neurons to 747s, fluid flow to ecosystems. Why not use it to describe cognitive processes as well?

The alternative, then, is the *dynamical* approach. Its core is the application of the mathematical tools of dynamics to the study of cognition. Dynamics provides for the dynamical approach what computer science provides for the computational approach: a vast resource of powerful concepts and modeling tools. But the dynamical approach is more than just powerful tools; like the computational approach, it is a worldview. The cognitive system is not a computer, it is a dynamical system. It is not the brain, inner and encapsulated; rather, it is the whole system comprised of nervous system, body, and environment. The cognitive system is not a discrete sequential manipulator of static representational structures; rather, it is a structure of mutually and simultaneously influencing *change*. Its processes do not take place in the arbitrary, discrete time of computer steps; rather, they take place in the *real* time of ongoing change in the environment, the body, and the nervous system. The cognitive system does not interact with other aspects of the world by passing messages or commands; rather, it continuously co-evolves with them.

The dynamical approach is not a new idea: dynamical theories have been a continuous undercurrent of cognitive science since the field began. It is not just a vision of the way things *might* be done; it's the way large amounts of groundbreaking research *has already* been carried out, and the amount of dynamical research undertaken grows every month. A great deal of the more recent work carried out under the connectionist banner is thoroughly dynamical; the same is true of such diverse areas as neural modeling, cognitive neuroscience, situated robotics, motor control, and ecological psychology. Dynamical models are increasingly prominent in cognitive psychology, developmental psychology, and even some areas of linguistics. In short, the dynamical approach is not just some new kid on the block; rather, to see that there is a dynamical approach is to see a new way of conceptually reorganizing cognitive science as it is currently practiced.

Here we provide a general overview of the dynamical approach: its essential commitments, its strengths, its relationship to other approaches, its history. We attempt to present the dynamical approach as a unified, coherent, plausible research paradigm. It should be noted, however, that dynamicists are a highly diverse group, and no single characterization would describe all dynamicists perfectly. Consequently, our strategy is to characterize a kind of *standard* dynamicist position, one which can serve as a useful point of reference in understanding dynamical research.[1]

Before proceeding we wish to stress that the primary concern of the dynamical approach is understanding *natural* cognitive systems – evolved biological systems such as humans and other animals. While the dynamical approach is generally critical of computational approaches to the study of natural cognition, it has no objection to investigations into the nature of computation itself, and into the potential abilities of computational systems such as take place in many branches of artificial intelligence (AI). While it is presumably *unlikely* that it will be possible to reproduce the kinds of intelligent capacity that are exhibited by natural cognitive systems without also reproducing their basic non–computational architecture, the dynamical approach need take no stand on whether it is possible to program computers to exhibit these, or other, intelligent capacities.

2   What Is the Dynamical Approach?

The heart of the dynamical approach can be succinctly expressed in the form of a very broad empirical hypothesis about the nature of cognition. For decades, the philosophy of cognitive science has been dominated by the *computational* hypothesis that cognitive systems are a special kind of computer. This hypothesis has been articulated in a number of ways, but perhaps the most famous statement is Newell and Simon's *Physical Symbol System Hypothesis*, the claim that physical symbol systems (computers) are necessary and sufficient for intelligent behavior (Newell and Simon, 1976). According to this hypothesis, natural cognitive systems are intelligent by virtue of being physical symbol systems of the right kind. At this same level of generality, dynamicists can be seen as embracing the *Dynamical Hypothesis*:

> *Natural cognitive systems are dynamical systems, and are best understood from the perspective of dynamics.*

Like its computational counterpart, the Dynamical Hypothesis forms a general framework within which detailed theories of particular aspects of cognition can be constructed. It can be empirically vindicated or refuted, but not by direct tests. We will only know if the Dynamical Hypothesis is true if, in the long run, the best theories of cognitive processes are expressed in dynamical terms.

The following sections explore the various components of the Dynamical Hypothesis in more detail.

2.1   *Natural cognitive systems are dynamical systems*

2.1.1   What are dynamical systems?   This notion occurs in a wide range of mathematical and scientific contexts, and as a result the term has come to be used in many different ways. In this section our aim is simply to characterize dynamical systems in the way that is most useful for understanding the dynamical approach to cognition.

Roughly speaking, we take dynamical systems to be systems with numerical states which evolve over time according to some rule. Clarity is critical at this stage, however, so this characterization needs elaboration and refinement.

To begin with, a *system* is a set of changing aspects of the world. The overall *state* of the system at a given time is just the way these aspects happen to be at that time. The *behavior* of the system is the change over time in its overall state. The totality of overall states the system might be in comprises its *state set*, commonly referred to as its *state space*. Thus the behavior of the system can be thought of as a sequence of points in its state space.

Not just any set of aspects of the world constitutes a system. A system is distinguished by the fact that its aspects somehow belong together. This really has two sides. First, the aspects must interact with each other; the way any one of them changes must depend on the way the others are. Second, if there is some *further* aspect of the world which interacts in this sense with anything in the set, then clearly it too is really part of the same system. In short, for a set of aspects to comprise a system, they must be interactive and self-contained: change in any aspect must depend on, and only on, other aspects in the set.

For example, the solar system differs from, say, the set containing just the color of my car and the position of my pencil, in that the position of any one planet makes a difference to where the other planets will be. Moreover, to a first approximation at least, the future positions of the planets are affected *only* by the positions, masses, etc., of the sun and other planets; there's nothing else we need take into account. By contrast, the position of my pencil is affected by a variety of other factors; in fact, it is unlikely that there is *any* identifiable system to which the position of my pencil (in all the vicissitudes of its everyday use) belongs.

Dynamical systems are special kinds of system. To see *what* kind, we first need another notion, that of *state-determined* systems (Ashby, 1952). A system is state-determined just in case its current state always determines a unique future behavior. Three features of such systems are worth noting. First, in such systems, the future behavior cannot depend in any way on whatever states the system might have been in *before* the current state. In other words, past history is irrelevant (or at least, past history only makes a difference insofar as it has left an effect on the current state). Second, the fact that the current state determines future behavior implies the existence of some *rule of evolution* describing the behavior of the system as a function of its current state. For systems we wish to understand, we always hope that this rule can be specified in some reasonably succinct and useful fashion. One source of constant inspiration, of course, has been Newton's formulation of the laws governing the solar system. Third, the fact that future behaviors are uniquely determined means that state space sequences can never fork. Thus, if we observe some system that proceeds in different ways at different times from the same state, we know we do not have a state-determined system.

The core notion of a state-determined system, then, is that of a self-contained, interactive set of aspects of the world such that the future states of the system are always uniquely determined, according to some rule, by the current state. Before proceeding, we should note an important extension of this idea, for cases in which changing factors external to the system do in fact affect how the system behaves. Suppose we have a set S of aspects $\{s_1, \ldots s\}$ whose change depends on some further aspect s_n of the world, but change in s_n does not in turn depend on the state of S, but on other things entirely. Then, strictly speaking, neither S nor $S + s_n$ form systems, since neither set is self-contained. Yet we can *treat* S as a state-determined system by thinking of the influence of s_n as built into its rule of evolution. Then the current state of the system *in conjunction with the rule* can be thought of as uniquely determining future behaviors, while the rule changes as a function of time. For example, suppose scientists discovered that the force of gravity has actually been fluctuating over time, though not in a way that depends on the positions and motions of the sun and planets. Then the solar system still forms a state-determined system, but one in which the rules of planetary motion must build in a gravitational constant which is changing over time. Technically, factors which affect, but are not in turn affected by, the evolution of a system are known as *parameters*. If a parameter changes over time, its changing effect can be taken into account in the rule of evolution, but then the rule itself is a function of time and the system is known as *non-homogeneous*.

Now, according to some (e.g., Giunti, 1995), *dynamical systems* are really just *state-determined systems*. This identification is certainly valuable for some purposes. In fact, it is really this very inclusive category of systems (or at least, its abstract mathematical counterpart) that is studied by that branch of mathematics known as *dynamical systems theory*. Nevertheless, if our aim is to characterize the dynamical approach to cognition – and in particular, to contrast it with the computational approach – it turns out that a narrower definition is more useful. This narrower definition focuses on specifically *numerical* systems.

The word "dynamical" is derived from the Greek *dynamikos*, meaning "forceful" or "powerful." A system that is dynamical in this sense is one in which changes are a function of the *forces* operating within it. Whenever forces apply, we have accelerations or decelerations; i.e., there is change in the *rate* at which the states are changing at any given moment. The standard mathematical tools for describing rates of change are *differential equations*. These can be thought of as specifying the way a system is changing at any moment as a function of its state at that moment.[2]

For example, the differential equation

$$\ddot{x} = -\frac{k}{m}x$$

describes the way (in ideal circumstances) a heavy object on the end of a spring will bounce back and forth by telling us the instantaneous acceleration ($\ddot{x}$) of the object as a function of its position (x); k and m are constants (parameters) for the spring tension and mass, respectively.

State-determined systems governed by differential equations are paradigm examples of dynamical systems in the current sense, but the latter category also includes other systems which are similar in important ways. Whenever a system can be described by differential equations, it has n aspects or features (position, mass, etc.) evolving simultaneously and continuously in real time. Each of these features at a given point in time can be *measured* as corresponding to some real number. Consequently we can think of the overall state of the system as corresponding to an ordered set of n real numbers, and the state space of the system as isomorphic to a space of real numbers whose n dimensions are magnitudes corresponding (via measurement) to the changing aspects of the system. Sometimes this numerical space is also known as the system's state space, but for clarity we will refer to it as the system's *phase space*[3] (figure 6.1). The evolution of the system over time corresponds to a sequence of points, or trajectory, in its phase space. These sequences can often be described mathematically as functions of an independent variable, time. These functions are *solutions* to the differential equations which describe the behavior of the system.

Now, phase space trajectories can be specified in a variety of ways. Differential equations constitute one particularly compact way of describing the shape of all possible trajectories in a given system. This kind of specification is useful for some purposes but not for others. A common alternative is to specify trajectories by means of a discrete mapping of any given point in the phase space onto another point. For example, perhaps the most-studied family of dynamical systems is the one whose rule is the "logistic equation" or "quadratic map" (Devaney, 1986)

$$F_m(x) = mx(1 - x)$$

For any particular value of the parameter m, this equation determines a particular mapping of every point x in the phase space onto another point $F_m(x)$. A mapping like this can be regarded as giving us the state of a system at a subsequent point in time ($t + 1$) if we know the state of the system at any given time (t).[4] When the rule is written so as to bring this out, it is known as a *difference equation*, taking the general form

$$x(t + 1) = F(x(t))$$

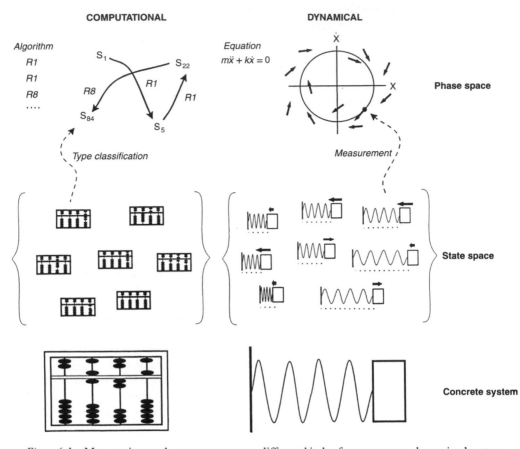

Figure 6.1 Mass–springs and computers are two different kinds of concrete state-determined system. (Our figure depicts an abacus; strictly speaking, the abacus would have to be automated to count as a computer.) Such systems are always in a particular state at a given point in time. This state is only one of many states that they *could* be in. The total set of possible states is commonly known as the system's *state space*. Corresponding to the state space is a set of abstract elements which is also commonly described as the system's state space, but which for clarity we refer to as the *phase space*. Possible states of the system are mapped onto elements of the phase space by some form of classification. In the computational case, tokens of symbols in the concrete system are classified into types, allowing the total state of the system to be classified as instantiating a particular configuration of symbol types. In the dynamical case, aspects of the system are measured (i.e., some yardstick is used to assign a number to each aspect), thereby allowing an ordered set of numbers to be assigned to the total state. Sequences of elements in the phase space can be specified by means of rules such as algorithms (in the computational case) and differential equations (in the dynamical case). A phase space and a rule are key elements of abstract state-determined systems. A concrete system realizes an abstract system when its states can be systematically classified such that the sequences of actual states it passes through mirror the phase space sequences determined by the rule. Typically, when cognitive scientists provide a model of some aspect of cognition, they provide an abstract state-determined system, such that the cognitive system is supposed to realize that abstract system or one relevantly like it

If we take any given point in the phase space and apply ("iterate") the mapping many times, we obtain a phase space trajectory.

Mathematicians and scientists often describe dynamical systems by means of discrete mappings rather than differential equations. In many cases these mappings are closely related to particular differential equations describing essentially the same behavior. This is not always the case, however. Consequently, a more liberal definition of *dynamical system* is: any state-determined system with a numerical phase space and a rule of evolution (including differential equations and discrete maps) specifying trajectories in this space.

These systems, while only a subset of state-determined systems in general, are the locus of dynamical research in cognitive science. They find their most relevant contrast with *computational* systems. These systems have states which are configurations of symbols, and their rules of evolution specify transformations of one configuration of symbols into another.[5] Whereas the phase space of a dynamical system is a *numerical* space, the phase space of a computational system is a space of configurations of *symbol types*, and trajectories are sequences of such configurations.

Why is it that dynamical systems (in our sense) are the ones chosen for study by dynamicists in cognitive science? Here we briefly return to the traditional idea that dynamics is a matter of forces, and therefore essentially involves rates of change. In order to talk about rates of change, we must be able to talk about *amounts* of change in *amounts* of time. Consequently, the phase space must be such as to allow us to say *how far* the state is changing, and the *time* in which states change must involve real *durations*, as opposed to a mere linear ordering of temporal points.

Now, these notions make real sense in the context of dynamical systems as defined here. Numerical phase spaces can have a metric which determines distances between points. Further, if the phase space is rich enough (e.g., dense) then between any two points in the phase space we can find other points, and so we can talk of the state of the system at any time between any two other times. Thus the notion of time in which the system operates is also one to which a substantial notion of "length" can be applied; in other words, it comes to possess some of the same key mathematical properties as *real* time. Note that neither of these properties is true of computational systems such as Turing Machines;[6] in them, there is no natural notion of distance between any two total states of the system, and "time" (t_1, t_2, etc.) is nothing more than order. Consequently it is impossible to talk of how fast the state of the system is changing, and as a matter of fact, nobody ever tries; the issue is in a deep way irrelevant.

The importance of being able to talk about rates of change is that all actual processes in the real world (including cognitive processes) do in fact unfold at certain rates in real time. Further, for many such systems (including cognitive systems) *timing* is essential: they wouldn't be able to function properly unless they got the fine details of the timing right. Therefore, in order to provide adequate scientific descriptions of the behavior of such systems, we need to understand them as systems in which the notion of rates of change makes sense (see section 3.1). Dynamicists in cognitive science propose dynamical models in the current sense because they are such systems. It may well be that there are other, less well-known mathematical frameworks within which one could model change in real time without using specifically numerical systems. As things stand, however, dynamical systems in cognitive science are in fact state-determined numerical systems.

A wide variety of fascinating questions can be raised about the relations between dynamical and computational systems. For example, what is the relationship between an ordinary digital computer and the underlying electrical dynamical system which in some sense makes it up? Or, what is the relation between a dynamical system and a computational simulation or emulation of it? Even more abstractly, how "powerful" is the class of dynamical systems, in comparison with computational systems? However, we must be very careful not to allow the fact that *there are* many such relationships, some of them quite intimate, to blind us to an important philosophical, and ultimately practical, truth: dynamical and computational systems are fundamentally different *kinds* of system, and hence the dynamical and computational approaches to cognition are fundamentally different in their deepest foundations.

2.1.2   Natural cognitive systems as dynamical systems   Describing natural phenomena as the behavior of some dynamical system lies at the very heart of modern science. The first truly dynamical theory – of the motions of the planets under the force of gravitational attraction – was developed by Newton in the seventeenth century. Ever since, scientists have been discovering more and more aspects of the natural world which constitute dynamical systems of one kind or another. Dynamicists in cognitive science are claiming that yet another naturally occurring phenomenon, namely *cognition*, is the behavior of an appropriate kind of dynamical system. They are thus making exactly the same kind of claim for cognitive systems as scientists have been making for so many other aspects of the natural world. In the Dynamical Hypothesis, this is expressed as the idea that natural cognitive systems *are* dynamical systems.

Demonstrating that some aspect of the world constitutes a dynamical system requires picking out a relevant set of magnitudes, and ways of measuring them, such that the resulting phase space trajectories conform to some specifiable rule. These trajectories must correspond to the behaviors of theoretical interest. So, if we are interested in *cognitive* systems, then the behaviors of interest are their *cognitive performances* (perceiving, remembering, conversing, etc.), and it is *these* behaviors, at their characteristic time scales, that must unfold in a way described by the rule of evolution. Consequently, the claim that cognitive systems are dynamical systems is certainly not trivial. Not everything is a dynamical system, and taking some novel phenomenon and showing that it *is* the behavior of a dynamical system is always a significant scientific achievement. If the Dynamical Hypothesis is in fact true, we will only know this as a result of much patient scientific work.[7]

Natural cognitive systems are enormously subtle and complex entities in constant interaction with their environments. It is the central conjecture of the Dynamical Hypothesis that these systems constitute single, unified dynamical systems. This conjecture provides a general theoretical orientation for dynamicists in cognitive science, but it has not been (and in fact may never be) demonstrated in detail, for nobody has specified the relevant magnitudes, phase space, and rules of evolution for the entire system. Like scientists confronting the physical universe as a whole, dynamicists in cognitive science strive to isolate particular aspects of the complex, interactive totality which are relatively self-contained and can be described mathematically. Thus, in practice, the Dynamical Hypothesis reduces to a series of more specific assertions, to the effect that particular aspects of cognition are the behavior of distinct, more localized systems. For example, Turvey and Carello (1995) focus on our ability to perceive the shape of an object such as a hammer simply by wielding it. They show how to think of the wielding itself as a dynamic system, and of perception of shape as attunement to key parameters of this system. The Dynamical Hypothesis that entire cognitive systems constitute dynamical systems is thus comparable to the Laplacean hypothesis that the entire physical world is a single dynamical system.

Many cognitive processes are thought to be distinguished from other kinds of process in the natural world by the fact that they appear to depend crucially on *knowledge* which must somehow be stored and utilized. At the heart of the computational approach is the idea that this knowledge must be *represented*, and that cognitive processes must therefore be operations on these representations.Further, the most powerful known medium of representation is symbolic, and hence cognitive processes must manipulate symbols, i.e., must be computational in nature.

In view of this rather compelling line of thought, it is natural to ask: how can dynamicists, whose models do *not* centrally invoke the notion of representation, hope to provide theories of paradigmatically *cognitive* processes? If cognition depends on *knowledge*, how can there be a dynamical approach to *cognition*? The answer is that, while dynamical models are not *based* on transformations of representational structures, they allow plenty of room for representation. A wide variety of aspects of dynamical models can be regarded as having a representational status: These include states, attractors, trajectories, bifurcations, and parameter settings. So dynamical systems can store knowledge and have this stored knowledge influence their behavior. The crucial difference between computational models and dynamical models is that in the former, the rules that govern how the system behaves are defined over the entities that have representational status, whereas in dynamical models, the rules are defined over numerical states.[8] That is, dynamical systems can be representational without having their rules of evolution defined over representations. For example, in simple connectionist associative memories such as that described in Hopfield (1982), representations of stored items are point attractors in the phase space of the system. Recalling or recognizing an item is a matter of settling into its attractor, a process which is governed by purely numerical dynamical rules.

2.1.3 The nature of cognitive systems The claim that cognitive systems are computers, and the competing claim that natural cognitive systems are dynamical systems, each forms the technical core of a highly distinctive vision of the nature of cognitive systems.

For the computationalist, the cognitive system is the brain, which is a kind of control unit located inside a body which in turn is located in an external environment. The cognitive system interacts with the outside world via its more direct interaction with the body. Interaction with the environment is handled by sensory and motor *transducers*, whose function is to translate between the *physical* events in the body and the environment, on one hand, and the *symbolic* states which are the medium of cognitive processing. Thus the sense organs convert physical stimulation into elementary symbolic representations of events in the body and in the environment; and the motor system converts symbolic representations of actions into movements of the muscles. Cognitive episodes take place in a cyclic and sequential fashion; *first* there is sensory input to the cognitive system, *then* the cognitive system algorithmically manipulates symbols, coming up with an output which *then* causes movement of the body; the whole cycle then begins again. Internally, the cognitive system has a modular, hierarchical construction; at the highest level, there are modules corresponding to vision, language, planning, etc., and each of these modules breaks down into simpler modules for more elementary tasks. Each module replicates in basic structure the cognitive system as a whole; thus, they take symbolic representations as inputs, algorithmically manipulate those representations, and deliver a symbolic specification as output. Note that because the cognitive system traffics only in symbolic representations, the body and the physical environment can be dropped from consideration; it is possible to study the cognitive system as an autonomous, bodiless, and worldless system whose function is to transform input representations into output representations.

Now, the dynamical vision differs from this picture at almost every point. As we have seen, dynamical systems are complexes of parts or aspects which are all evolving in a simultaneous and mutually determining fashion. If cognitive systems are dynamical systems, then they must likewise be complexes of interacting change. Since the nervous system, body and environment are all continuously evolving and simultaneously influencing each other, the cognitive system cannot be simply the encapsulated brain; rather, it is a single unified system embracing all three. The cognitive system does not interact with the body and the external world by means of periodic symbolic inputs and outputs;rather, inner and outer processes are *coupled*, so that both sets of processes are continually influencing each other. Cognitive processing is not cyclic and sequential, for all aspects of the cognitive system are undergoing change all the time. There is a *sense* in which the system is modular, since for theoretical purposes the total system can be broken down into smaller dynamical subsystems responsible for distinct cognitive phenomena. Standardly these smaller systems are coupled, and hence co-evolving, with others, but significant insight can be obtained by "freezing" this interaction and studying their independent dynamics. Of course, cognitive performances do exhibit many kinds of sequential character. Speaking a sentence, for example, is behavior that has a highly distinctive sequential structure. However, in the dynamical conception, any such sequential character is something that emerges over time as the overall trajectory of change in an entire system (or relevant subsystem) whose rules of evolution specify not sequential change but rather simultaneous, mutual co-evolution.

2.2   Natural cognitive systems are best understood using dynamics

In science, as in home repair, the most rapid progress is made when you have the right tools for the job. Science is in the business of describing and explaining the natural world, and has a very wide range of conceptual and methodological tools at its disposal. Computer science provides one very powerful collection of tools, and these are optimally suited for under-standing complex systems of a particular kind, namely *computational* systems. If *cognitive* systems are computational systems, then they will be best understood by bringing these tools to bear. If the Dynamical Hypothesis is right, however, then the most suitable conceptual tools will be those of *dynamics*. So, whereas in the previous sections we described *what it is* for natural cognitive systems to *be* dynamical systems, in the following sections we describe what is involved in applying dynamics in *understanding* such systems.

2.2.1   What is dynamics?   Dynamics is a very broad field overlapping both pure and applied mathematics. For current purposes, it can be broken down into two broad subdivisions. *Dynamical modeling* is describing natural phenomena *as* the behavior of a dynamical system in the sense outlined in the previous section. It involves finding a way of isolating the relevant system, a way of measuring the states of the system, and a mathematical rule, such that the phenomena of interest unfold in exactly the way described by the rule. Obviously, effective dynamical modeling involves considerable exploration of both the real system being studied, and the mathematical properties of the governing equations.

Dynamical systems theory is the general study of dynamical systems. As a branch of pure mathematics, it is not directly concerned with the empirical description of natural phenomena, but rather with abstract mathematical structures. Dynamical systems theory is particularly concerned with complex systems for which the *solutions* of the defining equations (i.e., functions which specify trajectories as a function of time) are difficult or impossible to write down. It offers a wide variety of powerful concepts and tools for describing the general properties of such systems. Perhaps the most distinctive feature of dynamical systems theory is that it provides a *geometric* form of understanding: behaviors are thought of in terms of locations, paths, and landscapes in the phase space of the system.[9]

Some natural phenomena can be described as the evolution of a dynamical system governed by particularly straightforward equations. For such systems, the traditional techniques of dynamical modeling are sufficient for most explanatory purposes. Other phenomena, however, can only be described as the behavior of systems governed by nonlinear equations for which solutions may be unavailable. Dynamical systems theory is essential for the study of such systems. With the rapid development in the twentieth century of the mathematics of dynamical systems theory, an enormous range of natural systems have been opened up to scientific description. There is no sharp division between dynamical modeling and dynamical systems theory, and gaining a full understanding of most natural systems requires relying on both bodies of knowledge.

2.2.2   *Understanding cognitive phenomena dynamically*

Dynamics is a large and diverse set of concepts and methods, and consequently there are many different ways that cognitive phenomena can be understood dynamically. Yet they all occupy a broadly dynamical perspective, with certain key elements.

At the heart of the dynamical perspective is *time*. Dynamicists always focus on the details of how behavior unfolds in real time; their aim is to describe and explain the temporal course of this behavior. The beginning point and the end point of cognitive processing are usually of only secondary interest, if indeed they matter at all. This is in stark contrast with the computationalist orientation, in which the primary focus is on input/output relations – i.e., on what output the system delivers for any given input.

A second key element of the dynamical perspective is an emphasis on *total state*. Dynamicists assume that all aspects of a system are changing simultaneously, and so think about the behavior of the system as a matter of how the total state of a system is changing from one time to the next. Computationalists, by contrast, tend to suppose that most aspects of a system (e.g., the symbols stored in memory) do *not* change from one moment to the next. Change is assumed to be a local affair, a matter of replacement of one symbol by another.

Because dynamicists focus on how a system changes from one total state to another, it is natural for them to think of that change as a matter of movements in the *space* of all possible total states of the system; and since the phase spaces of their systems are numerical, natural notions of *distance* apply. Thus, dynamicists conceptualize cognitive processes in *geometric* terms. The distinctive character of some cognitive process as it unfolds over time is a matter of how the total states the system passes through are spatially located with respect to each other and the dynamical landscape of the system.

2.2.3   *Quantitative modeling*

Precise, quantitative modeling of some aspect of cognitive performance is always the ultimate goal of dynamical theorizing in cognitive science. Such research always requires two basic components: data and model. The data takes the form of a time series: a series of measurements of the phenomenon to be understood, taken as that phenomenon unfolds over time. The model is a set of equations and associated phase space. The modeling process is a matter of distilling out the phenomenon to be understood, obtaining the time-series data, developing a model, and *interpreting* that model as capturing the data (i.e., setting up correspondences between the numerical sequences contained in the model those in the data). When carried out successfully, the modeling process yields not only precise *descriptions* of the existing data, but also *predictions* which can be used in evaluating the model.

For an excellent example of quantitative dynamical modeling, recall the process of reaching a decision described briefly in section 1. We saw that traditional computational (expected-utility theory) approaches to decision making have had some measure of success in accounting for what decisions are actually reached, but say nothing at all about any of the temporal aspects of the deliberation process. For Busemeyer and Townsend, by contrast, describing these temporal aspects is a central goal (Busemeyer and Townsend, 1993, 1995). Their model of decision making is a dynamical system with variables corresponding to quantities such as values of consequences and choice preferences. The model describes the multiple simultaneous *changes* that go on in an individual decision maker in the process of coming to a decision. It turns out that this model not only recapitulates the known data on *outcomes* as well as or better than traditional computational models; it also explains a range of temporal phenomena such as the dependence of preference on deliberation time, and makes precise predictions which can be experimentally tested.

2.2.4 Qualitative modeling Human cognitive performance is extraordinarily diverse, subtle, complex, and interactive. Every human behaves in a somewhat different way, and is embedded in a rich, constantly changing environment. For these kinds of reason (among others), science has been slow in coming to be able to apply to cognition the kinds of explanatory technique that have worked so successfully elsewhere. Even now, only a relatively small number of cognitive phenomena have been demonstrated to be amenable to precise, quantitative dynamical modeling. Fortunately, however, there are other ways in which dynamics can be used to shed light on cognitive phenomena. Both the data time series and the mathematical model that dynamical modeling requires can be very difficult to obtain. Even without an elaborate data time series, one can study a mathematical model which exhibits behavior that is at least *qualitatively* similar to the phenomena being studied. Alternatively, in the absence of a precise mathematical model, the language of dynamics can be used to develop qualitative dynamical descriptions of phenomena that may have been recorded in a precise data time series (section 2.2.5).

Cognitive scientists can often develop a sophisticated understanding of an area of cognitive functioning independently of having any elaborate data time series in hand. The problem is then to understand what kind of system might be capable of exhibiting that kind of cognitive performance. It can be addressed by specifying a mathematical dynamical model and comparing its behavior with the known empirical facts. If the dynamical model and the observed phenomena agree sufficiently in broad qualitative outline, then insight into the nature of the system has been gained.

Elman's investigations into language processing are a good example of qualitative dynamical modeling (Elman, 1991, 1995). In broad outline, at least, the distinctive complexity of sentences of natural language is well understood, and psycholinguistics has uncovered a wide range of information on human abilities to process sentences. For example, it is a widely known fact that most people have trouble processing sentences that have three or more subsidiary clauses embedded centrally within them. In an attempt to understand the internal mechanisms responsible for language use, Elman investigates the properties of a particular class of connectionist dynamical systems. When analyzed using dynamical concepts, these models turn out to be in broad agreement with a variety of general constraints in the data, such as the center-embedding limitation. This kind of agreement demonstrates that it is possible to think of aspects of our linguistic subsystems in dynamical terms, and to find there a basis for some of the regularities. This model does not make precise temporal predictions about the changing values of observable variables, but it does make testable *qualitative* predictions about human performance.

Often, the system one wishes to understand can be observed to exhibit any of a variety of highly distinctive *dynamical* properties: asymptotic approach to a fixed point, the presence or disappearance of maxima or minima, catastrophic jumps caused by small changes in control variables, oscillations, chaotic behavior, hysteresis, resistance to perturbation, and so on. Such properties can be observed even without knowing the specific equations which in fact govern the evolution of the system. They are, however, a particularly rich source of constraints for the process of qualitative dynamical modeling, for they narrow down considerably the classes of equations that can exhibit qualitatively similar behavior.

2.2.5 Dynamical description In another kind of situation, we may or may not have good time-series data available for modeling, but the complexity of the phenomena is such that laying down the equations of a formal model adequate to the data is currently not feasible. However, even here dynamics may hold the key to advances in understanding, because it provides a general conceptual apparatus for understanding the way systems – including in particular completely nonlinear systems – change over time. In this kind of scenario it is general *dynamical systems theory* which turns out to be particularly useful.

For example, Esther Thelen is concerned with understanding the development, over periods of months and even years, of basic motor skills such as reaching out for an object (Thelen, 1995). At this stage, no satisfactory mathematical model of this developmental process is available. Indeed, it is still a major problem to write down suitable equations describing just the basic movements themselves! Nevertheless, adopting a dynamical perspective can make possible descriptions which cumulatively amount to a whole new way of understanding how motor skills can emerge and change, and how the long-term developmental process is interdependent with the actual exercise of the developing skills themselves. From this perspective, particular actions are conceptualized as attractors in a space of possible bodily movements, and development of bodily skills is the emergence, and change in nature, of these attractors over time under the influence of factors such as bodily growth and practice of the action itself. Adopting this general perspective entails significant changes in research methods. For example, Thelen pays close attention to the exact shape of individual gestures at particular intervals in the development process, and focuses on the specific changes that occur in each individual subject rather than the gross changes that are inferred by averaging over many subjects. It is only in the fine detail of an individual subject's movements and their change over time that real shape of the dynamics of development is revealed.

3 Why Dynamics?

Why should we believe the Dynamical Hypothesis? Ultimately, as stressed already, the proof of the pudding will be in the eating. The Dynamical Hypothesis is correct only if sustained empirical investigation shows that the most powerful models of cognitive processes take dynamical form. Although there are already dynamical models – which are currently the best available in their particular area, the jury is still out on the general issue.[10] Even if the day of final reckoning is a long way off, however, we can still ask whether the dynamical approach is *likely* to be correct, and if so, why.

The dynamical approach certainly begins with a huge head-start. Dynamics provides a vast resource of extremely powerful concepts and tools. Their usefulness in offering the best scientific explanations of phenomena throughout the natural world has been proven again and again. It would hardly be a surprise if dynamics turned out to be the framework within which the most powerful descriptions of cognitive processes were also forthcoming. The conceptual resources of the computational approach, on the other hand, are known to describe only one category of things in the physical universe: manmade digital computers. Even this success is hardly remarkable: digital computers were designed and constructed by us in accordance with the computational blueprint. It is a bold and highly controversial speculation that these same resources might also be applicable to natural cognitive systems, which are evolved biological systems in constant causal interaction with a messy environment.

This argument for the dynamical approach is certainly attractive, but it is not grounded in any way in the specific nature of cognitive systems. What we really want to know is: what general things do we *already know* about the nature of *cognitive* systems that suggest that dynamics will be the framework within which the most powerful models are developed?

We know, at least, these very basic facts: that cognitive processes always unfold in real time; that their behaviors are pervaded by *both* continuities and discretenesses; that they are composed of multiple subsystems which are simultaneously active and interacting; that their distinctive kinds of structure and complexity are not present from the very first moment, but emerge over time; that cognitive processes operate over many time scales, and events at different time scales interact; and that they are embedded in a real body and environment. The dynamical approach provides a natural framework for the description and explanation of phenomena with these broad properties. The computational approach, by contrast, either ignores them entirely or handles them only in clumsy, ad hoc ways.[11]

3.1 Cognition and time

The argument of this section is simple. Cognitive processes always unfold in real time. Now, computational models specify only the *sequence* of states that a system passes through. Dynamical models, by contrast, specify in detail how processes unfold in real time *as well as* the sequence of states the system passes through. This enables dynamical models to explain a wider range of data for any cognitive functions, and to explain cognitive functions whose dependence on real time is essential (e.g., temporal pattern processing).

When we say that cognitive processes unfold in real time, we are really saying two distinct things. First, real time is a continuous quantity best measured by the real numbers, and for every point in time there is a state of the cognitive system. For an example of a process unfolding in real time, consider the movement of your arm as it swings beside you. At every one of an infinite number of instants in time from the beginning to the end of the motion, there is a position which your arm occupies. In other words, no matter how finely time is sampled, it makes sense to ask what position your arm occupies at every sampled point. Now, the same is true of cognitive processes. As you recognize a face, or reason through a problem, or throw a ball, various aspects of your total cognitive system are undergoing change in real time, and no matter how finely time is sampled, there is a state of the cognitive system at each point. This is really just an obvious and elementary consequence of the fact that cognitive processes are ultimately physical processes taking place in real biological hardware.

The second thing we mean by saying that cognitive processes unfold in real time is that – as a consequence of the first point – *timing* always matters. A host of questions about way the processes happen *in* time makes perfect sense; questions about rates, durations, periods, synchrony, and so forth. Because cognitive processes happen in time, they cannot take too little time or too much time. The system must spend an appropriate amount of time in the vicinity of any given state. The timing of any particular operation must respect the rate at which other cognitive, bodily, and environmental processes are taking place. There are numerous subtleties involved in correct timing, and they are all real issues when we consider real cognitive processing.

Since cognitive processes unfold in real time, any framework for the description of cognitive processes that hopes to be fully adequate to the nature of the phenomena must be able to describe not merely *what* processes occur but *how* those processes unfold in real time. Now, dynamical models based on differential equations are the pre-eminent mathematical framework science uses to describe how things happen in time. Such models specify how instantaneous change in state variables at any instant depends upon the current values of those variables themselves and other parameters. Solutions to the governing equations tell you the state that the system will be in at any point in time, as long as the starting state and the amount of elapsed time are known. The use of differential equations presupposes that the variables change smoothly and continuously, and that time itself is a real-valued quantity. It is, in short, of the *essence* of dynamical models of this kind to describe how processes unfold, moment by moment, in real time.

Computational models, by contrast, specify only a bare sequence of states that the cognitive system goes through, and tell us nothing about the timing of those states over and above their mere order. Consider, for example, that paradigm of computational systems, the Turing Machine. Every Turing Machine passes through a series of discrete symbolic states, one after another. We do talk about the state of the machine at time 1, time 2, and so forth. However, these "times" are not points in real time; they are merely indexes which help us keep track of the order that states fall in as the machine carries out its sequence of computational steps. We use the integers to index states because they have a very familiar order and there are always as many of them as we need. However, we mustn't be misled into supposing that we are talking about *amounts* of time or *durations* here. Any other ordered set (e.g., people who ran the Boston Marathon, in the order they finished) would, in theory, do just as well for indexing the states of a Turing Machine, though in practice they would be very difficult to use. To see that the integer "times" in the Turing Machine are not real times, consider the following questions: What state was the machine in at time 1.5? At time 14.253? How long was the machine in state 1? How long did it take for the machine to change from state 1 to state 2? *None of these questions is appropriate*, though they would be if we were talking about real amounts of time.

Now, let us suppose we have a particular Turing Machine which adds numbers, and we propose this machine as a model of the cognitive processes going on in real people when they add numbers in their heads. The model specifies a sequence of symbol manipulations, passing from one discrete state to another; we suppose that a person passes through essentially the same sequence of discrete states. Note, however, that the Turing Machine model is inherently incapable of telling us anything at all about the *timing* of these states and the transitions from one state to another. The model just tells us "first this state then that state . . ."; it makes no stand on how long the person will be in the first state, how fast the transition to the second state is, and so forth; it cannot even tell us what state the person will be in half-way between the time it enters the first state and the time it enters the second state, for questions such as these make no sense in the model.

Of course, even as far as computational models go, Turing Machines do not make good models of cognitive processes. But the same basic points hold true for all standard computational models. LISP programs, production systems, generative grammars, etc., are all intrinsically incapable of describing the fine temporal structure of the way cognitive processes unfold, because all they specify – indeed, all they *can* spccify – is *which* states the system will go through, and in what order. To see this, just try picking up any mainstream computational model of a cognitive process – of parsing, or planning, for example – and try to find any place where the model makes any commitment at all about such elementary temporal issues as how much time each symbolic manipulation takes. One quickly discovers that computational models simply aren"t in that business; they're not dealing with time. "Time" in a computational model is not real time, it is mere order.

Computationalists do sometimes attempt to extract from their models implications for the timing of the target cognitive processes. The standard and most appropriate way to do this is to assume that each computational step takes a certain chunk of real time (say, 10 ms).[12] By adding assumptions of this kind we can begin to make some temporal predictions, such as that a particular computational process will take a certain amount of time, and that a particular step will take place some number of milliseconds after some other event. Yet the additional temporal assumptions are completely ad hoc; the theorist is free to choose the step time, for example, in any way that renders the model more consistent with the psychological data.[13] In our opinion, it is futile to attempt to weld temporal considerations onto an essentially atemporal kind of model. If one professes to be concerned with temporal issues, one may as well adopt a modeling framework which builds temporal issues in from the very beginning – i.e., take up the dynamical approach.

One refuge for the computationalist from these arguments is to insist that certain physical systems are such that they can be described at an abstract level where temporal issues can be safely ignored, and that the most tractable descriptions of these systems must in fact take place at that level. This claim is clearly true of ordinary desktop digital computers; we standardly describe their behavior in algorithmic terms in which the precise details of timing are completely irrelevant, and these algorithmic descriptions are the most tractable given our high-level theoretical purposes. The computationalist *conjecture* is that cognitive systems will be like computers in this regard; high-level cognitive processes can, and indeed can *only* be tractably described in computational terms which ignore fine-grained temporal issues. Notice, however, that this response concedes that computational models are inherently incapable of being fully adequate to the nature of the cognitive processes themselves, since these processes always do unfold in real time. Further, this response concedes that *if there were* a tractable dynamical model of some cognitive process, it would be inherently superior, since it describes aspects of the processes which are out of reach of the computational model. Finally, computationalists have not as yet done enough to convince us that the only tractable models of these high-level processes will be computational ones. Dynamicists, at least, are still working on the assumption that it *will* someday be possible to produce fully adequate models of cognitive processes.

Computationalists sometimes point out that dynamical models of cognitive processes are themselves typically "run" or simulated on digital computers. Does this not establish that computational models are not inherently limited in the way these arguments seem to suggest? Our answer, of course, is no, and the reason is simple: A computational simulation of a dynamical model of some cognitive process is not itself a model of that cognitive process in anything like the manner of standard computational models in cognitive science. Thus, the cognitive system is not being hypothesized to pass through a sequence of symbol structures of the kind that evolve in the computational simulation, any more than a weather pattern is thought to pass through a sequence of discrete symbolic states just because we can simulate a dynamical model of the weather. Rather, all the computational simulation delivers is a sequence of symbolic *descriptions* of points in the dynamical model (and thereby, indirectly, of states of the cognitive system). What we have in such situations is a dynamical model plus an atemporal computational approximation to it.[14]

3.2   Continuity in state

Natural cognitive systems sometimes change state in continuous ways; sometimes, on the other hand, they change state in ways that can appear discrete. Dynamics provides a framework within which continuity *and* discreteness can be accounted for, even within the same model. The computational approach, by contrast, can only model a system as changing state from one discrete state to another.Consequently, the dynamical approach is inherently more flexible – and hence more powerful – than the computational approach.

This argument must be carefully distinguished from the previous one. There, the focus was continuity in *time*; the claim was that models must be to able specify the state of the system at every point in time. Here, the focus is continuity in *state*; the claim is that models must be capable of describing change from one state to another arbitrarily close to it, *as well as* sudden change from one state to another discretely distinct from it.

Standard computational systems only ever change from one discrete state to another.[15] Think again of a Turing Machine. Its possible (total) states are configurations of symbols on the tape, the condition of the head, and the position of the head. Every state transition is a matter of adding or deleting a symbol, changing the head condition, and changing its position. The possibilities, however, are all discrete; the system always jumps directly from one state to another without passing through any in between. There simply *are no* states in between; they are just not defined for the system. The situation is like scoring points in basketball: the ball either goes through the hoop or it doesn't. In basketball, you can't have fractions of points.

When a computational system is used as a model for a natural cognitive process, the natural cognitive system is hypothesized to go through the same state transitions as the model. So a computational model can only ever attribute discrete states, and discrete state transitions, to the cognitive system.

Now, quite often, state transitions in natural cognitive systems can be thought of as discrete. For example, in trying to understand how people carry out long division in their heads, the internal processes can be thought of as passing through a number of discrete states corresponding to stages in carrying out the division. However, there are innumerable kinds of task that cognitive systems face which appear to demand a continuum of states in any system that can carry them out. For example, most real problems of sensorimotor coordination deal with a world in which objects and events can come in any shape, size, position, orientation, and motion. A system which can flexibly deal with such a world must be able to occupy states that are equally rich and subtly distinct. Similarly, everyday words as simple as *truck* seem to know no limit in the fineness of contextual shading they can take on. Any system that can understand *Billy drove the truck* must be able to accommodate this spectrum of senses. Only a system that can occupy a continuum of states with respect to word meanings stands a real chance of success.

Dynamical systems, in the core sense that we have adopted in this introduction, change in continuous phase spaces, and so the dynamical approach is inherently well suited to describing how cognitive systems might change in continuous ways. However – and this is the key point – it can also describe discrete transitions, in a number of ways. The dynamical approach is therefore more flexible – and hence, again, more powerful – than the computational approach, which can only attribute discrete states to a system.

The dynamical approach can accommodate discrete state transitions in two ways. First, the concepts and tools of dynamics can be used to describe the behavior of systems with only discrete states. A dynamical model of an ecosystem, for example, assumes that its populations always come in discrete amounts; you can have 10 or 11 rabbits, but not 10.5 rabbits. However, perhaps the most interesting respect in which dynamics can handle discreteness is in being able to describe how a continuous system can undergo changes that look discrete from a distance. This is more interesting because cognitive systems appear to be thoroughly pervaded by *both* continuity and discreteness; the ideal model would be one which could account for both together. One kind of discrete change in a continuous system is a *catastrophe*: a sudden, dramatic change in the state of a system when a small change in the parameters of the equations defining the system leads to a qualitative change – a bifurcation – in the "dynamics" or structure of forces operating in that system (Zeeman, 1977; Petitot, 1995).[16] Thus, high-level, apparently discrete changes of state can be accounted for within a dynamical framework in which continuity and discreteness coexist; indeed, the former is the precondition and explanation for the emergence of the latter.

3.3   *Multiple simultaneous interactions*

Consider again the process of returning a serve in tennis. The ball is approaching; you are perceiving its approach, are aware of the other player's movements, are considering the best strategy for the return, and are shifting into position to play the stroke. *All this is happening at the same time.* As you move into place, your perspective on the approaching ball is changing, and hence so is activity on your retina and in your visual system. It is your evolving sense of how to play the point which is affecting your movement. The path of the approach ball affects which strategy would be best and hence how you move. *Everything is simultaneously affecting everything else.*

Consider natural cognitive systems from another direction entirely. Neurons are complex systems with hundreds, perhaps thousands of synaptic connections. There is some kind of activity in every one of these, all the time. From all this activity, the cell body manages to put together a firing rate. Each cell forms part of a network of neurons, all of which are active (to a greater or lesser degree) all the time, and the activity in each is directly affecting hundreds, perhaps thousands of others, and indirectly affecting countless more. The networks form into maps, the maps into systems, and systems into the CNS [central nervous system]; but at every level we have the same principle, that there is constant activity in all components at once, and components are simultaneously affecting each other. No part of the nervous system ever is ever completely inactive. As neurophysiologist Karl Lashley put it, "Every bit of evidence available indicates a dynamic, constantly active system, or, rather, a composite of many interacting systems" (Lashley, 1960).

Clearly, any fully adequate approach to the study of cognitive systems must be one that can handle multiple, simultaneous, interactive activity. Yet doing this is the essence of dynamics. Dynamical systems *are* just the simultaneous, mutually influencing activity of multiple parts or aspects. The dynamical approach is therefore inherently well suited to describe cognitive systems.

A classic example of a dynamical model in this sense is McClelland and Rumelhart's "interactive activation network" (McClelland and Rumelhart, 1981). This model was designed to account for how a letter embedded in the context of a five-letter word of English could be recognized faster than the same letter embedded within a nonword string of letters and even better than the single letter presented all by itself. This "word superiority effect" suggested that somehow the whole word was being recognized at the same time as the individual letters that make up the word. Thus, it implied a mechanism where recognition of the word and the letters takes place simultaneously and in such a way that each process influences the other. Rumelhart and McClelland proposed separate cliques of nodes in their network that mutually influence each other by means of coupled difference equations. The output activation of some nodes served as an excitatory or inhibitory input to certain other nodes. This model turned out to capture the word superiority effect and a number of other related effects as well.

Almost all computational approaches attempt to superimpose on this multiple, simultaneous, interactive behavior a sequential, step-by-step structure. They thereby appear to assume that nothing of interest is going on in any component other than the one responsible for carrying out the next stage in the algorithm. It is true, as computationalists will point out, that a computational model can – in principle – run in parallel, though it is devilishly difficult to write such code. The "blackboard model" of the HEARSAY-II speech recognition system (Erman et al., 1980) represents one attempt at approaching parallelism by working within the constraints of serial computationalism. The "blackboard", however, was just a huge, static data structure on which various independent analysis modules might asynchronously post messages, thereby making partial analyses of each module available for other modules to interpret. This is a step in the right direction, but it is a far cry from simultaneous interactive activation. Each module in HEARSAY-II can do no more than say "Here is what I have found so far, as stated in terms of my own vocabulary," rather than "Here is exactly how your activity should change on the basis of what has happened in my part of the system – the kind of interaction that components governed by coupled equations have with each other. Other methods of parallelism more sophisticated than this may certainly be postulated in principle, but apparently await further technological developments. In the long run, the computational approach is doomed to failure since in cognitive systems activity of any component is constantly influencing and being influenced by the activity of many other components.

3.4   Multiple time scales

Cognitive processes always take place at many time scales. Changes in the state of neurons can take just a few milliseconds, visual or auditory recognition half a second or less, coordinated movement a few seconds, conversation and story understanding minutes or even hours, and the emergence of sophisticated capacities can take months and years. Further, these time scales are interrelated; processes at one time scale affect processes at another. For example, Esther Thelen (1995) has shown how actually engaging in coordinated movement promotes the development of coordination, and yet development itself shapes the movements that are possible; it is in this interactive process, moreover, that we find the emergence of concepts such as *space* and *force*. At finer scales, what we see (at the hundreds of milliseconds time scale) affects how we move (at the seconds scale) and vice versa.

The dynamical approach provides ways of handling this variety and interdependence of time scales. For example, the equations governing a dynamical system typically include two kinds of variable: state variables and parameters. The way the system changes state depends on both, but only the state variables take on new values; the parameters are standardly fixed. However, it is possible to think of the parameters as not fixed but rather changing as well, though over a considerably longer time scale than the state variables. Thus we can have a single system with both a "fast" dynamics of state variables on a short time scale and a "slow" dynamics of parameters on a long time scale, such that the slow dynamics helps shape the fast dynamics. It is even possible to link the equations such that the fast dynamics shapes the slow dynamics; in such a case, we have true interdependence of time scales.

Note that it is other features of the dynamical approach, such as continuity in space and time, and multiple simultaneous interactive aspects, which make possible its account of the interdependence of time scales. The computational approach, by contrast, has no natural methods of handling this pervasive structural feature of natural cognitive systems.

3.5   Self-organization and the emergence of structure

Cognitive systems are highly structured, in both their behavior and their internal spatial and temporal organization. One kind of challenge for cognitive science is to *describe* that structure. Another kind of challenge is to explain *how it got to be there*. Since the computational framework takes inspiration from the organization of formal systems like logic and mathematics, the traditional framework characteristically tackles only the problem of describing the structure that exists. Models in this framework typically postulate some initial set of a priori structures from which more complex structures may be derived by application of rules. The question of *emergence* – of where the initial elements or structures come from – always remains a problem, usually ignored.

A major advantage of the dynamical approach is that dynamical systems are known to be able to create structure both in space and in time. By structure, we mean something nonrandom in form that endures or recurs in time. Thus an archetypal physical object, such as a chair, is invariant in form over time, while a transient event, like a breaking wave on a beach, may recur with temporal regularity. The words in human languages tend to be constructed out of units of speech sound that are reused in different sequences (e.g., *gnat*, *tan*, *ant*, etc.), much like the printed letters with which we write words down. But where do *any* such structures come from if they are not either assumed or somehow fashioned from pre-existing primitive parts? This is the question of "morphogenesis," the creation of forms. It has counterparts in many branches of science, including cosmology. Why are matter and energy not uniformly distributed in the universe? Study of the physics of relatively homogeneous physical systems, like the ocean, the atmosphere, or a tank of fluid, can begin to provide answers. Some form of energy input is required plus some appropriate dynamical laws. Under these circumstances most systems will tend to generate regular structure of some sort under a broad range of conditions.

The atmosphere exhibits not only its all-too-familiar chaotic properties, but can also display many kinds of highly regular spatiotemporal structure that can be modeled by the use of differential equations. For example, over the Great Plains in the summer, one sometimes observes long "streets" of parallel clouds with smooth edges like the waves of sand found in shallow water along a beach or in the corduroy ridges on a well-traveled dirt road. How can these parallel ridges be created? Probably not with any form of rake or plow. These patterns all depend on some degree of homogeneity of medium and a consistently applied influx of energy. In other conditions (involving higher energy levels), a fluid medium may, in small regions, structure itself into a highly regular tornado or whirlpool. Although these "objects" are very simple structures, it is still astonishing that any medium so unstructured and so linear in its behavior could somehow constrain itself over vast distances in such a way that regular structures in space and time are produced. The ability of one part of a system to "enslave" other parts, that is, to restrict the degrees of freedom of other, distant parts, is now understood at least for fairly simple systems (Haken, 1988, 1991; Kelso et al., 1992; Thom, 1975).

The demonstration that structure can come into existence without either a specific plan or an independent builder raises the possibility that many structures in physical bodies as well as in cognition might occur without any externally imposed shaping forces. Perhaps cognitive structures, like embryological structures, the weather and many other examples, simply *organize themselves* (Kugler and Turvey, 1987; Thelen and Smith, 1993). Dynamical models are now known to account for many spatial and temporal structures in a very direct way (Madore and Freeman, 1987; Murray, 1989). They enable us to understand how such apparently unlikely structures could come to exist and retain their morphology for some extended period of time. We assume that cognition is a particular structure in space and time – one that supports intelligent interaction with the world. So our job is to discover how such a structure could turn out to be a stable state of the brain in the context of the body and environment. The answer to this question depends both on structure that comes from the genes and on structure that is imposed by the world. No theoretical distinction need be drawn between learning and evolution – they are both, by hypothesis, examples of adaptation toward stable, cognitively effective states of a brain (or an artificial system). The primary difference is that they operate on different time scales.

In both computer science and in cognitive science, the role of adaptation as a source of appropriate structure is under serious development (Forrest, 1991; Holland, 1975; Kauffman, 1993). Most of these methods depend on differential or difference equations for optimization. Thus, a fifth reason to adopt the dynamical perspective is the possibility of eventually accounting for how the structures that support intelligent behavior could have come about. Detailed models for specific instances of structure creation present many questions and will continue to be developed. But the possibility of such accounts developing from dynamical models can no longer be denied.

3.6 *Embeddedness*

If we follow common usage and use the term "cognitive system" to refer primarily to the internal mechanisms that underwrite sophisticated performance, then cognitive systems are essentially embedded, both in a nervous system and, in a different sense, in a body and an environment. Any adequate account of cognitive functioning must be able to describe and explain this embeddedness. Now, the behavior of the nervous system, of bodies (limbs, muscles, bone, blood), and of the immediate physical environment are all best described in dynamical terms. An advantage of the dynamical conception of cognition is that, by describing cognitive processing in fundamentally similar terms, it minimizes difficulties in accounting for embeddedness.

The embeddedness of cognitive systems has two rather different aspects. The first is the relation of the cognitive system to its neural substrate. The cognitive system somehow *is* the central nervous system, but what are the architectural and processing principles, and level relationships, that allow us to understand how the one can be the other? The other aspect is the relation of the cognitive system to its essential surrounds – the rest of the body, and the physical environment. How do internal cognitive mechanisms "interact" with the body and the environment?

A computational perspective gives a very different kind of understanding of the behavior of a complex system than a dynamical perspective. Now, given that the behavior of the nervous system, the body, and the environment are best described in dynamical terms, adopting the computational perspective for internal cognitive mechanisms transforms the *issue* of embedding into a *problem*: how can two kinds of system, which are described in fundamentally different terms, be related? That is, describing cognition in computational terms automatically creates a theoretical gap between cognitive systems and their surrounds, a gap which must then somehow be bridged.

In the case of the embeddedness of the cognitive system in a nervous system, the problem is to account for how a system which is fundamentally dynamic at one level can simultaneously be a computational system considered at another level. The challenge for the computationalist is to show how such a dynamical system configures itself into a classical computational system at another level. It is a challenge because the two kinds of system are so deeply different. Of course, it is not *impossible* to meet a challenge of this kind; standard digital computers are systems which are continuous dynamical systems at one level and discrete computational systems at another, and we can explain how one realizes the other. However, this provides little reason to believe that a similar cross-level, cross-kind explanation will be feasible in the case of natural cognitive systems, since computers were constructed precisely so that the low-level dynamics would be severely, artificially constrained in exactly the right way. Finding the components of a computational cognitive architecture in the actual dynamical neural hardware of real brains is a challenge of an altogether different order. It is a challenge that computationalists have not even begun to meet.

The embeddedness of the cognitive system within a body and an environment is equally a problem for the computational approach. Again, the problem arises because we are trying to describe the relationship between two systems described in fundamentally different terms. The crux of the problem here is time. Most of what organisms deal with essentially happens in time. Most of the critical features of the environment which must be perceived – including events of "high-level" cognitive significance, such as linguistic communication – unfold over time, and so produce changes in the body over time. In action, the movement of the body, and its effects on the environment, happen in time. This poses a real problem for models of cognitive processes which are in a deep way atemporal. For the most part, computational approaches have dealt with this problem by simply avoiding it. They have assumed that cognition constitutes an autonomous domain that can be studied entirely independently of embeddedness. The problem of how an atemporal cognitive system interacts with a temporal world is shunted off to supposedly noncognitive transduction systems (i.e., somebody else's problem). When computationalists do face up to problems of embeddedness, the interaction of the cognitive system with the body and world is usually handled in ad hoc, biologically implausible ways. Thus inputs are immediately "detemporalized" by transformation into static structures, as when speech signals are transcribed into a spatial buffer. Outputs are handled by periodic intervention in the environment, with the hope that these interventions will keep nudging things in the right direction. Both methods require the addition to the model of some independent timing device or clock, yet natural cognitive systems don"t have clocks in anything like the required sense (Glass and

Mackey, 1988; Winfree, 1980). The diurnal clocks observed in many animals including humans do not help address the problem of rapid, regular sampling that would appear to be required to recognize speech (or a bird song or any other distinctive pattern that is complex in time) using a buffered representation in which time is translated into a labeled spatial axis.

The dynamical approach to cognition handles the embeddedness problem by refusing to create it. The same basic mathematical and conceptual tools are used to describe cognitive processes on one hand and the nervous system and the body and environment on the other. Though accounting for the embeddedness of cognitive systems is still by no means trivial, at least the dynamic approach to cognition does not face the problem of attempting to overcome the differences between two very different general frameworks. Thus the dynamics of central cognitive processes are nothing more than aggregate dynamics of low-level neural processes, redescribed in higher-level, lower-dimensional terms. Dynamical systems theory provides a framework for understanding these level relationships and the emergence of macroscopic order and complexity from microscopic behavior. Similarly, a dynamical account of cognitive processes is directly compatible with dynamical descriptions of the body and the environment, since the dynamical account never steps outside time in the first place. It describes cognitive processes as essentially unfolding over time, and can therefore describe them as occurring in the very same time frame as the movement of the body itself and physical events that occur in the environment.

That cognitive processes must, for this general reason, ultimately be understood dynamically can be appreciated by observing what happens when researchers attempt to build serious models at the interface between the internal cognitive system and the body and environment. Thus Port et al. (1995) aim to describe how it is possible to handle auditory patterns, with all their complexities of sequence, rhythm, and rate, without biologically implausible artificialities such as static input buffers or a rapid time-sampling system. They find that the inner, cognitive processes themselves must unfold over time with the auditory sequence, and that their qualitative properties (like invariance of perception despite change in rate of presentation) are best described in dynamical terms. In other words, attempting to describe how a cognitive system might perceive its essentially temporal environment drives dynamical conceptualizations inward, into the cognitive system itself. Similarly, researchers interested in the production of speech (Saltzman, 1995; Browman and Goldstein, 1995) find that to understand the control of muscle, jaw, etc., we need models of cognitive mechanisms underlying motor control which unfold dynamically in time. That is, attempts to describe how a cognitive system might control essentially temporal bodily movements also drives dynamics inward into the cognitive system. In short, whenever confronted with the problem of explaining how a natural cognitive system might interact with another system which is essentially temporal, one finds that the relevant aspect of the cognitive system itself must be given a dynamical account. It then becomes a problem how this dynamical component of the cognitive system interacts with even more "central" processes. The situation repeats itself, and dynamics is driven further inward. The natural outcome of this progression is a picture of cognitive processing in its entirety, from peripheral input systems to peripheral output systems and everything in between, as all unfolding dynamically in real time: *mind as motion*.[17]

NOTES

This research was supported by a Queen Elizabeth II Research Fellowship from the Australian Research Council to the first author, and Office of Naval Research grants N0001491-J-1261,

N0001493, and N0001492-J-1029 to the second author. Critical feedback from John Haugeland, Esther Thelen, and James Townsend was especially useful in its preparation.

1   Our discussion is generally pitched in quite abstract terms. Space limitations have prevented us from going into particular examples in much detail. We urge readers hungry for extended concrete illustrations of the general points to turn to actual examples of dynamical research in cognitive science, such as those contained in Port and van Gelder (1995).

2   Technically, a differential equation is any equation involving a function and one or more of its derivatives. For more details on differential equations, and the mass-spring equation in particular, see Norton (1995).

3   The notion of *phase*, like that of *dynamical system* itself, differs from one context to another. In some contexts, a phase space is taken to be one in which one of the dimensions is a time derivative such as velocity. In other contexts, phase is taken to refer to position in a periodic pattern, as when we talk of the phase of an oscillating signal. Our notion of phase here is a generalization of this latter sense. Since the rule governing a state-determined system determines a unique sequence of points for any given point, every point in the space can be understood as occupying a position (or "phase") in the total pattern (or "dynamic") fixed by the rule. Our use thus accords with the common description of diagrams which sketch the overall behavior of a dynamical system as *phase portraits* (see, e.g., Abraham and Shaw, 1982).

4   For an example of the use of forms of the logistic equation, as a difference equation, in cognitive modeling, see van Geert (1995).

5   In fact, the total state of a computational system is more than just a configuration of symbols. A Turing Machine, for example (see n. 6), has at any time a configuration of symbols on its tape, but it is also in a certain head state, and the head occupies a certain position; these must also be counted as components of the total state of the system.

6   Turing Machines are a particularly simple kind of computer, consisting of one long tape marked with squares that can contain symbols, and a "head" (a central processing unit) which moves from square to square making changes to the symbols. They are very often used in discussions of foundational issues in cognitive science because they are widely known and, despite their simplicity, can (in principle) perform computations just as complex as any other computational system. For a very accessible introduction to Turing Machines, see Haugeland (1985).

7   In particular, one could not demonstrate that cognitive systems are dynamical systems merely by showing that any given natural cognitive system is governed by some dynamical rule or other. Certainly, all people and animals obey the laws of classical mechanics; drop any one from a high place, and it will accelerate at a rate determined by the force of gravitational attraction. However, this does not show that *cognitive* systems are dynamical systems; it merely illustrates the fact that heavy objects belong to dynamical systems.

8   A more radical possibility is that dynamical systems can behave in a way that depends on knowledge without actually *representing* that knowledge by means of any particular, identifiable aspect of the system.

9   For a more detailed introduction to dynamics, see Norton (1995).

10 [Editors' note: See the anthology to which this essay is an introduction: K. Port and T. van Gelder (eds) (1995) *Mind as Motion: Explorations in the Dynamics of Cognition.* Cambridge, MA: MIT Press.]

11 Of course, a range of general and quite powerful arguments has been put forward as demonstrating that cognitive systems must be computational in nature (see, e.g., Fodor, 1975; Newell and Simon, 1976; Pylyshyn, 1984). Dynamicists remain unconvinced by these arguments, but we do not have space here to cover the arguments and dynamicists' responses to them.

12 One *inappropriate* way to extract temporal considerations from a computational model is to rely on the timing of operations that follow from the model's being *implemented* in real physical hardware. This is inappropriate because the particular details of a model's hardware implementation are irrelevant to the nature of the model, and choice of a particular implementation is theoretically completely arbitrary.

13 Ironically, these kinds of assumption have often been the basis for attacks on the plausibility of computational models. If you assume that each computational step must take some certain minimum amount of time, it is not difficult to convince yourself that the typical computational model has no hope of completing its operations within a psychologically realistic amount of time.

14 Precisely because discrete models are only an approximation to an underlying continuous one, there are hard limits on how well the continuous function can be modeled. Thus, it is well known to communications engineers that one must have at least two discrete samples for each event of interest in the signal (often called Nyquist's Theorem). The cognitive correlary of this is that to model dynamic cognitive events that last in the order of a half second and longer, one must discretely compute the trajectory at least four times a second. Anything less may result in artifactual characterization of the events. Since the time scale of cognitive events is relatively slow compared to modern computers, this limit on discrete modeling of cognition would not itself serve as a limiting constraint on real-time modeling of human cognitive processes.

15 This is true for computational systems when they are considered at the level at which we understand them as computational. The same object (e.g., a desktop computer) can be seen as undergoing continuous state changes when understood at some different level, e.g., the level of electric circuits.

16 Note that when continuous systems bifurcate there can be *genuinely* discrete changes in the attractor landscape of the system.

17 [Editors' note: In the original there follow two sections discussing the historical background and other approaches to cognition.]

REFERENCES

Abraham, R. and Shaw, C. D. (1982). *Dynamics: The Geometry of Behavior*. Santa Cruz, CA: Aerial Press.

Ashby, R. (1952). *Design for a Brain*. London: Chapman and Hall.

Basar, E. (ed.) (1990). *Chaos in Brain Function*. Berlin: Springer-Verlag.

Basar, E. and Bullock, T. H. (ed.) (1989). *Brain Dynamics: Progress and Perspectives*. Berlin: Springer-Verlag.

Beer, R. D. (1995). Computational and dynamical languages for autonomous agents. In R. Port and T. van Gelder (eds), *Mind as Motion: Explorations in the Dynamics of Cognition*. Cambridge, MA: MIT Press.

Bernstein, N. A. (1967). *The Control and Regulation of Movement*. London: Pergamon.

Bingham, G. (1995). Dynamics and the problem of event recognition. In R. Port and T. van Gelder (eds), *Mind as Motion: Explorations in the Dynamics of Cognition*. Cambridge, MA: MIT Press.

Browman, C. and Goldstein, L. (1995). Dynamics and articulatory phonology. In R. Port and T. van Gelder (eds), *Mind as Motion: Explorations in the Dynamics of Cognition*. Cambridge, MA: MIT Press.

Busemeyer, J. R. and Townsend, J. T. (1993). Decision field theory: a dynamic–cognitive approach to decision making in an uncertain environment. *Psychological Review*, 100: 432–59

Busemeyer, J. R. and Townsend, J. T. (1995). Dynamic representation of decision making. In R. Port and T. van Gelder (eds), *Mind as Motion: Explorations in the Dynamics of Cognition*. Cambridge, MA: MIT Press.

Devaney, R. L. (1986). *An Introduction to Chaotic Dynamical Systems*. Menlo Park, CA: Benjamin/ Cummings.

Dreyfus, H. L. (1992). *What Computers Still Can't Do: A Critique of Artificial Reason*. Cambridge, MA: MIT Press.

Elman, J. L. (1991). Distributed representations, simple recurrent networks, and grammatical structure. *Machine Learning*. 7: 195–225

Elman, J. (1995). Language as a dynamical system. In R. Port and T. van Gelder (eds), *Mind as Motion: Explorations in the Dynamics of Cognition*. Cambridge, MA: MIT Press.

Erman, L. D., Hayes-Roth, F., Lesser, V. R., and Reddy, D. R. (1980). The HEARSAY-II speech understanding system: integrating knowledge to resolve uncertainty. *Computing Surveys*, 12: 213–53

Fodor, J. A. (1975). *The Language of Thought*. Cambridge, MA: Harvard University Press.

Forrest, S. (ed.) (1991). *Emergent Computation: Self-organizing, Collective, and Cooperative Phenomena in Natural and Artificial Computing Networks*. Cambridge, MA: MIT Press.

Gibson, J. J. (1979). *The Ecological Approach to Visual Perception*. Boston: Houghton-Mifflin.

Giunti, M. (1995). Dynamical models of cognition. In R. Port and T. van Gelder (eds), *Mind as Motion: Explorations in the Dynamics of Cognition*. Cambridge, MA: MIT Press.

Glass, L. and Mackey, M. (1988). *From Clocks to Chaos: The Rhythms of Life*. Princeton, NJ: Princeton University Press.

Grossberg, S. (1995). Neural dynamics of motion perception, recognition learning and spatial attention. In R. Port and T. van Gelder (eds), *Mind as Motion: Explorations in the Dynamics of Cognition*. Cambridge, MA: MIT Press.

Haken, H. (1988). *Information and Self-Organization: A Macroscopic Approach to Complex Systems*. Berlin: Springer-Verlag.

Haken, H. (1991). *Synergetics, Computers and Cognition*. Berlin: Springer-Verlag.

Haugeland, J. (1985). *Artificial Intelligence: The Very Idea*. Cambridge, MA: MIT Press.

Hinton, G. E. and Anderson, J. A. (eds) (1981). *Parallel Models of Associative Memory*. Hillsdale, NJ: Erlbaum.

Holland, J. H. (1975). *Adaptation in Natural and Artificial Systems*. Ann Arbor: University of Michigan Press.

Hopfield, J. (1982). Neural networks and physical systems with emergent collective computational abilities. *Proceedings of the National Academy of Sciences USA*, 79: 2554–8

Kauffman, S. A. (1993). *The Origins of Order: Self-organization and Selection in Evolution*. New York: Oxford University Press.

Kelso, J. A. and Kay, B. A. (1987). Information and control: a macroscopic analysis of perception – action coupling. In H. Heuer and A. F. Sanders (eds), *Perspectives on Perception and Action*. Hillsdale, NJ: Erlbaum.

Kelso, J. A. S., Ding, M., and Schöner, G. (1992). Dynamic pattern formation: a primer. In J. E. Mittenthal and A. B. Baskin (eds), *Principles of Organization in Organisms*. Reading, MA: Addison-Wesley.

Kugler, P. N. and Turvey, M. T. (1987). *Information, Natural Law, and the Self-assembly of Rhythmic Movement*. Hillsdale, NJ: Erlbaum.

Lashley, K. S. (1960). The problem of serial order in behavior. In F. A. Beach, D. O. Hebb, C. T. Morgan, and H. W. Nissen (eds), *The Neuropsychology of Lashley*. New York: McGraw-Hill.

Madore, B. F. and Freeman, W. L. (1987). Self-organizing structures. *American Scientist*, 75: 253–9

McClelland, J. L. and Rumelhart, D. E. (1981). An interactive – activation model of context effects in letter perception: part 1, an account of basic findings. *Psychological Review*, 88: 375–407

McClelland, J. L. and Rumelhart, D. E. (eds) (1986). *Parallel Distributed Processing: Explorations in the Microstructure of Cognition. Vol. 2, Psychological and Biological Models*. Cambridge, MA: MIT Press.

McCulloch, W. S. (1965). *Embodiments of Mind*. Cambridge, MA: MIT Press.

Murray, J. D. (1989). *Mathematical Biology*. Berlin: Springer-Verlag.

Newell, A. and Simon, H. (1976). Computer science as empirical enquiry: symbols and search. *Communications of the Association for Computing Machinery*, 19: 113–26

Norton, A. (1995). Dynamics: an introduction. In R. Port and T. van Gelder (eds), *Mind as Motion: Explorations in the Dynamics of Cognition*. Cambridge, MA: MIT Press.

Petitot, J. (1985a). *Les Catastrophes de la Parole*. Paris: Maloine.

Petitot, J. (1985b). *Morphogenése du Sens*. Paris: Presses Universitaires de France.

Petitot, J. (1995). Morphodynamics and attractor syntax. In R. Port and T. van Gelder (eds), *Mind as Motion: Explorations in the Dynamics of Cognition*. Cambridge, MA: MIT Press.

Port, R. and van Gelder, T. (eds) (1995). *Mind as Motion: Explorations in the Dynamics of Cognition*. Cambridge, MA: MIT Press.

Port, R., Cummins, F., and McAuley, D. (1995). Modeling auditory recognition using attractor dynamics. In R. Port and T. van Gelder (eds), *Mind as Motion: Explorations in the Dynamics of Cognition*. Cambridge, MA: MIT Press.

Pylyshyn, Z. W. (1984). *Computation and Cognition: Toward a Foundation for Cognitive Science*. Cambridge, MA: Bradford/MIT Press.

Quinlan, P. (1991). *Connectionism and Psychology*. Chicago: University of Chicago Press.

Reidbord, S. and Redington, D. (1995). The dynamics of mind and body during clinical interviews: current trends, potential, and future directions. In R. Port and T. van Gelder (eds), *Mind as Motion: Explorations in the Dynamics of Cognition*. Cambridge, MA: MIT Press.

Rosenberg, C. R. and Sejnowski, T. J. (1987). Parallel networks that learn to pronounce English text. *Complex Systems*, 1: 145–68.

Rosenblatt, F. (1962). *Principles of Neurodynamics: Perceptrons and the Theory of Brain Mechanisms*. Washington, DC: Spartan Books.

Rumelhart, D. E. and McClelland, J. L. (eds) (1986). *Parallel Distributed Processing: Explorations in the Microstructure of Cognition. Vol. 1: Foundations*. Cambridge, MA: MIT Press.

Saltzman, E. (1995). Dynamics and coordinate systems in skilled sensorimotor activity. In R. Port and T. van Gelder (eds), *Mind as Motion: Explorations in the Dynamics of Cognition*. Cambridge, MA: MIT Press.

Shannon, C. E. and Weaver, W. (1949). *The Mathematical Theory of Communication*. Urbana, IL: University of Illinois Press.

Skarda, C. A. and Freeman, W. J. (1987). Brain makes chaos to make sense of the world. *Behavior and Brain Sciences*, 10, 161–95

Smolensky, P., Legendre, G., and Miyata, Y. (1992). Principles for an integrated connectionist/symbolic theory of higher cognition. No. CU-CS-600–92, Computer Science Department, University of Colorado at Boulder.

Thelen, E. (1995). Time scale dynamics and the development of an embodied cognition. In R. Port and T. van Gelder (eds), *Mind as Motion: Explorations in the Dynamics of Cognition*. Cambridge, MA: MIT Press.

Thelen, E. and Smith, L. B. (1993). *A Dynamics Systems Approach to the Development of Cognition and Action*. Cambridge, MA: MIT Press.

Thom, R. (1975). *Structural Stability and Morphogenesis* (trans. D.H. Fowler). Reading, MA: W. A. Benjamin.

Thom, R. (1983). *Mathematical Models of Morphogenesis*. Chichester: Ellis Horwood.

Touretzky, D. S. (1990). BoltzCONS: dynamic symbol structures in a connectionist network. *Artificial Intelligence*, 46: 5–46

Turvey, M. T. and Carello, C. (1995). Some dynamical themes in perception and action. In R. Port and T. van Gelder (eds), *Mind as Motion: Explorations in the Dynamics of Cognition*. Cambridge, MA: MIT Press.

van Geert, P. (1995). Growth dynamics in development. In R. Port and T. van Gelder (eds), *Mind as Motion: Explorations in the Dynamics of Cognition*. Cambridge, MA: MIT Press.

von Neumann, J. (1958). *The Computer and the Brain*. New Haven: Yale University Press.

Wiener, N. (1948). *Cybernetics: Or Control and Communication in the Animal and the Machine*. New York: John Wiley.

Wildgen, W. (1982). *Catastrophe Theoretic Semantics: An Elaboration and Extension of René Thom's Theory*. Amsterdam: John Benjamins.

Winfree, A. T. (1980). *The Geometry of Biological Time*. New York: Springer-Verlag.

Zeeman, C. (1977). *Catastrophe Theory: Selected Papers 1972–1977*. Redwood City: Addison-Wesley.

7

Mind and Environment

Introduction

We have already seen how language relates to the environment. It is now time to see how mind relates to the environment. We are primarily concerned with whether there are thoughts that, in some sense, presuppose the existence of other bodies and how that affects our treatment of thoughts. If my thoughts about Clinton presuppose, for instance, that Clinton exists and that I stand in some relationship with Clinton, is it then possible for an artificial mind to emulate this relationship?

In "Methodological Solipsism Considered as a Research Strategy in Cognitive Psychology," Jerry Fodor defends the view that mental states and processes are computational, i.e., that they are formal processes, specified without reference to such semantic properties of representations as truth, meaning, and reference (Fodor calls this the "formality condition"). Fodor's view implies that people who are doing machine simulations, including many cognitive psychologists and cognitive scientists, are not studying how language and thought relate to the world, which is what they claim to be doing. Instead, they are studying formal operations on symbols. If you ask a machine who the 42nd president of the US is and the machine replies "Bill Clinton is the 42nd president of the US," then Fodor's claim is that the machine's answer is not about Bill Clinton. You can choose to interpret the answer as being about Bill Clinton, but, as Fodor puts it, that is no business of the machine's. The machine has no access to the semantic information that "Bill Clinton" refers to Bill Clinton. When I claim that Clinton didn't inhale I am certainly thinking about Clinton. When the machine claims that Clinton didn't inhale it is simply manipulating uninterpreted symbols.

Fodor first draws a distinction between opaque and transparent taxonomies of mental states, where an opaque taxonomy, but not the transparent one, counts the belief that the Morning Star rises in the East as different from the belief that the Evening Star rises in the East. He then argues that it is typically opaquely taxonomized states that figure in explanations of behavior, so it is the opaquely taxonomized states that psychology is concerned with. But opaquely taxonomized states are exactly what the formality condition allows us to have, for the transparently taxonomized states but not the opaquely taxonomized ones require semantic properties such as reference. For if we count the beliefs that the Morning Star rises in the East as the same as the belief that the Evening Star rises in the East it can only be because "the Morning Star" and "the Evening Star" are coreferential. Fodor's view recognizes the intuition that transparently identical beliefs can have different behavioral effects because, when opaquely construed, they are formally different and thus have different functional and causal roles.

What, then, about the semantic notions of truth, reference, and meaning? Where do they belong? Fodor does not answer that question. All he wants to show is that the semantic notions are not psychological notions and that cognitive psychology should proceed without the semantic notions. In Putnam's terminology, cognitive psychology should only be concerned with narrow contents.

In "Individualism and Psychology" Tyler Burge argues that individualism, the position Fodor holds, is mistaken and that a person's intentional states could vary even though the person's physical and functional states, specified nonintentionally and individualistically, are held constant. Burge first discusses several different arguments individualists have used to support their views, and then presents a positive argument for anti-individualism. Burge has argued for anti-individualism by extending Putnam's examples in "The Meaning of 'Meaning'" to mental contents, but here his main argument is that an influential computational account of vision by David Marr is nonindividualistic. Since a theory of vision is important in psychology and since perceptual processes provide inputs for various cognitive processes, Burge thinks it is reasonable to believe that psychology is in fact not individualistic, even if some philosophers believe that it ought to be solipsistic.

According to Burge anti-individualism is guided by two very natural assumptions. The first is that there are psychological states that represent, or are about, an objective world, and the second is that we should give an account that explains our successes and failures in dealing with the world via communication, vision, hearing, and so on. Given these assumptions it seems clear that cognitive psychology should proceed with the semantic notions of meaning, reference, and truth, contrary to what Fodor argued.

This section leaves us with important questions about the nature of thought and questions about what is involved in emulating human thoughts. If the anti-individualists are right, then a study of computational manipulation of symbols leaves out an essential part of language (language and environment) and thought. If artificial minds cannot interact with the environment in order to acquire the "aboutness" captured by the anti-individualists, then it appears that an essential part of thought is missing. Is, then, the individualist simply biting the bullet?

Further Reading

Adams, F. and Fuller, G. (1992). Names, Contents and Causes. *Mind and Language* 7: 205–21.

Bach, K. (1982). *De Re* Belief and Methodological Solipsism. In *Thought and Object: Essays on Intentionality*. Ed. A. Woodfield. Oxford: Clarendon Press.

Burge, T. (1979). Individualism and the Mental. *Midwest Studies in Philosophy* 5: 73–122.

Davidson, D. (1987). Knowing One's Own Mind. *Proceedings and Addresses of the American Philosophical Association* 60: 441–58.

Fodor, J. (1987). *Psychosemantics*. Cambridge, MA: MIT Press.

Segal, G. (1989). Seeing What Is Not There. *Philosophical Review* 98: 189–214.

Stalnaker, R. (1989). On What's in the Head. *Philosophical Perspectives* 3: 287–316.

Stich, S. (1978). Autonomous Psychology and the Belief–Desire Psychology. *The Monist* 61: 573–91.

Methodological Solipsism Considered as a Research Strategy in Cognitive Psychology

JERRY A. FODOR

to form the idea of an object and to form an idea simply is the same thing; the reference of the idea to an object being an extraneous denomination, of which in itself it bears no mark or character.

Hume (1967), p. 20

Your standard contemporary cognitive psychologist – your thoroughly modern mentalist – is disposed to reason as follows. To think (e.g.) that Marvin is melancholy is to represent Marvin in a certain way; viz. as being melancholy (and not, for example, as being maudlin, morose, moody, or merely moping and dyspeptic). But surely we cannot represent Marvin as being melancholy except as we are in some or other relation to a representation of Marvin; and not just to *any* representation of Marvin, but, in particular, to a representation the content of which is *that* Marvin is melancholy, a representation which, as it were, expresses the proposition that Marvin is melancholy. So, a fortiori, at least some mental states/ processes are or involve at least some relations to at least some representations. Perhaps, then, this is the *typical* feature of such mental states/processes as cognitive psychology studies; perhaps all such states can be viewed as relations to representations and all such processes as operations defined on representations.

This is, prima facie, an appealing proposal, since it gives the psychologist two degrees of freedom to play with and they seem, intuitively, to be the right two. On the one hand, mental states are distinguished by the *content* of the associated representations, and we therefore can allow for the difference between thinking that Marvin is melancholy and thinking that Sam is (or that Albert isn't, or that it sometimes snows in Cincinnati); and, on the other hand, mental states are distinguished by the *relation* that the subject bears to the associated representation (so we can allow for the difference between thinking, hoping, supposing, doubting and pretending that Marvin is melancholy). It's hard to believe that a serious psychology could make do with fewer (or less refined) distinctions than these, and it's hard to believe that a psychology that makes these distinctions could avoid taking the notion of mental representation seriously. Moreover, the burden of argument is clearly upon anyone who claims that we need *more* degrees of freedom than just these two: the least hypothesis that is remotely plausible is that a mental state is (type) individuated by specifying a relation and a representation such that the subject bears the one to the other.[1]

I'll say that any psychology that takes this line is a version of the *representational theory of the mind*. I think that it's reasonable to adopt some such theory as a sort of working hypothesis, if only because there aren't any alternatives which seem to be even *remotely* plausible and because empirical research carried out within this framework has, thus far, proved interesting and fruitful.[2] However, my present concern is neither to attack nor to defend this view, but rather to distinguish it from something other – and stronger – that modern cognitive psychologists *also* hold. I shall put this stronger doctrine as the view that mental states and processes are *computational*. Much of what is characteristic of cognitive psychology is a consequence of adherence to this stronger view. What I want to do in this paper is to say something about what this stronger view is, something about why I think it's plausible, and, most of all, something about the ways in which it shapes the cognitive psychology we have.

I take it that computational processes are both *symbolic* and *formal*. They are symbolic because they are defined over representations, and they are formal because they apply to representations in virtue of (roughly) the *syntax* of the representations. It's the second of these conditions that makes the claim that mental processes are computational stronger than the representational theory of the mind. Most of this paper will be a meditation upon the consequences of assuming that mental processes are formal processes.

I'd better cash the parenthetical "roughly." To say that an operation is formal isn't the same as saying that it is syntactic since we could have formal processes defined over representations which don't, in any obvious sense, *have* a syntax. Rotating an image would be a timely example. What makes syntactic operations a species of formal operations is that being syntactic is a way of *not* being semantic. Formal operations are the ones that are specified without reference to such semantic properties of representations as, for example, truth, reference, and meaning. Since we don't know how to complete this list (since, that is, we don't know what semantic properties there are), I see no responsible way of saying what, in general, formality amounts to. The notion of formality will thus have to remain intuitive and metaphoric, at least for present purposes: formal operations apply in terms of the, as it were, shapes of the objects in their domains.[3]

To require that mental processes be computational (viz. formal-syntactic) is thus to require something not very clear. Still, the requirement has some clear consequences, and they are striking and tendentious. Consider that we started by assuming that the *content* of representations is a (type) individuating feature of mental states. So far as the *representational* theory of the mind is concerned, it's possibly the only thing that distinguishes Peter's thought that Sam is silly from his thought that Sally is depressed. But, now, if the *computational* theory of the mind is true (and if, as we may assume, content is a semantic notion *par excellence*) it follows that content alone cannot distinguish thoughts. More exactly, the computational theory of the mind requires that two thoughts can be distinct in content only if they can be identified with relations to formally distinct representations. More generally: fix the subject and the relation, and then mental states can be (type) distinct only if the representations which constitute their objects are formally distinct.

Again, consider that accepting a formality condition upon mental states implies a drastic narrowing of the ordinary ontology of the mental; all sorts of state which look, prima facie, to be mental in good standing are going to turn out to be none of the psychologist's business if the formality condition is endorsed. This point is one that philosophers have made in a number of contexts, and usually in a deprecating tone of voice. Take, for example, knowing that such-and-such, and assume that you can't know what's not the case. Since, on that assumption, knowledge is involved with truth, and since truth is a semantic notion, it's going to follow that there can't be a psychology of *knowledge* (even if it is consonant with the formality condition to hope for a psychology of *belief*). Similarly, it's a way of making a point of Ryle's to say that, strictly speaking, there can't be a psychology of perception if the formality condition is to be complied with. Seeing is an achievement; you can't see what's not there. From the point of view of the representational theory of the mind, this means that seeing involves relations between mental representations *and their referents*; hence, semantic relations within the meaning of the act.

I hope that such examples suggest (what, in fact, I think is true) that even if the formality condition isn't very clear, it is quite certainly very strong. In fact, I think it's not all *that* anachronistic to see it as the central issue which divides the two main traditions in the history of psychology: "rational psychology" on the one hand, and "naturalism" on the other. Since this is a mildly eccentric way of cutting the pie, I'm going to permit myself a semihistorical excursus before returning to the main business of the paper.

Descartes argued that there is an important sense in which how the world is makes no difference to one's mental states. Here is a well-known passage from the first *Meditation*:

> At this moment it does indeed seem to me that it is with eyes awake that I am looking at this paper; that this head which I move is not asleep, that it is deliberately and of set purpose that I extend my hand and perceive it . . . But in thinking over this I remind myself that on many occasions I have been deceived by similar illusions, and in dwelling on this reflection I see so manifestly that there are no certain indications by which we may clearly distinguish wakefulness from sleep that I am lost in astonishment. And my astonishment is such that it is almost capable of persuading me that I now dream. (1967, p. 146)

At least three sorts of reaction to this kind of argument are distinguishable in the philosophical literature. First, there's a long tradition, including both Rationalists and Empiricists, which takes it as axiomatic that one's experiences (and, a fortiori, one's beliefs) might have been just as they are even if the world had been quite different from the way that it is. See, for example, the passage from Hume which serves as an epigraph to this paper. Second, there's a vaguely Wittgensteinian mood in which one argues that it's just *false* that one's mental states might have been what they are had the world been relevantly different. For example, if there had been a dagger there, Macbeth would have been *seeing*, not just hallucinating. And what could be more different than that? If the Cartesian feels that this reply misses the point, he is at least under an obligation to say precisely which point it misses; in precisely *which* respects the way the world is irrelevant to the character of one's beliefs, experiences, etc. Finally there's a tradition which argues that – epistemology to one side – it is at best a strategic mistake to attempt to develop a psychology which individuates mental states without reference to their environmental causes and effects (e.g., which counts the state that Macbeth *was* in as type identical to the state he would have been in had the dagger been supplied). I have in mind the tradition which includes the American naturalists (notably Pierce and Dewey), all the learning theorists, and such contemporary representatives as Quine in philosophy and Gibson in psychology. The recurrent theme here is that psychology is a branch of biology, hence that one must view the organism as embedded in a physical environment. The psychologist's job is to trace those organism/environment interactions which constitute its behavior. A passage from William James (1890) will serve to give the feel of the thing:

> On the whole, few recent formulas have done more service of a rough sort in psychology than the Spencerian one that the essence of mental life and of bodily life are one, namely, "the adjustment of inner to outer relations." Such a formula is vagueness incarnate; but because it takes into account the fact that minds inhabit environments which act on them and on which they in turn react; because, in short, it takes mind in the midst of all its concrete relations, it is immensely more fertile than the old-fashioned "rational psychology" which treated the soul as a detached existent, sufficient unto itself, and assumed to consider only its nature and its properties. (p. 6)

A number of adventitious intrusions have served to muddy the issues in this long-standing dispute. On the one hand, it may well be that Descartes was relying on a specifically introspectionist construal of the claim that the individuation of mental states is independent of their environmental causes. That is, Descartes' point may have been that (1) mental states are (type) identical if and only if they are introspectively indistinguishable, and (2) introspection cannot distinguish (e.g.) perception from hallucination, or knowledge from belief. On the other hand, the naturalist, in point of historical fact, is often a behaviorist as well. He wants to argue not only that mental states are individuated by reference to organism/ environment relations, but also that such relations constitute the mental. In the context of the present discussion, he is arguing for the abandonment not just of the formality condition, but of the notion of mental representation as well.

If, however, we take the computational theory of the mind as what's central to the issue, we can reconstruct the debate between rational psychologists and naturalists in a way that does justice to both their points; in particular, in a way which frees the discussion from involvement with introspectionism on the one side and behaviorism on the other.

Insofar as we think of mental processes as computational (hence as formal operations defined on representations) it will be natural to take the mind to be, inter alia, a kind of computer. That is, we will think of the mind as carrying out whatever symbol manipulations are constitutive of the hypothesized computational processes. To a first approximation, we may thus construe mental operations as pretty directly analogous to those of a Turing Machine. There is, for example, a working memory (corresponding to a tape) and there are capacities for scanning and altering the contents of the memory (corresponding to the operations of reading and writing on the tape). If we want to extend the computational metaphor by providing access to information about the environment, we can think of the computer as having access to "oracles" which serve, on occasion, to enter information in the memory. On the intended interpretation of this model, these oracles are analogues to the senses. In particular, they are assumed to be transducers, in that what they write on the tape is determined solely by the ambient environmental energies that impinge upon them. (For elaboration of this sort of account, see Putnam, 1960; it is, of course, widely familiar from discussions in artificial intelligence.)

I'm not endorsing this model, but simply presenting it as a natural extension of the computational picture of the mind. Its present interest is that we can use it to see how the formality condition connects with the Cartesian claim that the character of mental processes is somehow independent of their environmental causes and effects. The point is that, so long as we are thinking of mental processes as purely computational, the bearing of environmental information upon such processes is exhausted by the formal character of whatever the oracles write on the tape. In particular, it doesn't matter to such processes whether what the oracles write is *true*; whether, for example, they really are transducers faithfully mirroring the state of the environment, or merely the output end of a typewriter manipulated by a Cartesian demon bent on deceiving the machine. I'm saying, in effect, that the formality condition, viewed in this context, is tantamount to a sort of methodological solipsism. If mental processes are formal, they have access only to the formal properties of such representations of the environment as the senses provide. Hence, they have no access to the *semantic* properties of such representations, including the property of being true, of having referents, or, indeed, the property of being representations *of the environment*.

That some such methodological solipsism really is implicated in much current psychological practice is best seen by examining what researchers actually do. Consider, for example, the well-known work of Professor Terry Winograd. Winograd was primarily interested in the computer simulation of certain processes involved in the handling of verbal information; asking and answering questions, drawing inferences, following instructions and the like. The form of his theory was a program for a computer which "lives in" and operates upon a simple world of block-like geometric objects. (Cf. Winograd, 1972.) Many of the capacities that the device exercises vis-à-vis its environment seem impressively intelligent. It can arrange the blocks to order, it can issue "perceptual" reports of the present state of its environment and "memory" reports of its past states, it can devise simple plans for achieving desired environment configurations, and it can discuss its undertakings (more or less in English) with whoever is running the program.

The interesting point for our purposes, however, is that the machine environment which is the nominal object of these actions and conversations actually isn't there. What actually happens is that the programmer so arranges the memory states of the machine that the available data are whatever they would be *if* there were objects for the machine to perceive and manipulanda for it to operate upon. In effect, the machine lives in an entirely notional world; all its beliefs are false. Of course, it doesn't matter to the machine that its beliefs are false since falsity is a semantic property and, *qua* computer, the device satisfies the formality condition; viz. it has access only to formal (nonsemantic) properties of the representations that it manipulates. In effect, the device is in precisely the situation that Descartes dreads; it's a mere computer which dreams that it's a robot.

I hope that this discussion suggests how acceptance of the computational theory of the mind leads to a sort of methodological solipsism as a part of the research strategy of contemporary cognitive psychology. In particular, I hope it's clear how you get that consequence from the formality condition alone, without so much as raising the introspection issue. I stress this point because it seems to me that there has been considerable confusion about it among the psychologists themselves. People who do machine simulation, in particular, very often advertise themselves as working on the question how thought (or language) is related to the world. My present point is that, whatever else they're doing, they certainly aren't doing *that*. The very assumption that defines their field – viz. that they study mental processes *qua* formal operations on symbols – guarantees that their studies won't answer the question how the symbols so manipulated are semantically interpreted. You can, for example, build a machine that answers baseball questions in the sense that (e.g.) if you type in "Who had the most wins by a National League pitcher since Dizzy Dean?" it will type out "Robin Roberts, who won 28." But you delude yourself if you think that a machine which in this sense answers baseball questions is thereby answering questions *about* baseball (or that the machine has somehow referred to Robin Roberts). If the *programmer* chooses to interpret the machine inscription "Robin Roberts won 28" as a statement about Robin Roberts (e.g., as the statement that he won 28), that's all well and good, but it's no business of the machine's. The machine has no access to that interpretation, and its computations are in no way affected by it. The machine doesn't know what it's talking about, and it doesn't care; *about* is a semantic relation.[4]

This brings us to a point where, having done some sort of justice to the Cartesian's insight, we can also do some sort of justice to the naturalist's. For, after all, mental processes are supposed to be operations on representations, and it is in the nature of representations to represent. We have seen that a psychology which embraces the formality condition is thereby debarred from raising questions about the semantic properties of mental representations; yet surely such questions ought *somewhere* to be raised. The computer which prints out "RR won 28" is not thereby referring to RR. But, surely, when I think *RR won 28*, I *am* thinking about RR, and if not in virtue of having performed some formal operations on some representations, then presumably in virtue of something else. It's perhaps borrowing the least tendentious fragment of causal theories of reference to assume that what fixes the interpretation of my mental representations of RR is something about the way that he and I are embedded in the world; perhaps not a causal chain stretching between us, but anyhow *some* facts about how he and I are causally situated; *Dasein*, as you might say. Only a *naturalistic* psychology will do to specify these facts, because here we are explicitly in the realm of organism/environment transactions.

We are on the verge of a bland and ecumenical conclusion: that there is room both for a computational psychology – viewed as a theory of formal processes defined over mental representations – *and* a naturalistic psychology, viewed as a theory of the (presumably causal) relations between representations and the world which fix their semantic interpretations of the former. I think that, in principle, this is the right way to look at things. In practice, however, I think that it's misleading. So far as I can see, it's overwhelmingly likely that computational psychology is the only one that we are going to get. I want to argue for this conclusion in two steps. First, I'll argue for what I've till now only assumed: that we must *at least* have a psychology which accepts the formality condition. Then I'll argue that there's good reason to suppose that that's the most that we can have; that a naturalistic psychology isn't a practical possibility and isn't likely to become one.

The first move, then, is to give reasons for believing that at least some part of psychology should honor the formality condition. Here too the argument proceeds in two steps. I'll argue first that it is typically under an *opaque* construal that attributions of propositional attitudes to organisms enter into explanations of their behavior; and second that the formality condition is intimately involved with the explanation of propositional attitudes so construed: roughly, that it's reasonable to believe that we can get such explanations only within computational theories. *Caveat emptor*: The arguments under review are, in large part, nondemonstrative. In particular, they will assume the perfectibility in principle of the kinds of psychological theory now being developed, and it is entirely possible that this is an assumption contrary to fact.

Thesis: When we articulate the generalizations in virtue of which behavior is contingent upon mental states, it is typically an opaque construal of the mental state attributions that does the work; for example, it's a construal under which believing that *a is F* is logically independent from believing that *b is F*, even in the case where $a = b$. It will be convenient to speak not only of opaque construals of propositional attitude ascriptions, but also of *opaque taxonomies* of mental state types; e.g., of taxonomies which, inter alia, count the belief that the Morning Star rises in the East as type distinct from the belief that the Evening Star does. (Correspondingly, *transparent* taxonomies are such as, inter alia, would count these beliefs as type identical.) So, the claim is that mental states are typically opaquely taxonomized for purposes of psychological theory.[5]

The point doesn't depend upon the examples, so I'll stick to the most informal sorts of case. Suppose I know that John wants to meet the girl who lives next door; and suppose I know that this is true when "wants to" is construed opaquely. Then, given even rough-and-ready generalizations about how people's behaviors are contingent upon their utilities, I can make some reasonable predictions (/guesses) about what John is likely to do: he's likely to say (viz. utter), "I want to meet the girl who lives next door." He's likely to call upon his neighbor. He's likely (at a minimum, and all things being equal) to exhibit next-door-directed behavior. None of this is frightfully exciting, but it's all I need for present purposes, and what more would you expect from folk psychology?

On the other hand, suppose that all I know is that John wants to meet the girl next door where "wants to" is construed transparently. I.e., all I know is that it's true of the girl next door that John wants to meet her. Then there is little or nothing that I can predict about how John is likely to proceed. And this is *not* just because rough-and-ready psychological generalizations want *ceteris paribus* clauses to fill them in; it's also for the deeper reason that I can't infer from what I know about John to any relevant description of the mental causes of his behavior. For example, I have no reason to predict that John will say such things as "I want to meet the girl who lives next door" since, let John be as cooperative and as truthful as you like, and let him be utterly a native speaker, still, he *may believe* that the girl he wants to meet languishes in Latvia. In which case, "I want to meet the girl who lives next door" is the last thing it will occur to him to say. (The contestant wants to say "suspender," for "suspender" is the magic word. Consider what we can predict about his probable verbal behavior if we take this (1) opaquely and (2) transparently. And, of course, the same sorts of point apply, *mutatis mutandis*, to the prediction of *non*verbal behavior.)

Ontologically, transparent readings are stronger than opaque ones; for example, the former license existential inferences which the latter do not. But psychologically, opaque readings are stronger than transparent ones; they tell us more about the character of the mental causes of behavior. The representational theory of mind offers an explanation of this anomaly. Opaque ascriptions are true in virtue of the way that the agent represents the objects of his wants (intentions, beliefs, etc.) *to himself*. And, by assumption, such representations function in the causation of the behaviors that the agent produces. So, for example, to say that it's true *opaquely* that Oedipus did such-and-such because he wanted to marry Jocasta, is to say something like (though not, perhaps, *very* like; see Fodor, 1978): "Oedipus said to himself, 'I want to marry Jocasta,' and his so saying was among the causes of his behavior." Whereas to say (only) that it's true transparently that O. wanted to marry J. is to say no more than that among the causes of his behavior was O.'s saying to himself "I want to marry . . ." where the blank was filled by *some* expression that denotes J.[6] But now, what O. *does*, how he in the proprietary sense behaves, will depend on which description he (literally) had in mind.[7] If it's "Jocasta," courtship behavior follows *ceteris paribus*. Whereas, if it's "my Mum," we have the situation towards the end of the play and Oedipus at Colonus eventually ensues.

I dearly wish that I could leave this topic here, because it would be very convenient to be able to say, without qualification, what I strongly implied above: the opaque readings of propositional attitude ascriptions tell us how people represent the objects of their propositional attitudes. What one would like to say, in particular, is that if two people are identically related to formally identical mental representations, then they are in opaquely type identical mental states. This would be convenient because it yields a succinct and gratifying characterization of what a computational cognitive psychology is about: such a psychology studies propositional attitudes opaquely taxonomized.

I think, in fact, that this is *roughly* the right thing to say, since what I think is *exactly* right is that the construal of propositional attitudes which such a psychology renders is non-transparent. (It's nontransparency that's crucial in all the examples we have been considering.) The trouble is that nontransparency isn't quite the same notion as opacity, as we shall now see.

The question before us is: "What are the relations between the pretheoretic notion of type identity of mental states opaquely construed and the notion of type identity of mental states that you get from a theory which strictly honors the formality condition?" And the answer is: complicated. For one thing, it's not clear that we have a pretheoretic notion of the opaque reading of a propositional attitude ascription: I doubt that the two standard tests for opacity (failure of existential generalization and failure of substitutivity of identicals) so much as pick out the same class of cases. But what's more important are the following considerations. While it's notorious that extensionally identical thoughts may be opaquely type distinct (e.g., thoughts about the Morning Star and thoughts about the

Evening Star), there are nevertheless some semantic conditions on opaque type identification. In particular:

1 there are some cases of formally distinct but coextensive token thoughts which count as tokens of the same (opaque) type (and hence as identical in content at least on one way of individuating contents); and
2 *non*coextensive thoughts are ipso facto type distinct (and differ in content at least on one way of individuating contents).

Cases of type (1): (a) I think I'm sick and you think I'm sick. What's running through my head is "I'm sick"; what's running through your head is "he's sick." But we are both having thoughts of the same (opaque) type (and hence of the same content). (b) You think: "that one looks edible"; I think: "this one looks edible." Our thoughts are opaquely type identical if we are thinking about the same one.

It connects with the existence of such cases that pronouns and demonstratives are typically (perhaps invariably) construed as referring, even when they occur in what are otherwise opaque constructions. So, for example, it seems to me that I can't report Macbeth's hallucination by saying: "Macbeth thinks that's a dagger" if Macbeth is staring at nothing at all. Which is to say that "that's a dagger" doesn't report Macbeth's mental state even though "that's a dagger" may be precisely what is running through Macbeth's head (precisely the representation his relation to which is constitutive of his belief).

Cases of type (2): (a) Suppose that Sam feels faint and Misha knows he does. Then what's running through Misha's head may be "he feels faint." Suppose too that Misha feels faint and Alfred knows he does. Then what's running through Alfred's head, too, may be "he feels faint." I have no, or rather no univocal, inclination to say, in this case, that Alfred and Misha are having type identical thoughts even though the principle of type individuation is, by assumption, opaque and even though Alfred and Misha have the same things running through their heads. But if this is right, then formal identity of mental representations cannot be sufficient for type identity of opaquely taxonomized mental states.[8] (There is an interesting discussion of this sort of case in Geach (1957). Geach says that Aquinas says that there is no "intelligible difference" between Alfred's thought and Misha's. I don't know whether this means that they are having the same thought or that they aren't.)

(b) Suppose that there are two Lake Eries (two bodies of water so-called). Consider two tokens of the thought "Lake Erie is wet," one of which is, intuitively speaking, about the Lake Erie in North America and one of which is about the other one. Here again, I'm inclined to say that the aboriginal, uncorrupted, pretheoretical notion of type-wise same thought wants these to be tokens of *different* thoughts and takes these thoughts to differ in content. In this case, though, as in the others, I think there's also a countervailing inclination to say that they count as type identical – and as identical in content – for some relevant purposes and in some relevant respects. How like aboriginal, uncorrupted, pretheoretical intuition!

I think, in short, that the intuitive opaque taxonomy is actually what you might call "semi-transparent." On the one hand, certain conditions on coreference are in force (Misha's belief that he's ill is type distinct from Sam's belief that *he's* ill, and my thought *this is edible* may be type identical to your thought *that is edible*. On the other hand, you don't get free substitution of coreferring expressions (beliefs about the Morning Star are type distinct from beliefs about the Evening Star) and existential generalization doesn't go through for beliefs about Santa Claus.

Apparently, then, the notion of same mental state that we get from a theory which honors the formality condition is related to, but not identical to, the notion of same mental state that unreconstructed intuition provides for opaque construals. And it would certainly be reasonable to ask whether we actually need both. I think the answer is probably: yes, if we want to capture *all* the intuitions. For, if we restrict ourselves to either one of the taxonomies we get consequences that we don't like. On the one hand, if we taxonomize *purely* formally, we get identity of belief compatible with difference of truth value. (Misha's belief that *he's* ill will be type identical to Sam's belief that be's ill, but one may be true while the other is false.) On the other hand, if we taxonomize solely according to the pretheoretic criteria, we get trouble with the idea that people act out of their beliefs and desires. We need, in particular, some taxonomy according to which Sam and Misha have the *same* belief in order to explain why it is that they exhibit the same behaviors. It is, after all, *part* of the pretheoretic notion of belief that difference in belief ought *ceteris paribus* to show up in behavior *somewhere* ("*ceteris paribus*" here means "given relevant identities among other mental states"), whereas it's possible to construct cases where differences like the one between Misha's belief and Sam's can't show up in behavior even in principle (see note 8). What we have, in short, is a tension between a partially semantic taxonomy and an entirely functional one, and the recommended solution is to use both.

Having said all this, I now propose largely to ignore it and use the term "opaque taxonomy" for principles of type individuation according to which Misha and Sam are in the same mental state when each believes himself to be ill. When I need to distinguish this sense of opaque taxonomy from the pretheoretic one, I'll talk about *full* opacity and fully opaque type identification.

My claim has been that, in doing our psychology, we want to attribute mental states fully opaquely because it's the fully opaque reading which tells us what the agent has in mind, and it's what the agent has in mind that causes his behavior. I now need to say something about how, precisely, all this is supposed to constitute an argument for the formality condition.

Point one: It's just as well that it's the fully opaque construal of mental states that we need since, patently, that's the only one that the formality condition permits us. This is because the formality condition prohibits taxonomizing psychological states by reference to the semantic properties of mental representations and, at bottom, transparency is a semantic (viz. nonformal; viz. nonsyntactic) notion. The point is sufficiently obvious: If we count the belief that the Evening Star is F as (type) identical to the belief that the Morning Star is F, that must be because of the coreference of such expressions as "the Morning Star" and "the Evening Star." But coreference is a semantic property, and not one which could conceivably have a formal *Doppelgänger*; it's inconceivable, in particular, that there should be a system of mental representations such that, in the general case, coreferring expressions are formally identical in that system. (This might be true for God's mind, but not, surely, for anybody else's (and not for God's either unless he is an Extensionalist; which I doubt).) So, if we want transparent taxonomies of mental states, we will have to give up the formality condition. So it's a good thing for the computational theory of the mind that it's not transparent taxonomies that we want.

What's harder to argue for (but might, nevertheless, be true) is point two: that the formality condition *can* be honored by a theory which taxonomizes mental states according to their content. For, barring caveats previously reviewed, it may be that mental states are distinct in content only if they are relations to formally distinct mental representations; in effect, that aspects of content can be reconstructed as aspects of form, at least insofar as appeals to content figure in accounts of the mental causation of behavior. The main thing to be said in favor of this speculation is that it allows us to explain, within the context of the representational theory of mind, how beliefs of different content *can* have different behavioral effects, even when the beliefs are transparently type identical. The form of explanation goes: it's because different content implies formally distinct internal representations (via the formality condition) and formally distinct internal representations can be functionally different – can differ in their causal role. Whereas, to put it mildly, it's hard to see how internal representations could differ in causal role *unless* they differed in form.

To summarize: Transparent taxonomy is patently incompatible with the formality condition; whereas taxonomy in respect of content *may* be compatible with the formality condition, plus or minus a bit. That taxonomy in respect of content is compatible with the formality condition, plus or minus a bit, is perhaps *the* basic idea of modern cognitive theory. The representational theory of mind and the computational theory of mind merge here for, on the one hand, it's claimed that psychological states differ in content only if they are relations to type distinct mental representations; and, on the other, it's claimed that only formal properties of mental representations contribute to their type individuation for the purposes of theories of mind/body interaction. Or, to put it the other way round, it's allowed that mental representations affect behavior in virtue of their content, but it's maintained that mental representations are distinct in content only if they are also distinct in form. The first clause is required to make it plausible that mental states are relations to mental representations and the second is required to make it plausible that mental processes are computations. (Computations just *are* processes in which representations have their causal consequences in virtue of their form.) By thus exploiting the notions of content and computation *together*, a cognitive theory seeks to connect the *intensional* properties of mental states with their *causal* properties vis-à-vis behavior. Which is, of course, exactly what a theory of the mind ought to do.

As must be evident from the preceding, I'm partial to programmatic arguments: ones which seek to infer the probity of a conceptual apparatus from the fact that it plays a role in some prima facie plausible research enterprise. So, in particular, I've argued that a taxonomy of mental states which honors the formality condition seems to be required by theories of the mental causation of behavior, and that that's a reason for taking such taxonomies very seriously.

But there lurks, within the general tradition of representational theories of mind, a deeper intuition: that it is not only *advisable* but actually *mandatory* to assume that mental processes have access only to formal (nonsemantic) properties of mental representations; that the contrary view is not only empirically fruitless but also conceptually unsound. I find myself in sympathy with this intuition, though I'm uncertain precisely how the arguments ought to go. What follows is just a sketch. I'll begin with a version that I *don't* like; an epistemological version.

> Look, it makes no *sense* to suppose that mental operations could apply to mental representations in virtue of (e.g.) the truth or falsity of the latter. For, consider: truth value is a matter of correspondence to the way the world is. To determine the truth value of a belief would therefore involve what I'll call "directly comparing" the belief with the world; i.e., comparing it with the way the world *is*, not just with the way the world is represented as being. And the

representational theory of mind says that we have access to the world only via the ways in which we represent it. There is, as it were, nothing that corresponds to looking around (behind? through? what's the right metaphor?) one's beliefs to catch a glimpse of the things they represent. Mental processes can, in short, compare representations, but they can't compare representations with what they're representations of. Hence mental processes can't have access to the truth value of representations or, *mutatis mutandis*, to whether they denote. Hence the formaity condition.

This line of argument could certainly be made a good deal more precise. It has been in, for example, some of the recent work of Nelson Goodman (see especially Goodman, 1978). For present purposes, however, I'm content to leave it *im*precise so long as it sounds familiar. For, I suspect that all versions of the argument suffer from a common deficiency: they assume that you can't run a *correspondence* theory of truth together with a coherence theory of evidence. Whereas, I see nothing compelling in the inference from "truth is a matter of the correspondence of a belief with the way the world is" to "*ascertaining* truth is a matter of 'directly comparing' a belief with the way the world is." Perhaps we ascertain the truth of our beliefs by comparing them with one another, appealing to inference to the best explanation whenever we need to do so.

Anyhow, it would be nice to have a *non*epistemological defense of the formality condition; one which saves the intuition that there's something conceptually wrong with its denial but doesn't acquire the skeptical/relativistic commitments with which the traditional epistemic versions of the argument have been encumbered. Here goes:

Suppose, just for convenience, that mental processes are algorithms. So, we have rules for the transformation of mental representations, and we have the mental representations which constitute their ranges and domains. Think of the rules as being like hypothetical imperatives; they have antecedents which specify conditions on mental representation, and they have consequents which specify what is to happen if the antecedents are satisfied. And now consider rules (a) and (b).

(a)   If it's the case that *P*, do such and such.

(b)   If you believe it's the case that *P*, do such and such.

Notice, to begin with, that the compliance conditions on these injunctions are quite different. In particular, in the case where *P* is *false but believed true*, compliance with (b) consists in doing such and such, whereas compliance with (a) consists in *not* doing it. But despite this difference in compliance conditions, there's something *very* peculiar (perhaps *pragmatically* peculiar, whatever precisely that may mean) about supposing that an organism might have different ways of going about attempting to comply with (a) and (b). The peculiarity is patent in (c):

(c)   Do such and if it's the case that *P*, *whether or not* you believe that it's the case that *P*.[9]

To borrow a joke from Professor Robert Jagger, (c) is a little like the advice: 'Buy low, sell high.' One knows just what it would be *like* to comply with either, but somehow knowing that doesn't help much.

The idea is this: When one has done what one can to establish that the belief that *P* is warranted, one has done what one can to establish that the antecedent of (a) is satisfied. And, conversely, when one has done what one can do to establish that the antecedent of (a) is satisfied, one has done what one can to establish the warrant of the belief that *P*. Now, I suppose that the following is at least *close* to being true: to have the belief that *P* is to have the belief that the belief that *P* is warranted; and conversely, to have the belief that the belief that *P* is warranted is to have the belief that *P*. And the upshot of *this* is just the formality condition all over again. Given that mental operations have access to the fact that *P* is believed (and hence that the belief that *P* is believed to be warranted, and hence that the belief that the belief that *P* is warranted is believed to be warranted, . . ., etc.) there's nothing further left to do; there is nothing that corresponds to the notion of a mental operation which one undertakes to perform just in case one's belief that *P* is *true*.

This isn't, by the way, any form of skepticism, as can be seen from the following: There's nothing wrong with Jones having one mental operation which he undertakes to perform if it's the case that *P* and another *quite different* mental operation which he undertakes to perform if *Smith* (≠ Jones) believes that it's the case that *P*. (Cf. "I promise . . . though I don't intend to . . ." vs. "I promise . . . though Smith doesn't intend to . . ."). There's a first person/third person asymmetry here, but it doesn't impugn the semantic distinction between "*P* is true" and "*P* is believed true." The suggestion is that it's the tacit recognition of this pragmatic asymmetry that accounts for the traditional hunch that you can't both identify mental operations with transformations on mental representations and at the same time flout the formality condition; that the representational theory of mind and the computational theory of mind are somehow conjoint options.

So much, then, for the formality condition and the psychological tradition which accepts it. What about naturalism? The first point is that none of the arguments *for* a rational psychology is, in and of itself, an argument *against* a naturalistic psychology. As I remarked above, to deny that mental operations have access to the semantic properties of mental representations is *not* to deny that mental representations *have* semantic properties. On the contrary, beliefs are *just* the kinds of thing which exhibit truth and denotation, and the naturalist proposes to make science out of the organism/environment relations which (presumably) fix these properties. Why, indeed, should he not?

This all *seems* very reasonable. Nevertheless, I now wish to argue that a computational psychology is the only one that we are likely to get; that *qua* research strategy, the attempt to construct a *naturalistic* psychology is very likely to prove fruitless. I think that the basis for such an argument is already to be found in the literature, where it takes the form of a (possibly inadvertent) reductio ad absurdum of the contrary view.

Consider, to begin with, a distinction that Professor Hilary Putnam introduces in "The Meaning of 'Meaning'" (1975) between what he calls "psychological states in the wide sense." and "psychological states in the narrow sense." A psychological state in the *narrow* sense is one the ascription of which does not "[presuppose] the existence of any individual other than the subject to whom that state is ascribed" (p. 136). All others are psychological states in the wide sense. So, for example, *x's jealousy of y* is a schema for expressions that denote psychological states in the wide sense, since such expressions presuppose the existence not only of the *x*s who are in the states, but also of the *y*s who are its objects. Putnam remarks that methodological solipsism (the phrase, by the way, is his) can be viewed as the requirement that only psychological states in the narrow sense are allowed as constructs in psychological theories.

But it is perhaps Putnam's main point that there are at least *some* scientific purposes (e.g., semantics and accounts of intertheoretical reference) which demand the wide construal. Here, rephrased slightly, is the sort of example that Putnam finds persuasive.

There is a planet (call it "Yon") where things are very much as they are here. In particular, by a cosmic accident, some of the people on Yon speak a dialect indistinguishable from English and live in an urban conglomerate indistinguishable from the Greater Boston Area. Still more, for every one of our Greater Bostonians there is a *Doppelgänger* on Yon who has precisely the same neurological structure down to and including microparticles. We can assume that so long as we're construing "psychological state" narrowly, this latter condition guarantees type identity of our psychological states with theirs.

However, Putnam argues, it doesn't guarantee that there is a corresponding identity of psychological states hither and Yon if we construe "psychological state" *widely*. Suppose that there is this difference between Yon and Earth, whereas, over here, the stuff we call "water" has the atomic structure H_2O, it turns out that the stuff that they call "water" over there has the atomic structure XYZ ($\neq H_2O$). And now, consider the mental state *thinking about water*. The idea is that, so long as we construe that state widely, it's one that we, but not our *Doppelgängers*, can reasonably aspire to. For, construed widely, one is thinking about water only if it is water that one is thinking about. But it's water that one's thinking about only if it is H_2O that one's thinking about; water *is* H_2O. But since, by assumption, they never think about H_2O over Yon, if follows that there's at least one wide psychological state that we're often in and they never are, however neurophysiologically like us they are, and however much our narrow psychological states converge with theirs.

Moreover, if we try to say what they speak about, refer to, mention, etc. – if, in short, we try to supply a semantics for their dialect – we will have to mention XYZ, not H_2O. Hence it would be wrong, at least on Putnam's intuitions, to say that they have a word for water. A fortiori, the chemists who work in what they call "MIT" don't have theories *about* water, even though what runs through their head when they talk about XYZ may be identical to what runs through our heads when we talk about H_2O. The situation is analogous to the one which arises for demonstratives and token reflexives, as Putnam insightfully points out.

Well, what are we to make of this? Is it an argument against methodological solipsism? And, if so, is it a *good* argument against methodological solipsism?

To begin with, Putnam's distinction between psychological states in the narrow and wide sense looks to be very intimately related to the traditional distinction between psychological state ascriptions opaquely and transparently construed. I'm a bit wary about this, since what Putnam *says* about wide ascriptions is only that they "presuppose the existence" of objects other than the ascribee; and, of course *a believes Fb and b exists* does not entail *b is such that a believes F of him*, or even $\exists x$ (*a believes Fx*). Moreover, the failure of such entailments is notoriously important in discussions of quantifying in. For all that, however, I don't *think* that it's Putnam's intention to exploit the difference between the existential generalization test for transparency and the presupposition of existence test for wideness. On the contrary, the burden of Putnam's argument seems to be precisely that "John believes (widely) that water is F" is true only if water (viz. H_2O) is such that John believes it's F. It's thus unclear to me why Putnam gives the weaker condition on wideness when it appears to be the stronger one that does the work.[10]

But whatever the case may be with the wide sense of belief, it's pretty clear that the narrow sense must be (what I've been calling) fully opaque. This is because it is only full opacity which allows type identity of beliefs that have different truth conditions (Sam's belief that he's ill with Misha's belief that *he* is; Yon beliefs about XYZ with hither beliefs about H_2O). I want to emphasize this correspondence between narrowness and full opacity, and not just in aid of terminological parsimony. Putnam sometimes writes as though he takes the methodological commitment to a psychology of narrow mental states to be a sort of vulgar prejudice: "Making this assumption is, of course, adopting a *restrictive program* – a program which deliberately limits the scope and nature of psychology to fit certain mentalistic preconceptions or, in some cases, to fit an idealistic reconstruction of knowledge and the world" (p. 137). But in light of what we've said so far, it should be clear that this is a methodology with malice aforethought. Narrow psychological states are those individuated in light of the formality condition; viz. without reference to such semantic properties as truth and reference. And honoring the formality condition is part and parcel of the attempt to provide a theory which explains (1) how the belief that the Morning Star is F could be different from the belief that the Evening Star is F despite the well-known astronomical facts; and (2) how the behavioral effects of believing that the Morning Star is F could be different from those of believing that the Evening Star is F, astronomy once again apparently to the contrary notwithstanding. Putnam is, of course, dubious about this whole project: "The three centuries of failure of mentalistic psychology is tremendous evidence against this procedure, in my opinion" (p. 137). I suppose this is intended to include everybody from Locke and Kant to Freud and Chomsky. I should have such failures.

So much for background. I now need an argument to show that a naturalistic psychology (a psychology of mental states transparently individuated; hence, presumably, a psychology of mental states in the wide sense) is, for practical purposes, out of the question. So far as I can see, however, Putnam has given that argument. For, consider: a naturalistic psychology is a theory of organism/environment transactions. So, to stick to Putnam's example, a naturalistic psychology would have to find some stuff S and some relation R, such that one's narrow thought that water is wet is a thought about S in virtue of the fact that one bears R to S. Well, *which* stuff? The natural thing to say would be: "Water, of course." Notice, however, that if Putnam is right, it may not even be *true* that the narrow thought that water is wet is a thought about water; it *won't* be true of tokens of that thought which occur on Yon. Whether the narrow thought that water is wet is about water depends on whether it's about H_2O; and whether it's about H_2O depends on "how science turns out" – viz. on what *chemistry* is true. (Similarly, mutatis mutandis, *"water" refers to water* is *not*, on this view, a truth of any branch of linguistics; it's *chemists* who tell us what it is that "water" refers to.) Surely, however, characterizing the objects of thought is methodologically prior to characterizing the causal chains that link thoughts to their objects. But the theory which characterizes the objects of thought is the theory of *everything*; it's all of science. Hence, the methodological moral of Putnam's analysis seems to be: The naturalistic psychologists will inherit the Earth, but only after everybody else is finished with it. No doubt it's alright to have a research strategy that says "wait awhile". But who wants to wait *forever*?

This sort of argument isn't novel. Indeed, it was anticipated by Bloomfield (1933). Bloomfield argues that, for all practical purposes, you can't do semantics. The reason you can't is that to do semantics you have to be able to say, for example, what "salt" refers to. But what "salt" refers to is NaCl, and that's a bit of chemistry, not linguistics:

> The situations which prompt people to utter speech include every object and happening in their universe. In order to give a scientifically accurate definition of meaning for every form of a language, we would have to have a scientifically accurate knowledge of everything in the speaker's world. The actual extent of human knowledge is very small compared to this. We can define the meaning of a speech-form accurately when this meaning has to do with some matter of which we possess scientific knowledge. We can define the names of minerals, as when we say

that the ordinary meaning of the English word *salt* is "sodium chloride (NaCl)," and we can define the names of plants or animals by means of the technical terms of botany or zoology, but we have no precise way of defining words like *love* or *hate*, which concern situations that have not been accurately classified . . . The statement of meanings is therefore the weak point in language-study, and will remain so until knowledge advances very far beyond its present state. (pp. 139–40)

It seems to me as though Putnam ought to endorse all of this *including the moral*: the distinction between wanting a naturalistic semantics (psychology) and not wanting any is real but academic.[11]

The argument just given depends, however, on accepting Putnam's analysis of his example. But suppose that one's intuitions run the other way. Then one is at liberty to argue like this:

1 They do too have water over Yon; all Putnam's example shows is that there could be two kinds of water, our kind ($= H_2O$) and their kind ($= XYZ$).
2 Hence, Yon tokens of the thought that water is wet are thoughts about water after all.
3 Hence, the way chemistry turns out is irrelevant to whether thoughts about water are about water.
4 Hence, the naturalistic psychology of thought need not wait upon the sciences of the objects of thought.
5 Hence, a naturalistic psychology may be in the cards after all.

Since the premises of this sort of reply may be tempting (since, indeed, they may be *true*), it's worth presenting a version of the argument which doesn't depend on intuitions about what *XYZ* is.

A naturalistic psychology would specify the relations that hold between an organism and an object in its environment when the one is thinking about the other. Now, think how such a theory would have to go. Since it would have to define its generalizations over mental states on the one hand and environmental entities on the other, it will need, in particular, some canonical way of referring to the latter. Well, *which* way? If one assumes that what makes my thought about Robin Roberts a thought *about Robin Roberts* is some causal connection between the two of us, then we'll need a description of *RR* such that the causal connection obtains in virtue of his satisfying that description. And *that* means, presumably, that we'll need a description under which the relation between him and me instantiates a law.

Generally, then, a naturalistic psychology would attempt to specify environmental objects in a vocabulary such that environment/organism relations are law-instantiating when so described. But here's the depressing consequence again: We have no access to such a vocabulary prior to the elaboration (completion?) of the nonpsychological sciences. "What Granny likes with her herring" isn't, for example, a description under which salt is law-instantiating; nor, presumably, is "salt". What we need is something like "NaCl", and descriptions like "NaCl" are available only *after* we've done our chemistry. What this comes down to is that, at a minimum, '*x*'s being *F* causally explains . . ." can be true only when "*F*" expresses nomologically necessary properties of the *x*s. Heaven knows it's hard to say what *that* means, but it presumably rules out both "Salt's being what Granny likes with her-ring . . ." and "Salt's being salt . . ."; the former for want of being necessary, and the latter for want of being nomological. I take it, moreover, that Bloomfield is right when he says (1) that we don't know relevant nomologically necessary properties of most of the things we can refer to (think about) and (2) that it isn't the linguist's (psychologist's) job to find them out.

Here's still another way to put this sort of argument. The way Bloomfield states his case invites the question: "Why *should* a semanticist want a definition of 'salt' that is 'scientifically accurate' in your sense? Why wouldn't a 'nominal' definition do?" There is, I think, some point to such a query. For example, as Hartry Field has pointed out (1972), it wouldn't make much difference to the way that truth conditional semantics goes if we were to say only "'salt' refers to whatever it refers to." All we need for this sort of semantics is some way or other of referring to the extension of "salt"; we don't, in particular, need a "scientifically accurate" way. It's therefore pertinent to do what Bloomfield notably does not: distinguish between the goals of *semantics* and those of a naturalistic psychology of language. The latter, by assumption, purports to explicate the organism/environment transactions in virtue of which relations like reference hold. It therefore requires, at a minimum, lawlike generalizations of the (approximate) form: *X's utterance of "salt" refers to salt if X bears relation R to Δ*. Since this whole thing *is* supposed to be lawlike, what goes in for "Δ" must be a projectible characterization of the extension of "salt." But in general we discover which descriptions are projectible only a posteriori, in light of how the sciences (including the nonpsychological sciences) turn out. We are back where we started. Looked at this way, the moral is that we can do (certain kinds of) semantics if we have a way of referring to the extension of "salt." But we can't do the naturalistic psychology of reference unless we have some way of saying what salt *is*; which of its properties determine its causal relations.

It's important to emphasize that these sorts of argument do *not* apply against the research program embodied in "rational psychology' – viz. to the program that envisions a psychology that honors the formality condition. The problem we've been facing is: Under what description does the object of thought enter into scientific generalizations about the relations between thoughts and their objects? It looks as though the naturalist is going to have to say: under a description that is law-instantiating – e.g., under physical description. But the rational psychologist has a quite different answer. What *he* wants is *whatever description the organism has in mind* when it thinks about the object of thought, construing "thinks about" fully opaquely. So for a theory of psychological states narrowly construed, we want such descriptions of Venus as, e.g., "the Morning Star," "The Evening Star," "Venus," etc., for it is these sorts of descriptions which we presumably entertain when we think that the Morning Star is *F*. In particular, it is our relation to these sorts of description which determine what psychological state type we're in insofar as the goal in taxonomizing psychological states is explaining how they affect behavior.

Final point under the general head: the hopelessness of naturalistic psychology. Practicing naturalistic psychologists have been at least dimly aware all along of the sort of bind that they're in. So, for example, the "physical specification of the stimulus" is just about invariably announced as a requirement upon adequate formulations of $S-R$ generalizations. We can now see why. Suppose, wildly contrary to fact, that there exists a human population (e.g., English speakers) in which pencils are, in the technical sense of the notion, discriminative stimuli controlling the verbal response "pencil". The point is that even if some such generalization were true, it wouldn't be among those enunciated by a naturalistic psychology; the generalizations of naturalistic psychology are presumably supposed to be nomological, and there aren't any *laws* about pencils *qua* pencils. That is, expressions like "pencil" presumably occur in no true, lawlike sentences. Of course, there presumably is *some* description in virtue of which pencils fall under the organism/environment laws of a naturalistic psychology, and everybody (except, possibly, Gibson) has always assumed that those descriptions are, approximately, physical descriptions. Hence, the naturalist's demand, perfectly warranted by his lights, that the stimulus should be physically specified.

But though their theory has been consistent, their practice has uniformly not. In practice, and barring the elaborately circumscribed cases that psychophysics studies, the requirement that the stimulus be physically specified has been ignored by just about *all* practitioners. And, indeed, they were well advised to ignore it; how else could they get on with their job? If they really had to wait for the physicists to determine the description(s) under which pencils are law-instantiators, how would the psychology of pencils get off the ground?

So far as I can see, there are really only two ways out of this dilemma:

1   We can fudge, the way that learning theorists usually do. That is, we can "read" the description of the stimulus from the character of the organism's response. In point of historical fact, this has led to a kind of naturalistic psychology which is merely a solemn paraphrase of what everybody's grandmother knows: e.g., to saying "pencils are discriminative stimuli for the utterance of 'pencil'" where Granny would have said "pencil" refers to pencils. I take it that Chomsky's review of *Verbal Behavior* demonstrated, once and for all, the fatuity of this course. What *would* be interesting – what would have surprised Grandmother – is a generalization of the form $\varDelta$ *is the discriminative stimulus for utterances of "pencil"* where $\varDelta$ is a description that picks out pencils in some projectable vocabulary (e.g., in the vocabulary of physics). Does anybody suppose that such descriptions are likely to be forthcoming in, say, the *next* three hundred years?

2   The other choice is to try for a computational psychology – which is, of course, the burden of my plaint. On this view, what we can reasonably hope for is a theory of mental states fully opaquely type individuated. We can try to say what the mental representation is, and what the relation to a mental representation is, such that one believes that the Morning Star is F in virtue of bearing the latter to the former. And we can try to say how that representation, or that relation, or both, differ from the representation and the relation constitutive of believing that the Evening Star is F. A naturalistic psychology, by contrast, remains a sort of ideal of pure reason; there must *be* such a psychology, since, presumably, we do sometimes think of Venus and, presumably, we do so in virtue of a causal relation between it and us. But there's no practical hope of making science out of this relation. And, of course, for methodology, practical hope is *everything*.

One final point, and then I'm through. Methodological solipsism isn't, of course, solipsism *tout court*. It's not part of the enterprise to assert, or even suggest, that you and I are actually in the situation of Winograd's computer. Heaven only knows what relation between me and Robin Roberts makes it possible for me to think of him (refer to him, etc.), and I've been doubting the practical possibility of a science whose generalizations that relation instantiates. But I *don't* doubt that there *is* such a relation or that I do sometimes think of him. Still more: I have reasons not to doubt it; precisely the sorts of reason I'd supply if I were asked to justify my knowledge claims about his pitching record. In short: It's true that Roberts won 28 and it's true that I know that he did, and nothing in the preceding tends to impugn these truths. (Or, contrariwise, if he didn't and I'm mistaken, then the reasons for my mistake are philosophically boring; they're biographical, not epistemological or ontological.) My point, then, is *of course* not that solipsism is true; it's just that truth, reference, and the rest of the semantic notions aren't psychological categories. What they are is: They're modes of *Dasein*. I don't know what *Dasein* is, but I'm sure that there's lots of it around, and I'm sure that you and I and Cincinnati have all got it. What more do you want?

NOTES

I've had a lot of help with this one. I'm particularly indebted to Professors Ned Block, Sylvain Bromberger, Janet Dean Fodor, Keith Gundersen, Robert Richardson, and Judith Thomson; and to Mr Israel Krakowski.

1 I shall speak of "type identity" (distinctness) of mental states to pick out the sense of "same mental state" in which, for example, John and Mary are in the same mental state if both believe that water flows. Correspondingly, I shall use the notion of "token identity" (distinctness) of mental state to pick out the sense of "same mental state" in which it's necessary that if x and y are in the same mental state, then $x = y$.

2 For extensive discussion, see Fordor (1975, 1978).

3 This is *not*, notice, the same as saying formal operations are the ones that apply mechanically; in this latter sense, *formality* means something like *explicitness*. There is no particular reason for using formal to mean both syntactic and explicit, though the ambiguity abound in the literature.

4 Some fairly deep methodological issues in AI are involved here. See Fodor (1978), where this surface is lightly scratched.

5 I'm told by some of my friends that this paragraph could be read as suggesting that there are *two kinds* of belief: opaque ones and transparent ones. That is not, of course, the way that it is intended to be read. The idea is rather that there are two kinds of condition that we can place on determinations that a pair of belief tokens count as tokens of the same belief type. According to one set of conditions (corresponding to transparent taxonomy), a belief that the Morning Star is such and such counts as the same belief as a belief that the Evening Star is such and such; whereas, according to the other set of conditions (corresponding to opaque taxonomy), it does not.

6 I'm leaving it open that it may be to say still less than this (e.g., because of problems about reference under false descriptions). For purposes of the present discussion, I don't need to run a line on the truth conditions for transparent propositional attitude ascriptions. Thank Heaven, since I do not have one.

7 It's worth emphasizing that the sense of behavior *is* proprietary, and that that's pretty much what you would expect. Not every true description of an act can be such that a theory of the mental causation of behavior will explain the act under that description. (In being rude to Darcy, Elizabeth is insulting the man whom she will eventually marry. A theory of the mental causation of her behavior might have access to the former description, but not, surely, to the latter.)

Many philosophers – especially since Wittgenstein – have emphasized the ways in which the description of behavior may depend upon its context, and it is a frequent charge against modern versions of rational psychology that they typically ignore such characterizations. So they do, but so what? You can't have explanations of everything under every description, and it's a question for empirical determination which descriptions of behavior reveal its systematicity vis-à-vis its causes. The rational psychologist is prepared to bet that – to put it *very* approximately – behavior will prove to be systematic under some of the descriptions under which it is intentional.

At a minimum, the present claim goes like this: there is a way of taxonomizing behaviors and a way of taxonomizing mental states such that, given these taxonomies, theories of the mental causation of behavior will be forthcoming. And that way of taxonomizing mental states construes them nontransparent.

8 One might try saying what counts for opaque type individuation is what's *in* your head, not just what's running through it. So for example, though Alfred and Misha are both thinking, "he feels faint", nevertheless different counterfactuals are true of them. Misha would cash his pronoun as "he, Sam," whereas Alfred would cash *his* pronoun as "he, Misha." The problem would then be

to decide which such counterfactuals are relevant, since, if we count all of them, it's going to turn out that there are few, if any, cases of distinct organisms having type identical thoughts.

I won't, in any event, pursue this proposal, since it seems clear that it won't, in principle, cope with all the relevant cases. Two people would be having different thoughts when each is thinking, "I'm ill" even if *everything* in their heads were the same.

9   I'm assuming, for convenience, that all the Ps are such that either they or their denials are believed. This saves having to relativize to time (e.g., having *b* and *c* read ". . . you believe or come to believe . . .").

10 I blush to admit that I had missed some of these complexities until Sylvain Bromberger kindly rubbed my nose in them.

11 It may be that Putnam *does* accept this moral. For example, the upshot of the discussion. (ca. p. 153 of his article appears to be that a Greek semanticist prior to Archimedes *could* not (in practice) have given a correct account of what (the Greek equivalent of) "gold" means – because the theory needed to specify the extension of the term was simply not available. Presumably *we* are in that situation vis-à-vis the objects of many of *our* thoughts and the meanings of many of our terms; and, presumably, we will continue to be so into the indefinite future. But then, what's the point of so defining psychology (semantics) that there can't be any?

References

Bloomfield, L. 1933. *Language*. London: Allen and Unwin.
Chomsky, N. 1959. "Review of Skinner's *Verbal Behavior*." *Language* 35: 26–56 [reproduced as part of ch. 8 in this volume].
Descartes, R. 1967. *Meditations on First Philosophy*. Trans. E. Haldane and G. R. T. Ross. Cambridge: Cambridge University Press.
Field, H. 1972. "Tarski's Theory of Truth." *Journal of Philosophy* 69:347–75.
Fodor, J. 1975. *Language of Thought*. New York: Thomas Y. Crowell.
Fodor J. 1978. "Tom Swift and his Procedural Grandmother." *Cognition* 6: 229–47.
Geach, P. 1957. *Mental Acts*. London: Routledge and Kegan Paul.
Goodman, N. 1978. *Ways of Worldmaking*. Hassocks: Harvester Press.
Hume, D. 1967. *Treatise on Human Nature*. Oxford: Clarendon Press.
James, W. 1890. *Principles of Psychology*. Vol. I. New York: Henry Holt (Reprinted New York: Dover, 1950).
Putnam, H. 1960. "Minds and Machines." In S. Hook, ed., *Dimensions of Mind*. New York: New York University Press.
Putnam, H. 1975. "The Meaning of 'Meaning'." In K. Gunderson, ed., *Minnesota Studies in the Philosophy of Science 7. Language, Mind and Knowledge*. Minneapolis: University of Minnesota Press [reproduced as ch. 3 in this volume].
Winograd, T. 1972. *Understanding Natural Language*. New York: Academic Press.

Individualism and Psychology

TYLER BURGE

Recent years have seen in psychology – and overlapping parts of linguistics, artificial intelligence, and the social sciences – the development of some semblance of agreement about an approach to the empirical study of human activity and ability. The approach is broadly mentalistic in that it involves the attribution of states, processes, and events that are intentional, in the sense of "representational." Many of these events and states are unconscious and inaccessible to mere reflection. Computer jargon is prominent in labeling them. But they bear comparison to thoughts, wants, memories, perceptions, plans, mental sets, and the like – ordinarily so-called. Like ordinary propositional attitudes, some are described by means of that-clauses and may be evaluated as true or false. All are involved in a system by means of which a person knows, represents, and utilizes information about his or her surroundings.

In the first part of this paper, I shall criticize some arguments that have been given for thinking that explanation in psychology is, and ought to be, purely "individualistic." In the second part of the paper, I shall discuss in some detail a powerful psychological theory that is not individualistic. The point of this latter discussion will be to illustrate a nonindividualistic conception of explanatory kinds. In a third section, I shall offer a general argument against individualism that centers on visual perception. What I have to say, throughout the paper, will bear on all parts of psychology that attribute intentional states. But I will make special reference to explanation in cognitive psychology.

Individualism is a view about how kinds are correctly individuated, how their natures are fixed. We shall be concerned primarily with individualism about the individuation of mental kinds. According to individualism about the mind, the mental natures of all a person's or animal's mental states (and events) are such that there is no necessary or deep individuative relation between the individual's being in states of those kinds and the nature of the individual's physical or social environments.

This view owes its prominence to Descartes. It was embraced by Locke, Leibniz, and Hume. And it has recently found a home in the phenomenological tradition and in the doctrines of twentieth-century behaviorists, functionalists, and mind–brain identity theorists. There are various more specific versions of the doctrine. A number of fundamental issues in traditional philosophy are shaped by them. In this paper, however, I shall concentrate on versions of the doctrine that have been prominent in recent philosophy of psychology.

Current individualistic views of intentional mental states and events have tended to take one of two forms. One form maintains that an individual's being in any given intentional state (or being the subject of such an event) can be *explicated* by reference to states and events of the individual that are specifiable without using intentional vocabulary and without presupposing anything about the individual subject's social or physical environments. The explication is supposed to specify – in nonintentional terms – stimulations, behavior, and internal physical or functional states of the individual. The other form of individualism is implied by the first, but is weaker. It does not attempt to explicate anything. It simply makes a claim of *supervenience*: an individual's intentional states and events (types and tokens) could not be different from what they are, given the individual's physical, chemical, neural, or functional histories, where these histories are specified nonintentionally and in a way that is independent of physical or social conditions outside the individual's body.

In other papers I have argued that both forms of individualism are mistaken. A person's intentional states and events could (counterfactually) vary, even as the individual's physical, functional (and perhaps phenomenological) history, specified nonintentionally and individualistically, is held constant. I have offered several arguments for this conclusion. Appreciating the strength of these arguments, and discerning the philosophical potential of a nonindividualist view of mind, depend heavily on reflecting on differences among these arguments. They both reinforce one another and help map the topography of a positive position.

For present purposes, however, I shall merely sketch a couple of the arguments to give their flavor. I shall not defend them or enter a variety of relevant qualifications. Consider a person A who thinks that aluminum is a light metal used in sailboat masts, and a person B who believes that he or she has arthritis in the thigh. We assume that A and B can pick out instances of aluminum and arthritis (respectively) and know many familiar general facts about aluminum and arthritis. A is, however, ignorant of aluminum's chemical structure and microproperties. B is ignorant of the fact that arthritis cannot occur outside of joints. Now we can imagine counterfactual cases in which A and B's bodies have their same histories considered in isolation of their physical environments, but in which there are significant environmental differences from the actual situation. A's counterfactual environment lacks aluminum and has in its places a similar-looking light metal. B's counterfactual environment is such that no one has ever isolated arthritis as a specific disease, or syndrome of diseases. In these cases, A would lack "aluminum thoughts" and B would lack "arthritis thoughts." Assuming natural developmental patterns, both would have different thoughts. Thus these differences from the actual situation show up not only in the protagonist's relations to their environments, but also in their intentional mental states and events, ordinarily so-called. The arguments bring out variations in obliquely (or intensionally) occurring expressions in literal mental state and event ascriptions, our primary means of identifying intentional mental states.[1]

I believe that these arguments use literal descriptions of mental events, and are independent of conversational devices that may affect the form of an ascription without bearing on the nature of the mental event described. The sort of argument that we have illustrated does not depend on special features of the notions of arthritis or aluminum. Such arguments go through for observational and theoretical notions, for percepts as well as concepts, for natural-kind and nonnatural-kind notions, for notions that are the special preserve of experts, and for what are known in the psychological literature as "basic categories." Indeed, I think that, at a minimum, relevantly similar arguments can be shown to go through with any notion that applies to public types of object, property, or event that are typically known by empirical means.[2]

I shall not elaborate or defend the arguments here. In what follows, I shall presuppose that they are cogent. For our purposes, it will be enough if one bears firmly in mind their conclusion: Mental states and events may in principle vary with variations in the environment, even as an individual's physical (functional, phenomenological) history, specified nonintentionally and individualistically, remains constant.

A common reaction to these conclusions, often unsupported by argument, has been to concede their force, but to try to limit their effect. It is frequently held that they apply to commonsense attributions of attitudes, but have no application to analogous attributions in psychology. Nonindividualistic aspects of mentalistic attribution have been held to be uncongenial with the purposes and requirements of psychological theory. Of course, there is a tradition of holding that ordinary intentional attributions are incapable of yielding any knowledge at all. Others have held the more modest view that mentalistic attributions are capable of yielding only knowledge that could not in principle be systematized in a theory.

I shall not be able to discuss all of these lines of thought. In particular I shall ignore generalized arguments that mentalistic ascriptions are deeply indeterminate, or otherwise incapable of yielding knowledge. Our focus will be on arguments that purport to show that nonindividualistic mentalistic ascriptions cannot play a systematic role in psychological explanation – *because* of the fact that they are not individualistic.

There are indeed significant differences between theoretical discourse in psychology and the mentalistic discourse of common sense. The most obvious one is that the language of theoretical psychology requires refinements on ordinary discourse. It not only requires greater system and rigor, and a raft of unconscious states and events that are not ordinarily attributed (though they are, I think, ordinarily allowed for). It also must distill out descriptive-explanatory purposes of common attributions from uses that serve communication at the expense of description and explanation. Making this distinction is already common practice. Refinement for scientific purposes must, however, be systematic and meticulous – though it need not eliminate all vagueness. I think that there are no sound reasons to believe that such refinement cannot be effected through the development of psychological theory, or that effecting it will fundamentally change the nature of ordinary mentalistic attributions.

Differences between scientific and ordinary discourse survive even when ordinary discourse undergoes the refinements just mentioned. Although commonsense discourse – both about macrophysical objects and about mental events – yields knowledge, I believe that the principles governing justification for such discourse differ from those that are invoked in systematic scientific theorizing. So there is, prima facie, room for the view that psychology is or should be fully individualistic – even though ordinary descriptions of mental states are not. Nevertheless, the arguments for this view that have been offered do not seem to me cogent. Nor do I find the view independently persuasive.

Before considering such arguments, I must articulate some further background assumptions, this time about psychology itself. I shall be taking those parts of psychology that utilize mentalistic and information-processing discourse pretty much as they are. I assume that they employ standard scientific methodology, that they have produced interesting empirical results, and that they contain more than a smattering of genuine theory. I shall not prejudge what sort of science psychology is, or how it relates to the natural sciences. I do, however, assume that its cognitive claims and, more especially, its methods and presuppositions are to be taken seriously as the best we now have in this area of inquiry. I believe that there are no good reasons for thinking that the methods or findings of this body of work are radically misguided.

I shall not be assuming that psychology *must* continue to maintain touch with commonsense discourse. I believe that such touch will almost surely be maintained. But I think that empirical disciplines must find their own way according to standards that they set for themselves. Quasi-a priori strictures laid down by philosophers count for little. So our reflections concern psychology as it is, not as it will be or must be.

In taking psychology as it is, I am assuming that it seeks to refine, deepen, generalize, and systematize some of the statements of informed common sense about people's mental activity. It accepts, for example, that people see physical objects with certain shapes, textures, and hues, and in certain spatial relations, under certain specified conditions. And it attempts to explain in more depth what people do when they see such things, and how their doing it is done. Psychology accepts that people remember events and truths, that they categorize objects, that they draw inferences, that they act on beliefs and preferences. And it attempts to find deep regularities in these activities, to specify mechanisms that underly them, and to provide systematic accounts of how these activities relate to one another. In describing and, at least partly, in explaining these activities and abilities, psychology makes use of interpreted that-clauses and other intensional constructions – or what we might loosely call "intentional content."[3] I have seen no sound reason to believe that this use is merely heuristic, instrumentalistic, or second class in any other sense.

I assume that intentional content has internal structure – something like grammatical or logical structure – and that the parts of this structure are individuated finely enough to correspond to certain individual abilities, procedures, or perspectives. Since various abilities, procedures, or perspectives may be associated with any given event, object, property, or relation, intentional content must be individuated more finely than the entities in the world with which the individual interacts. We must allow different ways (even, I think, different primitive ways) for the individual to conceive of or represent any given entity. This assumption about the fine-grainedness of content in psychology will play no explicit role in what follows. I note it here to indicate that my skepticism about individualism as an interpretation of psychology does not stem from a conception of content about which it is already clear that it does not play a dominant role in psychology.[4]

Finally, I shall assume that individualism is prima facie *wrong* about psychology, including cognitive psychology. Since the relevant parts of psychology frequently use attributions of intentional states that are subject to our thought experiments, the language actually used in psychology is not purely individualistic. That is, the generalizations with counterfactual force that appear in psychological theories, given their standard interpretations, are not all individualistic. For ordinary understanding of the truth conditions, or individuation conditions, of the relevant attributions suffices to verify the thought experiments. Moreover, there is at present no well-explained, well-understood, much less well-tested, individualistic language – or individualistic reinterpretation of the linguistic forms currently in use in psychology – that could serve as surrogate.

Thus individualism as applied to psychology must be revisionistic. It must be revisionistic at least about the language of psychological theory. I shall be developing the view that it is also revisionistic, without good reason, about the underlying presuppositions of the science. To justify itself, individualism must fulfill two tasks. It must show that the language of psychology should be revised by demonstrating that the presuppositions of the science are or should be *purely* individualistic. And it must explain a new individualistic language (attributing what is sometimes called "narrow content") that captures genuine theoretical commitments of the science.

These tasks are independent. If the second were accomplished, but the first remained unaccomplishable, individualism would be wrong; but it would have engendered a new level of explanation. For reasons I will mention later, I am skeptical about such wholesale supplementation of current theory. But psychology is not a monolith. Different explanatory tasks and types of explanation coexist within it. In questioning the view that psychology is individualistic, I am not *thereby* doubting whether there are some subparts of psychology that conform to the strictures of individualism. I am doubting whether all of psychology as it is currently practiced is or should be individualistic. Thus I shall concentrate on attempts to fulfill the first of the two tasks that face someone bent on revising psychology along individualistic lines. So much for preliminaries.

I

We begin by discussing a general argument against nonindividualistic accounts. It goes as follows. The behavior of the physiologically and functionally identical protagonists in our thought experiments is identical. But psychology is the science (only) of behavior. Since the behavior of the protagonists is the same, a science of behavior should give the *same* explanations and descriptions of the two cases (by some Ockhamesque principle of parsimony). So there is no room in the discipline for explaining their behavior in terms of different mental states.[5]

The two initial premises are problematic. To begin with the first: It is not to be assumed that the protagonists are behaviorally identical in the thought experiments. I believe that the only clear, general interpretation of "behavior" that is available and that would verify the first premise is "bodily motion." But this construal has almost no relevance to psychology as it is actually practiced. "Behavior" has become a catch-all term in psychology for observable activity on whose description and character psychologists can reach quick "pretheoretical" agreement. Apart from methodological bias, it is just not true that all descriptions that would count as "behavioral" in cognitive (social, developmental) psychology would apply to both the protagonists. Much behavior is intentional action; many action specifications are nonindividualistic. Thought experiments relevantly similar to those which we have already developed will apply to them.

For example, much "behavioral" evidence in psychology is drawn from what people say or how they answer questions. Subjects' utterances (and the questions asked them) must be taken to be interpreted in order to be of any use in the experiments; and it is often assumed that theories may be checked by experiments carried out in different languages. Since the protagonists' sayings in the thought experiments are different, even in nontransparent or oblique occurrences, it is prima facie mistaken to count the protagonists "behaviorally" identical. Many attributions of nonverbal behavior are also intentional and nonindividualistic, or even relational: she picked up the apple, pointed to the square block, tracked the moving ball, smiled at the familiar face, took the money instead of the risk. These attributions can be elaborated to produce nonindividualist thought experiments. The general point is that many relevant specifications of behavior in psychology are intentional, or relational, or both. The thought experiments indicate that these specifications ground nonindividualist mental attributions. An argument for individualism cannot reasonably *assume* that these specifications are individualistic or ought to be.

Of course, there are nonindividualistic specifications of behavior that are unsuitable for any scientific enterprise ("my friend's favorite bodily movement"). But most of these do not even appear to occur in psychology. The problem of providing reasonable specifications of behavior cannot be solved from an armchair. Sanitizing the notion of behavior to meet some antecedently held methodological principle is an old game, never won. One must look at what psychology actually takes as "behavioral" evidence. It is the responsibility of the argument to show that nonindividualistic notions have no place in psychology. Insofar as the argument assumes that intentional, nonindividualistic specifications of behavior are illegitimate, it either ignores obvious aspects of psychological practice or begs the question at issue.

The second step of the argument also limps. One cannot assume without serious discussion that psychology is correctly characterized as a science (only) of behavior. This is, of course, particularly so if behavior is construed in a restrictive way. But even disregarding how behavior is construed, the premiss is doubtful. One reason is that it is hardly to be assumed that a putative science is to be characterized in terms of its evidence as opposed to its subject matter. Of course, the subject matter is to some extent under dispute. But cognitive psychology appears to be about certain molar abilities and activities some of which are propositional attitudes. Since the propositional attitudes attributed do not seem to be fully individuable in individualistic terms, we need a direct argument that cognitive psychology is not a science of what it appears to be a science of.

A second reason for doubting the premiss is that psychology seems to be partly about relations between people, or animals, and their environment. It is hard to see how to provide a natural description of a theory of vision, for example, as a science of behavior. The point of the theory is to figure out how people do what they obviously succeed in doing – how they see objects in their environment. We are trying to explain relations between a subject and a physical world that we take ourselves to know something about. Theories of memory, of certain sorts of learning, of linguistic understanding, of belief formation, of categorization, do the same. It is certainly not obvious that these references to relations between subject and environment are somehow inessential to (all parts of) psychological theory. They seem, in fact, to be a large part of the point of such theory. In my view, these relations help motivate nonindividualistic principles of individuation (cf. section II). In sum, I think that the argument we have so far considered begs significant questions at almost every step.

There is a kindred argument worth considering: The determinants of behavior supervene on states of the brain. (If one is a materialist, one might take this to be a triviality: "brain states supervene on brain states.") So if propositional attitudes are to be treated as among the determinants of behavior, they must be taken to supervene on brain states. The alternative is to take propositional attitudes as behaviorally irrelevant.[6]

This argument can, I think, be turned on its head. Since prepositional attitudes are among the determinants of our "behavior" (where this expression is as openended as ever), and since propositional attitudes do not supervene on our brain states, not all determinants of our "behavior" supervene on our brain states. I want to make three points against the original argument, two metaphysical and one epistemic or methodological. Metaphysics first.

The ontological stakes that ride on the supervenience doctrine are far less substantial than one might think. It is simply not a "trivial consequence" of materialism about mental states and events that the determinants of our behavior supervene on the states of our brains. This is because what supervenes on what has at least as much to do with how the relevant entities are individuated as with what they are made of. If a mental event m is individuated partly by reference to normal conditions outside a person's body, then, regardless of whether m has material composition, m might vary even as the body remains the same.

Since intentional phenomena form such a large special case, it is probably misleading to seek analogies from other domains to illustrate the point. To loosen up the imagination, however, consider the Battle of Hastings. Suppose that we preserve every human body, every piece of turf, every weapon, every physical structure, and all the physical interactions among them, from the first confrontation to the last death or withdrawal on the day of the battle. Suppose that, counterfactually, we imagine all these physical events and props placed in California (perhaps at the same time in 1066). Suppose that the physical activity is artificially induced by brilliant scientists transported to earth by Martian film producers. The distal causes of the battle have nothing to do with the causes of the Battle of Hastings. I think it plausible (and certainly coherent) to say that in such circumstances, not the Battle of Hastings, but only a physical facsimile would have taken place. I think that even if the location in Hastings were maintained, sufficiently different counterfactual causal antecedents would suffice to vary the identity of the battle. The battle is individuated partly in terms of its causes. Though the battle does not supervene on its physical constituents, we have little hesitation about counting it a physical event.

Our individuation of historical battles is probably wrapped up with intentional states of the participants. The point can also be made by reference to cases that are clearly independent of intentional considerations. Consider the emergence of North America from the ocean.

Suppose that we delimit what count as constituent (say, micro-) physical events of this larger event. It seems that if the surrounding physical conditions and laws are artfully enough contrived, we can counterfactually conceive these same constituent events (or the constituent physical objects' undergoing physically identical changes in the same places) in such a way that they are embedded in a much larger land mass, so that the physical constituents of North America do not make up any salient part of this larger mass. The emergence of North America would not have occurred in such a case, even though its "constituent" physical events were, in isolation, physically identical with the actual events. We individuate the emergence of continents or other land masses in such a way that they are not supervenient on their physical constituents. But such events are nonetheless physical.

In fact, I think that materialism does not provide reasonable restrictions on theories of the role of mentalistic attributions in psychology. The relation of physical composition presently plays no significant role in any established scientific theory of mental events, or of their relations to brain events. The restrictions that physiological considerations place on psychological theorizing, though substantial, are weaker than those of any of the articulated materialisms, even the weak compositional variety I am alluding to. My point is just that rejecting individualistic supervenience does not entail rejecting a materialistic standpoint. So materialism per se does nothing to support individualism.[7]

The second "metaphysical" point concerns causation. The argument we are considering in effect simply assumes that propositional attitudes (type and token) supervene on physicochemical events in the body. But many philosophers appear to think that this assumption is rendered obvious by bland observations about the etiology of mental events and behavior. It is plausible that events in the external world causally affect the mental events of a subject only by affecting the subject's bodily surfaces; and that nothing (not excluding mental events) causally affects behavior except by affecting (causing or being a causal antecedent of causes of) local states of the subject's body. One might reason that in the anti-individualistic thought experiments these principles are violated insofar as events in the environment are alleged to differentially "affect" a person's mental events and behavior without differentially "affecting" his or her body: only if mental events (and states) supervene on the individual's body can the causal principles be maintained.

The reasoning is confused. The confusion is abetted by careless use of the term "affect," conflating causation with individuation. Variations in the environment that do not vary the impacts that causally "affect" the subject's body may "affect" the individuation of the information that the subject is receiving, of the intentional processes he or she is undergoing, or of the way the subject is acting. It does not follow that the environment causally affects the subject in any way that circumvents its having effects on the subject's body.

Once the conflation is avoided, it becomes clear that there is no simple argument from the causal principles just enunciated to individualism. The example from geology provides a useful countermodel. It shows that one can accept the causal principles and thereby experience no bewilderment whatsoever in rejecting individualism. A continent moves and is moved by local impacts from rocks, waves, molecules. Yet we can conceive of holding constant the continent's peripheral impacts and chemically constituent events and objects, without holding identical the continent or certain of its macrochanges – because the continent's spatial relations to other land masses affect the way we individuate it. Or take an example from biology. Let us accept the plausible principle that nothing causally affects breathing except as it causally affects local states of the lungs. It does not follow, and indeed is not true, that we individuate lungs and the various subevents of respiration in such a way as to treat those objects and events as supervenient on the chemically described objects and events that compose them. If the same chemical process (same from the surfaces of the lungs inside, and back to the surfaces) were embedded in a different sort of body and had an entirely different function (say, digestive, immunological, or regulatory), we would not be dealing with the same biological states and events. Local causation does not make more plausible local individuation, or individualistic supervenience.

The intended analogy to mental events should be evident. We may agree that a person's mental events and behavior are causally affected by the person's environment only through local causal effects on the person's body. Without the slightest conceptual discomfort we may individuate mental events so as to allow distinct events (types or tokens) with indistinguishable chemistries, or even physiologies, for the subject's body. Information from and about the environment is transmitted only through proximal stimulations, but the information is individuated partly by reference to the nature of normal distal stimuli. Causation is local. Individuation may presuppose facts about the specific nature of a subject's environment.

Where intentional psychological explanation is itself causal, it may well presuppose that the causal transactions to which its generalizations apply bear some necessary relation to some underlying physical transactions (or other). Without a set of physical transactions, none of the intentional transactions would transpire. But it does not follow that the kinds invoked in explaining causal interactions among intentional states (or between physical states and intentional states – for example, in vision or in action) supervene on the underlying physiological transactions. The same physical transactions in a given person may in principle mediate or underlie transactions involving different intentional states – if the environmental features that enter into the individuation of the intentional states and that are critical in the explanatory generalizations that invoke those states vary in appropriate ways.

Let us turn to our epistemic point. The view that propositional attitudes help determine behavior is well entrenched in common judgments and in the explanatory practices of psychology. Our arguments that a subject's propositional attitudes are not fixed purely by his or her brain states are based on widely shared judgments regarding *particular* cases that in relevant respects bring out familiar elements in our actual psychological and commonsense practices of attitude attribution. By contrast, the claim that none of an individual's propositional attitudes (or determinants of his behavior) could have been different unless some of his brain states were different is a metaphysical conjecture. It is a modal generalization that is not grounded in judgments about particular cases or (so far) in careful interpretation of the actual explanatory and descriptive practices of psychology. Metaphysical ideology should either conform to and illuminate intellectual praxis, or produce strong reasons for revising it.

What we know about supervenience must be derived, partly, from what we know about individuation. What we know about individuation is derived from reflecting on explanations and descriptions of going cognitive practices. Individuative methods are bound up with the explanatory and descriptive needs of such practices. Thus justified judgments about what supervenes on what are *derivative* from reflection on the nature of explanation and description in psychological discourse and common attitude attributions. I think that such judgments cannot be reasonably invoked to restrict such discourse. It seems to me therefore that, apart from further argument, the individualistic supervenience thesis provides no reason for requiring (pan-) individualism in psychology. In fact, the argument from individualistic supervenience begs the question. It *presupposes* rather than establishes that *individuation – hence explanation and description –* in psychology should be fully individualistic. It is simply the wrong sort of consideration to invoke in a dispute about explanation and description.

This remark is, I think, quite general. Not just questions of supervenience, but questions of ontology, reduction, and causation generally, are epistemically posterior to questions about the success of explanatory and descriptive practices.[8] One cannot reasonably criticize a purported explanatory or descriptive practice primarily by appeal to some prior conception of what a "good entity" is, or of what individuation or reference should be like, or of what the overall structure of science (or knowledge) should turn out to look like. Questions of what exists, how things are individuated, and what reduces to what, are questions that arise by reference to going explanatory and descriptive practices. By themselves, proposed answers to these questions cannot be used to criticize an otherwise successful mode of explanation and description.[9]

Of course, one might purport to base the individualist supervenience principle on what we know about good explanation. Perhaps one might hope to argue from inference to the best explanation concerning the relations of higher-level to more basic theories in the natural sciences that the entities postulated by psychology should supervene on those of physiology. Or perhaps one might try to draw analogies between nonindividualistic theories in psychology and past, unsuccessful theories. These two strategies might meet our methodological strictures on answering the question of whether nonindividualistic explanations are viable in a way that an unalloyed appeal to a supervenience principle does not. But philosophical invocations of inference to the best explanation tend to conceal wild leaps supported primarily by ideology. Such considerations must be spelled out into arguments. So far they do not seem very promising.

Take the first strategy. Inductions from the natural sciences to the human sciences are problematic from the start. The problems of the two sorts of science look very different, in a multitude of ways. One can, of course, reasonably try to exploit analogies in a pragmatic spirit. But the fact that some given analogy does not hold hardly counts against an otherwise viable mode of explanation. Moreover, there are nonindividualistic modes of explanation even in the natural sciences. Geology, physiology, and other parts of biology appeal to entities that are not supervenient on their underlying physical make-up. Kind notions in these sciences (plates, organs, species) presuppose individuative methods that make essential reference to the environment surrounding instances of those kinds.

The second strategy seems even less promising. As it stands, it is afflicted with a bad case of vagueness. Some authors have suggested similarities between vitalism in biology, or action-at-a-distance theories in physics, and nonindividualist theories in psychology. The analogies are tenuous. Unlike vitalism, nonindividualist psychology does not ipso facto appeal to a new sort of force. Unlike action-at-a-distance theories, it does not appeal to action at a distance. It is true that aspects of the environment that do not differentially affect the physical movement of the protagonists in the thought experiments do differentially affect the explanations and descriptions. This is not, however, because some special causal relation is postulated, but rather because environmental differences affect what kinds of law obtain, and the way causes and effects are individuated.

Let us now consider a further type of objection to applying the thought experiments to psychology. Since the actual and counterfactual protagonists are so impressively *similar* in so many psychologically relevant ways, can a theoretical language that cuts across these similarities be empirically adequate? The physiological and nonintensional "behavioral" similarities between the protagonists seem to demand similarity of explanation. In its stronger form this objection purports to indicate that nonindividualistic mentalistic language has no place in psychology. In its weaker form it attempts to motivate a new theoretical language that attributes intensional content, yet is individualistic. Only the stronger form would establish individualism in psychology. I shall consider it first.

The objection is that the similarities between the protagonists render implausible any theory that treats them differently. This objection is vague or enthymemic. Filling it out tends to lead one back toward the arguments that we have already rejected. On any view, there are several means available (neurophysiology, parts of psychology) for explaining in similar fashion those similarities that are postulated between protagonists in the thought experiments. The argument is not even of the right form to produce a reason for thinking that the differences between the protagonists should not be reflected somewhere in psychological theory – precisely the point at issue.

The objection is often coupled with the remark that nonindividualistic explanations would make the parallels between the behavior of the protagonists in the thought experiments "miraculous": explaining the same behavioral phenomena as resulting from different propositional attitudes would be to invoke a "miracle." The rhetoric about miracles can be deflated by noting that the protagonists' "behavior" is not straightforwardly identical, that nonindividualistic explanations postulate no special forces, and that there are physical differences in the protagonists' environments that help motivate describing and explaining their activity, at least at one level, in different ways.

The rhetoric about miracles borders on a fundamental misunderstanding of the status of the nonindividualistic thought experiments, and of the relation between philosophy and psychology. There is, of course, considerable empirical implausibility, which we might with some exaggeration call "miraculousness," in two persons' having identical individualistic physical histories but different thoughts. Most of this implausibility is an artifact of the two-person version of the thought experiments – a feature that is quite inessential. (One may take a single person in two counterfactual circumstances.) This point raises a caution. It is important not to think of the thought experiments as if they were describing actual empirical cases. Let me articulate this remark.

The kinds of a theory, and its principles of individuation, evolve in response to the world as it actually is found to be. Our notions of similarity result from attempts to explain actual cases. They are not necessarily responsive to preconceived philosophical ideals.[10] The kind terms of propositional attitude discourse are responsive to broad, stable similarities in the actual environment that agents are taken to respond to, operate on, and represent. If theory had been frequently confronted with physically similar agents in different environments, it might have evolved different kind terms. But we are so far from being confronted by even rough approximations to global physical similarities between agents that there is little plausibility in imposing individual physical similarity by itself as an ideal sufficient condition for sameness of kind terms throughout psychology. Moreover, I think that local physical similarities between the psychologically relevant activities of agents are so frequently intertwined with environmental constancies that a psychological theory that insisted on entirely abstracting from the nature of the environment in choosing its kind terms would be empirically emasculate.

The correct use of counterfactuals in the thought experiments is to explore the scope and limits of the kind notions that have been antecedently developed in attempts to explain actual empirical cases. In counterfactual reasoning we assume an understanding of what our language expresses and explore its application conditions through considering nonactual applications. The counterfactuals in the philosophical thought experiments illumine individuative and theoretical principles to which we are already committed.

The empirical implausibility of the thought experiments is irrelevant to their philosophical point – which concerns possibility, not plausibility. Unlikely but limiting cases are sometimes needed to clarify the modal status of presuppositions that govern more mundane examples. Conversely, the highly counterfactual cases are largely irrelevant to *evaluating* an empirical theory – except in cases (not at issue here) where they present empirical possibilities that a theory counts impossible. To invoke a general philosophical principle, like the supervenience principle, or to insist in the face of the thought experiments that only certain sorts of similarity can be relevant to psychology – without criticizing psychological theory on empirical grounds or showing how the kind notions exhibited by the thought experiments are empirically inadequate – is either to treat counterfactual circumstances as if they were actual, or to fall into apriorism about empirical science.

Let us turn to the weaker form of the worry that we have been considering. The worry purports to motivate a new individualistic language of attitude attribution. As I have noted, accepting such a language is consistent with rejecting (pan-) individualism in psychology. There is a variety of levels or kinds of explanation in psychology. Adding another will not alter the issues at stake here, but let us pursue the matter briefly.

There are in psychology levels of individualistic description above the physiological but below the attitudinal that play a role in systematic explanations. Formalistically described computational processes are appealed to in the attempt to specify an algorithm by which a person's propositional information is processed. I think that the protagonists in our thought experiments might, for some purposes, be said to go through identical algorithms formalistically described. Different information is processed in the "same" ways at least at this formal level of description. But then might we not want a whole level of description, between the formal algorithm and ordinary propositional attitude ascription, that counts "information" everywhere the same between protagonists in the thought experiments? This is a difficult and complex question, which I shall not attempt to answer here. I do, however, want to mention grounds for caution about supplementing psychology wholesale.

In the first place, the motivation for demanding the relevant additions to psychological theory is empirically weak. In recent philosophical literature, the motivation rests largely on intuitions about Cartesian demons or brains in vats, whose relevance and even coherence have been repeatedly challenged; on preconceptions about the supervenience of the mental on the neural that have no generalized scientific warrant; on misapplications of ordinary observations about causation; and on a sketchy and unclear conception of behavior unsupported by scientific practice.[11] Of course, one may reasonably investigate any hypothesis on no more than an intuitively based hunch. What is questionable is the view that there are currently strong philosophical or scientific grounds for instituting a new type of individualistic explanation.

In the second place, it is easy to underestimate what is involved in creating a relevant individualistic language that would be of genuine use in psychology. Explications of such language have so far been pretty makeshift. It does not suffice to sketch a semantics that says in effect that a sentence comes out true in all worlds that chemically identical protagonists in relevant thought experiments cannot distinguish. Such an explication gives no clear rules for the use of the language, much less a demonstration that it can do distinctive work in psychology. Moreover, explication of the individualistic language (or language component) only for the special case in which the languageuser's physiological or (individualistically specified) functional states are held constant is psychologically useless, since no two people are ever actually identical in their physical states.

To fashion an individualist language, it will not do to limit its reference to objective properties accessible to perception. For our language for ascribing notions of perceptually accessible physical properties is not individualistic. More generally, as I have argued elsewhere ("Intellectual Norms and Foundations of Mind"), any attitudes that contain notions for physical objects, events, and properties are nonindividualistic.[12] The assumptions about objective representation needed to generate the argument are very minimal. I think it questionable whether there is a coherent conception of objective representation that can support an individualistic language of intentional attitude attribution. Advocates of such a language must either explain such a conception in depth, or attribute intentional states that lack objective physical reference.

II

I have been criticizing arguments for revising the language of psychology to accord with individualism. I have not tried to argue for nonindividualistic psychological theories from a standpoint outside of psychology. The heart of my case is the observation that psychological theories, taken literally, are not purely individualistic, that there are no strong reasons for taking them nonliterally, and that we currently have no superior standpoint for judging how psychology ought to be done than that of seeing how it *is* done. One can, of course, seek deeper understanding of nonindividualistic aspects of psychological theory. Development of such understanding is a multifaceted task. Here I shall develop only points that are crucial to my thesis, illustrating them in some detail by reference to one theory.

Ascription of intentional states and events in psychology constitutes a type of individuation and explanation that carries presuppositions about the specific nature of the person's or animal's surrounding environment. Moreover, states and events are individuated so as to set the terms for specific evaluations of them for truth or other types of success. We can judge directly whether conative states are practically successful and cognitive states are veridical. For example, by characterizing a subject as visually representing an X, and specifying whether the visual state appropriately derives from an X in the particular case, we can judge whether the subject's state is veridical. Theories of vision, of belief formation, of memory, learning, decision making, categorization, and perhaps even reasoning all attribute states that are subject to practical and semantical evaluation *by reference to standards partly set by a wider environment.*

Psychological theories are not themselves evaluative theories. But they often individuate phenomena so as to make evaluation readily accessible *because* they are partly motivated by such judgments. Thus we judge that in certain delimitable contexts people get what they want, know what is the case, and perceive what is there. And we try to frame explanations that account for these successes, and correlative failures, in such a way as to illumine as specifically as possible the mechanisms that underlie and make true our evaluations.

I want to illustrate and develop these points by considering at some length a theory of vision. I choose this example primarily because it is a very advanced and impressive theory, and admits to being treated in some depth. Its information-processing approach is congenial with mainstream work in cognitive psychology. Some of its intentional aspects are well understood – and indeed are sometimes conceptually and mathematically far ahead of its formal (or syntactical) and physiological aspects. Thus the theory provides an example of a mentalistic theory with solid achievements to its credit.

The theory of vision maintains a pivotal position in psychology. Since perceptual processes provide the input for many higher cognitive processes, it is reasonable to think that if the theory of vision treats intentional states nonindividualistically, other central parts of cognitive psychology will do likewise. Information processed by more central capacities depends, to a large extent, on visual information.

Certain special aspects of the vision example must be noted at the outset. The arguments that I have previously published against individualism (cf. note 1) have centered on "higher" mental capacities, some of which essentially involve the use of language. This focus was motivated by an interest in the relation between thought and linguistic meaning and in certain sorts of intellectual responsibility. Early human vision makes use of a limited range of representations – representations of shape, texture, depth and other spatial relations, motion, color, and so forth. These representations (percepts) are formed by processes that are relatively immune to correction from other sources of information; and the representations of early vision appear to be fully independent of language. So the thought experiments that I have previously elaborated will not carry over simply to early human vision. (One would expect those thought experiments to be more relevant to social and developmental psychology, to concept learning, and to parts of "higher" cognitive psychology.) But the case against individualism need not center on higher cognitive capacities or on the relation between thought and language. The anti-individualistic conclusions of our previous arguments can be shown to apply to early human vision. The abstract schema which those thought experiments articulate also applies.

The schema rests on three general facts. The first is that what entities in the objective world one intentionally interacts with in the employment of many representational (intentional) types affects the semantic properties of those representational types, what they are, and how we individuate them.[13] A near consequence of this first fact is that there can be slack between, on the one hand, the way a subject's representational types apply to the world, and on the other, what that person knows about, and how he or she can react to, the way they apply. It is possible for representational types to apply differently, without the person's physical reactions or discriminative powers being different. These facts, together with the fact that many fundamental mental states and events are individuated in terms of the relevant representational types, suffice to generate the conclusion that many paradigmatic mental states and events are not individualistically individuated: they may vary while a person's body and discriminative powers are conceived as constant. For by the second fact one can conceive of the way a person's representational types apply to the objective world as varying, while that person's history, nonintentionally and individualistically specified, is held constant. By the first fact, such variation may vary the individuation of the person's representational types. And by the third, such variation may affect the individuation of the person's mental states and events. I shall illustrate how instances of this schema are supported by Marr's theory of vision.[14]

Marr's theory subsumes three explanatory enterprises: (1) a theory of the computation of the information, (2) an account of the representations used and of the algorithms by which they are manipulated, and (3) a theory of the underlying physiology. Our primary interest is in the first level, and in that part of the second that deals with the individuation of representations. Both of these parts of the theory are fundamentally intentional.

The theory of the computation of information encompasses an account of what information is extracted from what antecedent resources, and an account of the reference-preserving "logic" of the extraction. These accounts proceed against a set of biological background assumptions. It is assumed that visual systems have evolved to solve certain problems forced on them by the environment. Different species are set different problems and solve them differently. The theory of human vision specifies a general information-processing problem – that of generating reliable representations of certain objective, distal properties of the surrounding world on the basis of proximal stimulations.

The human visual system computes complex representations of certain visible properties, on the basis of light intensity values on retinal images. The primary visible properties that Marr's theory treats are the shapes and locations of things in the world. But various other properties – motion, texture, color, lightness, shading – are also dealt with in some detail. The overall computation is broken down into stages of increasing complexity, each containing modules that solve various subproblems.

The theory of computation of information clearly treats the visual system as going through a series of intentional or representational states. At an early stage, the visual system is counted as representing objective features of the physical world.[15] There is no other way to treat the visual system as solving the problem that the theory sees it as solving than by attributing intentional states that represent objective, physical properties.

More than half of Marr's book is concerned with developing the theory of the computation of information and with individuating representational primitives. These parts of the theory are more deeply developed, both conceptually and mathematically, than the account of the algorithms. This point is worth emphasizing because it serves to correct the impression, often conveyed in recent philosophy of psychology, that intentional theories are regressive and all of the development of genuine theory in psychology has been proceeding at the level of purely formal, "syntactical" transformations (algorithms) that are used in cognitive systems.

I now want, by a series of examples, to give a fairly concrete sense of how the theory treats the relation between the visual system and the physical environment. Understanding this relation will form essential background for understanding the nonindividualistic character of the theory. The reader may skip the detail and still follow the philosophical argument. But the detail is there to support the argument and to render the conception of explanation that the argument yields both concrete and vivid.

Initially, I will illustrate two broad points. The *first* is that the theory makes essential reference to the subject's distal stimuli and makes essential assumptions about contingent facts regarding the subject's physical environment. Not only do the basic questions of the theory refer to what one sees under normal conditions, but the computational theory and its theorems are derived from numerous explicit assumptions about the physical world.

The *second* point to be illustrated is that the theory is set up to explain the reliability of a great variety of processes and subprocesses for acquiring information, at least to the extent that they are reliable. Reliability is presupposed in the formulations of the theory's basic questions. It is also explained through a detailed account of how in certain specified, standard conditions, veridical information is derived from limited means. The theory explains not merely the reliability of the system as a whole, but the reliability of various stages in the visual process. It begins by assuming that we see certain objective properties and proceeds to explain particular successes by framing conditions under which success would be expected (where the conditions are in fact typical). Failures are explained primarily by reference to a failure of these conditions to obtain. To use a phrase of Bernie Kobes's, the theory is not success-neutral. The explanations and, as we shall later see, the kinds of theory presuppose that perception and numerous subroutines of perception are veridical in normal circumstances.

Example 1: In an early stage of the construction of visual representation, the outputs of channels or filters that are sensitive to spatial distributions of light intensities are combined to produce representations of local contours, edges, shadows, and so forth. The filters fall into groups of different sizes, in the sense that different groups are sensitive to different bands of spatial frequencies. The channels are primarily sensitive to sudden intensity changes, called "zero-crossings," at their scales (within their frequency bands). The theoretical question arises: How do we combine the results of the different-sized channels to construct representations with physical meaning – representations that indicate edge segments or local contours in the external physical world? There is no a priori reason why zero-crossings obtained from different-sized filters should be related to some one physical phenomenon in the environment. There is, however, a physical basis for their being thus related. This basis is identified by *the constraint of spatial localization*. Things in the world that give rise to intensity changes in the image, such as changes of illumination (caused by shadows, light sources) or changes in surface reflectance (caused by contours, creases, and surface boundaries), are spatially localized, not scattered and not made up of waves. Because of this fact, if a zero-crossing is present in a channel centered on a given frequency band, there should be a corresponding zero-crossing at the same spatial location in larger-scaled channels. If this ceases to be so at larger scales, it is because (1) two or more local intensity changes are being averaged together in the larger channel (for example, the edges of a thin bar may register radical frequency changes in small channels, but go undetected in larger ones); or (2) because two independent physical phenomena are producing intensity changes in the same area but at different scales (for example, a shadow superimposed on a sudden reflectance change; if the shadow is located in a certain way, the positions of the zero-crossings may not make possible a separation of the two physical phenomena). Some of these exceptions are sufficiently rare that the visual system need not and does not account for them – thus allowing for possible illusions; others are reflected in complications of the basic assumption that follows. The spatial coincidence constraint yields *the spatial coincidence assumption*:

> If a zero-crossing segment is present in a set of independent channels over a contiguous range of sizes, and the segment has the same position and orientation in each channel, then the set of such zero-crossing segments indicates the presence of an intensity change in the image that is due to a single physical phenomenon (a change in reflectance, illumination, depth, or surface orientation).

Thus the theory starts with the observation that physical edges produce roughly coincident zero-crossings in channels of neighboring sizes. The spatial coincidence assumption asserts that the coincidence of zero-crossings of neighboring sizes is normally sufficient evidence of a real physical edge. Under such circumstances, according to the theory, a representation of an edge is formed.[16]

Example 2: Because of the laws of light and the way our eyes are made, positioned, and controlled, our brains typically receive similar image signals originating from two points that are fairly similarly located in the respective eyes or images, at the same horizontal level. If two objects are separated in depth from the viewer, the relative positions of their image signals will differ in the two eyes. The visual system determines the distance of physical surfaces by measuring the angular discrepancy in position (disparity) of the image of an object in the two eyes. This process is called stereopsis. To solve the problem of determining distance, the visual system must select a location on a surface as represented by one image, identify the same location in the other image, and measure the disparity between the corresponding image points. There is, of course, no a priori means of matching points from the two images. The theory indicates how correct matches are produced by appealing to three *physical constraints* (actually the first is not made explicit, but is relied upon): (1) the two eyes produce similar representations of the same external items; (2) a given point on a physical surface has a unique position in space at any given time; (3) matter is cohesive – separated into objects, the surfaces of which are usually smooth in the sense that surface variation is small compared to overall distance from the observer. These three physical constraints are rewritten as three corresponding *constraints on matching*: (1) two representational elements can match if and only if they normally could have arisen from the same physical item (for example, in stereograms, dots match dots rather than bars); (2) nearly always, each representational element can match only one element from the other image (exceptions occur when two markings lie along the line of sight of one eye but are separately visible by the other causing illusions); (3) disparity varies smoothly almost everywhere (this derives from physical constraint (3) because that constraint implies that the distance to the visible surface varies, approximately continuously except at object boundaries, which occupy a small fraction of the area of an image). Given suitable precisifications, these matching constraints can be used to prove the *fundamental theorem of stereopsis*:

> If a correspondence is established between physically meaningful representational primitives extracted from the left and right images of a scene that contains a sufficient amount of detail (roughly 2 percent density for dot stereograms), and if the correspondence satisfies the three matching constraints, then that correspondence is physically correct – hence unique.

The method is again to identify general physical conditions that give rise to a visual process, then to use those conditions to motivate constraints on the form of the process that, when satisfied, will allow the process to be interpreted as providing reliable representations of the physical environment.[17]

These examples illustrate theories of the computation of information. The critical move is the formulation of general physical facts that limit the interpretation of a visual problem enough to allow one to interpret the machinations of the visual system as providing a unique and veridical solution, at least in typical cases. The primary aim of referring to contingent physical facts and properties is to enable the theory to explain the visual system's reliable acquisition of information about the physical world: to explain the success or veridicality of various types of visual representation. So much for the first two points that we set out to illustrate.

I now turn to a third that is a natural corollary of the second, and that will be critical for our argument that the theory is nonindividualistic: the information carried by representations – their intentional content – is individuated in terms of the specific distal causal antecedents in the physical world that the information is about and that the representations normally apply to. The individuation of the intentional features of numerous representations depends on a variety of physical constraints that our knowledge of the external world gives us. Thus the individuation of intentional content of representational types presupposes the veridicality of perception. Not only the explanations but the intentional kinds of the theory presuppose contingent facts about the subject's physical environment.

> *Example 3*: In building up informational or representational primitives in the primal sketch, Marr states six general physical assumptions that constrain the choice of primitives. I shall state some of these to give a sense of their character: (1) the visible world is composed of smooth surfaces having reflectance functions whose spatial structure may be complex; (2) markings generated on a surface by a single process are often arranged in continuous spatial structures – curves, lines, etc.; (3) if direction of motion is discontinuous at more than one point – for example, along a line – then an object boundary is present. These assumptions are used to identify the physical significance of – the objective information normally given by – certain types of pattern in the image. The computational theory states conditions under which these primitives form to carry information about items in the physical world (Marr, *Vision*, pp. 44–71). The theory in example 1 is a case in point: conditions are laid down under which certain patterns may be taken as representing an objective physical condition; as being edge boundary, bar, or blob detectors. Similar points apply for more advanced primitives.

> *Example 4*: In answering the question "what assumptions do we reasonably and actually employ when we interpret silhouettes as three-dimensional shapes?" Marr motivates a central representational primitive by stating physical constraints that lead to the proof of a theorem. *Physical*

constraints: (1) Each line of sight from the viewer to the object grazes the object's surface at exactly one point. (2) Nearby points on the contour in an image arise from nearby points on the contour generator on the viewed object. (That is, points that appear close together in the image actually are close together on the object's surface.) (3) The contour generator lies wholly in a single plane. Obviously, these are conditions of perception that may fail, but they are conditions under which we seem to do best at solving the problem of deriving three-dimensional shape descriptions from representations of silhouettes. *Definition: A generalized cone* is a three-dimensional object generated by moving a cross-section along an axis; the cross-section may vary smoothly in size, but its shape remains the same. (For example footballs, pyramids, legs, stalagmites are or approximate generalized cones.) *Theorem*: If the surface is smooth and if physical constraints (1)–(3) hold for all distant viewing positions in any one plane, then the viewed surface is a generalized cone. The theorem indicates a natural connection between generalized cones and the imaging process. Marr infers from this, and from certain psychophysical evidence, that representations of generalized cones – that is, representations with intentional content concerning, generalized cones – are likely to be fundamental among our visual representations of three-dimensional objects (Marr, *Vision*, pp. 215–25).

Throughout the theory, representational primitives are selected and individuated by considering specific, contingent facts about the physical world that typically hold when we succeed in obtaining veridical visual information about that world. The information or content of the visual representations is always individuated by reference to the physical objects, properties, or relations that are seen. In view of the success-orientation of the theory, this mode of individuation is grounded in its basic methods. If theory were confronted with a species of organism reliably and successfully interacting with a different set of objective visible properties, the representational types that the theory would attribute to the organism would be different, regardless of whether an individual organism's physical mechanisms were different.

We are now in a position to argue that the theory is not individualistic: (1) The theory is intentional. (2) The intentional primitives of the theory and the information they carry are individuated by reference to contingently existing physical items or conditions by which they are normally caused and to which they normally apply. (3) So if these physical conditions and, possibly, attendant physical laws were regularly different, the information conveyed to the subject and the intentional content of his or her visual representations would be different. (4) It is not incoherent to conceive of relevantly different physical conditions and perhaps relevantly different (say, optical) laws regularly causing the same nonintentionally, individualistically individuated physical regularities in the subject's eyes and nervous system. It is enough if the differences are small; they need not be wholesale. (5) In such a case (by (3)) the individual's visual representations would carry different information and have different representational content, though the person's whole nonintentional physical history (at least up to a certain time) might remain the same. (6) Assuming that some perceptual states are identified in the theory in terms of their informational or intentional content, it follows that individualism is not true for the theory of vision.

I shall defend the argument stepwise. I take it that the claim that the theory is intentional is sufficiently evident. The top levels of the theory are explicitly formulated in intentional terms. And their method of explanation is to show how the problem of arriving at certain veridical representations is solved.

The second step of the argument was substantiated through examples 3 and 4. The intentional content of representations of edges or generalized cones is individuated in terms of *specific* reference to those very contingently instantiated physical properties, on the assumption that those properties normally give rise to veridical representations of them.

The third step in our argument is supported both by the way the theory individuates intentional content (cf. the previous paragraph and examples 3 and 4), and by the explanatory method of the theory (cf. the second point illustrated above, and examples 1–2). The methods of individuation and explanation are governed by the assumption that the subject has adapted to his or her environment sufficiently to obtain veridical information from it under certain normal conditions. If the properties and relations that *normally* caused visual impressions were regularly different from what they are, the individual would obtain different information and have visual experiences with different intentional content. If the regular, lawlike relations between perception and the environment were different, the visual system would be solving different information-processing problems; it would pass through different informational or intentional states; and the explanation of vision would be different. To reject this third step of our argument would be to reject the theory's basic methods and questions. But these methods and questions have already borne fruit, and there are presently no good reasons for rejecting them.

I take it that step four is a relatively unproblematic counterfactual. There is no metaphysically necessary relation between individualistically individuated processes in a person's body and the causal antecedents of those processes in the surrounding world.[18] (To reject this step would be self-defeating for the individualist.) If the environmental conditions were different, the same proximal *visual* stimulations could have regularly had different distal causes. In principle, we can conceive of some regular variation in the distal causes of perceptual impressions with no variation in a person's individualistically specified physical processes, even while conceiving the person as *well adapted* to the relevant environment – though, of course, not uniquely adapted.

Steps three and four, together with the unproblematic claim that the theory individuates some perceptual states in terms of their intentional content or representational types, entail that the theory is nonindividualistic.

Steps two and three are incompatible with certain philosophical approaches that have no basis in psychological theory. One might claim that the information content of a visual representation would remain constant even if the physical conditions that lead to the representation were regularly different. It is common to motivate this claim by pointing out that one's visual representations remain the same, whether one is perceiving a black blob on a white surface or having an eidetic hallucination of such a blob. So, runs the reasoning, why should changing the distal causes of a perceptual representation affect its content? On this view, the content of a given perceptual representation is commonly given as that of "the distal cause of *this* representation," or "the property in the world that has *this* sort of visual appearance." The content of these descriptions is intended to remain constant between possible situations in which the microphysical events of a person's visual processes remain the same while distal causes of those processes are regularly and significantly different. For it is thought that the representations themselves (and our experiences of *them*) remain constant under these circumstances. So as the distal antecedents of one's perceptual representations vary, the reference of those representations will vary, but their intentional content will not.[19]

There is more wrong with this line than I have room to develop here. I will mention some of the more straightforward difficulties. In the first place, the motivation from perceptual illusion falls far short. One is indeed in the same perceptual state whether one is seeing or hallucinating. But that is because the intentional content of one's visual state (or representation) is individuated against a background in which the relevant state is *normally* veridical. Thus the fact that one's percepts or perceptual states remain constant between normal perception and hallucinations does not even tend to show that the intentional visual state remains constant between circumstances in which different physical conditions are the normal antecedents of one's perceptions.

Let us consider the proposals for interpreting the content of our visual representations. In the first place both descriptions ("the distal cause of *this* representation" et al.) are insufficiently specific. There are lots of distal causes and lots of things that might be said to appear "thus" (for example, the array of light striking the retina as well as the physical surface). We identify the relevant distal cause (and the thing that normally appears thus and so) as the thing that we actually see. To accurately pick out the "correct" object with one of these descriptions would at the very least require a more complex specification. But filling out the descriptive content runs into one or both of two difficulties: Either it includes kinds that are tied to a specific environment ("the convex, rough-textured object that is causing this representation"), in which case, the description is still subject to our argument, for these kinds are individuated by reference to the empirical environment; or it complicates the constraints on the causal chain to the extent that the complications cannot plausibly be attributed to the content of processes in the early visual system.

Even in their unrevised forms, the descriptions are overintellectualized philosophers' conceits. It is extremely implausible and empirically without warrant to think that packed into every perceptual representation is a distinction between distal cause and experiential effect, or between objective reality and perceptual appearance. These are distinctions developed by reflecting on the ups and downs of visual perception. They do not come in at the ground, animal level of early vision.

A further mistake is the view that our perceptual representations never purport to specify particular physical properties *as such*, but only via some relation they bear to inner occurrences, which are directly referred to. (Even the phrase "the convex object causing this percept" invokes a specification of objective convexity as such.) The view will not serve the needs of psychological explanation as actually practiced. For the descriptions of information are too in-specific to account for specific successes in solving problems in retrieving information about the actual, objective world.

The best empirical theory that we have individuates the intentional content of visual representations by specific reference to specific physical characteristics of visible properties and relations. The theory does not utilize complicated, self-referential, attributively used role descriptions of those properties. It does not individuate content primarily by reference to phenomenological qualities. Nor does it use the notions of cause or appearance in specifying the intentional content of early visual representations.[20]

The second and third steps of our argument are incompatible with the claim that the intentional content of visual representations is determined by their "functional role" in each person's system of dispositions, nonintentionally and individualistically specified. This claim lacks any warrant in the practice of the science. In the first place, the theory suggests no reduction of the intentional to the nonintentional. In the second, although what a person can do, nonvisually, constitutes evidence for what he or she can see, there is little ground for thinking that either science or common sense takes an individual person's nonvisual abilities fully to determine the content of his or her early visual experience. A person's dispositions and beliefs develop by adapting to what the person sees. As the person develops, the visual system (at least at its more advanced stages – those involving recognition) and the belief and language systems affect each other. But early vision seems relatively independent of these nonvisual systems. A large part of learning is accommodating one's dispositions to the information carried by visual representations. Where there are failures of adaptation, the person does not know what the visual apparatus is presenting to him or her. Yet the presentations are there to be understood.

III

There is a general argument that seems to me to show that a person's nonintentional dispositions could not fix (individuate) the intentional content of the person's visual presentations. The argument begins with a conception of objectivity. As long as the person's visual presentations are of public, objective objects, properties, or relations, it is possible for the person to have mistaken presentations. Such mistakes usually arise for a single sensory modality – so that when dispositions associated with other modalities (for example, touch) are brought into play, the mistake is rectified. But as long as the represented object or property is objective and physical, it is in principle possible, however unlikely, that there be a confluence of illusions such that all an individual person's sensory modalities would be fooled and all of the person's nonintentional dispositions would fail to distinguish between the normal condition and the one producing the mistaken sensory representations. This is our first assumption. In the argument, we shall employ a corollary: our concept of objectivity is such that no one objective entity that we visually represent is such that it must vary with, or be typed so as necessarily to match exactly, an individual's proximal stimuli and discriminative abilities. The point follows from a realistic, and even from a nonsubjectivistic, view of the objects of sight.[21]

We argued earlier that intentional representational types are not in general individuated purely in terms of an attributive role description of a causal relation, or a relation of appearance similarity, between external objects and qualitative perceptual representatives of them. For present purposes, this is our second assumption: Some objective physical objects and properties are visually represented as such; they are specifically specified.

Third, in order to be empirically informative, some visual representations that represent objective entities as such must have the representational characteristics that they have partly *because* instances regularly enter into certain relations with those objective entities.[22] Their carrying information, their having objective intentional content, consists partly in their being the normal causal products of objective entities. And their specific intentional content depends partly on their being the normal products of the specific objective entities that give rise to them. That is why we individuate intentional visual representations in terms of the objective entities that they normally apply to, for members of a given species. This is the core of truth in the slogan, sometimes misapplied I think, that mistakes presuppose a background of veridicality.

The assumptions in the three preceding paragraphs enable us to state a general argument against individualism regarding visual states. Consider a person P who normally correctly perceives instances of a particular objective visible property O. In such cases, let the intentional type of P's perceptual representation (or perceptual state) be O'. Such perceptual representations are normally the product of interaction with instances of O. But imagine that for P, perceptual representations typed O' are on some few occasions the product of instances of a different objective property C. On such occasions, P mistakenly sees an instance of C as an O; P's perceptual state is of type O'. We are assuming that O' represents any instance of O as such (as an O), in the sense of our second premiss, not merely in terms of some attributive role description. Since O' represents an objective property, we may, by our first premiss, conceive of P as lacking at his or her disposal (at every moment up to a given time) any means of discriminating the instances of C from instances of O.

Now hold fixed both P's physical states (up to the given time) and his or her discriminative abilities, nonintentionally and individualistically specified. But conceive of the world as lacking O altogether. Suppose that the optical laws in the counterfactual environment are such that the impressions on P's eyes and the normal causal processes that lead to P's visual representations are explained in terms of Cs (or at any rate, in terms of some objective; visible entities other than instances of O). Then by our third premise, P's visual representation (or visual state) would not be of intentional type O'. At the time when in the actual situation P is misrepresenting a C as an O, P may counterfactually be perceiving something (say, a C) correctly (as a C) – if the processes that lead to that visual impression are normal and of a type that normally produces the visual impression that P has on that occasion. So the person's intentional visual states could vary while his or her physical states and nonintentionally specified discriminative abilities remained constant.

The first premiss and the methodology of intentional-content individuation articulated in the third premise entail the existence of examples. Since examples usually involve shifts in optical laws, and they are hard to fill out in great detail. But it is easiest to imagine concrete cases taken from early but still conscious vision. These limit the number of an individual's dispositions that might be reasonably thought to bear on the content of his or her visual states. Early vision is relatively independent of linguistic or other cognitive abilities. It appears to be relatively modular.

Suppose that the relevant visible entities are very small and not such as to bear heavily on adaptive success. An O may be a shadow of a certain small size and shape on a gently contoured surface. A C may be a similarly sized, shallow crack. In the actual situation P sees Os regularly and correctly as Os: P's visual representations are properly explained and specified as shadow representations of the relevant sort. We assume that P's visual and other discriminative abilities are fairly normal. P encounters Cs very rarely and on those few occasions not only misperceives them as Os, but has no dispositions that would enable him or her to discriminate those instances from Os. We may assume that given P's actual abilities and the actual laws of optics, P would be capable, in ideal circumstances, of visually discriminating some instances of Cs (relevantly similar cracks) from instances of O (the relevant sort of shadows). But our supposition is that in the actual cases where P is confronted by instances of Cs, the circumstances are not ideal. All P's abilities would not succeed in discriminating those instances of relevant cracks, in those circumstances, from instances of relevant shadows. P may not rely on touch in cases of such small objects; or touch may also be fooled. P's ability to have such mistaken visual states is argued for by the objectivity premiss.

In the counterfactual case, the environment is different. There are no instances of the relevant shadows visible to P; and the laws of optics differ in such a way that P's physical visual stimulations (and the rest of P's physical make-up) are unaffected. Suppose that the physical visual stimulations that in the actual case are derived from instances of O – at the relevant sort of shadows – are counterfactually caused by and explained in terms of Cs, relevantly sized cracks. Counterfactually, the cracks take the places of the shadows. On the few occasions where, in the actual case, P misperceives shadows as cracks, P is counterfactually confronted with cracks; and the optical circumstances that lead to the visual impressions on those occasions are, we may suppose, normal for the counterfactual environment.[23] On such counterfactual occasions, P would be visually representing small cracks as small cracks. *P* would never have visual representations of the relevant sort of shadows. One can suppose that even if there were the relevant sort of shadow in the counterfactual environment, the different laws of optics in that environment would not enable *P* ever to see them. But since *P*'s visual states would be the normal products of normal processes and would provide as good an empirical basis for learning about the counterfactual environment as *P* has for learning about the actual environment, it would be absurd to hold that (counterfactually) *P* misperceives the prevalent cracks as shadows on gently contoured surfaces. Counterfactually, *P* correctly sees the cracks as cracks. So *P*'s intentional perceptual states differ between actual and counterfactual situations. This general argument is independent of the theory of vision that we have been discussing. It supports and is further supported by that theory.

IV

Although the theory of vision is in various ways special, I see no reason why its nonindividualistic methods will not find analogues in other parts of psychology. In fact, as we noted, since vision provides intentional input for other cognitive capacities, there is reason to think that the methods of the theory of vision are presupposed by other parts of psychology. These nonindividualistic methods are grounded in two natural assumptions. One is that there are psychological states that represent, or are about, an objective world. The other is that there is a scientific account to be given that presupposes certain successes in our interaction with the world (vision, hearing, memory, decision, reasoning, empirical belief formation, communication, and so forth), and that explains specific successes and failures by reference to these states.

The two assumptions are, of course, interrelated. Although an intention to eat meat is "conceptually" related to eating meat, the relation is not one of entailment in either direction, since the representation is about an objective matter. An individual may be, and often is, ignorant, deluded, misdirected, or impotent. The very thing that makes the nonindividualistic thought experiments possible – the possibility of certain sorts of ignorance, failure, and misunderstanding – helps make it possible for explanations using nonindividualistic language to be empirically informative. On the other hand, as I have argued above, some successful interaction with an objective world seems to be a precondition for the objectivity of some of our intentional representations.

Any attempt to produce detailed accounts of the relations between our attitudes and the surrounding world will confront a compendium of empirically interesting problems. Some of the most normal and mundane successes in our cognitive and conative relations to the world must be explained in terms of surprisingly complicated intervening processes, many of which are themselves partly described in terms of intentional states. Our failures may be explained by reference to *specific* abnormalities in operations or surrounding conditions. Accounting for environmentally specific successes (and failures) is one of the tasks that psychology has traditionally set itself.

An illuminating philosophy of psychology must do justice not only to the mechanistic elements in the science. It must also relate these to psychology's attempt to account for tasks that we succeed and fail at, *where these tasks are set by the environment and represented by the subject himself or herself.* The most salient and important of these tasks are those that arise through relations to the natural and social worlds. A theory that insists on describing the states of human beings purely in terms that abstract from their relations to any specific environment cannot hope to provide a completely satisfying explanation of our accomplishments. At present our best theories in many domains of psychology do not attempt such an abstraction. No sound reason has been given for thinking that the nonindividualistic language that psychology now employs is not an appropriate language for explaining these matters, or that explanation of this sort is impossible.

NOTES

A version of this paper was given at the Sloan Conference at MIT in May, 1984. I have benefited from the commentaries by Ned Block, Fred Dretske, and Stephen Stich. I have also made use of discussion with Jerry Fodor, David Israel, Bernie Kobes, and Neil Stillings; and I am grateful to the editors for several suggestions.

1 "Individualism and the Mental," *Midwest Studies* 4 (1979), pp. 73–121; "Other Bodies," in A. Woodfield, ed., *Thought and Object* (Oxford: Oxford University Press, 1982); "Two Thought Experiments Reviewed," *Notre Dame Journal of Formal Logic* 23 (1982), pp. 284–93; "Cartesian Error and the Objectivity of Perception," forthcoming in MacDowell and P. Pettit, eds, *Subject, Thought, and Context* (Oxford: Oxford University Press, 1986) published in R. H. Grimm and D. D. Merrill, eds, *Content and Thought* (Tucson: University of Arizona Press, 1988); "Intellectual Norms and Foundations of Mind", forthcoming, *Journal of Philosophy* [83 (1986), pp. 697–720]. The aluminum argument is adapted from an argument in Hilary Putnam, "The Meaning of 'Meaning'," in *Philosophical Papers*, vol. II (Cambridge: Cambridge University Press, 1975) [reproduced as ch. 3 in this volume]. What Putnam wrote in his paper was, strictly, not even compatible with this argument. (Cf. the first two cited papers in this note for discussion.) But the aluminum argument lies close to the surface of the argument he does give. The arthritis argument raises rather different issues, despite its parallel methodology.

2 On basic categories, cf., e.g., E. Rosch, C. Mervis, W. Gray, D. Johnson, P. Boyes-Bream, "Basic Objects in Natural Categories," *Cognitive Psychology* 8 (1976), pp. 382–439. On the general claim in the last sentence, cf. my "Intellectual Norms" and the latter portion of this paper.

3 Our talk of intentional "content" will be ontologically colorless. It can be converted to talk about how that-clauses (or their components) are interpreted and differentiated – taken as equivalent or nonequivalent – for the cognitive purposes of psychology. Not all intentional states or structures that are attributed in psychology are explicitly propositional. My views in this paper apply to intentional states generally.

4 Certain approaches to intensional logic featuring either "direct reference" or some analogy between the attitudes and necessity have urged that this practice of fine-structuring attitudinal content be revised. I think that for purely philosophical reasons these approaches cannot account for the attitudes. For example, they do little to illumine the numerous variations on Frege's "paradox of identity." They seem to have even less to recommend them as prescriptions for the language of psychology. Some defenses of individualism have taken these approaches to propositional content to constitute the opposition to individualism. I think that these approaches are not serious contenders as accounts of propositional attitudes and thus should be left out of the discussion.

5 Stephen Stich, *From Folk Psychology to Cognitive Science* (Cambridge, MA: MIT Press, 1983), ch. 8. Although I shall not discuss the unformulated Ockhamesque principle, I am skeptical of it. Apart from question-begging assumptions, it seems to me quite unclear why a science should be required to explain two instances of the same phenomenon in the same way, particularly if the surrounding conditions that led to the instances differ.

6 I have not been able to find a fully explicit statement of this argument in published work. It seems to inform some passages of Jerry Fodor's "Methodological Solipsism Considered as a Research Strategy in Cognitive Psychology" in Fodor's *Representations* (Cambridge, MA: MIT Press, 1981)

[reproduced as part of ch. 7 in this volume], e.g., pp. 228–32. It lies closer to the surface in much work influenced by Fodor's paper. Cf., e.g., Colin McGinn, "The Structure of Content," in Woodfield, *Thought and Object*. Many who, like McGinn, concede the force of the arguments against individualism utilize something like this argument to maintain that individualistic "aspects" of intentional states are all that are relevant to psychological explanation.

7   In "Individualism and the Mental," pp. 109–13, I argue that token identity theories are rendered implausible by the nonindividualistic thought experiments. But token identity theories are not the last bastion for materialist defense policy. Composition is what is crucial. It is coherent, but I think mistaken, to hold that propositional-attitude attributions nonrigidly pick out physical events: so the propositional attributions vary between the actual and counterfactual protagonists in the thought experiments, though the ontology of mental event tokens remains identical. This view is compatible with most of my opposition to individualism. But I think that there is no good reason to believe the very implausible thesis that mental events are not individuated ("essentially" or "basically") in terms of the relevant propositional-attitude attributions. (cf. ibid.) So I reject the view that the same mental events (types or tokens) are picked out under different descriptions in the thought experiments. These considerations stand behind my recommending, to the convinced materialist, composition rather than identity as a paradigm. (I remain unconvinced.)

8   The points about ontology and reference go back to Frege, *Foundations of Arithmetic*, trans. J. Austin (Evanston: Northwestern University Press, 1968). The point about reduction is relatively obvious, though a few philosophers have urged conceptions of the unity of science in a relatively aprioristic spirit. At least as applied to ontology, the point is also basic to Quine's pragmatism. There are, however, strands in Quine's work and in the work of most of his followers that seem to me to let a preoccupation with physicalism get in the way of the Fregean (and Quinean) pragmatic insight. It is simply an illusion to think that metaphysical or even epistemic preconceptions provide a standard for judging the ontologies or explanatory efforts of particular sciences, deductive or inductive.

9   Even more generally, I think that epistemic power in philosophy derives largely from reflections on particular implementations of successful cognitive practices. By a cognitive practice, I mean a cognitive enterprise that is stable, that conforms to standard conditions of intersubjective checkability, and that incorporates a substantial core of agreement among its practitioners. Revisionistic philosophical hypotheses must not, of course, be rejected out of hand. Sometimes, but rarely nowadays, such hypotheses influence cognitive practices by expanding theoretical imagination so as to lead to new discoveries. The changed practice may vindicate the philosophical hypothesis. But the hypothesis waits on such vindication.

10 For an interesting elaboration of this theme in an experimental context, see Amos Tversky, "Features of Similarity," *Psychological Review* 84 (1977), pp. 327–52. Cf. also Rosch et al., "Basic Objects in Natural Categories."

11 The most careful and plausible of several papers advocating a new language of individualist explanation is Stephen White, "Partial Character and the Language of Thought," *Pacific Philosophical Quarterly* 63 (1982), pp. 347–65. It seems to me, however, that many of the problems mentioned in the text here and below beset this advocacy. Moreover, the positive tasks set for the new language are already performed by the actual nonindividualist language of psychology. The brain-in-vat intuitions raise very complex issues that I cannot pursue here. I discuss them further in "Cartesian Error and the Objectivity of Perception."

12 See especially "Intellectual Norms and Foundations of Mind," but also "Individualism and the Mental," pp. 81–2.

13 "Representational type" (also "intentional type") is a relatively theory-neutral term for intentional content, or even intentional state kinds. Cf n. 3. One could about as well speak of concepts, percepts, and the representational or intentional aspects of thought contents – or of the counterpart states.

14 In what follows I make use of the important book *Vision*, by David Marr (San Francisco: W. H. Freeman, 1982). Marr writes:

The purpose of these representations is to provide useful descriptions of aspects of the real world. The structure of the real world therefore plays an important role in determining both the nature of the representations that are used and the nature of the processes that derive and maintain them. An important part of the theoretical analysis is to make explicit the physical constraints and assumptions that have been used in the design of the representations and processes. (p. 43)

It is of critical importance that the tokens [representational particulars] one obtains [in the theoretical analysis] correspond to real physical changes on the viewed surface; the blobs, lines, edges, groups, and so forth that we shall use must not be artifacts of the imaging process, or else inferences made from their structure backwards to the structures of the surface will be meaningless. (p. 44)

Marr's claim that the structure of the real world figures in determining the nature of the representations that are attributed in the theory is tantamount to the chief point about representation or reference that generates our nonindividualist thought experiments–the first step in the schema. I shall show that these remarks constitute the central theoretical orientation of the book.

Calling the theory Marr's is convenient but misleading. Very substantial contributions have been made by many others; and the approach has developed rapidly since Marr's death. Cf. for example, D. H. Ballard, G. E. Hinton, and T. J. Sejnowski, "Parallel Vision Computation," *Nature* 306 (November 1983), pp. 21–6. What I say about Marr's book applies equally to more recent developments.

15 It is an interesting question when to count the visual system as having gone intentional. I take it that information is, in a broad sense, carried by the intensity values in the retinal image; but I think that this is too early to count the system as intentional or symbolic. I'm inclined to agree with Marr that where zero-crossings from different-sized filters are checked against one another (cf. example 1), it is reasonable to count visual processes as representational of an external physical reality. Doing so, however, depends on seeing this stage as part of the larger system in which objective properties are often discriminated from subjective artifacts of the visual system.

16 Marr, *Vision*, pp. 68–70; cf. also Marr and E. C. Hildreth, "Theory of Edge Detection," *Proceedings of Royal Society of London* B 207 (1980), pp. 187–217, where the account is substantially more detailed.

17 Marr, *Vision*, pp. 111–16; Marr and T. Poggio, "A Computational Theory of Human Stereo Vision," *Proceedings of Royal Society of London* B 204 (1979), pp. 301–28. Marr, *Vision*, pp. 205–12; Shimon Ullman, *The Interpretation of Visual Motion* (Cambridge, MA: MIT Press, 1979).

18 As I have intimated above, I doubt that all biological, including physiological, processes and states in a person's body are individualistically individuated. The failures of individualism for these sciences involve different but related considerations.

19 Descartes went further in the same direction. He thought that the perceptual system, and indeed the intellect, could not make a mistake. Mistakes derived from the will. The underlying view is that we primarily perceive or make perceptual reference to our own perceptions. This position fails to account plausibly for various visual illusions and errors that precede any activity of the will, or even intellect. And the idea that perceptions are in general what we make perceptual reference to has little to recommend it and, nowadays, little influence. The natural and, I think, plausible view is that we have visual representations that specify external properties specifically, that these representations are predoxastic in the sense they are not themselves objects of belief, and that they sometimes fail to represent correctly what is before the person's eyes: when they result from abnormal processes.

20 Of course, at least in the earliest stages of visual representation, there are analogies between

qualitative features of representations in the experienced image and the features that those representations represent. Representations that represent bar segments are bar-shaped, or have some phenomenological property that strongly tempts us to call them "bar-shaped." Similarly for blobs, dots, lines, and so forth. (Marr and Hildreth, "Theory of Edge Detection," p. 211, remark on this dual aspect of representations.) These "analogies" are hardly fortuitous. Eventually they will probably receive rigorous psychophysical explanations. But they should not tempt one into the idea that visual representations in general make reference to themselves, much less into the idea that the content of objective representation is independent of empirical relations between the representations and the objective entities that give rise to them. Perhaps these qualitative features are constant across all cases where one's bodily processes, nonintentionally specified, are held constant. But the information they carry, their intentional content, may vary with their causal antecedents and causal laws in the environment.

21   There is no need to assume that the abnormal condition is unverifiable. Another person with relevant background information might be able to infer that the abnormal condition is producing a perceptual illusion. In fact, another person with different dispositions might even be able to perceive the difference.

22   Not all perceptual representations that specify objective·entities need have their representational characteristics determined in this way. The representational characters of *some* visual representations (or states) may depend on the subject's background theory or primarily on interaction among other representations. There are hallucinations of purple dragons. (Incidentally, few if any of the perceptual representations – even the conscious perceptual representations – discussed in Marr's theory depend in this way on the subject's conceptual background.) Here, I assume only that some visual representations acquire their representational characters through interaction. This amounts to the weak assumption that the formation of some perceptual representations is *empirical*.

Some of the interaction that leads to the formation and representational characters of certain innate perceptual tendencies (or perhaps even representations) may occur in the making of the species, not in the learning histories of individuals. Clearly this complication could be incorporated into a generalization of this third premiss – without affecting the anti-individualistic thrust of the argument.

23   What of the nonintentionally specified dispositions that in the actual environment(given the actual laws of optics) would have enabled P to discriminate Cs from Os in ideal circumstances? In the counterfactual environment, in view of the very different optical laws and different objects that confront P, one can suppose that these dispositions have almost any visual meaning that one likes. These dispositions would serve to discriminate Cs from some other sort of entity. In view of the objectivity premiss, the nonintentional dispositions can always be correlated with different, normal antecedent laws and conditions – in terms of which their intentional content may be explained.

The argument of this section is developed in parallel but different ways in "Cartesian Error and the Objectivity of Perception."

Part III

The Science of Mind and Language

8

Language and Cognition

Introduction

The study of the mind changed so dramatically in the late 1950s and early 1960s that some have dubbed this shift "the cognitive revolution." What happened was that behaviorist approaches to the mind gave way to cognitivism. Behaviorism came in various forms, but what the various forms had in common was a refusal to admit into their explanations any reference to mental states and processes that were internal to the mind. For the behaviorist, all mental states, including all intelligent and cognitive capacities, were to be understood as input – output relations between stimuli from the environment and external bodily behavior and dispositions to such behavior. Behaviorists believed that they could explain and characterize thinking, reasoning, speaking, understanding, desiring, and so on, without relying on the causal role of any internal mental states.

Cognitivists denied this and maintained that the sciences of the human mind cannot avoid referring to internal psychological states and processes that mediate between the stimuli from the environment and behavior. Many people and factors contributed to this turn toward internal psychological states, but the study of the capacity of human beings to comprehend and produce language played a pivotal role in the move away from behaviorism. Two leading contributors to this shift were the linguist Noam Chomsky and the psychologist George Miller.

George Miller has made many contributions, but he is often cited for his work on short-term memory presented in a paper called "The Magical Number Seven, Plus or Minus Two" (1956). He argued that our short-term memory is limited to seven, plus or minus two, unrelated items, such as letters, numbers, or words. He also calculated that an average English speaker can understand at least 1,020 sentences, and that it would take 100,000,000,000 centuries to hear them all. These facts about our memory and linguistic capacities suggested to him that the reinforcement we get from hearing sentences cannot be the only mechanism involved in language learning. What these mechanisms must be, and the general point of view of cognitivism, are outlined in Miller's programmatic essay that opens this section on language and cognition.

Chomsky's review of B. F. Skinner's behaviorist account of language in *Verbal Behavior* was seen by many as the deathblow to behaviorism. Chomsky argues in some detail that the behaviorists' favored mechanisms of stimulus, response, and reinforcement are not sufficient to explain verbal behavior. One of his important arguments is the poverty of stimulus argument. What the child actually hears is too meager to account for the verbal competence children acquire. Children can produce and comprehend countless new sentences that are physically quite dissimilar from anything they have experienced. To account for these and other phenomena Chomsky entertains the hypothesis that the human brain evolved so that it is capable of comprehending and producing language. Specifically, the brain has evolved so that by nature, and not through learning, it encodes a finite set of rules that is capable of generating the syntactic structures human languages can have.

Eleanor Rosch is important for her work on the nature of the concepts human beings use to categorize the variety of objects in the world around them. She has argued that human beings have psychologically basic concepts that are independent of language. In the essay reprinted here Rosch argues on the basis of experimental evidence that these concepts do not have strict boundaries. This work coincided with and helped bolster the philosophical thesis, due in part to the philosopher Ludwig Wittgenstein, that there are no necessary and sufficient conditions for most of the interesting concepts human beings use. Thus philosophers' search for the necessary and sufficient conditions of, say, knowledge or virtue – a search that goes as far back as Socrates and Plato – is misguided.

Although Wittgenstein would approve of the view that concepts do not have strict boundaries, he would not, at least in his later philosophy, accept the view that some concepts are prior to language. The thesis that public language determines our cognition, or linguistic relativism, has been associated with Wittgenstein and his notoriously difficult Private Language Argument, defended in his *Philosophical Investigations* (1953). Other important sources in this century for this view are Edward Sapir and Benjamin Whorf, whose views will be discussed in chapter 9.

One way of characterizing cognitivism and the turn in the study of the human mind that was introduced by the work of Chomsky and Miller is in terms of innate theories human beings have for some domain. For example, according to Chomsky, our linguistic abilities are in part due to the fact that we are born with a theory of universal grammar. Although we are not conscious of this theory, we nevertheless apply it when we produce and comprehend verbal behavior. A difficult task for this sort of view is to account for what appear to be the highly untheoretical and unstructured cognitive capacities we have. These capacities are extremely sensitive to the tremendous variety of unpredictable contexts in which human beings find themselves, and because these contexts are so diverse and unpredictable, it seems that they are best understood as being governed not by theories but by pragmatic rules of thumb. An example of this is our capacity to have a conversation. We have already encountered attempts to deal with conversation and communication in chapter 2, "Language and Communication."

Another such context-sensitive capacity is non-demonstrative, that is, non-deductive reasoning. In a valid deductive argument, if the premises are true, the conclusion cannot fail to be true. But there are many other kinds of good reasoning where this is not true, for example when we are trying to figure out what someone is saying or what they have in mind. In this kind of reasoning the truth of the premises does not guarantee the truth of the conclusion, but, if our reasoning is good, the truth of the premises only makes the truth of the conclusion more probable.

Dan Sperber and Deirdre Wilson have a long-standing interest in the role of rhetoric and pragmatics in communication, and here we reprint a summary of their influential book *Relevance: Communication and Cognition* (1988). Sperber and Wilson use Grice's Principle of Relevance, introduced in Grice's essay "Logic and Conversation," to account for both communication and nondemonstrative reasoning. The fundamental idea is that when we communicate with someone, for instance by saying something, it is presumed that what we say is sufficiently relevant to the hearer to make it worth her while to process what we are saying. Their account goes a long way to show that it is possible to have theories even of those domains that appear to be highly context-sensitive and untheoretical.

Sperber and Wilson's work also exemplifies a persistent theme in the science of the mind, namely that our views of the mind are deeply influenced by our views about our linguistic capacities. Chomsky and Miller ushered in a new way of understanding the mind on the grounds that the old theories could not account for verbal behavior. In Sperber and Wilson we see how a more context-sensitive view of mind and cognition develops on the basis of the context-sensitive and pragmatic nature of human communication.

FURTHER READING

Chomsky, N. (1957). *Syntactic Structures*. The Hague: Mouton.
D'Agostino, F. (1986). *Chomsky's System of Ideas*. Oxford: Oxford University Press.
Fodor, J. (1983). *The Modularity of Mind*. Cambridge, MA: MIT Press.
Hunt, E. and Agnoli, F. (1991). The Whorfian Hypothesis: A Cognitive Psychology Perspective. *Psychological Review* 90: 377–89.
Jackendoff, R. (1983). *Semantics and Cognition*. Cambridge, MA: MIT Press.
Karmiloff-Smith, A. (1992). *Beyond Modularity: A Developmental Perspective on Cognitive Science*. Cambridge, MA: MIT Press.
Keil, F. (1989). *Concepts, Kinds and Cognitive Development*. Cambridge, MA: MIT Press.
Liebermann, P. (1991). *Uniquely Human: The Evolution of Speech Thought, and Selfless Behavior*. Cambridge, MA: Harvard University Press.
Miller, G. A. and Johnson-Laird, P. N. (1976). *Language and Perception*. Cambridge, MA: Harvard University Press.
Newell, A. (1990). *Unified Theories of Cognition*. Cambridge, MA: Harvard University Press.
Pinker, S. (1993). Central Problems for the Psycholinguist. In *Conceptions of the Human Mind*. Ed. G. Harman. Hillsdale: Lawrence Erlbaum.
Wittgenstein, L. (1953). *Philosophical Investigations*. Oxford: Blackwell.

Some Preliminaries to Psycholinguistics

GEORGE A. MILLER

The success of behavior theory in describing certain relatively simple correlations between stimulation and response has encouraged experimental psychologists to extend and test their theories in more complicated situations. The most challenging and potentially the most important of these extensions, of course, is into the realm of linguistic behavior. Consequently, in recent years we have seen several attempts to characterize human language in terms derived from behavioristic investigations of conditioning and learning in animals. These proposals are well known, so I will make no attempt to summarize them here. I will merely say that, in my opinion, their results thus far have been disappointing.

If one begins the study of a new realm of behavior armed with nothing but hypotheses and generalizations based on experience in some quite different area, one's theoretical preconceptions can be badly misleading. Trivial features may be unduly emphasized, while crucially important aspects may be postponed, neglected, or even overlooked entirely. These hazards are particularly dangerous when we generalize across species, or from nonverbal to verbal behavior.

The impulse to broaden the range of phenomena to which our concepts can be applied is commendable. But when this enthusiasm is not guided by a valid conception of the new phenomena to be explained, much intelligent enterprise can end in frustration and discouragement. Human language is a subtle and complex thing; there are many aspects that, if not actually unique, are at least highly distinctive of our species, and whose nature could scarcely be suspected, much less extrapolated from the analysis of nonverbal behavior.

It was with such thoughts in mind that I decided to take this opportunity to summarize briefly seven aspects of human language that should be clearly understood by any psychologist who plans to embark on explanatory ventures in psycholinguistics. The ideas are familiar to most people working in the field, who could no doubt easily double or treble their number. Nevertheless, the seven I have in mind are, in my opinion, important enough to bear repeating and as yet their importance does not seem to have been generally recognized by other psychologists.

Without further apologies, therefore, let me begin my catalogue of preliminary admonitions to anyone contemplating language as a potential subject for his psychological ratiocinations.

A Point of View

It is probably safe to say that no two utterances are identical in their physical (acoustic and physiological) characteristics. Nevertheless, we regularly treat them as if they were. For example, we ask a subject to repeat something we say, and we count his response as correct even though it would be a simple matter to demonstrate that there were many physical differences between his vocal response and the vocal stimulus we presented to him. Obviously, not all physical aspects of speech are significant for vocal communication.

The situation is more complicated than that, however. There are also many examples – homophones being the most obvious – where stimuli that are physically identical can have different significance. Not only are physically different utterances treated identically, but physically identical utterances can be treated differently. It may often happen that the difference in significance between two utterances cannot be found in any difference of a physical nature, but can only be appreciated on the basis of psychological factors underlying the physical signal.

The problem of identifying significant features of speech is complicated further by the fact that some physical features are highly predictable in nearly all speakers, yet have no communicative significance. For example, when a plosive consonant occurs initially, as in the word *pen*, American speakers pronounce it with aspiration; a puff of air accompanies the *p* (which you can feel if you will pronounce *pen* holding the back of your hand close to your lips). When *p* occurs as a noninitial member of a consonant cluster, however, as in *spend*, this puff of air is reduced or absent. The same phoneme is aspirated in one position and unaspirated in the other. This physical feature, which is quite reliable in American speech, has no communicative significance, by which I mean that the rare person who does not conform is perfectly intelligible and suffers no handicap in communicating with his friends. Facts such as these, which are well known to linguists, pose interesting problems for psychologists who approach the acquisition of language in terms of laboratory experiments on discrimination learning.

In order to discuss even the simplest problems in speech production and speech perception, it is necessary to be able to distinguish significant from nonsignificant aspects of speech. And there is no simple way to draw this distinction in terms of the physical parameters of the speech signal itself. Almost immediately, therefore, we are forced to consider aspects of language that extend beyond the acoustic or physiological properties of speech, that is to say, beyond the objective properties of "the stimulus."

Since the concept of significance is central and unavoidable, it is important to notice that it has two very different senses, which for convenience, I shall call "reference" and "meaning."

For example, in most contexts we can substitute the phrase "the first President of the United States" for "George Washington," since both of these utterances refer to the same historical figure. At least since Frege's time, however, it has been customary to assume that such phrases differ in meaning even though their referent is the same. Otherwise, there would be no point to such assertions of identity as "George Washington was the first President of the United States." If meaning and reference were identical, such an assertion would be as empty as "George Washington was George Washington." Since "George Washington was the first President of the United States" is not a pointless assertion, there must be some difference between the significance of the name "George Washington" and of the phrase "the first President of the United States," and, since this difference in significance is not a difference of referent, it must be a difference in something else – something else that, for want of a better name, we call its meaning.

This distinction between reference and meaning becomes particularly clear when we consider whole utterances. An utterance can be significant even though it might be extremely difficult to find anything it referred to in the sense that "table" refers to a four-legged, flat-topped piece of furniture, etc. Sentences are meaningful, but their meaning cannot be given by their referent, for they may have none.

Of course, one might argue that psycholinguists should confine their attention to the significance of isolated words and avoid the complexities of sentences altogether. Such an approach would be marvelously convenient if it would work, but it would work only if words were autonomous units that combined in a particularly simple way. If the meaning of a sentence could in some sense be regarded as the weighted sum of the meanings of the words that comprise it, then once we knew how to characterize the meanings of individual words, it would be a simple matter to determine the meaning of any combination of words. Unfortunately, however, language is not so simple; a Venetian blind is not the same as a blind Venetian.

Perhaps the most obvious thing we can say about the significance of a sentence is that it is not given as the linear sum of the significance of the words that comprise it. The pen in "fountain pen" and the pen in "play pen" are very different pens, even though they are phonologically and orthographically identical. The words in a sentence interact.

In isolation most words can have many different meanings; which meaning they take in a particular sentence will depend on the context in which they occur. That is to say, their meaning will depend both on the other words and on their grammatical role in the sentence. The meanings to be assigned to word combinations can be characterized in an orderly way, of course, but not by some simple rule for linear addition. What is required is an elaborate description of the various ways in which words can interact in combination.

As soon as we begin to look carefully at the relations among words in sentences, it becomes obvious that their interactions depend on the way they are grouped. For example, in sentences like, "They are hunting dogs," one meaning results if we group "are hunting" together as the verb, but another meaning results if we group "hunting dogs" together as a noun phrase. We cannot assign meanings to words in a sentence without knowing how the words are grouped, which implies that we must take into account the syntactic structure of the sentence.

Moreover, when we consider the psychology of the sentence, the problem of productivity becomes unavoidable. There is no limit to the number of different sentences that can be produced in English by combining words in various grammatical fashions, which means that it is impossible to describe English by simply listing all its grammatical sentences. This fairly obvious fact has several important implications. It means that the sentences of English must be described in terms of *rules* that can generate them.

For psychologists, the implication of this generative approach to language is that we must consider hypothetical constructs capable of combining verbal elements into grammatical sentences, and in order to account for our ability to deal with an unlimited variety of possible sentences, these hypothetical constructs must have the character of linguistic rules.

Language is the prime example of rule-governed behavior, and there are several types of rule to consider. Not only must we consider syntactic rules for generating and grouping words in sentences; we must also consider semantic rules for interpreting word combinations. Perhaps we may even need pragmatic rules to characterize our unlimited variety of belief systems. Only on the assumption that a language user knows a generative system of rules for producing and interpreting sentences can we hope to account for the unlimited combinatorial productivity of natural languages.

Rules are not laws, however. They can be broken, and in ordinary conversation they frequently are. Still, even when we break them, we usually are capable of recognizing (under appropriate conditions) that we have made a mistake; from this fact we infer that the rules are known implicitly, even though they cannot be stated explicitly.

A description of the rules we know when we know a language is different from a description of the psychological mechanisms involved in our use of those rules. It is important, therefore, to distinguish here, as elsewhere, between knowledge and performance; the psycholinguist's task is to propose and test performance models for a language user, but he must rely on the linguist to give him a precise specification of what it is a language user is trying to use.

Finally, it is important to remember that there is a large innate component to our language-using ability. Not just any self-consistent set of rules that we might be able to invent for communicative purposes could serve as a natural language. All human societies possess language, and all of these languages have features in common – features that are called "language universals," but are in fact pre-linguistic in character. It is difficult to imagine how children could acquire language so rapidly from parents who understand it so poorly unless they were already tuned by evolution to select just those aspects that are universally significant. There is, in short, a large biological component that shapes our human languages.

These are the seven ideas I wished to call to your attention. Let me recapitulate them in order, this time attempting to say what I believe their implications to be for psycholinguistic research.

Some Implications for Research

1 *Not all physical features of speech are significant for vocal communication, and not all significant features of speech have a physical representation.* I take this to imply that the perception of speech involves grouping and interpreting its elements and so cannot be simply predicted from studies of our ability to discriminate among arbitrary acoustic stimuli. Such studies can be useful only in conjunction with linguistic information as to which distinctions are significant. Linguists seem generally agreed that the absolute physical characteristics of a particular phone are less important than the binary contrasts into which it enters in a given language. It is noteworthy that after many decades of acoustic phonetics, we are still uncertain as to how to specify all the physical dimensions of the significant features of speech, particularly those that depend on syntactic or semantic aspects of the utterance.

2 *The meaning of an utterance should not be confused with its reference.* I take this to imply that the acquisition of meaning cannot be identified with the simple acquisition of a conditioned vocalization in the presence of a particular environmental stimulus. It may be possible to talk about reference in terms of conditioning, but meaning is a much more complicated phenomenon that depends on the relations of a symbol to other symbols in the language.

3 *The meaning of an utterance is not a linear sum of the meanings of the words that comprise it.* I take this to imply that studies of the meanings of isolated words are of limited value, and that attempts to predict the meaning of word compounds by weighted averages of the meanings of their components – an analogy with the laws of color mixture – cannot be successful in general. In *Gestalt* terminology, the whole is greater than (or at least, different from) the sum of its parts.

4 *The syntactic structure of a sentence imposes groupings that govern the interactions between the meanings of the words in that sentence.* I take this to imply that sentences are hierarchically organized, and that simple theories phrased in terms of chaining successive responses cannot provide an adequate account of linguistic behavior. Exactly how concepts are combined to produce organized groupings of linguistic elements that can be uttered and understood is a central problem for psycholinguistics.

5 *There is no limit to the number of sentences or the number of meanings that can be expressed.* I take this to imply that our knowledge of a language must be described in terms of a system of semantic and syntactic rules adequate to generate the infinite number of admissible utterances. Since the variety of admissible word combinations is so great, no child could learn them all. Instead of learning specific combinations of words, he learns the *rules* for generating admissible combinations. If knowledge of these rules is to be described in our performance models as the language user's "habits," it is necessary to keep in mind that they are generative habits of a more hypothetical and less abstract nature than have generally been studied in animal learning experiments.

6 *A description of a language and a description of a language user must be kept distinct.* I take this to imply that psycholinguists should try to formulate performance models that will incorporate, in addition to a generative knowledge of the rules, hypothetical information-storage and information-processing components that can simulate the actual behavior of language users. In general, limitations of short-term memory seem to impose the most severe constraints on our capacity to follow our own rules.

7   *There is a large biological component to the human capacity for articulate speech.* I take this to imply that attempts to teach other animals to speak a human language are doomed to failure. As Lenneberg has emphasized, the ability to acquire and use a human language does not depend on being intelligent or having a large brain. It depends on being human.

In science, at least half the battle is won when we start to ask the right questions. It is my belief that an understanding of these seven general propositions and their implications can help to guide us toward the right questions and might even forestall ill-considered forays into psycholinguistics by psychologists armed only with theories and techniques developed for the study of nonverbal behavior.

A Critique

I have now stated twice my seven preliminary admonitions. In order to make sure that I am being clear, I want to repeat it all once more, this time in the form of a critical analysis of the way many experimental psychologists write about language in the context of current learning theory.

For the purposes of exposition, I have chosen a sentence that is part of the introduction to the topic of language in a well-known and widely used textbook on the psychology of learning. After remarking that, "language seems to develop in the same way as other instrumental acts," the author says:

> Certain combinations of words and intonations of voice are strengthened through reward and are gradually made to occur in appropriate situations by the process of discrimination learning.

This, I believe is fairly representative of what can be found in many other texts. I have chosen it, not because I bear any malice toward the author, but simply because I think that all seven of my admonitions are ignored in only 27 words. Let me spell them out one by one.

First, since infants are not born with a preconception of what words are, they could hardly be expected to begin acquiring language by uttering combinations of words. Perhaps the author was not thinking of infants when he wrote this sentence. If he had been, he would probably have written instead that, "Certain combinations of *sounds* and intonations of voice are strengthened through reward and made to occur by the process of discrimination learning." In either case, however, he ignores my first admonition that not all physical features of speech are significant and not all significant features are physical.

A child does not begin with sounds or words and learn to combine them. Rather, he begins by learning which features are significant, and progressively differentiates his utterances as he learns. It is conceivable, though not necessary, that he might acquire those significant distinctions that have some physical basis "by the process of discrimination learning," but it would require an extensive revision of what we ordinarily mean by discrimination learning in order to explain how he acquires significant distinctions that are not represented in the physical signal, or why he acquires those features (such as aspiration only on initial plosives) that are not significant and are not systematically rewarded or extinguished.

Second, as I have already admitted (too generously, perhaps), it is possible to argue that a referential relation might be established between a visual input and a vocalization "by the process of discrimination learning." I deny, however, that it is reasonable to speak of acquiring meaning in this way.

Exactly what should be included in the meaning of a word is open to debate, but any interpretation will have to say something about the relation of this word's meaning to the meanings of other words and to the contexts in which it occurs – and these are complicated, systemic interrelations requiring a great deal more cognitive machinery than is necessary for simple discrimination. Since the author says specifically that *words* are acquired by discrimination learning, and since words have meaning as well as reference, I can only assume that he has ignored my admonition not to confuse reference and meaning. Perhaps a more accurate interpretation, suggested by the phrase "occur in appropriate situations," would be that he has not really confused reference and meaning, but has simply ignored meaning entirely. In either case, however, it will not do as a basis for psycholinguistics.

There is unfortunate ambiguity in the phrase, "Certain combinations of words and intonations of voice." I am not sure whether the author meant that each word was learned with several intonations, or that we learn several intonations for word combinations, or that we learn both to combine words and to modulate the pitch of our voice. Consequently, I have been forced to cheat on you by examining the context. What I found was no help, however, because all the formal propositions referred simply to "words," whereas all the examples that were cited involved combinations of words.

Perhaps I am being unfair, but I think that this author, at least when he is writing on learning theory, is not deeply concerned about the difference between words and sentences. If this distinction, which seems crucial to me, is really of no importance to him, then he must be ignoring my third admonition that the meaning of words are affected by the sentences in which they occur.

My fourth admonition – that the syntactic structure of a sentence imposes groupings that govern the interactions between the meanings of its words – is also ignored. No matter how I interpret the ambiguous phrase about, "Certain combinations of words and intonations of voice," it must be wrong. If I read it one way, he has ignored the problem of syntax entirely and is concerned only with the conditioning of isolated word responses. Or, if I put a more generous interpretation on it and assume he meant that combinations of words are strengthened and made to occur by discrimination learning, then he seems to be saying that every word and every acceptable combination of words is learned separately.

By a rough but conservative calculation, there are at least 10^{20} sentences 20 words long, and if a child were to learn only these it would take him something on the order of 1,000 times the estimated age of the earth just to listen to them. Perhaps this is what the word "gradually" means? In this interpretation he has clearly violated my fifth admonition, that there is no limit to the number of sentences to be learned, and so has wandered perilously close to absurdity. Any attempt to account for language acquisition that does not have a generative character will encounter this difficulty.

Sixth, from the reference to responses being "strengthened" I infer that each word–object connection is to be characterized by an intervening variable, along the lines of habit strength in Hull's system. This is a rather simple model, too simple to serve as a performance model for a language user, but it is all our author has to offer. As for keeping his performance model distinct from his competence model, as I advise in my sixth admonition, he will have none of it. He says – and here I resort to the context once more – that language "is a complex set of responses [*and*] also a set of stimuli." It may be defensible to talk about speech as a set of responses and stimuli, but what a language user knows about his language cannot be described in these performance terms.

A language includes all the denumerable infinitude of grammatical sentences, only a tiny sample of which ever have occurred or ever will occur as actual responses or stimuli. The author would blush crimson if we caught him confusing the notions of sample and population in his statistical work, yet an analogous distinction between speech and language is completely overlooked.

Finally, we need to make the point that the kind of reinforcement schedule a child is on when he learns language is very different from what we have used in experiments on discrimination learning. No one needs to monitor a child's vocal output continually and to administer "good" and "bad" as rewards and punishments. When a child says something intelligible, his reward is both improbable and indirect. In short, a child learns language by using it, not by a precise schedule of rewards for grammatical vocalizations "in appropriate situations." An experimenter who used such casual and unreliable procedures in a discrimination experiment would teach an animal nothing at all.

The child's exposure to language should not be called "teaching." He learns the language, but no one, least of all an average mother, knows how to teach it to him. He learns the language because he is shaped by nature to pay attention to it, to notice and remember and use significant aspects of it. In suggesting that language can be taught "by the process of discrimination learning," therefore, our author has ignored my final admonition to remember the large innate capacity humans have for acquiring articulate speech.

In summary, if this sentence is taken to be a description of the fundamental processes involved in language acquisition, it is both incomplete and misleading. At best, we might regard it as a hypothesis about the acquisition of certain clichés or expressive embellishments. But as a hypothesis from which to derive an account of the most obvious and most characteristic properties of human language, it is totally inadequate.

This completes the third and final run through my list of preliminaries to psycholinguistics. If I sounded a bit too contentious, I am sorry, but I did not want to leave any doubt as to why I am saying these things or what their practical implications for psycholinguistic research might be.

My real interest, however, is not in deploring this waste of our intellectual resources, but in the positive program that is possible if we are willing to accept a more realistic conception of what language is.

If we accept a realistic statement of the problem, I believe we will also be forced to accept a more cognitive approach to it: to talk about hypothesis testing instead of discrimination learning, about the evaluation of hypotheses instead of the reinforcement of responses, about rules instead of habits, about productivity instead of generalization, about innate and universal human capacities instead of special methods of teaching vocal responses, about symbols instead of conditioned stimuli, about sentences instead of words or vocal noises, about linguistic structure instead of chains of responses – in short, about language instead of learning theory.

The task of devising a cognitive production model for language users is difficult enough without wearing blinders that prevent us from seeing what the task really is. If the hypothetical constructs that are needed seem too complex and arbitrary, too improbable and mentalistic, then you had better forgo the study of language. For language is just that – complex, arbitrary, improbable, mentalistic – and no amount of wishful theorizing will make it anything else.

In a word, what I am trying to say, what all my preliminary admonitions boil down to, is simply this: Language is exceedingly complicated. Forgive me for taking so long to say such a simple and obvious thing.

NOTE

This paper is based on research supported in part by funds granted by the Advanced Research Projects Agency, Department of Defense, Contract No. SD-187; by Public Health Service Research Grant No. MH-08083 from the National Institutes of Health; by National Science Foundation, Contract No. GS-192; and by Carnegie Corporation of New York Grant No. 8-3004, to the Center for Cognitive Studies, Harvard University.

A Review of B. F. Skinner's *Verbal Behavior*

NOAM CHOMSKY

I

A great many linguists and philosophers concerned with language have expressed the hope that their studies might ultimately be embedded in a framework provided by behaviorist psychology, and that refractory areas of investigation, particularly those in which meaning is involved, will in this way be opened up to fruitful exploration. Since this volume is the first large-scale attempt to incorporate the major aspects of linguistic behavior within a behaviorist framework, it merits and will undoubtedly receive careful attention. Skinner is noted for his contributions to the study of animal behavior. The book under review is the product of study of linguistic behavior extending over more than twenty years. Earlier versions of it have been fairly widely circulated, and there are quite a few references in the psychological literature to its major ideas.

The problem to which this book is addressed is that of giving a "functional analysis" of verbal behavior. By "functional analysis," Skinner means identification of the variables that control this behavior and specification of how they interact to determine a particular verbal response. Furthermore, the controlling variables are to be described completely in terms of such notions as *stimulus*, *reinforcement*, *deprivation*, which have been given a reasonably clear meaning in animal experimentation. In other words, the goal of the book is to provide a way to predict and control verbal behavior by observing and manipulating the physical environment of the speaker.

Skinner feels that recent advances in the laboratory study of animal behavior permit us to approach this problem with a certain optimism, since "the basic processes and relations which give verbal behavior its special characteristics are now fairly well understood . . . the results [of this experimental work] have been surprisingly free of species restrictions. Recent work has shown that the methods can be extended to human behavior without serious modification" (p. 3).[1]

It is important to see clearly just what it is in Skinner's program and claims that makes them appear so bold and remarkable. It is not primarily the fact that he has set functional analysis as his problem, or that he limits himself to study of *observables*, i.e., input–output relations. What is so surprising is the particular limitations he has imposed on the way in which the observables of behavior are to be studied, and, above all, the particularly simple nature of the *function* which, he claims, describes the causation of behavior. One would naturally expect that prediction of the behavior of a complex organism (or machine) would require, in addition to information about external stimulation, knowledge of the internal structure of the organism, the ways in which it processes input information and organizes its own behavior. These characteristics of the organism are in general a complicated product of inborn structure, the genetically determined course of maturation, and past experience. Insofar as independent neurophysiological evidence is not available, it is obvious that inferences concerning the structure of the organism are based on observation of behavior and outside events. Nevertheless, one's estimate of the relative importance of external factors and internal structure in the determination of behavior will have an important effect on the direction of research on linguistic (or any other) behavior, and on the kinds of analogy from animal behavior studies that will be considered relevant or suggestive.

Putting it differently, anyone who sets himself the problem of analyzing the causation of behavior will (in the absence of independent neurophysiological evidence) concern himself with the only data available, namely the record of inputs to the organism and the organism's present response, and will try to describe the function specifying the response in terms of the history of inputs. This is nothing more than the definition of his problem. There are no possible grounds for argument here, if one accepts the problem as legitimate, though Skinner has often advanced and defended this definition of a problem as if it were a thesis which other investigators reject. The differences that arise between those who affirm and those who deny the importance of the specific "contribution of the organism" to learning and performance concern the particular character and complexity of this function, and the kinds of observation and research necessary for arriving at a precise specification of it. If the contribution of the organism is complex, the only hope of predicting behavior even in a gross way will be through a very indirect program of research that begins by studying the detailed character of the behavior itself and the particular capacities of the organism involved.

Skinner's thesis is that external factors consisting of present stimulation and the history of reinforcement (in particular, the frequency, arrangement, and withholding of reinforcing stimuli) are of overwhelming importance, and that the general principles revealed in laboratory studies of these phenomena provide the basis for understanding the complexities of verbal behavior. He confidently and repeatedly voices his claim to have demonstrated that the contribution of the speaker is quite trivial and elementary, and that precise prediction of verbal behavior involves only specification of the few external factors that he has isolated experimentally with lower organisms.

Careful study of this book (and of the research on which it draws) reveals, however, that these astonishing claims are far from justified. It indicates, furthermore, that the insights that have been achieved in the laboratories of the reinforcement theorist, though quite genuine, can be applied to complex human behavior only in the most gross and superficial way, and that speculative attempts to discuss linguistic behavior in these terms alone omit from consideration factors of fundamental importance that are, no doubt, amenable to scientific study, although their specific character cannot at present be precisely formulated. Since Skinner's work is the most extensive attempt to accommodate human behavior involving higher mental faculties within a strict behaviorist schema of the type that has attracted many linguists and philosophers, as well as psychologists, a detailed documentation is of independent interest. The magnitude of the failure of this attempt to account for verbal behavior serves as a kind of measure of the importance of the factors omitted from consideration, and an indication of how little is really known about this remarkably complex phenomenon.

The force of Skinner's argument lies in the enormous wealth and range of examples for which he proposes a functional analysis. The only way to evaluate the success of his program and the correctness of his basic assumptions about verbal behavior is to review these examples in detail and to determine the precise character of the concepts in terms of which the functional analysis is presented. Section II of this review describes the experimental context with respect to which these concepts are originally defined. Sections III and IV deal with the basic concepts – *stimulus, response*, and *reinforcement* – and sections VI to X with the new descriptive machinery developed specifically for the description of verbal behavior. In section V we consider the status of the fundamental claim, drawn from the laboratory, which serves as the basis for the analogic guesses about human behavior that have been proposed by many psychologists. The final section (section XI) will consider some ways in which further linguistic work may play a part in clarifying some of these problems.

II

Although this book makes no direct reference to experimental work, it can be understood only in terms of the general framework that Skinner has developed for the description of behavior. Skinner divides the responses of the animal into two main categories. *Respondents* are purely reflex responses elicited by particular stimuli. *Operants* are emitted responses, for which no obvious stimulus can be discovered. Skinner has been concerned primarily with operant behavior. The experimental arrangement that he introduced consists basically of a box with a bar attached to one wall in such a way that when the bar is pressed, a food pellet is dropped into a tray (and the bar press is recorded). A rat placed in the box will soon press the bar, releasing a pellet into the tray. This state of affairs, resulting from the bar press, increases the *strength* of the bar-pressing operant. The food pellet is called a *reinforcer*; the event, a *reinforcing event*. The strength of an operant is defined by Skinner in terms of the rate of response during extinction (i.e., after the last reinforcement and before return to the pre-conditioning rate).

Suppose that release of the pellet is conditional on the flashing of a light. Then the rat will come to press the bar only when the light flashes. This is called *stimulus discrimination*. The response is called a *discriminated operant* and the light is called the *occasion* for its emission: this is to be distinguished from elicitation of a response by a stimulus in the case of the respondent.[2] Suppose that the apparatus is so arranged that bar pressing of only a certain character (e.g., duration) will release the pellet. The rat will then come to press the bar in the required way. This process is called *response differentiation*. By successive slight changes in the conditions under which the response will be reinforced, it is possible to shape the response of a rat or a pigeon in very surprising ways in a very short time, so that rather complex behavior can be produced by a process of successive approximation.

A stimulus can become reinforcing by repeated association with an already reinforcing stimulus. Such a stimulus is called a *secondary reinforcer*. Like many contemporary behaviorists, Skinner considers money, approval, and the like to be secondary reinforcers which have become reinforcing because of their association with food, etc.[3] Secondary reinforcers can be generalized by associating them with a variety of different primary reinforcers.

Another variable that can affect the rate of the bar-pressing operant is *drive*, which Skinner defines operationally in terms of hours of deprivation. His major scientific book,

Behavior of Organisms, is a study of the effects of food deprivation and conditioning on the strength of the bar-pressing response of healthy mature rats. Probably Skinner's most original contribution to animal behavior studies has been his investigation of the effects of intermittent reinforcement, arranged in various different ways, presented in *Behavior of Organisms* and extended (with pecking of pigeons as the operant under investigation) in the recent *Schedules of Reinforcement* by Ferster and Skinner (1957). It is apparently these studies that Skinner has in mind when he refers to the recent advances in the study of animal behavior.[4]

The notions *stimulus, response, reinforcement* are relatively well defined with respect to the bar-pressing experiments and others similarly restricted. Before we can extend them to real-life behavior, however, certain difficulties must be faced. We must decide, first of all, whether any physical event to which the organism is capable of reacting is to be called a stimulus on a given occasion, or only one to which the organism in fact reacts; and correspondingly, we must decide whether any part of behavior is to be called a response, or only one connected with stimuli in lawful ways. Questions of this sort pose something of a dilemma for the experimental psychologist. If he accepts the broad definitions, characterizing any physical event impinging on the organism as a stimulus and any part of the organism's behavior as a response, he must conclude that behavior has not been demonstrated to be lawful. In the present state of our knowledge, we must attribute an overwhelming influence on actual behavior to ill-defined factors of attention, set, volition, and caprice. If we accept the narrower definitions, then behavior is lawful by definition (if it consists of responses); but this fact is of limited significance, since most of what the animal does will simply not be considered behavior. Hence, the psychologist either must admit that behavior is not lawful (or that he cannot at present show that it is – not at all a damaging admission for a developing science), or must restrict his attention to those highly limited areas in which it is lawful (e.g., with adequate controls, bar pressing in rats; lawfulness of the observed behavior provides, for Skinner, an implicit definition of a good experiment).

Skinner does not consistently adopt either course. He utilizes the experimental results as evidence for the scientific character of his system of behavior, and analogic guesses (formulated in terms of a metaphoric extension of the technical vocabulary of the laboratory) as evidence for its scope. This creates the illusion of a rigorous scientific theory with a very broad scope, although in fact the terms used in the description of real-life and of laboratory behavior may be mere homonyms, with at most a vague similarity of meaning. To substantiate this evaluation, a critical account of his book must show that with a literal reading (where the terms of the descriptive system have something like the technical meanings given in Skinner's definitions) the book covers almost no aspect of linguistic behavior, and that with a metaphoric reading, it is no more scientific than the traditional approaches to this subject matter, and rarely as clear and careful.[5]

III

Consider first Skinner's use of the notions *stimulus* and *response*. In *Behavior of Organisms* (p. 9) he commits himself to the narrow definitions for these terms. A part of the environment and a part of behavior are called *stimulus* (eliciting, discriminated, or reinforcing) and *response*, respectively, only if they are lawfully related; that is, if the *dynamic laws* relating them show smooth and reproducible curves. Evidently, stimuli and responses, so defined, have not been shown to figure very widely in ordinary human behavior.[6] We can, in the face of presently available evidence, continue to maintain the lawfulness of the relation between stimulus and response only by depriving them of their objective character. A typical example of *stimulus control* for Skinner would be the response to a piece of music with the utterance *Mozart* or to a painting with the response *Dutch*. These responses are asserted to be "under the control of extremely subtle properties" of the physical object or event (p. 108). Suppose instead of saying *Dutch* we had said *Clashes with the wallpaper, I thought you liked abstract work, Never saw it before, Tilted, Hanging too low, Beautiful, Hideous, Remember our camping trip last summer?*, or whatever else might come into our minds when looking at a picture (in Skinnerian translation, whatever other responses exist in sufficient strength). Skinner could only say that each of these responses is under the control of some other stimulus property of the physical object. If we look at a red chair and say *red*, the response is under the control of the stimulus *redness*; if we say *chair*, it is under the control of the collection of properties (for Skinner, the object) *chairness* (p. 110), and similarly for any other response. This device is as simple as it is empty. Since properties are free for the asking (we have as many of them as we have nonsynonymous descriptive expressions in our language, whatever this means exactly), we can account for a wide class of responses in terms of Skinnerian functional analysis by identifying the *controlling stimuli*. But the word *stimulus* has lost all objectivity in this usage. Stimuli are no longer part of the outside physical world; they are driven back into the organism. We identify the stimulus when we hear the response. It is clear from such examples, which abound, that the talk of *stimulus control* simply disguises a complete retreat to mentalistic psychology. We cannot predict verbal behavior in terms of the stimuli in the speaker's environment, since we do not know what the current stimuli are until he responds. Furthermore, since we cannot control the property of a physical object to which an individual will respond, except in highly artificial cases, Skinner's claim that his system, as opposed to the traditional one, permits the practical control of verbal behavior[7] is quite false.

Other examples of *stimulus control* merely add to the general mystification. Thus, a proper noun is held to be a response "under the control of a specific person or thing" (as controlling stimulus, p. 113). I have often used the words *Eisenhower* and *Moscow*, which I presume are proper nouns if anything is, but have never been *stimulated* by the corresponding objects. How can this fact be made compatible with this definition? Suppose that I use the name of a friend who is not present. Is this an instance of a proper noun under the control of the friend as stimulus? Elsewhere it is asserted that a stimulus controls a response in the sense that the presence of the stimulus increases the probability of the response. But it is obviously untrue that the probability that a speaker will produce a full name is increased when its bearer faces the speaker. Furthermore, how can one's own name be a proper noun in his sense? A multitude of similar questions arise immediately. It appears that the word *control* here is merely a misleading paraphrase for the traditional *denote* or *refer*. The assertion (p. 115) that so far as the speaker is concerned, the relation of reference is "simply the probability that the speaker will emit a response of a given form in the presence of a stimulus having specified properties" is surely incorrect if we take the words *presence, stimulus*, and *probability* in their literal sense. That they are not intended to be taken literally is indicated by many examples, as when a response is said to be "controlled" by a situation or state of affairs as "stimulus." Thus, the expression *a needle in a haystack* "may be controlled as a unit by a particular type of situation" (p. 116); the words in a single part of speech, e.g., all adjectives, are under the control of a single set of subtle properties of stimuli (p. 121); "the sentence *The boy runs a store* is under the control of an extremely complex stimulus situation" (p. 335); "*He is not at all well* may function as a standard response under the control of a state of affairs which might also control *He is ailing*" (p. 325); when an envoy observes events in a foreign country and reports upon his return, his report is under "remote stimulus control" (p. 416); the statement *This is war* may be a response to a "confusing international situation" (p. 441); the suffix *ed* is controlled by that "subtle property of stimuli which we speak of as action-in-the-past" (p. 121) just as the *s* in *The boy runs* is under the control of such specific features of the situation as its "currency" (p. 332). No characterization of the notion *stimulus control* that is remotely related to the bar-pressing experiment (or that preserves the faintest objectivity) can be made to cover a set of examples like these, in which, for example, the *controlling stimulus* need not even impinge on the responding organism.

Consider now Skinner's use of the notion *response*. The problem of identifying units in verbal behavior has of course been a primary concern of linguists, and it seems very likely that experimental psychologists should be able to provide much needed assistance in clearing up the many remaining difficulties in systematic identification. Skinner recognizes (p. 20) the fundamental character of the problem of identification of a unit of verbal behavior, but is satisfied with an answer so vague and subjective that it does not really contribute to its solution. The unit of verbal behavior – the verbal operant – is defined as a class of responses of identifiable form functionally related to one or more controlling variables. No method is suggested for determining in a particular instance what are the controlling variables, how many such units have occurred, or where their boundaries are in the total response. Nor is any attempt made to specify how much or what kind of similarity in form or *control* is required for two physical events to be considered instances of the same operant. In short, no answers are suggested for the most elementary questions that must be asked of anyone proposing a method for description of behavior. Skinner is content with what he calls an *extrapolation* of the concept of operant developed in the laboratory to the verbal field. In the typical Skinnerian experiment, the problem of identifying the unit of behavior is not too crucial. It is defined, by fiat, as a recorded peck or bar press, and systematic variations in the rate of this operant and its resistance to extinction are studied as a function of deprivation and scheduling of reinforcement (pellets). The operant is thus defined with respect to a particular experimental procedure. This is perfectly reasonable and has led to many interesting results. It is, however, completely meaningless to speak of extrapolating this concept of operant to ordinary verbal behavior. Such "extrapolation" leaves us with no way of justifying one or another decision about the units in the "verbal repertoire."

Skinner specifies "response strength" as the basic datum, the basic dependent variable in his functional analysis. In the bar-pressing experiment, response strength is defined in terms of rate of emission during extinction. Skinner has argued[8] that this is "the only datum that varies significantly and in the expected direction under conditions which are relevant to the 'learning process.'" In the book under review, response strength is defined as "probability of emission" (p. 22). This definition provides a comforting impression of objectivity, which, however, is quickly dispelled when we look into the matter more closely. The term *probability* has some rather obscure meaning for Skinner in this book.[9] We are told, on the one hand, that "our evidence for the contribution of each variable [to response strength] is based on observation of frequencies alone" (p. 28). At the same time, it appears that frequency is a very misleading measure of strength, since, for example, the frequency of a response may be "primarily attributable to the frequency of occurrence of controlling variables" (p. 27). It is not clear how the frequency of a response can be attributable to anything *but* the frequency of occurrence of its controlling variables if we accept Skinner's view that the behavior occurring in a given situation is "fully determined" by the relevant controlling variables (pp. 175, 228). Furthermore, although the evidence for the contribution of each variable to response strength is based on observation of frequencies alone, it turns out that "we base the notion of strength upon several kinds of evidence" (p. 22), in particular (pp. 22–8): emission of the response (particularly in unusual circumstances), energy level (stress), pitch level, speed and delay of emission, size of letters etc. in writing, immediate repetition, and – a final factor, relevant but misleading – overall frequency.

Of course, Skinner recognizes that these measures do not co-vary, because (among other reasons) pitch, stress, quantity, and reduplication may have internal linguistic functions.[10] However, he does not hold these conflicts to be very important, since the proposed factors indicative of strength are "fully understood by everyone" in the culture (p. 27). For example, "if we are shown a prized work of art and exclaim *Beautiful!*, the speed and energy of the response will not be lost on the owner." It does not appear totally obvious that in this case the way to impress the owner is to shriek *Beautiful* in a loud, high-pitched voice, repeatedly, and with no delay (high response strength). It may be equally effective to look at the picture silently (long delay) and then to murmur *Beautiful* in a soft, low-pitched voice (by definition, very low response strength).

It is not unfair, I believe, to conclude from Skinner's discussion of response strength, the *basic datum* in functional analysis, that his *extrapolation* of the notion of probability can best be interpreted as, in effect, nothing more than a decision to use the word *probability*, with its favorable connotations of objectivity, as a cover term to paraphrase such low-status words as *interest*, *intention*, *belief*, and the like. This interpretation is fully justified by the way in which Skinner uses the terms *probability* and *strength*. To cite just one example, Skinner defines the process of confirming an assertion in science as one of "generating additional variables to increase its probability" (p. 425), and more generally, its strength (pp. 425–9). If we take this suggestion quite literally, the degree of confirmation of a scientific assertion can be measured as a simple function of the loudness, pitch, and frequency with which it is proclaimed, and a general procedure for increasing its degree of confirmation would be, for instance, to train machine guns on large crowds of people who have been instructed to shout it. A better indication of what Skinner probably has in mind here is given by his description of how the theory of evolution, as an example, is confirmed. This "single set of verbal responses . . . is made more plausible – is strengthened – by several types of construction based upon verbal responses in geology, paleontology, genetics, and so on" (p. 427). We are no doubt to interpret the terms *strength* and *probability* in this context as paraphrases of more familiar locutions such as "justified belief" or "warranted assertability," or something of the sort. Similar latitude of interpretation is presumably expected when we read that "frequency of effective action accounts in turn for what we may call the listener's 'belief'" (p. 88) or that "our belief in what someone tells us is similarly a function of, or identical with, our tendency to act upon the verbal stimuli which he provides" (p. 160).[11]

I think it is evident, then, that Skinner's use of the terms *stimulus*, *control*, *response*, and *strength* justify the general conclusion stated in the last paragraph of section II. The way in which these terms are brought to bear on the actual data indicates that we must interpret them as mere paraphrases for the popular vocabulary commonly used to describe behavior and as having no particular connection with the homonymous expressions used in the description of laboratory experiments. Naturally, this terminological revision adds no objectivity to the familiar mentalistic mode of description.

IV

The other fundamental notion borrowed from the description of bar-pressing experiments is *reinforcement*. It raises problems which are similar, and even more serious. In *Behavior of*

Organisms, "the operation of reinforcement is defined as the presentation of a certain kind of stimulus in a temporal relation with either a stimulus or response. A reinforcing stimulus is defined as such by its power to produce the resulting change [in strength]. There is no circularity about this: some stimuli are found to produce the change, others not, and they are classified as reinforcing and nonreinforcing accordingly" (p. 62). This is a perfectly appropriate definition[12] for the study of schedules of reinforcement. It is perfectly useless, however, in the discussion of real-life behavior, unless we can somehow characterize the stimuli which are reinforcing (and the situations and conditions under which they are reinforcing). Consider first of all the status of the basic principle that Skinner calls the "law of conditioning" (law of effect). It reads: "if the occurrence of an operant is followed by presence of a reinforcing stimulus, the strength is increased" (*Behavior of Organisms*, p. 21). As reinforcement was defined, this law becomes a tautology.[13] For Skinner, learning is just change in response strength.[14] Although the statement that presence of reinforcement is a sufficient condition for learning and maintenance of behavior is vacuous, the claim that it is a necessary condition may have some content, depending on how the class of reinforcers (and appropriate situations) is characterized. Skinner does make it very clear that in his view reinforcement is a necessary condition for language learning and for the continued availability of linguistic responses in the adult.[15] However, the looseness of the term *reinforcement* as Skinner uses it in the book under review makes it entirely pointless to inquire into the truth or falsity of this claim. Examining the instances of what Skinner calls *reinforcement*, we find that not even the requirement that a reinforcer be an identifiable stimulus is taken seriously. In fact, the term is used in such a way that the assertion that reinforcement is necessary for learning and continued availability of behavior is likewise empty.

To show this, we consider some examples of *reinforcement*. First of all, we find a heavy appeal to automatic self-reinforcement. Thus, "a man talks to himself . . . because of the reinforcement he receives" (p. 163); "the child is reinforced automatically when he duplicates the sounds of airplanes, streetcars" (p. 164); "the young child alone in the nursery may automatically reinforce his own exploratory verbal behavior when he produces sounds which he has heard in the speech of others" (p. 58); "the speaker who is also an accomplished listener 'knows when he has correctly echoed a response' and is reinforced thereby" (p. 68); thinking is "behaving which automatically affects the behaver and is reinforcing because it does so" (p. 438; cutting one's finger should thus be reinforcing, and an example of thinking); "the verbal fantasy, whether overt or covert, is automatically reinforcing to the speaker as listener. Just as the musician plays or composes what he is reinforced by hearing, or as the artist paints what reinforces him visually, so the speaker engaged in verbal fantasy says what he is reinforced by hearing or writes what he is reinforced by reading" (p. 439); similarly, care in problem solving, and rationalization, are automatically self-reinforcing (pp. 442–3). We can also reinforce someone by emitting verbal behavior as such (since this rules out a class of aversive stimulations, p. 167), by not emitting verbal behavior (keeping silent and paying attention, p. 199), or by acting appropriately on some future occasion (p. 152: "the strength of [the speaker's] behavior is determined mainly by the behavior which the listener will exhibit with respect to a given state of affairs"; this Skinner considers the general case of "communication" or "letting the listener know"). In most such cases, of course, the speaker is not present at the time when the reinforcement takes place, as when "the artist . . . is reinforced by the effects his works have upon . . . others" (p. 224), or when the writer is reinforced by the fact that his "verbal behavior may reach over centuries or to thousands of listeners or readers at the same time. The writer may not be reinforced often or immediately, but his net reinforcement may be great" (p. 206; this accounts for the great "strength" of his behavior). An individual may also find it reinforcing to injure someone by criticism or by bringing bad news, or to publish an experimental result which upsets the theory of a rival (p. 154), to describe circumstances which would be reinforcing if they were to occur (p. 165), to avoid repetition (p. 222), to "hear" his own name though in fact it was not mentioned or to hear nonexistent words in his child's babbling (p. 259), to clarify or otherwise intensify the effect of a stimulus which serves an important discriminative function (p. 416), and so on.

From this sample, it can be seen that the notion of reinforcement has totally lost whatever objective meaning it may ever have had. Running through these examples, we see that a person can be reinforced though he emits no response at all, and that the reinforcing *stimulus* need not impinge on the *reinforced person* or need not even exist (it is sufficient that it be imagined or hoped for). When we read that a person plays what music he likes (p. 165), says what he likes (p. 165), thinks what he likes (pp. 438–9), reads what books he likes (p. 163), etc., *because* he finds it reinforcing to do so, or that we write books or inform others of facts *because* we are reinforced by what we hope will be the ultimate behavior of reader or listener, we can only conclude that the term *reinforcement* has a purely ritual function. The phrase "*X* is reinforced by *Y* (stimulus, state of affairs, event, etc.)" is being used as a cover term for "*X* wants *Y*," "*X* likes *Y*," "*X* wishes that *Y* were the case," etc. Invoking the term *reinforcement* has no explanatory force, and any idea that this paraphrase introduces any new clarity or objectivity into the description of wishing, liking, etc., is a serious delusion. The only effect is to obscure the important differences among the notions being paraphrased. Once we recognize the latitude with which the term *reinforcement* is being used, many rather startling comments lose their initial effect for instance, that the behavior of the creative artist is "controlled entirely by the contingencies of reinforcement" (p. 150). What has been hoped for from the psychologist is some indication how the casual and informal description of everyday behavior in the popular vocabulary can be explained or clarified in terms of the notions developed in careful experiment and observation, or perhaps replaced in terms of a better scheme. A mere terminological revision, in which a term borrowed from the laboratory is used with the full vagueness of the ordinary vocabulary, is of no conceivable interest.

It seems that Skinner's claim that all verbal behavior is acquired and maintained in "strength" through reinforcement is quite empty, because his notion of reinforcement has no clear content, functioning only as a cover term for any factor, detectable or not, related to acquisition or maintenance of verbal behavior.[16] Skinner's use of the term *conditioning* suffers from a similar difficulty. Pavlovian and operant conditioning are processes about which psychologists have developed real understanding. Instruction of human beings is not. The claim that instruction and imparting of information are simply matters of conditioning (pp. 357–66) is pointless. The claim is true, if we extend the term *conditioning* to cover these processes, but we know no more about them after having revised this term in such a way as to deprive it of its relatively clear and objective character. It is, as far as we know, quite false, if we use *conditioning* in its literal sense. Similarly, when we say that "it is the function of predication to facilitate the transfer of response from one term to another or from one object to another" (p. 361), we have said nothing of any significance. In what sense is this true of the predication *Whales are mammals*? Or, to take Skinner's example, what point is there in saying that the effect of *The telephone is out of order* on the listener is to bring behavior formerly controlled by the stimulus *out of order* under control of the stimulus *telephone* (or the telephone itself) by a process of simple conditioning (p. 362)? What laws of conditioning hold in this case? Furthermore, what behavior is controlled by the stimulus *out of order*, in the abstract? Depending on the object of which this is predicated, the present state of motivation of the listener, etc., the behavior may vary from rage to pleasure, from fixing the object to throwing it out, from simply not using it to trying to use it in the normal way (e.g., to see if it is really out of order), and so on. To speak of "conditioning" or "bringing previously available behavior under control of a new stimulus" in such a case is just a kind of play-acting at science (cf. also n. 43).

V

The claim that careful arrangement of contingencies of reinforcement by the verbal community is a necessary condition for language learning has appeared, in one form or another, in many places.[17] Since it is based not on actual observation, but on analogies to laboratory study of lower organisms, it is important to determine the status of the underlying assertion within experimental psychology proper. The most common characterization of reinforcement (one which Skinner explicitly rejects, incidentally) is in terms of drive reduction. This characterization can be given substance by defining drives in some way independently of what in fact is learned. If a drive is postulated on the basis of the fact that learning takes place, the claim that reinforcement is necessary for learning will again become as empty as it is in the Skinnerian framework. There is an extensive literature on the question of whether there can be learning without drive reduction (latent learning). The "classical" experiment of Blodgett indicated that rats which had explored a maze without reward showed a marked drop in number of errors (as compared to a control group which had not explored the maze) upon introduction of a food reward, indicating that the rat had learned the structure of the maze without reduction of the hunger drive. Drive-reduction theorists countered with an exploratory drive which was reduced during the pre-reward learning, and claimed that a slight decrement in errors could be noted before food reward. A wide variety of experiments, with somewhat conflicting results, have been carried out with a similar design.[18] Few investigators still doubt the existence of the phenomenon. E. R. Hilgard, in his general review of learning theory,[19] concludes that "there is no longer any doubt but that, under appropriate circumstances, latent learning is demonstrable."

More recent work has shown that novelty and variety of stimulus are sufficient to arouse curiosity in the rat and to motivate it to explore (visually), and in fact, to learn (since on a presentation of two stimuli, one novel, one repeated, the rat will attend to the novel one),[20] that rats will learn to choose the arm of a single-choice maze that leads to a complex maze, running through this being their only "reward";[21] that monkeys can learn object discriminations and maintain their performance at a high level of efficiency with visual exploration (looking out of a window for 30 seconds) as the only reward;[22] and, perhaps most strikingly of all, that monkeys and apes will solve rather complex manipulation problems that are simply placed in their cages, and will solve discrimination problems with only exploration and manipulation as incentives.[23] In these cases, solving the problem is apparently its own "reward." Results of this kind can be handled by reinforcement theorists only if they are willing to set up curiosity, exploration, and manipulation drives, or to speculate somehow about acquired drives[24] for which there is no evidence outside of the fact that learning takes place in these cases.

There is a variety of other kinds of evidence that has been offered to challenge the view that drive reduction is necessary for learning. Results on sensory–sensory conditioning have been interpreted as demonstrating learning without drive reduction.[25] Olds has reported reinforcement by direct stimulation of the brain, from which he concludes that reward need not satisfy a physiological need or withdraw a drive stimulus.[26] The phenomenon of imprinting, long observed by zoologists, is of particular interest in this connection. Some of the most complex patterns of behavior of birds, in particular, are directed towards objects and animals of the type to which they have been exposed at certain critical early periods of life.[27] Imprinting is the most striking evidence for the innate disposition of the animal to learn in a certain direction and to react appropriately to patterns and objects of certain restricted types, often only long after the original learning has taken place. It is, consequently, unrewarded learning, though the resulting patterns of behavior may be refined through reinforcement. Acquisition of the typical songs of song birds is, in some cases, a type of imprinting. Thorpe reports studies that show "that some characteristics of the normal song have been learned in the earliest youth, before the bird itself is able to produce any kind of full song."[28] The phenomenon of imprinting has recently been investigated under laboratory conditions and controls with positive results.[29]

Phenomena of this general type are certainly familiar from everyday experience. We recognize people and places to which we have given no particular attention. We can look up something in a book and learn it perfectly well with no other motive than to confute reinforcement theory, or out of boredom, or idle curiosity. Everyone engaged in research must have had the experience of working with feverish and prolonged intensity to write a paper which no one else will read or to solve a problem which no one else thinks important and which will bring no conceivable reward – which may only confirm a general opinion that the researcher is wasting his time on irrelevancies. The fact that rats and monkeys do likewise is interesting and important to show in careful experiment. In fact, studies of behavior of the type mentioned above have an independent and positive significance that far outweighs their incidental importance in bringing into question the claim that learning is impossible without drive reduction. It is not at all unlikely that insights arising from animal behavior studies with this broadened scope may have the kind of relevance to such complex activities as verbal behavior that reinforcement theory has, so far, failed to exhibit. In any event, in the light of presently available evidence, it is difficult to see how anyone can be willing to claim that reinforcement is necessary for learning, if reinforcement is taken seriously as something identifiable independently of the resulting change in behavior.

Similarly, it seems quite beyond question that children acquire a good deal of their verbal and nonverbal behavior by casual observation and imitation of adults and other children.[30] It is simply not true that children can learn language only through "meticulous care" on the part of adults who shape their verbal repertoire through careful differential reinforcement, though it may be that such care is often the custom in academic families. It is a common observation that a young child of immigrant parents may learn a second language in the streets, from other children, with amazing rapidity, and that his speech may be completely fluent and correct to the last allophone, while the subtleties that become second nature to the child may elude his parents despite high motivation and continued practice. A child may pick up a large part of his vocabulary and "feel" for sentence structure from television, from reading, from listening to adults, etc. Even a very young child who has not yet acquired a minimal repertoire from which to form new utterances may imitate a word quite well on an early try, with no attempt on the part of his parents to teach it to him. It is also perfectly obvious that, at a later stage, a child will be able to construct and understand utterances which are quite new, and are, at the same time, acceptable sentences in his language. Every time an adult reads a newspaper, he undoubtedly comes upon countless new sentences which are not at all similar, in a simple, physical sense, to any that he has heard before, and which he will recognize as sentences and understand; he will also be able to detect slight distortions or misprints. Talk of "stimulus generalization" in such a case simply perpetuates the mystery under a new title. These abilities indicate that there must be fundamental processes at work quite independently of "feedback" from the environment. I have been able to find no support whatsoever for the doctrine of Skinner and others that slow and careful shaping of verbal behavior through differential reinforcement is an absolute necessity. If reinforcement theory really requires the assumption that there be such meticulous care, it seems best to regard this simply as a *reductio ad absurdum* argument against this approach. It is also not easy to find any basis (or, for that matter, to attach very much content) to the claim that reinforcing contingencies set up by the verbal community are the single factor responsible for maintaining the strength of verbal behavior. The sources of the "strength" of this behavior are almost a total mystery at present. Reinforcement undoubtedly plays a significant role, but so do a variety of motivational factors about which nothing serious is known in the case of human beings.

As far as acquisition of language is concerned, if seems clear that reinforcement, casual observation, and natural inquisitiveness (coupled with a strong tendency to imitate) are important factors, as is the remarkable capacity of the child to generalize, hypothesize, and "process information" in a variety of very special and apparently highly complex ways which we cannot yet describe or begin to understand, and which may be largely innate, or may develop through some sort of learning or through maturation of the nervous system. The manner in which such factors operate and interact in language acquisition is completely unknown. It is clear that what is necessary in such a case is research, not dogmatic and perfectly arbitrary claims, based on analogies to that small part of the experimental literature in which one happens to be interested.

The pointlessness of these claims becomes clear when we consider the well-known difficulties in determining to what extent inborn structure, maturation, and learning are responsible for the particular form of a skilled or complex performance.[31] To take just one example,[32] the gaping response of a nestling thrush is at first released by jarring of the nest, and, at a later stage, by a moving object of specific size, shape, and position relative to the nestling. At this later stage the response is directed toward the part of the stimulus object corresponding to the parent's head, and characterized by a complex configuration of stimuli that can be precisely described. Knowing just this, it would be possible to construct a speculative, learning-theoretic account of how this sequence of behavior patterns might have developed through a process of differential reinforcement, and it would no doubt be possible to train rats to do something similar. However, there appears to be good evidence that these responses to fairly complex "sign stimuli" are genetically determined and mature without learning. Clearly, the possibility cannot be discounted. Consider now the comparable case of a child imitating new words. At an early stage we may find rather gross correspondences. At a later stage, we find that repetition is of course far from exact (i.e., it is not mimicry, a fact which itself is interesting), but that it reproduces the highly complex configuration of sound features that constitute the phonological structure of the language in question. Again, we can propose a speculative account of how this result might have been obtained through elaborate arrangement of reinforcing contingencies. Here too, however, it is possible that ability to select out of the complex auditory input those features that are phonologically relevant may develop largely independently of reinforcement, through genetically determined maturation. To the extent that this is true, an account of the development and causation of behavior that fails to consider the structure of the organism will provide no understanding of the real processes involved.

It is often argued that experience, rather than innate capacity to handle information in certain specific ways, must be the factor of overwhelming dominance in determining the specific character of language acquistion, since a child speaks the language of the group in which he lives. But this is a superficial argument. As long as we are speculating, we may consider the possibility that the brain has evolved to the point where, given an input of observed Chinese sentences, it produces (by an *induction* of apparently fantastic complexity and suddenness) the *rules* of Chinese grammar, and given an input of observed English sentences, it produces (by, perhaps, exactly the same process of induction) the rules of English grammar; or that given an observed application of a term to certain instances, it automatically predicts the extension to a class of complexly related instances. If clearly recognized as such, this speculation is neither unreasonable nor fantastic; nor, for that matter, is it beyond the bounds of possible study. There is of course no known neural structure capable of performing this task in the specific ways that observation of the resulting behavior might lead us to postulate; but for that matter, the structures capable of accounting for even the simplest kinds of learning have similarly defied detection.[33]

Summarizing this brief discussion, it seems that there is neither empirical evidence nor any known argument to support any *specific* claim about the relative importance of "feedback" from the environment and the "independent contribution of the organism" in the process of language acquisition.

VI

We now turn to the system that Skinner develops specifically for the description of verbal behavior. Since this system is based on the notions *stimulus, response,* and *reinforcement,* we can conclude from the preceding sections that it will be vague and arbitrary. For reasons noted in section I, however, I think it is important to see in detail how far from the mark any analysis phrased solely in these terms must be and how completely this system fails to account for the facts of verbal behavior.

Consider first the term *verbal behavior* itself. This is defined as "behavior reinforced through the mediation of other person" (p. 2). The definition is clearly much too broad. It would include as *verbal behavior,* for example, a rat pressing the bar in a Skinner-box, a child brushing his teeth, a boxer retreating before an opponent, and a mechanic repairing an automobile. Exactly how much of ordinary linguistic behavior is *verbal* in this sense, however, is something of a question: perhaps, as I have pointed out above, a fairly small fraction of it, if any substantive meaning is assigned to the term *reinforced.* This definition is subsequently refined by the additional provision that the mediating response of the reinforcing person (the *listener*) must itself "have been conditioned *precisely in order to reinforce* the behavior of the speaker" (p. 225, italics his). This still covers the examples given above, if we can assume that the reinforcing behavior of the psychologist, the parent, the opposing boxer, and the paying customer are the result of appropriate training, which is perhaps not unreasonable. A significant part of the fragment of linguistic behavior covered by the earlier definition will no doubt be excluded be the refinement, however. Suppose, for example, that while crossing the street I hear someone shout *Watch out for the car* and jump out of the way. It can hardly be proposed that my jumping (the mediating, reinforcing response in Skinner's usage) was conditioned (that is, I was trained to jump) precisely in order to reinforce the behavior of the speaker; and similarly, for a wide class of cases. Skinner's assertion that with this refined definition "we narrow our subject to what is traditionally recognized as the verbal field" (p. 225) appears to be grossly in error.

VII

Verbal operants are classified by Skinner in terms of their "functional" relation to discriminated stimulus, reinforcement, and other verbal responses. A *mand* is defined as "a verbal
operant is which the response is reinforced by a characteristic consequence and is therefore
under the functional control of relevant conditions of deprivation or aversive stimulation"
(p. 35). This is meant to include questions, commands, etc. Each of the terms in this
definition raises a host of problems. A mand such as *Pass the salt* is a class of responses. We
cannot tell by observing the form of a response whether it belongs to this class (Skinner is
very clear about this), but only by identifying the controlling variables. This is generally
impossible. Deprivation is defined in the bar-pressing experiment in terms of length of time
that the animal has not been fed or permitted to drink. In the present context, however, it is
quite a mysterious notion. No attempt is made here to describe a method for determining
"relevant conditions of deprivation" independently of the "controlled" response. It is of no
help at all to be told (p. 32) that it can be characterized in terms of the operations of the
experimenter. If we define deprivation in terms of elapsed time, then an any moment a
person is in countless states of deprivation.[34] It appears that we must decide that the relevant
condition of deprivation was (say) salt deprivation, on the basis of the fact that the speaker
asked for salt (the reinforcing community which "sets up" the mand is in a similar predicament). In this case, the assertion that a mand is under the control of relevant deprivation is
empty, and we are (contrary to Skinner's intention) identifying the response as a mand
completely in terms of form. The word *relevant* in the definition above conceals some rather
serious complications.

In the case of the mand Pass the salt, the word deprivation is not out of place, thought it
appears to be of little use for functional analysis. Suppose however that the speaker says *Give
me the book*, *Take me for a ride*, or *Let me fix it*. What kinds of deprivation can be associated
with these mands? How do we determine or measure the relevant deprivation? I think we
must conclude in this case, as before, either that the notion *deprivation* is relevant at most to
a minute fragment of verbal behavior, or else that the statement "*X* is under *Y*-deprivation"
is just an odd paraphrase for "*X* wants *Y*," bearing a misleading and unjustifiable connotation of objectivity.

The notion *aversive control* is just as confused. This is intended to cover threats, beating,
and the like (p. 33). The manner in which aversive stimulation functions is simply described.
If a speaker has had a history of appropriate reinforcement (e.g., if a certain response was
followed by "cessation of the threat of such injury – of events which have previously been
followed by such injury and which are therefore conditioned aversive stimuli"), then he will
tend to give the proper response when the threat which had previously been followed by the
injury is presented. It would appear to follow from this description that a speaker will not
respond properly to the mand *Your money or your life* (p. 38) unless he has a past history of
being killed. But even if the difficulties in describing the mechanism of aversive control are
somehow removed by a more careful analysis, it will be of little use for identifying operants
for reasons similar to those mentioned in the case of deprivation.

It seems, then, that in Skinner's terms there is in most cases no way to decide whether a
given response is an instance of a particular mand. Hence it is meaningless, within the terms
of his system, to speak of the *characteristic* consequences of a mand, as in the definition above.
Furthermore, even if we extend the system so that mands can somehow be identified, we will
have to face the obvious fact that most of us are not fortunate enough to have our requests,

commands, advice, and so on characteristically reinforced (they may nevertheless exist in considerable *strength*). These responses could therefore not be considered mands by Skinner. In fact, Skinner sets up a category of "magical mands" (pp. 48–9) to cover the case of "mands which cannot be accounted for by showing that they have ever had the effect specified or any similar effect upon similar occasions" (the word ever in this statement should be replaced by *characteristically*). In these pseudo–mands, "the speaker simply describes the reinforcement appropriate to a given state of deprivation or aversive stimulation." In other words, given the meaning that we have been led to assign to *reinforcement* and *deprivation*, the speaker asks for what he wants. The remark that "a speaker appears to create new mands on the analogy of old ones" is also not very helpful.

Skinner's claim that his new descriptive system is superior to the traditional one "because its terms can be defined with respect to experimental operations" (p. 45) is, we see once again, an illusion. The statement "X wants Y" is not clarified by pointing out a relation between rate of barpressing and hours of fooddeprivation; replacing "X wants Y" by "X is deprived of Y" adds no new objectivity to the description of behavior. His further claim for the superiority of the new analysis of mands is that it provides an objective basis for the traditional classification into requests, commands, etc. (pp. 38–41). The traditional classification is in terms of the intention of the speaker. But intention, Skinner holds, can be reduced to contingencies of reinforcement, and, correspondingly, we can explain the traditional classification in terms of the reinforcing behavior of the listener. Thus, a question is a mand which "specifies verbal action, and the behavior of the listener permits us to classify it as a request, a command, or a prayer" (p. 39). It is a request if "the listener is independently motivated to reinforce the speaker" a command if "the listeners behavior is . . . reinforced by reducing a threat"; a prayer if the mand "promotes reinforcement by generating and emotional disposition." The mand is advice if the listener is positively reinforced by the consequences of mediating the reinforcement of the speaker; it is a warning if "by carrying out the behavior specified by the speaker, the listener escapes from aversive stimulation"; and so on. All this is obviously wrong if Skinner is using the words *request, command,*etc., in anything like the sense of the corresponding English words. The word *question* does not cover commands. *Please pass the salt* is a request (but not a question), whether or not the listener happens to be motivated to fulfill it; not everyone to whom a request is addressed is favorably disposed. A response does not cease to be a command if it is not followed; nor does a question become a command if the speaker answers it because of an implied or imagined threat. Not all advice is good advice, and a response does not cease to be advice if it is not followed. Similarly, a warning may be misguided; heeding it may cause aversive stimulation, and ignoring it might be positively reinforcing. In short, the entire classification is beside the point. A moment's thought is sufficient to demonstrate the impossibility of distinguishing between requests, commands, advice, etc., on the basis of the behavior or disposition of the particular listener. Nor can we do this on the basis of the typical behavior of all listeners. Some advice is never taken, is always bad, etc., and similarly with other kinds of mand. Skinner's evident satisfaction with this analysis of the traditional classification is extremely puzzling.

VIII

Mands are operants with no specified relation to a prior stimulus. A *tact*, on the other hand, is defined as "a verbal operant in which a response of given form is evoked (or at least strengthened) by a particular object or event or property of an object or event" (p. 81). The examples quoted in the discussion of stimulus control (section III) are all tacts. The obscurity of the notion *stimulus control* makes the concept of the tact rather mystical. Since, however, the tact is "the most important of verbal operants," it is important to investigate the development of this concept in more detail.

We first ask why the verbal community "sets up" tacts in the child–that is, how the parent is reinforced by setting up the tact. The basic explanation for this behavior of the parent (pp. 85–6) is the reinforcement he obtains by the fact that his contact with the environment is extended; to use Skinner's example, the child may later be able to call him to the telephone. (It is difficult to see, then, how first children acquire tacts, since the parent does not have the appropriate history of reinforcement.) Reasoning in the same way, we may conclude that the parent induces the child to walk so that he can make some money delivering newspapers. Similarly, the parent sets up an "echoic repertoire" (e.g., a phonemic system) in the child because this makes it easier to teach him new vocabulary, and extending the child's vocabulary is ultimately useful to the parent. "In all these cases we explain the behavior of the reinforcing listener by pointing to an improvement in the possibility of controlling the speaker whom he reinforces" (p. 56). Perhaps this provides this explanation for the behavior of the parent in inducing the child to walk: the parent is reinforced by the improvement in his control of the child when the child's mobility increases. Underlying these modes of explanation is a curious view that it is somehow more scientific to attribute to a parent a desire to control the child or enhance his own possibilities for action than a desire to see the child develop and extend his capacities. Needless to say, no evidence is offered to support this contention.

Consider now the problem of explaining the response of the listener to a tact. Suppose, for example, that *B* hears *A* say *fox* and reacts appropriately–looks around, runs away, aims his rifle, etc. How can we explain *B*'s behavior? Skinner rightly rejects analyses of this offered by J. B. Watson and Bertrand Russell. His own equally inadequate analysis proceeds as follows (pp. 87–8). We assume (1) "that in the history of [*B*] the stimulus *fox* has been an occasion upon which looking around has been followed by seeing a fox" and (2) "that the listener has some current 'interest in seeing foxes'–that behavior which depends upon a seen fox for its execution is strong, and that the stimulus supplied by a fox is therefore reinforcing." *B* carries out the appropriate behavior, then, because "the heard stimulus *fox* is the occasion upon which turning and looking about is frequently followed by the reinforcement of seeing a fox," i.e., his behavior is a discriminated operant. This explanation is unconvincing. *B* may never have seen a fox and may have no current interest in seeing one, and yet may react appropriately to the stimulus *fox*.[35] Since exactly the same behavior may take place when neither of the assumptions is fulfilled, some other mechanism must be operative here.

Skinner remarks several times that his analysis of the tact in terms of stimulus control is an improvement over the traditional formulations in terms of reference and meaning. This is simply not true. His analysis is fundamentally the same as the traditional one, though much less carefully phrased. In particular, it differs only by indiscriminate paraphrases of such notions as *denotation* (reference) and *connotation* (meaning), which have been kept clearly apart in traditional formulations, in terms of the vague concept *stimulus control*. In one traditional formulation a descriptive term is said to denote a set of entities and to connote or designate a certain property or condition that an entity must possess or fulfil if the term is to apply to it.[36] Thus, the term *vertebrate* refers to (*denotes, is true of*) vertebrates and connotes the property *having a spine* or something of the sort. This connoted defining property is called the meaning of the term. Two terms may have the same reference but different meanings. Thus, it is apparently true that the creatures with hearts are all and only the vertebrates. If so, then the term *creature with a heart* refers to vertebrates and designates the property *having a heart*. This is presumably a different property (a different general condition) from having a spine; hence the terms *vertebrate* and *creature with a heart* are said to have different meanings. This analysis is not incorrect (for at least one sense of meaning), but its many limitations have frequently been pointed out.[37] The major problem is that there is no good way to decide whether two descriptive terms designate the same property.[38] As we have just seen, it is not sufficient that they refer to the same objects. *Vertebrate* and *creature with a spine* would be said to designate the same property (distinct from that designated by *creature with a heart*). If we ask why this is so, the only answer appears to be that the terms are synonymous. The notion *property* thus seems somehow language-bound, and appeal to "defining properties" sheds little light on questions of meaning and synonymy.

Skinner accepts the traditional account *in toto*, as can be seen from his definition of a tact as a response under control of a property (stimulus) of some physical object or event. We have found that the notion *control* has no real substance and is perhaps best understood as a paraphrase of *denote* or *connote* or, ambiguously, both. The only consequence of adopting the new term *stimulus control* is that the important differences between reference and meaning are obscured. It provides no new objectivity. The stimulus controlling the response is determined by the response itself; there is no independent and objective method of identification (see section III). Consequently, when Skinner defines *synonymy* as the case in which "the same stimulus leads to quite different responses" (p. 118), we can have no objection. The responses *chair* and *red* made alternatively to the same object are not synonymous, because the stimuli are called different. The responses *vertebrate* and *creature with a spine* would be considered synonymous because they are controlled by the same property of the object under investigation; in more traditional and no less scientific terms, they evoke the same concept. Similarly, when metaphorical extension is explained as due to "the control exercised by properties of the stimulus which, though present at reinforcement, do not enter into the contingency respected by the verbal community" (p. 92; traditionally, accidental properties), no objection can be raised which has not already been levelled against the traditional account. Just as we could "explain" the response *Mozart* to a piece of music in terms of subtle properties of the controlling stimuli, we can, with equal facility, explain the appearance of the response *sun* when no sun is present, as in *Juliet is [like] the sun*. "We do so by noting that Juliet and the sun have common properties, at least in their effect on the speaker" (p. 93). Since any two objects have indefinitely many properties in common, we can be certain that we will never be at a loss to explain a response of the form *A is like B*, for arbitrary *A* and *B*. It is clear, however, that Skinner's recurrent claim that his formulation is simpler and more scientific than the traditional account has no basis in fact.

Tacts under control of private stimuli (Bloomfield's "displaced speech") form a large and important class (pp. 130–46), including not only such responses as *familiar* and *beautiful*, but also verbal responses referring to past, potential, or future events or behavior. For example, the responses *There was an elephant at the zoo* "must be understood as a response to current stimuli, including events within the speaker himself" (p. 143).[39] If we ask ourselves what proportion of the tacts in actual life are responses to (descriptions of) actual current outside stimulation, we can see just how large a role must be attributed to private stimuli. A minute amount of verbal behavior, outside the nursery, consists of such remarks as *This is red* and *There is a man*. The fact that *functional analysis* must make such a heavy appeal to obscure internal stimuli is again a measure of its actual advance over traditional formulations.

IX

Responses under the control of prior verbal stimuli are considered under a different heading from the tact. An *echoic operant* is a response which "generates a sound pattern similar to that of the stimulus" (p. 55). It covers only cases of immediate imitation.[40] No attempt is made to define the sense in which a child's echoic response is "similar" to the stimulus spoken in the father's bass voice; it seems, though there are no clear statements about this, that Skinner would not accept the account of the phonologist in this respect, but nothing else is offered. The development of an echoic repertoire is attributed completely to differential reinforcement. Since the speaker will do no more, according to Skinner, than what is demanded of him by the verbal community, the degree of accuracy insisted on by this community will determine the elements of the repertoire, whatever these may be (not necessarily phonemes). "In a verbal community which does not insist on a precise correspondence, an echoic repertoire may remain slack and will be less successfully applied to novel patterns." There is no discussion of such familiar phenomena as the accuracy with which a child will pick up a second language or a local dialect in the course of playing with other children, which seem sharply in conflict with these assertions. No anthropological evidence is cited to support the claim that an effective phonemic system does not develop (this is the substance of the quoted remark) in communities that do not insist on precise correspondence.

A verbal response to a written stimulus (reading) is called *textual behavior*. Other verbal responses to verbal stimuli are called *intraverbal operants*. Paradigm instances are the response *four* to the stimulus *two plus two* or the response *Paris* to the stimulus *capital of France*. Simple conditioning may be sufficient to account for the response *four* to *two plus two*,[41] but the notion of intraverbal response loses all meaning when we find it extended to cover most of the facts of history and many of the facts of science (pp. 72, 129); all word association and "flights of ideas" (pp. 73–76); all translations and paraphrases (p. 77); reports of things seen, heard, or remembered (p. 315); and, in general, large segments of scientific, mathematical, and literary discourse. Obviously, the kind of explanation that might be proposed for a student's ability to respond with *Paris* to *capital of France*, after suitable practice, can hardly be seriously offered to account for his ability to make a judicious guess in answering the questions (to him new): *What is the seat of the French government?*, . . . *the source of the literary dialect.?*, . . . *the chief target of the German blitzkrieg?*, etc., or his ability to prove a new theorem, translate a new passage, or paraphrase a remark for the first time or in a new way.

The process of "getting someone to see a point," to see something your way, or to understand a complex state of affairs (e.g., a difficult political situation or a mathematical proof) is, for Skinner, simply a matter of increasing the strength of the listener's already available behavior.[42] Since "the process is often exemplified by relatively intellectual scientific or philosophical discourse," Skinner considers it "all the more surprising that it may be reduced to echoic, textual, or intraverbal supplementation" (p. 269). Again, it is only the vagueness and latitude with which the notions *strength* and *intraverbal response* are used that save this from absurdity. If we use these terms in their literal sense, it is clear that understanding a statement cannot be equated to shouting it frequently in a high-pitched voice (high response strength), and a clever and convincing argument cannot be accounted for on the basis of a history of pairings of verbal responses.[43]

X

A final class of operants, called *autoclitics*, includes those that are involved in assertion, negation, quantification, qualification of responses, construction of sentences, and the "highly complex manipulations of verbal thinking." All these acts are to be explained "in terms of behavior which is evoked by or acts upon other behavior of the speaker" (p. 313). Autoclitics are, then, responses to already given responses, or rather, as we find in reading through this section, they are responses to covert or incipient or potential verbal behavior. Among the autoclitics are listed such expressions as *I recall, I imagine, for example, assume, let X equal . . .* , the terms of negation, the *is* of predication and assertion, *all, some, if, then,* and, in general, all morphemes other than nouns, verbs, and adjectives, as well as grammatical processes of ordering and arrangement. Hardly a remark in this section can be accepted without serious qualification. To take just one example, consider Skinner's account of the autoclitic *all* in *All swans are white* (p. 329). Obviously we cannot assume that this is a tact to all swans as stimulus. It is suggested, therefore, that we take *all* to be an autoclitic modifying the whole sentence *Swans are white. All* can then be taken as equivalent to *always,* or *always it is possible to say.* Notice, however, that the modified sentence *Swans are white* is just as general as *All swans are white.* Furthermore, the proposed translation of *all* is incorrect if taken literally. It is just as possible to say *Swans are green* as to say *Swans are white.* It is not always possible to say either (e.g., while you are saying something else or sleeping). Probably what Skinner means is that the sentence can be paraphrased "*X is white* is true, for each swan *X.*" But this paraphrase cannot be given within his system, which has no place for *true.*

Skinner's account of grammar and syntax as autoclitic processes (ch. 13) differs from a familiar traditional account mainly in the use of the pseudo-scientific terms *control* or *evoke* in place of the traditional *refer.* Thus, in *The boy runs,* the final *s* of *runs* is a tact under control of such "subtle properties of a situation" as "the nature of running as an activity rather than an object or property of an object."[44] (Presumably, then, in *The attempt fails, The difficulty remains, His anxiety increases,* etc., we must also say that the *s* indicates that the object described as the attempt is carrying out the activity of failing, etc.) In *the boy's gun,* however, the *s* denotes possession (as, presumably, in *the boy's arrival, . . . story, . . . age,* etc.) and is under the control of this "relational aspect of the situation" (p. 336). The "relational autoclitic of order" (whatever it may mean to call the order of a set of responses a response to them) in *The boy runs the store* is under the control of an "extremely complex stimulus situation," namely, that the boy is running the store (p. 335). *And* in *the hat and the shoe* is under the control of the property "pair." *Through* in *the dog went through the hedge* is under the control of the "relation between the going dog and the hedge" (p. 342). In general, nouns are evoked by objects, verbs by actions, and so on.

Skinner considers a sentence to be a set of key responses (nouns, verbs, adjectives) on a skeletal frame (p. 346). If we are concerned with the fact that Sam rented a leaky boat, the raw responses to the situation are *rent, boat, leak,* and *Sam.* Autoclitics (including order) which qualify these responses, express relations between them, and the like, are then added by a process called *composition* and the result is a grammatical sentence, one of many alternatives among which selection is rather arbitrary. The idea that sentences consist of lexical items placed in a grammatical frame is of course a traditional one, within both philosophy and linguistics. Skinner adds to it only the very implausible speculation that in the internal process of composition, the nouns, verbs, and adjectives are chosen first and then are arranged, qualified, etc., by autoclitic responses to these internal activities.[45]

This view of sentence structure, whether phrased in terms of autoclitics, syncate-gorematic expressions, or grammatical and lexical morphemes, is inadequate. *Sheep provide wool* has no (physical) frame at all, but no other arrangement of these words is an English sentence. The sequences *furiously sleep ideas green colorless* and *friendly young dogs seem harmless* have the same frames, but only one is a sentence of English (similarly, only one of the sequences formed by reading these from back to front). *Struggling artists can be a nuisance* has the same frame as *marking papers can be a nuisance*, but is quite different in sentence structure, as can be seen by replacing *can be* by *is* or *are* in both cases. There are many other similar and equally simple examples. It is evident that more is involved in sentence structure than insertion of lexical items in grammatical frames; no approach to language that fails to take these deeper processes into account can possibly achieve much success in accounting for actual linguistic behavior.

XI

The preceding discussion covers all the major notions that Skinner introduces in his descriptive system. My purpose in discussing the concepts one by one was to show that in each case, if we take his terms in their literal meaning, the description covers almost no aspect of verbal behavior, and if we take them metaphorically, the description offers no improvement over various traditional formulations. The terms borrowed from experimental psychology simply lose their objective meaning with this extension, and take over the full vagueness of ordinary language. Since Skinner limits himself to such a small set of terms for paraphrase, many important distinctions are obscured. I think that this analysis supports the view expressed in section I, that elimination of the independent contribution of the speaker and learner (a result which Skinner considers of great importance, cf. pp. 311–12) can be achieved only at the cost of eliminating all significance from the descriptive system, which then operates at a level so gross and crude that no answers are suggested to the most elementary questions.[46] The questions to which Skinner has addressed his speculations are hopelessly premature. It is futile to inquire into the causation of verbal behavior until much more is known about the specific character of this behavior; and there is little point in speculating about the process of acquisition without much better understanding of what is acquired.

Anyone who seriously approaches the study of linguistic behavior, whether linguist, psychologist, or philosopher, must quickly become aware of the enormous difficulty of stating a problem which will define the area of his investigations, and which will not be either completely trivial or hopelessly beyond the range of present-day understanding and technique. In selecting functional analysis as his problem, Skinner has set himself a task of the latter type. In an extremely interesting and insightful paper,[47] K. S. Lashley has implicitly delimited a class of problems which can be approached in a fruitful way by the linguist and psychologist, and which are clearly preliminary to those with which Skinner is concerned. Lashley recognizes, as anyone must who seriously considers the data, that the composition and production of an utterance is not simply a matter of stringing together a sequence of responses under the control of outside stimulation and intraverbal association, and that the syntactic organization of an utterance is not something directly represented in any simple way in the physical structure of the utterance itself. A variety of observations leads him to conclude that syntactic structure is "a generalized pattern imposed on the specific acts as they occur" (p. 512), and that "a consideration of the structure of the sentence and other motor sequences will show . . . that there are, behind the overtly expressed sequences, a multiplicity of integrative processes which can only be inferred from the final results of their activity" (p. 509). He also comments on the great difficulty of determining the "selective mechanisms" used in the actual construction of a particular utterance (p. 522).

Although present-day linguistics cannot provide a precise account of these integrative processes, imposed patterns, and selective mechanisms, it can at least set itself the problem of characterizing these completely. It is reasonable to regard the grammar of a language L ideally as a mechanism that provides an enumeration of the sentences of L in something like the way in which a deductive theory gives an enumeration of a set of theorems. (*Grammar*, in this sense of the word, includes phonology.) Furthermore, the theory of language can be regarded as a study of the formal properties of such grammars, and, with a precise enough formulation, this general theory can provide a uniform method for determining, from the process of generation of a given sentence, a structural description which can give a good deal of insight into how this sentence is used and understood. In short, it should be possible to derive from a properly formulated grammar a statement of the integrative processes and generalized patterns imposed on the specific acts that constitute an utterance. The rules of a grammar of the appropriate form can be subdivided into the two types, optional and obligatory; only the latter must be applied in generating an utterance. The optional rules of the grammar can be viewed, then, as the selective mechanisms involved in the production of a particular utterance. The problem of specifying these integrative processes and selective mechanisms is nontrivial and not beyond the range of possible investigation. The results of such a study might, as Lashley suggests, be of independent interest for psychology and neurology (and conversely). Although such a study, even if successful, would by no means answer the major problems involved in the investigation of meaning and the causation of behavior, it surely will not be unrelated to these. It is at least possible, furthermore, that such a notion as *semantic generalization*, to which such heavy appeal is made in all approaches to language in use, conceals complexities and specific structures of inference not far different from those that can be studied and exhibited in the case of syntax, and that consequently the general character of the results of syntactic investigations may be a corrective to oversimplified approaches to the theory of meaning.

The behavior of the speaker, listener, and learner of language constitutes, of course, the actual data for any study of language. The construction of a grammar which enumerates sentences in such a way that a meaningful structural description can be determined for each sentence does not in itself provide an account of this actual behavior. It merely characterizes abstractly the ability of one who has mastered the language to distinguish sentences from nonsentences, to understand new sentences (in part), to note certain ambiguities, etc. These are very remarkable abilities. We constantly read and hear new sequences of words, recognize them as sentences, and understand them. It is easy to show that the new events that we accept and understand as sentences are not related to those with which we are familiar by any simple notion of formal (or semantic or statistical) similarity or identity of grammatical frame. Talk of generalization in this case is entirely pointless and empty. It appears that we recognize a new item as a sentence not because it matches some familiar item in any simple way, but because it is generated by the grammar that each individual has somehow and in some form internalized. And we understand a new sentence, in part, because we are somehow capable of determining the process by which this sentence is derived in this grammar.

Suppose that we manage to construct grammars having the properties outlined. We can then attempt to describe and study the achievement of the speaker, listener, and learner. The speaker and the listener, we must assume, have already acquired the capacities characterized abstractly by the grammar. The speakers task is to select a particular compatible set of optional rules. If we know, from grammatical study, what choices are available to him and what conditions of compatibility the choices must meet, we can proceed meaningfully to investigate the factors that lead him to make one or another choice. The listener (or reader) must determine, from an exhibited utterance, what optional rules were chosen in the construction of the utterance. It must be admitted that the ability of a human being to do this far surpasses our present understanding. The child who learns a language has in some sense constructed the grammar for himself on the basis of his observation of sentences and nonsentences (i.e., corrections by the verbal community). Study of the actual observed ability of a speaker to distinguish sentences from nonsentences, detect ambiguities, etc., apparently forces us to the conclusion that this grammar is of an extremely complex and abstract character, and that the young child has succeeded in carrying out what from the formal point of view, at least, seems to be a remarkable type of theory construction. Furthermore, this task is accomplished in an astonishingly short time, to a large extent independently of intelligence, and in a comparable way by all children. Any theory of learning must cope with these facts.

It is not easy to accept the view that a child is capable of constructing an extremely complex mechanism for generating a set of sentences, some of which he has heard, or that an adult can instantaneously determine whether (and if so, how) a particular item is generated by this mechanism, which has many of the properties of an abstract deductive theory. Yet this appears to be a fair description of the performance of the speaker, listener, and learner. If this is correct, we can predict that a direct attempt to account for the actual behavior of speaker, listener, and learner, not based on a prior understanding of the structure of grammars, will achieve very limited success. The grammar must be regarded as a component in the behavior of the speaker and listener which can only be inferred, as Lashley has put it, from the resulting physical acts. The fact that all normal children acquire essentially comparable grammars of great complexity with remarkable rapidity suggests that human beings are somehow specially designed to do this, with data-handling or "hypothesis-formulating" ability of unknown character and complexity.[48] The study of linguistic structure may ultimately lead to some significant insights into this matter. At the moment the question cannot be seriously posed, but in principle it may be possible to study the problem of determining what the built-in structure of an information-processing (hypothesis-forming) system must be to enable it to arrive at the grammar of a language from the available data in the available time. At any rate, just as the attempt to eliminate the contribution of the speaker leads to a "mentalistic" descriptive system that succeeds only in blurring important traditional distinctions, a refusal to study the contribution of the child to language learning permits only a superficial account of language acquisition, with a vast and unanalyzed contribution attributed to a step called *generalization* which in fact includes just about everything of interest in this process. If the study of language is limited in these ways, it seems inevitable that major aspects of verbal behavior will remain a mystery.

NOTES

1 Skinner's confidence in recent achievements in the study of animal behavior and their applicability to complex human behavior does not appear to be widely shared. In many recent publications

of confirmed behaviorists there is a prevailing note of skepticism with regard to the scope of these achievements. For representative comments, see the contributions to *Modern Learning Theory* (by W. K. Estes, S. Koch, K. MacCorquodale, P. E. Mecal, C. G. Mueller Jr, W. N. Schoenfeld, and W. S. Verplanck; New York: Appleton-Century-Crofts, 1954); B. R. Bugelski, *Psychology of Learning* (New York: Holt, Rinehart & Winston, 1956); S. Koch, in *Nebraska Symposium on Motivation*, 58 (Lincoln, 1956); W. S. Verplanck, "Learned and Innate Behavior," *Psychological Review*, 52 (1955), 139. Perhaps the strongest view is that of H. Harlow, who has asserted ("Mice, Monkeys, Men, and Motives," *Psychological Review*, 60 (1953), 23–32) that "a strong case can be made for the proposition that the importance of the psychological problems studied during the last 15 years has decreased as a negatively accelerated function approaching an asymptote of complete indifference." N. Tinbergen, a leading representative of a different approach to animal behavior studies (comparative ethology), concludes a discussion of *functional analysis* with the comment that "we may now draw the conclusion that the causation of behavior is immensely more complex than was assumed in the generalizations of the past. A number of internal and external factors act upon complex central nervous structures. Second, it will be obvious that the facts at our disposal are very fragmentary indeed" – *The Study of Instinct* (Toronto: Oxford University Press, 1951), p. 74.

2   In *Behavior of Organisms* (New York: Appleton-Century-Crofts, 1938), Skinner remarks that "although a conditioned operant is the result of the correlation of the response with a particular reinforcement, a relation between it and a discriminative stimulus acting prior to the response is the almost universal rule" (pp. 178–9). Even emitted behavior is held to be produced by some sort a of "originating force" (p. 51) which, in the case of operant behavior, is not under experimental control. The distinction between eliciting stimuli, discriminated stimuli, and "originating forces" has never been adequately clarified and becomes even more confusing when private internal events are considered to be discriminated stimuli (see below).

3   In a famous experiment, chimpanzees were taught to perform complex tasks to receive tokens which had become secondary reinforcers because of association with food. The idea that money approval, prestige, etc., actually acquire their motivating effects on human behavior according to this paradigm is unproved, and not particularly plausible. Many psychologists within the behaviorist movement are quite skeptical about this (cf. n. 23). As in the case of most aspects of human behavior, the evidence about secondary reinforcement is so fragmentary, conflicting, and complex that almost any view can find some support.

4   Skinner's remark quoted above about the generality of his basic results must be understood in the light of the experimental limitations he has imposed. If it were true in any deep sense that the basic processes in language are well understood and free of species restriction, it would be extremely odd that language is limited to man. With the exception of a few scattered observations (cf. his article, "A Case History in Scientific Method," *American Psychologist*, 11 (1956), 221–33), Skinner is apparently basing this claim on the fact that qualitatively similar results are obtained with bar pressing of rats and pecking of pigeons under special conditions of deprivation and various schedules of reinforcement. One immediately questions how much can be based on these facts, which are in part at least an artifact traceable to experimental design and the definition of *stimulus* and *response* in terms of *smooth dynamic curves* (see below). The dangers inherent in any attempt to *extrapolate* to complex behavior from the study of such simple responses as bar pressing should be obvious and have often been commented on (cf., e.g., Harlow, "Mice, Monkeys, Men, and Motives"). The generality of even the simplest results is open to serious question. Cf. in this connection M. E. Bitterman, J. Wodinsky, and D. K. Candland, "Some Comparative Psychology," *American Journal of Psychology*, 71 (1958), 94–110, where it is shown that there are important qualitative differences in solution of comparable elementary problems by rats and fish.

5   An analogous argument, in connection with a different aspect of Skinner's thinking, is given by M. Scriven in *A Study of Radical Behaviorism*, University of Minnesota Studies in Philosophy of Science, I. Cf. Verplanck's contribution to *Modern Learning Theory*, pp. 283–8, for more general discussion of the difficulties in formulating an adequate definition of *stimulus* and *response*. He concludes, quite correctly, that in Skinner's sense of the word, stimuli are not objectively

identifiable independently of the resulting behavior, nor are they manipulable. Verplanck presents a clear discussion of many other aspects of Skinner's system, commenting on the untestability of many of the so-called "laws of behavior" and the limited scope of many of the others, and the arbitrary and obscure character of Skinner's notion of *lawful relation*; and, at the same time, noting the importance of the experimental data that Skinner has accumulated.

6   In *Behavior of Organisms*, Skinner apparently was willing to accept this consequence. He insists (pp. 41–2) that the terms of casual description in the popular vocabulary are not validly descriptive until the defining properties of stimulus and response are specified, the correlation is demonstrated experimentally, and the dynamic changes in it are shown to be lawful. Thus, in describing a child as hiding from a dog, "it will not be enough to dignify the popular vocabulary by appealing to essential properties of *dogness* or *hidingness* and to suppose them intuitively known." But this is exactly what Skinner does in the book under review, as we will see directly.

7   Pp. 253ff and elsewhere, repeatedly. As an example of how well we can control behavior using the notions developed in this book, Skinner shows here how he would go about evoking the response *pencil*. The most effective way, he suggests, is to say to the subject, "Please say *pencil*" (our chances would, presumably, be even further improved by use of "aversive stimulation," e.g., holding a gun to his head). We can also "make sure that no pencil or writing instrument is available, then hand our subject a pad of paper appropriate to pencil sketching, and offer him a handsome reward for a recognizable picture of a cat." It would also be useful to have voices saying *pencil* or *pen and* . . . in the background; signs reading *pencil* or *pen and* . . . ; or to place a "large and unusual pencil in an unusual place clearly in sight." "Under such circumstances, it is highly probable that our subject will say *pencil*." "The available techniques are all illustrated in this sample." These contributions of behavior theory to the practical control of human behavior are amply illustrated elsewhere in the book, as when Skinner shows (pp. 113–14) how we can evoke the response *red* (the device suggested is to hold a red object before the subject and say, "Tell me what color this is").

In fairness, it must be mentioned that there are certain nontrivial applications of *operant conditioning* to the control of human behavior. A wide variety of experiments has shown that the number of plural nouns (for example) produced by a subject will increase if the experimenter says "right" or "good" when one is produced (similarly, positive attitudes on a certain issue, stories with particular content, etc.; cf. L. Krasner, "Studies of the Conditioning of Verbal Behavior," *Psychological Bulletin*, 55 (1958), 148–70, for a survey of several dozen experiments of this kind, mostly with positive results). It is of some interest that the subject is usually unaware of the process. Just what insight this gives into normal verbal behavior is not obvious. Nevertheless, it is an example of positive and not totally expected results using the Skinnerian paradigm.

8   "Are Theories of Learning Necessary?", *Psychological Review*, 57 (1950), 193–216.

9   And elsewhere. In his paper "Are Theories of Learning Necessary?" Skinner considers the problem how to extend his analysis of behavior to experimental situations in which it is impossible to observe frequencies, rate of response being the only valid datum. His answer is that "the notion of probability is usually extrapolated to cases in which a frequency analysis cannot be carried out. In the field of behavior we arrange a situation in which frequencies are available as data, but we use the notion of probability in analyzing or formulating instances of even types of behavior which are not susceptible to this analysis" (p. 199). There are, of course, conceptions of probability not based directly on frequency, but I do not see how any of these apply to the cases that Skinner has in mind. I see no way of interpreting the quoted passage other than as signifying an intention to use the word *probability* in describing behavior quite independently of whether the notion of probability is at all relevant.

10 Fortunately, "In English this presents no great difficulty" since, for example, "relative pitch levels . . . are not . . . important" (p. 25). No reference is made to the numerous studies of the function of relative pitch levels and other intonational features in English.

11 The vagueness of the word *tendency*, as opposed to *frequency*, saves the latter quotation from the obvious incorrectness of the former. Nevertheless, a good deal of stretching is necessary. If *tendency* has anything like its ordinary meaning, the remark is clearly false. One may believe

strongly the assertion that Jupiter has four moons, that many of Sophocles' plays have been irretrievably lost, that the Earth will burn to a crisp in ten million years, and so on, without experiencing the slightest tendency to act upon these verbal stimuli. We may, of course, turn Skinner's assertion into a very unilluminating truth by defining "tendency to act" to include tendencies to answer questions in certain ways, under motivation to say what one believes is true.

12   One should add, however, that it is in general not the stimulus as such that is reinforcing, but the stimulus in a particular situational context. Depending on experimental arrangement, a particular physical event or object may be reinforcing, punishing, or unnoticed. Because Skinner limits himself to a particular, very simple experimental arrangement, it is not necessary for him to add this qualification, which would not be at all easy to formulate precisely. But it is of course necessary if he expects to extend his descriptive system to behavior in general.

13   This has been frequently noted.

14   See, for example, "Are Theories of Learning Necessary?", p. 199. Elsewhere, he suggests that the term *learning* be restricted to complex situations, but these are not characterized.

15   "A child acquires verbal behavior when relatively unpatterned vocalizations, selectively reinforced, gradually assume forms which produce appropriate consequences in a given verbal community" (p. 31). "Differential reinforcement shapes up all verbal forms, and when a prior stimulus enters into the contingency, reinforcement is responsible for its resulting control. . . . The availability of behavior, its probability or strength, depends on whether reinforcements *continue* in effect and according to what schedules" (pp. 203–4); elsewhere, frequently.

16   Talk of schedules of reinforcement here is entirely pointless. How are we to decide, for example, according to what schedules covert reinforcement is *arranged*, as in thinking or verbal fantasy, or what the scheduling is of such factors as silence, speech, and appropriate future reactions to communicated information?

17   See, for example, N. E. Miller and J. Dollard, *Social Learning and Imitation* (New York: Yale University Press, 1941), pp. 82–3, for a discussion of the "meticulous training" that they seem to consider necessary for a child to learn the meanings of words and syntactic patterns. The same notion is implicit in O. H. Mowrer's speculative account of how language might be acquired, in *Learning Theory and Personality Dynamics* (New York: Ronald Press, 1950), ch. 23. Actually, the view appears to be quite general.

18   For a general review and analysis of this literature, see D. L. Thistlethwaite, "A Critical Reviewiew of Latent Learning and Related Experiments," *Psychological Bulletin*, 48 (1951), 97–129. K. MacCorquodale and P. E. Meehl, in their contribution to *Modern Learning Theory*, carry out a serious and considered attempt to handle the latent learning material from the standpoint of drive-reduction theory, with (as they point out) not entirely satisfactory results. W. H. Thorpe reviews the literature from the standpoint of the ethologist, adding also material on homing and topographical orientation (*Learning and Instinct in Animals* (Cambridge, MA: Harvard University Press, 1956)).

19   E. R. Hilgard, *Theories of Learning* (New York: Appleton-Century-Crofts, 1956), p. 214.

20   O. E. Berlyne, "Novelty and Curiosity as Determinants of Exploratory Behavior," *British Journal of Psychology*, 41 (1950), 68–80, and "Perceptual Curiosity in the Rat," *Journal of Comparative Physiological Psychology*, 48 (1955), 238–46; W. R. Thompson and L. M. Solomon, "Spontaneous Pattern Discrimination in the Rat," *Journal of Comparative Physiological Psychology*, 47 (1954), 104–7.

21   K. C. Montgomery, "The Role of the Exploratory Drive in Learning," *Journal of Comparative Physiological Psychology*, 47 (1954), pp. 60–3. Many other papers in the same journal are designed to show that exploratory behavior is a relatively independent primary "drive" aroused by novel external stimulation.

22   R. A. Butler, "Discrimination Learning by Rhesus Monkeys to Visual-Exploration Motivation," *Journal of Comparative Physiological Psychology*, 46 (1953), 95–8. Later experiments showed that this "drive" is highly persistent, as opposed to derived drives which rapidly extinguish.

23   H. F. Harlow, M. K. Harlow, and D. R. Meyer, "Learning Motivated by a Manipulation Drive," *Journal of Experimental Psychology*, 40 (1950), 228–34, and later investigations initiated by

Harlow. Harlow has been particularly insistent on maintaining the inadequacy of physiologically based drives and homeostatic need states for explaining the persistence of motivation and rapidity of learning in primates. He points out, in many papers, that curiosity, play exploration, and manipulation are, for primates, often more potent drives than hunger and the like, and that they show none of the characteristics of acquired drives. Hebb also presents behavioral and supporting neurological evidence in support of the view that in higher animals there is a positive attraction in work, risk puzzle, intellectual activity, mild fear and frustration, and so on. ("Drives and the CNS." *Psychological Review*, 62 (1955), 243–54.) He concludes that "we need not work out tortuous and improbable ways to explain why men work for money, why children learn without pain, why people dislike doing nothing."

   In a brief note ("Early Recognition of the Manipulative Drive in Monkeys," *British Journal of Animal Behaviour*, 3 (1955), 71–2), W. Dennis calls attention to the fact that early investigators (G. J. Romanes, 1882; E. L. Thorndike, 1901), whose "perception was relatively unaffected by learning theory, did note the intrinsically motivated behavior of monkeys," although, he asserts no similar observations on monkeys have been made until Harlow's experiments. He quotes Romanes (*Animal Intelligence* (1882)) as saying that "much the most striking feature in the psychology of this animal, and the one which is least like anything met with in other animals, was the tireless spirit of investigation." Analogous developments, in which genuine discoveries have blinded systematic investigators to the important insights of earlier work, are easily found within recent structural linguistics as well.

24 Thus, J. S. Brown, in commenting on a paper of Harlow's in *Current Theory and Research in Motivation* (Lincoln: University of Nebraska Press, 1953), argues that "in probably every instance [of the experiments cited by Harlow] an ingenious drive-reduction theorist could find some fragment of fear, insecurity, frustration, or whatever, that he could insist was reduced and hence was reinforcing" (p. 53). The same sort of thing could be said for the ingenious phlogiston or ether theorist.

25 Cf. H. G. Birch and M. E. Bitterman, "Reinforcement and Learning: The Process of Sensory Integration," *Psychological Review*, 56 (1949), 292–308.

26 See, for example, his paper "A Physiological Study of Reward" in D. C. McClelland, ed., *Studies in Motivation* (New York: Appleton-Century-Crofts, 1955), pp. 134–43.

27 See Thorpe, *Learning and Instinct*, particularly pp. 115–18 and 337–76, for an excellent discussion of this phenomenon, which has been brought to prominence particularly by the work of K. Lorenz (cf. "Der Kumpan in der Umwelt des Vogels," parts of which are reprinted in English translation in C. M. Schiller, ed., *Instinctive Behavior* (New York: International Universities Press, 1957), pp. 83–128).

28 Thorpe, *Learning and Instinct*, p. 372.

29 See, e.g., J. Jaynes, "Imprinting: Interaction of Learned and Innate Behavior," *Journal of Comparative Physiological Psychology*, 49 (1956), 201–6, where the conclusion is reached that "the experiments prove that without any observable reward, young birds of this species follow a moving stimulus object and very rapidly come to prefer that object to others."

30 Of course, it is perfectly possible to incorporate this fact within the Skinnerian framework. If, for example, a child watches an adult using a comb and then, with no instruction, tries to comb his own hair, we can explain this act by saying that he performs it because he finds it reinforcing to do so, or because of the reinforcement provided by behaving like a person who is forcing to do so, or because of the reinforcement provided by behaving like a person who is "reinforcing" (cf. p. 164). Similarly, an automatic explanation is available for any other behavior. It seems strange at first that Skinner pays so little attention to the literature on latent learning and related topics, considering the tremendous reliance that he places on the notion of reinforcement; I have seen no reference to it in his writings. Similarly, F.S. Keller and W. N. Schoenfeld, in what appears to be the only text written under predominantly Skinnerian influence, *Principles of Psychology* (New York: Appleton-Century-Crofts, 1950), dismiss the latent learning literature in one sentence as "beside the point," serving only "to obscure, rather than clarify, a fundamental principle" (*the law of effect*, p. 41). However, this neglect is perfectly appropriate in Skinner's case. To the drive

reductionist, or anyone else for whom the notion *reinforcement* has some substantive meaning, these experiments and observations are important (and often embarrassing). But in the Skinnerian sense of the word, neither these results nor any conceivable others can cast any doubt on the claim that reinforcement is essential for the acquisition and maintenance of behavior. Behavior certainly has some concomitant circumstances, and whatever they are, we can call them *reinforcement*.

31   Tinbergen, *Study of Instinct*, ch. VI, reviews some aspects of this problem, discussing the primary role of maturation in the development of many complex motor patterns (e.g., flying, swimming) in lower organisms, and the effect of an "innate disposition to learn" in certain specific ways and at certain specific times. Cf. also P. Schiller, "Innate Motor Action as a Basis for Learning," in C. H. Schiller, ed., *Instinctive Behavior* (New York: International Press, 1957), pp. 265–88, for a discussion of the role of maturing motor patterns in apparently insightful behavior in the chimpanzee.

Lenneberg ("The Capacity for Language Acquisition," this volume [*Language*, 35 (1959)]) presents a very interesting discussion of the part that biological structure may play in the acquisition of language, and the dangers in neglecting this possibility.

32   From among many cited by Tinbergen, *Study of Instinct*, p. 85.

33   Cf. K. S. Lashley, "In Search of the Engram," *Symposium of the Society for Experimental Biology*, 4 (1950), 454–82. R. Sperry, "On the Neural Basis of the Conditioned Response," *British Journal of Animal Behavior*, 3 (1955), 41–4, argues that to account for the experimental results of Lashley and others, and for other facts that he cites, it is necessary to assume that high-level cerebral activity of the type of insight, expectancy, and so on is involved even in simple conditioning. He states that "we still lack today a satisfactory picture of the underlying neural mechanism" of the conditioned response.

34   Furthermore, the motivation of the speaker does not, except in the simplest cases, correspond in intensity to the duration of deprivation. An obvious counterexample is what D. O. Hebb has called the "salted-nut phenomenon" (*Organization of Behavior* (New York: John Wiley, 1949), p. 199). The difficulty is of course even more serious when we consider *deprivations* not related to physiological drives.

35   Just as he may have the appropriate reaction, both emotional and behavioral, to such utterances as *the volcano is erupting* or *there's a homicidal maniac in the next room* without any previous pairing of the verbal and the physical stimulus. Skinner's discussion of Pavlovian conditioning in language (p. 154) is similarly unconvincing.

36   J. S. Mill, *A System of Logic* (1843). R. Carnap gives a recent reformulation in "Meaning and Synonymy in Natural Languages," *Philosophical Studies*, 6 (1955), 33–47, defining the meaning (intension) of a predicate Q for a speaker X as "the general condition which an object y must fulfil in order for X to be willing to ascribe the predicate Q to y." The connotation of an expression is often said to constitue its "cognitive meaning" as opposed to its "emotive meaning," which is, essentially, the emotional reaction to the expression.

Whether or not this is the best way to approach meaning, it is clear that denotation, cognitive meaning, and emotive meaning are quite different things. The differences are often obscured in empirical studies of meaning, with much consequent confusion. Thus, Osgood has set himself the task of accounting for the fact that a stimulus comes to be a sign for another stimulus (a buzzer becomes a sign for food, a word for a thing, etc.). This is clearly (for linguistic signs) a problem of denotation. The method that he actually develops for quantifying and measuring meaning (cf. C. E. Osgood, G. Suci, and P. Tannenbaum, *The Measurement of Meaning* (Urbana: University of Illinois Press, 1957) applies, however, only to emotive meaning. Suppose, for example, that A hates both Hitler and science intensely, and considers both highly potent and "active," while B, agreeing with A about Hitler, likes science very much, although he considers it rather ineffective and not too important. Then, A may assign to "Hitler" and "science" the same position on the semantic differential, while B will assign "Hitler" the same position as A did, but "science" a totally different position. Yet, A does not think that "Hitler" and "science" are synonymous or that they have the same reference, and A and B may agree precisely on the cognitive meaning of "science." Clearly, it is the attitude toward the things (the emotive meaning of the words) that is being measured here.There is a gradual shift in Osgood's account from denotation to cognitive meaning to emotive meaning. The confusion is caused, no doubt, by the fact that the term *meaning* is used in all three senses (and others). (See J. Carroll's review of the book by Osgood, Suci, and Tannenbaum in *Language*, 35, no. 1 (1959).)

37   Most clearly by Quine. See *From a Logical Point of View* (Cambridge, MA: Harvard University Press, 1953), especially chs 2, 3, and 7.

38   A method for characterizing synonymy in terms of reference is suggested by Goodman, "On Likeness of Meaning," *Analysis*, 10 (1949), 1–7. Difficulties are discussed by Goodman, "On Some Differences about Meaning," *Analysis*, 13 (1953), 90–6. Carnap, "Meaning and Synonymy," presents a very similar idea (section 6), but somewhat misleadingly phrased, since he does not bring out the fact that only extensional (referential) notions are being used.

39   In general, the examples discussed here are badly handled, and the success of the proposed analyses is overstated. In each case, it is easy to see that the proposed analysis, which usually has an air of objectivity, is not equivalent to the analyzed expression. To take just one example, the response *I am looking for my glasses* is certainly not equivalent to the proposed paraphrases: "When I have behaved in this way in the past, I have found my glasses and have then stopped behaving in this way," or "Circumstances have arisen in which I am inclined to emit any behavior which in the past has led to the discovery of my glasses; such behavior includes the behavior of looking in which I am now engaged." One may look for one's glasses for the first time; or one may emit the same behavior in looking for ones glasses as in looking for one's watch, in which case *I am looking for my glasses* and *I am looking for my watch* are equivalent, under the Skinnerian paraphrase. The difficult questions of purposiveness cannot be handled in this superficial manner.

40   Skinner takes great pains, however, to deny the existence in human beings (or parrots) of any innate faculty or tendency to imitate. His only argument is that no one would suggest an innate tendency to read, yet reading and echoic behavior have similar "dynamic properties." This similarity, however, simply indicates the grossness of his descriptive categories.

In the case of parrots, Skinner claims that they have no instinctive capacity to imitate, but only to be reinforced by successful imitation (p. 59). Given Skinner's use of the word *reinforcement*, it is difficult to perceive any distinction here, since exactly the same thing could be said of any other instinctive behavior. For example, where another scientist would say that a certain bird instinctively builds a nest in a certain way, we could say in Skinner's terminology (equivalently) that the bird is instinctively reinforced by building the nest in this way. One is therefore inclined to dismiss this claim as another ritual introduction of the word *reinforce*. Though there may, under some suitable clarification, be some truth in it, it is difficult to see how many of the cases reported by competent observers can be handled if *reinforcement* is given some substantive meaning. Cf. Thorpe, *Learning and Instinct*, pp. 353ff; K. Lorenz, *King Solomon's Ring* (New York: Crowell, 1952), pp. 85–8; even Mowrer, who tries to show how imitation might develop through secondary reinforcement, cites a case, in *Learning Theory and Personality Dynamics*, p. 694, which he apparently believes, but where this could hardly be true. In young children, it seems most implausible to explain imitation in terms of secondary reinforcement.

41   Although even this possibility is limited. If we were to take these paradigm instances seriously, it should follow that a child who knows how to count from one to 100 could learn an arbitrary 10×10 matrix with these numbers as entries as readily as the multiplication table.

42   Similarly, "the universality of a literary work refers to the number of potential readers inclined to say the same thing" (p. 275; i.e., the most "universal" work is a dictionary of clichés and greetings); a speaker is "stimulating" if he says what we are about to say ourselves (p. 272); etc.

43   Similarly, consider Skinner's contention (pp. 362–5) that communication of knowledge or facts is just the process of making a new response available to the speaker. Here the analogy to animal experiments is particularly weak. When we train a rat to carry out some peculiar act, it makes sense to consider this a matter of adding a response to his repertoire. In the case of human communication, however, it is very difficult to attach any meaning to this terminology. If *A* imparts to *B* the information (new to *B*) that the railroads face collapse, in what sense can the response *The railroads face collapse* be said to be now, but not previously, available to *B*? Surely *B*

could have said it before (not knowing whether it was true), and known that it was a sentence (as opposed to *Collapse face railroads the*). Nor is there any reason to assume that the response has increased in strength, whatever this means exactly (e.g., *B* may have no interest in the fact, or he may want it suppressed). It is not clear how we can characterize this notion of "making a response available" without reducing Skinner's account of "imparting knowledge" to a triviality.

44   P. 332. On the next page, however, the *s* in the same example indicates that "the object described as the boy possesses the property of running." The difficulty of even maintaining consistency with a conceptual scheme like this is easy to appreciate.

45   One might just as well argue that exactly the opposite is true. The study of hesitation pauses has shown that these tend to occur before the large categories – noun, verb, adjective; this finding is usually described by the statement that the pauses occur where there is maximum uncertainty or information. Insofar as hesitation indicates ongoing composition (if it does at all), it would appear that the "key responses" are chosen only after the "grammatical frame." Cf. C. E. Osgood, unpublished paper; F. Goldman-Eisler, "Speech Analysis and Mental Processes," *Language and Speech*, 1 (1958), 67.

46   E.g., what are in fact the actual units of verbal behavior? Under what conditions will a physical event capture the attention (be a stimulus) or be a reinforcer? How do we decide what stimuli are in "control" in a specific case? When are stimuli "similar"? And so on. (It is not interesting to be told, e.g., that we say *Stop* to an automobile or billiard ball because they are sufficiently similar to reinforcing people (p. 46).)

The use of unanalyzed notions like *similar* and *generalization* is particularly disturbing, since it indicates an apparent lack of interest in every significant aspect of the learning or the use of language in new situations. No one has ever doubted that, in some sense, language is learned by generalization, or that novel utterances and situations are in some way similar to familiar ones. The only matter of serious interest is the specific "similarity." Skinner has, apparently, no interest in this. Keller and Schoenfeld, *Principles of Psychology*, proceed to incorporate these notions (which they identify) into their Skinnerian "modern objective psychology" by defining two stimuli to be similar when "we make the same sort of response to them" (p. 124; but when are responses of the "same sort"?). They do not seem to notice that this definition converts their "principle of generalization" (p. 116), under any reasonable interpretation of this, into a tautology. It is obvious that such a definition will not be of much help in the study of language learning or construction of new responses in appropriate situations.

47   "The Problem of Serial Order in Behavior," in L. A. Jeffress, ed., *Hixon Symposium on Cerebral Mechanisms in Behavior* (New York: John Wiley, 1951). Reprinted in F. A. Beach, D. O. Hebb, C. T. Morgan, and H. W. Nissen, eds, *The Neuropsychology of Lashley* (New York: McGraw-Hill, 1960). Page references are to the latter.

48   There is nothing essentially mysterious about this. Complex innate behavior patterns and innate "tendencies to learn in specific ways" have been carefully studied in lower organisms. Many psychologists have been inclined to believe that such biological structure will not have an important effect on acquisition of complex behavior in higher organisms, but I have not been able to find any serious justification for this attitude. Some recent studies have stressed the necessity for carefully analyzing the strategies available to the organism, regarded as a complex "information-processing system" (cf. J. S. Bruner, J. J. Goodnow, and G. A. Austin, *A Study of Thinking* (New York: John Wiley, 1956); A. Newell, J. C. Shaw, and H. A. Simon, "Elements of a Theory of Human Problem Solving," *Psychological Review*, 65 (1958), 151–66), if anything significant is to be said about the character of human learning. These may be largely innate, or developed by early learning processes about which very little is yet known. (But see Harlow, "The Formation of Learning Sets," *Psychological Review*, 56 (1949), 51–65, and many later papers, where striking shifts in the character of learning are shown as a result of early training; also Hebb, *Organization of Behavior*, pp. 109ff). They are undoubtedly quite complex. Cf. Lenneberg, "The Capacity for Language Acquisition", and R. B. Lees, review of Chomsky's *Syntactic Structures* in *Language*, 33 (1957), 406ff, for discussion of the topics mentioned in this section.

Family Resemblances: Studies in the Internal Structure of Categories

ELEANOR ROSCH AND CAROLYN B. MERVIS

As speakers of our language and members of our culture, we know that a chair is a more reasonable exemplar of the category *furniture* than a radio, and that some chairs fit our idea or image of a chair better than others. However, when describing categories analytically, most traditions of thought have treated category membership as a digital, all-or-none phenomenon. That is, much work in philosophy, psychology, linguistics, and anthropology assumes that categories are logical bounded entities, membership in which is defined by an item's possession of a simple set of criterial features, in which all instances possessing the criterial attributes have a full and equal degree of membership.

In contrast to such a view, it has been recently argued (see Lakoff, 1972; Rosch, 1973; Zadeh, 1965) that some natural categories are analog and must be represented logically in a manner which reflects their analog structure. Rosch (1973, 1975b) has further characterized some natural analog categories as internally structured into a prototype (clearest cases, best examples of the category) and nonprototype members, with nonprototype members tending toward an order from better to poorer examples. While the domain for which such a claim has been demonstrated most unequivocally is that of color (Berlin and Kay, 1969; Heider, 1971, 1972; Mervis, Catlin, and Rosch, 1975; Rosch, 1974, in press c, in press d), there is also considerable evidence that natural superordinate semantic categories have a prototype structure. Subjects can reliably rate the extent to which a member of a category fits their idea or image of the meaning of the category name (Rosch, 1973, 1975a), and such ratings predict performance in a number of tasks (Rips et al., 1973; Rosch, 1973, 1975a, 1975b, in press c; Smith, Rips, and Shoben, 1974; Smith, Shoben, and Rips, 1974).

However, there has, as yet, been little attention given to the problem of how internal structure arises. That is, what principles govern the formation of category prototypes and gradients of category membership? For some categories which probably have a physiological basis, such as colors, forms, and facial expressions of basic human emotions, prototypes may be stimuli which are salient prior to formation of the category, whose salience, at the outset, determines the categorical structuring of those domains (Ekman, 1971; McDaniel, 1972; Rosch, 1974, 1975b). For the artificial categories which have been used in prototype research – such as families of dot patterns (Posner, 1973) and artificial faces (Reed, 1972) – the categories have been intentionally structured and/or the prototypes have been defined so that the prototypes were central tendencies of the categories. For most domains, however, prototypes do not appear to precede the category (Rosch, in press a) and must be formed through principles of learning and information processing from the items given in the category. The present research was not intended to provide a processing model of the learning of categories or formation of prototypes; rather, our intention was to examine the stimulus relations which underlie such learning. That is, the purpose of the present research was to explore one of the major *structural* principles which, we believe, may govern the formation of the prototype structure of semantic categories.

This principle was first suggested in philosophy; Wittgenstein (1953) argued that the referents of a word need not have common elements in order for the word to be understood and used in the normal functioning of language. He suggested that, rather, a family resemblance might be what linked the various referents of a word. A family resemblance relationship consists of a set of items of the form AB, BC, CD, DE. That is, each item has at least one, and probably several, elements in common with one or more other items, but no, or few, elements are common to all items. The existence of such relationships in actual natural-language categories has not previously been investigated empirically.

In the present research, we viewed natural semantic categories as networks of overlapping attributes; the basic hypothesis was that members of a category come to be viewed as prototypical of the category as a whole in proportion to the extent to which they bear a family resemblance to (have attributes which overlap those of) other members of the category. Conversely, items viewed as most prototypical of one category will be those with least family resemblance to or membership in other categories. In natural categories of concrete objects, the two aspects of family resemblance should coincide rather than conflict, since it is reasonable that categories tend to become organized in such a way that they reflect the correlational structure of the environment in a manner which renders them maximally discriminable from each other (Rosch, in press a; Rosch et al., in press).

The present structural hypothesis is closely related to a cue-validity-processing model of classification in which the validity of a cue is defined in terms of its total frequency within a category and its proportional frequency in that category relative to contrasting categories. Mathematically, cue validity has been defined as a conditional probability – specifically, the frequency of a cue being associated with the category in question divided by the total frequency of that cue over all relevant categories (Beach, 1964; Reed, 1972). Unfortunately, cue validity has been treated as a model in conflict with a prototype model of category processing where prototypes are operationally defined solely as attribute means (Reed, 1972). If prototypes are defined more broadly – for example, as the abstract representation of a category, or as those category members to which subjects compare items when judging category membership, or as the internal structure of the category defined by subjects' judgments of the degree to which members fit their "idea or image" of the category – then prototypes should coincide rather than conflict with cue validity. That is, if natural categories of concrete objects tend to become organized so as to render the categories maximally discriminable from each other, it follows that the maximum possible cue validity of items within each category will be attained (Rosch et al., in press). The principle of family resemblance relationships can be restated in terms of cue validity since the attributes most distributed among members of a category and least distributed among members of contrasting categories are, by definition, the most valid cues to membership in the category in question. We use the term *family resemblance* rather than *cue validity* primarily to emphasize that we are dealing with a description of structural principles and not with a processing model. We believe that the principle of family resemblance relationships is a very general one and is applicable to categories regardless of whether or not they have features common to members of the category or formal criteria for category membership.

In all of the studies of the present research, family resemblances were defined in terms of discrete attributes such as *has legs*, *you drive it*, or *the letter B is a member*. These are the kinds of feature of natural semantic categories which can be most readily reported and the features normally used in definitions of categories by means of lists of formal criteria. Insofar as the context in which an attribute occurs as part of a stimulus may always affect perception and understanding of the attribute, discrete attributes of this type may be an analytic myth. However, in one sense, the purpose of the present research was to show that it is not necessary to invoke attribute interactions or higher-order *Gestalt* properties of stimuli (such as those used by Posner, 1973; Reed, 1972; Rosch et al., 1975) in order to analyze the prototype structure of categories. That is, even at the level of analysis of the type of discrete attributes normally used in definitions of categories by means of criterial features, we believe there is a principle of the structure of stimulus sets, family resemblances, which can be shown to underlie category prototype structure.

The present paper reports studies using three different types of category: superordinate semantic categories such as *furniture* and *vehicle*, basic-level semantic categories such as *chair* and *car*, and artificial categories formed from sets of letter strings. For each type of stimulus, both aspects of the family resemblance hypothesis (that the most prototypical members of categories are those with most attributes in common with other members of that category and are those with least attributes in common with other categories) were tested.

Superordinate semantic categories are of particular interest because they are sufficiently abstract that they have few, if any, attributes common to all members (Rosch et al., in press). Thus, such categories may consist almost entirely of items related to each other by means of family resemblances of overlapping attributes. In addition, superordinate categories have the advantage that their membership consists of a finite number of names of basic-level categories which can be adequately sampled. Superordinate categories have the disadvantage that they do not have contrasting categories (operationally defined below); thus, the second half of the family resemblance hypothesis (that prototypical members of categories have least resemblance to other categories) had to be tested indirectly by measuring membership in, rather than attributes in common with, other superordinate categories.

Basic-level semantic categories are of great interest because they are the level of abstraction at which the basic category cuts in the world may be made (Rosch, in press a; Rosch et al., in press). However, basic-level categories present a sampling problem since their membership consists of an infinite number of objects. On the positive side, basic-level categories do form contrast sets, thus making possible a direct test of the second part of the family resemblance hypothesis.

Artificial categories were needed because they made possible the study of prototype formation with adequate controls. In natural-language domains of any type, categories have long since evolved in culture and been learned by subjects. Both prototypes and the attribute structure of categories are independent variables; we can only measure their correlations. Artificial categories are of use because attribute structures can be varied in a controlled manner and the development of prototypes studied as a dependent variable.

1   Superordinate Semantic Categories

Experiment 1

Although it is always possible for an ingenious philosopher or psychologist to invent criterial attributes defining a category, earlier research has shown that actual subjects rate superordinate semantic categories as having few, if any, attributes common to all members (Rosch et al., in press). Thus, if the "categorical" nature of these categories was to be explained, it appeared most likely to reside in family resemblances between members. Part of the purpose of the present experiment was to obtain portraits of the distribution of attributes of members of a number of superordinate natural-language categories. Part of the hypothesis was that category members would prove to bear a family resemblance relationship to each other. The major purpose of the experiment, however, was to observe the relation between degree of relatedness between members of the category and the rated prototypicality of those members. The specific hypothesis was that a measure of the degree to which an item bore a family resemblance to other members of the category would prove significantly correlated with previously obtained prototypicality ratings of the members of the category.

Method **Subjects.** Subjects were 400 students in introductory psychology classes who received this 10-minute task as part of their classroom work.

Stimuli. The categories used were the six most common categories of concrete nouns in English, determined by a measure of word frequency (Kucera and Francis, 1967). All of the categories were ones for which norms for the prototypicality of items had already been obtained for 50–60 category members (Rosch, 1975a). These norms were derived from subjects' ratings of the extent to which each item fit their "idea or image" of the meaning of the category name. (The rating task and instructions were very similar to those used in experiment 3 of the present research. A complete account of the methods for deriving the six superordinate categories and complete norms for all items of the six categories are provided in Rosch, in press d.) The 20 items from each category used in the present experiment were chosen to represent the full range of goodness-of-example ranks. These items are listed, in their goodness-of-example order, in table 8.1.

Procedure. Each of the 120 items shown in table 8.1 was printed at the top of a page, and the pages assembled into packets consisting of six items, one from each superordinate category. Items were chosen randomly within a category such that each subject who received an item received it with different items from the other five categories and received the items representing each category in a different order. Each item was rated by 20 subjects. Each subject rated six items, one from each category.

Table 8.1 Superordinate categories and items used in experiments 1 and 2

			Category			
Item	Furniture	Vehicle	Fruit	Weapon	Vegetable	Clothing
1	Chair	Car	Orange	Gun	Peas	Pants
2	Sofa	Truck	Apple	Knife	Carrots	Shirt
3	Table	Bus	Banana	Sword	String beans	Dress
4	Dresser	Motorcycle	Peach	Bomb	Spinach	Skirt
5	Desk	Train	Pear	Hand grenade	Broccoli	Jacket
6	Bed	Trolley car	Apricot	Spear	Asparagus	Coat
7	Bookcase	Bicycle	Plum	Cannon	Corn	Sweater
8	Footstool	Airplane	Grape	Bow and arrow	Cauliflower	Underpants
9	Lamp	Boat	Strawberry	Club	Brussel sprouts	Socks
10	Piano	Tractor	Grapefruit	Tank	Lettuce	Pajamas
11	Cushion	Cart	Pineapple	Teargas	Beets	Bathing suit
12	Mirror	Wheelchair	Blueberry	Whip	Tomato	Shoes
13	Rug	Tank	Lemon	Icepick	Lima beans	Vest
14	Radio	Raft	Watermelon	Fists	Eggplant	Tie
15	Stove	Sled	Honeydew	Rocket	Onion	Mittens
16	Clock	Horse	Pomegranate	Poison	Potato	Hat
17	Picture	Blimp	Date	Scissors	Yam	Apron
18	Closet	Skates	Coconut	Words	Mushroom	Purse
19	Vase	Wheelbarrow	Tomato	Foot	Pumpkin	Wristwatch
20	Telephone	Elevator	Olive	Screwdriver	Rice	Necklace

Subjects were asked to list the attributes possessed by each item. Instructions were:

> This is a very simple experiment to find out the characteristics and attributes that people feel are common to and characteristic of different kinds of ordinary everyday objects. For example, for *bicycles* you might think of things they have in common like two wheels, pedals, handlebars, you ride on them, they don't use fuel, etc. For *dogs* you might think of things they have in common like having four legs, barking, having fur, etc.
>
> There are six pages following this one. At the top of each is listed the name of one common object. For each page, you'll have a minute and a half to write down all of the attributes of that object that you can think of. But try not to just free associate – for example, if bicycles just happen to remind you of your father, *don't* write down *father*.
>
> Okay – you'll have a minute and a half for each page. When I say turn to the next page, read the name of the object and write down the attributes or characteristics you think are characteristic of that object as fast as you can until you're told to turn the page again.

Measurement of family resemblance. To derive the basic measure of family resemblance, for each category, all attributes mentioned by subjects were listed and each item, for which an attribute had been listed, was credited with that attribute. Two judges reviewed the resulting table and indicated cases in which an attribute was clearly and obviously false. These attributes were deleted from the tabulation. The judges also indicated any attribute which had been listed for one or more items, but was clearly and obviously true of another item in the category for which it had not happened to be listed by any of the 20 subjects. These items were also credited with the relevant attribute. Judges were not permitted to list new attributes, and no item was credited with an attribute about which judges disagreed or about which either judge was uncertain. The total changes made by the judges were infrequent.

Each attribute received a score, ranging from 1 to 20, representing the number of items in the category which had been credited with that attribute. By this means, each attribute was weighted in accordance with the number of items in the category possessing it. The basic measure of degree of family resemblance for an item was the sum of the weighted scores of each of the attributes that had been listed for that item.

This basic measure of family resemblance possessed a source of potential distortion, however. In the measure, each additional item with which an attribute was credited added an equal increment of family resemblance. Thus, the measure depended upon the assumption that the numerical frequency of an attribute within a category was an interval measure of the underlying psychological weight of that attribute (e.g., the difference between an attribute which belonged to two items versus one item was equal to the difference between an attribute which belonged to 19 versus 18 items). Such an assumption is not necessarily reasonable; therefore, a second measure of family resemblance was also computed. To derive this measure, each attribute was weighted with the natural logarithm of the raw score representing the number of items in the category which had been credited with that attribute; the second measure, thus, consisted of the sum of the natural logarithms of the scores of each of the attributes that had been listed for an item.

Results and discussion   The purpose of the study was both to provide a portrait of the structure of the categories and to test the correlation between family resemblance and prototypicality of items. In terms of structure, figure 8.1 shows the mean frequency distribution for the number of attributes applied to each number (1–20) of items/category. As had been previously found when subjects listed attributes for superordinate category names

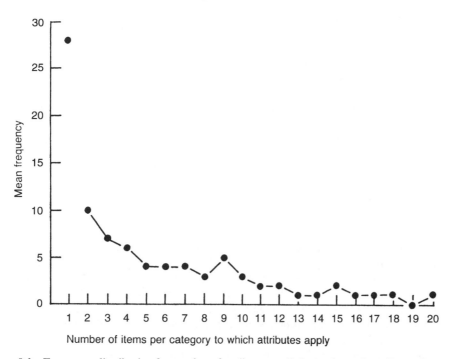

Figure 8.1 Frequency distribution for number of attributes applied to each number of items/category

(Rosch et al., in press), in the present study, few attributes were given which were true of all 20 members of the category – for four of the categories, there was only one such item; for two of the categories, none. Furthermore, the single attribute which did apply to all members, in three cases was true of many other items besides those within that superordinate (for example, "you eat it" for fruit). Thus, the salient attribute structure of these categories tended to reside, not in criterial features common to all members of the category which distinguished those members from all others, but in a large number of attributes true of some, but not all, category members.

Those attributes unique to a single member are not of primary interest for the present study since they do not contribute to the structure of the category per se. In actual fact, the number of unique attributes applicable to items was evenly distributed over members of the categories; for none of the six categories was the number of unique attributes significantly correlated with prototypicality. Of the attributes applicable to two or more members, figure 8.1 shows that the number of attributes decreases as the number of items to which the attribute is applicable increases. In summary: The majority of attributes listed for items in the six categories demonstrated a family resemblance relationship; that is, they were common to only some of the category members.

The major hypothesis of the experiment was that this family resemblance structure would prove significantly correlated with the prototypicality of items. Correlations were computed separately for each of the two measures of family resemblance and separately for each category. The measure of prototypicality was the mean rating on a seven-point scale of the extent to which items fit subjects' idea or image of the meaning of the category names

(Rosch, 1975a). The basic measure of degree of family resemblance for an item was the sum of the weighted raw scores of each of the attributes listed for the item. The logarithmic measure of family resemblance was the sum of the natural logarithms of the scores of each of the attributes that had been listed for an item. Items in each category were ranked 1–20 on the basis of prototypicality and were ranked 1–20 on the basis of each of the measures of family resemblance. Spearman rank-order correlations between the ranks of items on family resemblance and their ranks on prototypicality were performed separately for each of the measures of family resemblance and for each of the categories. These correlations, for the basic measure of family resemblance, were: furniture, 0.88; vehicle, 0.92; weapon, 0.94; fruit, 0.85; vegetable, 0.84; clothing, 0.91. These correlations for the logarithmic measure of family resemblance were: furniture, 0.84; vehicle, 0.90; weapon, 0.93; fruit, 0.88; vegetable, 0.86; clothing, 0.88. All were significant ($p < .001$).

Such results strongly confirm our hypothesis that the more an item has attributes in common with other members of the category, the more it will be considered a good and representative member of the category. Furthermore, the similarity in results obtained with the basic and the logarithmic measures of family resemblance argues that this relationship is not dependent upon the properties of the particular scale used in measurement. Specifically, items in a category tended to be credited with approximately equal numbers of attributes, but the less prototypical the item, the fewer other items in the category tended to share each attribute. Thus, the ranks for the basic and logarithmic measures of family resemblance were almost identical, and the correlations between family resemblance and prototypicality were scarcely affected by the change in measure. The relationship between degree of family resemblance and prototypicality for these categories thus appears to be a robust one.

A corollary of this finding may account for one of the persistent illusions concerning superordinate categories. Subjects, upon receiving feedback from the experiment, and audiences, upon being told of it, generally argue that they feel positive that there are many attributes common to all members of the category even when they cannot think of any specific attributes for which there are not counterexamples. If the more prototypical members of a category are those which have most attributes common to other members of the category it is probable that they are most likely to have attributes in common with each other. To investigate this possibility, the number of attributes common to the five most and five least prototypical items in each category were compared. The number of attributes are shown in table 8.2. It is clear from this count that, while category members as a whole may not have items in common, the five most typical items of each category tend to have many items in common. Thus, if subjects think of the best examples of the category when hearing the category name (Rosch, 1975a), the illusion of common elements is likely to arise and

Table 8.2 Number of attributes in common to five most and five least prototypical members of six categories

Category	Most typical members	Least typical members
Furniture	13	2
Vehicle	36	2
Fruit	16	0
Weapon	9	0
Vegetable	3	0
Clothing	21	0

persist – an illusion which may be what makes definition of categories in terms of criterial attributes appear so reasonable.

A second corollary of the finding of a strong relationship between family resemblance and prototypicality concerns the structure of the semantic space in which items of a category are embedded. Previous studies of the nature of the semantic spaces of superordinate categories have focused on the dimensionality of the space (Henley, 1969; Rips et al., 1973; Smith, Shoben, and Rips, 1974). However, there are other properties of semantic spaces which can be of interest. For example, items which are perceived as closest to all members of a group of items should fall in the center of the space defined by means of proximity scaling of those items. For purposes of the present study, we can predict that items with the greatest family resemblance should fall in the center of the semantic space defined by proximity scaling of the items in a category; such an effect can be predicted regardless of the dimensionality or lack of dimensionality of the semantic space. If, in addition, items are perceived as similar to each other in proportion to the number of attributes which they have in common, multidimensional scaling of the similarity judgments between all pairs of items in a category should result in a semantic space in which the distance of items from the origin of the space is determined by their degree of family resemblance.

A multidimensional scaling study of the categories *furniture, vehicle, weapon, fruit,* and *vegetable* was performed as part of a larger study.[1] Stimuli were the same 20 items in these categories shown in table 8.1 plus the superordinate category name. All possible pairs of the 21 items in each category were printed in a booklet and were rated on a nine-point scale for degree of similarity between the items. Fifteen subjects rated the items in each category. The similarity ratings were scaled by M-D scale (Shepard, 1962; Shepard et al., 1972, Vol. I). Results showed that, while the dimensionality of the scaling solutions was generally difficult to interpret, in all cases the category name and the most prototypical items appeared to be the most central in the scaling solution regardless of the number of dimensions or the rotation used. To check this finding, Spearman rank-order correlations between degree of family resemblance and distance of an item from the origin in the three-dimensional scaling solution with minimum stress were performed for the five categories. These correlations were: furniture, 0.89; vehicle, 0.94; weapon, 0.95; fruit, 0.92; and vegetable, 0.90. All were significant ($p < .001$).

In the use of proximity scaling for items in semantic categories, it is customary to rely for interpretation on dimensions which characterize the space as a whole (see Shepard et al., 1972, Vol. II). Such a trend is similar to the tradition of treating categories only in terms of logical defining features which are common to all members of the category. The present example of the use of scaling shows that, although family resemblance was defined in terms of discrete features no one of which was common to all category members, and although the dimensionality of the categories was not obvious in the scaling solutions, the property of centrality of items in the semantic space was still interpretable; that is, degree of family resemblance was highly predictive of centrality in a semantic space defined by global similarity ratings of the items in the category.

In summary: The hypotheses of experiment 1 were confirmed. For six superordinate categories, 20 members of the category were characterized by attributes which were common to some, but not all, members. The degree to which a given member possessed attributes in common with other members was highly correlated with the degree to which it was rated prototypical (representative) of the category name. In addition, degree of family resemblance predicted the centrality of items in the semantic space generated by multidimensional scaling of similarity ratings between items in the category.

Experiment 2

The initial hypothesis behind experiment 2 was the direct converse of that of experiment 1, namely that the most prototypical members of categories would not only have the greatest family resemblance to members of their category but would also be maximally distant from and, thus, have the least attributes in common with members of other categories at the same level of linguistic contrast. We found that this hypothesis could not be tested directly for supcordinate categories.

The standard empirical method for deriving linguistic contrast sets from research participants is some variant of the question, "If X is not a Y, what is it (might it be)?" (Frake, 1969). We pre-tested both the simple form of the question and the elaborated instructions used in experiment 4. However, for the six superordinate categories of the present research, such instructions failed to produce consistent responses from subjects; those subjects who were able to respond at all tended to produce individual creative answers which were not considered reasonable by other subjects to whom they were shown. For superordinate categories, we, therefore, turned to an indirect test of the hypothesis by means of measurement of overlap in category membership. If the best examples of superordinate categories are those with least in common with other categories they should be dominant members of few (or no) categories other than the superordinate in question. Thus, prototypicality should be correlated with a measure of the dominance of a category over its members (Loftus and Scheff, 1971). Subjects could readily list superordinates for category members. The hypothesis of experiment 2 was, thus, that the more prototypical a member of a superordinate category, the less dominant its membership would prove to be in categories other than the superordinate in question.

Method **Subjects.** Subjects were 400 students in introductory and upper-division psychology classes, none of whom had participated in experiment 1. They participated in the experiment as part of their classroom work.

Stimuli. Stimuli were the same members of five of the six most common superordinate categories of concrete nouns that had been used in experiment 1 (*clothing* was erroneously omitted). The items were assembled in the same manner as described for experiment 1. The only difference in format was that under each item, three lines labeled "1, 2, and 3" were printed on the page.

Procedure. Instructions were as follows:

> On each of the pages given you, you will see a noun and three lines. On each line, we want you to write a category to which the noun belongs. For example, if the noun were "collie," you might write *dog*, *animal*, or *pet* (etc.).
>
> Note that all of the words you see are to be interpreted as concrete nouns, not as verbs. For example, if you see the word "dress," interpret it as the article of clothing "dress" and not the action of getting dressed.
>
> Be sure to write three categories to which the noun belongs for each noun.

Computation of category membership score. Categories listed in first, second, and third place were weighted accordingly: three for first-place mention, two for second-place mention, one for third-place mention. Since our hypothesis concerned single versus multiple category memberships and salient category memberships in any category other than the designated superordinate, we required a measure of the degree of dominance of the designated superordinate over the other most frequently mentioned superordinates. For each item, this was the following weighted measure: (designated superordinate minus most frequently mentioned other superordinate) plus (designated superordinate minus second most frequently measured other superordinate). This produced a single measure of category dominance for each item.

Results and discussion Category dominance of each item was scored as described above; the items within each category were ranked in accordance with their relative degree of category dominance. A Spearman rank-order correlation was performed for each category between category dominance and prototypicality. These correlations were: fruit, 0.71; furniture, 0.83; vegetable, 0.67; vehicle, 0.82; weapon, 0.77. All were significant ($p < .001$).

Our hypothesis was that the more prototypical an item in a given category, the less it would bear a family resemblance to items in other categories, and, thus, the less likely it would be to have salient membership in those other categories. Membership in other categories was the variable which it proved possible to measure. The strong positive correlations between prototypicality and dominance of membership in the category for which prototypicality had been measured confirms this hypothesis.

2 Basic-level Categories

It has been previously argued (Rosch, in press a; Rosch et al., in press) that there is a basic level of abstraction at which the concrete objects of the world are most naturally divided into categories. A working assumption has been that, in the domains of both man-made and biological objects, there occur information-rich bundles of attributes that form natural discontinuities. These bundles are both perceptual and functional. It is proposed that basic cuts are made at this level. Basic objects (for example, *chair*, *car*) are the most inclusive level of abstraction at which categories can mirror the correlational structure (Garner, 1974) of the environment and the most inclusive level at which there can be many attributes common to all or most members of the categories. The more abstract combinations of basic level objects (e.g., categories such as *furniture* and *vehicle* used in experiments 1 and 2) are superordinates which share only a few attributes; the common attributes are rather abstract ones. Categories below the basic level are subordinates (e.g., *kitchen*, *chair*, *sports car*). Subordinates are also bundles of predictable attributes and functions, but contain little more information than the basic-level object to which they are subordinate. Basic categories are, thus, the categories for which the cue validity of attributes within categories is maximized: Superordinate categories have lower cue validity than basic because they have fewer common attributes within the category; subordinate categories have lower cue validity than basic because they share attributes with contrasting subordinate categories (e.g., *kitchen chair* shares most of its attributes with *living room chair*).

In a converging series of experiments (Rosch et al., in press), it was confirmed that basic objects are the most inclusive categories in which clusters of attributes occur which subjects agree are possessed by members of the category; sets of common motor movements are made when using or interacting with objects of that type; commonalities in the shape, and, thus, the overall look, of objects occur; it is possible to recognize an averaged shape of an object of that class; and it is possible to form a representation of a typical member of the class which is sufficiently concrete to aid in detection of the object in visual noise. In addition, basic objects were shown to be the first categorizations made by young children, and basic object names the level of abstraction at which objects are first named by children and usually named by adults.

The present research concerned the question of whether the family resemblances of items in basic-level categories were related to prototypicality in the way in which they had proved to be in the superordinate categories studied in experiments 1 and 2. Do subjects agree concerning which members of basic object categories are the more prototypical – do they agree, for example, about which cars more closely fit their idea or image of the meaning of *car*? And, if agreement in prototypicality ratings is obtained, does it hold, as it did in the case of superordinate categories, that the more prototypical category members are those with most resemblance to members of that category and least resemblance to other categories? In experiment 3, the hypothesis was tested that prototypicality ratings and degree of family resemblance were positively correlated. Experiment 4 tested the converse hypothesis that prototypicality ratings were negatively correlated with the degree to which an item possessed attributes which were also possessed by members of contrasting categories.

Experiment 3

Method   **Subjects.** Subjects were 182 paid undergraduate volunteers who participated as a part of a fundraising for a student organization. None had participated in the superordinate category experiments. Thirty-two subjects rated the stimuli for goodness-of-example; 150 listed attributes.

Stimuli. Superordinate categories have a finite number of members designable by words, with norms available for the frequency with which the members are listed by subjects (Battig and Montague, 1969). The members of basic-level categories, however, are actual objects, an essentially infinite population. Six categories were chosen for the present experiment, which had been shown to be at the basic level of abstraction by the convergent techniques used in Rosch et al. (in press). The categories were: car, truck, airplane, chair, table, and lamp. Each of these was a category for which pictures of many objects could be readily obtained and a category which had the property that the attributes of the object most listed by subjects (Rosch et al., in press) could be seen in pictures of the object. Pictures to be used in the present research were selected from a large sample of pictures (described in Rosch et al., in press); two judges chose 15 pictures by the following method – for each category, they first found the picture they felt most prototypical of the category, then the picture they felt was the worst example of the category (but still clearly called a ca, chair, etc.). They then selected 13 other pictures which they agreed spanned the distance between the two extreme pictures in as equal subjective steps as possible given the available pool of pictures. The 90 pictures, 15 in each category, chosen in this manner served as stimuli in the experiment.

Procedure. 1 *Prototypicality ratings.* Subjects were given essentially the same instructions as had been given subjects who rated the prototypicality of members of superordinate categories. Basically, subjects were asked to rate, on a seven-point scale, the extent to which an instance represented their idea or image of the meaning of the category name. Precise instructions were:

> This study has to do with what we have in mind when we use words which refer to categories. Let's take the word red as an example. Close your eyes and imagine a true red. Now imagine an orangish red . . . imagine a purple red. Although you might still name the orange-red or the

purple-red with the term red, they are not as good examples of red (as clear cases of what red refers to) as the clear "true" red. In short, some reds are redder than others. The same is true for other kinds of categories. Think of dogs. You all have some notion of what a "real dog," a "doggy dog" is. To me a Retriever or a German shepherd is a very doggy dog while a Pekingese is a less doggy dog. Notice that this kind of judgment has nothing to do with how well you like the thing; you can like a purple-red better than a true red but still recognize that the color you like is not a true red. You may prefer to own a Pekingese without thinking that it is the breed that best represents what people mean by dogginess.

In this study you are asked to judge how good an example of a category various instances of the category are. The members of the category are pictures; you will be told the name of the category and shown 15 pictures of items in the category. On your answer sheet are six columns of 15 numbers. After each number is a blank. You are to rate how good an example of the category each picture is on a 7-point scale. A 1 means that you feel the picture is a very good example of your idea or image of what the category is; a 7 means you feel the picture fits very poorly with your idea or image of the category (or is not a member at all). A 4 means you feel the picture fits moderately well. Use the other numbers of the 7-point scale to indicate intermediate judgments.

Don't worry about why you feel that something is or isn't a good example of the category. And don't worry about whether it's just you or people in general who feel that way. Just mark it the way you see it.

Slides of the 15 pictures in a category were shown the subjects once through rapidly in random order; then, each slide was shown the group for 30 seconds while subjects made their ratings. Means of the ratings of the 32 subjects in the experiment formed the basis for ranking the items.

2. *Attribute listing.* Subjects were given the same instructions for listing attributes as the subjects in experiment 1, with the exception that they were told they would be seeing pictures and were asked to list the attributes of the item in each picture. Each subject listed attributes for six pictures, one from each of the basic-level categories. Sets of pictures were assembled by the same principles as the sets of words had been in testing superordinate categories. Ten subjects listed attributes for each picture. Subjects were allowed 1.5 minutes to list attributes for each slide.

Results and discussion Methods used for computing family resemblance and for computing the correlation between family resemblance of attributes and prototypicality ratings were the same methods as had been used in experiment 1. As expected (Rosch et al., in press), basic-level categories differed from the subordinates in that many more attributes were common to all members of the basic level categories. However, there were also many attributes listed which were not common to all members. These attributes were used in the correlation between family resemblance and prototypicality. The Spearman rank-order correlations between the basic measure of family resemblance and prototypicality were: car, 0.94; truck, 0.84; airplane, 0.88; chair, 0.81; table, 0.88; and lamp, 0.69. The correlations between the logarithmic measure of family resemblance and prototypicality were: car, 0.86; truck, 0.88; airplane, 0.88; chair 0.79; table, 0.85; and lamp, 0.64. All were significant ($p < .01$). Thus, we have verified for pictures of basic-level objects, as well as for names of members of superordinate categories, the more prototypical items are those which have most attributes in common with other members of the category. As in the case of superordinate categories, this relationship was not dependent on the particular scale used to measure family resemblance.

Experiment 4

The purpose of both experiments 2 and 4 was to provide data complementary to that of experiments 1 and 3. The basic hypothesis of both experiments was that categories tend to become organized in such a way that they are maximally discriminable from other categories at the same level of contrast; hence, the most prototypical members of a category are those with least resemblance to, or membership in, other categories. For superordinate categories, it had not been possible to obtain contrast sets and, thus, not possible to measure commonality of attributes between contrasting categories directly; instead, the hypothesis had been tested indirectly by means of an item's membership in multiple categories. For members of basic-level categories, the hypothesis proved testable directly.

The basic design of the experiment was: (1) to determine which categories were seen in direct contrast to a sample of the basic-level categories for which we had obtained prototypicality ratings and attribute lists in Experiment 2, (2) to obtain lists of attributes for pictures representing items in the contrasting categories, and (3) to correlate the number of attributes which items shared with contrasting categories with prototypicality ratings for the items; a negative correlation was predicted.

Method   **Subjects.** Subjects were 44 students in psychology classes who performed the task as part of their classroom work; 24 of the subjects served in the contrast set portion of the experiment; 20 subjects listed attributes.

Stimuli and procedure. The first part of the experimental procedure required obtaining contrast sets of the basic-level categories to be used. Subjects were read the following instructions:

> Suppose that you are participating in a communication task experiment. Another person is describing "items" to you, and you have to figure out what kind of "item" he is describing. The person tells you about each item's *physical attributes* (what it looks like, what parts it has, etc.), and about its *functions* (what people do with it), and about its *actions* (what it does). Suppose, also, that you have guessed once for each item, and you have been told that your answer was not correct, but was very close to the correct one. Assume that each word I read was your first answer to one item. After I read each item, write down what your second answer would be. Remember that your first guess was very close to being correct. Think of something that has physical attributes, functions, and actions very similar to the ones your "first answer" had.

Subjects were then given the six names of basic-level items used in experiment 2 and asked to write their first guess as to what the item might be. Thirty seconds per item were allowed.

Subjects' responses were tallied. From the six basic-level categories, two were selected for which the most consistent responses had been given. These two, chair and car, were used for the second part of the experiment.

Stimuli for the attribute listing consisted of pictures of two examples of each of the three most frequently given contrast items for *chair* and *car*. These were: for chair – sofa, stool, and cushion; for car – truck, bus, and motorcycle. The pictures were chosen randomly from the pool of available pictures of these items, with the restriction that all of the pictures chosen had been rated (by two judges) as good examples of their category.

Attribute lists had already been obtained for the chair and car pictures in experiment 3. Attributes for the six contrast categories were obtained by the same procedures as used in experiment 3; subjects were read the same instructions as in experiment 3, were shown slides of the pictures in the contrast categories in random order, and were given 1.5 minures to list attributes for each picture. Each subject saw six pictures, one of each contrast item. Each picture was seen by 10 subjects.

Results and discussion For each of the 15 chair and 15 car pictures, a tally was made of the number of attributes listed for that picture, which had also been listed for at least one of the pictures of one of the three contrast categories. This tally was used as the measure of amount of overlap between the attributes of a given item and the attributes of items in the closest contrasting categories. A Spearman rank-order correlation was performed between the prototypicality and attribute overlap ranks of the 15 chair and 15 car pictures. Results were: chairs $r = -.67$; cars, $r = -.86$. Both were significant ($p < .01$). In short, it was clearly confirmed for two basic-level categories that the more prototypical of the category a picture had been rated, the fewer attributes it shared with categories in direct contrast with that category.[2]

General Discussion

The results of the present study confirmed the hypothesis that the most prototypical members of common superordinate, basic-level, and artificial categories are those which bear the greatest family resemblance to other members of their own category and have the least overlap with other categories. In probabilistic language, prototypicality was shown to be a function of the cue validity of the attributes of items. In the particular studies in this paper, we defined and measured family resemblance in terms of discrete attributes; however, previous studies indicate that the principle can be applied, to some extent, to other types of category, such as dot patterns distorted around a prototype and categories consisting of items composed of continuous attributes which have a metric (Posner, 1973; Reed, 1972; Rosch et al., 1975). In such categories, the prototype dot pattern and the pattern with attributes at mean values have more in common with (are more like) the other items in the category than are items further from the prototype or the mean. Family resemblances (even broadly defined) are undoubtedly not the only principle of prototype formation – for example, the frequency of items and the salience of particular attributes or particular members of the categories (perceptual, social, or memorial salience), as well as the as yet undefined *Gestalt* properties of stimuli and stimulus combinations, undoubtedly contribute to prototype formation (Rosch, 1975b) – however, the results of the present study indicate that family resemblance is a major factor.

Such a finding is important in six ways: (1) It suggests a structural basis for the formation of prototypes of categories; (2) it argues that in modeling natural categories, prototypes and cue validity are not conflicting accounts, but, rather, must be incorporated into a single model; (3) it indicates a structural rationale for the use of proximity scaling in the study of categories, even in the absence of definable category dimensionality; (4) it offers a principle by which prototype formation can be understood as part of the general processes through which categories themselves may be formed; (5) it provides a new link between adult and children's modes of categorization; and (6) it offers a concrete alternative to criterial attributes in understanding the logic of categorical structure.

Family resemblance as a structural basis for prototype formation

The origin of prototypes of categories is an issue because, as outlined in the introduction, there is now considerable evidence that the extent to which members are conceived typical of a category appears to be an important variable in the cognitive processing of categories (Rosch, 1975a, 1975b, in press a, in press b, in press c, in press d). From that previous work alone, it could be argued that ratings of prototypicality are only measures of the associative linkage between an item and the category name and that it is such associative strength which determines the effects of typicality on processing tasks such as those used in semantic memory. While in a processing model, associative strength may, by definition, be directly related to typicality effects, associative strength need not be conceived only as the result of the frequency of (arbitrary or accidental) pairings of the item with the category name. The present experiments have attempted to provide a structural principle for the formation of prototypes; family resemblance relationships are not in contradiction to, but, rather, themselves offer a possible structural reason behind associative strength.

The principle of family resemblance is similar but not identical to two recent accounts of prototype effects: the attribute frequency model (Neumann, 1974) and an element tag model (Reitman and Bower, 1973). Both of these models were designed to account, without recourse to an "abstraction process," for the findings of several specific previous experiments – primarily those of Bransford and Franks (1971) and Franks and Bransford (1971). Both models predict memory (particularly the mistaken memory for prototype items which were not actually presented) from the frequency with which elements appear in a learning set.

A family resemblance account of prototypes is of greater generality than these models. In the first place, it accounts for prototypes in terms of distributions of attributes rather than in terms of the simple frequency of attributes (a factor which also distinguishes family resemblances from a narrow definition of cue validity). In the second place, it includes an account of the distribution of attributes over contrasting categories rather than focusing only on the category in question. That it is distribution rather than simple frequency of attributes which is most relevant to prototypes in natural categories is argued by two facts: (1) The measure of distribution used in the present study was highly correlated with ratings of prototypicality for superordinate categories, whereas a measure of the frequency of items (which is necessarily correlated with frequency of attributes) in the category is not correlated with prototypicality (Mervis, Rosch, and Catlin, 1975); and (b) the overlap of attributes with contrasting categories is itself a distributional property not a property of simple frequency. (In the artificial categories of experiment 5 of the present paper, distributional and simple frequency were equivalent; however, in the other experiments, they were not – clarification of the relations between distribution and frequency of attributes is an issue which requires further research. [Experiments 5 and 6 are discussed in a section on artificial categories not reproduced here.]) That the distribution of attributes over contrasting categories is as important a principle of prototype formation as distribution of attributes within a category is argued by the results of experiments 2, 4, and 6.

At this point, it should be reiterated that the principle of family resemblance, as defined in the present research, is a descriptive, not a processing, principle. Family resemblances are related to process models in two ways: (1) Any account of the processes by which humans convert stimulus attributes into mental or behavioral prototypes (such as an attribute tag model) should be able to account for the family resemblance attribute structure of categories outlined by the present research; and (2) classification by computation of cue validity and classification by matching to a prototype have been treated as alternative process models which are in conflict; however, the principle of family resemblance suggests that, for natural categories, both should be aspects of the same processing model.

Family resemblance as an argument for the compatibility of cue validity and prototype models

Probability models, such as cue validity, and distance models, such as matching to a prototype, have been treated as two fundamentally different forms of categorization model whose conflicting validities must be tested by empirical research (Reed, 1972). However, the present study has shown that empirically defined prototypes of natural categories are just those items with highest cue validity. Such a structure of categories would, in fact, appear to provide the means for maximally efficient processing of categories. Computation and summation of the validities of individual cues is a laborious cognitive process. However, since cue validity appears to be the basis of categories (Rosch et al., in press), it is ecologically essential that cue validities be taken into account, in some manner, in categorization. If prototypes function cognitively as representatives of the category and if prototypes are items with the highest cue validities, humans can use the efficient processing mechanism of matching to a prototype without sacrificing attention to the validity of cues. (Note that such an account is similar to the compromise model which ultimately proved the most predictive for Reed's 1972 categories of schematic faces – a prototype matching model in which the importance of each feature in the prototype was weighted in accordance with its cue validity.) In short, humans probably incorporate probabilistic analysis of cues and computation of distance from a representation of the category into the same process of categorization; future research on categorization would do well to attempt to model the ways in which that incorporation can occur rather than to treat cue validity and prototypes as conflicting models.

Family resemblance as a basis for proximity scaling

Just as it has been customary to treat categories in terms of logical defining features which were assumed to be common to all members of the category, it is also not uncommon to treat proximity scaling of items in categories only as a means of determining the general dimensions along which items of the category are seen to differ. However, the results of the multidimensional scaling of the items of the superordinate categories in experiment 1 (performed with Smith, Shoben, and Rips) indicated that family resemblance was predictive of centrality of items in the derived similarity space regardless of interpretability of dimensions or of item clusters. It should, in general, be the case that the more that items have in common with other items in a class (the closer the items are to all other items irrespective of the basis of closeness), the more central those items will be in a space derived from proximity measures. The demonstration of the importance of family resemblances (and of prototypicality) in classification provided by the present research suggests that the dimension of centrality may itself be an important aspect of and deserve to be a focus of attention in the analysis of proximity spaces.

Family resemblance as a part of the general process of category formation

The concept of family resemblances is also of general use because it characterizes prototype formation as part of the general process by which categories themselves are formed. It has been argued by Rosch et al. (in press) that division of the world into categories is not arbitrary. The basic category cuts in the world are those which separate the information-rich bundles of attributes which form natural discontinuities. Basic categories have, in fact, been shown to be the most inclusive categories in which all items in the category possess significant numbers of attributes in common, and, thereby, are used by means of similar sequences of motor movements and are like each other in overall appearance. Basic categories are the categories for which the cue validity of attributes within categories is maximized, since superordinate categories have fewer common attributes within the category than do basic categories, and subordinate categories share more attributes with contrasting categories than do basic categories. Basic categories are, thus, the categories which mirror the correlational structure of the environment.

The present study has shown that formation of prototypes of categories appears to be likewise nonarbitrary. The more prototypical a category member, the more attributes it has in common with other members of the category and the less attributes in common with contrasting categories. Thus, prototypes appear to be just those members of the category which most reflect the redundancy structure of the category as a whole. That is, categories form to maximize the information-rich clusters of attributes in the environment and, thus, the cue validity of the attributes of categories; when prototypes of categories form by means of the principle of family resemblance, they maximize such clusters and such cue validity still further within categories.

Family resemblance as a link with children's classifications

The principle of family resemblances in adult categories casts a new perspective on children's classifications. Young children have been shown to classify objects or pictures by means of complexive classes; that is, classes in which items are related to each other by attributes not shared by all members of the class (Bruner, et al. 1966; Vygotsky, 1962). For example, Vygotsky (1962) speaks of the child in the "phase of thinking in complexes" starting with a small yellow triangle, putting with it a red triangle, then a red circle – in each case matching the new item to one attribute of the old. Bruner et al. describe the young child's tendency to classify by means of "complexive structures," for example, "banana and peach are yellow, peach and potato round. . . ." Such complexive classes have been considered logically more primitive than the adult preferred method of grouping taxonomically by "what a thing is"; that is, grouping by superordinate classes and justifying groups by their superordinate names. However, the present research has shown that family resemblance, a form of complexive grouping, appears to be one of the structural principles in the composition of the superordinate classes themselves, and, thus, one of the structural principles in adult classification. Since adult taxonomic classes, such as furniture or chair, themselves consist of complexive groupings of attributes, it would appear appropriate to study the development of the integration of complexive into taxonomic categories rather than the replacement of the former by the latter.

Family resemblance as a logical alternative to criterial attributes

There is a tenacious tradition of thought in philosophy and psychology which assumes that items can bear a categorical relationship to each other only by means of the possession of common criterial attributes. The present study is an empirical confirmation of Wittgenstein's (1953) argument that formal criteria are neither a logical nor a psychological necessity; the categorical relationship in categories which do not appear to possess criterial attributes, such as those used in the present study, can be understood in terms of the principle of family resemblance.

NOTES

1   The larger study was performed in collaboration with E. E. Smith, E. J. Shoben, and L. J. Rips of Stanford University. Half of the subjects were tested at the University of California, Berkeley, half at Stanford University. The multidimensional scaling was performed entirely at Stanford.
2   [Editors' note: There follows the section on artificial categories. The results are summarized in the general discussion that concludes the article.]

REFERENCES

Battig, W. F. and Montague, W. E. (1969). Category norms for verbal items in 56 categories: a replication and extension of the Connecticut category norms. *Journal of Experimental Psychology*, 80: 1–46.

Beach, L. R. (1964). Cue probabilism and inference behavior. *Psychological Monographs*, 78: 1–20.

Berlin, B. and Kay, P. (1969). *Basic Color Terms: Their Universality and Evolution*. Berkeley: University of California Press.

Bransford, J. D. and Franks, J. J. (1971). Abstraction of linguistic ideas. *Cognitive Psychology*, 2: 331–50.

Bruner, J. S., Oliver, R. R., and Greenfield, P. M. (1966). *Studies in Cognitive Growth*. New York: John Wiley.

Ekman, P. (1971). Universals and cultural differences in facial expressions of emotion. In J. K. Cole (ed.), *Nebraska Symposium on Motivation*. Lincoln, NE: University of Nebraska Press.

Frake, C. O. (1969). The ethnographic study of cognitive systems. In S. A. Tyler (ed.), *Cognitive Anthropology*. New York: Holt, Rinehart, & Winston.

Franks, J. J. and Bransford, J. D. (1971). Abstraction of visual patterns. *Journal of Experimental Psychology*, 90: 65–74.

Garner, W. R. (1974). *The Processing of Information and Structure*. New York: Halsted Press.

Heider, E. R. (1972). Universals in color naming and memory. *Journal of Experimental Psychology*, 93: 10–20.

Henley, N. M. (1969). A psychological study of the semantics of animal terms. *Journal of Verbal Learning and Verbal Behavior*, 8: 176–84.

Kucera, H. K. and Francis, W. N. (1967). *Computational Analysis of Present-day American English*. Providence, RI: Brown University Press.

Lakoff, G. (1972). Hedges: a study in meaning criteria and the logic of fuzzy concepts. *Papers from the Eighth Regional Meeting, Chicago Linguistics Society*. Chicago: University of Chicago Linguistics Department.

Loftus, E. F. and Scheff, R. W. (1971). Categorization norms for fifty representative instances. *Journal of Experimental Psychology*, 91: 355–64.

McDaniel, C. K. (1972). Hue perception and hue naming. Unpublished BA thesis, Harvard College.

Mervis, C. B. Catlin, J., and Rosch, E. (1975). Development of the structure of color categories. *Developmental Psychology*, 11: 54–60.

Mervis, C. B., Rosch, E., and Catlin, J. (1975). Relationships among goodness-of-example, category norms, and word frequency. Unpublished manuscript. (Available from the second author.)

Neumann, P. G. (1974). An attribute frequency model for the abstraction of prototypes. *Memory and Cognition*, 2: 241–8.

Posner, M. I. (1973). *Cognition: An Introduction*. Glencoe, IL: Scott, Foresman.

Reed, S. K. (1972). Pattern recognition and categorization. *Cognitive Psychology*, 3: 382–407.

Reitman, J. S. and Bower, G. H. (1973). Storage and later recognition of concepts. *Cognitive Psychology*, 4: 194–206.

Rips, L. J., Shoben, E. J. and Smith, E. E. (1973). Semantic distance and the verification of semantic relations. *Journal of Verbal Learning and Verbal Behaviors*, 12: 1–20.

Rosch, E. (1973). On the internal structure of perceptual and semantic categories. In T. E. Moore (ed.), *Cognitive Development and the Acquisition of Language*. New York: Academic Press.

Rosch, E. (1974). Linguistic relativity. In A. Silverstein (ed.), *Human Communications: Theoretical Perspectives*. New York: Halsted Press.

Rosch, E. (1975a). Cognitive representations of semantic categories. *Journal of Experimental Psychology: General*, 104: 192–233.

Rosch, E. (1975b). Universals and cultural specifics in human categorization. In R. Brislin, S. Bochner, and W. Lonner (eds), *Cross-cultural Perspectives on Learning*. New York: Halsted Press.

Rosch, E. (in press, a). Classifications of real-world objects: origins and representations in cognition. *Bulletin de Psychologie*.

Rosch, E. (in press, b). Cognitive reference points. *Cognitive Psychology* [7 (1975), 532–47].

Rosch, E. (in press c). Human categorization. In N. Warren (ed.), *Advances in Cross-cultural Psychology*. Vol. 1. London: Academic Press. [1977].

Rosch, E. (in press, d). Cognitive representations of semantic categories. *Journal of Experimental Psychology: Human Perception and Performance* [104 (1975), 192–233].

Rosch, E. (in press, e). The nature of mental codes for color categories. *Journal of Experimental Psychology: Human Perception and Performance* [1 (1975), 303–22].

Rosch, E., Mervis, C. B., Gray, W., Johnson, D., and Boyes-Bream, P. (in press) Basic objects in natural categories. *Cognitive Psychology* [8 (1976), 382–439].

Rosch, E., Simpson, C., and Miller, R. S. (1975). Structural bases of typicality effects. Manuscript submitted for publication.

Shepard, R. N. (1962). The analysis of proximities: multidimensional scaling with an unknown distance function. I and II. *Psychometrika*, 27: 125–40, 219–46.

Shepard, R. N., Romney, A. K., and Nerlove, S. B. (1972). *Multidimensional Scaling: Theory and Applications in the Behavioral Sciences*. Vols I and II. New York: Seminar Press.

Smith, E. E., Rips, L. J., and Shoben, E. J. (1974). Semantic memory and psychological semantics. In G. H. Bower (ed.), *The Psychology of Learning and Motivation*. Vol. 8. New York: Academic Press.

Smith, E. E., Shoben, E. J., and Rips, L. J. (1974). Structure and process in semantic memory: a featural model for semantic decisions. *Psychological Review*, 81: 214–41.

Vygotsky, L. S. (1962). *Thought and Language*. New York: John Wiley.

Wittgenstein, L. (1953). *Philosophical Investigations*. New York: Macmillan.

Zadeh, L. A. (1965). Fuzzy sets. *Information and Control*, 8: 338–53.

Précis of *Relevance: Communication and Cognition*

DAN SPERBER AND DEIRDRE WILSON

In *Relevance: Communication and Cognition* (Sperber and Wilson, 1986a, henceforth *Relevance*), we present a new approach to the study of human communication. This approach, outlined in the first chapter, is grounded in the general view of human cognition developed in the second and third chapters. Human attention and thought, we argue, automatically turn toward information which seems relevant: To communicate is to claim someone's attention, hence to communicate is to imply that the information communicated is relevant. We call this thesis the *principle of relevance*, and show in the fourth chapter how it is enough on its own account of linguistic meaning with contextual factors in utterance interpretation.

In this précis, we will follow the general plan of the book. However, we have had to leave out several steps in the argumentation, many side issues, most examples, almost all discussion of other approaches, and all traces of wit.

1   Communication

1.1   The code model and its limits

Communication is a process involving two information-processing devices. One device modifies the physical environment of the other. As a result the second device constructs representations similar to representations already stored in the first device. Oral communication, for instance, is a modification by the speaker of the hearer's acoustic environment, as a result of which the hearer entertains thoughts similar to the speaker's own.

The question is: How can a physical stimulus bring about the required similarity of representations when there is no similarity whatsoever between the stimulus (e.g., sound patterns) on the one hand and the representations (e.g., human thoughts) it brings into correspondence on the other? From Aristotle through to modern semiotics, all theories of communication were based on a single model, which we call the *code model*. A *code* is a system which pairs internal messages with external signals, thus enabling two information-processing devices (organisms or machines) to communicate.

Linguistic utterances – the most important means of human communication – do succeed in communicating thoughts; the hypothesis that utterances are signals that encode thoughts seems to explain this fact. However, it is descriptively inadequate: Comprehension involves more than the decoding of a linguistic symbol. Although a language can be seen as a code which pairs phonetic and semantic representations of sentences, much recent work in psycholinguistics, pragmatics, and the philosophy of language[1] shows that there is a gap between the semantic representations of sentences and the thoughts actually communicated by utterances. The gap is filled not by mere coding but by inference.

The study of the semantic representation of sentences belongs to grammar; the study of the interpretation of utterances belongs to what is now known as *pragmatics*. Among its tasks, pragmatics must explain how hearers resolve ambiguities, complete elliptical or otherwise semantically incomplete sentences, identify intended references, identify illocutionary force, recognize tropes, and recover implicit import. These are some of the ways in which the context-independent semantic representation of a sentence falls short of determining the interpretation of an utterance of that sentence in context.

To justify the code model of verbal communication, it would have to be shown that the interpretation of utterances in context can be accounted for by adding an extra pragmatic level of decoding to the linguistic level provided by the grammar. Much recent work in pragmatics has assumed that this can be done.[2] At the programmatic level, pragmatics has been described, on the analogy of phonology, syntax, and semantics, as a code-like mental device underlying a distinct level of linguistic ability. In practice, however, most pragmaticians have described comprehension as an inferential process.

Inferential and decoding processes are quite different. An *inferential process* takes a set of premises as input and yields as output a set of conclusions which follow logically from, or at least are warranted by, the premises. A *decoding process* takes a signal as input and yields as output a message associated with the signal by an underlying code. In general, conclusions are not associated with their premises by a code, and signals do not warrant the messages they convey. Does it follow that pragmaticians who hold to the code model but describe comprehension in inferential terms are being inconsistent? Not necessarily: It is formally conceivable that a decoding process should contain an inferential process as a subpart. However, for this to be possible, speaker and hearer must use not only the same language but also the same set of premises, because what makes the code model explanatory is that symmetrical operations are performed at the emitting and receiving ends.

The set of premises used in interpreting an utterance constitutes what is generally known (see Gazdar, 1979; Johnson-Laird, 1983) as the *context*. A context is a psychological construct, a subset of the hearer's assumptions about the world. Each new utterance, though drawing on the same grammar and the same inferential abilities as previous utterances, requires a rather different context (if only because the interpretation of the previous utterance has become part of the context). A central problem for pragmatic theory is to describe how the hearer constructs a new context for every new utterance.

For code theorists, the context used by the hearer should always be identical to the one envisaged by the speaker. Can this condition be met? Because any two people are sure to share at least a few assumptions about the world, they might be expected to use only these shared assumptions. However, this cannot be the whole answer in that it immediately raises a new question: How are the speaker and hearer to distinguish the assumptions they share from those they do not? For that, they must make second-order assumptions about which first-order assumptions they share; but then they had better make sure that they share these second-order assumptions, which calls for third-order assumptions, and so on indefinitely. Assumptions or knowledge of this infinitely regressive sort was first identified by Lewis (1969) as "common knowledge" and by Schiffer (1972) as "mutual knowledge."

Within the framework of the code model, mutual knowledge is a necessity. However, pragmaticians have offered no independent support for the claim that individuals engaging in verbal communication can and do distinguish mutual from nonmutual knowledge. In *Relevance*, we present several arguments to show that the mutual knowledge hypothesis is psychologically implausible. We therefore reject the code model of verbal communication that implies it.[3]

1.2   The inferential model

In 1957, Paul Grice published an article, "Meaning," which has been the object of a great many controversies, interpretations, and revisions.[4] In it Grice analyzed what it is for an individual to mean something by an utterance in terms of intentions and the recognition of intentions, and tried to extend this analysis of "speaker's meaning" into such areas of traditional semantic concern as the analysis of "sentence meaning" and "word meaning." Grice's analysis provides the point of departure for a new model of communication, the *inferential model*, and this is how we use it in *Relevance*. We look in detail at Grice's own proposal, as well as at some of the objections that have been raised and some of the reformulations that have been proposed, notably by Strawson (1964), Searle (1969), and Schiffer (1972). Here we will give a short, informal account of the basic idea before outlining some developments of our own.

Suppose that Mary intends to inform Peter of the fact that she has a sore throat. All she has to do is let Peter hear her hoarse voice, thus providing him with salient and conclusive evidence that she has a sore throat. Suppose now that Mary intends, on June 2, to inform

Peter that she had a sore throat on the previous Christmas Eve. This time she is unlikely to be able to produce *direct* evidence of her past sore throat. What she can do though is give him direct evidence, not of her past sore throat, but of her present intention to inform him of it. She may do this, for instance, by saying "I had a sore throat on Christmas Eve," or by nodding when he asks her if she did. Mary's utterance or nod is directly caused by her present intention to inform Peter of her past sore throat and is therefore direct evidence of this intention. Suppose now that Peter assumes that Mary is sincere and well informed. Then the fact that she intends to inform him that she had a sore throat on that date provides indirect but nevertheless conclusive evidence that she had one. Mary's intention to inform Peter of her past sore throat is fulfilled by making him recognize her intention.

This example shows that information can be conveyed in two different ways. One way is to provide direct evidence for it. This should not in itself be regarded as a form of communication: Any state of affairs provides direct evidence for a variety of assumptions without necessarily *communicating* those assumptions in any interesting sense. Another way of conveying information is to provide direct evidence of one's intention to convey it. The first method can be used only with information for which direct evidence can be provided. The second method can be used with any information at all, as long as direct evidence of the communicator's intentions can be provided. This second method is clearly a form of communication; it can be called *inferential communication* because the audience infers the communicator's intention from evidence provided for this precise purpose.

A communicator intentionally engaging in inferential communication perceptibly modifies the physical environment of her[5] audience – that is, she produces a stimulus. She does so with two characteristic intentions: the *informative intention*, to inform the audience of something, and the *communicative intention*, to inform the audience of her informative intention. Note that the communicative intention is itself a second-order informative intention.

This description of communication in terms of intentions and inferences is, in a way, commonsensical. As speakers, we intend our hearers to recognize our intention to inform them of some state of affairs. As hearers we try to recognize what it is that the speaker intends to inform us of. The idea that communication exploits the well-known ability of humans to attribute intentions to each other should appeal to cognitive and social psychologists. To justify this appeal, however, what is needed is not merely a descriptive account, but a genuine explanation of communicative success.

How are informative intentions recognized? The key to an answer is again suggested by Grice (1975, 1978), who argues that a rational communicator tries to meet certain general standards. Grice describes these standards as a "cooperative principle" and nine associated "maxims." From knowledge of these standards, observation of the communicator's behaviour, and the context, the audience can normally infer the communicator's informative intention. In *Relevance*, we discuss in detail both Grice's proposal and its elaborations by others. Here a brief illustration must suffice.

Consider the following dialogue:

(1) *Peter:* Do you want coffee?
     Mary: Coffee would keep me awake.

Unless some further assumptions are made, Mary's answer fails to satisfy one of Grice's maxims: "Be relevant." However, Peter should take for granted that Mary is not flouting the maxim; he can justify this assumption by assuming, further, that she intends him to infer from her answer that she does not want to stay awake and hence does not want any coffee. These contextually inferred assumptions, recovered by reference to the cooperative principle and maxims, are what Grice calls *implicatures* of her utterance. Such implicatures are communicated not by coding, but by providing evidence of the fact that the speaker intends to convey them.

Although more systematic than the reconstructions that can be elicited from unsophisticated speakers, the analyses of implicature proposed by Grice and his followers have shared with these reconstructions the defect of being almost entirely *ex post facto*. Given that an utterance in context is found to carry particular implicatures, what both the hearer and the pragmatician can do is to show how, in intuitive terms, an argument based on the context, the utterance, and general expectations about the behaviour of speakers justifies the particular interpretation chosen. What they fail to show is that, on the same basis, an equally well-formed argument could not have been given for a quite different and in fact implausible interpretation.

Grice's idea that the very act of communicating creates expectations which it then exploits provides a starting point. Beyond that, the inferential model needs radical reworking in order to become truly explanatory. A psychologically realistic answer must be given to such basic questions as these: What shared information is exploited in communication? What forms of inference are used? What is relevance and how is it achieved? What role does the search for relevance play in communication?

1.3   *Cognitive environments and mutual manifestness*

In analyzing the nature of the shared information involved in communication, we introduce the notion of a cognitive environment (analogous, at a conceptual level, to notions of visual or acoustic environment at a perceptual level):

> A *cognitive environment* of an individual is a set of facts that are manifest to him.
>
> A fact is *manifest* to an individual at a given time if, and only if, the individual is capable at that time of representing it mentally and accepting its representation as true or probably true.

To be manifest, then, is to be perceptible or inferable. An individual's total cognitive environment consists not only of all the facts that he is aware of, but of all the facts that he is capable of becoming aware of at that time and place. Manifestness so defined is a property not only of facts but, more generally, of true or false assumptions. It is a relative property: Facts and assumptions can be more or less strongly manifest. Because *manifest* is weaker than *known* or *assumed*, a notion of mutual manifestness can be developed that does not suffer from the same psychological implausibility as mutual knowledge.

The same facts and assumptions may be manifest in the cognitive environments of several people. In that case, these cognitive environments intersect, and their intersection is a cognitive environment that the people in question share. One thing that can be manifest in a shared cognitive environment is a characterization of those who have access to it. For instance, every Freemason has access to a number of secret assumptions, which include the assumption that all Freemasons have access to these same secret assumptions. In other words, all Freemasons share a cognitive environment that contains the assumption that all Freemasons share this environment. Any shared cognitive environment in which it is manifest which people share it is what we call a *mutual cognitive environment*. For every manifest assumption, in a mutual cognitive environment, the fact that it is manifest to the people who share the environment is itself manifest. In a mutual cognitive environment, therefore, every manifest assumption is *mutually manifest*.

If a cognitive environment is merely a set of assumptions that an individual is capable of mentally representing and accepting as true, the question becomes: Which of these assumptions will the individual actually make? This question is of interest not only to the psychologist, but also to every ordinary communicator who wants to modify the thoughts of her audience but can directly affect only its cognitive environment.

1.4   Relevance and ostension

Most discussions of information processing, whether in experimental psychology or in artificial intelligence, have been concerned with the achievement of pre-set goals. However, many cognitive tasks consist not in reaching a fixed state, but in increasing the value of some parameters. Human cognition as a whole is a case in point: It is aimed at improving the quantity, quality, and organization of the individual's knowledge. To achieve this goal as efficiently as possible, the individual must at each moment try to allocate his processing resources to the most *relevant* information: that is, as we will shortly show, information likely to bring about the greatest improvement of knowledge at the smallest processing cost. Our claim is that this is done automatically and that an individual's particular cognitive goal at a given time is always consistent with the more general goal of maximizing the relevance of the information processed.

Human cognition is relevance-oriented. As a result, and to the extent that one knows the cognitive environment of an individual – which one does when the environment is mutual – one can infer which assumptions he is actually likely to entertain and how a change in that environment might affect his train of thoughts. This makes it possible to affect people's thoughts in a partly predictable way by modifying their cognitive environment.

Peter and Mary are sitting on a park bench. He points in a direction where she had not so far noticed anything in particular. This time, she takes a closer look and sees their acquaintance Julius in the distance, sitting on the grass. In other words, as a result of Peter's behaviour, the presence of Julius, which was weakly manifest in Mary's cognitive environment, has become more manifest, to the point of being actually noticed. Moreover, it has become manifest that Peter had himself noticed Julius and intended her to notice him too. Such behaviour – which makes manifest an intention to make something manifest – we call *ostension*.

How does ostension work? For instance, how does Mary discover, when Peter points in a certain direction, which of the many phenomena visible in that direction he intended her to notice? Any request for attention, and hence any act of ostension, conveys a presumption of relevance; it does so because attention goes only to what is presumed relevant. By pointing, Peter conveys to Mary that by paying attention she will gain some relevant information. This makes it reasonable for her to pay more attention that she had before; discovering the presence of Julius, she may reasonably assume that Peter thought it would be relevant to her, and, moreover, that this was part of his reason for bringing it to her attention.

Ostension provides two layers of information to be picked up: The first consists of the information that has been pointed out; the second consists of the information that the first layer of information was intentionally pointed out. In our example, the first basic layer of information – Julius's presence – was already manifest and is merely made more manifest by the ostension. In other cases, all the evidence displayed in an act of ostension bears on the agent's intentions and on nothing else directly. In these cases, it is only by discovering the agent's intentions that the audience can also discover, indirectly, the basic information that the agent intended to make manifest. As we show in *Relevance*, there is a continuum of cases between those that provide full direct evidence for the basic information made manifest (i.e., they "show something") and those that provide only indirect evidence (e.g., by "saying something"). We argue that inferential communication and ostension are one and the same process, but seen from two different points of view: that of the communicator who is involved in ostension and that of the audience who is involved in inference.

1.5   Ostensive-inferential communication

Most accounts of communication take "saying that" as their paradigm case, and assume that the communicator's intention is to induce certain specific thoughts in an audience. We want to suggest that the communicator's informative intention is better described as an intention to modify directly not the thoughts but the cognitive environment of the audience, with only partly foreseeable effects on the audience's actual thoughts. We therefore reformulate the notion of an informative intention:

> *Informative intention:* the intention to make manifest or more manifest to the audience a certain set of assumptions.

Why should someone who has an informative intention bother to make it known to the audience? In other words, what are the reasons for engaging in ostensive communication? So far we have discussed only one of these reasons: Making one's informative intention known is often the best way, or the only way, of fulfilling it. There is another major reason for engaging in ostensive communication. Mere informing alters the cognitive environment of the audience. True communication is "overt" in Strawson's sense (Strawson, 1964); in our terms, it takes place in the mutual cognitive environment of the audience and the communicator. Mutual manifestness may be of little cognitive importance, but it is of crucial social or interpersonal importance. A change in the mutual cognitive environment of two people is a change in the possibilities of interaction (and, in particular, in their possibilities of further communication). This is why we redefine the communicative intention as follows:

> *Communicative intention:* the intention to make mutually manifest to audience and communicator the communicator's informative intention.

Ostensive-inferential communication, which, incidentally, need not be intentional, can itself be defined as follows:

> *Ostensive-inferential communication:* The communicator produces a stimulus which makes it mutually manifest to communicator and audience that the communicator intends, by means of the stimulus, to make manifest or more manifest to the audience a certain set of assumptions.

Instead of treating an assumption as either communicated or not communicated, we have a set of assumptions which, as a result of communication, become manifest or more manifest to varying degrees. We can think of communication itself, then, as a matter of degree. When the communicator makes strongly manifest her informative intention to make some particular assumption strongly manifest, then that assumption is strongly communicated. An example would be answering a clear "Yes," when asked "Will you take John So-and-so as your lawful wedded husband?" When the communicator's intention is to increase simultaneously the manifestness of a wide range of assumptions, so that her intention concerning each of these assumptions is itself weakly manifest, then each of them is weakly communicated. An example would be sniffing ecstatically and ostensively at the fresh seaside air. Often in human interaction weak communication is found sufficient or even preferable to the stronger forms.

Nonverbal communication is often of the weaker kind. One of the advantages of verbal communication is that it allows the strongest possible form of communication to take place; it enables the hearer to pin down the speaker's intentions about the explicit content of her utterance to a single, strongly manifest candidate, with no alternative worth considering at all. On the other hand, what is implicitly conveyed in verbal communication is generally weakly communicated. Because all communication has been seen as strong communication, descriptions of nonverbal communication have been marred by spurious attributions of definite meaning; and in the case of verbal communication, the vagueness of most implicatures and of nonliteral forms of expression has been idealized away. Our approach, we believe, provides a way of giving a precise description and explanation of the weaker effects of communication.

We began this section by asking how communication is possible. Our answer is that it is possible in at least two very different ways: by means of a code shared by communicator and audience, or by means of ostensive stimuli providing the audience with evidence from which the communicator's informative intention can be inferred. We argue against upgrading either model to the status of a general theory of communication. It is particularly important to keep the distinction between the two modes of communication in mind when it comes to describing how they can combine, as they do in human verbal communication.

2 Inference

In the second chapter of *Relevance,* we outline a model of the main inferential abilities involved in verbal comprehension. This model is concerned with only one type of inferential process that of nondemonstrative inference from assumptions to assumptions, which, we claim, takes place automatically and unconsciously during comprehension. We do not discuss conscious reasoning, which sometimes plays a role in comprehension; we merely suggest how unconscious inference may be exploited in conscious reasoning.

In presenting this model of inference, our aims are twofold. First, we claim that the general notion of relevance is instantiated differently in each particular inferential system. By describing one system, however sketchily, we make it possible to give a detailed example of such an instantiation. If future research shows that human inferential abilities not only are much more complex and varied than our model (which of course they are), but also radically different from that model, this illustrative purpose would still be served.

Our second aim is to show how the study of inferential comprehension may shed light on central thought processes. We accept in broad outline Jerry Fodor's view of the modularity of mind (Fodor, 1983, 1985); like him, we see linguistic decoding as modular. Unlike him, however, we see the inferential tier of verbal comprehension as the application of unspecialized central thought processes to the output of the existing decoding module. We argue that verbal comprehension is more typical of central processes, and much more amenable to investigation, than scientific theorizing, which, for Fodor, is the paradigm case of a central thought process. Like all other models of human inference, the sketch we offer is tentative: The evidence available so far is compatible with very different approaches. However, as we try to show, the requirement that such a model should help account for inferential communication is both constraining and suggestive.

2.1   Nondemonstrative inference and strength of assumptions

Inference is the process by which an assumption is accepted as true or probably true on the strength of the truth or probable truth of other assumptions. In *demonstrative inference*, the only form of inference that is well understood, the truth of the premises guarantees the truth of the conclusions. In *nondemonstrative inference*, the truth of the premises merely makes the truth of the conclusions probable. Clearly, the process of inferential comprehension is nondemonstrative: The evidence provided by the communicator never amounts to a proof of her informative intention.

According to what may be called the "logical view" of human nondemonstrative inference, every assumption resulting from such an inference consists of two representations. The first is a representation of a state of affairs: for instance, (2a) below. The second is a representation of the probability or confirmation value of the first representation: for instance, (2b):

(2)   (a)   Jane likes caviar.
       (b)   The confirmation value of (a) is 0.95.

How are these two representations arrived at? The first, so the story goes, is the output of a nonlogical cognitive process of assumption formation. The second is the output of a process of logical computation which takes as input the assumption to be confirmed on the one hand, and the available evidence on the other.

According to the "functional view," which we put forward, an assumption consists of a single representation, such as (2a). The confidence with which this assumption is held – what we call its *strength* – is a result of its processing history and not of some special computation. The initial strength of an assumption depends on the way it is acquired. For instance, assumptions based on a clear perceptual experience tend to be very strong; assumptions based on the acceptance of somebody's word have a strength commensurate with one's confidence in the speaker; the strength of assumptions arrived at by deduction depends on the strength of the premises from which they were derived. Thereafter, it might be that the strength of an assumption is increased every time it helps in processing some new information and is diminished every time it makes the processing of new information more difficult. According to this view, the strength of an assumption is a functional property, just like, say, its accessibility; it need not be represented in the mind (though it can be). We argue moreover that the strength of an assumption, unlike its confirmation value, is, in the terms of Carnap (1950), a comparative rather than a quantitative feature: It allows only gross absolute judgments, and finer comparisons of closely related cases.

2.2   Deduction and its role in nondemonstrative inference

By its very definition, a nondemonstrative inference cannot *consist* in a deduction. Many authors seem to make the much stronger and unwarranted hypothesis that a non-demonstrative inference cannot *contain* a deduction as one of its subparts. The recovery of implicatures, for example, is a paradigm case of nondemonstrative inference, and it is becoming a commonplace of the pragmatic literature that deduction plays little if any role in this process.[6] We maintain, on the contrary, that the spontaneous and essentially unconscious formation of assumptions by deduction is a key process in nondemonstrative inference. More generally, the ability to perform deductions provides the mind with a uniquely adapted means of extracting more information from information it already possesses, of deriving the maximum cognitive benefit from new information, and of checking the mutual consistency of its assumptions.

To model this unconscious deductive ability, we describe a *deductive device* which takes as input a set of assumptions and systematically deduces all the conclusions it can get from them. If this device were equipped with a standard logic, it would derive an infinity of conclusions from any given set of premises; its operations would therefore never come to an end. However, most of these conclusions would be of a trivial sort (e.g., (P and Q), ((P and Q) and Q), deduced from P and Q by the standard rule of *and*-introduction). On the other hand, many deductions which do play a role in ordinary thinking would not be made at all; for example, the deduction from premises (3) and (4a) to the conclusion (5) would not be performed, because it requires a nonstandard rule of concept logic allowing (4b) to be deduced from (4a):

(3) If a relative of Peter's was present, he must have been happy.
(4) (a) Peter's mother was present.
     (b) A relative of Peter's was present.
(5) Peter must have been happy.

One gets a more adequate picture of human deductive abilities by assuming that the rules available to the deductive device are not those of a standard logic but are *elimination rules* attached to concepts. We treat concepts as triples of (possibly empty) entries – logical, lexical, and encyclopaedic filed at a single address. The *logical entry* of a concept consists of deductive rules that apply only to sets of premises in which that concept occurs, yielding only conclusions from which that occurrence has been eliminated. Examples of such elimination rules are the standard *and*-elimination rule, or *Modus ponendo ponens* (eliminating "if . . . then"), and the rules of concept logic which determine deductions from "he ran" to "he moved," from "the glass is red" to "the glass is coloured," or from (4a) to (4b). The *encyclopaedic entry* of a concept contains information about the objects, events, or properties that instantiate it. The *lexical entry* contains information about the word or phrase of natural language that expresses the concept. The *address* of a concept, when it appears in the logical structure of an assumption, gives access to these three types of entry.

We show how the deductive device, drawing on elimination rules attached to concepts, will, from a finite set of premises, automatically deduce a finite set of nontrivial conclusions. We distinguish not only trivial from nontrivial implications, but also analytic from synthetic implications, and discuss their respective role in comprehension. We are particularly concerned with the effect of deductions in which the initial set of assumptions placed in the memory of the deductive device can be partitioned into two subsets, corresponding respectively to some item of new information and to the context in which the new information is processed. Such a deduction may yield conclusions not derivable from either the new information or the context alone. These we call the *contextual implications* of the new information in the context. A contextual implication is thus a synthesis of old and new information. We see it as a central function of the deductive device to derive, spontaneously, automatically, and unconsciously, the contextual implications of any newly presented information in a context of old information.

The information processed by the deductive device, whether new and derived from input systems or old and derived from memory, comes in the form of assumptions with variable strength. We discuss in detail how conclusions inherit their strength from premises. This allows us to characterize three types of *contextual effect* that the processing of new information in a context may bring about: the first, already considered, is the derivation of new assumptions as contextual implications; the second is the strengthening of old assumptions; and the third is the elimination of old assumptions in favour of stronger new assumptions which contradict them. The notion of a contextual effect is essential to a characterization of relevance.

3   Relevance

3.1   Degrees of relevance: effect and effort

It should be clear that we are not trying to define the ordinary and rather fuzzy English word *relevance*. We believe, though, that there is an important psychological property – a property involved in mental processes – which the ordinary notion of *relevance* roughly approximates, and which it is therefore appropriate to call by that name, using it in a technical sense.

As we show in the book, the notion of a contextual effect can be used to state a necessary and sufficient condition for relevance: An assumption is *relevant* in a context if, and only if, it has some contextual effect in that context. This captures the intuition that, to be relevant in a context, an assumption must connect with that context in some way; and it clarifies this intuition by specifying the nature of the connection required. Such a definition, however, is insufficient for at least two reasons: The first is that relevance is a matter of degree and the definition says nothing about how degrees of relevance are determined; the second reason is that it defines relevance as a relation between an assumption and a context, whereas we might want to be able to describe the relevance of any kind of information to any kind of information-processing device, and more particularly to an individual. At the moment, then, we have simply defined a formal property, leaving its relation to psychological reality undescribed.

Consider first the question of degrees of relevance. What we propose is a kind of cost/benefit analysis. We argue that the contextual effects of an assumption in a given context are only one of two factors to be taken into account. Contextual effects are brought about by mental processes; mental processes, like all biological processes, involve a certain effort. This processing effort is the second factor involved. We then define:

Relevance:

Extent condition 1: An assumption is relevant in a context to the extent that its contextual effects in that context are large.

Extent condition 2: An assumption is relevant in a context to the extent that the effort required to process it in that context is small.

This definition of relevance is comparative rather than quantitative. It makes clear comparisons possible only in some cases: Other things being equal, an assumption with greater contextual effects is more relevant; and, other things being equal, an assumption requiring a smaller processing effort is more relevant. When effect and effort vary in the same direction, comparison may be impossible.

Relevance could be defined not just as a comparative but as a quantitative concept, which might be of some interest to logicians and AI specialists. However, the notion needed by psychologists is the comparative one. It is highly implausible that individuals *compute* the size of cognitive effects and mental efforts. We assume rather that the mind assesses its own efforts and their effects by monitoring physicochemical changes in the brain. We argue then that effect and effort are nonrepresentational dimensions of mental processes: That is, they exist whether or not they are represented; and when they are represented, it is in the form of intuitive comparative judgments. The same holds for relevance, which is a function of effect and effort.

3.2   *The relevance of a phenomenon to an individual*

In much of the pragmatic literature, relevance is seen as a variable to be assessed in a predetermined context. This is psychologically unrealistic. As we amply illustrate, the context is not given but chosen. Moreover, humans are not in the business of simply assessing the relevance of new information. They try to process information as relevantly as possible; that is, they try to obtain from each new item of information as great a contextual effect as possible for as small as possible a processing effort. For this, they choose a context which will maximize relevance. In verbal communication in particular, relevance is more or less treated as given and context is treated as a variable.

At any moment, an individual has at his disposal a particular set of accessible contexts. There is first an *initial context* consisting of the assumptions used or derived in the last deduction performed. This initial context can be expanded in three directions: by adding to its assumptions used or derived in preceding deductions, by adding to its chunks of information taken from the encyclopaedic entries of concepts already present in the context or in the assumption being processed, and by adding input information about the perceptual environment. Thus each concept except the initial one includes other contexts: The set of accessible contexts is partly ordered by the inclusion relation. This formal relation has a psychological counterpart: Order of inclusion corresponds to order of accessibility.

Treating relevance as a property of propositions or assumptions (as is often done in the pragmatic literature) involves a considerable abstraction: Individuals do not directly pick up an assumption from an utterance, or, more generally, from perceptible phenomena in their environment. Each phenomenon may give rise to a wide range of assumptions or be left unattended. If relevance theory is to explain ostensive-inferential communication, it must explain how attention is directed to a particular phenomenon, and which assumption is likely to be constructed to describe it. For this, we need to define not just the relevance of an assumption, but more generally the relevance of a phenomenon.

Note that the choice, or construction, of an adequate context by expanding the initial context requires some effort, and so does the construction of an assumption about a phenomenon on the basis of the sensory stimulation it provides. To convert our definition of the relevance of an assumption in a context into a definition of the relevance of a phenomenon to an individual, all we have to do, then, is add on the effort side the effort required to arrive at an assumption and a context:

Relevance of a phenomenon to an individual:

Extent condition 1: A phenomenon is relevant to an individual to the extent that the contextual effects achieved in processing is are large.

Extent condition 2: A phenomenon is relevant to an individual to the extent that the effort required to process it is small.

One could leave this definition as it stands and take the relevance of a phenomenon to vary according to how it is actually processed. We propose instead to take the relevance of a phenomenon to an individual to be the relevance achieved when it is optimally processed: that is, when the best possible representation and context are constructed, and by the most economical method. In *Relevance*, we suggest that this proposal, together with the assumption that human cognition is relevance-oriented, yields new insight into the focusing of attention, the choice of a particular representation for a given phenomenon, and the organization of memory.

3.3   The principle of relevance

When paying attention to an ordinary phenomenon, the individual may have hopes of relevance. What makes these hopes reasonable is that humans have a number of heuristics, some of them innate, others developed through experience, aimed at picking out relevant phenomena. Even so, hopes of relevance sometimes turn out to be unjustified; and when they are justified, they are justified to a greater or lesser extent: There can be no general expectation of a steady and satisfactory level of relevance in individual experience.

With an ostensive stimulus, however, the addressee can have not only hopes but also fairly precise expectations of relevance. It is manifest that an act of ostensive communication cannot succeed unless the addressee pays attention to the ostensive stimulus. It is also manifest that people will pay attention to a phenomenon only if it seems relevant to them. It is manifest, then – mutually manifest in normal conditions – that a communicator must intend to make it manifest to the addressee that the ostensive stimulus is relevant to him. In other words, an act of ostensive communication automatically communicates a *presumption of relevance*. We argue that the presumption of relevance is different on the effect and effort sides. On the effect side, the presumption is that the level of achievable effects is never lower than is needed to make the stimulus worth processing; on the effort side, it is that the level of effort required is never gratuitously higher than is needed to achieve these effects.

The level of relevance thus presumed to exist takes into account the interests of both communicator and audience. Let us call it a level of *optimal relevance*. We can now spell out the presumption of optimal relevance communicated by every act of ostensive communication:

Presumption of optimal relevance:
(a)   The set of assumptions *I* that the communicator intends to make manifest to the addressee is relevant enough to make it worth the addressee's while to process the ostensive stimulus.
(b)   The ostensive stimulus is the most relevant one the communicator could have used to communicate *I*.

What we call the *principle of relevance* is the thesis that every act of ostensive communication communicates the presumption of its own optimal relevance. We argue that the principle of relevance explains how the production of an ostensive stimulus can make the communicator's informative intention mutually manifest, thus leading to the fulfillment of the communicative intention. Several inferential steps are involved. In *Relevance*, we discuss how the stimulus can be recognized as ostensive, and how its structure, in the case of both coded and noncoded stimuli, makes accessible a range of hypotheses about the communicator's informative intention. Here we consider only how the principle of relevance provides a sufficient criterion for selecting one of these hypotheses.

Once the ostensive nature of a stimulus is manifest, it is also manifest that the communicator has the informative intention of making manifest to the addressee some set of assumptions *I*. What the principle of relevance does is identify one member of *I:* namely, the presumption of relevance. The presumption of relevance is not just a member of *I*, it is also *about I*. As a result, it can be confirmed or disconfirmed by the contents of *I*. A rational communicator (who genuinely intends to communicate rather than, say, distract an audience) must expect the identification of *I* to confirm the presumption of relevance. To recognize the communicator's informative intention, the addressee must then discover for which set *I* the communicator had reason to expect that *I* would confirm the presumption of relevance. We argue that this is all he has to do.

Let us say that an interpretation is *consistent with the principle of relevance* if and only if a rational communicator might expect it to be optimally relevant to the addressee. Imagine an addressee who tests hypotheses about the contents of *I* in order of accessibility. Suppose he arrives at a hypothesis that is consistent with the principle of relevance. Should he stop there, or go on and test the next hypothesis on the ground that it too may be consistent with the principle of relevance? Suppose he does go on, and finds another hypothesis that verifies the first part of the presumption of relevance: The putative set *I* is relevant enough. In these circumstances, the second part of the presumption of relevance is almost invariably falsified: The communicator should have used a stimulus that would have saved the addressee the effort of first accessing two hypotheses consistent with the principle of relevance, and then having to choose between them. Thus, the principle of relevance warrants the selection of the first accessible interpretation consistent with the principle. If there is such an interpretation and it is the one intended, communication succeeds. Otherwise it fails.

The principle of relevance does, with much greater explicitness, all the explanatory work of Grice's maxims, and more. There is, however, a radical difference between the principle of relevance and Grice's maxims. Grice's cooperative principle and maxims are norms which communicators and audience must know in order to communicate adequately. Although communicators generally keep to the norms, they may also violate them to achieve particular effects; and the audience uses its (presumably learned) knowledge of the norms in interpreting communicative behaviour.

The principle of relevance, by contrast, is a generalization about ostensive-inferential communication. Communicators and audience need no more know the principle of relevance to communicate than they need to know the principles of genetics to reproduce. It is not the general principle but the fact that a particular presumption of relevance has been communicated, by and about a particular act of communication, that the audience uses in inferential comprehension. Communicators do not "follow" the principle of relevance; and they could not violate it even if they wanted to. The principle of relevance applies without exception: Every act of ostensive communication communicates a presumption of relevance. Note, though, that the presumption of relevance carried by a particular act of communication does not have to be true or accepted as true: The communicator may fail to be relevant. It is enough that the presumption of relevance should be communicated – and it always is – to fulfil its most important role: determining the interpretation of the ostensive stimulus.

4 Aspects of Verbal Communication

Verbal communication, we argue, involves two types of communication process: one based on coding and decoding, the other on ostension and inference. The coded communication is of course linguistic: A linguistic stimulus triggers an automatic process of decoding. The semantic representations uncovered by decoding are *logical forms* which, like the logician's open sentences, but in more ways, fall short of determining a single proposition. These logical forms, we claim, never surface to consciousness. Instead, they act as assumption schemas which can be inferentially completed into fully *propositional forms*, each determining a single proposition and serving as a tentative identification of the intended explicit content of the utterance. This explicit content alone has contextual effects and is therefore worthy of conscious attention.

The coded communication process, then, serves as a source of hypotheses and evidence for the second communication process, the inferential one. If comprehension is defined as a process of identifying the speaker's informative intention, linguistic decoding is better seen not as part of comprehension proper, but rather as providing the main input to the comprehension process. Unlike most pragmaticians, who see the inferential tier of comprehension as governed by a variety of specialized rules constituting a kind of pragmatic "module," we argue that it involves only the application of nonspecialized inference rules rules that apply as well to all conceptually represented information. We see pragmatics as the study, not of a distinct mental device, but of the interaction between a linguistic input module and central inferential abilities.[7]

4.1 The identification of explicit content

The first task in inferential comprehension is to complete the logical form recovered by decoding and identify the explicit content of the utterance.[8] This in turn involves three subtasks: disambiguation (when, as is usual, the decoding yields a choice of logical forms); identification of the referents of referring expressions; and enrichment of the schema selected – a subtask less often considered, of which we analyze several examples.

These subtasks could in principle yield a variety of outcomes. By what criterion does the hearer recognize the right explicit content, that is, the one he was intended to choose? Although there is a considerable literature on disambiguation and reference assignment, this question has not been seriously addressed. The aims of psycholinguists lie elsewhere: They want to describe not the criteria used in disambiguation, but the procedure by which it is achieved. The only criterion generally considered, and apparently confirmed by much experimental evidence, is one of economy, something like a principle of least effort.

Could the answer simply be that the right explicit content is the one obtained by going through some effort-saving procedure? The existence of so-called garden-path utterances (e.g., "I saw that gasoline can explode. And a brand new can it was too") strongly suggests that whatever regular procedures are available for disambiguation, reference assignment, and enrichment yield at best a tentative identification, one that will be rejected if it turns out not to meet some as yet unspecified criterion. We show, with examples, that the correct criterion is consistency with the principle of relevance. This answer does not eliminate considerations of effort; on the contrary, it integrates them by suggesting that the least effort-consuming, and therefore the potentially most relevant interpretation, should be considered first (although it should be abandoned if it fails to yield the expected effect).

4.2   *The identification of implicatures*

We introduce a distinction between two kinds of implicature: *implicated premises* and *implicated conclusions.* Implicated conclusions are deduced from the explicit content of an utterance and its context. What makes it possible to identify such conclusions as implicatures is that the speaker must have expected the hearer to derive them, or some of them, given that she intended her utterance to be manifestly relevant to the hearer. Implicated premises are added to the context by the hearer, who either retrieves them from memory or constructs them ad hoc. What makes it possible to identify such premises as implicatures is that the speaker must have expected the hearer to supply them, or some of them, in order to be able to deduce the implicated conclusions and thereby arrive at an interpretation consistent with the principle of relevance.

To illustrate, consider dialogue (6):

(6)   (a) *Peter:* Would you drive a Mercedes?
       (b) *Mary:* I wouldn't drive *any* expensive car.

The explicit content of Mary's reply does not directly answer Peter's question. However, processed in a context containing (7), (6b) yields the contextual implication (8):

(7)   A Mercedes is an expensive car.
(8)   Mary would not drive a Mercedes.

We have a situation, then, in which Mary, in producing (6b), has not directly and explicitly answered Peter's question, but has made manifest a contextually implied answer, that is, (8). Given that she could not expect her utterance to be relevant unless it made manifest such an answer, this implied answer is manifestly intentional: It is an implicated conclusion of her utterance. Since it is manifest that Peter would not have deduced this conclusion without adding (7) to the context, (7) is an implicated premise of Mary's utterance.

Implicatures (7) and (8) have two properties which many pragmaticians think of as shared by all implicatures. In the first place, they are fully determinate. Mary expects Peter to supply not merely something *like* premise (7) and conclusion (8), but a premise and conclusion with just this logical content. Second, Mary guarantees their truth. Suppose that before (6b) was produced, Peter had not known that Mercedes cars were expensive; then (6b) would give him as much reason to think they are as if Mary had explicitly asserted it. There has been a tendency in modern pragmatics to treat *all* implicatures as fully determinate assumptions for which the speaker is just as responsible as if she had asserted them directly. According to this approach, utterance comprehension consists in the recovery of an enumerable set of assumptions, some explicitly expressed, others implicitly conveyed, but all individually intended by the speaker. We argue that this is a mistake, or, at best, a counterproductive idealization.

Consider, for instance, the exchange in (9):

(9)   *Peter:* What do you intend to do today?
       Mary: I have a terrible headache.

What does Mary implicate? That she will not do anything? That she will do as little as possible? That she will do as much as she can? That she does not yet know what she will do?

There is no precise assumption, apart from the one explicitly expressed, which she can be said to intend Peter to share. Yet there is more to her utterance than its explicit content; she manifestly intends Peter to draw some conclusions from what she said, and not just any conclusions. Quite ordinary cases such as (9) are never discussed in the pragmatic literature. Moreover, even in cases such as (6)–(8), the implicit import of the utterance is usually not exhausted by clear implicatures such as (7) and (8). Mary's reply (6b) suggests, but only in a vaguer way, that she would not drive, say, a Jaguar, that she finds driving an expensive car objectionable, and so on. What pragmatics needs   and relevance theory provides – is a precise account of these vaguer effects.

In our framework, the greater the mutual manifestness of the informative intention to make manifest some particular assumption, the more strongly this assumption is communicated. Using this approach, the indeterminacy of implicatures presents no particular formal problem. An utterance that forces the hearer to supply a very specific premiss or conclusion to arrive at an interpretation consistent with the principle of relevance has a very strong implicature. An utterance that can be given an interpretation consistent with the principle of relevance on the basis of different – though of course related – sets of premises and conclusions has a wide range of weak implicatures. Clearly, the weaker the implicatures, the less confidence the hearer can have that the particular premises or conclusions he supplies closely reflect the speaker's thoughts, and this is where the indeterminacy lies. However, people may entertain different thoughts and come to have different beliefs on the basis of the same cognitive environment. The aim of communication in general, we claim, is to increase the mutuality of cognitive environments and thereby the similarity of thoughts, rather than to guarantee a (generally unreachable) strict duplication of thoughts.

4.3   Explicit content and style: presuppositional effects

It might seem that two utterances with the same linguistically determined truth conditions must have identical implicatures. We argue that this is not so: They may differ in the processing effort they require, which, given the principle of relevance, can lead to different effects. This, we claim, is the key to an explanatory theory of style. In *Relevance*, we discuss two classes of stylistic effects: presuppositional effects at some length and poetic effects more briefly. Here we will merely indicate the relevance of relevance theory to these two aspects of style.

Presuppositional effects result from the fact that a sentence is decoded not as a single symbol, in one go, but in steps, as a structured string of constituents (some of which may be highlighted by stress – an important aspect left out of this précis). Each constituent provides some information by allowing analytic implications to be deduced. Among these, we distinguish *foreground implications*, which contribute to relevance by having contextual effects, and *background implications*, which contribute to relevance by saving effort. Background implications save effort in particular by making more accessible the context in which foreground implications will produce contextual effects. In general (and we show that exceptions are predicted by relevance theory), an optimally relevant utterance will have its effort-saving background implications made available by initial constituents, and its effect-carrying foreground implications made available by its final constituents: Thus the construction of the context will be well underway, or even over, when the last word is uttered, and effect can be achieved at the smallest processing cost.

Processing an utterance as economically as possible, the hearer normally treats the implications made available by the initial constituents as background, the implications made available by the last constituents as foreground, and expects the foreground implications to carry their effects in the context made accessible by the background implications. Thus two utterances with the same truth conditions but different word order lead to the construction of different contexts and the search for different effects. Compare for instance:

(10)   Leo sold Peter a painting.
(11)   Peter bought a painting from Leo.

In (10) the hearer's expectation is that the utterance will be relevant in a context of information about Leo. If it were mutually manifest, for instance, that Leo desperately needed money, a key implicature would be that he has just made some. In (11), the hearer's expectation is that the utterance will be relevant in a context of information about Peter; for instance, if it were mutually manifest that Peter did not care for Leo's painting but knew he needed money, (11) would implicate that Peter behaved generously. In other words, even though (10) and (11) have the same truth conditions and the hearer could in principle draw the same contextual implications from either, not all of the implications are implicated, or implicated to the same degree, by both utterances. This is because the two utterances organize the hearer's efforts differently.

We argue in *Relevance* that all the stylistic effects discussed in the literature in terms of presupposition and focus, presupposition and assertion, topic and comment, given and new, theme and rhyme, and so on,[9] can be explained with greater generality, simplicity, and predictive power in terms of background and foreground. Unlike these other distinctions, which purport to describe linguistic or pragmatic properties registered by a competent speaker, the foreground/background distinction is not something that speakers need to have built into either their grammar or their inferential abilities. Given that utterances have constituent structure, internal order, and focal stress and are processed over time, backgrounding and foregrounding arise as automatic effects of the hearer's tendency to maximize relevance and the speaker's exploitation of that tendency.

4.4   Implicatures and style: poetic effects

Style arises, we maintain, in the pursuit of relevance. In allocating the information she wants to communicate between the explicit content and the implicatures of her utterance, in relying on stronger or weaker implicatures, the speaker makes manifest her assessment of the tenor and quality of mutual understanding between her audience and herself. She thereby gives her utterance its particular style.

Here we will briefly illustrate this point with an example of the simplest of all the classical figures of speech: epizeuxis or repetition. Compare the interpretation of (12) and (13):

(12)   My childhood days are gone.
(13)   My childhood days are gone, gone.

Both have the same truth conditions and therefore potentially the same contextual implications. What (13) has is more *implicatures* than (12): that is, more contextual assumptions and implications that receive some degree of backing from the speaker. The repetition of "gone" causes some extra processing effort. Given the principle of relevance, this extra effort should be justified by some extra effect. Having thought of all the implicatures that the speaker could reasonably have expected him to derive from the first occurrence of "gone," the hearer may assume that there is a whole range of still further premises and conclusions which the speaker wants to implicate. For this, he must expand the context. Thus (13) may encourage the hearer to compare the speaker's childhood and her present condition, to assume that she herself is reminiscing and making a similar comparison, and to imagine the feelings this may invoke in her. What the repetition produces, then, is many very weak implicatures.

We suggest that the peculiar effect of an utterance that achieves most of its relevance through a wide array of weak implicatures is properly called a *poetic effect*. How do poetic effects affect the mutual cognitive environment of speaker and hearer? They do not add entirely new assumptions which are strongly manifest in this environment. Instead, they marginally increase the manifestness of a great many weakly manifest assumptions. In other words, poetic effects create common impressions rather than common knowledge. Utterances with poetic effects can be used precisely in this sense of apparently affective rather than cognitive mutuality. What we are suggesting is that, if you look at these affective effects through the microscope of relevance theory, you see a wide array of minute cognitive effects.

4.5   Descriptive and interpretive dimensions of language use

There is a considerable literature on illocutionary force and speech acts, and an even more considerable one on tropes. There is very little overlap between the two, as if it went without saying that these are two essentially different aspects of language use. In both cases, the literature is centrally concerned with problems of classification and offers little in the way of explanation. We propose a new, more integrated and more explanatory approach, based on a fundamental distinction between interpretation and description.[10]

The relationship between a representation and the object it represents can be of two kinds: It can be based on resemblance or on truth. Any object in the world can, under appropriate conditions, be used as a representation of some other object that it resembles. You ask me what is the shape of Brazil, and by way of reply, I point to an appropriately shaped cloud in the sky. Resemblance raises well-known philosophical and psychological problems: How are degrees of resemblance assessed? That is, how can the representation inform one about the object it resembles? At least when resemblance is used ostensively, relevance theory provides the key to an answer: Consider hypotheses in their order of accessibility (salient features first, etc.) and select the first hypothesis that the producer of the representation may have thought would be relevant enough.

An object with a propositional content – an utterance, for example – can be used to represent in two quite different ways. It can represent some state of affairs by virtue of being true of that state of affairs; in this case we will say that the representation is a *description*, or that it is used *descriptively*. Or, like any object, it can represent something it resembles, and in particular some other representation with a similar propositional content; in this case we will say that the first representation is an *interpretation* of the second one, or that it is used *interpretively*. Two representations resemble one another interpretively when they share analytic and contextual implications.[11]

The only generally acknowledged interpretive use of utterances is in the reporting of speech or thought, as in quotations and summaries. However, there are others. Utterances can be used interpretively to represent utterance types, or thoughts worth considering for their intrinsic properties, rather than because they can be attributed to Peter, Mary, or public opinion. We argue that there is an even more essential interpretive use of utterances: On a more fundamental level, *every* utterance is used interpretively to represent a thought of the speaker's. One of the assumptions a speaker intends to make manifest is that she is entertaining a thought with some particular attitude: It is on this ground that the hearer may be led to entertain a similar thought with a similar attitude. You may well tell me that you will come tomorrow, but you will not make me believe it unless you first make me believe that you believe it too. This much is hardly controversial. In our terms, it means that an utterance is, or purports to be, in the first instance, an interpretation of the thought of the speaker.

Actually, an even stronger claim is generally made. Most pragmaticians and philosophers of language take for granted that there is a convention, principle, or presumption to the effect that the propositional content of the utterance must be a literal expression – that is, a strictly faithful interpretation – of a thought of the speaker's.[12] We argue that this claim is too strong. How close the interpretation is, and in particular when it is literal, can be inferentially determined by the hearer.

What does the thought interpretively represented by an utterance itself represent, and how? A mental representation, like any representation, can be used descriptively or interpretively. When it is used descriptively, it can be a description of an actual state of affairs, or it can be a description of a desirable state of affairs. When it is used interpretively, it can be an interpretation of an attributed thought or utterance, or it can be an interpretation of a relevant, hence desirable thought. There may be other possibilities, and one might consider what the thoughts interpreted by thoughts might represent in their turn and how; but let us leave it at that, and use figure 8.2 to show the representations and relationships considered so far.

Any utterance involves at least two levels of representation: It interpretively represents a thought of the speaker's which itself descriptively represents some state of affairs, or interpretively represents some further representation. All the basic relationships involved in tropes and illocutionary forces are represented in figure 8.2: Metaphor involves an interpretive relation between the propositional form of an utterance and the thought it represents; irony involves an interpretive relation between the speaker's thought and attributed thoughts or utterances; assertion involves a descriptive relation between the speaker's thought and a state of affairs in the world; requesting or advising involves a descriptive relation between the speaker's thought and a desirable state of affairs; interrogatives and exclamatives involve an interpretive relation between the speaker's thought and a relevant – that is, desirable – thought. Our book develops all of these ideals; here we shall briefly consider only the potentially more controversial interpretive cases: those of metaphor, irony, interrogatives, and exclamatives.

4.6 Literalness, looseness, and metaphor

An utterance, we claim, is an interpretation of one of the speaker's thoughts, that is, both share a number of implications. This means that, in order to communicate a set of assumptions I which are the essential implications of some thought of hers, the speaker must produce an utterance whose explicit content logically or contextually implies I. An utterance that implies exactly I and nothing else may not be available, or it may be available but not economical. However, the speaker may freely use an utterance that implies many other assumptions she does not want to endorse, as long as the hearer has some way of recognizing the intended implications which are members of I. In our framework, all the hearer has to do is start computing, in order of accessibility, those implications which are or which the speaker would consider to be relevant to him, and continue to add them to the overall interpretation of the utterance until it is, or might have seemed to the speaker, relevant

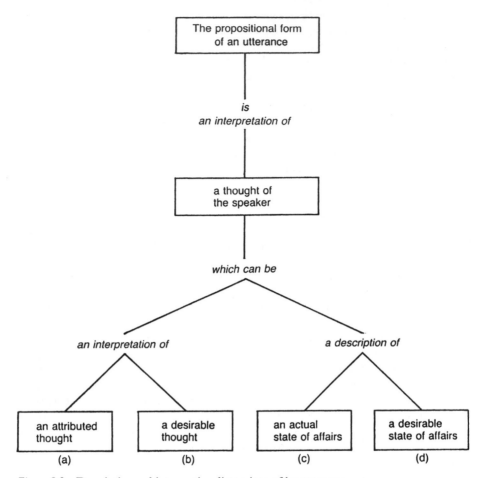

Figure 8.2   Descriptive and interpretive dimensions of language use

enough to be consistent with the principle of relevance. At this point, the sorting will have been accomplished as a by-product of the search for relevance: It will require no specific effort of its own.

The comprehension of every utterance involves such a process of identifying relevant implications. When the proposition expressed is itself among the implications on which optimal relevance depends, the result is a literal interpretation. According to this view, literalness is simply maximal resemblance, and enjoys no privileged status. In general though, some looseness of expression is to be expected. For example, the speaker may spare the hearer some processing effort, and thereby optimize relevance, by saying "It's half-past five" rather than "It's twenty-eight minutes past five" (even though she knows that the latter is true) when the relevance-producing effects of her utterance do not depend on a strictly literal reading. Similarly, if the speaker says "I'm exhausted," no one will stop to wonder whether exhausted is exactly what she is, as long as there is an acceptable range of implications which makes her utterance relevant enough. This is again true if the speaker says, in the same circumstances, "I'm dead" – a clear metaphor this time.

In *Relevance*[13] we show that there is no discontinuity between literal uses, loose uses, and metaphors. According to this approach, metaphor (like a variety of related tropes such as hyperbole, metonymy, and synecdoche) requires no special interpretive abilities or procedures: The fact that some utterances are interpreted metaphorically, just as others are interpreted literally, results from the same standard process of comprehension.

4.7 Echoic utterances and irony

We argue that irony and a variety of related tropes such as meiosis and litotes fall together with a range of cases not normally regarded as figurative at all. What unites these cases is the fact that the thought of the speaker, which is interpreted by the utterance, in itself an interpretation. What it interprets is a thought of someone (or some group) other than the speaker – or of the speaker in the past. That is, these utterances are second-degree interpretations of someone else's thought, as illustrated by path (a) in figure 8.2 above.

How do interpretations of someone else's thought achieve relevance? In the best-known case, that of "reported speech," they achieve relevance by informing the hearer of the fact that so-and-so has said something or thinks something. In other cases, these interpretations achieve relevance by informing the hearer of the fact that the speaker has in mind what some individual or individuals say or think and has a certain attitude to it. When interpretations achieve relevance in this way, we say that they are *echoic*.

By representing a thought that is not her own in a manifestly skeptical, amused, surprised, triumphant, approving, or reproving way, the speaker can express her own attitude to it. There is no limit to the attitudes that a speaker can express to an opinion echoed. In particular, she may indicate her agreement or disagreement. Compare (14) and (15):

(14) (a) *He:* It's a lovely day for a picnic.
          (They go for a picnic and the sun shines.)
      (b) *She* (happily): A lovely day for a picnic, indeed!
(15) (a) *He:* It's a lovely day for a picnic.
          (They go for a picnic and it rains.)
      (b) *She* (sarcastically): A lovely day for a picnic, indeed!

In both (14b) and (15b) there is an echoic allusion to be picked up. In the circumstances described, it is clear that the speaker of (14b) endorses the opinion echoed, whereas the speaker of (15b) rejects it with scorn. These utterances are interpreted on exactly similar patterns, the only difference being in the attitudes they express: (14b) has not been thought by rhetoricians to be worthy of special attention; (15b) is, of course, a case of verbal irony.

An ironical attitude is of the disapproving kind. From the display of such an attitude, the hearer can infer, if it was not already obvious to him, that the speaker believes the opposite of the opinion echoed: Thus the speaker of (15b) manifestly believes that it is *not* a lovely day for a picnic. However, against classical approaches to irony, we argue that this is not the "figurative meaning" of the ironical utterance. At most, it is one of its implicatures: More relevant implicatures might be that her companion's judgment has been unsound, that they should never have set out, that it was his fault that their day has been ruined, and so on. The recovery of these implicatures depends, first, on a recognition of the utterance as echoic, second, on an identification of the source of the opinion echoed, and third, on a recognition that the speaker's attitude to the opinion echoed is one of disapproval. We argue that these are the key factors in the interpretation of all ironical utterances.[14]

We are arguing that on the one hand the metaphors and ironies are not essentially different from other types of utterance but that, on the other hand, they are not essentially similar to one another. Metaphor plays on the relationship between the propositional form of an utterance and that of the speaker's thought; irony plays on the relationship between the speaker's thought and a thought it interprets. This suggests that the classical notion of a trope, which covers metaphor and irony and distinguishes both from "nonfigurative" utterances, should be abandoned altogether: It groups together phenomena which are not closely related and fails to group together phenomena which are.

4.8   Speech acts: interrogatives and exclamatives

Our book questions some of the basic assumptions of current speech-act theory, and sketches an alternative approach which puts a much greater load on inference than on decoding in the identification of illocutionary force. Given the principle of relevance, we argue that illocutionary-force indicators such as declarative or imperative mood or interrogative word order have to make manifest only a rather abstract property of the speaker's informative intention: the direction in which the relevance of the utterance is to be sought. Here, we will take the case of interrogatives and exclamatives as an illustration of this general approach.

Speech-act theorists tend to analyze interrogative utterances as a special subtype of directive speech act: specifically, as requests for information (see Bach and Harnish 1979, p. 48; Searle 1969, p. 69). As a result, rhetorical questions such as (16), expository questions such as (17), and self-addressed questions such as (18), all require ad hoc separate treatment:

(16)   When did you say you were going to give up smoking?
(17)   What are the main objectives to this approach? First . . .
(18)   Why do we have to die?

We argue that what the interrogative word order signals is a much more abstract property than that of being a request for information. It signals that the utterance represents (not descriptively but interpretively, of course) an assumption which would be relevant if true. In other words, a question is an interpretation of a desirable thought – the piece of knowledge which would answer it; it follows path (b) on figure 8.2. In the case of a yes – no interrogative, the propositional form of the utterance is like a quotation of the relevant-if-true assumption. In the case of a wh-question (who-which-what-why and so on), the logical form of the utterance is not fully propositional; it is an incomplete interpretive representation of the relevant-if-true assumption.

On this account, this is all the interrogative word order signals. Decisions about who would find the assumption represented relevant, and about whether the speaker expects an answer, are left to the hearer to infer on the basis of the principle of relevance. For example, rhetorical questions such as (16) are often reminders, designed to prompt the retrieval of an assumption the speaker regards as relevant to the hearer. Expository questions such as (17) are analyzable as questions whose answers the speaker not only regards as relevant to the hearer but is about to provide herself. Regular requests for information, by contrast, are analyzable as questions whose answers the speaker regards as relevant to her and, moreover, expects the hearer to supply. In pure speculations such as (18), the suggestion is that the answer would be relevant to the speaker, or to both speaker and hearer, but there is no expectation that anyone will be in a position to supply it. There is thus no need to analyze all questions as requests for information, no need to set up special speech-act categories to handle offers of information, rhetorical questions, expository questions, and so on.

One advantage of this approach is that it suggests a way of explaining the striking syntactic parallels between interrogative and exclamative sentences such as (19) and (20):

(19)   How clever is Jane?
(20)   How clever Jane is!

In traditional speech-act terms, since interrogatives are requests for information and exclamatives are emphatic assertions, it is hard to account for the consistent cross-linguistic parallelisms (see Grimshaw, 1979; Sadock and Zwicky, 1985) between these two utterance types. On our approach, exclamatives, like interrogatives and unlike declaratives, are specialized for interpretive rather than descriptive use, and also follow path (b) of figure 8.2. Whereas a speaker who asks a question such as (19) indicates that some true completion of the incomplete thought represented by her utterance is relevant, a speaker who produces an exclamation such as (20) indicates that some relevant completion of the incomplete thought represented by her utterance is true. In other words, the speaker of (20) indicates that Jane is high enough on the scale of cleverness for this to be worth drawing attention to. Thus, the intuition that exclamatives are like emphatic assertions and the striking parallelisms between exclamative and interrogative form are simultaneously explained.

5   Concluding Remark

We are well aware that the view developed in *Relevance* and summarized here is very speculative and, as it stands, too general to determine directly either specific experimental tests or computer simulations. In assessing a new approach to human communication, however, the following questions should be kept in mind. How does it compare with other current approaches in terms of explicitness, plausibility, generality, and explanatory power? Does it throw new light both on the very rich and diverse data available to all of us as individuals involved in communication and on the narrower but more reliable data gathered by scholars? Does it suggest new empirical research? Is it relevant to more than one of the many disciplines involved in the study of human communication – linguistics, pragmatics, philosophy, cognitive psychology, artificial intelligence, social psychology, literary studies, anthropology, and sociology – and could it foster fruitful interactions among them?

NOTES

1   See, for example, Bach and Harnish (1979); Clark (1977); Clark and Carlson (1981); Green and Morgan (1981); Leech (1983); Lewis (1979); Sag (1981).
2   Notably Gazdar (1979). For recent surveys of the pragmatics literature, see Brown and Yule (1983); Levinson (1983).
3   For a general discussion of the mutual knowledge issue, see Smith (1982), in particular contributions by Clark and Carlson, Johnson-Laird, and Sperber and Wilson.
4   See Armstrong (1971); Bach and Harnish (1979); Bennett (1976); Blackburn (1984); Davidson, (1984); Davies (1981); Grice (1957, 1968, 1969, 1982); Harman (1968); Lewis (1969); Loar (1976, 1981); McDowell (1980); Patton and Stampe (1969); Recanati (1979, forthcoming); Schiffer (1972); Searle (1969, 1983); Strawson (1964, 1969, 1971); Wright (1975); Yu (1979); Ziff (1967).

5   For ease of exposition, we will talk of a female communicator and a male addressee.
6   See Leech (1983, pp. 30–1); Levinson (1983, pp. 115–16); Bach and Harnish (1979, pp. 92–3); Brown and Yule (1983, p. 33); de Beaugrande and Dressler (1981, pp. 93–4).
7   On the issue of modularity, see also Wilson and Sperber (1986).
8   In *Relevance*, we do not talk of "explicit content"; but we distinguish the "propositional form" of an utterance and its "explicatures." We also propose a redefinition of the explicit/implicit contrast, and provide both a classificatory and a comparative criterion of explicitness. For reasons of space, we leave these issues out of this précis.
9   See Brown and Yule (1983, chs 3–5); Chafe (1976); Clark and Haviland (1977); Givon (1979); Halliday (1967–8); Jackendoff (1972); Lyons (1977, ch. 12.7); Oh and Dinneen (1979); Prince (1981); Reinhart (1981); Rochemont (1988); Taglicht (1984, chs 1–3).
10 A distinction relevant also to the philosophy of the social sciences, as argued in Sperber (1985).
11 See Wilson and Sperber (1986) for further discussion.
12 See Bach and Harnish (1979); Lewis (1975); Searle (1969).
13 See also Wilson and Sperber (1986).
14 For further discussion see Sperber and Wilson (1981); Sperber (1984). For an experimental approach, see Jorgensen et al. (1984).

REFERENCES

Armstrong, D. (1971). Meaning and Communication. *Philosophical Review* 80: 427–47.
Bach K. and Harnish R. (1979). *Linguistic Communication and Speech Acts*. Cambridge, MA: MIT Press.
de Beaugrande, R. and Dressler, W. (1981). *Introduction to Text Linguistics*. London: Longman.
Bennett, J. (1976). *Linguistic Behavior*. Cambridge: Cambridge University Press.
Blackburn, S. (1984). *Spreading the Word*. Oxford: Oxford University Press.
Brown, G. and Yule, G. (1983). *Discourse Analysis*. Cambridge: Cambridge University Press.
Carnap, R. (1950). *The Logical Foundations of Probability*. London: Routledge and Kegan Paul.
Chafe, W. (1976). Givenness, Contrastiveness, Definiteness, Subjects, Topics and Points of View. In C. Li, ed., *Subject and Topic*. New York: Academic Press.
Clark, H. (1977). Bridging. In P. Johnson-Laird and P. Wason, eds, *Thinking: Readings in Cognitive Science*. Cambridge: Cambridge University Press.
Clark, H. and Carlson, T. (1981). Context for Comprehension. In J. Long and A. Baddley, eds, *Attention and Performance IX*. Hillsdale, NJ: Lawrence Erlbaum.
Clark, H. and Haviland, S. (1977). Comprehension and the Given – New Contract. In R. Freedle, ed., *Discourse Production and Comprehension*. Norwood, NJ: Ablex.
Cole, P. (ed.) (1981). *Radical Pragmatics*. New York: Academic Press.
Cole, P. and Morgan, J. (eds) (1975). *Syntax and Semantics 3: Speech Acts*. New York: Academic Press.
Davidson, D. (1984). Communication and Convention. In *Truth and Interpretation*. Oxford: Clarendon Press.
Davies, M. (1981). *Meaning Quantification and Necessity: Themes in Philosophical Logic*. London: Routledge and Kegan Paul.
Fodor, J. A. (1983). *The Modularity of the Mind*. Cambridge, MA: MIT Press.
Fodor, J. A. (1985). Précis of *The Modularity of the Mind*. *Behavioral and Brain Sciences* 8: 1–42.
Gazdar, G. (1979). *Pragmatics: Implicature, Presupposition and Logical Form*. New York: Academic Press.
Givon, T. (ed.) (1979). *Syntax and Semantics 12: Discourse and Syntax*. New York: Academic Press.
Green, G. and Morgan, J. (1981). *Pragmatics, Grammar and Discourse*. In Cole 1981.
Grice, H. P. (1957). Meaning. *Philosophical Review* 66: 377–88 [reproduced as part of ch. 2 in this volume].

Grice, H. P. (1968). Utterer's Meaning, Sentence Meaning, and Word Meaning. *Foundations of Language* 4: 225–42.

Grice, H. P. (1969). Utterer's Meaning and Intentions. *Philosophical Review* 78: 147–77.

Grice, H. P. (1975). Logic and Conversation. In Cole and Morgan 1975 [reproduced as part of ch. 2 in this volume].

Grice, H. P. (1982). Meaning Revisited. In Smith 1982.

Grimshaw, J. (1979). Complement Selection and the Lexicon. *Linguistic Inquiry* 10(2): 279–326.

Halliday, M. (1967–8). Notes on Transitivity and Theme in English. *Journal of Linguistics* 3: 37–81, 199–244; 4: 179–215.

Harman, G. (1968). Three Levels of Meaning. *Journal of Philosophy* 65: 590–602.

Jackendoff, R. (1972). *Semantic Interpretation and Generative Grammar*. Cambridge, MA: MIT Press.

Johnson-Laird, P. (1983). *Mental Models*. Cambridge: Cambridge University Press.

Jorgensen, J., Miller, G. and Sperber, D. (1984). Test of the Mention Theory of Irony. *Journal of Experimental Psychology: General* 113.1: 112–20.

Leech, G. (1983). *Principles of Pragmatics*. London: Longman.

Levinson, S. (1983). *Pragmatics*. Cambridge: Cambridge University Press.

Lewis, D. (1969). *Convention*. Cambridge, MA: Harvard University Press.

Lewis, D. (1975). Languages and Language. In K. Gunderson, ed., *Language, Mind and Knowledge*. Minneapolis: University of Minnesota Press [reproduced as part of ch. 2 in this volume].

Lewis, D. (1979). Scorekeeping in a Language Game. In R. Bäuerle, U. Egli, and A. von Stechow, eds, *Semantics from a Different Point of View*. Berlin: Springer Verlag.

Loar, B. (1976). Two Theories of Meaning. In G. Evans and J. McDowell, eds, *Truth and Meaning*. Oxford: Oxford University Press.

Loar, B. (1981). *Mind and Meaning*. Cambridge: Cambridge University Press.

Lyons, J. (1977). *Semantics*. Cambridge: Cambridge University Press.

McDowell, J. (1980). Meaning, Communication and Knowledge. In Z. van Straaten, ed., *Philosophical Subjects*. Oxford: Clarendon Press.

Oh, C.-K. and Dinneen, D. (eds) (1979). *Syntax and Semantics 11: Presupposition*. New York: Academic Press.

Patton, T. and Stampe, D. (1969). The Rudiments of Meaning: On Ziff and Grice. *Foundations of Language* 5.1: 2–16.

Prince, E. (1981). Towards a Taxonomy of Given – New Information. In Cole 1981.

Recanati, F. (1979). *La Transparence et l'Énonciation*. Paris: Seuil.

Recanati, F. (forthcoming). *Performative Utterances*. Cambridge: Cambridge University Press. [Published as *Meaning and Force: The Pragmatics of Performative Utterances* (1987).]

Reinhart, T. (1981). Pragmatics and Linguistics: An Analysis of Sentence Topics. *Philosophica* 27: 53–94.

Rochemont, M. (1988). *Focus on Generative Grammar*. Amsterdam: Benjamin.

Sadock, J. and Zwicky, A. (1985). Sentence Types. In T. Shopen, ed., *Language Typology and Syntactic Description*. Cambridge: Cambridge University Press.

Sag, I. (1981). Formal Semantics and Extralinguistic Context. In Cole 1981.

Schiffer, S. (1972). *Meaning*. Oxford: Clarendon Press.

Searle, J. (1969). *Speech Acts*. Cambridge: Cambridge University Press.

Searle, J. (1983). *Intentionality*. Cambridge: Cambridge University Press.

Smith, N. (1982). *Mutual Knowledge*. London: Academic Press.

Sperber, D. (1984). Verbal Irony: Pretense or Echoic Mention. *Journal of Experimental Psychology: General* 113.1: 130–6.

Sperber, D. (1985). *On Anthropological Knowledge*. Cambridge: Cambridge University Press.

Sperber, D. and Wilson, D. (1981). Irony and the Use–Mention Distinction. In Cole 1981.

Sperber, D. and Wilson, D. (1986). *Relevance: Communication and Cognition*. Cambridge, MA: Harvard University Press.

Strawson, P. F. (1964). Intention and Convention in Speech Acts. *Philosophical Review* 73: 439–60.

Strawson, P. F. (1969). Meaning and Truth. Inaugural lecture at the University of Oxford. In Strawson 1971.

Strawson, P. F. (1971). *Logico-linguistic Papers*. London: Methuen.

Taglicht, J. (1984). *Message and Emphasis: On Focus and Scope in English*. London: Longman.

Wilson, D. and Sperber, D. (1986). Inference and Implicature. In C. Travis, ed., *Meaning and Interpretation*. Oxford: Blackwell.

Wright, R. (1975). Meaning-nn and Conversational Implicature. In Cole and Morgan 1975.

Yu, P. (1979). On the Gricean Program about Meaning. *Linguistics and Philosophy* 3.2: 273–88.

Ziff, P. (1967). On H. P. Grice's Account of Meaning. *Analysis* 28: 1–8.

9

Artificial Intelligence

Introduction

When Turing asked whether machines can think he quickly refocused his question on language/communication abilities. The ability to communicate in a human-like way seemed a sure sign of machine intelligence. It was the machine's output that signaled intelligence, not how it processed data or how slow/fast it was. Subsequent attempts to model intelligence have, until very recently, assumed that a mind is a unified system; it was assumed to be either a rule-based model or, more recently, a connectionist model.

How a computer processes data is partly a function of its architecture. Classical artificial intelligence relied on rule-based processes that depend on read-and-write operations to transform symbols and symbol structures into new symbols and symbol structures. Such a system is a physical symbol system, and classical artificial intelligence pursued the hypothesis that such a system has the necessary and sufficient means for general intelligent action. On this view, the brain's mind is a physical symbol system that produces an evolving set of symbol structures (Newell and Simon, 1976). New connectionism, which took off in the early 1980s, rejects this approach to cognition and attempts to work with an architecture that more closely resembles the activity of neurons in the central nervous system. The two approaches to creating machine intelligence exhibit different strengths and different internal functions.

One of the practical obstacles to building intelligence in a machine is the threat of exponential explosion of search trees. A capable human chess player does not consider every possible move on the chessboard; she only considers the plausible moves. She is selective. How can such selectivity be built into brute machines?

Rule-based machines seem to think by manipulating symbols, zeros and ones or on and off states, according to structure-sensitive rules. Traditionally, this approach made the use of public language into a peripheral process in the service of cognition. A consequence of this was that linguistic relativism, namely the view that public language forms our thinking, appeared not to mix very well with classical artificial intelligence and, more generally, cognitivism. However, it turns out classical rule-based approaches can accommodate some features of linguistic relativism. In "The Role of Language in Cognition: A Computational Inquiry" Lehman, Newell, Polk, and Lewis argue that their rule-based model – Soar – actually allows public language to at least partially determine cognition. Specifically, linguistic principles can play a role in syllogistic reasoning. Although they don't mention this, theirs is a faint echo of an old view defended by the seventeenth-century philosopher Thomas Hobbes, namely that scientific reasoning depends on language.

"On Learning the Past Tenses of English Verbs" is a direct challenge to both rule-based architecture and the view that assumes that children learn languages by generalizing from implicit linguistic rules. The alternative Rumelhart and McClelland propose is that while the mechanisms that process language can be characterized by rules, the rules are nowhere written in explicit form in the system that processes the language. Rumelhart and McClelland chose to model the acquisition of the English past tense, a rather well-studied case. Children seem to go through three stages when acquiring the past tense. In stage 1 children learn the past tense of a few verbs, some of which are regular but most of which are irregular. In stage 2 they learn to form the past tense of a large number of verbs and show evidence of acquiring a rule for generating the past tense. Children often overgeneralize in this stage, producing an incorrect past tense of irregular verbs (e.g., *comed* or *camed* instead of *came*). In stage 3 the children produce the correct form of both regular and irregular verbs. The learning curve of irregular verbs thus has a U shape because the verbs are generally correct in the first and third stage but incorrect in the second stage. Rumelhart and McClelland's goal was to simulate with a connectionist network many of the characteristics of the children's acquisition of the past tense. On the basis of their experiments with the model they concluded that it is possible with a relatively simple network and without any explicit encoding of rules to simulate the learning process of children learning the past tense of English verbs. However, the Rumelhart McClelland model, perhaps because it directly challenged rule-based accounts of language learning, has become a prime target of critics of connectionism.

One of the criticisms is that connectionist models cannot handle the finer aspects of linguistic structure. Jeffrey L. Elman replies to those charges. In "Grammatical Structure and Distributed Representations" Elman describes a connectionist model that encodes compositional relationships between linguistic elements. We need to account for both the sameness and the difference of meaning in the contribution of "rock" to the following sentences:

1 The boy broke the window with the rock.
2 The rock broke the window.

Elman compares the results of his work with more traditional approaches to compositionality and concludes that, while much work remains to be done, the study shows that the networks have properties that are very plausible for the processing of natural languages and that at the very least connectionist models can be structuresensitive.

Steven Pinker, along with his colleague Alan Prince, was one of the first to raise questions about how much linguistic structure Rumelhart and McClelland's model for language learning could handle. In the selection printed here Pinker reflects on the virtues of and faults of both connectionist models and the rule-based models, and reaches a fair-minded conclusion. He argues that while both excel at some aspects of language learning there are features in it that neither can account for. Pinker, like Rumelhart and McClelland, focuses on the learning of the past tense in his study. For example, the rule-based systems cannot adequately account for the partial systematicity of irregular verbs (sing-sang, ring-rang, spring-sprang), while the connectionist systems cannot explain how languages can contain semantically unrelated homophones with different past tense forms (ring-rang, wring-wrung). Pinker's solution calls for a syntheses of the two approaches to language learning. We need both connectionism and rule-based accounts. The mind might not, after all, be a homogeneous system.

Just as the study of language was a major driving force behind the cognitive revolution that toppled behaviorism, it appears that the study of language again forces linguists, psychologists, philosophers, and other cognitive scientists to rethink their positions about the nature of cognition and seek new models and explanations that overcome old positions and oppositions.

FURTHER READING

Bechtel, W. and Abrahamsen, A. (1991). *Connectionism and the Mind: An Introduction to Parallel Processing in Networks*. Oxford: Blackwell.

Clark, A. (1990). *Microcognition: Philosophy, Cognitive Science and Parallel Distributed Processing*. Cambridge, MA: MIT Press.

Clark, A. and Karmiloff-Smith, A. (1993). The Cognizer's Innards: A Psychological and Philosophical Perspective on the Development of Thought. *Mind and Language* 8: 487–519.

Fodor, J. and Pylyshyn, Z. (1988). Connectionism and Cognitive Architecture: A Critical Analysis. *Cognition* 28: 3–71.

Johnson-Laird, P. N. (1988). *The Computer and the Mind*. Cambridge, MA: Harvard University Press.

Marr, D. (1982). *Vision: A Computational Investigation into the Human Representation and Processing of Visual Information*. New York: W. H. Freeman.

Newell, A. and Simon, H. (1976). Computer Science as Empirical Inquiry. In *Mind Design*. Ed. J. Haugeland. Cambridge, MA: MIT Press.

Pinker, S. and Prince, A. (1988). On Language and Connectionism: Analysis of a Parallel Distributed Processing Model of Language Acquisition. *Cognition* 28: 73–193.

Pylyshyn, Z. W. (1984). *Computation and Cognition: Toward a Foundation for Cognitive Science*. Cambridge, MA: MIT Press.

Rumelhart, D. E. and McClelland, J. L. (1986). *Parallel Distributed Processing: Explorations in the Microstructure of Cognition*. 2 vols. Cambridge, MA: MIT Press.

Smolensky, P. (1987). The Constituent Structure of Mental States: A Reply to Fodor and Pylyshyn. *Southern Journal of Philosophy* 26: 137–60.

Smolensky, P. (1988). On a Proper Treatment of Connectionism. *Behavioral and Brains Sciences* 11: 1–74.

The Role of Language in Cognition: A Computational Inquiry

JILL FAIN LEHMAN, ALLEN NEWELL, THAD POLK, AND RICHARD L. LEWIS

We were asked to "tell George Miller how the mind works from our particular standpoint." We have chosen, instead, to answer the question, "What is the role of language in cognition?" We decided not to tell George how the mind works, because one of us has recently composed a statement of considerable length on just that topic (Newell, 1990). Yet, the core of the detailed answer given there, namely, Soar as a unified theory of cognition, seems to many cognitive scientists to be rooted primarily in artificial intelligence (AI) and cognitive psychology, hence, not rooted in language. George would surely object if that were really so. The relationship between language and cognition has been a central concern for George throughout his career. We are sure that he takes an answer to our question as central to any theory of mind – as central to "how the mind works." We agree with him. So much so that we thought the most interesting thing we could do was to tackle that relationship from "our particular standpoint," which is to say, from a standpoint that is grounded in computation and cognition.

Benjamin Lee Whorf (1956) casts a long shadow over questions about the role of language in cognition, much as one might like to have it otherwise. His striking claim was that our habitual language determines our everyday thought, thereby trapping the members of a culture within the worldview implicit in their linguistic structures.[1] After it became clear from many attempts at verification that no such determining effect could be discerned (Hoijer, 1954), a distinction was drawn between the original conception of linguistic relativity, the Strong Whorfian Hypothesis, and a more modest version, the Weak Whorfian Hypothesis. In the weakest of all its forms, the latter states simply that language has effects on cognition, although exactly what effects remains unclear. That the notion of linguistic relativity is alive and well is attested to by a recent article (Hunt and Agnoli, 1991), which takes the astounding (to us) view that because chronometric psychologists typically take 50-millisecond differences in their experimental results to be significant, any linguistic treatment effect that shows a 50-millisecond difference in a cognitive variable supports the Weak Whorfian Hypothesis. With this criterion in hand, the authors then make a grand tour through the literature of language/cognition experiments and show that language affects cognition almost everywhere.

So the Weak Hypothesis holds pervasively. Yet, surely there is much more to the role of language in cognition. Surely there must be strong effects, if only we knew where to look for them. Surely there are other ways to ask the question.

Our standpoint is computational. It is not to examine or test a hypothesis – here, Whorf, weak or strong. We start with Whorf because we think that helps to provide an overall context for the question, although it is clear that other theories address our question as well (e.g., modularity; Fodor, 1983). Our methodology in exploring the issue is to reason from the architecture and to examine existing systems, looking for clues about how language and cognition might relate. We begin our discussion of the role of language in cognition by examining the prevailing computational point of view.

Language as Transducer

A basic tenet of cognitive science is the *internal task-operation* view of mental activity, which states that thinking occurs in internal, task-oriented spaces that use internal, task-oriented operators on internal representations of the situation. This characterization of cognition is one of the field's great contributions. It allowed computation to be brought to the enterprise of understanding the nature of mind. It still allows us to see how thinking could actually occur. Illustrations of its usefulness are everywhere: the work in logic in AI and formal semantics, the formulation in AI of toy tasks such as the blocks world as well as real-world tasks found in expert systems, and the positing of *mentalese*, an internal language of thought, by Fodor (1983). Indeed, the view is essentially coextensive with the *computational view of mind* (Pylyshyn, 1984).

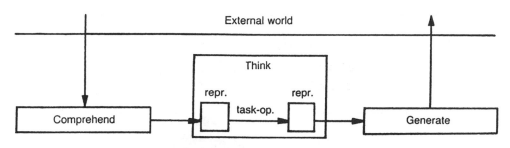

Figure 9.1   The transducer model

When applied to our question, the internal task-operation view yields the paradigm of *language as transducer*, in which language comprehension and language generation act, essentially, as peripheral processes in the service of cognition (see figure 9.1). The process of comprehension transforms utterances from the external world into the internal representation of their meaning that task-oriented operators require. Suitable, goal-oriented manipulations occur; then the complementary process of generation transforms the result of those task operations back into external linguistic forms. Thus, in this view, linguistic processes are peripheral in both the word's senses: existing at the periphery where cognition meets the environment and somehow unessential to the stuff of thinking itself.

The transducer paradigm is as pervasive as the internal task-operation model. In psychological modeling, this is how the UNDERSTAND theory of problem acquisition works (Hayes and Simon, 1975). In AI, the transducer paradigm is epitomized by the natural-language front end.

What does the transducer paradigm say about the role of language in cognition? It provides a simple and direct answer. Language and cognition share a structure, which we call the *situation model*. By delivering a nonlinguistic representation of the situation to the task, language has its effect on cognition through the encoding of their shared model and through any subsequent structures added to long-term memory based on that encoding. The transducer paradigm supports a form of the Weak Whorfian Hypothesis: Language influences cognition, but does not determine it. Language's effects are pervasive, just because its encodings provide the starting points for thought. Yet, considering cognition's general force toward veridical and useful encodings, the effects of language per se will only occasionally be crucial. Given this long-standing response to our question, is any other answer possible? We go to the architecture and ask.

The Architecture Replies

The Soar architecture has been described elsewhere (Newell, 1990). Figure 9.2 summarizes it briefly. Following the numbers in parentheses, the architecture consists of a long-term *recognition memory* (1) composed of patterns that deliver their associations to a *working memory* (2) whenever the current knowledge in working memory matches the pattern.[2] Working memory defines the current problem-solving context. Problem solving itself occurs in *problem spaces*, shown as triangles (3), by a process of state-to-state transition from an initial state to a desired state. Transitions occur via the application of *operators*, one transition per *decision cycle* (4). Long-term patterns match during the elaboration phase of a decision cycle, resulting in the flow of knowledge from recognition memory into working memory (5).

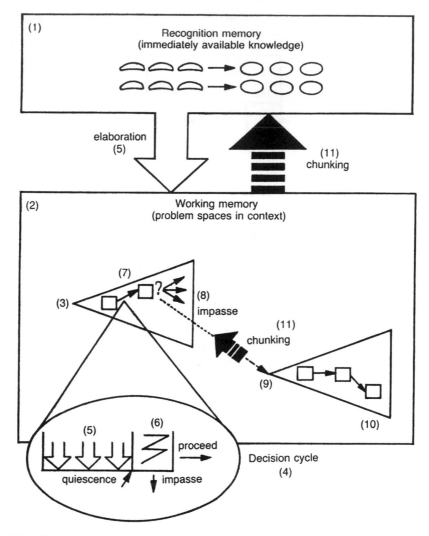

Figure 9.2 The Soar architecture

This knowledge includes preferences for new problem spaces, operators, or states. Once all patterns have delivered their associations, a fixed decisions procedure is invoked (6). If there is an unequivocal next step, it is taken (7). Otherwise, the architecture *impasses* (8) and a new *goal* is established to attain the knowledge to resolve the impasse. The new goal gives rise to a new problem space (9), and problem solving continues. Once the impasse is resolved by reaching a desired state in the subspace (10), Soar's learning mechanism combines the pattern of conditions that lead to the impasse with the results of problem solving into an association for that pattern. These *chunks* are added to long-term memory (11).

To understand the architecture's reply to the question of the role of language in cognition, let us first separate cognition from language by reifying the former in a *task problem space* defined by task operators, and the latter in a *language problem space* defined by comprehension and generation operators (figure 9.3). This reification is just shorthand for the sets of problem spaces that actually realize a language or task capability. Of course, some of the task problem space's task operators will be *transduction operators* to allow information to flow between the task space and the environment, because doing so is part of the task. These transduction operators are not implemented in the task space, however; they are only evoked there, for they involve the language capabilities of the system (and so are implemented in the language space). All of this simply follows from the desire to represent language and thought within the Soar architecture. From this beginning, we can then imagine the typical, hierarchical goal stack that arises in Soar as a result of impasses during problem solving. As shown in figure 9.3, within the goal stack we can, in general, find either or both of the two possible relationships between language and thought: A task space may impasse into a language space, or a language space may impasse into a task space. This is purely a structural reply from the architecture. However, it is not without functional consequences.

An examination of the impasse from task to language (figure 9.3(A)) reveals Soar's version

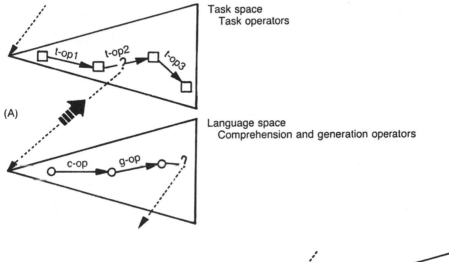

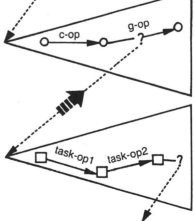

Figure 9.3 Possible relationships between language and cognition

of the transducer paradigm. The mapping is straightforward; we trace it out in figure 9.4. The task space, in this case the blocks-world space, contains task operators that perform task-related transformations on the state. For example, in panel A task-op1 creates an initial situation model containing red and green blocks on a table. Some of the task space operators are transduction operators, used when linguistic input appears from the external world. Panel B of the figure shows the application of task-op2 in the context established by the initial situation model. Task-op2 performs a transduction of the sentence *Put the red block on the green block* into its nonlinguistic representation in the situation model. Because the transduction requires linguistic knowledge, task-op2 is implemented by com-

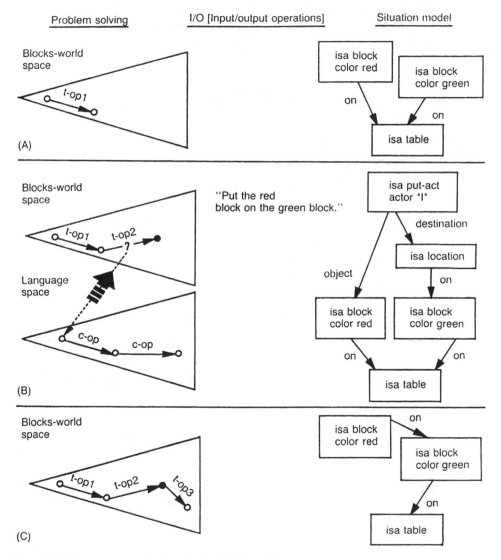

Figure 9.4   Language transductions in the blocks world

prehension operators in the language space, giving an instance of the structural configuration in figure 9.3(A). Once the content of the utterance has been transduced, operators in the task space may continue to transform the state in the service of the task. Panel C of figure 9.4 shows task-op3, which actually moves the red block (mentally, if not through motor commands as well).[3] Of course, a similar process occurs when transduction is required for generation.

The role of language here is essentially ancillary. Granted, a Weak Whorfian view is supported by the architecture, because task operations proceed based on the situation model delivered by language. However, if there were some other method for generating the relevant piece of situation model (such as remembering it or looking at it), then no impasse would arise, and task operations alone would be adequate to reach a desired state. The Weak Whorfian Hypothesis is weakened further by the observation that, whatever language operations are used, they may occur in the context of, and be influenced by, a pre-existing situation model that has resulted solely from task operations.

That the transducer paradigm can be found among the potential behaviors of the Soar architecture should not be surprising. Soar clearly takes the internal task-operation view; it is from this view that the transducer paradigm naturally evolves. The question now becomes whether this is the end of the story. Surprisingly, the structural reply in figure 9.3 produces two other functional possibilities, each very different.

From Task to Language: Linguistic Thinking Operators

In the preceding example, and in the transducer paradigm in general, there are two types of operation: (1) thinking, and (2) transduction. As shown in figure 9.4(A) and (C), thinking operations are carried out by task operators that are proposed and implemented in the task space using task knowledge to take an existing state into a new state. As shown in panel B, transduction operators are carried out by a distinct subclass of the task operators, the transduction operators, that are proposed in the task space, but implemented by linguistic operators in the language space using linguistic knowledge. Some transduction operators take an existing situation model and a linguistic input from the external environment into a new situation model; others take an existing situation model and produce a linguistic output.

The characterization of thinking operations as nonlinguistic is an assumption of the transducer paradigm, not the Soar architecture. Indeed, as shown in the second panel of figure 9.5, the architecture admits the possibility of *linguistic-thinking operators* (LTOs) – task operators implemented in the language space that use knowledge about language to take existing situation models directly to new situation models without the presence of an external utterance. Of course, we know what linguistic knowledge is needed to implement a transduction. At this point in the discussion, it is unclear what linguistic knowledge is needed to implement an LTO.

Observing that the architecture admits the possibility of LTOs is a far cry from either demonstrating that LTOs exist or explaining what LTOs mean. To do so, we must look beyond the architecture's reply and employ our second methodological tool of examining existing Soar systems. Thus, we turn to VR-Soar, a system that solves syllogisms, to find answers.

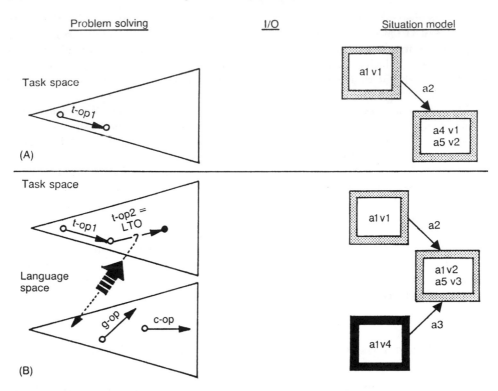

Figure 9.5   Linguistic thinking operators

A brief digression: VR-Soar and the categorical syllogism task

The syllogism task is probably familiar: Given two premises, state a conclusion that relates the terms unique to each premise and that necessarily follows from the premises. Two specific syllogisms and their general forms are shown:

Premiss 1:	All artists are barbers	All A are B
Premiss 2:	*All barbers are chefs*	*All B are C*
Response:	All artists are chefs	All A are C
Premiss 1:	All artists are barbers	All A are B
Premiss 2:	*Some barbers are chefs*	*Some B are C*
Response:	?	?

VR-Soar is a computational theory of human syllogistic reasoning.[4] By predicting individual behavior on all 64 premiss pairs, the theory seeks to explain both the regularities humans show in syllogistic behavior and their individual differences (Polk and Newell, 1988; Polk et al., 1989). As is clear in the examples, some syllogisms are easy and some are not, the latter providing evidence that solving syllogisms is a genuine reasoning task. As such, we expect to find task operators as well as transduction operators. Indeed, computational theories of this task fit the transducer paradigm. One family of theories claims that humans use a *propositional representation* and reason by means of *logical inference operations* (Braine,

1978; Rips, 1983). These theories use content-independent rules to derive additional propositions from the collection that is already available. Another family of theories claims that humans use *mental-model representations* and reason by means of *semantic validity operations* that construct alternative models (in the model-theoretic sense) to show that the results are true in all models of the premises (Johnson-Laird and Bara, 1984; Johnson-Laird and Byrne, 1991). In both families the externally provided premises which, of course, are linguistic – are encoded into the central representation (propositions or mental models, as the case may be) and manipulated by task operators. The conclusion, formed in the task space, is then generated as a linguistic expression.

VR-Soar is a member of the mental-model family. The general organization of the system is shown in figure 9.6. The static impasse structure in the figure makes it clear that there are ample opportunities for task to language impasses during actual problem solving. The task space has two task operators, generate-conclusion and negate-conclusion, and two transduction operators, read and respond. The two task operators do not strictly follow our previous definition, because they are not completely implemented in the task space. Nevertheless, both generate-conclusion and negate-conclusion are task operators. To understand why, observe that in VR-Soar the language generation capability is spread across these two operators and respond. Generate-conclusion produces a nonemitted linguistic form that obeys the task constraint of relating the terms unique to each premiss. Therefore, it uses task knowledge to change the state by adding to it an internal representation of a linguistic form – it performs both a task operation and a piece of the transduction.[5] Respond then performs the remainder of the transduction by emitting the internal linguistic form to the external world. Negate-conclusion also requires task knowledge that is independent of the operator's participation in the transduction process. It is proposed for the task-specific purpose of checking whether the conclusion necessarily follows from the premises. It changes the state by taking an internal linguistic form and producing a new internal linguistic form. Although

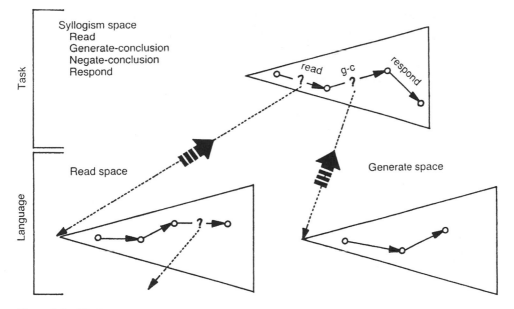

Figure 9.6 VR-Soar, a system for solving syllogisms

generate-conclusion and negate-conclusion perform part of the transduction process in the VR–Soar implementation, this need not have been the case. The transduction effects of these operators could have been separated out and implemented by other operators, but their task effects could not.[6] In short, both generate-conclusion and negate-conclusion have essential roles to play in the thinking part of the syllogism task.

VR–Soar uses two different methods to solve syllogisms: (1) a basic method, and (2) a falsification method. In the basic method, the system simply generates a statement that involves the two unique terms from the cumulative situation model created by reading the premises. Consider the first example we saw and the situation model produced after each premise:

Operators	*Situation model*
Read: "All artists are barbers."	[(artist barber)]
Read: "All barbers are chefs."	[(artist barber chef)]
Generate-conclusion: All artists are chefs.	
Respond: "All artists are chefs."	

Reading the first premiss produces a model with a single person that has the properties of being both an artist and a barber. Reading the second premiss in the context of the existing model augments the single person with the property of being a chef (that is, comprehension of the premiss results in every barber already in the model being made a chef). From this cumulative model it is straightforward to generate the conclusion *All artists are chefs* and respond accordingly.

Often the basic method leads to situation models that support conclusions that don't necessarily follow from the premises. Some of these conclusions can be filtered out by the falsification method and its use of the negated-conclusion operator. Falsification will filter out those conclusions whose negations lead to a contradiction in the situation model established by the premises. Consider how this method is used in our second example:

Operators	*Situation*
Read: "All artists are barbers."	[(artist barber)]
Read: "Some barbers are chefs."	[(artist barber)
	(artist barber chef)]
Generate-conclusion: Some artists are chefs.	
Negate-conclusion: No artists are chefs.	
Read: No artists are chefs.	[(artist barber not–chef)
	(artist barber not–chef)]
(Re)read: All artists are barbers.	no change
(Re)read: Some barbers are chefs.	[(artist barber not–chef)
	(artist barber not–chef)]
Respond: "No valid conclusion."	

As in the previous example, reading the first premiss creates the model of a single person who is an artist and barber, which is then augmented by reading the second premiss. How a person interprets the word *some* is considered a source of individual differences. In the interpretation shown here, the meaning of some is that at least one but not all of the barbers that are being talked about are chefs. This interpretation results in the addition to the situation model of a barber/artist who is a chef. From this cumulative model, a conclusion relating the unique terms can be generated: *Some artists are chefs.* At this point in the basic method, VR-Soar would respond with the generated, albeit incorrect, conclusion. Using falsification, however, the next step is, instead, to negate the conclusion. Comprehending the negated conclusion then augments the model further – the artists are no longer chefs. Finally, the system rereads the two premises. The first premise is consistent with the model and produces no changes. The second premise is consistent as well, and augments the model further. Because no inconsistency arises with respect to the situation model during reread-ing, the system correctly responds *No valid conclusion.*

Several interesting things occur in these two examples. In the first syllogism, solved by the basic method, treating the language processes as transducers was sufficient for the task. In fact, transduction processes alone were enough to accomplish most of the task. In the second syllogism, however, falsification required two additional thinking operations: (1) incorporating the negated conclusion into the situation model, and (2) testing that situation model against the premises. These thinking operations were accomplished using language processes. This is exactly what LTOs are all about.

LTOs: reprise

Before the digression, we established two features of LTOs:

1   We defined an LTO as a task operator implemented in the language space.
2   We noted that an LTO is distinct from a transduction operator because it does not require input from the external environment in order to produce a change to the state.

At that point in the discussion, it remained unclear how LTOs could be implemented in the language space, whether they really exist, and, most importantly, what they mean.

If we look closely at the series of task events that take place in VR-Soar during problem solving by the falsification method, we find two instances of LTOs. The first occurs in the sequence of operations that transforms the initial situation model produced by reading the premises into the new situation model that incorporates the negated conclusion. As required, this sequence of operations changes the situation model through linguistic means, but without the existence of an utterance from the external environment. Specifically, the change comes about through a piece of language generation followed by a piece of language comprehension. The generation is performed jointly by the generate-conclusion and negate-conclusion operators; the comprehension is performed by read.[7]

The second (and third) instance of an LTO can be found in the rereading operations that test the validity of the cumulative situation model. Here there is one LTO for each premiss tested, and the acts of generation and comprehension are performed during the implemen-tation of a single operator. These LTOs are a bit harder to recognize for two reasons. First, the regeneration of each premiss happens via reading, which seems to be a case of bringing in an utterance from the external environment, and, therefore, is not a case of an LTO. Functionally, however, the rereading is an internal activity – that the premises are read was necessary the first time (the transduction), but that they are read is incidental the second time. They could, for example, have simply been remembered. To make the point a bit differently, suppose we had heard the premises initially and written them down. The act of writing them down is functionally equivalent to memorizing them. Thus, if recovering them in the latter case is an internal act of generation, then it is functionally internal in the former case as well. The second difficulty in recognizing the rereading operations as LTOs is that in the first rereading there is no apparent change to the situation model, as required by our definition (the second rereading is fine in this respect). Again, we must look past the implementation details to the functional issues being played out. Although no change to the content of the model occurs, the observation that the premise is not in contradiction with the model must nevertheless leave some mark (or how else can we know we have performed a test?).

We have found two examples of LTOs in VR-Soar and discovered their implementation in language to consist of an act of generation followed by an act of comprehension. What, to answer our final question, do LTOs mean? By virtue of performing task operations that are not mere transductions, using LTOs is truly thinking in language. Do LTOs therefore vindicate the Strong Whorfian Hypothesis that language determines thought? If LTOs were the only kind of thinking operator available, the answer would be yes. Clearly, if all thinking had to be done via language, then the structure of the language would have strong effects on thinking. Yet we have not established how widely LTOs can be used, and there are certainly many nonlinguistic spaces for tasks as well. Spaces based on the visual world are available from the very beginning. We also teach ourselves many spaces for calculation, diagram interpretation, and so on. All these spaces are filled with nonlinguistic thinking operators. Thus, whereas LTOs may take their rightful place in the cognitive repertoire, they are but one of the techniques available for thinking.

From Language to Task: Taskification

In looking at the blocks-world example and VR-Soar, we found two functional implications of the structural configuration produced by an impasse from task to language. Language can influence thinking by being the transducer of knowledge from linguistic form into the situation model – the Weak Whorfian Hypothesis. Alternatively, language can actually perform the task; that is, thinking can occur in language – what we might call the LTO-Whorfian Hypothesis. The impasse from task to language being only half the story, we now turn our attention to the other half of the architecture's reply.

Consider the configuration shown previously in figure 9.3(B). There, an operator in the language space (in this case a comprehension operator) gives rise to an impasse that can only be resolved through task knowledge. To understand how such a configuration can occur, and what taskification means, we must digress once again, this time to understand how language comprehension occurs in Soar.

A brief digression: NL-Soar and the language-comprehension task

NL-Soar is the current realization of Soar's language space. It is the set of problem spaces and operators that provide Soar with a comprehension capability that responds to the real-time constraint of 200 to 300 milliseconds per word (Lehman et al., 1991a, 1991b). In the mapping of Soar onto human cognition (Newell, 1990), the real-time constraint corresponds to a processing constraint of two to three operators per word. Meeting this processing constraint requires *recognitional comprehension* via total integration of the relevant knowledge sources: syntax, semantics, pragmatics, and discourse. This total integration is achieved in

NL-Soar by a *comprehension operator* that is learned automatically through chunking, thereby also becoming recognitional.

A graphical trace of the operation of NL-Soar is shown in figure 9.7. Comprehension is recognitional whenever the comprehension operator contains the knowledge of what to do with the given word in the given context. Under those circumstances, all knowledge is brought to bear in a single operator application, incrementally augmenting NL-Soar's utterance and situation models. The utterance model captures the structure of the incoming utterance, whereas the situation model captures its meaning. When the comprehension operator is inadequate for the current context, an impasse arises, and the remaining problem spaces in NL-Soar implement the comprehension operator through deliberate problem

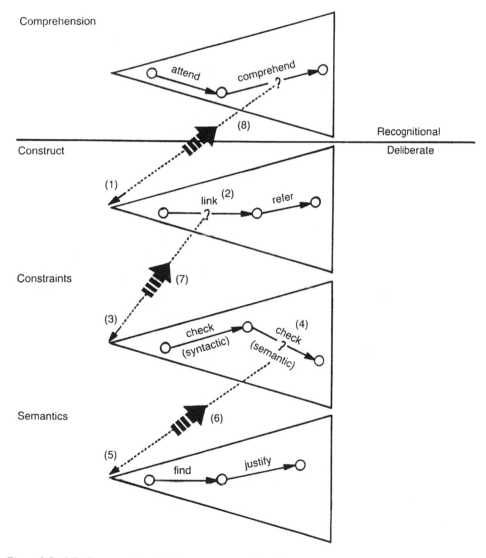

Figure 9.7 NL-Soar, a system for language comprehension

solving. The problem spaces accessible via the impasse bring syntactic, semantic, and pragmatic knowledge to bear by the sequential application of relevant operators. When the impasse is resolved, chunks are built that avoid the impasse in analogous contexts in the future. These chunks become part of the comprehension operator, integrating in a single operation all the knowledge that was applied sequentially during the problem solving to resolve the impasse.

Suppose NL-Soar is given the sentence *The artist is a barber* and assume the comprehension operator is undefined for *barber* in the context created by *The artist is a*. Following the numbers in parentheses in figure 9.7, consider the processing done by the system for that word when it is encountered in that context. Extrapolating from the examples previously discussed, we know that at the point that *barber* is processed, the situation model contains only a single person with the property of being an artist. The lack of comprehension operator knowledge for barber creates an impasse in the comprehension space (1). As a result, a link operator is proposed in the construct space to tie *barber* into the utterance model as a predicate nominative (2). Before the link can be established, it must meet certain syntactic, semantic, and pragmatic conditions. Thus, another impasse arises leading to further processing in the constraints space (3). In constraints, NL-Soar performs a number of syntactic checks, for example, to make sure there is number agreement between the subject and the predicate nominative. Then the system must make certain that the link makes sense, that is, that artists are, in fact, the sorts of thing that can be barbers (4).

Suppose that the knowledge that satisfied this semantic constraint is unavailable in the constraints space. Then an impasse arises (5), and operators in the semantics space are brought to bear that show this constraint to be satisfied.[8] All of this processing has assembled the knowledge that the proposed link for *barber* can be made. Yet, assembling that knowledge is only the first half of the process. As each impasse resolves, chunking occurs. Through chunking, knowledge from semantics becomes immediately available in constraints in analogous contexts in the future (6). Similarly, as the impasse from construct to constraints is resolved, chunking moves syntactic, semantic, and pragmatic knowledge into the higher space (7). Once the situation model has been augmented by the refer operator in construct, the impasse from comprehension to construct is resolved, and chunking creates a new piece of the comprehension operator for *barber* (8). The association that is learned during this last impasse resolution tests for all the conditions that determined the word's meaning in the general context, including the semantic condition that justified making the artist a barber. When those conditions are present in the future, the comprehension-operator chunks will produce their changes to the utterance and situation models directly, including the change that adds the property of being a barber. In other words, chunking has moved linguistic knowledge from the lower spaces up into recognitional comprehension. Because chunking is a general, uniform mechanism, the integration of any knowledge source into the comprehension process is accomplished in the same way. This is exactly what the impasse from language to task is all about.

Taskification: reprise

Before our second digression, we raised two questions regarding the impasse from language to task: How could it arise? What would it mean? The NL-Soar example shows the process by which independent knowledge sources become part of the conditions of the comprehension operator, and, thus, part of the relevant context for assigning a particular meaning. Because this process is essentially invariant over knowledge sources, we are now in a position to answer our questions: A language to task impasse arises whenever the task constrains the meaning of a word. The result of such an event is the incorporation of task-specific knowledge into the comprehension operator, a process we call *taskification*.

To make the idea of taskification concrete, let us consider two examples. In our first example, we reconsider the second premise of the second syllogism discussed in the section headed "A brief digression", *Some barbers are chefs*. It is certainly possible to assume, as we did implicitly earlier, that the interpretation a person gives to *some* in this task is whatever the meaning of *some* would normally be for that person. It is also possible, however, to instruct someone to use a particular meaning of *some*, as in, *by "some" we mean that there is at least one that is not*. How could these instructions be used by someone who did not, naturally, interpret *some* in this way? Figure 9.8 demonstrates.

The instruction defining the meaning of *some* creates a task constraint that is part of the context of the syllogism task. Reading the premiss occurs as a regular transduction in this context (1). If the comprehension operator is already sensitive to this context, comprehension for *some* proceeds recognitionally, otherwise an impasse occurs (2). The action proposed in construct is the normal one for *some*: to link the word via the qualifier role to an expectation in the utterance model. The expectation simultaneously holds a place for the subsequent head noun and its referent and acts as a repository for constraints that the head noun and its referent must meet. The proposed link must undergo constraint checking as part of the normal deliberate processing (3), and the task constraint must be passed just like all of the linguistic constraints. The proposal of this constraint causes an impasse (4), just as the semantics constraint did. This time, however, the language space does not have the knowledge to resolve the impasse. Because the task space does have the knowledge, the impasse that arises goes from language to task. Once the task space has done whatever is needed to satisfy the task constraint (e.g., by using an LTO to change the proposed situation model to include two referents (5)), the language-to-task impasse is resolved and the goal stack itself begins to unwind. As we follow chunking back up the problem-space hierarchy ((6) through (8)), task knowledge will move up into the language space. When we resolve the final impasse (9), the new piece of the comprehension operator for *some* will implement the variant form of the situation model directly.

As a second example of taskification, we reconsider the transition from panel B to panel C in the blocks-world example of figure 9.4. During our previous discussion, we noted the distinction between establishing the meaning of a sentence in context and acting to realize that meaning. In response to this distinction, we argued that the situation model in panel B was the proper result of comprehension, requiring an additional task operation beyond the transduction to arrive at the situation model in panel C. We also noted, however, that the Soar architecture affords the possibility of producing the model in panel C directly during comprehension. It is now clear how that could occur – through a language-to-task impasse during constraint checking. If such an impasse were to occur, the task space could, in response, perform exactly the transformation shown in the figure, but perform it on the *proposed* situation model. By bringing task knowledge to bear within the comprehension process (rather than after it), the subsequent knowledge added to the comprehension operator via chunking would directly realize the mental action.

What these examples do not quantify is the limits of taskification. Given the real-time character of comprehension, there is simply not enough time for arbitrary numbers of task operations (arbitrary amounts of thinking) during the process. The question that remains – how much work can the task do in influencing comprehension? – is a natural one for which we have, as yet, no response.[9] Nevertheless, we can make a more general statement about

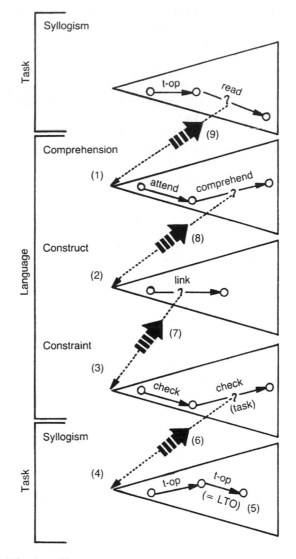

Figure 9.8 The taskification of language

what taskification means in cases in which the task does constrain meaning. As more task contexts arise, more and more of the task will move up into the language space. Over time, the comprehension operator will contain more and more task-specific knowledge for the vocabulary of the task. Thus, as the taskification of the person's language proceeds, the apparent modularity between task and language disappears.

Beyond Whorf: Predictions from the Architecture

We began our exploration of the role of language in cognition by observing that the current practice is to view language as merely a transducer, distinct from cognition and with limited potential for influencing cognition's path. We then countered this Weak Whorfian view by appealing to the architecture. What we found – LTOs and taskification – predicts a decidedly more active role for language than the common view allows.

In essence, LTOs show us that thinking in language is possible. This, in itself, appears noteworthy. Although we have not done an exhaustive scan of the literature, it is our impression that no one else has described how thinking in language is possible – though it is assumed in many contexts. Indeed, the transducer model claims thinking in language is not possible, because there must always be task operations to do the work of thinking.

Although LTOs might seem to lead to a dominating role for language in cognition – the Strong Whorfian Hypothesis that language determines thought – that simple conclusion is unwarranted. LTOs are not required for thought; they are only one possible method for performing task operations. To the extent that nonlinguistic means are used during problem solving, language will have only the weak influence it has as a transducer. Thus, the existence of LTOs creates the potential for a determining role for language: the LTO-Whorf Hypothesis, stronger than the Weak Whorfian view but weaker than the Strong.

How much stronger? How much weaker? In part, taskification decides. If we assume that an LTO is used only when it can do the job, then the more taskified the language is, the more often LTOs are applicable and the stronger the influence of language on cognition. At the same time, taskification means that the language through which the LTOs are implemented is, itself, partly task dependent, once again weakening language's role. The role of the language in thinking is also limited by the structure of language, that is, by the kinds of change comprehension can make in a situation model. The nature of these limits is hardly apparent from our discussion. What we have shown in this chapter is only a provocative beginning for the full story of thinking in language.

What the Soar architecture tells us, then, is twofold: Language can, in fact, determine thought, but its power to do so independent of the task itself varies over time and context. It is not clear that such conclusions would follow from other architectures. Strong modularity, for example, precludes the possibility of taskification and is essentially antithetical to the idea that task and language slowly blend into one. Thus, the architecture yields two novel predictions. These do not fully answer the question we posed at the beginning: "What is the role of language in cognition?" Yet, they open up the question to new avenues of investigation. They also show that an architecture grounded in both AI and cognitive psychology can contain fundamental insights about language: Cognitive science need not be split forever into its core disciplines of AI, linguistics, and cognitive psychology. George Miller would surely approve of that.

NOTES

1   Actually it is difficult to determine to whom to attribute the forcefulness of the statement – Whorf or his mentor Sapir.

2   These patterns-with-associations are usually described as *productions* in the Soar literature. This is technically correct, but has proven confusing, because productions are often taken in the sense used within the expert systems literature. Productions in Soar form a type of associative memory. Productions in expert systems correspond to the operators of problem spaces.

3   It may seem strange that the act of comprehending the given sentence does not result in the situation model in panel C. It is important to note that in this example we have separated the act of establishing the meaning of a sentence in context from the act of realizing that meaning; that is, we have separated recognizing a command to perform an act of putting from the actual moving of the block. The act of establishing meaning is the responsibility of comprehension; the realization

of the meaning is considered to be outside of comprehension and the responsibility of the task. Later in the chapter, we examine what it would mean to produce the situation model in the bottom panel directly through comprehension and demonstrate how the Soar architecture affords both possibilities.

4   The version discussed here differs in some ways from the final version, which is still under minor modification and evaluation (Polk, 1992).

5   The test for the unique premiss terms is that part of the operator's implementation that is in the task space (Newell et al., 1991).

6   We could, for example, have had generate-conclusion simply annotate two elements of the situation model as being the unique terms in the premises, leaving the production of the internal linguistic form connecting those two terms to another operator.

7   It should not be considered problematic that the LTO whose purpose is to incorporate the negated conclusion appears in VR-Soar as a sequence of operators rather than a single operator. Operators can generally be realized atomically or as a composition of suboperations. Expressed differently, operators can usually be implemented as methods, and methods can usually be implemented as single operators. To understand this structural distinction in the current context, consider a version of figure 9.6 in which the task space contains an incorporate-negated-conclusion operator that is implemented in a lower space by the operators generate-conclusion, negate-conclusion, and read.

8   Although it is not obvious from the discussion, pragmatic knowledge is brought to bear in semantics as well.

9   Although we observe that it seems, in general character, quite similar to the question of how much inference can occur during the process of bringing semantic constraints to bear during comprehension.

REFERENCES

Braine, M. D. S. (1978). On the relation between the natural logic of reasoning and standard logic. *Psychological Review*, 85 (1), 1–21.

Fodor, J. A. (1983). *Modularity of Mind: An Essay on Faculty Psychology*. Cambridge, MA: MIT Press.

Hayes, J. R. and Simon, H. A. (1975). Understanding written problem instructions. In L. W. Gregg (ed.), *Knowledge and Cognition*, pp. 167–200. Hillsdale, NJ: Lawrence Erlbaum.

Hoijer, H. (ed.) (1954). *Language in Culture: Conference on the Interrelations of Language and Other Aspects of Culture*. Chicago, IL: University of Chicago Press.

Hunt, E. and Agnoli, F. (1991). The Whorfian hypothesis: a cognitive psychology perspective. *Psychological Review*, 90 (3), 377–89.

Johnson-Laird, P. N. and Bara, B. G. (1984). Syllogistic inference. *Cognition*, 16, 1–61.

Johnson-Laird, P. N. and Byrne, R. M. J. (1991). *Deduction*. Hillsdale, NJ: Lawrence Erlbaum.

Lehman, J. F., Lewis, R. L., and Newell, A. (1991a). Integrating knowledge sources in language comprehension. *Proceedings of the Thirteenth Annual Conference of the Cognitive Science Society*, pp. 461–6.

Lehman, J. F., Lewis, R. L., and Newell, A. (1991b). *Natural Language Comprehension in Soar* (Tech. Rep. CMU–CS–91-117). Pittsburgh, PA: Carnegie Mellon University.

Newell, A. (1990). *Unified Theories of Cognition*. Cambridge, MA: Harvard University Press.

Newell, A., Yost, G., Laird, J. E., Rosenbloom, P. S., and Altmann, E. (1991). Formulating the problem-space computational model. In R. F. Rashid (ed.), *CMU Computer Science: A 25th Anniversary Commemorative*, pp. 255–93. New York: ACM Press Anthology Series.

Polk, T. A. (1992). *A Verbal Reasoning Theory for Categorical Syllogisms* (Tech. Rep. CMU–CS–92-178). Pittsburgh, PA: Carnegie Mellon university.

Polk, T. A. and Newell, A. (1988). Modeling human syllogistic reasoning in Soar. *Proceedings of the Tenth Annual Conference of the Cognitive Science Society*, pp. 181–7.

Polk, T. A., Newell, A., and Lewis, R. L. (1989). Toward a unified theory of immediate reasoning in Soar. *Proceedings of the Eleventh Annual Conference of the Cognitive Science Society*, pp. 506–13.

Pylyshyn, Z. W. (1984). *Computation and Cognition: Toward a Foundation for Cognitive Science.* Cambridge, MA: Bradford Books/MIT Press.

Rips, L. J. (1983). Cognitive processes in propositional reasoning. *Psychological Review*, 90 (1), 38–71.

Whorf, B. L. (1956). *Language, Thought, and Reality: Selected Writings.* Cambridge, MA: Technology Press of MIT.

On Learning the Past Tenses of English Verbs

DAVID E. RUMELHART AND JAMES L. MCCLELLAND

The Issue

Scholars of language and psycholinguistics have been among the first to stress the importance of rules in describing human behavior. The reason for this is obvious. Many aspects of language can be characterized by rules, and the speakers of natural languages speak the language correctly. Therefore, systems of rules are useful in characterizing what they will and will not say. Though we all make mistakes when we speak, we have a pretty good ear for what is right and what is wrong – and our judgments of correctness – or grammaticality – are generally even easier to characterize by rules than actual utterances.

On the evidence that what we will and won't say and what we will and won't accept can be characterized by rules, it has been argued that, in some sense, we "know" the rules of our language. The sense in which we know them is not the same as the sense in which we know such "rules" "as *i* before *e* except after *c*," however, since we need not necessarily be able to state the rules explicitly. We know them in a way that allows us to use them to make judgments of grammaticality, it is often said, or to speak and understand, but this knowledge is not in a form or location that permits it to be encoded into a communicable verbal statement. Because of this, this knowledge is said to be *implicit*.

So far there is considerable agreement. However, the exact characterization of implicit knowledge is a matter of great controversy. One view, which is perhaps extreme but is nevertheless quite clear, holds that the rules of language are stored in explicit form as propositions, and are used by language production, comprehension, and judgment mechanisms. These propositions cannot be described verbally only because they are sequestered in a specialized subsystem which is used in language processing, or because they are written in a special code that only the language-processing system can understand. This view we will call the *explicit inaccessible rule* view.

On the explicit inaccessible rule view, language acquisition is thought of as the process of inducing rules. The language mechanisms are thought to include a subsystem – often called the *language acquisition device* (LAD) – whose business it is to discover the rules. A considerable amount of effort has been expended on the attempt to describe how the LAD might operate, and there are a number of different proposals which have been laid out. Generally, though, they share three assumptions:

- The mechanism hypothesizes explicit inaccessible rules.
- Hypotheses are rejected and replaced as they prove inadequate to account for the utterances the learner hears.
- The LAD is presumed to have *innate* knowledge of the possible range of human languages and, therefore, is presumed to consider only hypotheses within the constraints imposed by a set of *linguistic universals*.

The recent book by Pinker (1984) contains a state-of-the-art example of a model based on this approach.

We propose an alternative to explicit inaccessible rules. We suggest that lawful behavior and judgments may be produced by a mechanism in which there is no explicit representation of the rule. Instead, we suggest that the mechanisms that process language and make judgments of grammaticality are constructed in such a way that their performance is characterizable by rules, but that the rules themselves are not written in explicit form anywhere in the mechanism. An illustration of this view, which we owe to Bates (1979), is provided by the honeycomb. The regular structure of the honeycomb arises from the interaction of forces that wax balls exert on each other when compressed. The honeycomb can be described by a rule, but the mechanism which produces it does not contain any statement of this rule.

In our earlier work with the interactive activation model of word perception (McClelland and Rumelhart, 1981; Rumelhart and McClelland, 1981, 1982), we noted that lawful behavior emerged from the interactions of a set of word and letter units. Each word unit stood for a particular word and had connections to units for the letters of the word. There were no separate units for common letter clusters and no explicit provision for dealing differently with orthographically regular letter sequences – strings that accorded with the rules of English – as opposed to irregular sequences. Yet the model did behave differently with orthographically regular nonwords than it behaved with words. In fact, the model simulated rather closely a number of results in the word perception literature relating to the finding that subjects perceive letters in orthographically regular letter strings more accurately than they perceive letters in irregular, random letter strings. Thus, the behavior of the model was lawful even though it contained no explicit rules.

It should be said that the pattern of perceptual facilitation shown by the model did not correspond exactly to any system of orthographic rules that we know of. The model produced as much facilitation, for example, for special nonwords like *SLNT*, which are clearly irregular, as it did for matched regular nonwords like *SLET*. Thus, it is not correct to say that the model exactly mimicked the behavior we would expect to emerge from a system which makes use of explicit orthographic rules. However, neither do human subjects. Just like the model, they showed equal facilitation for vowelless strings like *SLNT* as for regular nonwords like *SLET*. Thus, human perceptual performance seems, in this case at least, to be characterized only approximately by rules.

Some people have been tempted to argue that the behavior of the model shows that we can do without linguistic rules. We prefer, however, to put the matter in a slightly different light. There is no denying that rules still provide a fairly close characterization of the performance of our subjects. And we have no doubt that rules are even more useful in characterizations of sentence production, comprehension, and grammaticality judgments. We would only suggest that parallel distributed processing (PDP) models may provide a mechanism suffcient to capture lawful behavior, without requiring the postulation of explicit but inaccessible rules. Put succinctly, our claim is that PDP models provide an alternative to the explicit but inaccessible rules account of implicit knowledge of rules.

We can anticipate two kinds of argument against this kind of claim. The first kind would claim that although certain types of rule-guided behavior might emerge from PDP models, the models simply lack the computational power needed to carry out certain types of operation which can be easily handled by a system using explicit rules. We believe that this argument is simply mistaken. We discuss the issue of computational power of PDP models in chapter 4.[1] Some applications of PDP models to sentence processing are described in chapter 19. The second kind of argument would be that the details of language behavior, and, indeed, the details of the language acquisition process, would provide unequivocal evidence in favor of a system of explicit rules.

It is this latter kind of argument we wish to address in the present chapter. We have selected a phenomenon that is often thought of as demonstrating the acquisition of a linguistic rule. And we have developed a parallel distributed processing model that learns in a natural way to behave in accordance with the rule, mimicking the general trends seen in the acquisition data.

The Phenomenon

The phenomenon we wish to account for is actually a sequence of three stages in the acquisition of the use of past tense by children learning English as their native tongue. Descriptions of development of the use of the past tense may be found in Brown (1973), Ervin (1964), and Kuczaj (1977).

In stage 1, children use only a small number of verbs in the past tense. Such verbs tend to be very high-frequency words, and the majority of these are irregular. At this stage, children tend to get the past tenses of these words correct if they use the past tense at all. For example, a child's lexicon of past-tense words at this stage might consist of *came*, *got*, *gave*, *looked*, *needed*, *took*, and *went*. Of these seven verbs, only two are regular – the other five are generally idiosyncratic examples of irregular verbs. In this stage, there is no evidence of the use of the rule – it appears that children simply know a small number of separate items.

In stage 2, evidence of implicit knowledge of a linguistic rule emerges. At this stage, children use a much larger number of verbs in the past tense. These verbs include a few more irregular items, but it turns out that the majority of the words at this stage are examples of the *regular* past tense in English. Some examples are *wiped* and *pulled*.

The evidence that the stage 2 child actually has a linguistic rule comes not from the mere fact that he or she knows a number of regular forms. There are two additional and crucial facts:

- The child can now generate a past tense for an invented word. For example, Berko (1958) has shown that if children can be convinced to use *rick* to describe an action, they will tend to say *ricked* when the occasion arises to use the word in the past tense.
- Children now *incorrectly* supply regular past-tense endings for words which they used correctly in stage 1. These errors may involve either adding *ed* to the root as in *comed* /k^md/, or adding *ed* to the irregular past tense form as in *camed*/kʌmd/[2] (Ervin, 1964; Kuczaj, 1977).

Such findings have been taken as fairly strong support for the assertion that the child at this stage has acquired the past-tense "rule". To quote Berko (1958):

> If a child knows that the plural of *witch* is *witches*, he may simply have memorized the plural form. If, however, he tells us that the plural of *gutch* is *gutches*, we have evidence that he actually knows, albeit unconsciously, one of those rules which the descriptive linguist, too, would set forth in his grammar. (p. 151)

In stage 3, the regular and irregular forms coexist. That is, children have regained the use of the correct irregular forms of the past tense while they continue to apply the regular form to new words they learn. Regularizations persist into adulthood – in fact, there is a class of words for which a regular and an irregular version are both considered acceptable – but for the commonest irregulars such as those the child acquired first, they tend to be rather rare. At this stage there are some clusters of exceptions to the basic, regular past-tense pattern of English. Each cluster includes a number of words that undergo identical changes from the present to the past tense. For example, there is a *ing/ang* cluster, an *ing/ung* cluster, an *eet/it* cluster, etc. There is also a group of words ending in /d/ or /t/ for which the present and past are identical.

Table 9.1 summarizes the major characteristics of the three stages.

Table 9.1   Characteristics of the three stages of past tense acquisition

Verb type	Stage 1	Stage 2	Stage 3
Early verbs	Correct	Regularized	Correct
Regular	–	Correct	Correct
Other irregular	–	Regularized	Correct or regularized
Novel	–	Regularized	Regularized

Variability and gradualness

The characterization of past-tense acquisition as a sequence of three stages is somewhat misleading. It may suggest that the stages are clearly demarcated and that performance in each stage is sharply distinguished from performance in other stages.

In fact, the acquisition process is quite gradual. Little detailed data exists on the transition from stage 1 to stage 2, but the transition from stage 2 to stage 3 is quite protracted and extends over several years (Kuczaj, 1977). Further, performance in stage 2 is extremely variable. Correct use of irregular forms is never completely absent, and the same child may be observed to use the correct past of an irregular, the base+ed form, and the past+ed form, within the same conversation.

Other facts about past-tense acquisition

Beyond these points, there is now considerable data on the detailed types of error children make throughout the acquisition process, both from Kuczaj (1977) and more recently from Bybee and Slobin (1982). We will consider aspects of these fmdings in more detail below. For now, we mention one intriguing fact: According to Kuczaj (1977), there is an interesting difference in the errors children make to irregular verbs at different points in stage 2. Early on, regularizations are typically of the base+ed form, like *goed*; later on, there is a large increase in the frequency of past+ed errors, such as *wented*.

The Model

The goal of our simulation of the acquisition of past tense was to simulate the three-stage performance summarized in table 9.1, and to see whether we could capture other aspects of acquisition. In particular, we wanted to show that the kind of gradual change characteristic of normal acquisition was also a characteristic of our distributed model, and we wanted to see whether the model would capture detailed aspects of the phenomenon, such as the change in error type in later phases of development and the change in differences in error patterns observed for different types of word.

We were not prepared to produce a full-blown language processor that would learn the past tense from full sentences heard in everyday experience. Rather, we have explored a very simple past-tense learning environment designed to capture the essential characteristics necessary to produce the three stages of acquisition. In this environment, the model is presented, as learning experiences, with pairs of inputs – one capturing the phonological structure of the root form of a word and the other capturing the phonological structure of the correct past-tense version of that word. The behavior of the model can be tested by giving it just the root form of a word and examining what it generates as its "current guess" of the corresponding past-tense form.

Structure of the model

The basic structure of the model is illustrated in figure 9.9. The model consists of two basic parts: (1) a simple *pattern* associator network similar to those studied by Kohonen (1977, 1984; see chapter 2) which learns the relationships between the base form and the past-tense form, and (2) a decoding network that converts a featural representation of the past-tense form into a phonological representation. All learning occurs in the pattern associator; the decoding network is simply a mechanism for converting a featural representation which may be a near miss to any phonological pattern into a legitimate phonological representation. Our primary focus here is on the pattern associator. We discuss the details of the decoding network in the appendix.

Units The pattern associator contains two pools of units. One pool, called the input pool, is used to represent the input pattern corresponding to the root form of the verb to be learned. The other pool, called the output pool, is used to represent the output pattern generated by the model as its current guess as to the past tense corresponding to the root form represented in the inputs.

Each unit stands for a particular feature of the input or output string. The particular features we used are important to the behavior of the model, so they are described in a separate section below.

Connections The pattern associator contains a modifiable connection linking each input unit to each output unit. Initially, these connections are all set to 0 so that there is no influence of the input units on the output units. Learning, as in other PDP models described

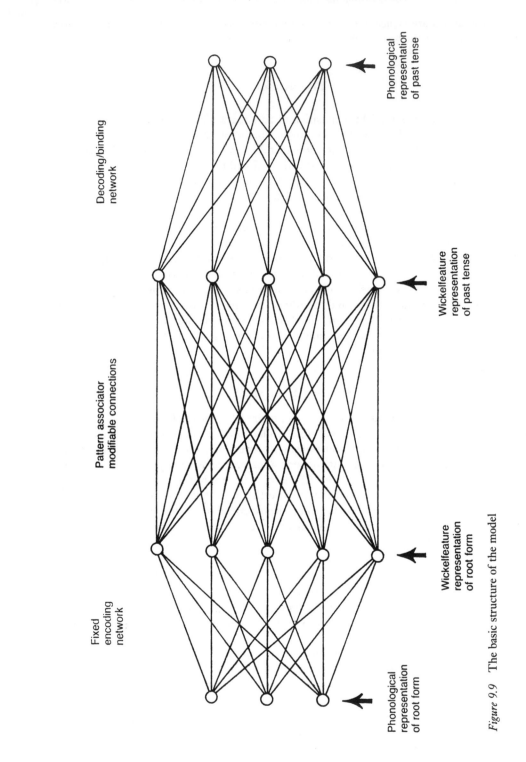

Decoding/binding network

Phonological representation of past tense

Wickelfeature representation of past tense

Pattern associator
modifiable connections

Fixed encoding network

Wickelfeature representation of root form

Phonological representation of root form

Figure 9.9   The basic structure of the model

in this book, involves modification of the strengths of these interconnections, as described below.

Operation of the model

On test trials, the simulation is given a phoneme string corresponding to the root of a word. It then performs the following actions. First, it encodes the root string as a pattern of activation over the input units. The encoding scheme used is described below. Node activations are discrete in this model, so the activation values of all the units that should be on to represent this word are set to 1, and all the others are set to 0. Then, for each output unit, the model computes the net input to it from all of the weighted connections from the input units. The net input is simply the sum over all input units of the input unit activation times the corresponding weight. Thus, algebraically, the net input to output unit i is

$$net = \Sigma a_j w_{ij}$$

where a_j represents the activation of input unit j, and w_{ij} represents the weight from unit j to unit i.

Each unit has a threshold, θ, which is adjusted by the learning procedure that we will describe in a moment. The probability that the unit is turned on depends on the amount the net input exceeds the threshold. The logistic probability function is used here as in the Boltzmann machine and in harmony theory to determine whether the unit should be turned on. The probability is given by

$$p\,(a_i = 1) = \frac{1}{1 + e^{-(net_i - \theta_i)/T}} \tag{1}$$

where T represents the temperature of the system. The logistic function is shown in figure 9.10. The use of this probabilistic response rule allows the system to produce different responses on different occasions with the same network. It also causes the system to learn more slowly, so the effect of regular verbs on the irregulars continues over a much longer period of time. As discussed in chapter 2, the temperature, T, can be manipulated so that at very high temperatures the response of the units is highly variable; with lower values of T, the units behave more like *linear threshold units*.

Since the pattern associator built into the model is a one-layer net with no feedback connections and no connections from one input unit to another or from one output unit to another, iterative computation is of no benefit. Therefore, the processing of an input pattern is a simple matter of first calculating the net input to each output unit and then setting its activation probabilistically on the basis of the logistic equation given above. The temperature T only enters in setting the variability of the output units; a fixed value of T was used throughout the simulations.

To determine how well the model did at producing the correct output, we simply compare the pattern of output Wickelphone activations to the pattern that the correct response would have generated. To do this, we first translate the correct response into a target pattern of activation for the output units, based on the same encoding scheme used for the input units. We then compare the obtained pattern with the target pattern on a unit-by-unit basis. If the output perfectly reproduces the target, then there should be a 1 in the

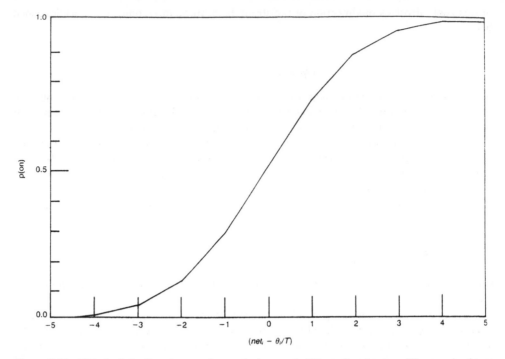

Figure 9.10 The logistic function used to calculate probability of activation. The *x*-axis shows values of $(net_i - \theta_i/T)$, and the *y*-axis indicates the corresponding probability that unit i will be activated

output pattern wherever there is a 1 in the target. Such cases are called *hits*, following the conventions of signal detection theory (Green and Swets, 1966). There should also be a 0 in the output whenever there is a 0 in the target. Such cases are called *correct rejections*. Cases in which there are 1s in the output but not in the target are called *false alarms*, and cases in which there are 0s in the output that should be present in the input are called *misses*. A variety of measures of performance can be computed. We can measure the percentage of output units that match the correct past tense, or we can compare the output to the pattern for any other response alternative we might care to evaluate. This allows us to look at the output of the system independently of the decoding network. We can also employ the decoding network and have the system synthesize a phonological string. We can measure the performance of the system either at the featural level or at the level of strings of phonemes. We shall employ both of these mechanisms in the evaluation of different aspects of the overall model.

Learning

On a learning trial, the model is presented with both the root form of the verb and the target. As on a test trial, the pattern associator network computes the output it would generate from the input. Then, for each output unit, the model compares its answer with the target. Connection strengths is adjusted using the classic *perceptron convergence procedure* (Rosenblatt, 1962). The perceptron convergence procedure is simply a discrete variant of the delta rule presented in chapter 2 and discussed in many places in this book. The exact procedure is as follows: We can think of the target as supplying a teaching input to each output unit, telling it what value it ought to have. When the actual output matches the target output, the model is doing the right thing and so none of the weights on the lines coming into the unit is adjusted. When the computed output is 0 and the target says it should be 1, we want to increase the probability that the unit will be active the next time the same input pattern is presented. To do this, we increase the weights from all of the input units that are active by a small amount η. At the same time, the threshold is also reduced by η. When the computed output is 1 and the target says it should be 0, we want to decrease the probability that the unit will be active the next time the same input pattern is presented. To do this, the weights from all of the input units that are active are reduced by η, and the threshold is increased by η. In all of our simulations, the value of η is simply set to 1. Thus, each change in a weight is a unit change, either up or down. For nonstochastic units, it is well known that the perceptron convergence procedure will find a set of weights that will allow the model to get each output unit correct, provided that such a set of weights exists. For the stochastic case, it is possible for the learning procedure to find a set of weights that will make the probability of error as low as desired. Such a set of weights exists if a set of weights exists that will always get the right answer for nonstochastic units.

Learning regular and exceptional patterns in a pattern associator

In this section, we present an illustration of the behavior of a simple pattern associator model. The model is a scaled-down version of the main simulation described in the next section. We describe the scaled-down version first because in this model it is possible to actually examine the matrix of connection weights, and from this to see clearly how the model works and why it produces the basic three-stage learning phenomenon characteristic of acquisition of the past tense. Various aspects of pattern associator networks are described in a number of places in this book (chapters 1, 2, 8, 9, 11, and 12, in particular) and elsewhere (Anderson, 1973, 1977; Anderson et al., 1977; Kohonen, 1977, 1984). Here we focus our attention on their application to the representation of rules for mapping one set of patterns into another.

For the illustration model, we use a simple network of eight input and eight output units and a set of connections from each input unit to each output unit. The network is illustrated in figure 9.11. The network is shown with a set of connections sufficient for associating the pattern of activation illustrated on the input units with the pattern of activation illustrated on the output units. (Active units are darkened; positive and negative connections are indicated by numbers written on each connection.) Next to the network is the matrix of connections abstracted from the actual network itself, with numerical values assigned to the positive and negative connections. Note that each weight is located in the matrix at the point where it occurred in the actual network diagram. Thus, the entry in the ith row of the jth column indicates the connection w_{ij} from the jth input unit to the ith output unit.

Using this diagram, it is easy to compute the net inputs that will arise on the output units when an input pattern is presented. For each output unit, one simply scans across its rows and adds up all the weights found in columns associated with active input units. (This is exactly what the simulation program does!) The reader can verify that when the input pattern illustrated in the left-hand panel is presented, each output unit that should be on in the output pattern receives a net input of $+45$; each output unit that should be off receives a net input of -45.[3] Plugging these values into equation (1), using a temperature of 15,[4] we

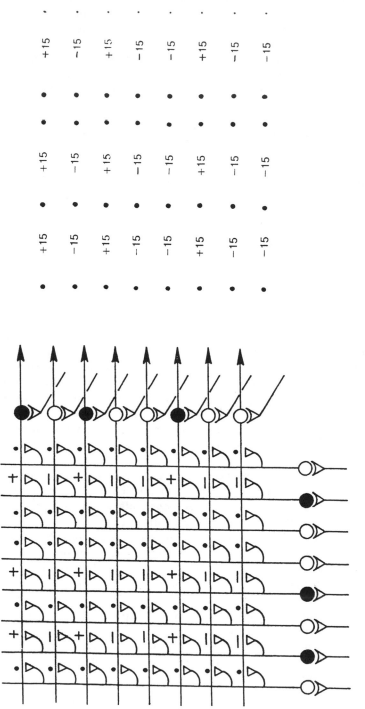

Figure 9.11 Simple network used in illustrating basic properties of pattern associator networks; excitatory and inhibitory connections needed to allow the active input pattern to produce the illustrated output patterns are indicated with + and −. Next to the network is the matrix of weights indicating the strengths of the connections from each input unit to each output unit. Input units are indexed by the column they appear in; output units are indexed by row

can compute that each output unit will take on the correct value about 95% of the time. The reader can check this in figure 9.10; when the net input is $+45$, the exponent in the denominator of the logistic function is 3, and when the net input is -45, the exponent is -3. These correspond to activation probabilities of about .95 and .05, respectively.

One of the basic properties of the pattern associator is that it can store the connections appropriate for mapping a number of different input patterns to a number of different output patterns. The perceptron convergence procedure can accommodate a number of arbitrary associations between input patterns and output patterns, as long as the input patterns form a linearly independent set. Table 9.2 illustrates this aspect of the model. The first two cells of the table show the connections that the model learns when it is trained on each of the two indicated associations separately. The third cell shows connections learned by the model when it is trained on both patterns in alternation, first seeing one and then seeing the other of the two. Again, the reader can verify that if either input pattern is presented to a network with this set of connections, the correct corresponding output pattern is reconstructed with high probability; each output unit that should be on gets a net input of at least $+45$, and each output unit that should be off gets a net input below -45.

The restriction of networks such as this to linearly independent sets of patterns is a severe one since there are only N linearly independent patterns of length N. That means that we could store at most eight unrelated associations in the network and maintain accurate performance. However, if the patterns all conform to a general rule, the capacity of the network can be greatly enhanced. For example, the set of connections shown in table 9.2D is capable of processing all of the patterns defined by what we call the *rule of 78*. The rule is described in table 9.3. There are 18 different input/output pattern pairs corresponding to this rule, but they present no difficulty to the network. Through repeated presentations of examples of the rule, the perceptron convergence procedure learned the set of weights

Table 9.2 Weights in the 8-unit network after various learning experiences

A Weights acquired in learning $(2\ 4\ 7) \rightarrow (1\ 4\ 6)$

```
.   15   .   15   .   .   15   .
.  -16   .  -16   .   .  -16   .
.  -17   .  -17   .   .  -17   .
.   16   .   16   .   .   16   .
.  -16   .  -16   .   .  -16   .
.   17   .   17   .   .   17   .
.  -16   .  -16   .   .  -16   .
.  -17   .  -17   .   .  -17   .
```

B Weights acquired in learning $(3\ 4\ 6) \rightarrow (3\ 6\ 7)$

```
.   .  -16  -16   .  -16   .   .
.   .  -17  -17   .  -17   .   .
.   .   17   17   .   17   .   .
.   .  -16  -16   .  -16   .   .
.   .  -17  -17   .  -17   .   .
.   .   16   16   .   16   .   .
.   .   17   17   .   17   .   .
.   .  -17  -17   .  -17   .   .
```

C Weights acquired in learning A and B together

```
.   24  -24    .   .  -24   24   .
.  -13  -13  -26   .  -13  -13   .
.  -23   24    1   .   24  -23   .
.   24   25    1   .  -25   24   .
.  -13  -13  -26   .  -13  -13   .
.   13   13   26   .   13   13   .
.  -25   24   -1   .   24  -25   .
.  -12  -13  -25   .  -13  -12   .
```

D Weights acquired in learning the rule of 78

```
.   61  -37  -37   -5   -5   -3   -6   -7
.  -35   60  -38   -4   -6   -3   -5   -8
.  -39  -35   61   -4   -5   -4   -7   -6
.   -6   -4   -5   59  -37  -37   -8   -7
.   -5   -5   -4  -36   60  -38   -7   -7
.   -5   -4   -6  -37  -38   60   -8   -7
.    .    1    .    1    .    .  -50   51
.    .    .   -1   -2    1    .   49  -50
```

Table 9.3 The rule of 78

Input patterns consist of one active unit from each of the following sets:	(1 2 3) (4 5 6) (7 8)
The output pattern paired with a given input pattern consists of:	The same unit from (1 2 3) The same unit from (4 5 6) The other unit from (7 8)
Examples:	$2\,4\,7 \to 2\,4\,8$ $1\,6\,8 \to 1\,6\,7$ $3\,5\,7 \to 3\,5\,8$
An exception:	$1\,4\,7 \to 1\,4\,7$

shown in cell D of table 9.2. Again, the reader can verify that it works for any legal association fitting the rule of 78. (Note that for this example, the "regular" pairing of (1 4 7) with (1 4 8) was used rather than the exceptional mapping illustrated in table 9.3.)

We have, then, observed an important property of the pattern associator: If there is some structure to a set of patterns, the network may be able to learn to respond appropriately to all of the members of the set. This is true, even though the input vectors most certainly do not form a linearly independent set. The model works anyway because the response that the model should make to some of the patterns can be predicted from the responses that it should make to others of the patterns.

Now let's consider a case more like the situation a young child faces in learning the past tenses of English verbs. Here, there is a regular pattern, similar to the rule of 78. In addition, however, there are exceptions. Among the first words the child learns are many exceptions, but as the child learns more and more verbs, the proportion that are regular increases steadily. For an adult, the vast majority of verbs are regular.

To examine what would happen in a pattern associator in this kind of a situation, we first presented the illustrative 8−unit model with two pattern pairs. One of these was a regular example of the 78 rule [(2 5 8) → (2 5 7)]. The other was an exception to the rule [(1 4 7) → (1 4 7)]. The simulation saw both pairs 20 times, and connection strengths were adjusted after each presentation. The resulting set of connections is shown in cell A of table 9.4. This number of learning trials is not enough to lead to perfect performance; but after this much experience, the model tends to get the right answer for each output unit close to 90 percent of the time. At this point, the fact that one of the patterns is an example of a general rule and the other is an exception to that rule is irrelevant to the model. It learns a set of connections that can accommodate these two patterns, but it cannot generalize to new instances of the rule.

This situation, we suggest, characterizes the situation that the language learner faces early on in learning the past tense. The child knows, at this point, only a few high-frequency verbs, and these tend, by and large, to be irregular, as we shall see below. Thus each is treated by the network as a separate association, and very little generalization is possible.

But as the child learns more and more verbs, the proportion of regular verbs increases. This changes the situation for the learning model. Now the model is faced with a number of examples, all of which follow the rule, as well as a smattering of irregular forms. This new

Table 9.4 Representing exceptions: weights in the 8-unit network

A After 20 exposures to
(1 4 7) → (1 4 7), (2 5 8) → (2 5 7)

12	−12	.	12	−12	.	12	−12
−11	13	.	−11	13	.	−11	13
−11	−11	.	−11	−11	.	−11	−11
12	−12	.	12	−12	.	12	−12
−11	11	.	−11	11	.	−11	11
−11	−12	.	−11	−12	.	−11	−12
12	11	.	12	11	.	12	11
−11	−13	.	−11	−13	.	−11	−13

B After 10 more exposure to all 18 associations

44	−34	−26	−2	−10	−4	−8	−8
−32	46	−27	−11	2	−4	−9	−4
−30	−24	43	−5	−5	−1	−2	−9
−1	−7	−7	45	−34	−26	−4	−11
−8	−3	−3	−31	44	−27	−7	−7
−6	−8	−3	−31	−28	42	−7	−10
11	−2	−6	11	−2	−6	−35	38
−9	−4	7	−13	1	6	36	−42

C After 30 more exposures to all 18 associations

61	−38	−38	−6	−5	−4	−6	−9
−38	62	−39	−6	−5	−4	−8	−7
−37	−38	62	−5	−5	−3	−7	−6
−4	−6	−6	62	−40	−38	−8	−8
−5	−5	−4	−38	62	−38	−7	−7
−6	−4	−5	−38	−39	62	−8	−7
20	−5	−4	22	−5	−6	−50	61
−19	8	5	−18	5	7	54	−60

D After a total of 500 exposures to all 18 associations

64	−39	−39	−5	−4	−5	−7	−7
−39	63	−39	−5	−5	−5	−7	−8
−39	−40	64	−5	−5	−5	−8	−7
−5	−5	−5	64	−40	−39	−8	−7
−5	−5	−5	−39	63	−39	−7	−8
−5	−5	−5	−39	−39	63	−8	−7
71	−28	−29	70	−28	−28	−92	106
−70	27	28	−70	27	28	91	−106

situation changes the experience of the network, and thus the pattern of interconnections it contains. Because of the predominance of the regular form in the input, the network learns the regular pattern, temporarily "overregularizing" exceptions that it may have previously learned.

Our illustration takes this situation to an extreme, perhaps, to illustrate the point. For the second stage of learning, we present the model with the entire set of 18 input patterns consisting of one active unit from (1 2 3), one from (4 5 6), and one from (7 8). All of these patterns are regular except the one exception already used in the first stage of training.

At the end of 10 exposures to the full set of 18 patterns, the model has learned a set of connection strengths that predominantly captures the "regular pattern."to At this point, its response to the exceptional pattern is *worse* than it was before the beginning of phase 2; rather than getting the right output for units 7 and 8, the network is now *regularizing* it.

The reason for this behavior is very simple. All that is happening is that the model is continually being bombarded with learning experiences directing it to learn the rule of 78. On only one learning trial out of 18 is it exposed to an exception to this rule.

In this example, the deck has been stacked very strongly against the exception. For several learning cycles, it is in fact quite difficult to tell from the connections that the model is being exposed to an exception mixed in with the regular pattern. At the end of 10 cycles, we can see that the model is building up extra excitatory connections from input units 1 and 4 to output unit 7 and extra inhibitory strength from units 1 and 4 to unit 8, but these are not strong enough to make the model get the right answer for output units 7 and 8 when the (1 4 7) input pattern is shown. Even after 40 trials (panel C of table 9.4), the model still gets the wrong answer on units 7 and 8 for the (1 4 7) pattern more than half the time. (The reader can still be checking these assertions by computing the net input to each output unit that would result from presenting the (1 4 7) pattern.)

It is only after the model has reached the stage where it is making very few mistakes on the 17 regular patterns that it begins to accommodate to the exception. This amounts to making the connection from units 1 and 4 to output unit 7 strongly excitatory and making the connections from these units to output unit 8 strongly inhibitory. The model must also make several adjustments to other connections so that the adjustments just mentioned do not cause errors on regular patterns similar to the exceptions, such as (1 5 7), (2 4 7), etc. Finally, in panel D, after a total of 500 cycles through the full set of 18 patterns, the weights are sufficient to get the right answer nearly all of the time. Further improvement would be very gradual since the network makes errors so infrequently at this stage that there is very little opportunity for change.

It is interesting to consider for a moment how an association is represented in a model like this. We might be tempted to think of the representation of an association as the difference between the set of connection strengths needed to represent a set of associations that includes the association and the set of strengths needed to represent the same set excluding the association of interest. Using this definition, we see that the representation of a particular association is far from invariant. What this means is that learning that occurs in one situation (e.g., in which there is a small set of unrelated associations) does not necessarily transfer to a new situation (e.g., in which there are a number of regular associations). This is essentially why the early learning our illustrative model exhibits of the (1 4 7) → (1 4 7) association in the context of just one other association can no longer support correct performance when the larger ensemble of regular patterns is introduced.

Obviously, the example we have considered in this section is highly simplified. However, it illustrates several basic facts about pattern associators. One is that they tend to exploit regularity that exists in the mapping from one set of patterns to another. Indeed, this is one of the main advantages of the use of distributed representations. Second, they allow exceptions and regular patterns to coexist in the same network. Third, if there is a predominant regularity in a set of patterns, this can swamp exceptional patterns until the set of connections has been acquired that captures the predominant regularity. Then further, gradual tuning can occur that adjusts these connections to accommodate both the regular patterns and the exception. These basic properties of the pattern associator model lie at the heart of the three-stage acquisition process, and account for the gradualness of the transition from stage 2 to stage 3.

Featural representations of phonological patterns

The preceding section describes basic aspects of the behavior of the pattern associator model and captures fairly well what happens when a pattern associator is applied to the processing of English verbs, following a training schedule similar to the one we have just considered for the acquisition of the rule of 78. There is one caveat, however: The input and target patterns – the base forms of the verbs and the correct past tenses of these verbs – must be represented in the model in such a way that the features provide a convenient basis for capturing the regularities embodied in the past-tense forms of English verbs. Basically, there were two considerations:

- We needed a representation that permitted a differentiation of all of the root forms of English and their past tenses.
- We wanted a representation that would provide a natural basis for generalizations to emerge about what aspects of a present tense correspond to what aspects of the past tense.

A scheme which meets the first criterion, but not the second, is the scheme proposed by Wickelgren (1969). He suggested that words should be represented as sequences of context-sensitive phoneme units, which represent each phone in a word as a triple, consisting of the phone itself, its predecessor, and its successor. We call these triples *Wickelphones*. Notationally, we write each Wickelphone as a triple of phonemes, consisting of the central phoneme, subscripted on the left by its predecessor and on the right by its successor. A phoneme occurring at the beginning of a word is preceded by a special symbol (#) standing for the word boundary; likewise, a phoneme occurring at the end of a word is followed by #. The word /kat/, for example, would be represented as $_{\#}k_a$, $_ka_t$, and $_at_\#$. Though the Wickelphones in a word are not strictly position specific, it turns out that (1) few words contain more than one occurrence of any given Wickelphone, and (2) there are no two words we know of that consist of the same sequence of Wickelphones. For example, /slit/ and /silt/ contain no Wickelphones in common.

One nice property of Wickelphones is that they capture enough of the context in which a phoneme occurs to provide a sufficient basis for differentiating between the different cases of the past-tense rule and for characterizing the contextual variables that determine the subregularities among the irregular past-tense verbs; for example, the word-final phoneme that determines whether we should add /d/, /t/ or /^d/ in forming the regular past. And it is the sequence $_iN_\#$ which is transformed to $_aN_\#$ in the *ing* → *ang* pattern found in words like *sing*.

The trouble with the Wickelphone solution is that there are too many of them, and they are too specific. Assuming that we distinguish 35 different phonemes, the number of Wickelphones would be 35^3, or 42,875, not even counting the Wickelphones containing word boundaries. And, if we postulate one input unit and one output unit in our model for each Wickelphone, we require rather a large connection matrix (4.3 × 10⁴ squared, or about 2×10^9) to represent all their possible connections.

Obviously, a more compact representation is required. This can be obtained by representing each Wickelphone as a distributed pattern of activation over a set of feature detectors. The basic idea is that we represent each phoneme, not by a single Wickelphone, but by a pattern of what we call *Wickelfeatures*. Each Wickelfeature is a conjunctive, or context-sensitive, feature, capturing a feature of the central phoneme, a feature of the predecessor, and a feature of the successor.

Details of the Wickelfeature representation   For concreteness, we will now describe the details of the feature coding scheme we used. It contains several arbitrary properties, but it also captures the basic principles of coarse, conjunctive coding described in chapter 3. First, we will describe the simple feature representation scheme we used for coding a single phoneme as a pattern of features without regard to its predecessor and successor. Then we describe how this scheme can be extended to code whole Wickelphones. Finally, we show how we "blur" this representation, to promote generalization further.

To characterize each phoneme, we devised the highly simplified feature set illustrated in table 9.5. The purpose of the scheme was (1) to give as many of the phonemes as possible a distinctive code, (2) to allow code similarity to reflect the similarity structure of the phonemes in a way that seemed sufficient for our present purposes, and (3) to keep the number of different features as small as possible.

The coding scheme can be thought of as categorizing each phoneme on each of four dimensions. The first dimension divides the phonemes into three major types: interrupted consonants (stops and nasals), continuous consonants (fricatives, liquids, and semivowels), and vowels. The second dimension further subdivides these major classes. The interrupted consonants are divided into plain stops and nasals; the continuous consonants into fricatives and sonorants (liquids and semivowels are lumped together); and the vowels into high and low. The third dimension classifies the phonemes into three rough places of articulation –

Table 9.5 Categorization of phonemes on four simple dimensions

		Place					
		Front		Middle		Back	
		V/L	*U/S*	*V/L*	*U/S*	*V/L*	*U/S*
Interrupted	*Stop*	b	p	d	t	g	k
	Nasal	m	–	n	–	N	–
Cont. consonant	*Fric.*	v/D	f/T	z	s	Z/j	S/C
	Liq/SV	w/l	–	r	–	y	h
Vowel	*High*	E	i	O	^	U	u
	Low	A	e	I	a/α	W	*/o

Key: N = ng in *sing*; D = th in *the*; T = th in *with*; Z = z in *azure*; S = sh in *ship*; C = ch in *chip*; E = ee in *beet*; i = i in *bit*; O = oa in *boat*; ^ = u in *but* or schwa; U = oo in *boot*; u = oo in *book*; A = ai in *bait*; e = e in *bet*; I = i e in *bite*; a = a in *bat*; α = a in *father*; W = ow in *cow*; * = aw in *saw*; o = o in *hot*.

front, middle, and back. The fourth subcategorizes the consonants into voiced vs. voiceless categories and subcategorizes the vowels into long and short. As it stands, the coding scheme gives identical codes to six pairs of phonemes, as indicated by the duplicate entries in the cells of the table. A more adequate scheme could easily be constructed by increasing the number of dimensions and/or values on the dimensions.

Using the above code, each phoneme can be characterized by one value on each dimension. If we assigned a unit for each value on each dimension, we would need 10 units to represent the features of a single phoneme, since two dimensions have three values and two have two values. We could then indicate the pattern of these features that corresponds to a particular phoneme as a pattern of activation over the 10 units.

Now, one way to represent each Wickelphone would simply be to use three sets of feature patterns: one for the phoneme itself, one for its predecessor, and one for its successor. To capture the word-boundary marker, we would need to introduce a special eleventh feature. Thus, the Wickelphone $_{\#}k_a$ can be represented by

$$[(000)\ (00)\ (000)\ (00)\ 1]$$
$$[(100)\ (10)\ (001)\ (01)\ 0]$$
$$[(001)\ (01)\ (010)\ (01)\ 0].$$

Using this scheme, a Wickelphone could be represented as a pattern of activation over a set of 33 units.

However, there is one drawback with this. The representation is not sufficient to capture more than one Wickelphone at a time. If we add another Wickelphone, the representation gives us no way of knowing which features belong together.

We need a representation, then, that provides us with a way of determining which features go together. This is just the job that can be done with detectors for Wickelfeatures – triples of features, one from the central phoneme, one from the predecessor phoneme, and one from the successor phoneme.

Using this scheme, each detector would be activated when the word contained a Wickelphone containing its particular combination of three features. Since each phoneme of a Wickelphone can be characterized by 11 features (including the word-boundary feature) and each Wickelphone contains three phonemes, there are $11 \times 11 \times 11$ possible Wickelfeature detectors. Actually, we are not interested in representing phonemes that cross word boundaries, so we only need 10 features for the center phoneme.

Though this leaves us with a fairly reasonable number of units ($11 \times 10 \times 11$ or 1,210), it is still large by the standards of what will easily fit in available computers. However, it is possible to cut the number down still further without much loss of representational capacity, since a representation using all 1,210 units would be highly redundant; it would represent each feature of each of the three phonemes 16 different times, one for each of the conjunctions of that feature with one of the four features of one of the other phonemes and one of the four features of the other.

To cut down on this redundancy and on the number of units required, we simply eliminated all those Wickelfeatures specifying values on two different dimensions of the predecessor and the successor phonemes. We kept all the Wickelfeature detectors for all combinations of different values on the same dimension for the predecessor and successor phonemes. It turns out that there are 260 of these (ignoring the word-boundary feature), and each feature of each member of each phoneme triple is still represented four different times. In addition, we kept the 100 possible Wickelfeatures combining a preceding word-boundary feature with any feature of the main phoneme and any feature of the successor; and the 100 Wickelfeatures combining a following word-boundary feature with any feature of the main phoneme and any feature of the successor. All in all then, we used only 460 of the 1,210 possible Wickelfeatures.

Using this representation, a verb is represented by a pattern of activation over a set of 460 Wickelfeature units. Each Wickelphone activates 16 Wickelfeature units. Table 9.6 shows the 16 Wickelfeature units activated by the Wickelphone $_k A_m$, the central Wickelphone in the word *came*. The first Wickelfeature is turned on whenever we have a Wickelphone in which the preceding contextual phoneme is an interrupted consonant, the central phoneme is a vowel, and the following phoneme is an interrupted consonant. This Wickelfeature is turned on for the Wickelphone $_k A_m$ since /k/ and /m/, the context phonemes, are both interrupted consonants and /A/, the central phoneme, is a vowel. This same Wickelfeature would be turned on in the representation of $_b i_d$, $_p \wedge_t$, $_m a_p$, and many other Wickelfeatures. Similarly, the sixth Wickelfeature listed in the table will be turned on whenever the preceding phoneme is made in the back, and the central and following phonemes are both made in the front. Again, this is turned on because /k/ is made in the back and /A/ and /m/ are both made in the front. In addition to $_k A_m$ this feature would be turned on for the Wickelphones $_g i_v$, $_g A_p$, $_k A_p$, and others. Similarly, each of the 16 Wickelfeatures stands for a conjunction of three phonetic features and occurs in the representation of a large number of Wickelphones.

Now, words are simply lists of Wickelphones. Thus, words can be represented by simply turning on all of the Wickelfeatures in any Wickelphone of a word. Thus, a word with three Wickelphones (such as *came*, which has the Wickelphones $_\# k_A$, $_k A_m$, and $_a m_\#$) will have at most 48 Wickelfeatures turned on. Since the various Wickelphones may have some Wickelfeatures in common, typically there will be less than 16 times the number of Wickelfeatures turned on for most words. It is important to note the temporal order is entirely implicit in this representation. All words, no matter how many phonemes in the word, will be represented by a subset of the 460 Wickelfeatures.

Table 9.6   The sixteen Wickelfeatures for the Wickelphone $_kA_m$

Feature	Preceding context	Central phoneme	Following context
1	Interrupted	Vowel	Interrupted
2	Back	Vowel	Front
3	Stop	Vowel	Nasal
4	Unvoiced	Vowel	Voiced
5	Interrupted	Front	Vowel
6	Back	Front	Front
7	Stop	Front	Nasal
8	Unvoiced	Front	Voiced
9	Interrupted	Low	Interrupted
10	Back	Low	Front
11	Stop	Low	Nasal
12	Unvoiced	Low	Voiced
13	Interrupted	Long	Vowel
14	Back	Long	Front
15	Stop	Long	Nasal
16	Unvoiced	Long	Voiced

Blurring the Wickelfeature representation   The representational scheme just outlined constitutes what we call the *primary* representation of a Wickelphone. In order to promote faster generalization, we further blurred the representation. This is accomplished by turning on, in addition to the 16 primary Wickelfeatures, a randomly selected subset of the similar Wickelfeatures, specifically, those having the same value for the central feature and one of the two context phonemes. That is, whenever the Wickelfeature for the conjunction of phonemic features f_1, f_2, and f_3 is turned on, each Wickelfeature of the form $<?f_2 f_3>$ and $<f_1 f_2?>$ may be turned on as well. Here "?" stands for "any feature." This causes each word to activate a larger set of Wickelfeatures, allowing what is learned about one sequence of phonemes to generalize more readily to other similar but not identical sequences.

To avoid having too much randomness in the representation of a particular Wickelphone, we turned on the same subset of additional Wickelfeatures each time a particular Wickelphone was to be represented. Based on subsequent experience with related models, we do not believe this makes very much difference.

There is a kind of trade-off between the discriminability among the base forms of verbs that the representation provides and the amount of generalization. We need a representation which allows for rapid generalization while at the same time maintaining adequate discriminability. We can manipulate this factor by manipulating the probability p that any one of these similar Wickelfeatures will be turned on. In our simulations we found that turning on the additional features with fairly high probability (.9) led to adequate discriminability while also producing relatively rapid generalization.

Although the model is not completely immune to the possibility that two different words will be represented by the same pattern, we have encountered no difficulty decoding any of the verbs we have studied. However, we do not claim that Wickelfeatures necessarily capture all the information needed to support the generalizations we might need to make for this or other morphological processes. Some morphological processes might require the use of units that were further differentiated according to vowel stress or other potential distinguishing characteristics. All we claim for the present coding scheme is its sufficiency for the task of representing the past tenses of the 500 most frequent verbs in English and the importance of the basic principles of distributed, coarse (what we are calling blurred), conjunctive coding that it embodies.

Summary of the structure of the model

In summary, our model contained two sets of 460 Wickelfeature units, one set (the input units) to represent the base form of each verb and one set (the output units) to represent the past-tense form of each verb.

The model is tested by typing in an input phoneme string, which is translated by the fixed encoding network into a pattern of activation over the set of input units. Each active input unit contributes to the net input of each output unit, by an amount and direction (positive or negative) determined by the weight on the connection between the input unit and the output unit. The output units are then turned on or off probabilistically, with the probability increasing with the difference between the net input and the threshold, according to the logistic activation function. The output pattern generated in this way can be compared with various alternative possible output patterns, such as the correct past-tense form or some other possible response of interest, or can be used to drive the decoder network described in the appendix.

The model is trained by providing it with pairs of patterns, consisting of the base pattern and the target, or correct, output. Thus, in accordance with common assumptions about the nature of the learning situation that faces the young child, the model receives only correct input from the outside world. However, it compares what it generates internally to the target output, and when it gets the wrong answer for a particular output unit, it adjusts the strength of the connection between the input and the output units so as to reduce the probability that it will make the same mistake the next time the same input pattern is presented. The adjustment of connections is an extremely simple and local procedure, but it appears to be sufficient to capture what we know about the acquisition of the past tense.

NOTES

1   [Editors' note: Cross-references in this extract are to *Parallel Distributed Processing: Explorations in the Microstructure of Cognition*, eds D. E. Rumelhart and J. L. McClelland (Cambridge, MA: MIT Press, 1986).]

2   The notation of phonemes used in this chapter is somewhat nonstandard. It is derived from the computer-readable dictionary containing phonetic transcriptions of the verbs used in the simulations. A key is given in table 9.5.

3   In the examples we will be considering in this section, the thresholds of the units are fixed at 0. Threshold terms add an extra degree of freedom for each output unit and allow the unit to come on in the absence of input, but they are otherwise inessential to the operation of the model. Computationally, they are equivalent to an adjustable weight to an extra input unit that is always on.

4   For the actual simulations of verb learning, we used a value of T equal to 200. This means that for a fixed value of the weight on an input line, the effect of that line being active on the unit's probability of firing is much lower than it is in these illustrations. This is balanced by the fact that in the verb-learning simulations, a much larger number of inputs contribute to the activation of each output unit. Responsibility for turning a unit on is simply more distributed when larger input patterns are used.

REFERENCES

Anderson, J. A. (1973). A theory for the recognition of items from short memorized lists. *Psychological Review*, 80: 417–38.

Anderson, J. A. (1977). Neural models with cognitive implications. In D. LaBerge and S. J. Samuels (eds), *Basic Processes in Reading: Perception and Comprehension*. Hillsdale, NJ: Lawrence Erlbaum.

Anderson, J. A., Silverstein, J. W., Ritz, S. A., and Jones, R. S. (1977). Distinctive features, categorical perception, and probability learning: some applications of a neural model. *Psychological Review*, 84: 413–51.

Bates, E. (1979). *Emergence of Symbols*. New York: Academic Press.

Berko, J. (1958). The child's learning of English morphology. *Word*, 14: 150–77.

Brown, R. (1973). *A First Language*. Cambridge, MA: Harvard University Press.

Bybee, J. L. and Siobin, D. I. (1982). Rules and schemas in the development and use of the English past tense. *Language*, 58: 265–89.

Ervin, S. (1964). Imitation and structural change in children's language. In E. Lenneberg (ed.), *New Directions in the Study of Language*. Cambridge, MA: MIT Press.

Green, D. M. and Swets, J. A. (1966). *Signal Detection Theory and Psychophysics*. New York: John Wiley.

Kohonen, T. (1977). *Associative Memory: A System Theoretical Approach*. New York: Springer.

Kohonen, T. (1984). *Self-organization and Associative Memory*. Berlin: Springer-Verlag.

Kuczaj, S. A. (1977). The acquisition of regular and irregular past tense forms. *Journal of Verbal Learning and Verbal Behavior*, 16: 589–600.

McClelland, I. L. and Rumelhart, D. E. (1981). An interactive activation model of context effects in letter perception: part 1. An account of basic findings. *Psychological Review*, 88, 375–407.

Pinker, S. (1984). *Language Learnability and Language Development*. Cambridge, MA: Harvard University Press.

Rosenblatt, F. (1962). *Principles of Neurodynamics*. New York: Spartan.

Rumelhart, D. E. and McClelland, J. L. (1981). Interactive processing through spreading activation. In A. M. Lesgold and C. A. Perfetti (eds), *Interactive Processing in Reading*. Hillsdale, NJ: Lawrence Erlbaum.

Rumelhart, D. E. and McClelland, J. L. (1982). An interactive activation model of context effects in letter perception: part 2. The contextual enhancement effect and some tests and extensions of the model. *Psychological Review*, 89: 60–94.

Wickelgren, W. A. (1969). Context-sensitive coding, associative memory, and serial order in (speech) behavior. *Psychological Review*, 76: 1–15.

Grammatical Structure and Distributed Representations

JEFFREY ELMAN

Introduction

Neural networks have a number of properties which make them attractive computational systems for modelling cognitive behavior (McClelland et al., 1986; Rumelhart and McClelland, 1986). One of the useful characteristics is their sensitivity to contextual factors, and another is their ability to seek a solution which satisfies multiple constraints.

For example, work by Kawamoto and McClelland (1986) and by St John and McClelland (in press) has shown how grammatical cues can be combined with context information to make inferences about events. Elman (in press) demonstrated that sequential context can provide the basis for adducing the category structure of internal representations of lexical items. Mikkulainen and Dyer (in press) showed how a similar effect could be achieved for external representations (i.e., forms which could then be used by other processing modules).

In these studies, *distributed representations* (Hinton, 1988; Hinton et al., 1986; van Gelder, in press) play a key role. Distributed representations provide a high-dimensional, continuously valued space which can support finely graded, multidimensional distinctions. This is clearly useful for language. However, there are other requirements for language processing, and it is not self-evident that distributed representations can meet these requirements.

Consider the problem of how to represent complex grammatical structure and, in particular, hierarchical constituent structure. In Elman (in press), for instance, a network developed an internal representation for the lexical item "rock," which captured the fact that this item (as used in the language environment to which the network was exposed) was a *noun*, *inanimate*, and of the class of things which may be used to break other things. This representation was induced solely from the behavior of this word across many contexts; the input form itself was a basis vector (i.e., a vector with a single randomly assigned bit turned on and orthogonal to all other vectors used to represent lexical items).

Although this is a useful result, other issues arise as we consider what sort of lexical representations might be required in sentences such as the following.

(1a)   The boy threw the *rock*.
(1b)   The boy broke the window with the *rock*.
(1c)   The *rock* broke the window.
(1d)   The boy who threw the *rock* later had to fix the window.

In a simple sense, the word "rock" has, in all of these sentences, the same meaning. One would, therefore, want a model to reflect this by having representations which are more or less the same across the four sentences. At the same time, the usage of the word differs across contexts. In (1a) "rock" is the direct object (patient, or theme). In (1b) "rock" is used as the instrument of an action. In (1c) the word is still the instrument but also functions as the grammatical subject. Finally, "rock" is used in (1d) in a context which is very similar to that in (1a); however, (1d) is a complex sentence and the representation of rock *qua* object must include the fact that this role occurs in the subordinate clause (in order to distinguish it from the object role in the main clause). Thus, while there is some aspect to the meaning of the word "rock" which is fixed across usage, the way in which the word is construed is also dependent on its context.

One way of dealing with such phenomena would be to posit sharp distinctions between the various types of information which might be relevant to sentence interpretation and to assign information to different levels of representation. Thus, one might posit levels for phonological, morphological, lexical, syntactic, semantic, discourse, and pragmatic information (and possibly others).

Although this approach, which emphasizes the autonomy of levels, has enjoyed great popularity in the generative linguistic tradition, it is not without its shortcomings (cf. Langacker, 1987: ch. 1). At the very least, this approach leaves unanswered the question of how – lacking a shared vocabulary – information is to be exchanged between different levels. The problem is nontrivial. Furthermore, although many phenomena can be described superficially in purely syntactic or lexical (or semantic, morphological, phonological, etc.) terms, such encapsulation often requires glossing over important details or ignoring trouble-some exceptions. For instance, morphology is usually defined as the level of representation at which minimal sound/meaning correspondences are encoded. There are, however, sound/meaning relationships ("sound symbolism") which are never fully productive nor easily described and which occur at what might seem to be submorphological levels. And although one might think that the existence of a lexical level should not be controversial (certainly all languages have words?), in reality it turns out to be difficult, and perhaps impossible, to define the concept *word* in any way which is consistent within a language (let alone across languages). The distinction between words, compounds, and phrases (e.g., "tooth," "teeth-mark," "man-in-street"), can be very tenuous.

Nonetheless, although there may be controversy regarding the appropriate way of representing the context-dependent role of the word "rock" in the above sentences, it is clear that the representations in the different contexts must somehow be different. The representations must reflect facts about rocks in general as well as the usage in the specific contexts. These usage distinctions include the various roles filled by the rock and also the part of the sentence of which "rock" is a constituent (e.g., the difference between "rock" in (1a) and (1d)). This latter issue has been raised forcefully by Fodor and Pylyshyn (1988). They argued that the ability to represent compositional relations is fundamental to a theory of cognition, but they also claimed that such representations can only be supported by the so-called classical theories (more precisely, the language of thought; Fodor 1976).

I take Fodor and Pylyshyn's first claim (regarding the importance of compositionality) as relatively uncontroversial. What is less clear is that compositional relationships can only be achieved by the so-called classical theories or by connectionist models which implement those theories. Fodor and Pylyshyn present a regrettably simplistic picture of current linguistic theory. What they call the classical theory actually encompasses a heterogeneous set of theories, not all of which are obviously compatible with the language of thought. Furthermore, there have, in recent years, been well-articulated linguistic theories in which composition figures prominently but which do not share the basic premises of the language of thought (e.g., Chafe, 1970; Fauconnier, 1985; Fillmore, 1982; Givon, 1984; Hopper and Thompson, 1980; Kuno, 1987; Lakoff, 1987; Langacker, 1987). Thus the two alternatives presented by Fodor and Pylyshyn, that connectionism must either implement the language of thought or fail as a cognitive model, are unnecessarily bleak and do not exhaust the range of possibilities.

In what follows, I ask whether connectionist models can in fact encode compositional relationships between linguistic elements. The investigation proceeds in two parts. First, the question is raised indirectly by seeing whether it is possible to produce in a network behaviors which may plausibly be thought to require representations that reflect com–positional relationships. This is similar to the strategy employed by linguists, who infer abstract mental representations based on observable behavior. The second approach is more direct. Because networks are artificial systems, one can inspect them directly and examine the mechanisms being used to produce the behavior. Having done this, we may then be in a position to raise the more interesting question, which is how such representations differ (or are similar to) the available alternatives.

Although I cannot at present give a definitive answer to this question, I will suggest some ways in which connectionist representations (at least, of the sort described here) differ from the so-called classical representations. Two characteristics in particular stand out. First, the connectionist representation of composition seems to be inherently more efficient at encoding contextual dependencies and at handling interactions among constituents (what, Langacker, 1987, calls accommodation) than are classical alternatives. Secondly, the connectionist state representation of hierarchical relations involves what might be called "leaky recursion." This differs from the "true recursion" afforded by stack machines. Leaky recursion allows information to spread more easily between levels of organization; this makes it unnecessary to assume movement of constituents, traces, etc. It also raises the possibility that when information coordination (i.e., long-distance dependencies) is blocked in certain situations, it is, for processing reasons, very different than in a stack machine, which relies on percolation and subjacency constraints. These issues will be explored in the discussion section.

I should emphasize that the work described below, whatever its merits, should not be taken as a *theory* of language. A theory of language will require certain properties of a processing mechanism which implements it, and I wish to know whether or not connectionist models are viable candidates. The current work thus should be seen as an exploration in the representational characteristics of a class of connectionist models in order to determine their relevancy for language. But for various reasons (in part having to do with the artificiality of the task they are taught), the models here do not provide a complete account of natural language use.

The remainder of this paper is organized in two sections, the first of which reports empirical results. After reviewing a related simulation from Elman (in press), I describe a task in which a network has to construct abstract representations which encode grammatical relations, including embedding relations. The trained network is studied in terms of performance. Then the internal representations are analyzed in order to understand how the network has solved the task. These results are discussed at greater length in the second section and are related to the broader question of the usefulness of the connectionist framework for modeling cognitive phenomena. Finally, I compare a connectionist model with classical representations.

Simulations

Language is structured in a number of ways. One important kind of structure has to do with the structure of the categories of language elements (e.g., words). The first simulation addressed the question of whether a connectionist model can induce the lexical category structure underlying a set of stimuli. A second way in which language is structured has to do with the possible ways in which strings can be combined (e.g., the grammatical structure). The second simulation addresses that issue.

Lexical category structure

Words may be categorized with respect to many factors. These include traditional notions such as *noun*, *verb*, etc., the argument structure they are associated with, and their semantic features. One of the consequences of lexical category structure is word order. Not all classes of words may appear in any position. Furthermore, certain classes of words, e.g., transitive verbs, tend to co–occur with other words. (As we shall see in the next simulation, these co-occurrent facts can be quite complex.)

The goal of the first simulation was to see if a network could learn the lexical category structure which was implicit in a language corpus. The overt form of the language items was arbitrary in the sense that the form of the lexical items contained no information about their lexical category. However, the behavior of the lexical items – defined in terms of co-occurrence restrictions – reflected their membership in implicit classes and subclasses. The question was whether or not the network could induce these classes.

Network architecture. Time is an important element in language, and so the question of how to represent serially ordered inputs is crucial. Various proposal have been advanced (for reviews, see Elman, in press; Mozer, 1988). The approach taken here involves treating the network as a simple dynamical system in which previous states are made available as an additional input (Jordan 1986). In Jordan's work the prior state was derived from the output units on the previous time cycle. In the work here, the prior state comes from the hidden unit patterns on the previous cycle. Because the hidden units are not taught to assume specific values in the course of learning a task, they can develop representations which encode the temporal structure of that task. In other words, the hidden units learn to become a kind of memory which is very task-specific.

The type of network used in the first simulation is shown in figure 9.12. This network is basically a three–layer network with the customary feed-forward connections from *input units* to *hidden units* and from *hidden units* to *output units*. There is an additional set of units, called *context units*, which provide for limited recurrence (and so this may be called a *simple recurrent network*). These context units are activated on a one-for-one basis by the hidden unit, with a fixed weight of 1.0.

The result is that at each time cycle the hidden unit activations are copied into the context units; on the next time cycle, the contexts combine with the new input to activate the hidden units. The hidden units therefore take on the job of mapping new inputs and prior states to the output; and because they themselves constitute the prior state, they must develop representations which facilitate the input/output mapping. The simple recurrent network has been studied in a number of tasks (Elman, in press; Hare et al., 1988; Servan-Schreiber et al., 1988). In this first simulation, there were 31 input units, 150 hidden and context units, and 31 output units.

Stimuli and task. A lexicon of 29 nouns and verbs was chosen. Words were represented as 31-bit binary vectors (two extra bits were reserved for another purpose). Each word was randomly assigned a unique vector in which only one bit was turned on. A sentence-generating program was then used to create a corpus of 10,000 two-and three-word sentences. The sentences reflected certain properties of the words. For example, only animate nouns occurred as the subject of the verb *eat*, and this verb was only followed by edible substances. Finally, the words in successive sentences were concatenated so that a stream of 27,354 vectors was created. This formed the input set.

The task was simply for the network to take successive words from the input stream and to predict the subsequent word (by producing it on the output layer). After each word was input, the output was compared with the actual next word, and the back-propagation of error learning algorithm (Rumelhart et al., 1986) was used to adjust the network weights. Words were presented in order, with no breaks between sentences. The network was trained on six passes through the corpus.

The prediction task was chosen for several reasons. First, it makes minimal assumptions about special knowledge required for training. The teacher function is simple and the

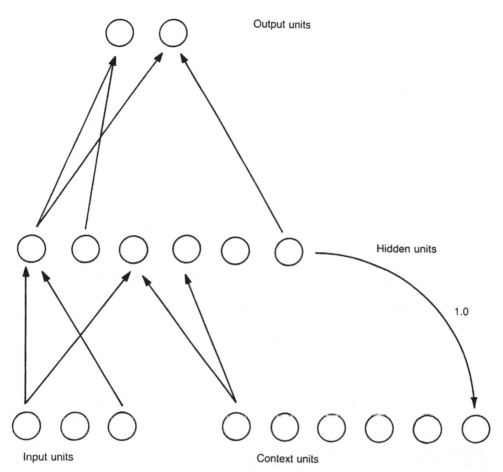

Figure 9.12 Network used in first simulation. Hidden unit activations are copied along fixed weights (of 1.0) into linear context units on a one-to-one basis; on the next time step the context units feed into hidden units on a distributed basis

information provided is available in the world at any moment. Thus, there are no a priori theoretical commitments which might bias the outcome. Second, although the task is simple and should not be taken as a model of comprehension, it does seem to be the case that much of what listeners do involves anticipation of future input (Grosjean, 1980; Marslen-Wilson and Tyler, 1980; Salasoo and Pisoni, 1985).

Results. Because the sequence is nondeterministic, short of memorizing the sequence, the network cannot succeed in exact predictions. That is, the underlying grammar and lexical category structure provides a set of constraints on the form of sentences, but the sentences themselves involve a high degree of optionality. Thus, measuring the performance of the network in this simulation is not straightforward. Root mean squared (rms) error at the conclusion of training had dropped to 0.88, but this result is not particularly positive in and of itself. In simulations where output vectors are sparse, as were those used in this simulation (only one bit out of 31 output bits is turned on for any particular patten), the network quickly learns to reduce error dramatically by turning all the output units off. This drops error from the initial random value of ~15.5 to 1.0, which is close to the final rms error value of 0.88.

Although the prediction task is nondeterministic, it is also true that word order is not random or unconstrained. For any given sequence of words there are a limited number of possible successors.Under these circumstances, it would seem more appropriate to ask whether or not the network has learned what the class of valid successors is at each point in time. We therefore might expect that the network should learn to activate the output nodes to some value proportional to the probability of occurrence of each word in that context.

Therefore, rather than evaluating final network performance using the rms error calculated by comparing the network's output with the actual next word, we can compare the output with the probability of occurrence of possible successors. These values can be derived empirically from the training data base (for details see Elman 1989); such calculation yields a likelihood output vector which is appropriate for each input and which reflects the context-dependent expectations given the training base (where context is defined as extending from the beginning of the sentence to the input). Note that it is appropriate to use these likelihood vectors only for the evaluation phase. Training must be performed on the actual successor words, because the point is to force the network to learn the context-dependent probabilities for itself.

Evaluated in this manner, the error on the training set is 0.053 (sd: 0.100). The cosine of the angle between output vectors and likelihood vectors provides another measure of performance (which normalizes for length differences in the vectors); the mean cosine is 0.916 (sd: 0.123), indicating that the two vectors on average have very similar shapes. Objectively, the performance appears to be quite good.

Lexical categories   The question to be asked now is how this performance has been achieved. One way to answer this is to see what sorts of internal representation the network develops in order to carry out the prediction task. This is particularly relevant, given the focus of the current paper. The internal representations are instantiated as activation patterns across the hidden units which are evoked in response to each word in its context. These patterns were saved at a testing phase, during which no learning took place. For each of the 29 unique words, a mean vector was computed and averaged across all occurrences of the word in various contexts. These mean vectors were then subjected to hierarchical clustering analysis. Figure 9.13 shows the tree constructed from the hidden unit patterns for the 29 lexical items.The tree in figure 9.13 shows the similarity structure of the internal representations of the 29 lexical items. The form of each item is randomly assigned (and orthogonal to all other items), and so the basis for the similarity in the internal representations is the way in which these words "behave" with regard to the task.

The network has discovered that there are several major categories of words. One large category corresponds to *verbs*; another category corresponds to *nouns*. The verb category is broken down into groups which require a direct object (d.o.); which are intransitive; and for which a direct object is optional. The noun category is divided into major groups for *animates* and *inanimates*. Animates are divided into *human* and *human*; the *nonhumans* are subdivided into *large animals* and *small animals*. Inanimates are divided into *breakables, edibles*, and *miscellaneous*.

This category structure reflects facts about the possible sequential ordering of the inputs. The network is not able to predict the precise order of specific words, but it recognizes that (in this corpus) there is a class of inputs (viz., verbs) which typically follow other inputs (viz.,

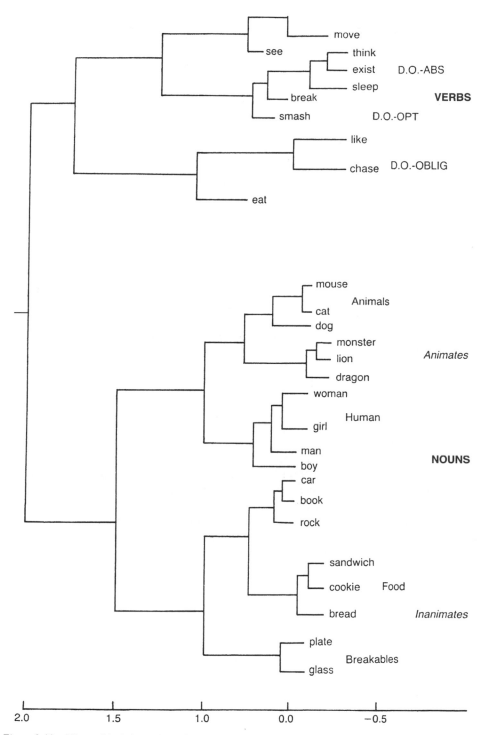

Figure 9.13 Hierarchical clustering of mean hidden unit vectors following presentation of each of the lexical items (in context). The similarity structure of the space reflects distributional properties of the lexical items

nouns). This knowledge of class behavior is quite detailed; from the fact that there is a class of items which always precedes *chase*, *break*, and *smash*, it infers a category of large animals (or, possibly, aggressors).

Several points should be emphasized. First, the category structure appears to be hierarchical. *Dragons* are large animals, but also members of the class [−human, +animate] nouns. The hierarchical interpretation is achieved through the way in which the spatial relations of the representations are organized. Representations which are near one another in representational space form classes, and higher-level categories correspond to larger and more general regions of this space.

Second, it is also the case that the hierarchicality and category boundaries are "soft". This does not prevent categories from being qualitatively distinct by being far from each other in space with no overlap. But there may also be entities which share properties of otherwise distinct categories, so that in some cases category membership maybe marginal or ambiguous.

Finally, the content of the categories is not known to the network. The network has no information available which would ground the structural information in the real world. This is both a plus and a minus. Obviously, a full account of language processing needs to provide such grounding. On the other hand, it is interesting that the evidence for category structure can be inferred so readily on the basis of language internal evidence alone.

Type–token distinctions   The tree shown in figure 9.13 was constructed from activation patterns averaged across context. It is also possible to cluster activation patterns evoked in response to words in the various contexts in which they occur. When the context-sensitive hidden units patterns are clustered, it is found that the large-scale structure of the tree is identical to that shown in figure 9.13. However, each terminal leaf is now replaced with further arborization for all occurrences of the word. (There are no instances of lexical items appearing on inappropriate branches.)

This finding bears on the type–token problem in an important way. In this simulation, the context makes up an important part of the internal representation of a word. Indeed, it is somewhat misleading to speak of the hidden unit representations as word representations in the conventional sense, since these patterns also reflect the prior context. As a result, it is literally the case that every occurrence of a lexical item has a separate internal representation. We cannot point to a canonical representation for *John*; instead there are representations for *John 1*, *John 2*, . . . *John*. These are the tokens of *John*, and the fact that they are different is the way the system marks what may be subtle but important meaning differences associated with the specific token. The fact that these are all tokens of the same type is not lost, however. These tokens have representations which are extremely close in space closer to each other by far than to any other entity. Even more interesting is that the spatial organization within the token space is not random but reflects differences in context which are also found among tokens of other items. The tokens of "boy" which occur in subject position tend to cluster together as distinct from tokens of "boy" which occur in object position. This distinction is marked in the same way for tokens of other nouns. Thus, the network has learned not only about types and tokens, categories and category members; it has also learned a grammatical role distinction which cuts across lexical items.

This simulation has involved a task in which the category structure of inputs was an important determinant of their behavior. The category structure was apparent only in their behavior; their external form provided no useful information. We have seen that the network makes use of spatial organization in order to capture this category structure. We turn next to a problem in which the lexical category structure provides only one part of the solution, and in which the network must learn abstract grammatical structure.

Representation of grammatical structure

In the previous simulation there was little interesting structure of the sort that related words to one another. Most of the relevant information regarding sequential behavior was encoded in terms of invariant properties of items. Although lexical information plays an important role in language, it actually accounts for only a small range of facts. Words are processed in the contexts of other words; they inherit properties from the specific grammatical structure in which they occur. This structure can be quite complex, and it is not clear that the kind of category structure supported by the spatial distribution of representations is sufficient to capture the structure which belongs, not to individual words, but to particular configurations of words.

As we consider this issue, we also note that till now we have neglected an important dimension along which structure may be manifest, that is, time. The clustering technique used in the previous simulation informs us of the similarity relations along spatial dimensions. The technique tells us nothing about the patterns of movement through space. This is unfortunate, since the networks we are using are dynamical systems whose states change over time. Clustering groups states according to the metric of Euclidean distance but, in so doing, discards the information about whatever temporal relations may hold between states. This information is clearly relevant if we are concerned about grammatical structure.

Consider the sentences

(1a) The man saw the *car*.
(1b) The man who saw the *car* called the cops.

On the basis of the results of the previous simulation, we would expect that the representations for the word *car* in these two sentences would be extremely similar. Not only are they the same lexical type, but they both appear in clause-final position as the object of the same verb. But we might also wish to have their representations capture an important structural difference between them. *Car* in sentence (1a) occurs at the end of the sentence; it brings us to a state from which we should move into another class of states that is associated with the onset of new sentences. In sentence (1b), *car* is also at the end of a clause but occurs in a matrix sentence which has not yet been completed. There are grammatical obligations which remain unfulfilled. We would like the state that is associated with *car* in this context to lead us to the class of states which might conclude the main clause. The issue of how to understand the temporal structure of state trajectories will thus figure importantly in our attempts to understand the representation of grammatical structure.

Stimuli and task. The stimuli in this simulation were based on a lexicon of 23 items. These included 8 nouns, 12 verbs, the relative pronoun *who*, and an end-of-sentence indicator, " . ". Each item was represented by a randomly assigned 26-bit vector in which a single bit was set to one (three bits were reserved for another purpose). A phrase structure grammar, shown in table 9.7, was used to generate sentences. The resulting sentences possessed certain important properties, which include the following:

Table 9.7

S → NP VP "."
NP → PropN | N | N RC
VP → V (NP)
RC → *who* NP VP | *who* VP (NP)
N → *boy* | *girl* | *cat* | *dog* | *boys* | *girls* | *cats* | *dogs*
PropN → *John* | *Mary*
V → *chase* | *feed* | *see* | *hear* | *walk* | *live* | *chases* | *feeds* | *sees* | *hears* | *walks* | *lives*

Additional restrictions:
- number agreement between N and V within clause and (where appropriate) between head N and subordinate V
- verb arguments:
  hit, feed → require a direct object
  see, hear → optionally allow a direct object
  walk, live → preclude a direct object
  (observed also for head/verb relations in relative clauses)

Agreement Subject nouns agree with their verbs. Thus, for example, (2a) is grammatical but (2b) is not. (The training corpus consisted of positive examples only; thus the starred examples below did not occur.)

>   (2a)   John feeds dogs.
>   (2b)   *Boys sees Mary.

Words are not marked for number (singular/plural), form class (verb/noun, etc.), or grammatical role (subject/object, etc.). The network must learn first that there are items which function as what we would call nouns, verbs, etc.; then it must learn which items are examples of singular and plural; and then it must learn which nouns are subjects and which are objects (since agreement only holds between subject nouns and their verbs).

Verb argument structure Verbs fall into three classes: those that require direct objects, those that permit an optional direct object, and those that preclude direct objects. As a result, sentences (3a–d) are grammatical, whereas sentences (3e–f) are ungrammatical.

>   (3a)   Girls feed dogs. (*D.o. required*)
>   (3b)   Girls see boys. (*D.o. optional*)
>   (3c)   Girls see. (*D.o. optional*)
>   (3d)   Girls live. (*D.o. precluded*)
>   (3e)   *Girls feed.
>   (3f)   *Girls live dogs.

Again, the type of verb is not overtly marked in the input, and so the class membership needs to be inferred at the same time as the co-occurrence facts are learned.

Interactions with relative clauses Both the agreement and the verb argument facts are complicated in relative clauses. While direct objects normally follow the verb in simple sentences, some relative clauses have the direct object as the head of the clause, in which case the network must learn to recognize that the direct object has already been filled (even though it occurs before the verb). Thus, the normal pattern in simple sentences (3a–d) appears also in (4a) but contrasts with (4b).

(4a) Dog _{who chases cat} ^{sees girl.}

(4b) Dog _{who cat chases} ^{sees girl.}

Sentence (4c), which seems to conform to the pattern established in (3), is ungrammatical.

(4c) *Dog _{who cat chases dog} ^{sees girl.}

Similar complications arise for the agreements facts. In simple sentences agreement involves N1–V1. In complex sentences, such as (5a), that regularity is violated, and any straight-forward attempt to generalize it to sentences with multiple clauses would lead to the ungrammatical (5b).

(5a) Dog _{who boys feed} ^{sees girl.}

(5b) *Dog who _{boys feeds} ^{see girl.}

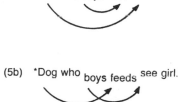

Recursion The grammar permits recursion through the presence of relative clauses (which expand to noun phrases which may introduce yet other relative clauses, etc.). This leads to sentences such as (6) in which the grammatical phenomena noted in (a–c) may be extended over a considerable distance.

(6) Boys _{who girls} _{who dogs chase} ^{see} ^{hear.}

Viable sentences One of the literals inserted by the grammar is ".". This mark occurs at the end of sentences and can, of course, potentially occur anywhere in a string where a sentence is viable (in the sense that it is grammatically well formed and may at that point be terminated). Thus in sentence (7), the carets indicate positions where a "." might legally occur.

(7)   Boys see $\wedge$ dogs $\wedge$ who see $\wedge$ girls $\wedge$ who hear $\wedge$.

The data in (4–7) are examples of the sorts of phenomenon which linguists argue cannot be accounted for without abstract representations; it is these representations, rather than the surface strings, on which the correct grammatical generalizations are made.

   A network of the form shown in figure 9.14 was trained on the prediction task (layers are shown as rectangles; numbers indicate the number of nodes in each layer). The training data were generated from the phrase structure grammar given in table 9.7. At any given point during training, the training set consisted of 10,000 sentences, which were presented to the network five times. (As before, sentences were concatenated so that the input stream proceeded smoothly, without breaks between sentences.) However, the composition of these sentences varied over time. The following training regimen was used in order to provide for incremental training. The network was trained on five passes through each of the following four corpora.

   Phase 1: The first training set consisted exclusively of simple sentences. This was accomplished by eliminating all relative clauses. The result was a corpus of 34,605 words forming

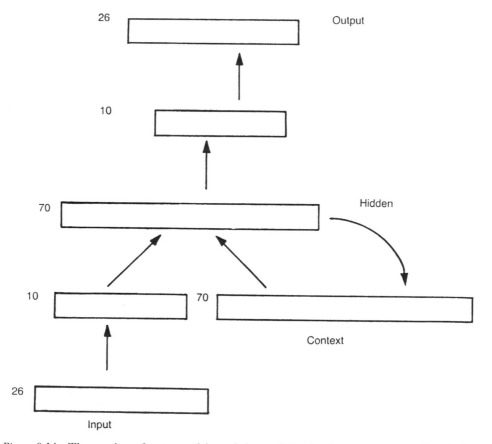

Figure 9.14   The number of notes used in each layer of the simple recurrent network trained to predict the grammatical structures of simple sentences and sentences with relative clauses

10,000 sentences (each sentence includes the terminal "."). Phase 2: The network was then exposed to a second corpus of 10,000 sentences which consisted of 25 percent complex sentences and 75 percent simple sentences (complex sentences were obtained by permitting relative clauses). Mean sentence length was 3.92 (minimum three words, maximum 13 words). Phase 3: The third corpus increased the percentage of complex sentences to 50 percent, with mean sentence length of 4.38 (minimum three words, maximum 13 words). Phase 4: The fourth consisted of 10,000 sentences, 75 percent complex, 25 percent simple. Mean sentence length was 6.02 (minimum three words, maximum 16 words).

This staged learning strategy was developed in response to results of earlier pilot work. In this work, it was found that the network was unable to learn the task when given the full range of complex data from the beginning of training. However, when the network was permitted to focus on the simpler data first, it was able to learn the task quickly and then move on successfully to more complex patterns. The important aspect to this was that the earlier training constrained later learning in a useful way; it forced the network to focus on canonical versions of the problems, which apparently created a good basis for then solving the more difficult forms of the same problems.

Results. At the conclusion of the fourth phase of training, the weights were frozen at their final values and network performance was tested on a novel set of data, which was generated in the same way as the last training corpus. The technique described in the previous simulation was used, and context-dependent likelihood vectors were generated for each word in every sentence. These vectors represented the empirically derived probabilities of occurrence for an possible predictions, given the sentence context up to that point. The rms error of network predictions, compared against the likelihood vectors, was 0.177 (sd: 0.463); the mean cosine of the angle between the vectors was 0.852 (sd: 0.259). Although this performance is not as good as in the previous simulation, it is still quite good. And the task is obviously much more difficult.

These gross measures of performance, however, do not tell us how well the network has done in each of the specific problem areas posed by the task. Let us look at each area in turn.

Agreement in simple sentences   Agreement in simple sentences is shown in figures 9.15a and 9.15b. The network's predictions following the word *boy* are that either a singular verb will follow (words in all three singular verb categories are activated, since it has no basis for predicting the type of verb), or the next word may be the relative pronoun *who*. Conversely, when the input is the word *boys*, the expectation is that either a verb in the plural or a relative pronoun will follow. Similar expectations hold for the other nouns in the lexicon.

Verb argument structure in simple sentences   Figure 9.16 shows network predictions following an initial noun and then a verb from each of the three different verb types. When the verb is *lives*, the network's expectation is that the following item will be "." (which is in fact the only successor permitted by the grammar in this context). The verb *sees*, on the other hand, may be followed either by a "." or by a direct object (which may be a singular or plural noun, or proper noun). Finally, the verb *chases* requires a direct object, and the network learns to expect a noun following this and other verbs in the same class.

Interactions with relative clauses   The examples so far have all involved simple sentences? The agreement and verb argument facts are more complicated in complex sentences. Figure 9.17 shows the network predictions for each word in the sentence *boys who Mary chases feed*

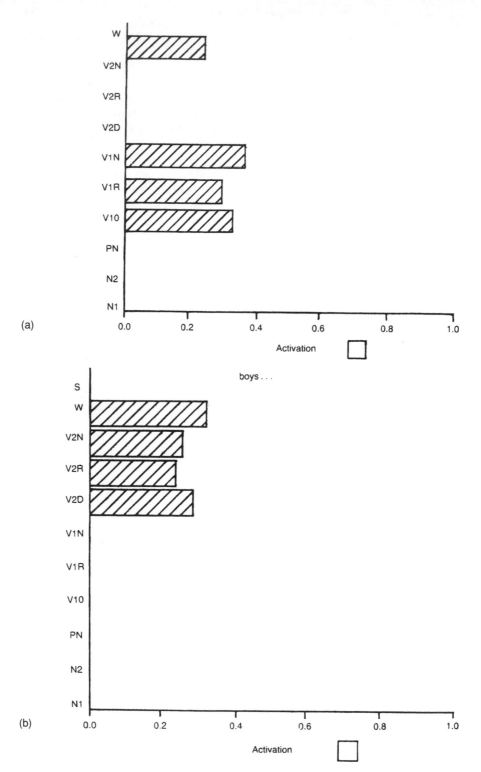

boys . . .

Figure 9.15a Graph of network predictions following presentation of the word *boy*. Predictions are shown as activations for words grouped by category. *S* stands for end-of-sentence ("."); *W* stands for who; *N* and *v* represent nouns and verbs; *1* and *2* indicate singular or plural; and type of verb is indicated by *N, R, O* (direct object not possible, required, or optional)

Figure 9.15b Graph of network predictions following presentation of the word *boys*

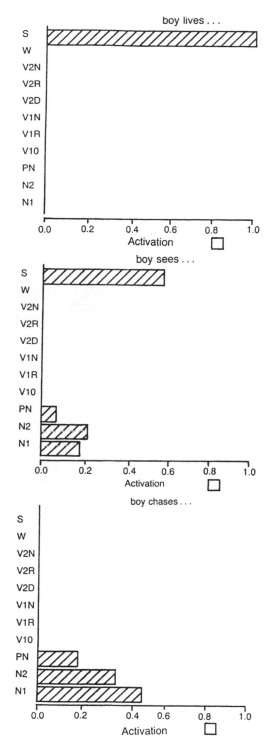

Figure 9.16 Graph of network predictions following the sequences *boy lives . . .* ; *boy sees . . .* ; and *boy chases . . .* (the first precludes a direct object, the second optional permits a direct object, and the third requires a direct object)

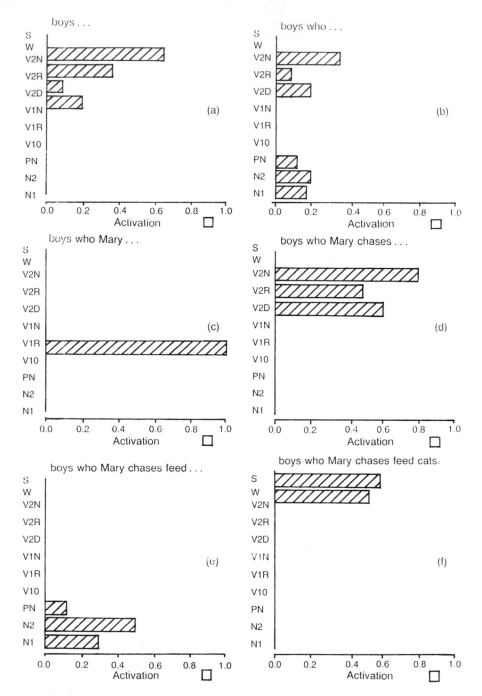

Figure 9.17 Graph of network predictions after each word in the sentence *boys who Mary chases feed cats* is input

cats. If the network were generalizing the pattern for agreement found in the simple sentences, we might expect the network to predict a singular verb following *Mary chases* (insofar as it predicts a verb in this position at all; conversely, it might be confused by the pattern *N1 N2 V1*). But, in fact, the prediction (9.17d) is, correctly, that the next verb should be in the singular in order to agree with the first noun. In so doing, it has found some mechanism for representing the long-distance dependency between the main clause noun and main clause verb, despite the presence of an intervening noun and verb (with their own agreement relations) in the relative clause.

Note that this sentence also illustrates the sensitivity to an interaction between verb argument structure and relative clause structure. The verb *chases* takes an obligatory direct object. In simple sentences the direct object follows the verb immediately; this is also true in many complex sentences (e.g., *boys who chase Mary feed cats*). In the sentence displayed, however, the direct object (boys) is the head of the relative clause and appears before the verb. This requires that the network learn (1) there are items which function as nouns, verbs, etc.; (2) which items fall into which classes; (3) there are subclasses of verbs which have different co-occurrence relations with nouns, corresponding to verb–direct object restrictions; (4) which verbs fall into which classes; and (5) when to expect that the direct object will follow the verb and when to know that it has already appeared. The network appears to have learned this, because in panel (d) of figure 9.17 we see that it expects that *chases* will be followed by a verb (the main clause verb, in this case) rather than a noun.

An even subtler point is demonstrated in (9.17c). The appearance of boys followed by a relative clause containing a different subject (*who Mary*) primes the network to expect that the verb which follows must be of the class that requires a direct object, precisely because a direct object filler has already appeared. In other words, the network correctly responds to the presence of a filler (*boys*) not only by knowing where to expect a gap (following *chases*); it also learns that when this filler corresponds to the object position in the relative clause, a verb is required which has the appropriate argument structure.

Network analysis. The natural question to ask at this point is how the network has learned to accomplish the task. It was initially assumed that success in this task would constitute prima facie evidence for the existence of internal representations which possessed abstract structure. That is, it seemed reasonable to believe that in order to handle agreement and argument structure facts in the presence of relative clauses, the network would be required to develop representations which reflected constituent structure, argument structure, grammatical category, grammatical relations, and number.

Having achieved success in the task, we would now like to test this assumption. In the previous simulation, hierarchical clustering was used to reveal the use of spatial organization at the hidden unit level for categorization purposes. However, the clustering technique makes it difficult to see patterns which exist over time. Some states may have significance not simply in terms of their similarity to other states but with regard to the ways in which they constrain movement into subsequent state space (recall the examples in (1)). Because clustering ignores the temporal information, it hides this information. It would be more useful to look at the trajectories, through state space over time, which correspond to the internal representations evoked at the hidden unit layer as a network processes a given sentence.

Phase-state portraits of this sort are commonly limited to displaying not more than a few state variables at once, simply because movement in more than three dimensions is difficult to graph. The hidden unit activation patterns in the current simulation take place over 70 variables. These patterns are distributed, in the sense that none of the hidden units alone provides useful information; the information instead lies along hyperplanes which cut across multiple units.

However, it is possible to identify these hyperplanes using principle component analysis. This involves passing the training set through the trained network (with weights frozen) and saving the hidden unit pattern produced in response to each new input. The covariance matrix of the set of hidden unit vectors is calculated, and then the eigen-vectors for the covariance matrix are found. The eigen-vectors are ordered by the magnitude of their eigen-values and are used as the new basis for describing the original hidden unit vectors. This new set of dimensions has the effect of giving a somewhat more localized description to the hidden unit patterns, because the new dimensions now correspond to the location of meaningful activity (defined in terms of variance) in hyperspace. Furthermore, since the dimensions are ordered in terms of variance accounted for, we can now look at phase state portraits of selected dimensions, starting with those with the largest eigen-values.

Agreement   The sentences in (8) were presented to the network, and the hidden unit patterns captured after each word were processed in sequence.

> (8a)   boys hear boys.
> (8b)   boy hears boys.
> (8c)   boy who boys chase chases boy.
> (8d)   boys who boys chase chase boy.

(These sentences were chosen to minimize differences due to lexical content and to make it possible to focus on differences to grammatical structure. (8a) and (8b) were contained in the training data; (8c) and (8d) were novel and had never been presented to the network during learning.) By examining the trajectories through state space along various dimensions, it was apparent that the second principal component played an important role in marking the number of the main clause subject.

Figure 9.18 shows the trajectories for (8a) and (8b); the trajectories are overlaid so that the differences are more readily seen. The paths are similar and diverge only during the first word, indicating the difference in the number of the initial noun. The difference is slight and is eliminated after the main (i.e., second *chase*) verb has been input. This is apparently because, for these two sentences (and for the grammar), number information does not have any relevance for this task once the main verb has been received.

It is not difficult to imagine sentences in which number information may have to be retained over an intervening constituent; sentences (8c) and (8d) are such examples. In both these sentences there is an identical relative clause which follows the initial noun (which differs with regard to number in the two sentences). This material, *who boys chase*, is irrelevant as far as the agreement requirements for the main clause verb are concerned. The trajectories through state space for these two sentences have been overlaid and are shown in figure 9.19; as can be seen, the differences in the two trajectories are maintained until the main clause verb is reached, at which point the states converge.

Verb argument structure   The representation of verb argument structure was examined by probing sentences containing instances of the three different classes of verbs. Sample sentences are shown in (9).

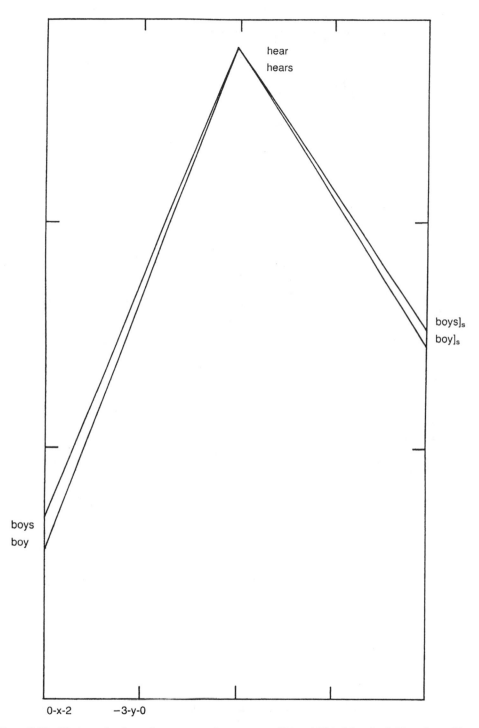

0-x-2   −3-y-0

Figure 9.18 Trajectories through state space for sentences (8a) and (8b). After the indicated word has been input, each point marks the position along the second principle component of hidden unit space. Magnitude of the second principle component is measured along the ordinate; time (i.e., order of words in sentence) is measured along the abscissa. In this and subsequent graphs the sentence-final word is marked with a]ₛ

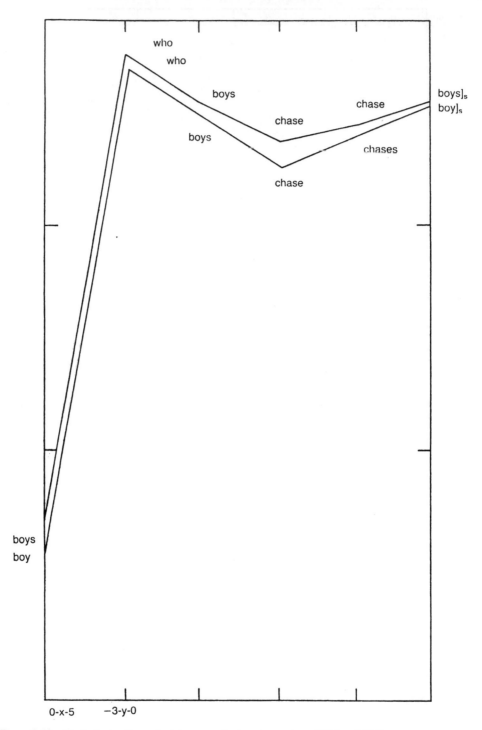

Figure 9.19 Trajectories through state space during processing of (8c) and (8d)

(9a) boy walks.
(9b) boy sees boy.
(9c) boy chases boy.

The first of these contains a verb which may not take a direct object; the second takes an option direct object; and the third requires a direct object. The movement through state space as these three sentences are processed is shown in figure 9.20, which illustrates how the network encodes several aspects of grammatical structure. Nouns are distinguished by role; subject nouns for all three sentences appear in the upper right portion of the space, and object nouns appear below them. (Principal component 4, not shown here, encodes the distinction between verbs and nouns, collapsing across case.) Verbs are differentiated with regard to their argument structure. *Chases* requires a direct object, *sees* takes an optional direct object, and *walks* precludes an object. The difference is reflected in a systematic displacement in the plane of principal components 1 and 3.

Relative clauses   The presence of relative clauses introduces a complication into the grammar in that the representations of number and verb argument structure must be clause-specific. It would be useful for the network to have some way to represent the constituent structure of sentences. The trained network was given the following sentences.

(10a) boy chases boy.
(10b) boy chases boy who chases boy.
(10c) boy who chases boy chases boy.
(10d) boy chases boy who chases boy who chases boy.

The first sentence is simple; the other three are instances of embedded sentences. Sentence 10a was contained in the training data; sentences 10c, 10d, and 10e were novel and had not been presented to the network during the learning phase.

The trajectories through state space for these four sentences (principal components 1 and 11) are shown in figure 9.21. Panel (a) there shows the basic pattern associated with what is in fact the matrix sentences for all four sentences. Comparison of this figure with panels (b) and (c) shows that the trajectory for the matrix sentence appears to be the same when the matrix subject noun is in the lower left region of state space, the matrix verb appears above it and to the left, and the matrix object noun is near the upper middle region. (Recall that we are looking at only two of the 70 dimensions; along other dimensions the noun–verb distinction this preserved categorically.) The relative clause appears to involve a replication of this basic pattern but is displaced toward the left and moved slightly downward relative to the matrix constituents. Moreover, the exact position of the relative clause elements indicates which of the matrix nouns are modified Thus, the relative clause modifying the subject noun is closer to it, as is the relative clause modifying the object noun. This trajectory pattern was found for all sentences with the same grammatical form; the pattern is thus systematic.

Figure 9.21 shows what happens when there are multiple levels of embedding. Successive embeddings are represented in a manner which is similar to the way that the first embedded clause is distinguished from the main clause; the basic pattern for the clause is replicated in the region of state space, which is displaced from the matrix material. This displacement provides a systematic way for the network to encode the depth of embedding in the current state. However, the reliability of the encoding is limited by the precision with which states are represented, which in turn depends on factors such as the number of hidden units and

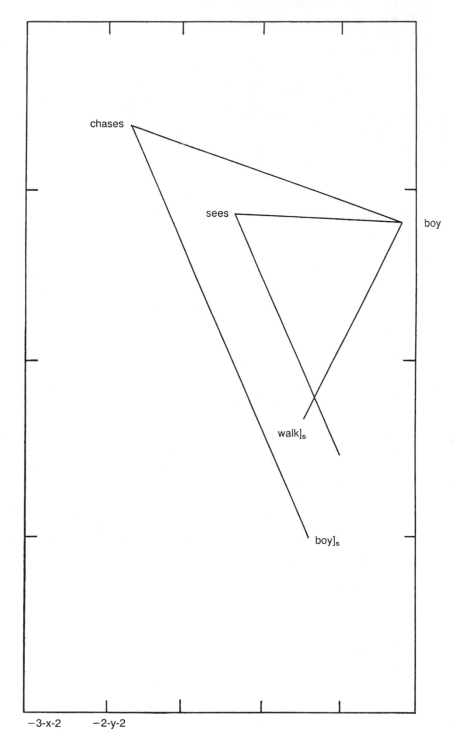

chases

sees

boy

walk]ₛ

boy]ₛ

−3-x-2   −2-y-2

Figure 9.20 Trajectories through state space for sentences (9a), (9b), and (9c). Principal component 1 is plotted along the abscissa; principal component 3 is plotted along the ordinate

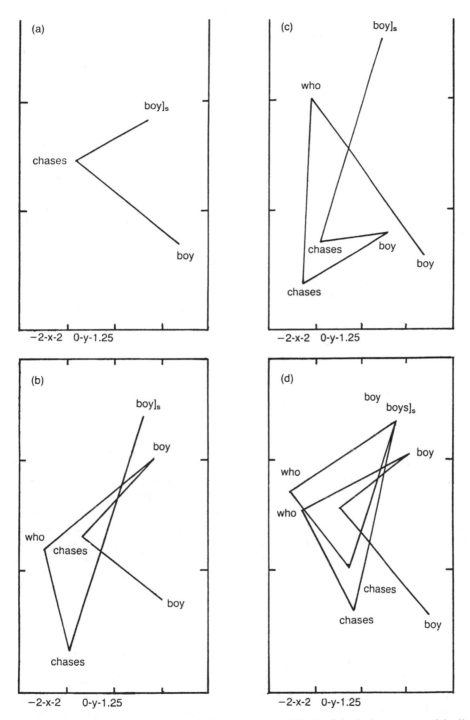

Figure 9.21 Trajectories through state space for sentences (10a–d). Principal component 1 is displayed along the abscissa; principal component 11 is plotted along the ordinate. It is interesting, although not a key point of this paper, that these abstract compositional relations are in fact learned by the network rather than innately specified. I assume that any theory of language must be learnable. How much is learned by individual language learners in their lifetime, and how much is "learned" through evolutionary mechanisms, is an interesting question but orthogonal to the issues currently at hand

the precision of the numerical values. In the current simulation, the representation degraded after about three levels of embedding. The consequences of this degradation on performance (in the prediction task) are different for different types of sentences. Sentences involving centre embedding (e.g., 8c and 8d), in which the level of embedding is crucial for maintaining correct agreement, are more adversely affected than are sentences involving so-called tail recursion (e.g., 10d). In these latter sentences the syntactic structures, in principle, involve recursion, but in practice the level of embedding is not relevant for the task (i.e., does not affect agreement or verb argument structure in any way).

Figure 9.21 is interesting in another respect. Given the nature of the prediction task, it is actually not necessary for the network to carry forward any information from prior clauses. It would be sufficient for the network to represent each successive relative clause as an iteration of the previous pattern. Yet the two relative clauses are differentiated. Similarly, Servan-Schreiber et al. (in press) found that when a simple recurrent network was taught to predict inputs that had been generated by a finite state automaton (FSA), the network developed internal representations which corresponded to the FSA states; however, it also redundantly made finer-grained distinctions which encoded the path by which the state had been achieved, even though this information was not used for the task. It thus seems to be a property of these networks that while they are able to encode state in a way which minimizes context as far as behaviour is concerned, their nonlinear nature allows them to remain sensitive to context at the level of internal representation.

Discussion

I began by asking whether distributed representations could be used to encode grammatical relations, and, in particular, whether they could represent the embedding relaonships in relative clauses. The results of the second simulation are encouraging and suggest that the networks of the sort studied here can support compositional relationships.

At this point it is reasonable to see if we can more precisely understand the nature of the mechanism that is used to represent the part–whole hierarchies. Does the mechanism differ from the traditional approach? If so, are the differences desirable or not? These are difficult questions, and only tentative suggestions can be made at this time. However, two aspects stand out with particular salience. First, the representational apparatus used by these networks has definite limitations. The representations have a finite precision, and they degrade over time (since they are continually recycled and passed through a nonlinear squashing function). Second, the representations are highly context sensitive. Even when contextual information is not needed, there is a tendency for the states of the system to reflect the path that was taken to get there.

The finite precision and tendency to degrade over time are, in fact, consistent with the observed abilities of language users. The representations, while continuously valued (in multidimensional space), have a finite precision. Locations in this space that are sufficiently close will be treated as identical. Furthermore, because these representations are repeatedly cycled arough the nonlinear activation function of the hidden units (which tends to push them toward the centre of representational space), information cannot be heldindefinitely.This limitation accounts for the difficulty the network has in processing centre-embedded sentences compared with right-branching structures; compare (11a) with (11b):

  (11a)   The boy who the girl who the cat sees knows walks.
  (11b)   The boy likes the girl who knows the cat who walks.

Information in the network degrades equally over time in both sentences; but it is only in the centre-embedded sentence that early information is needed in later parts of the sentence; the right-brancing structures can continue indefinitely, because the network does not need to refer back to earlier (lost) information. Note that this is not to say that the network cannot process centre-embedded sentences, only that its ability to do so is limited (and less than for right-branching sentences).

This characteristic of the network – its finite state quality – is interesting in light of Chomsky's (1957) argument against the sufficiency of Finite State Markov processes (or automata) as models for natural language grammar. There were actually two arguments advanced.

The strong argument rested on the observation that natural languages (such as English) contain classes of sentences (such as relative clauses) which permit infinite recursion. Such infinite recursion is beyond the capacity of FSAs. Of course, in reality, sentences do not take advantage of infinite recursion. There are no English sentences which are infinitely long. If one is willing to abitrarily fix an upper limit to the degree of recursion (or sentence length), choosing a limit sufficiently high that all sentences in the history of the language could be generated, then, in fact, it is possible to devise an FSA which could generate this set.

Consideration of this point leads to the second argument against the sufficiency of FSAs as models of natural language. This fallback position is that although the construction of an FSA, given an arbitrary limit on sentence length, would not literally be impossible, it "will be so complex that it will be of little use or interest" (Chomsky 1957: 23). An example of such a grammar would be a list of the sentences of the language. "In general, the assumption that languages are infinite is made in order to simplify the description of the language. If a grammar does not have recursive devices it will be prohibitively complex. If it does have recursive devices of some sort, it will produce infinitively many sentences" (ibid.: 24–5). Savitch (in press) has made a similar point and argued that there are classes of languages which are more perspicuously treated as "essentially infinite," even though they may have a finite number of sentences.

This second argument is, technically, the weaker of the two, since it depends on ill-defined and controversial notions of simplicity. But the intuitive appeal of this position should nonetheless be clear. Leaving aside the definition or even desirability of simplicity as a goal, I take it as at least desirable that grammars should provide insight into languages. Chomsky's claim was that FSAs – as understood at that time – cannot in principle offer such insight. The current work provides an example of a machine which is a finite state device, yet which may well satisfy the desideratum for a mechanism whose form explicates the systematic properties of the language it produces. The machine is not literally recursive, both because of limited depth and, more importantly, because of leakage across levels (see below); but it allows structures to be combined hierarchically in what could be called (following Savitch's terminology) an "essentially recursive" manner.

Let us now turn to the second way in which the networks appear to differ from conventional devices. This second characteristic may represent a more significant departure from the traditional approach. As noted earlier, Servan-Schreiber et al. (in press) found that, although their task only required that the network encode information in terms of a finite number of discrete states (in order to act like an FSA), the representations reflected the path information as well.

A similar effect can be found in the networks studied here. For example, the language learned by these networks contained classes of sentences such as (12):

(12)   {boy, girl cat, dog, John, Mary} chases . . .

In this language, there were no meaningful consequences attendant upon the choice of subject; in fact the state of the network when it receives the verb *chases* is different from what it is as a function of the subject. The difference is systematic across verbs. The subject *Mary*, for example, perturbs the state of the network when it processes *chases* in a way that affects the representation of other verbs. In other words, the precise representation of the verb reflects not only properties of the verb but who the subject is as well.

At first, this seems odd, and it is certainly at variance with the classical approach to compositionality. In classical theories, complex representations are constructed following a building-block metaphor. Each element is positioned in a larger structure and functions like a building block; that is to say, elements are not affected by their position nor do they interact in any way. The mechanism here, on the other hand, is highly interactive. Representational elements are subject to subtle adjustments as they combine. The resulting structure is not just the sum of the parts; it reflects interactions between those parts as well.

This sort of context sensitivity appears to be very similar to the notion of *accommodation*, as developed by Langacker (1987), for cognitive grammar. Because this view of how composition works differs significantly from generative accounts, it is worth citing Langacker's comments at length.

> It must be emphasized that syntagmatic combination involves more than the simple addition of components. A composite structure is an integrated system formed by coordinating its components in a specific, often elaborate manner. In fact, it often has properties that go beyond what one might expect from its components alone. Two brief observations should make it clear why this is so. First, composite structures originate as targets in specific usage events. As such they are often characterized relative to particular context with properties not predictable from the specifications of their components as manifested in other environments. A related point is that one component may need to be adjusted in certain details when integrated with another to form a composite structure; I refer to this as accommodation. For example, the meaning of *run* as applied to humans must be adjusted in certain respects when extended to four-legged animals such as horses, dogs, and cats (since the bodily motion observed in two-legged running is not identical to that in four-legged running); in a technical sense, this extension creates a new semantic variant of the lexical item. (Langacker 1987: 76–7)

It is true that current work does not take advantage of the network's propensity to combine elements in a highly context-sensitive manner; but it should not be difficult to imagine ways in which it could. If anything, the emergence of this property, despite not being utilized by the task that is taught, illustrates that it is central to the mechanism. This sensitivity to context also occurs across levels of organization. Not only may the verb in the main clause be represented in a manner which reflects the main clause subject, but embedded material may also be colored by elements in other clauses. Thus, the representation of hierarchical structure does not use "true" recursion, in which information at each level of processing is encapsulated and unaffected by information at other levels.

Again, one can ask whether this is good or bad. Certainly, there are many situations in which one wants the informational encapsulation afforded by true recursion. Many programming languages, for instance, depend crucially on the assumption that a procedure may be re-entered without contamination from earlier invocations. But, for natural language, I think a strong argument can be made for the desirability of what I will call the "leaky recursion" provided by simple recurrent networks.

The implicit claim of strict recursion – or more generally of a machine which uses a stack mechanism to construct hierarchically organized structures – is that, normally, information at different levels of a complex structure should be processed autonomously, and that there will be minimal interaction with information at other levels. But this is rarely the case for linguistic structures. Relative clauses, for instance, typically have an elaborative function; they provide information about a head noun phrase (which is at a higher level of organization). Adverbial clauses perform a similar function for main clause verbs. In general subordination involves *conceptual dependence* between clauses (Langacker in press: ch. 10). Thus, it may be more important that a language-processing mechanism facilitate interactions across levels of organization rather than impede the flow of information.

As one extreme example, consider the case of long-distance dependency relations. These are cases where one element in a sentence is in some way dependant on another element in the sentence, but the two are separated in linear order and also, possibly, across different levels of organization. Information which in some sense coheres is broken; and the problem for the listener, presumably, is to recognize the dependency in spite of the (apparent) dislocation.

(12a)   Who does Jeremy suspect Emily wanted me to invite to the party?
(12b)   It's the one on the left I want.
(12c)   I saw the car that Mary said a thief had broken into.
(12d)   Under which toadstool did you say there's a pot of gold?

In (12a) *who* refers to the person whom Emily invited to the party; in the clefted sentence (12b), the object phrase occurs at the beginning of the sentence; in (12c) the head of the relative clause (*car*) is also the object of the verb at the end of the sentence; and in (12d), the prepositional phrase has been topicalized and thus appears at the beginning of the sentence. In many cases the dependency has a morphological reflex; thus in (12a) the form of the interrogative pronoun is determined by the fact that it is a person and not a thing, animal, concept, etc., that can be invited to a party. In some dialects, the pronoun would, additionally, be marked in the accusative.

The dependency may range over a considerable distance and may span multiple levels of organization. This raises an interesting and difficult problem for a system which utilizes a stack device to construct complex hierarchies, as do (at least implicitly) generative grammars. Stacks have an important limitation: Information is stored in them by pushing the current contents "down" one level (like a stack of dishes) and storing new information on top; and information on the top may be pulled off, causing the contents below to pop up. In other implementations, information may be pulled off the bottom, according to the principle of "first-in-first-out." In either event, information in the middle (or at the wrong end) must percolate up or drip down one level at a time.

This limitation has curious consequences when one wants to account for long-distance dependencies of the sort illustrated in (12). As we have seen, the form of the pronoun is determined by information which occurs in a subordinate clause (two levels down). But in a stack, information is not normally available across levels. The implementation of this restriction in generative linguistics is subjacency, which constrains movement of constituents, as shown in (13) (Chomsky, 1973). A constituent in position Y may not move to position X, where X and Y are separated by more than one nesting level, as defined by a bounding node. (What constitutes a bounding node is a matter of some dispute.)

(13)   Constraint on subjacency:

$$\ldots X \ldots [\alpha \ldots [\beta \ldots Y \ldots \beta] \ldots \alpha] \ldots X \ldots$$

where $\alpha, \beta = [\bar{S} \text{ or NP}]$

The solution that is proposed to this dilemma is quite clever. Let us suppose that one has a sentence such as (14).

(14)   Who do you think the fans believe the umpire should fine?

We might imagine that this sentence has the structural configuration shown in figure 9.22, and that *who* originates in the position it would have as direct object of the verb *fine*. Then we can account for the fact that it has the form appropriate to its grammatical usage. We derive the question by percolating the interrogative pronoun up successive layers of the hierarchy (i.e., letting it move up the stack) one level at a time.

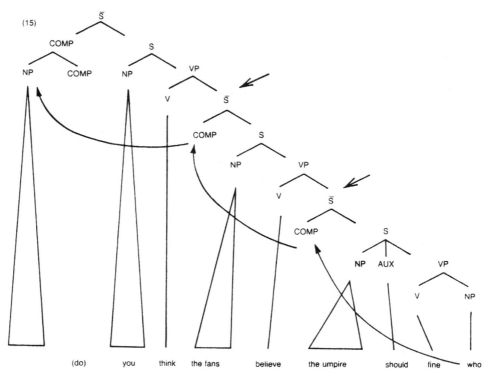

Figure 9.22

Such analyses, in which constituents are moved around in the course of deriving a sentence, are common in many generative theories. Although this notion of deriving a sentence through (among other things) moving constituents around may strike us as contrived and unnatural, we can see that it is entirely consistent with – indeed, is strongly encouraged by – the stack machine which implicitly underlies much of generative linguistic theory.

In contrast, the network architecture described here uses a representational mechanism in which there is no movement of constituents. There is no notion of derivation of sentences through intermediate forms. Still, sentences may have a hierarchical structure, and there may be long-distance dependencies between distal elements in a sentence. Recall, for example, that the simulation reported here involved relative clauses, in which there is a long-distance conceptual dependency between the head noun and the embedded clause. The network learned this dependency, with the consequence that its expectations regarding noun/verb number agreement and location of arguments were correct (see figure 9.17). But there is no movement of elements.

The key to the network's ability to encode a conceptual dependence between hierarchically disjoint elements is actually quite simple, but gets to the heart of the difference between the state representation of hierarchy and the stack representation. As we have already seen, information in a stack is encapsulated. In the state representation, on the other hand, all of the information about hierarchical structure is contained in a state vector (realized here as the context layer). This state vector is *entirely visible to the processor*. Thus, all the information is available simultaneously. (Simplistically, one can think of the state representation as a bit like what one would have if one took a traditional stack, replaced the walls with transparent material, and turned the entire device on its side; the result would be a kind of horizontal glass stack. This metaphor is not entirely accurate, since the state representation encodes information along many dimensions simultaneously; and the state representation facilitates interactions between dimensions in a way which is not conveyed by the image of the horizontal glass stack. But it conveys the idea that information from all levels of processing is available.) Because the information is visible in this manner, there is no need to move constituents around. They may all jointly participate in shaping the interpretation of the sentence.

I take this property to constitute perhaps the most striking difference from traditional language-processing mechanisms. It suggests a conception of composition which emphasizes integration and interaction. These are, I believe, desirable traits for a language processor; they are also highly compatible with the theory of language that has been developed by Langacker (1988).

It is obvious that the current work raises many questions. For example, although the state vectors contain information that spans hierarchical structure (while respecting it), the relative accessibility of this information remains to be determined. The fact that the entire state is visible to the processing mechanism does not mean that all information is equally available. There are known constraints on what information can be coordinated in natural language; thus, certain grammatical forms seem to impede or block access to information (e.g., the infelicity of *Who do you like the fact that she said no to?*). A project is currently directed toward trying to understand whether the state representations developed in simple recurrent networks have consequences for processing which might explain such facts.

While much work remains to be done, the current work is encouraging. The networks studied here have properties which seem to be genuinely different from those of traditional processing mechanisms but which are very plausible for the processing of natural languages.

NOTE

I am grateful for many useful discussions on this topic with Jay McClelland, Dave Rumelhart, Ron Langacker, Elizabeth Bates, Steve Stich, and members of the UCSD PDP/NLP Research Group. This research was supported by contracts N0001485K0076 from the Office of Naval Research and contract DAAB0787CH027 from Army Avionics, Ft Monmouth. Requests for reprints should be sent to the Center for Research in Language, 0126; University of California, San Diego; La Jolla, CA 92093-0126. The author can be reached via electronic mail at elman@amos.ucsd.edu.

REFERENCES

Bates, E. and MacWhinney, B. (1982). Functionalist approaches to grammar. In E. Wanner and L. Gleitman (eds), *Language Acquisition: The State of the Art*. New York: Cambridge University Press.

Chafe, W. (1970). *Meaning and the Structure of Language*. Chicago: University of Chicago Press.

Chomsky, N. (1957). *Syntactic Structures*. The Hague: Mouton.

Chomsky, N. (1973). Conditions on transformations. In S. R. Anderson and P. Kiparsky (eds), *A Festschrift for Morris Halle*. New York: Holt, Rinehart and Winston.

Dolan, C. and Dyer, M. G. (1987). Symbolic schemata in connectionist memories: role binding and the evolution of structure. Technical Report UCLAAI8711. Artificial Intelligence Laboratory, University of California, Los Angeles.

Dolan, C. and Smolensky, P. (1988). Implementing a connectionist production system using tensor products. Technical Report UCLAAI8815. Artificial Intelligence Laboratory, University of California, Los Angeles.

Elman, J. L. (1989). *Representation and Structure in Connectionist Systems*. CRL Technical Report. Center for Research in Language, University of California, San Diego.

Elman, J. L. (in press). Finding structure in time. *Cognitive Science* [14 (1990): 179–211].

Fauconnier, G. (1985). *Mental Spaces*. Cambridge, MA: MIT Press.

Feldman, J. A. and Ballard, D. H. (1982). Connectionist models and their proper ties. *Cognitive Science* 6: 205–54.

Fillmore, C. J. (1982). Frame semantics. In *Linguistics in the Morning Calm*. Seoul: Hansin.

Fodor, J. (1976). *The Language of Thought*. Brighton: Harvester Press.

Fodor, J. and Pylyshyn, Z. (1988). Connectionism and cognitive architecture: a critical analysis. In S. Pinker and J. Mehler (eds), *Connections and Symbols*. Cambridge, MA: MIT Press.

Forster, K.I. (1979). Levels of processing and the structure of the language processor. In W. E. Cooper and E. Walker (eds), *Sentence Processing: Psycholinguistic Studies Presented to Merrill Garrett*. Hilldale, NJ: Lawrence Erlbaum.

Givon, T. (1984). *Syntax: A Functional-Typological Introduction*. Amsterdam: Benjamins.

Grosjean, F. (1980). Spoken word recognition processes and the gating paradigm. *Perception and Psychophysics* 28: 267–83.

Hanson, S. J. and Burr, D. J. (1987). Knowledge representation in connectionist networks. Morristown, NJ: Bell Communications Research.

Hare, M., Corina, D., and Cottrell, G. (1988). Connectionist perspective on prosodic structure. CRL Newsletter 3:2. Center for Research in Language, University of California, San Diego.

Hinton, G. E. (1988). Representing part–whole hierarchies in connectionist networks. Technical Report CRGTR882, Connectionist Research Group, University of Toronto.

Hinton, G. E., McClelland, J. L., and Rumelhart, D. E. (1986). Distributed representations. In D. E. Rumelhart and J. L. McClelland (eds), *Parallel Distributed Processing: Explorations in the Microstructure of Cognition 1*. Cambridge, MA: MIT Press.

Hopper, P. J. and Thompson, S. A. (1980). Transitivity in grammar and discourse. *Language* 56: 251–99.

Hornik, K., Stinchcombe, M., and White, H. (in press). Multilayer feedforward networks are universal approximators. *Neural Networks*.

Jordan, M. I. (1986). Serial order: a parallel distributed processing approach. Institute for Cognitive Science Report 8604. University of California, San Diego.

Kawamoto, A. H. (1988). Distributed representations of ambiguous words and their resolution in a connectionist network. In S. L. Small, G. W. Cottrell, and M. K. Tanenhaus (eds), *Lexical Ambiguity Resolution: Perspectives from Psycholinguistics, Neuropsychology, and Artificial Intelligence*. San Mateo, CA: Morgan Kaufmann.

Kuno, S. (1987). *Functional Syntax: Anaphora, Discourse and Empathy*. Chicago: University of Chicago Press.

Lakoff, G. (1987). *Women, Fire, and Dangerous Things: What Categories Reveal about the Mind*. Chicago: University of Chicago Press

Langacker, R. W. (1987). *Foundations of Cognitive Grammar: Theoretical Perspectives*. Vol. 1. Stanford: Stanford University Press.

Langacker, R. W. (1988). A usage-based model. *Current Issues in Linguistic Theory* 50: 127–61.

Langacker, R. W. (in press). *Concept, Image, and Symbol: The Cognitive Basis of Grammar*. [New York: De Gruyter, 1990.]

Marslen-Wilson, W. and Tyler, L. K. (1980). The temporal structure of spoken language understanding. *Cognition* 8: 1–71.

McClelland, J. L. (1987). The case for interactionism in language processing. In M. Coltheart (ed.), *Attention and Performance XII: The Psychology of Reading*. London: Lawrence Erlbaum.

McClelland, J. L., Rumelhart, D. E., and Hinton, G. E. (1986). The appeal of parallel distributed processing. In D. E. Rumelhart and J. L. McClelland (eds), *Parallel Distributed Processing: Explorations in the Microstructure of Cognition 1*. Cambridge, MA: MIT Press.

McClelland, J. L., St John, M., and Taraban, R. (1989). Sentence comprehension: a parallel distributed processing approach. Manuscript. Department of Psychology, Carnegie – Mellon University.

McMillan, C. and Smolensky, P. (1988). Analyzing a connectionist model as a system of soft rules. Technical Report CUC530388. Department of Computer Science, University of Colorado, Boulder.

Mozer, M. (1988). A focused back-propagation algorithm for temporal pattern recognition. Technical Report CRGTR883. Departments of Psychology and Computer Science, University of Toronto.

Mozer, M. C. and Smolensky, P. (1989). Skeletonization: a technique for trimming the fat from a network via relevance assessment. Technical Report CUCS42189. Department of Computer Science, University of Colorado, Boulder.

Oden, G. (1978). Semantic constraints and judged preference for interpretations of ambiguous sentences. *Memory and Cognition* 6: 26–37.

Pollack, J. B. (1988). Recursive autoassociative memory: vevising compositional distributed representations. *Proceedings of the Tenth Annual Conference of the Cognitive Science Society*. Hillsdale, NJ: Lawrence Erlbaum.

Ramsey, W. (1989). The philosophical implications of connectionism. PhD thesis. University of California, San Diego.

Rumehart, D. E. and McClelland, J. L. (1986). On learning the past tenses of English verbs. In D. E. Rumelhart and J. L. McClelland (eds), *Parallel Distributed Processing: Explorations in the Microstructure of Cognition 1*. Cambridge, MA: MIT Press [reproduced as part of ch. 9 in this volume].

Rumelhart, D. E., Hinton, G. E., and Williams, R. J. (1986). Learning internal representations by error propagation. In D. E. Rumelhart and J. L. McClelland (eds), *Parallel Distributed Processing: Explorations in the Microstructure of Cognition 1*. Cambridge, MA: MIT Press.

Salasoo, A. and Pisoni, D. B. (1985). Interaction of knowledge sources in spoken word identification. *Journal of Memory and Language* 24: 210–31.

Sanger, D. (1989). Contribution analysis: a technique for assigning responsibilities to hidden units in connectionist networks. Technical Report CUC543589. Department of Computer Science, University of Colorado, Boulder.

Savitch, W. J. (in press). Infinity is in the eye of the beholder. In C. Georgopoulous and R. Ishihara (eds), *Interdisciplinary Approaches to Language: Essays in Honor of S. Y. Kuroda*. Dordrecht: Kluwer Academic.

Sejnowski, T. J. and Rosenberg, C. R. (1987). Parallel networks that learn to pronounce English text. *Complex Systems* 1: 145–68.

Servan-Schreiber, D., Cleeremans, A., and McClelland, J. L. (1988). Encoding sequential structure in simple recurrent networks. Technical Report CMUCS88183. Computer Science Department, Carnegie – Mellon University.

Servan-Schreiber, D., Cleeremans, A., and McClelland, J. L. (in press). Graded state machines: the representation of temporal contingencies in simple recurrent networks. *Machine Learning* [7 (1991): 161–94].

Shastri, L. and Ajjanagadde, V. (1989). A connectionist system for rule based reasoning with multiplace predicates and variables. Technical Report MSCIS8905. Computer and Information Science Department, University of Pennsylvania.

Smolensky, P. (1987a). On variable binding and the representation of symbolic structures in connectionist systems. Technical Report CUCS35587. Department of Computer Science, University of Colorado, Boulder.

Smolensky, P. (1987b). On the proper treatment of connectionism. Technical Report CUCS37787. Department of Computer Science, University of Colorado, Boulder.

St John, M. and McClelland, J. L. (in press). Learning and applying contextual constraints in sentence comprehension. Technical Report. Department of Psychology, Carnegie–Mellon University.

van Gelder, T. (in press). Compositionality: a connectionist variation on a classical theme. *Cognitive Science* [14 (1990): 355–84].

Rules of Language

STEVEN PINKER

Language and cognition have been explained as the products of a homogeneous associative memory structure or, alternatively, of a set of genetically determined computational modules in which rules manipulate symbolic representations. Intensive study of one phenomenon of English grammar and how it is processed and acquired suggests that both theories are partly right. Regular verbs (*walk–walked*) are computed by a suffixation rule in a neural system for grammatical processing; irregular verbs (*run–ran*) are retrieved from an associative memory.

Every normal human can convey and receive an unlimited number of discrete messages through a highly structured stream of sound or, in the case of signed languages, manual gestures. This remarkable piece of natural engineering depends upon a complex code or grammar implemented in the brain that is deployed without conscious effort and that develops, without explicit training, by the age of four. Explaining this talent is an important goal of the human sciences.

Theories of language and other cognitive processes generally fall into two classes. Associationism describes the brain as a homogeneous network of interconnected units modified by a learning mechanism that records correlations among frequently co–occurring input patterns.[1] (Hume, 1955; Hebb, 1949; Rumelhart and McClelland, 1986). Rule-and-representation theories describe the brain as a computational device in which rules and principles operate on symbolic data structures (Leibniz, 1989; Newell and Simon, 1961; Fodor, 1983). Some rule theories further propose that the brain is divided into modular computational systems that have an organization that is largely specified genetically, one of the systems being language (Fodor, 1983; Chomsky, 1980; Lenneberg, 1967).

During the last 35 years, there has been an unprecedented empirical study of human language structure, acquisition, use, and breakdown, allowing these centuries-old proposals to be refined and tested. I will illustrate how intensive multidisciplinary study of one linguistic phenomenon shows that both associationism and rule theories are partly correct, but about different components of the language system

Modules of Language

A grammar defines a mapping between sounds and meanings, but the mapping is done not in a single step but through a chain of intermediate data structures, each governed by a subsystem. Morphology is the subsystem that computes the forms of words. I focus on a single process of morphology: English past tense inflection in which the physical shape of the verb varies to encode the relative time of occurrence of the referent event and the speech act. Regular past tenses marking (for example, *walk–walked*) is a rulelike process resulting in addition of the suffix *−d*. In addition there are about 180 irregular verbs that mark the past tense in other ways (for example, *hit–hit, come–came, feel–felt*).

Past tense inflection is an isolable subsystem in which grammatical mechanisms can be studied in detail, without complex interactions with the rest of language. It is computed independently of syntax, the subsystem that defines the form of phrases and sentences: The syntax of English forces its speakers to mark tense in every sentence, but no aspect of syntax works differently with regular and irregular verbs. Past tense marking is also insensitive to lexical semantics (Pinker and Prince, 1988; Kim et al., 1991): the regular–irregular distinction does not correlate with any feature of verb meaning. For example, *hit–hit, strike–struck*, and *slap–slapped* have similar meanings, but three different past tense forms; *stand–stood, stand me up–stood me up*, and *understand understood*, have unrelated meanings but identical past tense forms. Past marking is also independent of phonology, which determines the possible sound sequences in a language: the three pronunciations of the regular suffix (in *ripped, ribbed*, and *ridded*) represent not three independent processes but a single suffix *−d* modified to conform with general laws of English sound patterning (Pinker and Prince, 1988).

Rulelike Processes in Language

English inflection can illustrate the major kinds of theory used to explain linguistic processes. Traditional grammar offers the following first approximation: Regular inflection, being fully predictable, is computed by a rule that concatenates the affix *−d* to the verb stem. This allows a speaker to inflect an unlimited number of new verbs, an ability seen both in adults, who easily create past forms for neologisms like *faxed*, and in pre-schoolers, who, given a novel verb like *to rick* in experiments, freely produced *ricked* (Berko, 1958). In contrast, irregular verb forms are unpredictable: compare *sit–sat* and *hit–hit, sing–sang* and *string–strung, feel–felt* and *tell–told*. Therefore they must be individually memorized. Retrieval of an irregular form from memory ordinarily blocks application of the regular rule, although in children retrieval occasionally fails, yielding "overregularization" errors like *breaked* (Kuczaj, 1977; Bybee and slobin, 1982; Marcus et al., 1990).

The rule–rote theory, although appealingly straightforward, is inadequate. Rote memory, if thought of as a list of slots, is designed for the very rare verbs with unrelated past tense forms, like *be–was* and *go–went*. But for all other irregular verbs, the phonological content of the stem is largely preserved in the past form, as in *swing–swung* (Pinker and Prince 1988; Chomsky and Halle, 1990). Moreover, a given irregular pattern such as a vowel change is typically seen in a family of phonetically similar items, such as *sing–sang, ring–rang, spring–sprang, shrink–shrank*, and *swim–swam*, or *grow–grew, blow–blew, throw–threw*, and *fly–flew* (Pinker and Prince, 1988; Bybee and Slobin, 1982; Chomsky and Halle, 1990). The rote theory cannot explain why verbs with irregular past forms come in similarity families, rather than belonging to arbitrary lists. Finally, irregular pairs are psychologically not a closed list, but their patterns can sometimes be extended to new forms on the basis of similarity to existing forms. All children occasionally use forms such as *bring–brang* and *bite–bote* (Pinker and Price, 1988; Bybee and Slobin, 1982). A few irregular past forms have entered the language historically under the influence of existing forms. *Quit, cost, catch* are from French, and *fling, sling, stick* have joined irregular clusters in the last few hundred years (Jesparson, 1961); such effects are obvious when dialects are compared (for example, *help–holp, rise–riz, drag–drug, climb–clome*; Mencken, 1936). Such analogizing can be demonstrated in the laboratory: faced with inflecting nonsense verbs like *spling*, many adults produce *splung* (Kim et al., 1991; Berko, 1958; Bybee and Modor, 1983; Prasada and Priker unpublished)

The partial systematicity of irregular verbs has been handled in opposite ways by modern rule and associationist theories. One version of the theory of generative phonology (Chomsky and Halle, 1990) posits rules for irregular verbs (for example, change *i* to *a*) as well as for regular ones. The theory is designed to explain the similarity between verb stems and their past tense forms: If the rule just changes a specified segment, the rest of the stem comes through in the output untouched by default, just as in the fully regular case. But the rule theory does not address the similarity among different verbs in the input set and people's tendency to generalize irregular patterns. If an irregular rule is restricted to apply to a list of words, the similarity among the words in the list is unexplained. But if a common pattern shared by the words is identified and the rule is restricted to apply to all and only the verbs displaying that pattern (for example, change *i* to *a* when it appears after a consonant cluster and precedes *ng*), the rule fails because the similarity to be accounted for is one of family resemblance rather than necessary or sufficient conditions (Pinker and Prince, 1988; Bybee and Slobin, 1982; Bybee and Modor, 1983; Bybee, 1985): Such a rule, while successfully applying to *spring, shrink, drink*, would incorrectly apply to *bring–brought* and *fling–flung* and would fail to apply to *begin–began* and *swim–swam*, where it should apply.

Associationist theories also propose that regular and irregular patterns are computed by a single mechanism, but here the mechanism is an associative memory. A formal implementation in neural net terms is the "connectionist" model of Rumelhart and McClelland (1986), which consists of an array of input units, an array of output units, and a matrix of modifiable weighted links between every input and every output. None of the elements or links corresponds exactly to a word or rule. The stem is represented by turning on a subset of input nodes, each corresponding to a sound pattern in the stem. This sends a signal across each of the links to the output nodes, which represent the sounds of the past tense form. Each output node sums its incoming signals and turns on if the sum exceeds a threshold; the output form is the word most compatible with the set of active output nodes. During the learning phase, the past tense form computed by the network is juxtaposed with the correct version provided by a "teacher", and the strengths of the links and thresholds are adjusted so as to reduce the difference. By recording and superimposing associations between stem sounds and past sounds, the model improves its performance and can generalize to new forms to the extent that their sounds overlap with old ones. This process is qualitatively the same for regular and irregular verbs: *stopped* is produced because input *op* units were linked to output *opped* units by previous verbs; *clung* is produced because *ing* was linked to *ung*. As a result such models can imitate people's analogizing of irregular patterns to new forms.

The models, however, are inadequate in other ways (Pinker and Prince, 1988; Lachter and Bever, 1988).[1] The precise patterns of inflectional mappings in the world's languages are unaccounted for: The network can learn input–output mappings found in no human language, such as mirror-reversing the order of segments, and cannot learn mappings that are common, such as reduplicating the stem. The actual outputs are often unsystematic blends such as *mail–membled* and *tour–tourder*. Lacking a representation of words as lexical entries, distinct from their phonological or semantic content, the model cannot explain how languages can contain semantically unrelated homophones with different past tense forms such as *lie–lied* (prevaricate) and *lie–lay* (recline), *ring–rang* and *wring–wrung*, *meet–met* and *mete–meted*.

These problems call for a theory of language with both a computational component, containing specific kinds of rule and representation, and an associative memory system, with certain properties of connectionist models (Pinker and Prince, 1988; Kicm et al., 1991; Marcus et al., 1990). In such a theory, regular past tense forms are computed by a rule that concatenates an affix with a variable standing for the stem. Irregulars are memorized pairs of words, but the linkages between the pair members are stored in an associative memory structure fostering some generalization by analogy (Bybee and Slobin, 1982; Bybee and Modor, 1983; Bybee, 1985): although *string* and *strung* are represented as separate linked words, the mental representation of the pair overlaps in part with similar forms like *sling* and *bring*, so that the learning of *slung* is easier and extensions like *brung* can occur as the result of noise or decay in the parts of the representation that code the identity of the lexical entry.

Because it categorically distinguishes regular from irregular forms, the rule-association hybrid predicts that the two processes should be dissociable from virtually every point of view. With respect to the psychology of language use, irregular forms, as memorized items, should be strongly affected by properties of associative memory such as frequency and similarity, whereas regular forms should not. With respect to language structure, irregular forms, as memory-listed words, should be available as the input to other word-formation processes, whereas regular forms, being the final outputs of such processes, should not. With respect to implementation in the brain, because regular and irregular verbs are subserved by different mechanisms, it should be possible to find one system impaired while the other is spared. The predictions can be tested with methods ranging from reaction-time experiments to the grammatical analysis of languages to the study of child development to the investigation of brain damage and genetic deficits.

Language Use and Associative Laws

Frequency

If irregular verbs are memorized items, they should be better remembered the more they are encountered. Indeed, children make errors like *breaked* more often for verbs their parents use in the past tense forms less frequently (Bybee and Slobin, 1982; Marcus et al., 1990).[2] To adults, low-frequency irregular past tense forms like *smote*, *bade*, *slew*, and *strode* sound odd or stilted and often coexist with regularized counterparts such as *slayed* and *strided* (Pinker and Prince, 1988; Bybee, 1985; Ullman and Pinker, 1991).[3] As these psychological effects accumulate over generations, they shape the language. Old English had many more irregular verbs than Modern English, such as *abide–abode, chide–chid, gild–gilt*; the ones used with lower frequencies have become regular over the centuries (Bybee, 1985). Most surviving irregular verbs are used at high frequencies, and the 13 most frequent verbs in English – *be, have, do, say, make, go, take, come, see, get, know, give, find* – are au irregular (Francis and Kucera, 1982).

Although any theory positing a frequency-sensitive memory can account for frequency effects on irregular verbs (with inverse effects on their corresponding regularized versions; Ullman and Pinker, 1991), the rule – associative-memory hybrid model predicts that regular inflection is different. If regular past tense forms can be computed on-line by concatenation of symbols for the stem and affix, they do not require prior storage of a past tense entry and thus need not be harder or stranger for low-frequency verbs than higher ones.[4]

Judgments by native English speakers of the naturalness of word forms bear this prediction out. Unlike irregular verbs, novel or low-frequency regular verbs, although they may sound unfamiliar in themselves, do not accrue any increment of oddness or uncertainty when put in the past tense: *infarcted* is as natural a past tense form of *infarct* as *walked* is of *walk* (Pinker and Prince, 1988). The contrast can be seen clearly in idioms and clichés, because they can contain a verb that is not unfamiliar itself but that appears in the idiom exclusively in the present or infinitive form. Irregular verbs in such idioms can sound strange when put in the past tense: Compare *You'll excuse me if I forgo the pleasure of reading your paper before it's published* with *Last night I forwent the pleasure of reading student papers*, or *I don't know how she can bear the guy* with *I don't know how she bore the guy*. In contrast, regular verbs in nonpast idioms do not sound worse when put in the past: compare *She doesn't suffer fools gladly* with *None of them ever suffered fools gladly*. Similarly, some regular verbs like *afford* and *cope* usually appear with *can't*, which requires the stem form, and hence have common stems but very low-frequency past tense forms (Francis and Kucera, 1982). But the uncommon *I don't know how he afforded it (coped)* does not sound worse than *He can't afford it (cope)*.

These effects can be demonstrated in quantitative studies (Ullman and Prinker, 1991): Subject's ratings of regular past tense forms of different verbs correlate significantly with their ratings of the corresponding stems ($r = 0.62$) but not with the frequency of the past form (-0.14, partialing out stem rating). In contrast, ratings of irregular past tense forms correlate less strongly with their stem ratings (0.32), and significantly with past frequency (0.29, partialing out stem rating).

Experiments on how people produce and comprehend inflected forms in real time confirm this difference. When subjects see verb stems on a screen and must utter the past form as quickly as possible, they take significantly less time (16–29-msec difference) for irregular verbs with high past frequencies than irregular verbs with low past frequencies (stem frequencies equated), but show no such difference for regular verbs (<2-msec difference; Prasaola et al., 1990).[5] When recognizing words, people are aided by having seen the word previously on an earlier trial in the experiment; their mental representation of the word has been "primed" by the first presentation. Presenting a regular past tense form speeds up subsequent recognition of the stem no less than presenting the stem itself (181- versus 166-msec reduction), suggesting that people store and prime only the stem and analyze a regular inflected form as a stem plus a suffix. In contrast, prior presentation of an irregular form is significantly less effective at priming its stem than presentation of the stem itself (39- versus 99-msec reduction), suggesting that the two are stored as separate but linked items (Stanners et al., 1982).[6]

Similarity

Irregular verbs fall into families with similar stems and similar past tense forms, partly because the associative nature of memory makes it easier to memorize verbs in such families. Indeed, children make fewer overregularization errors for verbs that fall into families with more numerous and higher-frequency members (Pinker and Prince, 1988; Kuczaj, 1977; Bybee and Slobin, 1982; Marcus et al., 1990).[7] As mentioned above, speakers occasionally extend irregular patterns to verbs that are highly similar to irregular families (*brang*), and such extensions are seen in dialects (Mencker, 1936). A continuous effect of similarity has been measured experimentally: subjects frequently (44 percent) convert *spling* to *splung* (based on *string, sling*, etc.), less often (24 percent) convert *shink* to *shunk*, and rarely (7 percent) convert *sid* to *sud* (Bybee and Modor, 1983).

The rule–associative-memory theory predicts that the ability to generate regular past tense forms should not depend on similarity to existing regular verbs: The regular rule applies as a default, treating all nonirregular stems as equally valid instantiations of the mental symbol verb. Within English vocabulary, we find that a regular "verb" can have any sound pattern, rather than falling into similarity clusters that complement the irregulars (Pinker and Prince, 1988): for example, need–needed coexists with *bleed–bled* and *feed–fed*, *blink–blinked* with *shrink–shrank* and *drink–drank*. Regular – irregular homophones such as *lie–lay; lie–lied, meet–met; mete–meted*, and *hang–hung; hang–hanged* are the clearest examples. Moreover verbs with highly unusual sounds are easily provided with regular pasts. Although no English verb ends in −*ev* or a neutral vowel (Francis and Kueera, 1982), novel verbs with these patterns are readily inflectable as natural past tense forms, such as *Yeltsin out-Gorbachev'ed Gorbachev* or *We rhumba'd all night*. Children are no more likely to overregularize an irregular verb if it resembles a family of similar regular verbs than if it is dissimilar from regulars, suggesting that regulars, unlike irregulars, do not form attracting clusters in memory (Marcus et al., 1990; and see n. 7). Adults, when provided with novel verbs, do not rate regular past forms of unusual sounds like *ploamphed* as any worse, relative to the stem, than familiar sounds like *plipped* (similar to *clip, flip, slip*, etc.), unlike their ratings for irregulars (Prasado and Pinker, unpublished).[8] In contrast, in associationist models both irregular and regular generalizations tend to be sensitive to similarity. For example the Rumelhart – McClelland model could not produce any output for many novel regular verbs that did not resemble other regulars in the training set (Pinker and Prince, 1988; Prasada and Pinker, unpublished; Lachter and Bever, 1988).

Organization of Grammatical Processes

Grammars divide into fairly autonomous submodules in which blocks of rules produce outputs that serve (or cannot serve) as the input for other blocks of rules. Linguistic research suggests an information flow of lexicon to derivational morphology (complex word formation) to regular inflection with regular and irregular processes encapsulated within different subcomponents (Aronoff, 1983; Andersen, 1988; Kiparsky, 1982). If irregular past tense forms are stored in memory as entries in the mental lexicon, then like other stored words they should be the input to rules of complex word formation. If regular past tense forms are computed from words by a rule acting as a default, they should be formed from the outputs of complex word formation rules. Two phenomena illustrate this organization.

A potent demonstration of the earlier point that regular processes can apply to any sound whatsoever, no matter how tightly associated with an irregular pattern, is "regularization-through-derivation": verbs intuitively perceived as derived from nouns or adjectives are always regular, even if similar or identical to an irregular verb. Thus one says *grandstanded*, not *grandstood*; *flied out* in baseball (from a fly (ball)), not *flew out*; *high-sticked* in hockey, not *high-stuck* (Pinker and Prince ,1988; Kim et al. ,1991; Kiparsky, 1982). The explanation is that irregularity consists of a linkage between two word roots, the atomic sound – meaning pairings stored in the mental lexicon; it is not a link between two words or sound patterns directly. *High-stuck* sounds silly because the verb is tacitly perceived as being based on the noun root (*hockey*) *stick*, and noun roots cannot be listed in the lexicon as having any past tense form (the past tense of a noun makes no sense semantically), let alone an irregular one. Because its root is not the verb *stick* there is no data pathway by which *stuck* can be made available; to obtain a past tense form, the speaker must apply the regular rule, which serves as the default. Subjects presented with novel irregular-sounding verbs (for example, to *line-drive*) strongly prefer the regular past tense form (*line-drived*) if it is understood as being based on a noun ("to hit a line drive"), but not in a control condition for unfamiliarity where the items were based on existing irregular verbs ("to drive along a line"); here the usual irregular form is preferred (Kim et al., 1991).

The effect, moreover, occurs in experiments testing subjects with no college education (Kim et al., 1991) and in pre-school children (Kim et al., in press). This is consistent with the fact that many of these lawful forms entered the language from vernacular speech and were opposed by language mavens and guardians of "proper" style (Kim et al., 1991; Mencken, 1936). "Rules of grammar" in the psycholinguists' sense, and their organization into components, are inherent to the computational systems found in all humans, not just those with access to explicit schooling or stylistic injunctions. These injunctions, involving a very different sense of "rule" as something that ought to be followed, usually pertain to minor differences between standard written and nonstandard spoken dialects.

A related effect occurs in lexical compounds, which sound natural when they contain irregular noun plurals, but not regular noun plurals: Compare *mice-infested* with *rats-infested*, *teethmarks* with *clawsmarks*, *men-bashing* with *guys-bashing* (Kiparsky ,1982). Assume that this compounding rule is fed by stored words. Irregulars are stored words, so they can feed compounding; regulars are computed at the output end of the morphology system, not stored at the input end, so they do not appear inside lexical compounds. This constraint has been documented experimentally in 3–5-year-old children (Gordor, 1985):[9] when children who knew the word *mice* were asked for a word for a "monster who eats mice," they responded with *mice-eater* 90 percent of the time; but when children who knew *rats* were asked for a word for "monster who eats rats," they responded *rats-eater* only 2 percent of the time. The children could not have learned the constraint by recording whether adults use irregular versus regular plurals inside compounds. Adults do not use such compounds often enough for most children to have heard them: the frequency of English compounds containing any kind of plural is indistinguishable from zero (Francis and Kucera, 1982; Gordor, 1985). Rather, the constraint may be a consequence of the inherent organization of the children's grammatical systems.

Developmental and Neurological Dissociations

If regular and irregular patterns are computed in different subsystems, they should dissociate in special populations. Individuals with undeveloped or damaged grammatical systems and intact lexical memory should be unable to compute regular forms but should be able to handle irregulars. Conversely, individuals with intact grammatical systems and atypical lexical retrieval should handle regulars properly but be prone to overregularizing irregulars. Such double dissociations, most clearly demonstrated in detailed case studies, are an important source of evidence for the existence of separate neural subsystems. Preliminary evidence suggests that regular and irregular inflection may show such dissociations.

Children

Most of the grammatical structure of English develops rapidly in the third year of life (Brown, 1973). One conspicuous development is the appearance of overregularizations like *comed*. Such errors constitute a worsening of past marking with time; for months beforehand, all overtly marked irregular past forms are correct (Marcus et al., 1990). The phenomenon is not due to the child becoming temporarily overwhelmed by the regular pattern because of an influx of regular verbs, as connectionist theories (Rumelhart and McClelland, 1986) predict (Pinker and Prince, 1988; Marcus et al., 1990).[10] Instead it accompanies the appearance of the regular tense-marking process itself: overregularizations appear when the child ceases using bare stems like *walk* to refer to past events (Kuczaj, 1977; Marcus et al., 1990). Say memorization of verb forms from parental speech, including irregulars, can take place as soon as words of any kind can be learned. But deployment of the rule system must await the abstraction of the English rule from a set of word pairs juxtaposed as nonpast and past versions of the same verb. The young child could possess memorized irregulars, produced probabilistically but without overt error, but no rule; the older child, possessing the rule as well, would apply it obligatorily in past tense sentences whenever he failed to retrieve the irregular, resulting in occasional errors.

Aphasics

A syndrome sometimes called agrammatic aphasia can occur after extensive damage to Broca's area and nearby structures in the left cerebral hemisphere. Labored speech, absence of inflections and other grammatical words, and difficulty comprehending grammatical distinctions are frequent symptoms. Agrammatics have trouble reading aloud regular inflected forms: *smiled* is pronounced as *smile*, *wanted* as *wanting*. Nonregular plural and past forms are read with much greater accuracy, controlling for frequency and pronounceability (Marin et al., 1976).[11] This is predicted if agrammatism results from damage to neural circuitry that executes rules of grammar, including the regular rule necessary for analyzing regularly inflected stimuli, but leaves the lexicon relatively undamaged, including stored irregulars which can be directly matched against the irregular stimuli.

Specific language impairment (SLI)

SLI refers to a syndrome of language deficits not attributable to auditory, cognitive, or social problems. The syndrome usually includes delayed onset of language, articulation difficulties in childhood, and problems in controlling grammatical features such as tense, number, gender, case, and person. One form of SLI may especially impair aspects of the regular inflectional process (Gopnik, 1990a, 1990b; Gopnik and Crago, in press). Natural speech includes errors like "We're go take a bus; I play musics; One machine clean all the two arena." In experiments, the patients have difficulty converting present sentences to past (32 percent for SLI; 78 percent for sibling controls). The difficulty is more pronounced for regular verbs than irregulars. Regular past forms are virtually absent from the children's spontaneous speech and writing, although irregulars often appear. In the writing samples of two children examined quantitatively, 85 percent of irregular pasts but 30 percent of regular pasts were correctly supplied. The first written regular past tense forms are for verbs with past tense frequencies higher than their stem frequencies; subsequent ones are acquired one at a time in response to teacher training, with little transfer to nontrained verbs. Adults' performance improves and their speech begins to sound normal but they continue to have difficulty inflecting nonsense forms like *zoop* (47 percent for SLI; 83 percent for controls). It appears as if their ability to apply inflectional rules is impaired relative to their ability to memorize words: irregular forms are acquired relatively normally, enjoying their advantage of high frequencies; regular forms are memorized as if they were irregular.

SLI appears to have an inherited component. Language impairments have been found in 3 percent of first-degree family members of normal probands but 23 percent of language-impaired probands (Tomblin, 1989; Tallal et al., 1989). The impairment has been found to be 80 percent concordant in monozygotic twins and 35 percent concordant in dizygotic twins (Tomblin unpublished). One case study (Gopnik, 1990a, 1990b; Gopnik and Crago, in press) investigated a three-generation, 30-member family, 16 of whom had SLI; the syndrome followed the pattern of a dominant, fully penetrant autosomal gene. This constitutes evidence that some aspects of use of grammar have a genetic basis.

Williams' syndrome

Williams' syndrome (WS), associated with a defective gene expressed in the central nervous system involved in calcium metabolism, causes an unusual kind of mental retardation (Bellugi et al., 1990). Although their intelligence quotient is measured at around 50, older children and adolescents with WS are described as hyperlinguistic with selective sparing of syntax, and grammatical abilities are close to normal in controlled testing (Bellugi et al., 1990). This is one of several kinds of dissociation in which language is preserved despite severe cognitive impairments, suggesting that the language system is autonomous of many other kinds of cognitive processing.

WS children retrieve words in a deviant fashion (Bellugi et al. 1990). When normal or other retarded children are asked to name some animals, they say *dog*, *cat*, *pig*; WS children offer *unicorn*, *tyrandon*, *yak*, *ibex*. Normal children speak of *pouring water*; WS children speak of *evacuating a glass*. According to the rule – associative-memory hybrid theory, preserved grammatical abilities and deviant retrieval of high-frequency words are preconditions for overregularization. Indeed, some WS children overregularize at high rates (16 percent), one of their few noticeable grammatical errors (Bellugi et al., 1990: Klima and Bellugi, unpublished).

Conclusion

For hundreds of years, the mind has been portrayed as a homogeneous system whose complexity comes from the complexity of environmental correlations as recorded by a general-purpose learning mechanism. Modern research on language renders such a view increasingly implausible. Although there is evidence that the memory system used in language acquisition and processing has some of the properties of an associative network, these properties do not exhaust the computational abilities of the brain. Focusing on a single rule of grammar, we find evidence for a system that is modular, independent of real-world meaning, nonassociative (unaffected by frequency and similarity), sensitive to abstract formal distinctions (for example, root versus derived, noun versus verb), more sophisticated than the kinds of "rule" that are explicitly taught, developing on a schedule not timed by environmental input, organized by principles that could not have been learned, possibly with a distinct neural substrate and genetic basis.

NOTES

I thank my collaborators A. Prince, G. Hickok, M. Hollander, J. Kim, G. Marcus, S. Prasada, A. Senghas, and S. Ullman, and thank T. Bever, N. Block, N. Etcoff, and especially A. Prince for comments. Supported by NIH grant HD18381.

1   More sophisticated connectionist models of past tense formation employing a hidden layer of nodes have computational limitations similar to those of the Rumelhart–McClelland model.
2   In speech samples from 19 children containing 9,684 irregular past tense forms (marcus et al. 1990), aggregate overregularization rate for 39 verbs correlated -0.37 with aggregate log frequency in parental speech. All correlations and differences noted herein are significant at $p = 0.05$ or less.
3   Data represent mean ratings by 99 subjects of the naturalness of the past and stem forms of 142 irregular verbs and 59 regular verbs that did not rhyme with any irregular, each presented in a sentence in counterbalanced random order.
4   Such effects can also occur in certain connectionist models that lack distinct representations of words and superimpose associations between the phonological elements of stem and past forms. After such models are trained on many regular verbs, any new verb would activate previously trained phonological associations to the regular pattern and could yield a strong regular form; the absence of prior training on the verb itself would not necessarily hurt it. However, the existence of homophones with different past tense forms (*lie–lay* versus *lie–lied*) makes such models psychologically unrealistic; representations of individual words are called for, and they would engender word familiarity effects.
5   The effects obtained in three experiments, each showing 32–40 subjects the stem forms of verbs on a screen for 300 msec and measuring their vocal response time for the past tense form. Thirty to 48 irregular verbs and 30–48 regular verbs were shown, one at a time in random order; every verb had a counterpart with the same stem frequency but a different past tense frequency (Francis and Kucesa, 1982). In control experiments, 40 subjects generated third person singular forms of stems, read stems aloud, or read past tense forms aloud, and the frequency difference among irregulars did not occur; this shows the effect is not due to inherent differences in access or articulation times of the verbs.
6   The effect was not an artifact of differences in phonological or orthographic overlap between the members of regular and irregular pairs.
7   For 17 of 19 children studied in Marcus et al. (1990), the higher the frequencies of the other irregulars rhyming with an irregular, the lower its overregulation rate (mean correlation -0.07, significantly less than 0). For the corresponding calculation with regulars rhyming with an irregular, no consistency resulted and the mean correlation did not differ significantly from zero.
8   Twenty-four subjects read 60 sentences containing novel verbs, presented in either stem form, a past form displaying an English irregular vowel change, or a past form containing the regular suffix. Each subject rated how good the verb sounded with a seven-point scale; each verb was

rated in each of the forms by different subjects. For novel verbs highly similar to an irregular family, the irregular past form was rated 0.8 points worse than the stem; for novel verbs dissimilar to the family, the irregular past form was rated 2.2 points worse. For novel verbs resembling a family of regular verbs, the regular past form was rated 0.4 points better than the stem; for novel verbs dissimilar to the family, the regular past form was rated 1.5 points better. This interaction was replicated in two other experiments.

9   The effect is not an artifact of pronounceability, as children were willing to say *pants-eater* and *scissors-eater*, containing s-final nouns that are not regular plurals.

10 The proportion of regular verb tokens in children's and parents' speech remains unchanged throughout childhood, because high-frequency irregular verbs (*make, put, take*, etc.) dominate conversation at any age. The proportion of regular verb types in children's vocabulary necessarily increases because irregular verbs are a small fraction of English vocabulary, but this growth does not correlate with overregularization errors (Fodor, 1983; Kuozaj, 1977).

11 For example, regular *misers, clues, buds* were read by three agrammatic patients less accurately than phonologically matched plurals that are not regular because they lack a corresponding singular, like *trousers, news, suds* (45 percent versus 90 percent) even though a phonologically well-formed stem is available in both cases. In another study, when verbs matched for past and base frequencies and pronounceability were presented to an agrammatic patient, he read 56 percent of irregular past forms and 13 percent of regular past forms successfully

REFERENCES

Andersen, S., in *Linguistics: The Cambridge Survey* (Cambridge University Press, New York, 1988), vol. 1, pp. 146–91.
Aronoff, M., *Annual Review of Anthropology* 12, 355 (1983).
Bellugi, U., Bihrle, A., Jernigan, T., Trauner, D., and Doherty, S., *American Journal of Medical Genetics, Supplement* 6, 115 (1990).
Berko, J., *Word* 14, 150 (1958).
Brown, R., *A First Language* (Harvard University Press, Cambridge, MA, 1973).
Bybee, J., *Morphology* (Benjamins, Philadelphia, 1985).
Bybee, J. and Modor, C., *Language* 59, 251 (1983).
Bybee, J. and Slobin, D., *Language* 58, 265 (1982).
Chomsky, N., *Rules and Representations* (Columbia University Press, New York, 1980).
Chomsky, N. and Halle, M., *Sound Pattern of English* (MIT Press, Cambridge, MA, 1990).
Curtiss, S., in L. Obler and D. Fein, eds, *The Exceptional Brain* (Guilford, New York, 1988).
Egedi, D. and Sproat, R., unpublished data.
Fodor, J., *Modularity of Mind* (MIT Press, Cambridge, MA, 1983).
Francis, N. and Kucera, H., *Frequency Analysis of English Usage* (Houghton Mifflin, Boston, 1982).
Gopnik, M., *Nature* 344, 715 (1990a).
Gopnik, M., *Language Acquisition* 1, 139 (1990b).
Gopnik, M. and Crago, M., *Cognition*, in press [39 (1991)].
Gordon, P., *Cognition* 21, 73 (1985).
Hebb, D. *Organization of Behavior* (John Wiley, New York, 1949).
Hickok G. and Pinker S., unpublished data.
Hume, D., *Inquiry Concerning Human Understanding* (Bobbs-Merril, Indianapolis, 1955);
Jesperson, O., *A Modern English Grammar on Historical Principles* (Allen and Unwin, London, 1961).
Kempley, S. and Morton, J., *British Journal of Psychology* 73, 441 (1982).
Kim, J., Marcus, G., Hollander, M., and Pinker, S., *Papers and Reports on Child Language Development*, in press. [Published as "Sensitivity of children's inflection to grammatical structure," *Journal of Child Language* 21 (1994).]
Kim, J., Pinker, S., Prince, A., and Prasada, S., *Cognitive Science* 15, 173 (1991).

Kiparsky, P., in H. van der Hulst and N. Smith, eds, *The Structure of Phonological Representations* (Foris, Dordrecht, 1982).

Klima, E. and Bellugi, U., unpublished data.

Kuczaj, S., *Journal of Verbal Learning and Verbal Behavior* 16, 589 (1977).

Lachter, J. and Bever, T., *Cognition* 28, 197 (1988).

Leibniz, G., *Philosophical Essays* (Hackett, Indianapolis, 1989).

Lenneberg, E., *Biological Foundations of Language* (John Wiley, New York, 1967).

Marin, O., Saffran, E., and Schwartz, M., *Annals of the New York Academy of Science* 280, 868 (1976).

Marcus, G., Ullman, M., Pinker, S., Hollander, M., Rosen, T., and Xu, F., Occasional Papers (MIT Centre for Cognitive Science, 41 (Cambridge, MA, 1990).

Mencken, H., *The American Language* (Knopf, New York, 1936).

Newell, A. and Simon, H., *Science* 134, 2011 (1961).

Pinker, S. and Prince, A., *Cognition* 28, 73 (1988).

Prasada S. and Pinker, S., unpublished data.

Prasada, S., Pinker, S., and Snyder, W., paper presented at the 31st Annual Meeting of the Psychonomic Society, New Orleans, 16–18 November 1990.

Rumelhart, D. and McClelland, J., eds, *Parallel Distributed Processing* (MIT Press, Cambridge, MA, 1986).

Rumelhart, D. and McClelland, J., in Rumelhart and McClelland (1986), pp. 216–71.

Stanners, R., Neiser, J., Hernon, W., and Hall, R., *Journal of Verbal Learning and Verbal Behavior* 18, 399 (1979).

Tallal, P., Ross, R., and Curtiss, S., *Journal of Speech and Hearing Disorder* 54, 167 (1989).

Tomblin, J., *Journal of Speech and Hearing Disorder* 54, 287 (1989).

Tomblin, J., unpublished data.

Ullman, M. and Pinker, S., paper presented at the Spring Symposium of the AAAI, Stanford, 26–8 March 1991.

Index